Lecture Notes in Computer Science   5140

Commenced Publication in 1973
Founding and Former Series Editors:
Gerhard Goos, Juris Hartmanis, and Jan van Leeuwen

José Meseguer   Grigore Roşu (Eds.)

Algebraic Methodology and Software Technology

12th International Conference, AMAST 2008
Urbana, IL, USA, July 28-31, 2008
Proceedings

 Springer

Volume Editors

José Meseguer
University of Illinois at Urbana-Champaign
Urbana, IL, USA
E-mail: meseguer@cs.uiuc.edu

Grigore Roşu
University of Illinois at Urbana-Champaign
Urbana, IL, USA
E-mail: grosu@cs.uiuc.edu

Library of Congress Control Number: 2008930999

CR Subject Classification (1998): F.3-4, D.2, C.3, D.1.6, I.2.3, I.1.3

LNCS Sublibrary: SL 2 – Programming and Software Engineering

ISSN 0302-9743

ISBN 978-3-540-79979-5 Springer Berlin Heidelberg New York

Springer is a part of Springer Science+Business Media

springer.com

© Springer-Verlag Berlin Heidelberg 2008

Typesetting: Camera-ready by author, data conversion by Scientific Publishing Services, Chennai, India
Printed on acid-free paper   SPIN: 12444250   06/3180   5 4 3 2 1 0

Preface

This volume contains the proceedings of AMAST 2008, the 12th International Conference on Algebraic Methodology and Software Technology, held during July 28–31, 2008, in Urbana, Illinois, USA.

The major goal of the AMAST conferences is to promote research toward setting software technology on a firm, mathematical basis. Work toward this goal is a collaborative, international effort with contributions from both academia and industry. The envisioned virtues of providing software technology developed on a mathematical basis include: *correctness*, which can be proved mathematically; *safety*, so that developed software can be used in the implementation of critical systems; *portability*, i.e., independence from computing platforms and language generations; and *evolutionary change*, i.e., the software is self-adaptable and evolves with the problem domain.

The previous AMAST conferences were held in: Iowa City, Iowa, USA (1989, 1991 and 2000); Twente, The Netherlands (1993); Montreal, Canada (1995); Munich, Germany (1996); Sydney, Australia (1997); Manaus, Brazil (1998); Reunion Island, France (2002); Stirling, UK (2004, colocated with MPC 2004); Kuressaare, Estonia (2006, colocated with MPC 2006).

For AMAST 2008 there were 58 submissions, which were thoroughly evaluated by the Program Committee. Each submission had an average of five reviews. Following a lively electronic meeting, the Program Committee selected 28 papers to be presented at the conference, including 5 tool papers. In addition to the accepted papers, the conference also featured invited talks by three distinguished speakers: Rajeev Alur (University of Pennsylvania), Jayadev Misra (University of Texas at Austin), and Teodor Rus (University of Iowa). This volume includes all the accepted papers, as well as abstracts or full papers by invited speakers.

AMAST 2008 was the result of a considerable effort by a number of people. We express our gratitude to the AMAST 2008 Program Committee and additional referees for their expertise and diligence in reviewing the submitted papers, and to the AMAST Steering Committee for its guidance. Special thanks go to Francesca Bell, Mark Hills, Ralf Sasse and Andrea Whitesell for helping with local organization. Additional warmest thanks go to Ralf Sasse for help with the preparation of this volume. We are also grateful to Springer for its continued support in the publication of the proceedings in the LNCS series, and to Andrei Voronkov for providing the EasyChair system, which was used to manage the submissions, the review process, the electronic PC meeting, and to assemble the proceedings. Finally, we thank the Department of Computer Science of the University of Illinois at Urbana-Champaign for hosting AMAST 2008.

May 2008

José Meseguer
Grigore Roşu

Organization

AMAST 2008 was organized by the department of Computer Science of the University of Illinois at Urbana-Champaign.

Steering Committee

Michael Johnson	Macquarie University, Sydney, Australia (Chair)
Egidio Astesiano	Università degli Studi di Genova, Italy
Robert Berwick	MIT, Cambridge, USA
Zohar Manna	Stanford University, USA
Michael Mislove	Tulane University, New Orleans, USA
Anton Nijholt	University of Twente, The Netherlands
Maurice Nivat	Universite Paris 7, France
Charles Rattray	University of Stirling, UK
Teodor Rus	University of Iowa, Iowa City, USA
Giuseppe Scollo	Università di Catania, Italy
Michael Sintzoff	Universite Catholique de Louvain, Belgium
Jeannette Wing	Carnegie Mellon University, Pittsburgh, USA
Martin Wirsing	Ludwig-Maximilians-Universität München, Germany

Program Committee Chairs

José Meseguer	University of Illinois at Urbana-Champaign, USA
Grigore Roşu	University of Illinois at Urbana-Champaign, USA

Program Committee

Gilles Barthe	INRIA Sophia-Antipolis, France
Michel Bidoit	INRIA Saclay - Ile-de-France, France
Manfred Broy	Technische Universität München, Germany
Roberto Bruni	University of Pisa, Italy
Mads Dam	Royal Institute of Technology (KTH), Stockholm, Sweden
Răzvan Diaconescu	Institute of Mathematics (IMAR), Bucharest, Romania
Jose Fiadeiro	University of Leicester, UK
Rob Goldblatt	Victoria University, Wellington, New Zealand
Bernhard Gramlich	Vienna University of Technology, Austria
Radu Grosu	State University of New York at Stony Brook, USA
Anne Haxthausen	Technical University of Denmark, Lyngby, Denmark

Rolf Hennicker   Ludwig-Maximilians-Universität München, Germany
Michael Johnson   Macquarie University, Sydney, Australia
Hélène Kirchner   INRIA Loria, Nancy, France
Paul Klint   CWI and Universiteit van Amsterdam,
                          The Netherlands
Gary T. Leavens   University of Central Florida, Orlando, USA
Narciso Martí-Oliet   Universidad Complutense de Madrid, Spain
Michael Mislove   Tulane University, New Orleans, USA
Ugo Montanari   University of Pisa, Italy
Larry Moss   Indiana University, Bloomington, USA
Till Mossakowski   DFKI Bremen, Germany
Peter Mosses   Swansea University, UK
Fernando Orejas   Technical University of Catalonia, Barcelona, Spain
Dusko Pavlovic   Kestrel Institute and Oxford University, USA
Jan Rutten   CWI and Vrije Universiteit Amsterdam,
                          The Netherlands
Lutz Schröder   DFKI Bremen/Universität Bremen, Germany
Wolfram Schulte   Microsoft Research, Seattle, USA
Giuseppe Scollo   Università di Catania, Italy
Henny Sipma   Stanford University, USA
Doug Smith   Kestrel Institute, Palo Alto, USA
Carolyn Talcott   SRI International, Menlo Park, USA
Andrzej Tarlecki   Warsaw University, Poland
Varmo Vene   University of Tartu, Estonia
Martin Wirsing   Ludwig-Maximilians-Universität München, Germany
Uwe Wolter   University of Bergen, Norway

Organizing Committee

Mark Hills, José Meseguer, Grigore Roşu, Ralf Sasse (University of Illinois at
Urbana-Champaign, USA)

Referees

Kamal Aboul-Hosn	Guillaume Bonfante	Jacek Chrzaszcz
Marc Aiguier	Michele Boreale	Corina Cirstea
Irem Aktug	Jewgenij Botaschanjan	Horatiu Cirstea
Musab AlTurki	Christiano Braga	Mihai Codescu
Oana Andrei	Mario Bravetti	Mika Cohen
Paolo Baldan	Franck van Breugel	Véronique Cortier
Anindya Banerjee	Marzia Buscemi	Pierre Courtieu
Ezio Bartocci	Josep Carmona	Silvano Dal Zilio
Hubert Baumeister	Maria V. Cengarle	Stéphanie Delaune
Beatrice Berard	Maura Cerioli	Denisa Diaconescu
Sascha Böhme	Julien Charles	Dominique Duval

Juhan Ernits
Ingo Feinerer
Gianluigi Ferrari
Wan Fokkink
David de Frutos-Escrig
Fabio Gadducci
Daniel Gaina
Samir Genaim
Sergey Goncharov
Dilian Gurov
Stefan Haar
Daniel Hausmann
Mark Hills
Clement Hurlin
Ethan Jackson
Bart Jacobs
Einar Broch Johnsen
Steffen Jost
Bartek Klin
Alexander Knapp
Piotr Kosiuczenko
Clemens Kupke
Ivan Lanese
Francois Laroussinie
Daan Leijen
Alberto Lluch Lafuente
Antonia Lopes
Michele Loreti
Hans Henrik Løvengreen
Etienne Lozes
Dorel Lucanu

Dominik Luecke
Andreas Lundblad
Christoph Lüth
Christian Maeder
M. Majster-Cederbaum
Florian Mangold
Claude Marché
Grzegorz Marczynski
Paulo Mateus
Catherine Meadows
Hernan Melgratti
Patrick Meredith
José Meseguer
Peter Müller
Markey Nicolas
Hitoshi Ohsaki
Sam Owre
Anne Pacalet
Luca Padovani
Miguel Palomino
Wiesław Pawłowski
Marius Petria
Henrik Pilegaard
Andrei Popescu
Daniel Ratiu
Bernhard Reus
Oliviero Riganelli
Sabine Rittmann
Camilo Rocha
Grigore Roşu
Ando Saabas

Jorge Luis Sacchini
Ralf Sasse
Christoph Schubert
Traian Serbanuta
Alexandra Silva
Ana Sokolova
Maria Spichkova
Katharina Spies
Gheorghe Stefanescu
Meng Sun
Chris Tartamella
René Thiemann
Veronika Thurner
David Trachtenherz
Emilio Tuosto
Mathieu Turuani
Tarmo Uustalu
Viktor Vafeiadis
Vasco Vasconcelos
Alberto Verdejo
Luca Vigano
Jørgen Villadsen
Erik de Vink
Vesal Vojdani
Dennis Walter
Michael Westergaard
James Worrell
Pei Ye
Artur Zawlocki
Benjamin Zorn

Table of Contents

Marrying Words and Trees

Rajeev Alur

University of Pennsylvania

We discuss the model of *nested words* for representation of data with both a
linear ordering and a hierarchically nested matching of items. Examples of data
with such dual linear-hierarchical structure include annotated linguistic data,
executions of structured programs, and HTML/XML documents. Nested words
generalize both words and ordered trees, and allow both word and tree operations. We define *nested word automata*—finite-state acceptors for nested words,
and show that the resulting class of regular languages of nested words has all
the appealing theoretical properties that the classical regular word languages
enjoy such as determinization, closure under a variety of operations, decidability
of emptiness as well as equivalence, and characterization using monadic second
order logic. The linear encodings of nested words gives the class of *visibly push-
down languages* of words, and this class lies between balanced languages and
deterministic context-free languages. We argue that for algorithmic verification
of structured programs, instead of viewing the program as a context-free language over words, one should view it as a regular language of nested words (or
equivalently, as a visibly pushdown language), and this would allow model checking of many properties (such as stack inspection, pre-post conditions) that are
not expressible in existing specification logics. We also study the relationship
between ordered trees and nested words, and the corresponding automata: while
the analysis complexity of nested word automata is the same as that of classical
tree automata, they combine both bottom-up and top-down traversals, and enjoy
expressiveness and succinctness benefits over tree automata. There is a rapidly
growing literature related to nested words, and we will briefly survey results on
languages infinite nested words, nested trees, temporal logics over nested words,
and new decidability results based on visibility.

More information about nested words and references can be found at
http://www.cis.upenn.edu/~alur/nw.html

J. Meseguer and G. Roşu (Eds.): AMAST 2008, LNCS 5140, p. 1, 2008.
© Springer-Verlag Berlin Heidelberg 2008

Simulation Using Orchestration
(Extended Abstract)

David Kitchin, Evan Powell, and Jayadev Misra

The University of Texas at Austin

Abstract. The real world is inherently concurrent and temporal. For simulating physical phenomena of the real world, one prefers frameworks which easily express concurrency and account for the passage of time. We propose *Orc*, a structured concurrent calculus, as a framework for writing simulations. Orc provides constructs to orchestrate the concurrent invocation of services while managing time-outs, priorities, and failures of services or communication. Orc's treatment of time is of particular interest in simulation. We propose an abstract notion of time and show its utility in coding simulations. We also show how Orc's structure allows us to compute statistics from a simulation.

1   Introduction

Orc[3,4] is a language for structured concurrent programming. It is based on the premise that structured concurrent programs should be developed much like structured sequential programs, by decomposing a problem and combining the solutions with the combinators of the language. Naturally, Orc combinators support concurrency: parallel subcomputations, spawning of computations and blocking or termination of subcomputations. Orc has a number of algebraic properties which make it amenable to formal analysis.

Physical phenomena in the real world are inherently concurrent and temporal. Simulations of physical phenomena typically involve describing concurrent entities, their interactions and passage of real time. The structure of Orc makes such descriptions extremely modular. This paper presents a preliminary report of our experience with coding simulations in Orc.

In Section 2, we give a brief overview of Orc, followed by example Orc programs in Section 3. Portions of Sections 2 and 3 have appeared previously in [3,4]. Section 4 presents an abstraction of time, in which we treat both physical (Newtonian) time and logical time analogously. In Section 5, we describe the implementation of simulations in Orc using logical timers. Section 6 describes how to compute statistics from a simulation. Section 7 includes plans for future research.

2   Overview of Orc

An Orc program consists of a *goal* expression and a set of definitions. The goal expression is evaluated in order to run the program. The definitions are used in the goal and in other definitions.

J. Meseguer and G. Roşu (Eds.): AMAST 2008, LNCS 5140, pp. 2–15, 2008.

An expression is either primitive or a combination of two expressions. A primitive expression is a call to an existing service, a *site*, to perform its computations and return a result; we describe sites in Section 2.1. Two expressions can be combined to form a composite expression using Orc combinators; we describe the combinators in Section 2.2. We allow expressions to be named in a definition, and these names may then be used in other expressions. Naming permits us to define an expression recursively by using its own name in the definition. Definitions and recursion are treated in Section 2.3. We give a complete formal syntax in Figure 2 of Section 2.4. Practical Orc examples use a modest set of syntactic extensions, discussed in Section 2.5. Orc examples appear in Section 3.

During its evaluation, an Orc expression calls sites and publishes values. Below, we describe the details of calls and publications.

2.1 Sites

A primitive Orc expression is a *site call* $M(\bar{p})$, where M is a site name and $\bar{p}$ a list of actual parameters. A site is an external program, like a web service. The site may be implemented on the client's machine or a remote machine. A site call elicits at most one response; it is possible that a site never responds to a call. For example, evaluation of $CNN(d)$, where CNN is a news service site and d is a date, calls CNN with parameter value d; if CNN responds (with the news page for the specified date), the response is published.

Site calls are *strict*, i.e., a site is called only if all its parameters have values.

We list a few sites in Figure 1 that are fundamental to effective programming in Orc (in the figure, a *signal* represents a unit value and has no additional information).

Site *if* is used for conditional evaluation. Site *Rtimer* is used to introduce delays and impose time-outs, and is essential for time-based computations. Site *Signal*() is a special case of *if*.

if(b):	Returns a signal if b is *true*, and otherwise does not respond.
Rtimer(t):	Returns a signal after exactly t, $t \geq 0$, time units.
Signal():	Returns a signal immediately. Same as *if*(*true*).
0:	Blocks forever. Same as *if*(*false*).

Fig. 1. Fundamental Sites

2.2 Combinators

There are three combinators in Orc for combining expressions. Given expressions f and g, they are: symmetric parallel composition, written as $f \mid g$; sequential composition with respect to variable x, written as $f >x> g$; and asymmetric parallel composition with respect to variable x, written as $f <x< g$.

To evaluate $f \mid g$, we evaluate f and g independently. The sites called by f and g are the ones called by $f \mid g$ and any value published by either f or g is published by $f \mid g$. There is no direct communication or interaction between these two computations. For example, evaluation of $CNN(d) \mid BBC(d)$ initiates two independent computations; up to two values will be published depending on which sites respond.

In $f >x> g$, expression f is evaluated and each value published by it initiates a fresh instance of g as a separate computation. The value published by f is bound to x in g's computation. Evaluation of f continues while (possibly several) instances of g are run. If f publishes no value, g is never instantiated. The values published by $f >x> g$ are the ones published by all the instances of g (values published by f are consumed within $f >x> g$). This is the only mechanism in Orc similar to spawning threads.

As an example, the following expression calls sites CNN and BBC in parallel to get the news for date d. Responses from either of these calls are bound to x and then site $email$ is called to send the information to address a. Thus, $email$ may be called 0, 1 or 2 times.

$$(CNN(d) \mid BBC(d)) >x> email(a, x)$$

Expression $f \gg g$ is short-hand for $f >x> g$, where x is not free in g.

As a short example of time-based computation, $Rtimer(2) \gg M()$ delays calling site M for two time units, and $M() \mid (Rtimer(1) \gg M()) \mid (Rtimer(2) \gg M())$ makes three calls to M at unit time intervals.

To evaluate $(f <x< g)$, start by evaluating both f and g in parallel. Evaluation of parts of f which do not depend on x can proceed, but site calls in which x is a parameter are suspended until x has a value. If g publishes a value, then x is assigned the (first such) value, g's evaluation is then terminated and the suspended parts of f can proceed. The values published by $(f <x< g)$ are the ones published by f. Any response received for g after its termination is ignored. This is the only mechanism in Orc to block or terminate parts of a computation.

As an example, in $((M() \mid N(x)) <x< R())$ sites M and R are called immediately (thus, M is called immediately, even before x may have a value). Once R responds with a value, x is bound to that value and $N(x)$ is then called. Contrast the following two expressions; in the first one $email$ is called at most once, whereas the second one (shown earlier) may call $email$ twice.

$$email(a, x) <x< (CNN(d) \mid BBC(d))$$
$$(CNN(d) \mid BBC(d)) >x> email(a, x)$$

2.3   Definitions and Recursion

Declaration $E(\bar{x}) \triangleq f$ defines expression E whose formal parameter list is $\bar{x}$ and body is expression f. We assume that only the variables $\bar{x}$ are free in f. A call $E(\bar{p})$ is evaluated by replacing the formal parameters $\bar{x}$ by the actual parameters $\bar{p}$ in the body of the definition f. Sites are called by value, while definitions are called by name.

A definition may be recursive (or mutually recursive): a call to E may occur in f, the body of the expression, yielding a recursively defined expression. Such expressions are used for encoding bounded as well as unbounded computations. Below, *Metronome* publishes a signal every time unit starting immediately.

$$Metronome() \; \underline{\Delta} \; Signal() \mid (Rtimer(1) \gg Metronome())$$

2.4 Formal Syntax

The formal syntax of Orc is given in Figure 2.[1] Here M is the name of a site and E a defined expression. An actual parameter p may be a variable x or a value m, and $\bar{p}$ denotes a list of actual parameters.

The syntax also allows actual parameters (variables x and values m) to appear alone as primitive expressions. The primitive expression m simply publishes m. The primitive expression x waits for the variable x to become bound, and then publishes the value bound to x.[2]

$$
\begin{aligned}
f, g, h \;\in\; & Expression ::= M(\bar{p}) \mid E(\bar{p}) \mid p \mid f >x> g \mid f \mid g \mid f <x< g \\
p \;\in\; & Actual \quad ::= x \mid m \\
& Definition ::= E(\bar{x}) \; \underline{\Delta} \; f
\end{aligned}
$$

Fig. 2. Syntax of Orc

Notation. The combinators are listed Figure 2 in decreasing order of precedence, so $f <x< g \mid h$ means $f <x< (g \mid h)$, and $f >x> g \mid h$ means $(f >x> g) \mid h$. Expression $f >x> g >y> h$ means $f >x> (g >y> h)$, i.e., $>x>$ is right-associative, and $f <x< g <y< h$ means $(f <x< g) <y< h$, i.e., $<x<$ is left-associative.

2.5 Syntax Extensions

In practice, Orc programs often incorporate syntactic sugar, to simplify and condense expressions. These constructs do not fundamentally extend the calculus; they are simply more compact representations.

Tuples. In additional to the fundamental sites shown earlier, it is also helpful to have site support for constructing and examining data structures. We allow the syntax $(\bar{p})$, as a shorthand for $tuple(\bar{p})$, where $tuple$ is a site which creates a single tuple value out of its argument values and publishes it. In order to examine these tuples, we extend the syntax of the combinators $>x>$ and $<x<$ with *pattern matching;* instead of binding a value to a variable, a combinator may bind a tuple of values to a tuple of variables.

For example, the following expression publishes the values 6 and 7:

$$((3, 6) \mid (4, 7)) >(x, y)> y$$

---

[1] Previous presentations of Orc have used the notation f **where** $x :\in g$ instead of $f <x< g$.
[2] Previous presentations of Orc used $let(x)$ to publish the value of x.

Dot Notation. In some cases, especially when writing code in an object-oriented style, it is helpful to have a special notation for calls. We write $M.name$ as syntactic sugar for $M(\textbf{name})$, where **name** is a message, and M maps messages to values. We use this notation to express both field accesses, written as $x.field$, and method calls, written as $x.method(\bar{p})$, which is a shorthand for $x.method >m> m(\bar{p})$.

Arithmetic and Logical Expressions. Orc does not include any operators for data manipulation; so, $3+4$ is an illegal expression in Orc. We get the same effect by calling a predefined site $Sum(3, 4)$. To simplify coding, we write arithmetic and logical expressions in the standard way, like $3 + 4$, which are compiled into appropriate site calls.

3   Examples

We give a number of small examples in this section to familiarize the reader with the Orc style of programming. Most of these examples have appeared earlier, in [3] and [4].

Time-Out. The following expression publishes the first value published by f if it is available before time t; otherwise it publishes 3. It evaluates f and $Rtimer(t) \gg 3$ in parallel and takes the first value published by either:

$$z <z< (f \mid Rtimer(t) \gg 3)$$

A typical programming paradigm is to call site M and publish a pair (x, b) as the value, where b is $true$ if M publishes x before the time-out, and $false$ if there is a time-out. In the latter case, the value of x is irrelevant. Below, z is the pair (x, b).

$$z <z< (\quad M() >x> (x, true) \\ \mid Rtimer(t) >x> (x, false))$$

Fork-Join Parallelism. In concurrent programming, one often needs to spawn two independent threads at a point in the computation, and resume the computation after both threads complete. Such an execution style is called *fork-join* parallelism. There is no special construct for fork-join in Orc, but it is easy to code such computations. Below, we define *forkjoin* to call sites M and N in parallel and publish their values as a tuple after they both complete their executions.

$$forkjoin() \quad \Delta \quad (x, y) <x< M() \\ <y< N()$$

Synchronization. There is no special machinery for synchronization in Orc; the $<x<$ combinator provides the necessary ingredients for programming synchronizations. Consider $M \gg f$ and $N \gg g$; we wish to execute them independently, but synchronize f and g by starting them only after *both* M and N have completed. We evaluate *forkjoin* (as described above), and start $f \mid g$ after *forkjoin* publishes.

$$forkjoin() \gg (f \mid g)$$

Delay. The following expression publishes N's response as soon as possible, but after at least one time unit. This is similar to a fork-join on $Rtimer(1)$ and N.

$$Delay() \; \triangleq \; (Rtimer(1) \gg y) \; <y< \; N()$$

Priority. Call sites M and N simultaneously. If M responds within one time unit, take its response, otherwise pick the first response. Using *Delay* defined above,

$$x \; <x< \; (M() \mid Delay())$$

Iterative Process and Process Networks. A process in a typical network-based computation repeatedly reads a value from a channel, computes with it and writes the result to another channel. Below, c and e are channels, and $c.get$ and $e.put$ are the methods to read from c and write to e. Below, $P(c, e)$ repeatedly reads from c and writes to e, and $Net(c, d, e)$ is a network of two such processes which share the output channel.

$$
\begin{aligned}
P(c, e) \;\; &\triangleq \;\; c.get() \;\; >x> \;\; Compute(x) \\
&\qquad\qquad\quad >y> \;\; e.put(y) \\
&\qquad\qquad\quad \gg \qquad P(c, e) \\
Net(c, d, e) \;\; &\triangleq \;\; P(c, e) \mid P(d, e)
\end{aligned}
$$

Parallel-or. A classic problem in non-strict evaluation is *parallel-or*. Suppose sites M and N publish booleans. We desire an expression that publishes *true* as soon as either site returns *true*, and *false* only if both return *false*. Otherwise, the expression never publishes. In the following solution, site $or(x, y)$ returns $x \vee y$.

$$
\begin{aligned}
z \;\; &<z< \;\; if(x) \gg true \mid if(y) \gg true \mid or(x, y) \\
&<x< \;\; M() \\
&<y< \;\; N()
\end{aligned}
$$

4   Timers

The site *Rtimer* is a powerful tool for orchestration. It is used mainly for orchestrating events that happen in real time, including interruptions (time-outs). However, the actual value of real time is never used in a computation. In this section, we consider a small combinatorial problem —computing the shortest path between two designated nodes in a weighted directed graph— for which we present a simple algorithm based on actual time values. Next, we introduce a more abstract version of timer, which is *logical* (or *virtual*) that mimics the (physical) real-time timer. We show that the shortest path problem can be solved using logical timers.

4.1   Shortest Path Algorithm Using Real Time

Given is a directed graph each edge of which has a non-negative weight denoting the distance between the two nodes. There are two special nodes, designated *source* and *sink*. It is required to find a shortest path from the source to sink, i.e., one with the least total distance. Henceforth, we simply calculate the length of the shortest path; the actual shortest path can be computed by an easy extension.

The traditional algorithm for solving this problem, due to Dijkstra [1], involves inherently sequential computation. Consider, instead, the following real-time, concurrent algorithm. From the source node, transmit a ray of light to each of its neighbors. Rays propagate along each edge at constant speed in real time; the weight of each edge is the time taken by the ray to traverse the edge. When a node receives its first ray, it transmits a ray to each of its own neighbors.[3] Subsequent rays received by that node are ignored. The length of the shortest path is the total elapsed time from the start of the computation to the point where the sink node receives its first ray.

We code three different versions of this algorithm, with varying levels of refinement. First, we abstract the structure of the graph using expression *succ*:

$succ(u)$: Publish all pairs (v, d) where (u, v) is an edge with weight d.

The graph structure is completely characterized by the identities of the source and the sink, and expression *succ*.

First Solution. We must note when a node first receives a ray, and be sure to ignore subsequent rays. To implement this behavior, we associate a "write-once" variable with each node in the graph, and use two sites to manipulate these variables: For every node u in the graph, $write(u, t)$ writes t into u. Writing is once-only for each u; all subsequent writes block. And, $read(u)$ blocks until u is written; it never blocks subsequently, and returns the written value.

In the following algorithm, the first time $eval1(u, t)$ is called for any u, (1) the relative time in the evaluation is t, and (2) t is the length of the shortest path to u from the source. Note that $eval1$ does not publish.

$eval1(u, t) \;\underline{\Delta}\; write(u, t) \gg Succ(u) >(v, d)> Rtimer(d) \gg eval1(v, t + d)$

$eval1(source, 0) \mid read(sink)$

---

[3] Assume that the amount of time to receive and rebroadcast a ray is inconsequential.

Here, we write the value for the source at time 0. For any other node v, whose predecessor along the shortest path (from the source) is u, we write the value d time units after writing the value for u, where d is the weight of edge (u, v). And, we read the value written for the sink as soon as possible. We have assumed that executions of *Succ*, *read* and *write* do not consume any real time.

Second Solution. The previous solution does not quite implement the real-time algorithm described for the problem. In particular, the path lengths are explicitly passed as parameter values; a node does not consult the elapsed time to record the length of the shortest path to it.

To this end, we associate real-time timers with computations. In the current implementation of Orc, calling *RealTimer* site generates a new real-time timer and initializes its value to 0. Every generated timer runs in real time. Therefore, *Rtimer* measures the progress of every real-time timer. To evaluate f with timer rt, write $RealTimer \gg rt \gg f$. Also, for each such timer rt, there is a site $rt.C$ that returns the current time of rt. The current time of rt is 0 when rt is created.

The following version of the shortest path algorithm is a more faithful rendering of the initial description. We have replaced $eval1(u, t)$ with $eval2(u, rt)$, where t can be computed from timer rt.

$$eval2(u, rt) \;\; \underline{\Delta} \;\; rt.C() >t> write(u, t) \gg$$
$$Succ(u) >(v, d)> Rtimer(d) \gg eval2(v, rt)$$

$$RealTimer >rt> (eval2(source, rt) \mid read(sink))$$

Third Solution. The previous solution records a time value for each node, whereas our interest is only in the shortest path to the sink. Therefore, we may simplify the recording for the nodes. Instead of $write(u, t)$, we use $mark(u)$ which merely notes that a node has been reached by a ray of light. Similarly, instead of $read(u)$, we employ $scan(u)$ which responds with a signal if u has been marked. The length of the shortest path is the value of $rt.C()$ when the sink is marked.

$$eval3(u, rt) \;\; \underline{\Delta} \;\; mark(u) \gg Succ(u) >(v, d)> Rtimer(d) \gg eval3(v, rt)$$

$$RealTimer >rt> (eval3(source, rt) \mid scan(sink) \gg rt.C())$$

4.2   Logical or Virtual Timers

Each of the shortest path algorithms given in the previous section waits for real time intervals. The running time of each algorithm is proportional to the actual length of the shortest path. This is quite inefficient. Additionally, We have assumed that executions of *Succ*, *read* and *write* do not consume any real time, which is unrealistic. To overcome these problem, we explore the use of logical (virtual) timers to replace real-time timers.

There are three essential properties of real-time timers that we have used in the previous section. Let rt be a real-time timer, and, as before, $rt.C()$ returns the current value of this timer.

1. (Monotonicity) The values returned by successive calls to $rt.C()$ are non-decreasing.
2. (Relativity) Using a notation similar to Hoare-triples, where $rt.C()$ denotes the value returned by a call to $rt.C()$,

$$\{rt.C() = n\}\ Rtimer(t)\ \{rt.C() = n + t\}$$

3. (Weak Progress) Some call to $Rtimer(.)$ responds eventually.

Monotonicity guarantees that $s \leq t$ in $rt.C()\ >s>\ \cdots rt.C()\ >t>\ \cdots$. Relativity says that if $Rtimer(t)$ is called when a timer value is n, the response to the call is received at time $n + t$. This property establishes the essential relationship between $rt.C$ and $Rtimer$. The progress property is a weak one, merely postulating the passage of time. Typically, we need a Strong Progress property: *every* call to $Rtimer(t)$ responds eventually. However, it can not be met in arbitrary Orc programs where infinite number of events may take place within bounded time, as in the following examples.

$$Met()\ \underline{\Delta}\ \ Signal\ |\ Rtimer(0) \gg Met()$$
$$M()\ \underline{\Delta}\ \ N()\ |\ M()$$

It is the obligation of the programmer to ensure that only a finite number of events occur during any finite time interval. A sufficient condition is that every recursive call is preceded by a call $Rtimer(t)$, where t is a positive integer. Then we can guarantee the Strong Progress property.

A logical (or virtual) timer is generated by a call to site $VirtTimer()$. There are two site calls associated with a logical timer lt: $lt.C()$ and $lt.R(t)$. These calls are analogous to $rt.C()$ and $Rtimer(t)$ for real-time timers. Further, logical timers obey the requirements of Monotonicity, Relativity and Weak Progress, as for the real-time timers. They also obey the Strong Progress property under analogous assumptions. We show in Section 4.3 how logical timers may be implemented.

There is one key difference between real-time and virtual-time timers. For site M other than a timer site, no logical time is consumed between calling the site and receiving its response, whereas real time may be consumed. Conversely, no real time is consumed in any interval where logical time is consumed.

We can rewrite the solutions to the shortest path problem using logical timers. Below, we do so for the third solution in Section 4.1, using $VirtTimer()$ to generate a virtual timer.

$$eval4(u, lt)\ \underline{\Delta}\ \ mark(u) \gg Succ(u)\ >(v, d)>\ lt.R(d) \gg eval4(v, lt)$$

$$VirtTimer()\ >lt>\ (eval4(source, lt)\ |\ scan(sink) \gg lt.C())$$

Observe that $mark$, $scan$ and $Succ$ may consume real time, though they do not consume any logical time. Further, the actual computation time is now decoupled from the length of the shortest path. Dijkstra's shortest path algorithm [1] is a sequential simulation of this algorithm that includes an efficient implementation of the logical timer.

4.3   Implementing Logical Timer

Let lt be a logical timer. Associate a value n with lt. Initially (when lt is created) $n = 0$. A call to $lt.C()$ responds with n. Call $lt.R(t)$ is assigned a *rank* $n + t$ and queued (in a priority queue). Eventually, the timer responds with a signal for the item of the lowest rank r in the queue, if an item exists, and removes it from the queue. Simultaneously, it sets n to r.

It is easy to see that Monotonicity holds, that n never decreases: we have the invariant $n \leq s$, for any rank s in the queue, and that the latest response to $lt.C()$ is n. Similarly, Relativity is also easy to see. The requirement of Weak Progress is met by eventually removing an item from the queue. Further, if only a finite number of events occur in any bounded logical time interval, the Strong Progress property is also met.

Note that the specification of a timer only ensures that the timer's responses are properly ordered with respect to each other. The relationship between a timer's responses and the behavior of other sites (or timers) is unspecified. This gives us a great deal of flexibility in implementing timers.

4.4   Stopwatch

A *stopwatch* is a site that is aligned with some timer, real or virtual. We will see some of its uses in simulation in Section 5.

A stopwatch is in one of two states, *running* or *stopped*, at any moment. It supports 4 methods: (1) *reset*: is applicable when the stopwatch is stopped, and then its value is set to 0; (2) *read*: returns the current value of the stopwatch; (3) *start*: changes the state from stopped to running; and (4) *stop*: changes the state from running to stopped.

A stopwatch can be implemented by having the variables *running* (boolean) and m, n (integer). The current state is given by *running*. If $\neg running$ holds (i.e., the state is stopped), then m is the value of the stopwatch and n's value is irrelevant. If *running* holds, then m is the value of the stopwatch when it was last started, and n is the value of lt, the timer with which the stopwatch is aligned, when the stopwatch was last started. Initially, *running* is *false* and both m and n are zero. The methods are implemented (in imperative-style) as follows.

$reset$: $m := 0$
$read$: **if** *running* **then** $\text{return}(m + lt.C() - n)$ **else** $\text{return}(m)$
$start$: *running* := *true*; $n := lt.C()$
$stop$: *running* := *false*; $m := m + lt.C() - n$

Note: Only the *read* method responds to its caller. The other methods do not respond, though they update the internal state of the stopwatch.

5 Simulation

The work reported in this section is at a preliminary stage.

A *simulation* is an abstraction of real-world processes. The goal of simulation is to observe the behaviors of the abstract processes, and compute statistics. A faithful simulation can predict the behavior of the real-world processes being simulated. A simulation language supports descriptions of the real-world processes, their interactions and the passage of real time. We contend that Orc is an effective tool for writing simulations. We can describe the individual processes as expressions in Orc. As we have demonstrated with the shortest path example in Section 4, replacing real-time timer with a logical timer can efficiently simulate the passage of time while maintaining the expected causal order among events.

Orc also simplifies data collection and statistics computation of the simulated processes because of its structured approach to concurrency. Since the lexical structure of the program reflects the dynamic structure of the computation, it is easy to identify points in the program at which to add observations and measurements. In an unstructured model of concurrency, this can be a more challenging task.

We show two small examples of simulation in Orc in this section. The examples, though small, are typical of realistic simulations. We consider data collection in the following section.

5.1 Example: Serving Customers in a Bank

Consider a bank that has two tellers to serve customers. A stream of customers arrive at the bank according to some arrival distribution. Each customer joins a queue on entering the bank. A teller asks the next customer to step forward whenever she is free. The service time for a customer is determined by the type of transaction. It is required to determine the average wait time for a customer, the queue length distribution, and the percentage of time that a teller is idle. In this section, we merely represent the system using Orc; computation of statistics is covered in the following section.

We represent the bank as consisting of three concurrent activities, customers and two tellers. We define each of these activities by an expression. Customers are generated as a stream by expression *Source* according to some given distribution. This expression also specifies the service time of each customer. We do not code *Source* though a complete simulation would have to include it.

The goal expression, given at the top of Figure 3, starts a logical timer *lt*, runs expression *Bank* for *simtime* logical time units (using the time-out paradigm), and then publishes the statistics by calling *Stats*(). Observe that expression *Bank*() does not publish, which is ensured by sequential composition with **0**, permitting us to use the time-out paradigm.

The Orc definitions have mostly described a physical system; therefore it is extremely succinct. The description is modular, which allows for experimentation with a variety of policies (e.g., assigning one teller to handle short jobs, for

$$VirtTimer() >lt>$$
$$(z <z< Bank(lt) \mid lt.R(simtime)) \gg$$
$$Stats()$$

$$Bank(lt) \quad \triangle \quad (Customers() \mid Teller(lt) \mid Teller(lt)) \gg 0$$
$$Customers() \quad \triangle \quad Source() >c> enter(c)$$
$$Teller(lt) \quad \triangle \quad next() >c>$$
$$lt.R(c.ServTime) \gg$$
$$Teller(lt)$$
$$enter(c) \quad \triangle \quad q.put(c)$$
$$next() \quad \triangle \quad q.get()$$

Fig. 3. Bank simulation

instance) and different mixes of system parameters (e.g., hiring more tellers). Further, there is no explicit mention of simulation in the definitions, only in the goal expression. Advancing of the logical timer will be automatically handled by the implementation.

5.2 Example: Serving Customers in a Fast Food Restaurant

The next example, serving customers in a fast food restaurant, is similar to that of the bank, though there are key differences. As in the bank example, we have a steady stream of customers entering a queue, and we have a single cashier in place of tellers. Rather than servicing customers' orders directly, the cashier processes the orders and puts them in another queue to be handled by one of the

$$VirtTimer() >lt>$$
$$(z <z< Restaurant(lt) \mid lt.R(simtime)) \gg$$
$$Stats()$$

$$Restaurant(lt) \quad \triangle \quad (Customers() \mid Cashier(lt) \mid Cook(lt) \mid Cook(lt)) \gg 0$$
$$Customers() \quad \triangle \quad Source() >c> enter(c)$$
$$Cashier(lt) \quad \triangle \quad next() >c>$$
$$lt.R(c.ringupTime) \gg$$
$$orders.put(c.order) \gg$$
$$Cashier(lt)$$
$$Cook(lt) \quad \triangle \quad orders.get() >order>$$
$$($$
$$(e,s,d)$$
$$<e< prepTime(order.entree) >t> lt.R(t)$$
$$<s< prepTime(order.side) \quad >t> lt.R(t)$$
$$<d< prepTime(order.drink) >t> lt.R(t)$$
$$) \gg$$
$$Cook(lt)$$
$$enter(c) \quad \triangle \quad q.put(c)$$
$$next() \quad \triangle \quad q.get()$$

Fig. 4. Fast food restaurant simulation

two cooking stations. Cooking stations prepare the main entree, side dish and the drink parts of an order in parallel, where each part takes some amount of time to complete. An order is complete only after all its parts have been completed. Unlike the bank example where each customer carried its service time with it, we let the restaurant decide the service time for each customer c, by calling $ringupTime(c)$ to determine the cashier's time, and $prepTime(c.drink)$ for the time required to prepare the drink order for c (and, similarly, for the other parts of the order).

Figure 4 describes the simulation of the restaurant for $simtime$ logical time units. Note that $Cook$ uses the fork-join strategy discussed in Section 3 (we have abbreviated a cooking station by $Cook$). Both q and $orders$ are FIFO channels which we use for our queues. Analogous to $enter(c)$ and $next()$, we could have entered and removed orders indirectly in queue $orders$ rather than directly as we do in Figure 4.

6   Measurement

The typical purpose of simulation is to measure the behaviors exhibited by the simulated processes. These measurements are especially useful when they incorporate information about the passage of time in the simulation, such as the total amount of time that a participant remained idle or the average delay experienced by some process waiting on another process.

The current time associated with logical timer lt is $lt.C$. We use this value to report the times at which certain events occur in the simulation. We also use differences between observed times to determine the duration of some activity.

Consider a fragment of the bank example, where we are adding customers to the queue and later removing them:

$$enter(c) \quad \triangleq \quad q.put(c)$$
$$next() \quad \triangleq \quad q.get()$$

We augment this part of the simulation with measurements to determine the amount of time each customer spends waiting in line. We report the waiting time with the site $reportWait$.

$$enter(c) \quad \triangleq \quad lt.C >s> q.put(c, s)$$
$$next() \quad \triangleq \quad q.get() >(c, t)>$$
$$lt.C >s>$$
$$reportWait(s - t) \gg$$
$$c$$

Histogram. We can also compute histograms or queue length distribution, as follows. Let t_i, where $0 \leq i < N$, be the duration during simulation for which the length of q has been i. We create $N + 1$ stopwatches, $sw[0..N]$, at the beginning of simulation. The final value of $sw[i]$, $0 \leq i < N$, is t_i. And, $sw[N]$ is the duration for which the queue length is at least N.

Now, modify $enter(c)$ and $next()$ to ensure that whenever the queue length is i, $0 \leq i < N$, $sw[i]$ is running and all other stopwatches are stopped (similarly for $sw[N]$). Therefore, initially, only $sw[0]$ is running. Whenever a new item is added to a queue of length i, $0 \leq i < N$, we stop $sw[i]$ and start $sw[i+1]$; for $i = N$, nothing needs to be done. Similarly, after removing an item if the queue length is i, $0 \leq i < N$, we start $sw[i]$ and stop $sw[i+1]$.

The modifications to $enter(c)$ and $next()$ are shown below. Assume $q.length$ returns the current length of q. Note that the code fragment
$q.length >i> if(i < N) \gg (sw[i].stop \mid sw[i+1].start)$
does not publish.

$$
\begin{aligned}
enter(c) \quad &\Delta \quad lt.C >s> q.put(c,s) \gg \\
&\quad q.length >i> if(i < N) \gg (sw[i].stop \mid sw[i+1].start) \\
next() \quad &\Delta \quad q.get() >(c,s)> \\
&\quad (\; lt.C >t> reportWait(s-t) \gg c \\
&\quad \mid q.length >i> if(i < N) \gg (sw[i].start \mid sw[i+1].stop) \\
&\quad)
\end{aligned}
$$

7 Summary and Conclusions

This paper reports some preliminary work on coding simulations in Orc. Orc supports descriptions of concurrent activities and real time, which make it possible to describe many physical systems. We have introduced logical timers in this paper to facilitate computations that do not need to synchronize with the wall clock. We have described some of the properties of logical timers and shown their use in solving a combinatorial problem (shortest path) as well as in coding simulations.

Orc cannot succinctly express certain simulations because it does not have the fundamental notion of *guarded choice*, as found in the π-calculus [2] and other concurrent calculi. For example, a *Teller* that watches two queues and takes a customer whenever either queue becomes non-empty is difficult to code without such a choice combinator. The addition of guarded choice to Orc is a topic of ongoing research.

References

1. Dijkstra, E.: A note on two problems in connection with graphs. Numerische Mathematik 1, 83–89 (1959)
2. Milner, R.: Communicating and Mobile Systems: the π-Calculus. Cambridge University Press, Cambridge (1999)
3. Misra, J., Cook, W.R.: Computation orchestration: A basis for wide-area computing. Journal of Software and Systems Modeling (May 2006), http://dx.doi.org/10.1007/s10270-006-0012-1
4. Wehrman, I., Kitchin, D., Cook, W.R., Misra, J.: A timed semantics of orc. Theoretical Computer Science (to appear, 2008)

Liberate Computer User from Programming

Teodor Rus[*]

Department of Computer Science
The University of Iowa, Iowa City, IA, USA

Abstract. This paper is about computer-based problem solving methodology. The issue addressed is: *can we develop a computer-based problem-
solving methodology which is not based on computer programming?* The
answer we provide to this question is YES. This raises the next question:
*if we do not use programming how do we communicate problem solving
algorithms to the computer?* The answer to this question is: (1) develop
software tools that support domain algorithm execution in the problem
domain environment (no programming as usual) and (2) allow problem-
domain experts to express their problem-solving algorithms using the
natural language of their problem domains. We achieve this computer-
based problem solving methodology by computational emancipation of
the application domain, which consists of:

1. Characterize the application domain in terms of concepts that are
   universal in the domain, have standalone computing meaning, and
   are composable.
2. Structure the application domain using an ontology where terms denoting domain characteristic concepts are associated with computer
   artifacts implementing them.
3. Develop a domain-dedicated virtual machine that executes domain
   algorithms expressed in the natural language of the domain (without asking to encode them into programs) and implement it on the
   physical computers existent in the computer-network.

With this methodology computers execute algorithms whose expressions
are conceptual, similar to the way human brain would execute them.

1   Introduction

The computer is a wonderful problem-solving tool that performs computations
faster and more reliably than the human brain. But in the end the computer
is just a tool that can help people solve problems providing that they learn
how to use it. The biggest hurdle people face when using computers to solve
their problems is determined by the current computer-based problem solving
methodology which requires the computer user to perform the following two
steps:

[*] I acknowledge Donald Curtis and Cuong Bui contributions to the research reported
in this paper.

J. Meseguer and G. Roşu (Eds.): AMAST 2008, LNCS 5140, pp. 16–35, 2008.

1. Develop a conceptual model of the problem and its solution algorithm[1].
2. Map the solution algorithm into a program in computer memory.

Program execution is then carried out by the computer. For the purpose of this paper the computer can be seen as a tuple $\langle PC, Execute(), Next() \rangle$ where:

- PC is a program counter register that points to the memory location holding the operation to be executed;
- Execute() is the wired action carried out by the machine while performing the operation shown by PC;
- Next() is the wired action that uses the current instruction to select the next instruction to be executed by the computer.

The process by which machine instructions are carried out by the computer while executing a program is further referred to as the program execution loop (PEL):

```
PC = First(Instruction);
while(not halt){Execute(PC); PC = Next(PC);}
```

Irrespective of its level of abstraction a program represents sequence of machine instructions and data encoded as bits and bytes that are further referred to as "machine computation". On the other hand the conceptual model and the solution algorithm represent concepts, i.e., problem domain abstractions fabricated by people's mind. Because the essence of programming is program creation and the essence of problem solving is conceptual modeling, the difference between programming and problem solving, further referred to as the *semantic gap*, is irreconcilable. It is the cause of the difficulties encountered by computer user with current computer-based problem solving methodology. Depending upon computer user expertise, computer programming can be a nightmare (for a non expert) or a delight (for computer experts). Computer technology was developed as software tools to support program development (using high-level notations of machine computations) and to control program execution (handling computer resources required by PEL and treating events that may occur during PEL). Success stories of computer use for solving difficult problems in all aspects of human life have led to an explosion of computer technology. Following the *cognition-process spiral* we observe that *computer technology increases the human cognition power which in turn increases the demand for more computer technology*. The consequences are many. Two of these consequences are: (a) complexity of software tools increases with the number and the diversity of problem domains using the computer, and (b) difficulty of computer use increases with software complexity. We use these consequences here to motivate the issues addressed by this paper.

1.1 Using Computers without Programming

The effort of developing a computer-based problem solving methodology that is not programming-based is justified by the observation that software tools meant to make programming easier are programs. A computer user who is not a computer

---

[1] We use here the term algorithm with an intuitive well-defined meaning, which may depend upon the problem domain.

expert may have the same kind of difficulties in using such tools as she would have with program development in the first place. In addition, looking at other technologies we may observe that, in general, they do not require their users to be their experts. A tractor driver needs not be a tractor designer. Software tools are aimed at making programming easier for programmers who are computer experts (sometimes referred to as IT experts). But current computer technology is ubiquitously used in all aspects of human life by people who are not programmers. Therefore, to set the standard of computer use to the same requirements as other technologies, computer technology needs to drop the requirement of using computers by programming. We need to allow a computer user to interact with her computer using her natural language. We claim that this interaction is feasible with the computer technology of today by making the computer↔user communication language be the *natural language of the user's problem domain.*

The difficulties encountered with natural language processing are alleviated by appropriate structuring of problem domains. The model of this structuring is provided by the scripting languages (such as job control languages and shells) that are used by computer experts while they interact with their problem domain, which happens to be software development. The unit of action in these languages is a command which tells the language interpreter to locate some previously developed program and to execute it on given parameters. For computer experts these programs implement software tools. For application domain (AD) experts these programs may implement AD concepts, and may be previously developed by expert programmers. Such programs can be executed by the interpretation of natural language terms associated with them, similar to scripting language command interpretation. This association can be set as the basis for bridging the semantic gap. A fragment of natural language developed on top of the terms denoting these concepts used as lexicon becomes the Natural Language of the Domain (NLD) to be used by AD experts to represent problem models and solution algorithms. Note that NLDs developed on this scheme are fragments of natural language dedicated to computer application domains. In this paper we show how to identify and structure the characteristic knowledge of an AD such that their terms to become the vocabulary of its NLD, and how to execute the domain algorithms in the domain, without programming them. The software tools we need to develop in order to support this manner of computer usage provide a breakthrough in computer technology which open a huge market for Application Driven Software (ADS) development.

1.2   Handling Software Complexity

The cognition-process spiral justifies the increasing demand to develop new software tools and to integrate them within the software tools previously developed. The resulting software complexity makes current computer-based problem solving a nightmare even for computer experts and has reached a level at which it threatens to *kill the information technology* [Kri], [IBM02]. Current computer technology solutions to the problems raised by increasing software complexity are based on the development of new and even more complex software tools, thus creating more software complexity.

Addressing the issue of *software tool complexity* we observe that current computer-based problem solving methodology makes no distinction between various problem domains. Yet experts of different problem domains may use different mechanisms for the development of their problem models and algorithms. The integration of this continuously increasing diversity of problem domains and solution algorithms within the current "one-size-fits-all" problem solving pattern of computer program generation is the main source of software complexity. The solution to the problem raised by software complexity is to remove the source of complexity. This means that we need to develop a computer-based problem-solving methodology where each problem domain may have its own computer-based problem solving pattern which can grow with the domain. That is, we actually want to follow the principle of adapting the computer to the problem domain rather than adapting the problem domain to the computer. This cannot be carried by problem domain expert or by computer expert independent of each other. This requires a cooperation along the following lines:

1. Problem domain expert characterizes her application domain in terms of well-defined concepts that have computational meaning and (a) are universal over the problem domain, (b) are standalone, and (c) are composable. This allows her to outsource the problem of creating computer artifacts (including programs) to the computer expert.
2. Computer expert develops implementations of the concepts that characterize the AD and broadcasts them to the domain using appropriate URIs [BL98].
3. Problem domain expert and computer expert structure the application domain using an application domain ontology [SS04] where concepts are associated with the URIs of the computer artifacts implementing them.

The process of computer-based problem solving may be further shared between domain expert and computer expert by the following protocol:

- The AD expert collaborates with the computer expert to create the NLD to be used for problem modeling and algorithm development. We discuss this language in Section 2.3 of the paper.
- Computer expert creates a domain-dedicated virtual machine that can execute domain algorithms in the AD environment. This is discussed in Section 2.4 of the paper.
- AD expert and computer expert collaborate to create the software tools that optimize and automate the problem solving process. These are creativity support tools [Shn07] that allow NLD evolution with the domain ontology. Some of these tools are discussed in Section 3.

1.3 Related Work

The entire research on programming is actually dedicated to making programming easier and is consequently related to our work. Therefore we need to be very specific in identifying the differences we make. For that we start with the observation that programming per say is not a goal, it is a mean to achieve the goal. The goal is problem solving. Of course, program creation is by itself a problem to solve and thus a goal which has a special place in the hierarchy of goals called *computer-based problem solving process*. The link which binds together the entire research on making programming easier is the process of *raising the level of abstraction of program notation to match the programmer interest and the problem to solve*. The raising of the abstraction level led from machine code to assembly, Fortran, Cobol, and further to Object Oriented. The matching of programmer interest to problem to solve led to Fortran for easy evaluation of numerical formulas, to Cobol for easy data manipulation, to Object Orientation to increase programming productivity, and further to today's DSL [MJS05]. Many of these accomplishments have been achieved by "liberating programming from various straitjackets" [Har08, Bac78, Apt96, Sim95] which suggested the title of this paper. In all these papers programming is "liberated". That is, in order to use the computer, the computer user is still required to program her problem solving algorithm. Since the goal is problem solving using computers the real problem is actually the computer user's liberation from programming.

Our main contribution is then the development of abstractions that liberate computer user from programming. This means that we advocate the creation of languages dedicated to problem solving not to program development. Of course, if the problem to solve is program development then the language we advocate is dedicated to program development. Since different problem domains may use different mechanisms for modeling their problem solving process, first we create the framework that allows computer user to employ her problem domain specific language while developing problem models and solution algorithms. To ensure the viability of this language we develop tools that make it coincide with the natural language used by a large class of domain experts during problem solving process. Finally, to eliminate programming requirement from computer use we create software tools that support the NLD algorithm development and execution in the problem domain. With the research we reported in [RC07, CR08] we have shown how can this methodology be used in linear algebra and chemistry. If the special train set in [SC98] is seen as a domain ontology, then we have another example of NLD use to *make programming easier for children*. The contribution of this paper is the development of the framework that shows that we can achieve the dream of using computers without programming with current computer technology for any *computationally emancipated application domain*.

Similar accomplishments are Microsoft tabletop systems, IBM Business Process Execution Language[ACD+], Mathematica, Language Oriented Programming [War94], Meta Programming System [Dim], etc. The difference is that in all these applications the goal is *easy computer program generation*. There may be other similar achievements which we are not aware of.

2   Computational Emancipation of Application Domains

The problem solving paradigm we discuss here relies on deep understanding of the problem domain. This is accomplished by computational emancipation of the application domain (CEAD) which is a dynamic process that consist of:

1. Identifying domain characteristic concepts whose computational meaning is: (a) universal in the domain, (b) standalone, and (c) composable.
2. Organizing domain characteristic concepts identified at (1) using a domain ontology [NM] which evolves with the domain knowledge evolution.
3. Developing a notation to be used by the domain expert to express problem models and solution algorithms and allow domain algorithm execution in the domain environment.

2.1   Domain Characteristic Concepts

Domain characteristic concepts represent domain perennial knowledge that characterize domain cognition process. Usually these concepts belong to the natural language and are taken as granted by all domain experts. For computational emancipation of the application domain they need to be explicitly identified and organized using an appropriate domain ontology [GO94, GMJE05] because: (a) they form the vocabulary of the NLD, (b) they are associated with computer artifacts implementing them thus providing the mechanism to bridge the semantic gap, and (c) their computation meanings are composed during the problem solving process generating new characteristic concepts of the domain, thus ensuring ontology evolution in sync with the domain's cognition process. The collection of terms used in the domain ontology to denote domain characteristic concepts is also enriched with computer-technology terms whose usage transcended from programming languages to natural language, preserving their meanings, and thus achieving the goal of the *computational thinking process* [Win06, TW07].

The meaning of the terms used in the domain ontology is informally specified as the *domain abstractions which domain experts denote by these terms*. Formally, these terms represent domain concepts that have a computational meaning which is: universal in the domain, standalone, and composable. For example, in high-school algebra, integer addition, denoted $+ : I \times I \to I$, is:

1. universal over the set I of integer numbers because $n_1 + n_2 \in I$ for any $n_1, n_2 \in I$,
2. standalone because the computation of the number $n_1 + n_2$ depends only of the numbers n_1, n_2,
3. composable because it can be composed with other operations, that is, $\forall n_1, n_2, n_3 \in I$, $(n_1 + n_2) + n_3 \in I$, that is, $+$ is the same operation, regardless of how do we define its arguments.

These kind of abstractions are well-known in mathematics but their properties are not always preserved in programming languages. For example, a standard library of a given programming language (PL) contains functions denoting computations that may be universal with respect to PL, but usually are not standalone because they can be used only in the context of a valid program of the PL, and are composable only through the composition rules defined by the PL. Hence, these abstractions do not characterize the domain; they characterize the machine-computations that implement the AD abstractions.

2.2 Domain Ontology

A domain ontology is a repository of information which plays a double role during the problem solving process. On the one hand it allows the domain expert to consistently use her knowledge for problem modeling and algorithm development. On the other hand it provides the framework used by the virtual machine that executes domain algorithms in the domain environment. Current approaches for knowledge representation and structuring for semantic web development [McB04] use a graph-representation for domain ontology structuring. Due to the dynamic of problem solving process, evolving as problem domains and sub-domains, it is important that domain ontology representation to capture the topological nature of knowledge evolution. In other words, the dynamic of problem solving process is characterized by non-metric information, captured by the topological notion of connectedness, rather than by shape, location, distance, size, etc. Therefore we suggest domain ontology representation by *higraphs* [Har88], whose nodes are *blobs*. Following higraph definition each blob is regarded as denoting a *certain kind of set of knowledge* provided with a nesting relationship that represent *set inclusion*, not set membership. Blobs are represented in the higraph by closed curves labeled by the terms used to denote the concept they represent. If there is no need to distinguish between a blob and its sub-blobs (as will be the case in the example below) then we my simple use the term denoting the concept as the blob representation of the node rather than using any geometric figure.

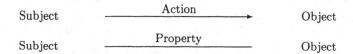

Fig. 1. The unit of action on a domain-ontology

The nodes of the domain ontology higraph represent data concepts and are labeled by the terms used in natural language to designate these concepts. The edges of the domain ontology higraph represent property and action concepts and are labeled by the terms used in natural language to designate the properties and the actions they represent. Here we distinguish between the two kind of edges in a domain ontology graph: line-edges which represent properties of data concepts and arrow-edges which represent actions that input data objects of the type represented by the term that sits at the source of the arrow and output data objects of the type represented by the term that sits at the top of the arrow. Labels on the line-edges are natural language terms that represent concepts denoting properties and labels on the arrow-edges are natural language terms denoting concepts that represent the actions performed by the edge. The unit of action problem solver manipulates during problem solving process is expressible through a simple-phrase that has the structure ⟨*Subject, Property/Action, Object*⟩ and is represented in the domain ontology higraph as shown in Figure 1.

Here we illustrate the concept of a domain ontology with a sub-domain of the natural language processing. Figure 2 shows the domain ontology of a subset of the natural language processing domain that deals with the problem known as the *recognizing textual entailment* [BM05], further referenced as the RTE problem. RTE problem is stated as follows: *Given two text phrases, T and H, and a knowledge database such as* WORD-NET, *develop an algorithm that decides whether T implies H or not.*

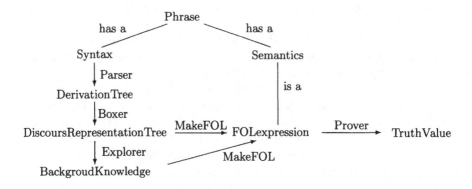

Fig. 2. Example domain-ontology

The terms Phrase, Syntax, Semantics, DerivationTree, DiscoursRepresentationTree, BackgroudKnowledge, TruthValue, used in the ontology in Figure 2 to represent data concepts, are all universal in natural language processing because they denote mathematically well-defined abstractions and all natural language experts may use them with the same meaning. The concepts Parser, Boxer, Explorer (knowledge explorer) and MakeFOL (make First Order Language expression) represent computational actions used in natural language processing which are universal (i.e., perform the same functions in all aspects of natural language processing) and standalone because the behavior they represent depends only on the arguments they take in order to perform their tasks. Further, they are composable because the computations they perform can be composed with one another according to their input/output behavior patterns, thus defining larger computations that represent valid concepts in the natural language of the domain. For example, Parser, Boxer, Explorer, and Prover (theorem prover) can be composed to form a Textual Entailment Recognizer. Note, in this ontology the concept represented by the term *Prover* represents a theorem prover, it is universal, standalone, and composable because in the RTE problem its meaning is a computation that for any logical expression of the form $T \to H$ it returns the truth-value of the logical implication $T \to H$.

For any domain, the domain ontology is ever-expanding, that is, it is built up "interactively and inter-subjectively" by the language used to communicate between domain experts based on their "commonsense" ontology [Bat93]. New terms of the language come from the interaction between domain experts during their communication process, from the interaction between domain experts and their domain ontology during problem solving process, and by inheritance from other domains. For example, the RTE domain contains the terms: *Phrase, Derivation-Tree, DiscourseRepresentationStructure* which denote concepts created in the RTE domain, while the term *Prover* is inherited from mathematical logic. Other terms (not shown in the domain ontology) such as *assignment* and *variable* are inherited from computer technology and mathematics. Usually the terms inherited by a domain from another domain may already exists in the domain that inherits them with a different semantics. Here we assume that terms in NLD inherited from computer technology (through computational thinking process) are used in the NLD with the meaning they have in the computer technology. In addition, we assume that the domain expert, during problem solving process, may create new terms as she needs them for the development of problem model and solution algorithm.

2.3   Natural Language of the Application Domain

Domain experts use NLD to express their ideas. To automate NLD processing domain experts still need to learn some syntax in order to express their ideas. This is easy because they use *the syntax of their natural language.* The meaning of their communication is specified by the domain ontology and therefore the semantics of NLD is dynamic and is totally controlled by the domain experts. During problem solving process the domain experts also use the NLD to communicate with the domain experts of other domains, such as computer technology experts, whose NLDs are programming languages. How can this interaction be performed without asking AD experts to learn PL or IT experts to learn NLD? The answer to this question is provided by the process of bridging the semantic gap performed by AD and IT experts through computational emancipation of the application domains. Since domain concepts are universal over the domain, are standalone, and are composable, they are implemented by the IT experts on computer platforms of choice and are associated with the terms of the ontology using URI-s. This allows domain experts and computer experts to bridge the semantic gap between natural language and computer language. Examples of such implementations would be libraries of functions that are universal (i.e., could be called from any programming environment), are standalone (i.e., their execution would depend only on their arguments), and are composable (i.e., they could be freely composed with other such functions). We believe that current function-libraries developed for given programming language environments could be easily transformed into functions satisfying these properties. The consequence is that with a CEAD-ed domain, the domain experts can communicate among them and with the IT experts using the terms of the ontology because the communication gap is bridged by the URI of the computer-artifacts associated with the NLD terms in the domain ontology.

To keep NLD simple, the above informal discussion can be formalized by the following three layers of NLD specification: vocabulary, simple phrase, and phrase.

1. **Vocabulary:** the vocabulary (or lexicon) of the NLD is a finite set of terms $V_D \cup A_D$, where V_D is the set of terms used to denote concepts in the domain

ontology and A_D is the set of terms inherited from IT or invented by domain expert to express *actions/properties* used to develop problem models and solution algorithms. For example, the term *assignment* (symbol :=) is used to express the process that evaluates a domain concept and gives the result as the value to a domain variable (unknown). Consistency of this use is ensured by the relationships provided by the domain ontology. For example, the simple phrase *"Parse Phrase: Y giving DerivationTree: X"* can be naturally expressed by *"DerivationTree X := Parser(Phrase Y)"*. Every term of the vocabulary is associated with three properties: arity, signature, and types:.

- The arity of a terms t shows the number of arguments t takes in order to express an action or a property.
- The signature of a term t shows the order and the type of the arguments t takes in order to express an action or a property.
- The type of a term t is the type of the concept created by the action/property t performs.

Note that if t is a term in the vocabulary and its arity is 0 (zero) then it represents a concept in the ontology and the action or property it expresses is well defined by the URI associated with it.

2. **Simple phrase:** a simple phrase of NLD is any action or property specified by a sequence $t_0 t_1 \ldots t_k$ where $arity(t_0) = k$, $sig(t_0) = t_1, t_2, \ldots, t_k$, and the $type(t_0 \ t_1 \ldots t_k) = type(t_0)$. Here the term t_0 represents the action/property and may be freely distributed over its arguments as is the case of $if \ then \ else$ inherited from PLs, or of the parentheses inherited from mathematics. Semantically a simple phrase represents a unit of action employed by the domain expert to denote a step of her solution algorithm. For example, $v := n_1 + n_2$ denotes the action of adding two numbers and giving the result as the value to the variable v.

3. **Phrase:** a phrase in NLD is either a simple phrase or an action $t_0 \ t_1 \ldots t_k$ where $arity(t_0) = k$, $k \geq 1$, and $t_1, \ldots, t_k$ are phrases. Semantically a phrase is a composed action. That is, a phrase represents a solution algorithm.

The BNF syntax of the NLD language whose semantics is specified above follows:

```
S = "AlgName:" [I";"][O";"] ActionList
I = "Input:" DL
O = "Output:"DL
DL= D | D "," DL
D = "ConceptType" VarList
VarList = Var | Var "," VarList
ActionList = Action | Action "compose" ActionList
Action = "Perform:" PhraseList
PhraseList = Phrase | Phrase ";" PhraseList
Phrase = Concept | Concept ArgList | "itOperator" Phrase
ArgList = "("Arg")" | "("Arg "," ArgList")"
Arg = Phrase | Concept
Var = "usersId"
Concept = "noun" | "verb"
```

where terminals are in quotes and nonterminals are capitalized.

The RTEdecider algorithm that solves RTE problem has the following expression in the NLD of the RTE domain:

```
RTEdecider:
   Input: T, H : Phrase;
   Output: Result: Phrase;
   Perform
      treeT = Parser(T); treeH = Parser(H);
      drsT  = Boxer(treeT); drsH = Boxer(treeH);
      bk    = Explorer (drsT,drsH);
      ET =  MakeFOL(drsT); EH = MakeFOL(drsH);
      Result = Prover((bk and ET) implies EH))
```

To emphasize the simplicity of this version of natural language processing we show below the derivation of RTEdecider from the BNF rules specifying its languages syntax:

```
S ---> RTEdecider: I; O; ActionList
  ---> Input: T, H : Phrase; O; ActionList
  ---> Input: T, H : Phrase;
        Output: Result: Phrase; ActionList
  ---> Input: T, H : Phrase;
        Output: Result: Phrase;
        Perform PhraseList
 --->* Input: T, H : Phrase;
        Output Result: Phrase;
        Perform
            treeT  = Parser(T); treeH = Parser(H);
            drsT   = Boxer(treeT); drsH = Boxer(treeH);
            bk     = Explorer (drsT,drsH);
            ET     =  MakeFOL(drsT); EH = MakeFOL(drsH);
            Result = Prover((bk and ET) implies EH))
```

A natural language expert can read and understand this algorithm without any other explanation because the concepts used are those in the domain ontology. Moreover, the domain expert understands the computation performed by the NLD algorithms without thinking at the machine that may execute them because each of the concepts used in the NLD algorithms has a well-defined meaning for her at her natural language level. The computations expressed by these algorithms are conceptually carried out by the domain expert handling them. In other words, in order to execute these algorithms the domain expert rely only on her domain knowledge. To carry out these computations she may use the virtual machine dedicated to her problem domain, as we will explain in Section 2.4, but she does not need to know where and how this computation is physically done.

2.4   Executing Natural Language Algorithms

Natural language algorithms are executed by a Domain Dedicated Virtual Machine (DDVM). This machine is virtual because its instructions perform actions associated with the concepts in the domain ontology in a similar way in which a Virtual Machine Monitor (VMM)[PG74] performs privileged operations of a real computer platform. DDVM is dedicated to the domain because the only operations it can execute are those defined in the domain ontology. In the hands of a domain expert, this machine behaves as a very large pocket-calculator provided with a picture of a domain ontology on which the user can select and press keys according to the actions she wants to execute. As with any pocket-calculator, the user identifies the function she needs using the term written on the key-board (which happens to be a term in the domain ontology). The user doesn't care who and how is actually performing that function, exactly as she doesn't really care who and how performs an arithmetic function of the pocket-calculator when she uses one. Instead of being a universal abstract state machine[Gur00] meant to define the concept of an algorithm, DDVM is a pragmatic machine, dedicated to the domain, and different ADs are usually provided with different DDVMs.

For the purpose of this paper a DDVM is an abstraction that consists of: a *Concept Counter* (CC), an *Abstract Processor* (AP), and a mechanism called *Next()*. Given a CEAD-ed domain ontology (DO) the DDVM(DO) performs as follows:

1. CC points to a concept in the DO.
2. AP executes the computation associated with the $CC(DO)$, if any.
3. Next(CC) determines the next concept of the DO to be performed.

To underline the similarity of DDVM with a universal computer described by the PEL-loop in Section 1, we denote the behavior of the DDVM(DO) by Domain Execution Loop (DEL) and describe it by the following pseudo-code:

```
CC = StartConcept(DO);
while(CC not END){Execute(AP,CC); CC = Next(CC);}
```

The DEL we describe mimics the behavior of the PEL-loop performed by real computers, but there are major differences. The concept counter (CC) of the DEL-loop is similar to the program counter (PC) of the PEL-loop in that it keeps track of what is to be performed. But rather than pointing to memory containing machine instructions, CC points to concepts on the emancipated domain ontology. Additionally, the concept pointed to by CC is evaluated by the abstract processor that performs the action Execute(AP,CC). By computational emancipation of the application domain, the concept shown by CC in the ontology may be associated with a standalone computer artifact identified by an URI. In this case Execute(AP,CC) creates a computer process and instructs it to execute that computer artifact. Thus, Execute(AP,CC) is *not* carrying out machine instructions. Machine instructions involved in this computation, if any, are performed by the computer process generated by Execute(AP,CC). Hence, from a domain expert viewpoint Execute(AP,CC) is actually a computational process performed by the brain, with or without the assistance of a real computer platform. The Next() component of the virtual machine is responsible for selecting the next component to be executed by the virtual machine. This is similar to the Next() function performed by PEL. Exactly as in the case of a real computer, we make the assumption that the next-operation performed by DDVM is *encoded in its current operation*. Consequently, an NLD algorithm is executed by DEL walking on the domain ontology in a similar way a program is executed by PEL walking the memory of a real computer.

For an AD expert to solve a problem without programming she follows a four step approach similar to Polya's [Pol73] four steps methodology:

1. Formulate the problem;
2. Develop a domain algorithm that solves the problem;
3. Type the algorithm, i.e., input the algorithm in the computer;
4. Execute the algorithm by a command that sets CC to the first concept to be evaluated by the DDVM while performing the algorithm.

To demonstrate this approach of problem solving we consider the example of high-school algebra. Suppose that the following assignment is given by the teacher: *students, develop an algorithm to solve the quadratic equation* $ax^2 + bx + c = 0$, *where* a, b, c *are real numbers and* $a \neq 0$, *and then apply your algorithm for the case of* $a = 1, b = 4, c = 4$.

1. The problem is formalized as a formal equality $ax^2 + bx + c = 0$ in the language of high-school algebra.
2. Using the properties of equality the students develop the solution: $x_{1,2} = \frac{-b + | - \sqrt{b^2 - 4*a*c}}{2*a}$. Now the students organize computations to be performed by $DDVM(HighSchoolAlgebra)$ as the following high-school algebra algorithm:

```
Solver:
  Input real a, b, c where a not zero;
  Output: real x1, x2; Local real t;
  t := b^2 - 4*a*c;
  if t >= 0 then
    x1 := (-b + sqrt(t))/2*a; x2 := (-b - sqrt(t))/2*a;
  else no real solutions
```

3. Input the algorithm (as a text) in their computers.
4. Initiate the algorithm by typing Start Solver.

The solution is obtained using a computer/user dialog where computer prompts the student using usual terms of high-school algebra. Assuming that the computer prompt is % this dialog could be:

```
%Enter a (student types 1)
%Enter b (student types 4)
%Enter c (student types 4)
```

In few fractions of second the computer prints: % Solution: x1 = -2, x2 = -2.

There are a few key things to note. The first is that we initiate the virtual machine by giving it the component of the domain algorithm to start the computation. In example above this is done by telling the DDVM to perform "Solver". The concepts used in the domain algorithm, such as $+, -,$ ' $sqrt$ are associated with computer artifacts implementing them on a real computer. The other concepts, such as Let, if, else, :=, in, out, etc., are terms inherited from computer technology in the language of high-school algebra. Students use them because they belong to their natural language and DDVM understand them by the software supporting this problem solving methodology.

As computer scientists the concepts used in this example are *trivial* because they are also computer operations. But there is a very clear distinction between the two. The algebraic concepts used in the above solution are concepts of high-school algebra and *not* references to the computer code which performs (approximations) of the computations represented by these concepts. That is, in high-school algebra the operations $+, -,$ ' $sqrt, etc.$ are *not* the operations which are utilized by a programming language such as C or Fortran. Rather, these terms represent universal, standalone, composable computational processes used by high-school students. It just happens that in this case these symbols represent terms that IT experts are accustomed to seeing in their favorite programming language.

This paradigm of algorithm execution does not imply that *computer programming disappears*. It only implies that computer programming is done by professional programmers while AD experts develop and run domain algorithms using domain concepts. Domain experts are not required to be aware of what or where the computer that performs the computation is. This means, students learning algebra may focus on algebra not on Fortran, C, or any other language that may be used to implement the concepts of high-school algebra.

To further the discussion of how NLD algorithms are carried out by the virtual machine, and also to show that this paradigm of problem solving is universal (i.e., it is no different when we move from one domain to another), we consider the example of the RTE problem discussed in Section 2.3 and its RTE solution given as RTEdecider. So, suppose we have two phrases: Bill is a man and Bill is human and we want to check whether Bill is a man *implies* Bill is human. Using RTEdecider this is obtained by the following dialog with the machine on which the computationally emancipated RTE domain, whose ontology is in Figure 2, is implemented:

% Start RTEdecider:

% Input phrase T: Bill is a man

% Input phrase H: Bill is a human

After a few fractions of a second the computer answer: % True

As usual, the text after the prompt is typed by the machine and the typewriter text is typed by the user.

As with the high-school algebra example, at the domain level the domain expert does not care how these concepts are performed, just that they are performed and they generate results. The whole point of this work is to utilize

the computer as a mind-tool [Jon00]. The CEADed ontology allows the AD
expert to do that by letting the computer carry out the concepts in the ontology rather than relying on the brain. From the viewpoint of a domain expert
using this paradigm of problem solving, the use of the computer is no different from the using a pocket-calculator. The difference is that while the usual
pocket-calculator performs simple arithmetical operations, the DDVM performs
complex algorithms associated with concepts in the domain ontology.

3   Optimization of NLD Algorithm Execution

Carrying out an NLD algorithm incurs the cost of searching the domain ontology for concepts used in the solution algorithm. The challenge to IT is then
twofold: (a) computer experts need to develop the computer artifacts that implement the concepts that populate the AD ontology, and (b) computer experts
need to develop software tools that support and optimize the process of NLD
algorithm execution. The computer artifacts involved at (a) are defined by the
properties of the domain characteristic concepts. The tools involved at (b) above
operate on NLD algorithms and the domain ontology, collect the ontology concepts involved, perform any validation that may occur, and produce a solution
algorithm that eliminates the search process at algorithm execution time. This
optimization can be done by the domain expert "manually", going from concept
to concept, collecting the URIs associated with each concept and generating an
expression of the domain algorithm using these URIs [RC06, RC07], similar to
what a translator of a natural language is performing. Due to the simple structure of the NLD, this can also be carried by a conventional compiler that maps
NLD into a process execution language where processes to be executed are completely defined in the ontology. The Software Architecture Description Language
(SADL) [RC06, RC07] was designed for this purpose and the SADL interpreter
was created as an automaton that executes SADL expressions representing NLD
algorithms.

3.1   SADL and SADL Interpreter

SADL is a process-description language similar to a shell scripting language.
The lexical elements of SADL are commands denoted by the terms from NLD
vocabulary. The semantics of the command denoted by a term t is the process
performing the software artifact associated with t in the domain ontology, or
the process that implements the meaning of the term t, if t is inherited. A
SADL simple process is a computer process that performs a command. A SADL
composed process consists of compositions of one or more SADL simple processes
that implement an NLD algorithm. The syntax of SADL is built on the extensible
markup language (XML). The two types of SADL processes are represented by
the two types of XML elements:

- A SADL simple process is represented by an empty XML element of the form $<op\ atr_1 = val_1 \ldots atr_n = val_n\ />$ where the tag op is an element of the NLD vocabulary and $atr_1, \ldots, atr_n$ are the attributes that define the process associated with that tag, such as the URI of the code.
- A SADL composed process is represented by a content XML element of the form $<op\ atr_1 = val_1 \ldots atr_n = val_n>\ p_1 \ldots p_n\ </op>$ where the tag op is an element of NLD vocabulary inherited from the computer technology representing a process that composes the processes $p_1 \ldots p_n$ using the attributes $atr_1, \ldots, atr_n$ to determine the behavior of the resulting composition.

Expressions in SADL contain all the necessary information to carry out the domain algorithms without the need to search the domain ontology.

The SADL interpreter uses the DEL loop to carry out domain algorithms by creating, composing, executing, and controlling the processes specified by SADL commands. This is easily accomplished using systems, such as Unix-5, that provide mechanisms supporting process creation, process execution, and controlling process interaction. We illustrate this using the solution algorithm for RTE problem discussed above, whose SADL expression follows:

```
<?xml version="1.0" ?>
<sadl>
  <RTEdecider input="URI(T) URI(H)" output="URI(result)">
    <Parser uri="URI(Parser)" input="URI(T)" output="URI(treeT)" />
    <Parser uri="URI(Parser)" input="URI(H)" output="URI(treeH)" />
    <Boxer  uri="URI(Boxer)"  input="URI(treeT)" output="URI(drsT)" />
    <Boxer  uri="URI(Boxer)"  input="URI(treeH)" output="URI(drsH)" />
    <Explorer uri="URI(Explorer)"
              input="URI(drsT),URI(drsH)"  output="URI(bk)" />
    <MakeFOL uri="URI(MakeFOL)" input="URI(drsT)" output="URI(ET)" />
    <MakeFOL uri="URI(MakeFOL)" input="URI(drsH)" output="URI(EH)" />
    <And uri="URI(and)"input="URI(bk) URI(ET)"output="URI(antecedent)"/>
    <Implies uri="URI(Implies)" input="URI(EH)" output="URI(wff)" />
    <Prover uri="URI(Prover)"input="URI(wff)"output="URI(result)"/>
  </RTE>
</sadl>
```

To increase readability here we use the notation "URI(concept)" instead of using the real URI of the concept in the ontology. Note however that SADL and SADL interpreter are designed and implemented by IT experts as software support for NLD algorithm executions and are invisible to the AD experts.

3.2 Mapping NLD Algorithms into SADL

The mapping of the NLD algorithms into SADL can be done by the domain expert by hand. This is feasible for toy problems. For more sophisticated problems it is beneficial to automate this process. This is another class of software tools that IT is challenged to develop in order to support computer user liberation from programming. The development of a translator mapping NLD algorithms into SADL expressions is facilitated by the following facts:

1. The lexicons of the source language (i.e., the NLD) and the target language (i.e., the SADL) are finite and one-to-one connected. However, notice that these lexicons evolves with the domain expert cognition process. For that, only the domain ontology needs to be updated.
2. As we have seen in Section 2.3, we can design the NLD language to have a very simple syntax, that avoids the usual ambiguities present in natural language. A Generalized Phrase Structure Grammar [HU93] is appropriate for this purpose. This allows us to use TICS tools[RKS+] to automatically generate the parser we need and to label the abstract syntax trees generated by this parser with the URIs of the concepts in the ontology and the IT operators encountered in the NLD algorithm.
3. The SADL expression is thus automatically generated by walking the abstract syntax tree generated by the parser. No intricacies implied in code generation for actual machines is involved. We encapsulate the NLD algorithm translation into the command: `Map2SADL DomainAlgorithm`.

Since only the vocabularies of different NLD-s are different, the evolving of NLD with the domain cognition process, or the porting of the `Map2SADL` translator from one NLD to another NLD, can be done by the domain expert by updating NLD vocabulary specification. Only the scanner needs to be reimplemented, which is automatically generated from the NLD vocabulary specification [RH00].

4   Conclusions

Feasibility of computer use without programming is demonstrated by many software tools in use today that expand from using a computer as a typewriter to the enterprise management systems. But there is no recognized trend of liberating computer user from programming. The ubiquitous expansion of computer use (with and without programming) cannot be sustained without a systematic research program toward liberating computer user from programming. This does not mean that research on programming would disappear, only that the computer science community needs to differentiate more carefully between computer users and computer experts, and consequently it needs to balance the research on software support for the two classes of experts. Once this is realized, it will be easy to observe that the software needs of computer users depend on application domains and domain expertise. In other words, the idea of liberating computer user from programming means actually the liberation of computer technology from the "one-size-fits-all" pattern imposed by current problem solving methodology. This pattern evolved from the Hilbert program [HPr] and characterizes the syntactic computation encapsulated in the concept of an algorithms, which correspond to the fixed rules of inference of a formalized axiomatic procedure. Its limitations are theoretically justified by Gödel's incompleteness theorem [NN01]. We believe that computer user liberation from the "straitjackets" imposed by programming language syntax, thus making the computer a mind-tool, opens the era of semantic computation, and consequently, will lead to a new explosion in computer technology.

Why do we want to present this research to AMAST community? The answer to this question resides in the history of AMAST. AMAST has been created to pursue the tendency of using algebraic (formal) thinking as mechanism of discovery and innovation in software development. Twenty some years ago software development had as the objective the development of tools to control the computing power embodied in computer hardware while providing it as services to computer users. The computer was seen as a universal tool that provides universal services. But by the ubiquitous computer use the universe seems to become too large and threatens to crush the computer. Human cognition power increases with computer use and requires the diversification of service types provided by the computer, thus leading to the need to abandon the "one-size-fits-all" pattern of computer usage. To sustain this aspect of the human cognition-process software tools need to evolve with the human cognition process and this can be achieved only by looking at the computer as a cognitive tool, in the hands of computer users. That is, the computer needs to be *a tool in the hands of its users* rather than being *a tool in the hands of its creators*. This can be achieved by moving computational thinking created by the development of software technology[TW07] back into the application domain. We believe that it is now time to continue the evolutionary view of algebraic methodology from $AM \rightarrow ST$ to $AM \rightarrow ST \rightarrow AD$. This is where the AMAST following may play a key role. Due to the thinking inertia created by the successes of computer technology developed so far, we expect that the main foes of this new paradigm of computer technology will be the computer experts themselves. The AMAST following is probably best prepared to understand, to accept, and to handle this situation. The AMAST community evolved as a class of computer experts supporting the setting of software technology on firm, mathematical basis. Now the AMAST-ers are called to collaborate with application domain experts to set computer application domains on firm, mathematical basis, by their computational emancipation, thus contributing to the creation of new software technology meant to liberate computer user from programming.

References

[ACD+]   Andrews, T., et al.: Business process execution language for web services, http://www-106.ibm.com/developerworks/webservices/library/ws-bpel/

[Apt96]   Apt, K.: From Logic Programming to PROLOG. Prentice Hall, Englewood Cliffs (1996)

[Bac78]   Backus, J.: Can Programming be Liberated from the von Neumann Style? A Functional Style and its Algebra of Programs. Comm. ACM 21(8), 613–641 (1978)

[Bat93]   Bateman, J.A.: Ontology construction and natural language. In: Proceedings of the International Workshop on Formal Ontology, Padova, Italy, pp. 83–93 (March 1993)

[BL98]   Berners-Lee, T., et al.: Rfc 2396: Uniform Resource Identifiers (URI): Generic Syntax (1998), www.ietf.org/rfc/rfc2396.txt

[BM05]   Bos, J., Markert, K.: Recognizing textual entailment with logical inference. In: HLT 2005: Proceedings of the conference on Human Language Technology and Empirical Methods in Natural Language Processing, Morristown, NJ, USA, pp. 628–635 (2005)

[CR08]   Curtis, D.E., Rus, T.: Application driven software for chemistry. In: 2008 IEEE International Conference on Electro/Information Technology, Proceedings, Iowa State University, IA, USA (2008)

[Dim]   Dimitriev, S.: Language Oriented Programming: The Next Programming Paradigm, http://www.onboard.jetBrains.com

[GMJE05]   Gal, A., Modica, G., Jamil, H., Eyal, A.: Automatic ontology matching using application semantics. AI Magazine, 21–31 (2005)

[GO94]   Gruber, T.R., Olsen, G.R.: An ontology for engineering mathematics. In: Proceedings of the 4th International Conference on Principles of Knowledge Representation and Reasoning (KR 1994), Bonn, Germany, May 24-27, 1994, pp. 258–269. Morgan Kaufmann, San Francisco (1994)

[Gur00]   Gurevich, Y.: Sequential Abstract-State Machines capture Sequential Algorithms. ACM Transactions on Computational Logic 1(1), 77–111 (2000)

[Har88]   Harel, D.: On Visual Formalisms. Comm. of the ACM 31(5), 514–529 (1988)

[Har08]   Harel, D.: Can Programming Be Liberated, Period? Computer 41(1), 28–37 (2008)

[HPr]   Hilbert's program. Stanford Encyclopedia of Philosophy, http://plato.stanford.edu/entries/hilbert-propgram

[HU93]   Hans, K., Uwe, R.: From Discourse To Logic. Kluwer Academic Publishers, Dordrecht (1993)

[IBM02]   IBM. Autonomic Computing, www.research.ibm.com/autonomic/

[Jon00]   Jonassen, D.H., Carr, C.S.: Mindtools: Affording Multiple Knowledge Representations for Learning. In: Computers as Cognitive Tools. No More Walls, vol. 2, pp. 165–196. Lawrence Erlbaum Associates, Mahwah (2000)

[Kri]   Krill, P.: Complexity is killing IT, say analysts, http://www.techworld.com

[McB04]   McBride, B.: The Resource Description Framework (RDF) and its Vocabulary Description Language RDFS. In: Handbook on Ontologies, pp. 51–65. Springer, Heidelberg (2004)

[MJS05]   Mernik, M., Heering, J., Soane, A.M.: When and how to develop domain-specific languages. ACM Computing Surveys 37(4), 316–344 (2005)

[NM]   Noy, N.F., McGuinness, D.L.: A guide to creating your first ontology, http://ksl.stanford.edu/people/dlm/papers/ontology-tutorial-noy-mcguinness-abstract.html

[NN01]   Nagel, E., Newman, J.R.: Gödel's Proof. New York University Press (2001)

[PG74]   Popek, G.J., Goldberg, R.P.: Formal requirements for virtualizable third generation architectures. Comm. of the A.C.M. 17(7), 412–421 (1974)

[Pol73]   Polya, G.: How To Solve It. Princeton University Press, Princeton (1973)

[RC06]   Rus, T., Curtis, D.E.: Application driven software development. In: International Conference on Software Engineering Advances, Proceedings, Tahiti (2006)

[RC07]   Rus, T., Curtis, D.E.: Toward application driven software technology. In: The 2007 World Congress in Computer Science, Computer Engineering, and Applied Computing, WORLDCOMP 2007, Las Vegas, USA (2007)

[RKS+]   Rus, T., et al.: TICS: A component based language processing environment, http://www.cs.uiowa.edu/~rus

[Rus]   Rus, T.: IPCsem: An Interactive LR Parser Construction with Semantic
          Functions, http://www.cs.uiowa.edu/~rus
[RH00]   Rus, T., Halverson, T.: A Language Independent Scanner Generator,
          http://www.cs.uiowa.edu/~rus
[SC98]   Smith, D.C., Cypher, A.: Making programming easier for children. Morgan
          Kaufmann Series In Interactive Technologies (1998)
[Shn07]   Shneiderman, B.: Creativity support tools – accelerating discovery and
          innovation. Comm. of the ACM 50(12), 10–31 (2007)
[Sim95]   Simonyi, C.: The Death of Computer Languages, The Birth of Intentional
          Programming. Technical Report MSR–TR–95–52, Microsoft (1995)
[SS04]   Staab, S., Studer, R. (eds.): Handbook on Ontologies. Springer, Heidelberg
          (2004)
[TW07]   Tekinay, S., Wing, J.: Cyber-enabled discovery and innovation. Computing
          Research News 19(5) (November 2007)
[War94]   Ward, M.P.: Language-Oriented Programming. Software — Concepts and
          Tools 15(4), 147–161 (1994)
[Win06]   Wing, J.M.: Computational thinking. Comm. of the ACM 49(3), 33–35
          (2006)

An Algebra for Features and Feature Composition

Sven Apel[1], Christian Lengauer[1], Bernhard Möller[2], and Christian Kästner[3]

[1] Department of Informatics and Mathematics, University of Passau
{apel,lengauer}@uni-passau.de
[2] Institute of Computer Science, University of Augsburg
moeller@informatik.uni-augsburg.de
[3] School of Computer Science, University of Magdeburg
kaestner@iti.cs.uni-magdeburg.de

Abstract. *Feature-Oriented Software Development (FOSD)* provides a multitude of formalisms, methods, languages, and tools for building variable, customizable, and extensible software. Along different lines of research, different notions of a feature have been developed. Although these notions have similar goals, no common basis for evaluation, comparison, and integration exists. We present a feature algebra that captures the key ideas of feature orientation and provides a common ground for current and future research in this field, in which also alternative options can be explored.

1 Introduction

Feature-Oriented Software Development (FOSD) is a paradigm that provides formalisms, methods, languages, and tools for building variable, customizable, and extensible software. The main abstraction mechanism of FOSD is the *feature*. A feature reflects a stakeholder's requirement and is an increment in functionality; features are used to distinguish between different variants of a program or software system [1]. *Feature composition* is the process of composing code associated with features consistently.

Research along different lines has been undertaken to realize the vision of FOSD [1, 2, 3, 4, 5]. While there are the common notions of a feature and feature composition, present approaches use different techniques, representations, and formalisms. For example, AspectJ[1] and AHEAD[2] can both be used to implement features, but they provide different language constructs: on the one hand pointcuts, advice, and inter-type declarations, and on the other hand collaborations and refinements [5]. A promising way of integrating the separate lines of research is to provide an encompassing abstract framework that captures many of the common ideas like introductions, refinements, or quantification and hides (what we feel are) distracting differences.

We propose a first step toward such a framework for FOSD: a *feature algebra*. Firstly, the feature algebra abstracts from the details of different programming languages and environments used in FOSD. Secondly, alternative design decisions in the algebra, e.g., allowing terminal composition or not, reflect variants and alternatives in concrete programming language mechanisms. Thirdly, the algebra is useful for describing, beside

---

[1] http://www.eclipse.org/aspectj/
[2] http://www.cs.utexas.edu/~schwartz/ATS.html

J. Meseguer and G. Roşu (Eds.): AMAST 2008, LNCS 5140, pp. 36–50, 2008.

composition, also other operations on features formally and independently of the language, e.g., type checking [6] and interaction analysis [7]. Fourthly, the algebraic description of a software system can be taken as an architectural view. External tools can use the algebra as a basis for feature expression optimization [4, 8].

We introduce a uniform representation of features, outline the properties of the algebra, and explain how the algebra models the key concepts of FOSD.

2   What Is a Feature?

Different researchers have been proposing different views of what a feature is or should be. A definition that is common to most (if not all) work on FOSD is: *a feature is a structure that extends and modifies the structure of a given program in order to satisfy a stakeholder's requirement, to implement a design decision, and to offer a configuration option.* This informal definition guides our work on a formal framework of FOSD.

Typically, a series of features is composed to form a final program, which is itself a feature. This way, a feature can be either a complete program which can be executed or a program increment which requires further features to form a complete program.

Mathematically, we describe feature composition by the operator •, which is defined over the set F of features. Typically, a program p (which is itself a feature) is composed of a series of simpler features:

$$\bullet : F \times F \to F \qquad\qquad p = f_n \bullet f_{n-1} \bullet \ldots \bullet f_2 \bullet f_1 \qquad\qquad (1)$$

The order of features in a composition matters since feature composition is not commutative, and parenthesization does not matter since feature composition is associative, as we will show.

For simplicity, we restrict feature composition such that each single feature can appear only once in a feature expression. Multiple instances of a single feature would be possible but do not add anything new.

3   The Structure of Features

We develop our model of features in several steps and – even though the algebra is language-independent – explain the details of the algebra and its implications by means of Java code. First, a simple form of features, which we call *basic features*, are introduced as trees that describe the collection of elementary components of an artifact, such as classes, fields, or methods in Java (Sec. 3–5.1). In the next step, we introduce *modifications* that act as rewrites on basic features (Sec. 5.2). Finally, *full features* are defined as tuples, called *quarks*, consisting of both, a basic feature and modifications (Sec. 6). Quarks can be composed to describe complex features in a structured way as compositions of sequences of simpler features.

A basic feature consists of one or more source code artifacts, each of which can have an internal structure. We model the structure of a basic feature as a tree, called *feature structure tree (FST)*, that organizes the feature's structural elements, e.g., classes, fields, or methods, hierarchically. Figure 1 depicts an excerpt of the Java implementation of

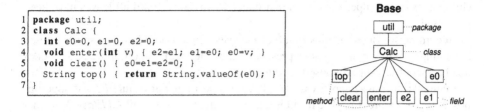

```
1  package util;
2  class Calc {
3    int e0=0, e1=0, e2=0;
4    void enter(int v) { e2=e1; e1=e0; e0=v; }
5    void clear() { e0=e1=e2=0; }
6    String top() { return String.valueOf(e0); }
7  }
```

Fig. 1. Implementation and FST of the feature *Base*

a feature *Base* and its representation in form of an FST. One can think of an FST as a stripped-down abstract syntax tree; however, it contains only the information that is necessary for the specification of the structure of a basic feature. The nature of this information depends on the degree of granularity at which software artifacts shall be composed, as we discuss below.

For example, the FST we use to represent Java code contains nodes that denote packages, classes, interfaces, fields, and methods, etc. It does not contain information about the internal structure of methods, etc. A different granularity would be to represent only packages and classes but not methods or fields as FST nodes, or to represent statements or expressions as well [9]. However, this decision does not affect our description of the algebra.

Furthermore, a name[3] and type information is attached to each node of an FST. This helps to prevent the composition of incompatible nodes during feature composition, e.g., the composition of two classes with different names, or of a field with a method of the same name.

The rightmost child of a node represents the topmost element in the lexical order of an artifact, e.g., the first member in a class is represented by the rightmost child node. Note that in the chosen granularity for Java the order could be arbitrary, but this is different at a finer granularity (the order of statements matters) and may differ in other languages (the order of XHTML elements matters).

4   Feature Composition

How does the abstract description of a feature composition $g \bullet f$ map to the concrete composition at the structural level? That is, how are FSTs composed in order to obtain a new FST? Our answer is by *FST superimposition* [10, 11, 12, 3].

4.1   Tree Superimposition

The basic idea is that two trees are superimposed by superimposing their subtrees, starting from the root and proceeding recursively. Two nodes are superimposed to form a new node (a) when their parents have been superimposed previously or both are root nodes and (b) when they have the same name and type. If two nodes have been superimposed, the whole process proceeds with their children. If not, they are added as separate

---

[3] Depending on the language, a name could be a simple identifier, a signature, etc.

child nodes to the superimposed parent node. This recurses until all leaves have been processed.

According to the semantics of FSTs (see Sec. 3), the children are superimposed beginning with the rightmost node preserving the order in the superimposed FST; nodes that have not been superimposed are added to the left.

Figure 2 illustrates the process of FST superimposition; our feature *Base* is superimposed with a feature *Add*. The result is a new feature, which we call *AddBase*. Note that the new method add appears to the left in *AddBase*.

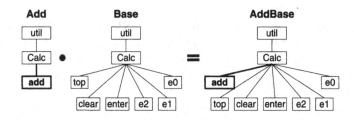

Fig. 2. An example of FST superimposition (*Add* • *Base* = *AddCalc*)

4.2   Terminal and Non-terminal Nodes

Independently of any particular language, an FST is made up of two different kinds of nodes:

Non-terminal nodes are the inner nodes of an FST. The subtree rooted at a non-terminal node reflects the structure of some implementation artifact of a feature. The artifact structure is regarded as *transparent* (substructures are represented by child nodes) and is subject to the recursive superimposition process. A non-terminal node has only a name and a type, i.e., no superimposition of additional content is necessary.

Terminal nodes are the leaves of an FST. Conceptually, a terminal node may also be the root of some structure, but this structure is regarded as *opaque* in our model (substructures are not represented by child nodes). The content of a terminal is not shown in the FST. A terminal node has a name, a type, and usually some content.

While superimposition of two non-terminals continues the recursive descent in the FSTs, the superimposition of two terminals terminates the recursion and requires a special treatment that may differ for each type of node.

Let us illustrate these concepts for Java. In Java, packages, classes, and interfaces are represented by non-terminals. The implementation artifacts they contain are represented by child nodes, e.g., a package contains several classes and classes contain inner classes, methods, and fields. Two compatible non-terminals are superimposed by superimposing their child nodes, e.g., two packages with equal names are merged into one package that contains the superimposition of the child elements (classes, interfaces, subpackages) of the two original packages. In contrast, Java methods, fields, imports, modifier lists, and extends, implements, and throws clauses are represented by terminals (the leaves of an FST), at which the recursion terminates. For each type of terminal node there needs to be a language-specific rule for superimposing their content.

4.3 Superimposition of Terminals

In order to superimpose terminals, each terminal type has to provide its own rule for superimposition. Here are four examples for Java and similar languages:
- Two methods can be superimposed if it is specified how the method bodies are superimposed (e.g., by overriding and calling the original method by using the keywords `original` [13] or `Super` [3] inside a method body). It is a question of programming style whether to allow or disallow replacement of method bodies (i.e., overriding without calling the original method).
- Two fields are superimposed by replacing one initializing variable declaration with the other or by requiring that at most one of the fields may have an initial value.
- Two `implements`, `extends`, or `throws` clauses are superimposed by concatenating their entries and removing duplicates.
- Two modifier lists are superimposed by a specific algorithm, e.g., `public` replaces `private`, but not vice versa; a modifier list containing `static` superimposed with one not containing `static` is an error; and so on.

Terminal types that do not provide a rule cannot be composed – an error is displayed.

4.4 Discussion

Superimposition of FSTs requires several properties of the language in which the elements of a feature are expressed:
1. The substructure of a feature must be hierarchical, i.e., a general tree.
2. Every structural element of a feature must have a name and type that become the name and type of the node in the FST.
3. An element must not contain two or more direct child elements with the same name and type.
4. Elements that do not have a hierarchical substructure (terminals) must provide superimposition rules, or cannot be superimposed.

These constraints are usually satisfied by contemporary programming languages. But also other (non-code) languages align well with them [3, 14]. Languages that do not satisfy these constraints are not "feature-ready", since they do not provide sufficient structural information. However, it may be possible to make them so by extending them with an overlaying module structure [14].

FST superimposition is associative only if the superimposition of the individual subtrees is associative and, to this end, if merging terminal content is associative. In order to retain associativity, we add a further constraint: superimposition rules of terminals must be associative. This constraint, too, is typically satisfied by contemporary programming languages.

5 Feature Algebra

Our feature algebra models features and their composition on top of FSTs. The elements of an algebraic expression correspond to the elements of an FST. The manipulation of an expression implies a manipulation of one or more FSTs. The changes of an algebraic expression are propagated to the associated feature implementations at code level.

An important design decision is that there is a one-to-one correspondence between an FST and its algebraic expression.[4] That is, the expression is a formal means for reasoning about the FST. Thus, FSTs can be converted, without information loss, to algebraic expressions and vice versa. Our laws for algebraic expressions describe what is allowed and disallowed when manipulating FSTs.

5.1 Introductions

For the purpose of expressing basic features and their composition, we use the notion of an atomic introduction. An *atomic introduction* is a constituent of the implementation of a basic feature that corresponds to a node in the FST, e.g., a method, field, class, or package. When composing two basic features, introductions are the elementary units of difference of one feature composed with another feature. A basic feature is represented by the superimposition of all paths / atomic introductions in its FST. We model the superimposition of FSTs via the operation of *introduction sum*.

Introduction Sum. Introduction sum $\oplus$ is a binary operation defined over the set I of introductions. The result of an introduction sum is again an (non-atomic) introduction. Thus, an FST can be represented in two ways: by the individual (atomic) summands and by a metavariable that represents the sum:

$$\oplus : I \times I \to I \qquad\qquad i_2 \oplus i_1 = i \qquad\qquad (2)$$

During composition, for each metavariable i, the individual atomic summands $i_2 \oplus i_1$ are preserved. That is, introduction sum retains information about the summands, which is useful for expression manipulation and code generation. Since the nodes of an FST are unique, the atomic summands of a sum of introductions are unique as well, as we will explain shortly.

In order to process algebraic expressions of features, we flatten the hierarchical structure of FSTs. That is, we convert the tree representation of an FST into a set of atomic introductions, one per FST node. But, in order not to lose information about which structural elements contain which other elements, we preserve the paths of the FST nodes.

Specifically, we use a simple prefix notation to identify an atomic introduction, similar to fully qualified names in Java: the name of the FST node is prefixed with the name of all its parent nodes, separated by dots.[5] The leftmost prefix contains the name of the feature an introduction belongs to, followed by an '::', although, for brevity, the prefix does not appear in the FST. Our feature *Base* (cf. Fig. 2) is denoted in path notation as follows:

$$Prog = Base :: util.Calc.top \oplus Base :: util.Calc.clear \oplus Base :: util.Calc.enter$$
$$\oplus\ Base :: util.Calc.e2 \oplus Base :: util.Calc.e1 \oplus Base :: util.Calc.e0$$
$$\oplus\ Base :: util.Calc \oplus Base :: util$$

---

[4] A one-to-one correspondence for Java was only possible by ordering the children of a node based on their lexical order (see Sec. 3).

[5] To be specific, the fully qualified name of an atomic introduction must also include the type of each path element. For lack of space and because there are no ambiguities in our examples, we omit the type information here.

The leftmost leaves of an FST become the leftmost summands of its introduction sum. Note that not every sum represents a valid FST. A well-formedness rule is, that for every dot-separated prefix of a summand, there is a summand with the same name, e.g., the prefix $Base :: util$ of $Base :: util.Calc$ is itself a summand.

Two features are composed by adding their atomic introductions. Since each atomic introduction preserves the path of the corresponding FST node, it is always known from which feature an introduction was added during the manipulation of an algebraic expression, e.g., $Base$ in $Base :: util.Calc$. Furthermore, we can convert each algebraic expression (containing a sum of introductions with prefixes) straightforwardly back to a tree, either to the original FSTs or to a new composed FST. When converting an introduction sum into a composed FST, it is associated with a new (composed) feature. Two atomic introductions with the same fully qualified name, that belong to different features, are composed via superimposition, as explained informally in Section 4.

For example, the introduction sum that represents the non-terminal superimposition of Figure 2 is as follows:

$$Add :: util.Calc.add \oplus \ldots \oplus Base :: util.Calc.top \oplus Base :: util.Calc.clear \oplus \ldots$$

It follows that the above sum represents a composed FST consisting of a package `util` with a class `Calc` that contains four methods (including `add`) and three fields.

For example, the superimposition of the two methods `enter` is represented in the corresponding introduction sum as:

$$Count :: util.Calc.enter \oplus \ldots \oplus Base :: util.Calc.enter \oplus \ldots$$

This sum represents a composed FST (only an excerpt is shown) consisting of a package `util` with a class `Calc` that contains three methods and three fields, and the bodies of the two `enter` methods are merged (similarly for `clear`).

Algebraic Properties. Introduction sum $\oplus$ over the set I of introductions forms a *non-commutative idempotent monoid* $(I, \oplus, \xi)$:[6]

Associativity: $(k \oplus j) \oplus i = k \oplus (j \oplus i)$ — Introduction sum is associative because FST superimposition is associative. This applies for terminals and non-terminals.

Identity: $\xi \oplus i = i \oplus \xi = i$ — ξ is the empty introduction, i.e., an FST without nodes.

Non-commutativity: Since we consider superimposition of terminals, introduction sum is not generally commutative. We consider the right operand to be introduced first, the left one is added to it.

Idempotence: $i \oplus j \oplus i = j \oplus i$ — Only the rightmost occurrence of an introduction i is effective in a sum, because it has been introduced first. That is, duplicates of i have no effect, as stressed at the end of Section 2. We refer to this rule as *distant idempotence*. For $j = \xi$, direct idempotence ($i \oplus i = i$) follows.

---

[6] All standard definitions of algebraic structures and properties are according to Hebisch and Weinert [15].

5.2   Modification

Beside superimposition also other techniques for feature composition have been proposed, most notably *composition by quantification* [16, 5]. The idea is that, when expressing the changes that a feature causes to another feature, we specify the points at which the two features are supposed to be composed. This idea has been explored in depth in work on *subject-oriented programming* [17] and *aspect-oriented programming* [18]. The process of determining where two features are to be composed is called *quantification* [19]. In the remainder, we distinguish between two approaches of composition: *composition by superimposition* and *composition by quantification*. Our definition of feature composition (•) incorporates both (see Sec. 6).

In order to model composition by quantification, we introduce the notion of a modification. A *modification* consists of two parts:
1. A specification of the nodes in the FST at which a feature affects another feature during composition.
2. A specification of how features are composed at these nodes.

In the context of our model, a modification is performed as an FST walk that determines the nodes which are being modified and applies the necessary changes to these nodes. The advantage of composition by quantification is that the specification of where a program is extended is declarative. Querying an FST can return more than one node at a time. This allows us to specify the modification of a whole set of nodes at once without having to reiterate it for every set member.

Note that composition by superimposition and composition by quantification are siblings. Quantification enables us to address parts of a feature more generically than superimposition. But, once it is known which points have to be changed, the two kinds of composition become equivalent. We have observed their conceptual duality before, but at the level of two concrete programming techniques [5]. The feature algebra makes it explicit at a more abstract level.

Semantics of Modification. A modification m consists of a query q that selects a subset of the atomic introductions of an introduction sum and a definition of change c that will be used to effect the desired changes:

$$m = (q, c) \tag{3}$$

Query. A simple query can be represented by an FST in which the node names may contain wildcards.[7] For example, the query q with the search expression '$util.Calc.*$' applied to our example would return the sum of all introductions that are members of the class Calc. This motivates the following definition.

Formally, a query applied to an atomic introduction returns either the same introduction or the empty introduction:

$$q(i) = \begin{cases} i, & \text{when } i \text{ is matched by } q \\ \xi, & \text{when } i \text{ is not matched by } q \end{cases} \tag{4}$$

---

[7] In practice, queries with regular expressions or queries over types might be useful.

A query applied to an introduction sum queries each summand:

$$q(i_n \oplus \ldots \oplus i_2 \oplus i_1) = q(i_n) \oplus \ldots \oplus q(i_2) \oplus q(i_1) \tag{5}$$

Definition of change. An introduction i selected by a query is modified according to the modification's definition of change c; c is a rewrite that is able to apply two kinds of changes: (a) it can add a new child to a given non-terminal and (b) it can alter the content of a terminal; the application of c distributes over introduction sum:

$$c(i_n \oplus \ldots \oplus i_2 \oplus i_1) = c(i_n) \oplus \ldots \oplus c(i_2) \oplus c(i_1) \qquad c(i_j) = \tau_c(i_c, i_j) \oplus i_j \tag{6}$$

The *atomic* introduction i_c represents a new child or the change applied to a terminal. It has to be provided by the programmer in the form of a generic piece of code or some other kind of specification. The function τ_c takes the generic definition of change i_c and the atomic introduction i_j to be changed and generates the final non-generic definition of change. That is, τ_c eliminates the genericity of i_c by substituting missing parts with details of the program to which c is applied.

For example, suppose a feature *Count* applies two modifications m_1 and m_2 to the introductions of *Base*, with c_1 adding a new field and c_2 altering the method `enter`:

$$\begin{aligned}
c_1(Base::util.Calc) &= \tau_{c_1}(count, util.Calc) \oplus Base::util.Calc \\
&= Count::util.Calc.count \oplus Base::util.Calc
\end{aligned}$$

$$\begin{aligned}
c_2(Base::util.Calc.enter) &= \tau_{c_2}(enter, util.Calc.enter) \oplus Base::util.Calc.enter \\
&= Count::util.Calc.enter \oplus Base::util.Calc.enter
\end{aligned}$$

Of course, applying c_1 and c_2 to a different feature (say $Base_2$) results in a different program. Since change is expressed as an introduction sum, a modification cannot delete nodes. The changes a feature can make via modifications are similar to the ones possible via introduction sum, but expressed differently.

Modification Application and Composition. For simplicity, we usually hide the steps of querying and applying the changes. We define an operator *modification application* ($\odot$) over the set M of modifications and the set I of introductions. A modification applied to an introduction returns either the introduction again or the introduction that has been changed:

$$\odot : M \times I \to I \qquad m \odot i = (q, c) \odot i = \begin{cases} c(i), & q(i) = i \wedge i \neq \xi \\ i, & q(i) = \xi \end{cases} \tag{7}$$

A consequence of this definition is that a modification cannot extend the empty introduction, i.e., the empty program. This is different from introduction sum which we can use to extend empty programs. While this fact is just a result of our definition, it reflects what contemporary languages that support quantification are doing, e.g., AspectJ's advice and inter-type declarations cannot extend the empty program.

A modification is applied to a sum of introductions by applying it to each introduction in turn and summing the results:

$$m \odot (i_n \oplus \ldots \oplus i_2 \oplus i_1) = (m \odot i_n) \oplus \ldots \oplus (m \odot i_2) \oplus (m \odot i_1) \tag{8}$$

The successive application of changes of a modification to an introduction sum implies the left distributivity of $\odot$ over $\oplus$.

Furthermore, the operator $\odot$ is overloaded.[8] With two modifications as arguments, it denotes the operation *modification composition*. The semantics of modification composition is that the right operand is applied to an introduction, and then the left operand to the result:

$$\odot : M \times M \to M \qquad\qquad (m_2 \odot m_1) \odot i = m_2 \odot (m_1 \odot i) \qquad (9)$$

Here, the leftmost of the four occurrences of $\odot$ is modification composition, all others are modification application.

A fully precise definition of modification composition requires an elaborate construction for combining the queries involved. Due to lack of space, we refer the reader to a technical report [20, pp. 14ff].

Using modification composition, a series of modifications can be applied to an introduction step by step:

$$(m_n \odot \ldots \odot m_2 \odot m_1) \odot i = m_n \odot (\ldots \odot (m_2 \odot (m_1 \odot i))\ldots) \qquad (10)$$

Note that the application of a modification may add new introductions that can be changed subsequently by other modifications. But, as prescribed by Equation 6, it is not possible to change an introduction sum such that some introductions are removed and the modifications applied subsequently cannot affect them anymore. This design decision is justified by the design of current languages that support feature composition, e.g., AspectJ's aspects or AHEAD's refinements [3] cannot remove members or classes.

Algebraic Properties. We define two modifications m_1 and m_2 as *equivalent* if they act identically on all introductions, i.e., if $m_1 \odot i = m_2 \odot i$ for all i. In the following, we write M also for the set of equivalence classes of modifications and $\odot$ for the corresponding induced operation on them. This induces a *non-commutative non-idempotent monoid* $(M, \odot, \zeta)$:

Associativity: $(o \odot n) \odot m = o \odot (n \odot m)$ — Modification composition is associative by the definition of modification application.

Identity: $\zeta \odot m = m \odot \zeta = m$ — ζ is the equivalence class of empty modifications. ζ does not change a given introduction.

Non-commutativity: Modification composition is not commutative because introduction sum is not commutative.

Non-idempotence: Although the changes made by a modification reduce to introduction sum (cf. Eq. 6), and introduction sum is distantly idempotent, the consecutive application of several modifications is *not* idempotent. The reason is that a modification m can add an introduction that is selected and changed by itself when applied repeatedly.

---

[8] We reuse the symbol $\odot$ because introduction sum and modification application and composition become all integrated into one algebraic structure with identical operator symbols for application and composition (see Sec. 5.3).

5.3   Introductions and Modifications in Concert

In order to describe feature composition, our algebra integrates our two algebraic structures $(I, \oplus, \xi)$ and $(M, \odot, \zeta)$ by means of the operation of modification application.

$(I, \oplus, \xi)$ induces a non-commutative idempotent monoid and $(M, \odot, \zeta)$ induces a non-commutative non-idempotent monoid. A notable property of $(I, \oplus, \xi)$ is that it is a *semimodule over the monoid* $(M, \odot, \zeta)$ since the distributive and associative laws (8) and (9) hold. In fact, the operation of modification application induces the semimodule on top of the individual operations introduction sum and modification composition. A semimodule over a monoid is related to a vector space but weaker (modification application plays the role of the scalar product) [15]. In a vector space, there would be an operation of *modification sum* that adds modifications similarly to introduction sum. In prior work, we have explored and integrated modification sum into the feature algebra [20] but, due to lack of space, we omit its description here. Moreover, the additive and multiplicative operations in vector spaces are commutative and there are inverse elements with respect to addition and multiplication. Nevertheless, the semimodule property guarantees a pleasant and useful flexibility of feature composition, which is manifested in the associativity and distributivity laws.

6   The Quark Model

So far, we have introduced two sets (I and M) and three operations ($\oplus : I \times I \rightarrow I$, $\odot : M \times M \rightarrow M$, and $\odot : M \times I \rightarrow I$) for feature composition. Now we integrate them in a compact and concise notation. This way, we allow *full features* that involve both introductions and modifications. Furthermore, we need to distinguish between local and global modifications. For this purpose, we introduce the *quark model*.[9]

A *quark* is a triple that represents a full feature, which consists of a composition g of *global* modifications, a sum i of introductions, and a further composition l of *local* modifications:

$$f = \langle g, i, l \rangle = \langle g_j \odot \ldots \odot g_1, i_k \oplus \ldots \oplus i_1, l_m \odot \ldots \odot l_1 \rangle \tag{11}$$

Here, i is the introduction sum of feature f and represents an FST; l and g contain the modifications that the feature f can make. A basic feature is represented in the quark model as a triple $\langle \zeta, i, \zeta \rangle$ where ζ is the empty modification. The application of quark q to introduction i is defined as the composition $q \bullet \langle \zeta, i, \zeta \rangle$.

When two quarks are composed, a new quark is constructed following certain composition rules. The new introduction part of the quark is constructed using modification application and introduction sum, while the new modification parts result by modification composition. We distinguish between two kinds of modifications because there are two options of using modifications when composing quarks: (a) *Local modifications* (l) can affect only already present introductions of features. (b) *Global modifications* (g)

---

[9] The idea and name of the quark model are due to Don Batory. Subsequently, the model was developed further in cooperation with us [20]. The term 'quark' was chosen as an analogy to the physical particles in quantum chromodynamics. Originally, quarks have been considered to be fundamental, but newer theories, e.g., preon or string theory, predict a further substructure.

can affect also introductions that are just being constructed during the composition. For quarks that represent basic features (g and l are empty) both definitions (a) and (b) yield $\langle \zeta, i_2, \zeta \rangle \bullet \langle \zeta, i_1, \zeta \rangle = \langle \zeta, i_2 \oplus i_1, \zeta \rangle$, which in retrospect justifies our use of $\bullet$ also for FST superimposition in Section 4.

The difference between local and global modifications requires a special treatment of composition of full quarks. When composing a sequence of quarks, we can apply the local modifications immediately. We cannot apply the global modifications immediately. We have to wait until all introductions and local modifications in a series of quarks have been composed; only then we can apply all global modifications. So, we generalize the binary operator $\bullet$ to an n-ary one:

$$
\begin{aligned}
f_n \bullet \ldots \bullet f_2 \bullet f_1 &= \langle g_n, i_n, l_n \rangle \bullet \ldots \bullet \langle g_2, i_2, l_2 \rangle \bullet \langle g_1, i_1, l_1 \rangle \\
&= \langle g_n \odot \ldots \odot g_1, (g_n \odot \ldots \odot g_1) \odot \\
&\quad (i_n \oplus (l_n \odot (\ldots (i_2 \oplus (l_2 \odot i_1))))), l_n \odot \ldots \odot l_1 \rangle \quad (12)
\end{aligned}
$$

This does not mean that the associativity properties of introduction sum and modification composition are useless. Associativity is necessary to make the application of local modifications to sums of introductions work smoothly.

7   Related Work

Lopez-Herrejon, Batory, and Lengauer model features as functions and feature composition as function composition [21, 7]. They distinguish between introductions and advice, which correspond roughly to our introductions and modifications. However, in their work there is no semantic model that defines precisely what introductions and advice are. In our feature algebra, we define introductions in terms of FSTs and modifications in terms of tree walks. This enables us to bridge the gap between algebra and implementation.

Möller et al. have developed an algebra for expressing software and hardware variabilities in the form of features [22]. This has recently been extended [23] to express a limited form of feature interaction. However, their algebra does not consider the structure and implementation of features.

There are some calculi that support feature-like structures and composition by superimposition [24, 25, 26, 27, 28, 29]. These calculi are typically tailored to Java-like languages and emphasize the type system. Instead, our feature algebra enables reasoning about feature composition on a more abstract level. We emphasize the structure of features and their static composition, independently of a particular language.

Several languages support features and their composition by superimposition [30, 31, 13, 32, 3]. Our algebra is a theoretical backbone that underlies and unifies all these languages. It reveals the properties a language must have in order to be feature-ready. Several languages exploit the synergistic potential of superimposition and quantification [16, 17, 32, 5]. The feature algebra allows us to study their relationship and integration, independently of a specific language.

Features are implemented not only by source code. Some tools support the feature-based composition of non-source code artifacts [3, 33, 14]. Our algebra is general enough to describe a feature containing these non-code artifacts since all their representations can be mapped to FSTs.

Finally, we have implemented a tool, called *FSTComposer*, that implements feature composition as described by our algebra [34]. With it, we have been able to demonstrate that such different languages as Java, XML, or Bali can be treated uniformly and the composition scales to medium-sized software projects. The integration of a new language requires only marginal effort because most information can be inferred from the language's grammar.

8   Conclusions and Perspectives

We have presented a model of FOSD in which features are represented as FSTs and feature composition is expressed by tree superimposition and tree walks. This reflects the state of the art in programming languages and composition models that favor superimposition and quantification. Our algebra describes precisely what their properties are and how such concepts from FOSD languages like aspects, collaborations, or refinements can be integrated. Though some of these approaches were integrated before in concrete languages, e.g., in FeatureC++ [32], aspectual feature modules [5], or Caesar [16], the algebra integrates these approaches for the first time formally and exposes fundamental concepts like the distinction of local vs. global modifications that prompted controversial discussions in earlier work, e.g., [21].

Our feature algebra forms a semimodule over a monoid, which is a weaker form of a vector space. The flexibility of this algebraic structure suggests that our decisions regarding the semantics of introductions and modifications and their operations are not arbitrary. With the presented configuration of our algebra, we achieve a high flexibility in feature composition, which is manifested in the associativity and distributivity laws.

Although our algebra is quite flexible, we also made several restrictive decisions. For example, introduction sum is idempotent and modifications are only allowed to add children and to compose content of terminals. An advantage of an algebraic approach is that we can evaluate the effects of our and alternative decisions directly by examining the properties of the resulting algebra. For example, if we forbid superimposition of terminals we can achieve commutativity of feature composition. Although this design decision might appear trivial, it is not obvious from contemporary programming languages but rather appears to be a byproduct of integrating other language constructs. With our formalization, such consequences become obvious and are helpful for carefully balancing expressiveness and composition flexibility when designing a new language. In our algebra, we decided to abandon commutativity in order to increase the expressive power of introduction sum by including overriding. Likewise, disallowing modifications to remove nodes from an FST guarantees that the targets of a feature remain present in a composition. Exploring the implications of our and alternative decisions is a promising avenue of further work.

Finally, with the feature algebra, we provide a framework for feature composition that is independent of a concrete language. Based on this framework, we have built the language-independent composition tool FSTComposer. Uniformity in feature composition has been a long-standing goal of FOSD [3] but, until now, feature composition tools for new languages were usually developed ad-hoc. In future work, we will also use the algebra for reasoning about types [6] and for interaction analysis [7] independently of concrete language mechanisms, e.g., of AspectJ or AHEAD.

Acknowledgments

We thank Don Batory, Tony Hoare, and Peter Höfner for helpful comments.

References

1. Kang, K., Cohen, S., Hess, J., Novak, W., Peterson, A.: Feature-Oriented Domain Analysis (FODA) Feasibility Study. Technical Report CMU/SEI-90-TR-21, SEI, CMU (1990)
2. Prehofer, C.: Feature-Oriented Programming: A Fresh Look at Objects. In: Proc. Europ. Conf. Object-Oriented Progr. (1997)
3. Batory, D., Sarvela, J., Rauschmayer, A.: Scaling Step-Wise Refinement. IEEE Trans. Softw. Eng. 30(6) (2004)
4. Czarnecki, K., Eisenecker, U.: Generative Programming: Methods, Tools, and Applications. Addison-Wesley, Reading (2000)
5. Apel, S., Leich, T., Saake, G.: Aspectual Feature Modules. IEEE Trans. Softw. Eng. 34(2) (2008)
6. Thaker, S., Batory, D., Kitchin, D., Cook, W.: Safe Composition of Product Lines. In: Proc. Int'l. Conf. Generative Program. and Component Eng. (2007)
7. Liu, J., Batory, D., Lengauer, C.: Feature-Oriented Refactoring of Legacy Applications. In: Proc. Int'l. Conf. Softw. Eng. (2006)
8. Batory, D.: From Implementation to Theory in Product Synthesis (Keynote). In: Proc. Int'l. Symp. Principles of Program. Lang. (2007)
9. Kästner, C., Apel, S., Kuhlemann, M.: Granularity in Software Product Lines. In: Proc. Int'l. Conf. Softw. Eng. (2008)
10. Chandy, M., Misra, J.: An Example of Stepwise Refinement of Distributed Programs: Quiescence Detection. ACM Trans. Program. Lang. Syst. 8(3) (1986)
11. Ossher, H., Harrison, W.: Combination of Inheritance Hierarchies. In: Proc. Int'l. Conf. Object-Oriented Progr., Syst., Lang., and App. (1992)
12. Bosch, J.: Super-Imposition: A Component Adaptation Technique. Information and Software Technology 41(5) (1999)
13. Bergel, A., Ducasse, S., Nierstrasz, O.: Classbox/J: Controlling the Scope of Change in Java. In: Proc. Int'l. Conf. Object-Oriented Progr. Syst. Lang. and App. (2005)
14. Anfurrutia, F., Díaz, O., Trujillo, S.: On Refining XML Artifacts. In: Proc. Int'l. Conf. Web Eng. (2007)
15. Hebisch, U., Weinert, H.: Semirings. World Scientific, Singapore (1998)
16. Mezini, M., Ostermann, K.: Variability Management with Feature-Oriented Programming and Aspects. In: Proc. Int'l. Symp. Foundations of Softw. Eng. (2004)
17. Tarr, P., Ossher, H., Harrison, W., Sutton Jr., S.: N Degrees of Separation: Multi-Dimensional Separation of Concerns. In: Proc. Int'l. Conf. Softw. Eng. (1999)
18. Masuhara, H., Kiczales, G.: Modeling Crosscutting in Aspect-Oriented Mechanisms. In: Proc. Europ. Conf. Object-Oriented Progr. (2003)
19. Filman, R., Friedman, D.: Aspect-Oriented Programming Is Quantification and Obliviousness. In: Aspect-Oriented Software Development. Addison-Wesley, Reading (2005)

20. Apel, S., Lengauer, C., Batory, D., Möller, B., Kästner, C.: An Algebra for Feature-Oriented Software Development. Technical Report MIP-0706, Department of Informatics and Mathematics, University of Passau (2007)
21. Lopez-Herrejon, R., Batory, D., Lengauer, C.: A Disciplined Approach to Aspect Composition. In: Proc. Int'l. Symp. Partial Evaluation and Semantics-Based Program Manipulation (2006)
22. Höfner, P., Khedri, R., Möller, B.: Feature Algebra. In: Proc. Int'l. Symp. Formal Methods (2006)
23. Höfner, P., Khedri, R., Möller, B.: Algebraic View Reconciliation. Technical Report 2007-13, Institute of Computer Science, University of Augsburg (2007)
24. Apel, S., Kästner, C., Lengauer, C.: An Overview of Feature Featherweight Java. Technical Report MIP-0802, Department of Informatics and Mathematics, University of Passau (2008)
25. Hutchins, D.: Eliminating Distinctions of Class: Using Prototypes to Model Virtual Classes. In: Proc. Int'l. Conf. Object-Oriented Progr. Syst. Lang. and App. (2006)
26. Ernst, E., Ostermann, K., Cook, W.: A Virtual Class Calculus. In: Proc. Int'l. Symp. Principles of Program. Lang. (2006)
27. Flatt, M., Krishnamurthi, S., Felleisen, M.: Classes and Mixins. In: Proc. Int'l. Symp. Principles of Program. Lang. (1998)
28. Findler, R., Flatt, M.: Modular Object-Oriented Programming with Units and Mixins. In: Proc. Int'l. Conf. Functional Program (1998)
29. Odersky, M., Cremet, V., Röckl, C., Zenger, M.: A Nominal Theory of Objects with Dependent Types. In: Proc. Europ. Conf. Object-Oriented Progr. (2003)
30. Odersky, M., Zenger, M.: Scalable Component Abstractions. In: Proc. Int'l. Conf. Object-Oriented Progr. Syst. Lang. and App. (2005)
31. McDirmid, S., Flatt, M., Hsieh, W.: Jiazzi: New-Age Components for Old-Fashioned Java. In: Proc. Int'l. Conf. Object-Oriented Progr. Syst. Lang. and App. (2001)
32. Apel, S., Leich, T., Rosenmüller, M., Saake, G.: FeatureC++: On the Symbiosis of Feature-Oriented and Aspect-Oriented Programming. In: Proc. Int'l. Conf. Generative Program. and Component Eng. (2005)
33. Alves, V., Gheyi, R., Massoni, T., Kulesza, U., Borba, P., Lucena, C.: Refactoring Product Lines. In: Proc. Int'l. Conf. Generative Program. and Component Eng. (2006)
34. Apel, S., Lengauer, C.: Superimposition: A Language-Independent Approach to Software Composition. In: Proc. Int'l. Symp. Softw. Comp. (2008)

Petri Nets Are Dioids[*]

Paolo Baldan[1] and Fabio Gadducci[2]

[1] Dipartimento di Matematica Pura e Applicata, Università Padova
Via Trieste 63, 35121 Padova, Italia
[2] Dipartimento di Informatica, Università di Pisa
Polo "Guglielmo Marconi", via dei Colli 90, 19100 La Spezia, Italia
baldan@math.unipd.it, gadducci@di.unipi.it

Abstract. In a seminal paper Montanari and Meseguer showed that an algebraic interpretation of Petri nets in terms of commutative monoids can be used to provide an elegant characterisation of the deterministic computations of a net, accounting for their sequential and parallel composition. Here we show that, along the same lines, by adding an (idempotent) operation and thus taking dioids (commutative semirings) rather than monoids, one can faithfully characterise the non-deterministic computations of a Petri net.

Introduction

Petri nets [12] are one of the best studied and most widely known models for concurrent systems. Due to the conceptual simplicity of the model and its intuitive graphical presentation, since their introduction, which dates back to the 60's [11], Petri nets have attracted the interest of both theoreticians and practitioners.

The basic operational behaviour of a Petri net can be straightforwardly defined in terms of the so-called token game and of firing sequences. Concurrency in computations can be made explicit by resorting to a semantics given in terms of *(non-sequential) deterministic processes* à la Goltz-Reisig [5]. A process describes the events occurring in a computation and their mutual dependency relations. Concretely, a deterministic processes is an acyclic, deterministic net whose structure induces a partial order on transitions which can be seen as occurrences of transition firings in the original net. A deterministic process thus captures an abstract notion of concurrent computation, in the sense that it can be seen as a representative of a full class of firing sequences differing only for the order of independent events, i.e., all the firing sequences corresponding to linearisations of the underlying partial ordering.

Different (concurrent) computations can be merged into a single non-deterministic process [3], a structure which, besides concurrency, captures also the intrinsic non-deterministic nature of Petri nets. A non-deterministic process is again a special Petri net, satisfying suitable acyclicity requirement, but where, roughly speaking, transitions can compete for the use of tokens, thus leading to a branching structure.

[*] Supported by the EU IST-2004-16004 SENSORIA and the MIUR Project ART.

J. Meseguer and G. Roşu (Eds.): AMAST 2008, LNCS 5140, pp. 51–66, 2008.

The concurrent nature of Petri net computations has been expressed in an elegant algebraic way in the so-called "Petri nets are monoids" approach [10]. A Petri net N is seen as a kind of signature Σ, and the computational model of the net is characterised as a symmetric monoidal category $\mathcal{P}(N)$ freely generated from N, in the same way as the cartesian category $\mathcal{L}(\Sigma)$ of terms and substitutions is freely generated from Σ. As (tuples of) terms in the free algebra $T_\Sigma(X)$ are arrows of $\mathcal{L}(\Sigma)$, processes of N are arrows of $\mathcal{P}(N)$. The functoriality of the monoidal operator $\otimes$ is shown to capture the essence of concurrency in net computations. The construction of $\mathcal{P}(N)$ provides a concise description of the concurrent operational semantics of P/T nets, and, as $\mathcal{P}(N)$ can be finitely axiomatized, one also gets an axiomatization of deterministic processes.

After the original paper, further proposals for adding suitable operators to the category of (deterministic) net computations were introduced, as summed up in [9]. However, to the best of our knowledge, no explicit connection was drawn from a categorical model to any set-theoretical notion of non-deterministic process, thus re-establishing the same connection as with $\mathcal{P}(N)$ and the deterministic processes of N. In this paper we show how the algebraic approach of [10] can be naturally generalised in order to capture the non-deterministic computations of Petri nets. The algebraic model of a net described above is extended by adding a second monoidal operator $\oplus$ which is intended to exactly model the non-deterministic composition of computations.

The presence of two symmetric monoidal operators $\otimes$ and $\oplus$, where the former distributes over the latter, naturally leads to consider the so-called *bimonoidal* (or *rig*) categories which, roughly speaking, are the categorical counterpart of semirings (or rigs) pretty much as monoidal categories corresponds to monoids. Additionally, the branching structure of non-deterministic computations is captured by the presence of a natural transformation $\nabla_a : a \to a \oplus a$. As this recalls the idempotency axioms of $\oplus$ in tropical semirings or dioids, we denoted the corresponding categorical structure as a *diodal category*.

More in detail, we introduce a category of concatenable non-deterministic processes $\mathbf{CNP}(N)$ for a Petri net N which generalises the category of deterministic processes originally defined in [2,14]. Then we show that the category of concatenable non-deterministic processes can be characterised as the free diodal category $\mathcal{NP}(N)$ built over N. As a consequence the non-deterministic processes of a net N, as introduced in [3], turn out to be in one to one correspondence with a suitable class of arrows of $\mathcal{NP}(N)$, quotiented under natural axioms.

The rest of the paper is organised as follows. In Section 1, after recalling some basics about Petri nets, we review the notions of deterministic and non-deterministic process. In Section 2 we present the construction of the category of concatenable non-deterministic processes for a Petri net. Section 3 recalls some basic notions on symmetric monoidal categories, introduces diodal categories and presents the main theorem, concerning the correspondence between non-deterministic processes and arrows of a free diodal category. The paper is rounded up with some remarks on our construction and pointers to further works.

1   Petri Nets and Non-deterministic Processes

Given a set X, we denote by $X^\otimes$ the free commutative monoid over X (finite multisets over X) with unit the empty set $\emptyset$. Furthermore, given a function $f : X \to Y^\otimes$ we denote by $f^\otimes : X^\otimes \to Y^\otimes$ its commutative monoidal extension. Given $u \in X^\otimes$, we denote by $[u]$ the underlying subset of X defined in the obvious way. When set relations are used over multisets, we implicitly refer to the underlying set. E.g., for $u, v \in X^\otimes$ by $x \in u$ we mean $x \in [u]$ and similarly $u \cap v$ means $[u] \cap [v]$.

Definition 1 (P/T net). *A P/T Petri net is a tuple* $N = (\zeta_0, \zeta_1, S, T)$, *where S is a set of* places, *T is a set of* transitions, *and $\zeta_0, \zeta_1 : T \to S^\otimes$ are functions assigning multisets called* source *and* target, *respectively, to each transition.*

Hereafter, for any net N we assume $N = (\zeta_0, \zeta_1, S, T)$, with subscripts and superscripts carrying over the names of the components. In order to simplify the presentation, we require that for any net N, for all $t \in T$, $\zeta_0(t) \neq \emptyset \neq \zeta_1(t)$.

Given a net N, a multiset $u \in S^\otimes$, representing a state of the net, is often referred to as a *marking* of N. It is called *safe* if any place occurs at most once in it, i.e., $u = [u]$.

The notion of net morphism naturally arises from an algebraic view, where places and transitions play the role of sorts and operators.

Definition 2 (net morphism). *A Petri net morphism* $f = \langle f_s, f_t \rangle : N \to N'$ *is a pair where $f_s : S^\otimes \to S'^\otimes$ is a monoid homomorphism, and $f_t : T \to T'$ is a function such that $\zeta'_i \circ f_t = f_s \circ \zeta_i$, for any $i \in \{0, 1\}$. The category of P/T nets (as objects) and their morphisms (as arrows) is denoted by* **Petri**.

In the sequel, when the meaning is clear from the context, we omit the subscripts from the morphism components, thus writing f instead of f_s and f_t.

Let N be a P/T net. The *causality relation* is the least transitive relation $<_N \subseteq (S \cup T) \times (S \cup T)$ such that

      i. if $s \in \zeta_0(t)$ then $s <_N t$;   ii. if $s \in \zeta_1(t)$ then $t <_N s$.

Given a place or transition $x \in S \cup T$, the set of *causes* of x in T is defined as $\lfloor x \rfloor = \{t \in T \mid t <_N x\} \cup \{t\}$; and, for $X \subseteq S \cup T$, $\lfloor X \rfloor = \bigcup_{x \in X} \lfloor x \rfloor$. The *conflict relation* $\#_N \subseteq (S \cup T) \times (S \cup T)$ is the least symmetric relation such that

i. if $t \neq t'$ and $\zeta_0(t) \cap \zeta_0(t') \neq \emptyset$ then $t \#_N t'$;
ii. if $x \#_N x'$ and $x' <_N x''$ then $x \#_N x''$.

Definition 3 (occurrence net). *An occurrence net is a P/T net N where $\zeta_0(t), \zeta_1(t)$ are safe for all $t \in T$ and (i) causality $<_N$ is a strict partial order and, for any transition t, the set of causes $\lfloor t \rfloor$ is finite; (ii) there are no backward conflicts, i.e., for any $t \neq t'$, $\zeta_1(t) \cap \zeta_1(t') = \emptyset$; (iii) conflict $\#_N$ is irreflexive. The sets of minimal and maximal places of N w.r.t. $<_N$ are denoted by $\min(O)$ and $\max(O)$. An occurrence net is* deterministic *if it has no forward conflicts, i.e., for any $t \neq t'$, $\zeta_0(t) \cap \zeta_0(t') = \emptyset$.*

A monomorphism $e : O_1 \to O_2$ such that $e^\otimes(\min(O_1)) = \min(O_2)$ is referred to as an embedding *of O_1 in O_2.*

An occurrence O net can be seen as the representation of a possibly non-deterministic computation starting from $\min(O)$. Reachable states in O can be characterised statically by using the dependency relation.

Definition 4 (cuts). *Let O be an occurrence Petri net. A cut in O is a maximal subset X of places such that neither $s <_O s'$ nor $s \# _O s'$ for all $s, s' \in X$. The set of cuts of O is denoted by $cuts(O)$. A subset of cuts $W \subseteq cuts(O)$ is called a covering of O if $T = \bigcup\{\lfloor X \rfloor : X \in W\}$.*

It can be shown that any cut $X \in cuts(O)$ is reachable by executing all the transitions in $\lfloor X \rfloor$ in any order compatible with $<_O$. The only nonstandard notion is that of covering: if a subset W of cuts is intended to represent the final states of a set of possible computations of O, then W is a covering for O if any possible transition in O is used in one of those computations.

We next review the notion of deterministic and non-deterministic process for P/T nets. A process is represented as a morphism $\pi : O \to N$ from an occurrence Petri net O to the original net N [5]. Since morphisms are simulations, the morphism maps computations of O into computations of N in such a way that the process can be seen as a representative of a set of possible computations of N. The occurrence net makes explicit the causal structure of such computations since each transition is fired at most once and each place is filled with at most one token during each computation. In this way transitions and places of O can be thought of, respectively, as firing of transitions and tokens in places of the original net. Actually, to allow for such an interpretation, some further restrictions have to be imposed on the morphism π, namely it must map places into places (rather than into multisets of places).

Let us call a net morphism $f : N \to N'$ *elementary* if for any $s \in S$, $f_s(s) \in S'$ (places are sent to single places rather than to proper multisets).

Definition 5 (process). *Let N be a P/T net. A non-deterministic process of N is an elementary net morphism $\pi : O \to N$ where O is a finite occurrence net and if $\pi(t) = \pi(t')$ and $\zeta_0(t) = \zeta_0(t')$ then $t = t'$ for any $t, t' \in T_O$ (irredundancy).*

The process π is deterministic *if the underlying occurrence net O is so. For a finite process π we write $\min(\pi)$, $\max(\pi)$ and $cuts(\pi)$ to refer to the sets $\min(O)$, $\max(O)$ and $cuts(O)$ in the underlying occurrence net. We also write $\zeta_0(\pi)$ for $\pi^{\otimes}(\min(\pi))$ and $\zeta_1(\pi)$ for $\pi^{\otimes}(\max(\pi))$.*

Intuitively, a process π represents a set of possible computations starting at the marking $\zeta_0(\pi)$. Not every elementary morphism is a process, as it might fail to satisfy the irredundancy condition, which essentially imposes that the non-deterministic composition of a computation with itself gives back the original computation [3]. However we can easily show that the following result holds.

Proposition 1 (collapsing). *Let N be a P/T net, O an occurrence net and $\xi : O \to N$ an elementary morphism. Then there exists a unique (up to isomorphism) factorisation $\xi = \beta; \pi(\xi)$, where β is epi and $\pi(\xi)$ is a process such that $\zeta_0(\pi(\xi)) = \xi^{\otimes}(\min(O))$. The process $\pi(\xi)$ is called the collapsing of ξ.*

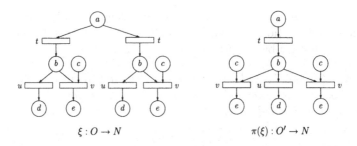

$$\xi : O \to N \qquad\qquad \pi(\xi) : O' \to N$$

Fig. 1. An elementary morphism and its collapsing

Intuitively, the collapsing of ξ is obtained from ξ by merging pairs of transitions which violate the irredundancy requirement. As an example, Fig. 1 presents on the left an elementary morphism from an occurrence net to a Petri net, and on the right its collapsing. The morphism is represented by labelling places and transitions of the occurrence net by their images over N (and the net N which they are mapped to is not relevant here and thus omitted).

2   Concatenable Processes

In this section, after reviewing the theory of concatenable deterministic process [2,14], we propose a notion of concatenable non-deterministic process. This leads to a category $\mathbf{CNP}(N)$ of non-deterministic processes for a net N, where objects are states and arrows model non-deterministic computations of N.

2.1   Concatenable Deterministic Processes

Concatenable processes for Petri nets have been introduced in [2,14] as a refinement of Goltz-Reisig deterministic processes, endowed with operations of sequential and parallel composition that are consistent with the causal structure of computations. In order to properly define such operations we need to impose a suitable ordering over the places in $\min(\pi)$ and $\max(\pi)$ for each process π. Such an ordering allows to distinguish among "interface" places of O_π which are mapped to the same place of the original net, a capability which is essential to track causal dependencies.

Definition 6. *Let A, B be sets and $f : A \to B$ a function. An f-indexed ordering is a family $\alpha = \{\alpha_b \mid b \in B\}$ of bijections $\alpha_b : f^{-1}(b) \to [|f^{-1}(b)|]$, where $[i]$ denotes the subset $\{1, \ldots, i\}$ of $\mathbb{N}$, and $f^{-1}(b) = \{a \in A \mid f(a) = b\}$.*

The f-indexed ordering α is often identified with the function from A to $\mathbb{N}$ that it naturally induces (formally defined as $\bigcup_{b \in B} \alpha_b$). Let $f_1 : A_1 \to B$ and $f_2 : A_2 \to B$, with $A_1 \cap A_2 = \emptyset$, so that $f = f_1 \cup f_2 : A_1 \cup A_2 \to B$ is a function. Consider two f_i-indexed orderings α_i, $i \in \{1, 2\}$. Then we denote by $\alpha_1 \otimes \alpha_2$ the f-indexed ordering defined by $\alpha_1 \otimes \alpha_2(a) = \alpha_1(a)$ if $a \in A_1$ and $\alpha_1 \otimes \alpha_2(a) = \alpha_2(a) + |f_1^{-1}(f_2(a))|$, otherwise.

Definition 7 (concatenable process). *A concatenable process of a net N is a triple $\delta = \langle \mu, \pi, \nu \rangle$, where π is a deterministic process of N, μ is a π-indexed ordering of $\min(\pi)$ and ν is a π-indexed ordering of $\max(\pi)$.*

Isomorphism of concatenable processes is defined in the usual way (see e.g. [2]) and an isomorphism class of processes is called *(abstract) concatenable process* and denoted by $[\delta]$, for δ is a member of the class. Often the word "abstract" is omitted and δ denotes the corresponding isomorphism class.

Definition 8 (sequential and parallel composition). *Let $\delta_1 = \langle \mu_1, \pi_1, \nu_1 \rangle$ and $\delta_2 = \langle \mu_2, \pi_2, \nu_2 \rangle$ be two concatenable processes of a net N.*

- *Let $\zeta_1(\pi_1) = \zeta_0(\pi_2)$. Suppose $T_1 \cap T_2 = \emptyset$ and $S_1 \cap S_2 = \max(\pi_1) = \min(\pi_2)$, with $\pi_1(s) = \pi_2(s)$ and $\nu_1(s) = \mu_2(s)$ for each $s \in S_1 \cap S_2$. Then $\delta_1; \delta_2$ is the concatenable process $\delta = \langle \mu_1, \pi, \nu_2 \rangle$, where the process π is the (component-wise) union of π_1 and π_2.*
- *Suppose $T_1 \cap T_2 = S_1 \cap S_2 = \emptyset$. Then $\delta_1 \otimes \delta_2$ is the concatenable process $\delta = \langle \mu, \pi, \nu \rangle$, where the process π is the (component-wise) union of π_1 and π_2, $\mu = \mu_1 \otimes \mu_2$ and $\nu = \nu_1 \otimes \nu_2$.*

The premise of the first item means that δ_1 and δ_2 overlap only on $\max(\pi_1) = \min(\pi_2)$, and on such places the labelling on the original net and the ordering coincide. Then, their concatenation is the process obtained by gluing the maximal places of π_1 and the minimal places of π_2 according to their ordering. Parallel composition is instead obtained simply by juxtaposing the two processes.

Concatenation and parallel composition clearly induce well-defined operations on abstract processes, independent of the choice of representatives.

Definition 9 (category of concatenable processes). *Let N be a net. The category of (abstract) concatenable processes of N, denoted by $\mathbf{CP}(N)$, is defined as follows. Objects are multisets of places of N, namely elements of $S^{\otimes}$. Each (abstract) concatenable process $[\langle \mu, \pi, \nu \rangle]$ of N is an arrow from $\zeta_0(\pi)$ to $\zeta_1(\pi)$. Parallel composition $\otimes$ makes $\mathbf{CP}(N)$ a symmetric monoidal category.*

2.2 Concatenable Non-deterministic Processes

Intuitively, a concatenable non-deterministic process is a set of non-deterministic processes, which, starting from a set of possible initial states, produces a set of possible final states. For technical reasons, it is preferable to consider sequences of processes rather than sets. Additionally, as in the deterministic case, in order to allow for a sequential composition of computations keeping track of the causal dependencies, initial and final states of computations are decorated.

Definition 10 (concatenable non-deterministic process). *Let N be a net. A concatenable non-deterministic process for N is a triple of finite non-empty lists $\eta = \langle \alpha, \boldsymbol{\pi}, \omega \rangle$ with*

- *$\boldsymbol{\pi} = \pi_1 \ldots \pi_n$, where each π_i is a non-deterministic process;*

- $\alpha = \alpha_1 \ldots \alpha_n$, where each α_i is a π_i-indexed ordering of $\min(\pi_i)$;
- $\omega = \omega_1 \ldots \omega_\ell$, where

  - for each $j \in \{1, \ldots, \ell\}$, $\omega_j : X \to \mathbb{N}$ with $X \in cuts(\pi_i)$ for some i and ω_j a π_i-indexed ordering of X;
  - for any i the cuts of O_i which occur in ω, i.e., $\{X \in cuts(\pi_i) \mid \exists j. \, \omega_j : X \to \mathbb{N}\}$, are a covering of O_i.

The source of η is the list $\zeta_0(\eta) = \zeta_0(\pi_1) \ldots \zeta_0(\pi_n)$, i.e., the list of the sources of the component processes, while the target of η is $\zeta_1(\eta) = u_1 \ldots u_\ell$ where $u_j = \pi_i^\otimes(X)$ if $\omega_j : X \to \mathbb{N}$ and $X \in cuts(O_i)$.

In order to ease notation we fix a naming scheme. We assume concatenable non-deterministic processes to be of the kind $\eta = \langle \alpha, \boldsymbol{\pi}, \omega \rangle$, with $\boldsymbol{\pi} = \pi_1 \ldots \pi_n$ and $n = |\boldsymbol{\pi}|$. In turn, for each process π_i in $\boldsymbol{\pi}$ we assume $\pi_i : O_i \to N$, where O_i has S_i and T_i as place and transition sets. Processes π_i are supposed to be pairwise disjoint. Superscripts carry over the name of the components.

Two concatenable non-deterministic processes $\eta = \langle \alpha, \boldsymbol{\pi}, \omega \rangle$, $\eta' = \langle \alpha', \boldsymbol{\pi}', \omega' \rangle$ are *isomorphic* if $|\boldsymbol{\pi}| = |\boldsymbol{\pi}'|$ and there exist non-deterministic process isomorphisms between π_i and π_i', with $i \in \{1, \ldots, |\boldsymbol{\pi}|\}$, consistent with the decorations and the ordering of sources and targets. Abstract concatenable non-deterministic processes, i.e., isomorphism classes of processes, are often identified with one of the representatives, i.e., we write η to refer to the corresponding abstract process.

Graphically, a concatenable non-deterministic process $\eta = \langle \alpha, \boldsymbol{\pi}, \omega \rangle$, with $\boldsymbol{\pi} = \langle \pi_1 \ldots \pi_n \rangle$, is represented by enclosing in a box the list of the nets $O_1, \ldots, O_n$, underlying the component subprocesses, separated by vertical bars. Places and transitions of O_i are labelled by their images through π_i (the net N which they are mapped to is not relevant here and thus omitted). The decoration of the source of each process π_i is represented by listing on the top of the process itself the places in $\min(\pi_i)$ in an order compatible with α_i, i.e., if $s, s' \in \min(O_i)$ and $\pi_i(s) = \pi_i(s')$ and $\alpha_i(s) < \alpha_i(s')$ then s is listed first. Similarly, in the bottom part of the box, we represent $w = w_1 \ldots w_\ell$ as a list of elements, one for each ω_j. If $\omega_j : X \to \mathbb{N}$, with $X \in cuts(\pi_i)$, then the corresponding element is itself a sequence which lists the places in X in an order compatible with ω_j. A process $\eta = \langle \alpha_1 \alpha_2, \pi_1 \pi_2, \omega_1 \omega_2 \omega_3 \rangle$ consisting of two component processes π_1 and π_2, with three targets can be found in Fig. 2. In this case, for instance, α_1 is the function $\alpha_1(s_1) = 0$, $\alpha_1(s_2) = 0$ and $\alpha_1(s_3) = 1$. Concerning the targets, $\{s_5, s_3\}, \{s_6, s_7\} \in cuts(\pi_1)$ and $\{s_{10}\} \in cuts(\pi_2)$. It is easy to see that the cuts $\{s_5, s_3\}, \{s_6, s_7\}$ form a covering of O_1, and similarly $\{s_{10}\}$ is a covering for O_2.

Sequential and parallel composition for concatenable non-deterministic processes can be defined as follows.

Definition 11 (sequential composition). *Let $\eta = \langle \alpha, \boldsymbol{\pi}, \omega \rangle$ and $\eta' = \langle \alpha', \boldsymbol{\pi}', \omega' \rangle$ be two concatenable non-deterministic processes of a net N such that $\zeta_1(\eta) = \zeta_0(\eta')$, and thus $|\omega| = |\alpha'|$. Suppose that for any i, j it holds $T_i \cap T_j' = \emptyset$ and, for all j, if $\omega_j : X \to \mathbb{N}$, with $X \in cuts(\pi_i)$ then $S_i \cap S_j' = X = \min(\pi_j')$,*

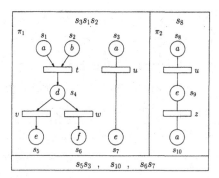

Fig. 2. A concatenable non-deterministic process

with $\pi_i(s) = \pi'_j(s)$ and $\omega_i(s) = \alpha'_j(s)$ for each $s \in X$. Then $\eta_1; \eta_2$ is the concatenable process $\eta = \langle \alpha, \pi'', \omega' \rangle$, where $\pi'' = \pi''_1 \dots \pi''_{|\pi|}$ and each process π''_i is obtained as follows: take the (component-wise) union of π_i with all processes π'_j such that $\omega_j : X \to \mathbb{N}$ with $X \in cuts(\pi_i)$ thus getting an elementary morphism $\xi_i : O''_i \to N$ and then consider the collapsing $\pi(\xi_i)$ of such morphism.

Roughly, for any $j \in \{1, \dots, |\omega|\}$, if $\omega_j : X \to \mathbb{N}$ where X is a cut in π_i, then the process π'_j in η' must be attached to the set of places X in π_i. Assuming that π_i and π'_j overlap only on $X = \min(\pi'_j)$, and on such places the labelling on the original net and the ordering imposed by the two processes coincide, then attaching π_j to π_i reduces to taking their component-wise union. Therefore the composition has $|\pi|$ components, each one obtained as the component-wise union of each π_i with all π'_j which must be connected to π_i.

Definition 12 (parallel composition). Let $\eta = \langle \alpha, \pi, \omega \rangle$ and $\eta' = \langle \alpha', \pi', \omega' \rangle$ be two concatenable non-deterministic processes. Suppose $|\pi| = n$, $|\pi'| = n'$, and $T_i \cap T'_j = S_i \cap S'_j = \emptyset$ for any i, j. Then $\eta \otimes \eta'$ is the concatenable process $\eta'' = \langle \alpha'', \pi'', \omega'' \rangle$, with

$$\pi'' = \pi_{1,1} \dots \pi_{n,1} \pi_{1,2} \dots \pi_{n,2} \dots \pi_{n',1} \dots \pi_{n',n}$$

where each $\pi_{i,j}$ is the (component-wise) union of π_i and π'_j. Similarly $\alpha'' = \alpha_{1,1} \dots \alpha_{n',n}$ with $\alpha_{i,j} = \alpha_i \otimes \alpha'_j$ and $\omega'' = \omega_{1,1} \dots \omega_{\ell',\ell}$ with $\omega_{i,j} = \omega_i \otimes \omega'_j$.

Note that when composing in parallel two non-deterministic processes η and η', we compose each component of η with each component of η'. Intuitively, this means that parallel composition distributes over non-deterministic composition.

Finally, we can easily define a notion of non-deterministic composition, which is obtained by juxtaposing the two processes.

Definition 13 (non-deterministic composition). Let $\eta = \langle \alpha, \pi, \omega \rangle$ and $\eta' = \langle \alpha', \pi', \omega' \rangle$ be concatenable non-deterministic processes. Then $\eta \oplus \eta' = \langle \alpha\alpha', \pi\pi', \omega\omega' \rangle$, where the juxtaposition of two lists denotes their concatenation.

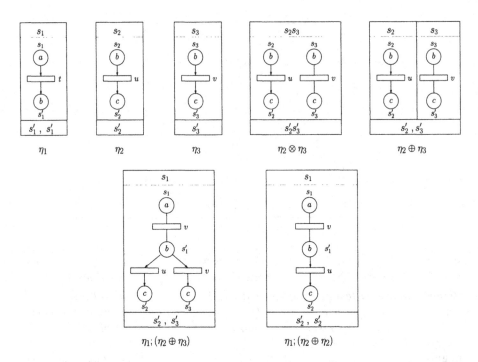

Fig. 3. Three simple concatenable non-deterministic processes η_1, η_2, η_3 and some processes arising from their composition

It can be shown that, as in the deterministic case, concatenation and parallel composition induce well-defined operations on abstract processes, independent of the particular choice of the representatives.

As an example consider the three simple processes η_1, η_2, η_3 in Fig. 3, consisting of one transition only. Note that η_1 nondeterministically offers two copies of s_1' as target. The same figure reports the parallel composition $\eta_2 \otimes \eta_3$, the nondeterministic composition $\eta_2 \oplus \eta_3$, the processes $\eta_1 ; (\eta_2 \oplus \eta_3)$ and $\eta_1 ; (\eta_2 \oplus \eta_2)$. For the last process observe that the two non-deterministic copies of u are joined as an effect of the composition (yet the composite process still non-deterministically offers two copies of s_2' as target).

Definition 14 (category of concatenable non-deterministic processes).
Let N be a net. The category of (abstract) concatenable non-deterministic processes of N, denoted by **CNP**(N), *is defined as follows. Objects are finite non-empty lists of elements of $S^{\otimes}$. Each (abstract) concatenable non-deterministic process of N is an arrow. Both parallel $\otimes$ and non-deterministic $\oplus$ composition make* **CNP**(N) *a symmetric monoidal category.*

Obviously, the non-deterministic processes of a net N, as given in Definition 5, correspond to the arrows of **CNP**(N) consisting of a single process $\eta = \langle \alpha_1, \pi_1, \omega \rangle$, once we forget the decoration.

3   Embedding Processes into Terms

This section presents the main result of the paper, namely, the description of the abstract concatenable non-deterministic processes of a net N, as defined in Section 2, as terms of a suitable algebra. Along the *Petri nets are monoids* paradigm, this is a sort of monoidal category, freely generated from the net itself.

3.1   Categorical Notions

Here we introduce the relevant categorical notions that are needed for the algebraic description of processes. Most definitions are standard: for the presentation of monoidal categories we closely follow [1].

Definition 15 (monoidal categories). *A (strict) monoidal category is a triple $\langle C, \_ \oplus \_, e \rangle$, where C is the underlying category, the tensor product $\_ \oplus \_ : C \times C \longrightarrow C$ is a functor satisfying the law $(t_1 \oplus t_2) \oplus t_3 = t_1 \oplus (t_2 \oplus t_3)$, and e is an object of C satisfying the law $t \oplus e = t = e \oplus t$, for all arrows $t, t_1, t_2, t_3 \in C$.*

A symmetric monoidal category is a 4-tuple $\langle C, \_ \oplus \_, e, \gamma \rangle$, where $\langle C, \_ \oplus \_, e \rangle$ is a monoidal category, and $\gamma : \_{-1} \oplus \_{-2} \Rightarrow \_{-2} \oplus \_{-1} : C \times C \longrightarrow C$ is a natural isomorphism[1] satisfying the coherence axioms $\gamma_{a,e} = a$ and

A i-monoidal category is a 5-tuple $\langle C, \_ \oplus \_, e, \gamma, \nabla \rangle$, where $\langle C, \_ \oplus \_, e, \gamma \rangle$ is a symmetric monoidal category and $\nabla : \_{-1} \Rightarrow \_{-1} \oplus \_{-1} : C \longrightarrow C$ is a natural transformation satisfying the coherence axioms $\nabla_e = e$ and

While symmetric monoidal categories are a staple of theoretical computer science, at least since the seminal work by Meseguer and Montanari [10], we introduced i-monoidality in order to capture the idempotency of the additive operator. Making each object s a cosemigroup object (not yet a comonoid object, since the arrow $s \to e$ is missing [8]) and requiring the naturality of ∇ are suggested by the need of equating somehow the addition of terms, yet banning the identity $t = t \oplus t$: we offer further remarks in the concluding section.

---

[1] Given functors $F, G : \mathcal{A} \to \mathcal{B}$, a *natural transformation* $\tau : F \Rightarrow G : \mathcal{A} \to \mathcal{B}$ is a family of arrows of $\mathcal{B}$ indexed by objects of $\mathcal{A}$, $\tau = \{\tau_a : F(a) \to G(a) \mid a \in O_{\mathcal{A}}\}$, such that for every arrow $f : a \to a'$ in $\mathcal{A}$, $\tau_a; G(f) = F(f); \tau_{a'}$ in $\mathcal{B}$. We say that τ is an *isomorphism* if all its components τ_a's are so.

Definition 16 (diodal categories). *A* bimonoidal category *is a 8-tuple* $\langle \mathcal{C}, \_\oplus$
$\_, e, \gamma, \_\otimes\_, o, \rho, \delta \rangle$*, where* $\langle \mathcal{C}, \_\oplus\_, e, \gamma \rangle$ *and* $\langle \mathcal{C}, \_\otimes\_, o, \rho \rangle$ *are symmetric monoidal*
categories satisfying the law $t \otimes e = e$ *for all arrows* $t \in \mathcal{C}$ *and the coherence*
axiom $\rho_{a,e} = e$*, and* $\delta : \_1 \otimes (\_2 \oplus \_3) \Rightarrow (\_1 \otimes \_2) \oplus (\_1 \otimes \_3) : \mathcal{C} \otimes \mathcal{C} \otimes \mathcal{C} \longrightarrow \mathcal{C}$ *is*
a natural isomorphism satisfying the axioms $\delta_{o,b,c} = b \oplus c$*,* $\delta_{a,b,e} = a \otimes b$ *and*

$$
\begin{array}{ccc}
a \otimes (b \oplus c) & \xrightarrow{\;\delta_{a,b,c}\;} & (a \otimes b) \oplus (a \otimes c) \\
{\scriptstyle a \otimes \gamma_{b,c}} \downarrow & & \uparrow {\scriptstyle \gamma_{a \otimes c, a \otimes b}} \\
a \otimes (c \oplus b) & \xrightarrow[\;\delta_{a,c,b}\;]{} & (a \otimes c) \oplus (a \otimes b)
\end{array}
$$

Finally, a diodal category *is a 9-tuple* $\langle \mathcal{C}, \_\oplus\_, o, \rho, \nabla, \_\otimes\_, e, \gamma, \delta \rangle$*, where*
$\langle \mathcal{C}, \_\oplus\_, o, \rho, \nabla \rangle$ *is a i-monoidal category and* $\langle \mathcal{C}, \_\oplus\_, o, \rho, \_\otimes\_, e, \gamma, \delta \rangle$ *is a*
bimonoidal category, satisfying the coherence axiom

$$
\begin{array}{ccc}
a \otimes b & \xrightarrow{\;a \otimes \nabla_b\;} & a \otimes (b \oplus b) \\
& {\scriptstyle \nabla_{a \otimes b}} \searrow & \downarrow {\scriptstyle \delta_{a,b,b}} \\
& & (a \otimes b) \oplus (a \otimes b)
\end{array}
$$

Bimonoidal categories, and their coherence laws, have been considered quite early
on in the literature [7]. Recently they surfaced, sometimes with the name *rig* or
semiring categories, in the definition of models for quantum programming [6].

We introduced diodal categories in order to obtain a categorical counterpart of
dioids, i.e., semirings where the additive operator is idempotent. In the following,
we consider diodal categories satisfying an additional requirement.

Definition 17 (bipermutative and dipermutative categories). *A* bipermutative category *is a bimonoidal category such that* δ *is an identity, so that the*
objects $a \otimes (b \oplus c)$ *and* $(a \otimes b) \oplus (a \otimes c)$ *coincide; and moreover* $\rho_{a, b \oplus c} = \rho_{a,b} \oplus \rho_{a,c}$*.*
Dipermutative categories *are diodal categories based on bipermutative categories.*

3.2 Categories of Processes

In this part we introduce a concrete category, out of the transitions of the net, and
we prove that it forms a diodal category. More importantly, those arrows exactly
correspond to non-deterministic processes, along the lines of the characterisation
of deterministic processes via the category $\mathcal{P}(N)$ in [2].

Notation. Given a monoid $\langle M, \otimes, 1 \rangle$, we denote by $M^\oplus$ the free monoid over M
(finite non-empty lists over M): the unit of $\oplus$ is the list $\langle 1 \rangle$ containing only the
unit of the monoid. Note that the $\otimes$ operator can be extended set-wise to the
monoid $M^\oplus$, resulting in a semiring (not yet a dioid, since $\oplus$ is not idempotent).
So, assuming that M is $X^\otimes$, the resulting structure is denoted simply as $X^{\otimes, \oplus}$,
and it coincides with the free $\otimes$-commutative semiring on X.

Definition 18 (a category for deterministic processes). *Let N be a P/T*
net. Then, $\mathcal{DP}(N)$ is the category whose objects are markings of N (i.e., elements

$$\frac{s \in S_N^{\otimes,\oplus}}{id_s : s \to s \in \mathcal{NP}(N)} \qquad \frac{t \in T_N}{t : \zeta_0(t) \to \zeta_1(t) \in \mathcal{NP}(N)} \qquad \frac{s, s' \in S_N^{\otimes,\oplus}}{\rho_{s,s'} : s \otimes s' \to s' \otimes s \in \mathcal{NP}(N)}$$

$$\frac{t : s \to s', t_1 : s' \to s_1 \in \mathcal{NP}(N)}{t; t_1 : s \to s_1 \in \mathcal{NP}(N)} \qquad \frac{t : s \to s', t_1 : s_1 \to s_1' \in \mathcal{NP}(N)}{t \otimes t_1 : s \otimes s_1 \to s' \otimes s_1' \in \mathcal{NP}(N)}$$

Fig. 4. The deterministic fragment of the set of inference rules generating $\mathcal{NP}(N)$

$$t; id_{s'} = t = id_s; t \quad t = t \otimes id_\emptyset \quad (t_1 \otimes t_2); (t_3 \otimes t_4) = (t_1; t_3) \otimes (t_2; t_4)$$

$$\rho_{s,s'}; \rho_{s',s} = id_{s \otimes s'} = id_s \otimes id_{s'} \quad \rho_{s,s' \otimes s''} = (id_s \otimes \rho_{s',s''}); (\rho_{s,s''} \otimes id_{s'}) \quad \rho_{s,\emptyset} = id_s$$

$$\rho_{s_1,s_2}; (t_1 \otimes t_2) = (t_2 \otimes t_1); \rho_{s_2',s_1'} \quad \rho_{a,b} = id_{a \otimes b} \text{ for } a \neq b \in S_N \quad \rho; t = t; \rho' \text{ for } t \in T_N$$

Fig. 5. The set of axioms for deterministic processes quotienting $\mathcal{DP}(N)$

of $S_N^\otimes$), while the arrows are freely generated according to the rules in Fig. 4, subject to the axioms in Fig. 5.[2]

Since the composition operator ; is partial, axioms in Fig. 5 hold when both sides are defined; additionally, note that a, b denote places in S_N, instead of elements of $S_N^\otimes$. The objects of $\mathcal{DP}(N)$ are thus markings of N, representing sources and targets of deterministic processes. Its arrows are equivalence classes of concrete elements generated by the set of inference rules in Fig. 4, modulo the equations making it a symmetric monoidal category.

The further equations $\rho_{a,b} = id_a \otimes id_b$ and $\rho; t = t; \rho'$ (for permutations ρ, ρ', i.e., arrows built out of identities and $\rho_{a,b}$'s) represent a well-known idiosyncrasy of the concrete representation of deterministic processes [13], so that e.g. for transitions t_1 and t_2 with distinct sources and targets, the processes $t_1 \otimes t_2$ and $t_2 \otimes t_1$ have to be identified, since, as discussed for concrete processes, the order of distinct places is irrelevant. Analogous issues appear in the category below, extending the former in order to include non-determinism.

Definition 19 (a category for non-deterministic processes). *Let N be a P/T net. Then, $\mathcal{NP}(N)$ is the category whose objects are finite non-empty lists of markings of N (i.e., elements of $S_N^{\otimes,\oplus}$), while the arrows are freely generated according to the rules in Fig. 4 and 6, subject to the axioms in Fig. 5 and 7.*

Given a net N, the objects of $\mathcal{NP}(N)$ are lists of markings of N, each one representing the source of one non-deterministic component of the non-deterministic process. Instead, arrows are equivalence classes of elements generated by the inference rules in Fig. 4 and 6, modulo a set of equations making it a dipermutative category. Note the lack of the equation $\gamma_{a,b} = id_{a \oplus b}$.

---

[2] For the sake of space saving, we overloaded some symbols, so that for the current definition $S_N^{\otimes,\oplus}$ and $\mathcal{NP}(N)$ in Fig. 4 should read as $S_N^\otimes$ and $\mathcal{DP}(N)$.

$$\frac{s, s' \in S_N^{\otimes \oplus}}{\gamma_{s,s'} : s \oplus s' \to s' \oplus s \in \mathcal{NP}(N)} \qquad \frac{s \in S_N^{\otimes, \oplus}}{\nabla_s : s \to s \oplus s \in \mathcal{NP}(N)}$$

$$\frac{t : s \to s', t_1 : s_1 \to s_1' \in \mathcal{NP}(N)}{t \oplus t_1 : s \oplus s_1 \to s' \oplus s_1' \in \mathcal{NP}(N)}$$

Fig. 6. The inference rules for non-determinism generating $\mathcal{NP}(N)$

$$t = t \oplus id_{\langle \emptyset \rangle} \qquad (t_1 \oplus t_2); (t_3 \oplus t_4) = (t_1; t_3) \oplus (t_2; t_4)$$

$$\gamma_{s,s'}; \gamma_{s',s} = id_{s \oplus s'} = id_s \oplus id_{s'} \quad \gamma_{s,s' \oplus s''} = (id_s \oplus \gamma_{s',s''}); (\gamma_{s,s''} \oplus id_{s'}) \quad \gamma_{s,\langle \emptyset \rangle} = id_s$$

$$\nabla_s; \gamma_{s,s} = \nabla_s \quad \nabla_s; (id_s \otimes \nabla_s) = \nabla_s; (\nabla_s \otimes id_s) \quad \nabla_{s \oplus s} = (\nabla_s \oplus \nabla_s); (id_s \oplus \gamma_{s,s} \oplus id_s)$$

$$\gamma_{s_1,s_2}; (t_1 \oplus t_2) = (t_2 \oplus t_1); \gamma_{s_2',s_1'} \quad \nabla_{\langle \emptyset \rangle} = id_{\langle \emptyset \rangle} = \rho_{s,\langle \emptyset \rangle} \quad id_s \otimes \nabla_{s'} = \nabla_{s \otimes s'}$$

$$t \otimes (t_1 \oplus t_2) = (t \otimes t_1) \oplus (t \otimes t_2) \qquad \rho_{s,s' \oplus s''} = \rho_{s,s'} \oplus \rho_{s,s''}$$

Fig. 7. The set of axioms quotienting $\mathcal{NP}(N)$

The objects of $\mathcal{NP}(N)$ are obtained by constructing the free $\otimes$-commutative semiring, out of the initial set of places of the net N. As for arrows, the analogy with the semiring construction out of a monoid is confirmed by the characterization result stated below. For a marking s, we let s^k denote the k-times composition $s \oplus \ldots \oplus s$; while we let ∇_s^k denote the unique arrow with source s and target s^k, inductively built as $\nabla_s^1 = id_s$ and $\nabla_s^{k+1} = \nabla_s^k; (id_s \oplus \nabla_s)$.

Proposition 2. *Let* $s_1, \ldots, s_l \in S_N^{\otimes}$ *and* $t \in \mathcal{NP}(N)$ *an arrow with source* $s_1 \oplus \ldots \oplus s_l$. *Then,* t *can be decomposed as* $(\nabla_{s_1}^{k_1} \oplus \ldots \oplus \nabla_{s_l}^{k_l}); \gamma; (t_1 \oplus \ldots \oplus t_n)$, *for* $n = k_1 + \ldots + k_l$, γ *a permutation and* t_i's *in* $\mathcal{DP}(N)$.

The permutation γ is just an arrow built out of identities and $\gamma_{a,b}$'s. The normal form can be proved unique, up-to a syntactic ordering on arrows. The corollary below exploits the axiom equating $\nabla_s; \gamma_{s,s}$ to ∇_s for $s \in S_N^{\otimes}$.

Corollary 1. *Let* $s \in S_N^{\otimes}$ *and* $t \in \mathcal{NP}(N)$ *an arrow with source* s. *Then,* t *can be decomposed as* $\nabla_s^k; (t_1 \oplus \ldots \oplus t_k)$, *for* t_i's *in* $\mathcal{DP}(N)$.

As shown above, and hinted at in the beginning of the section, the insertion of the $\oplus$ operator mimics the well-known generation of a semiring from a monoid. The arrows of the resulting category $\mathcal{NP}(N)$ can indeed be seen as suitable list of arrows of $\mathcal{DP}(N)$. Recalling that $\mathcal{DP}(N)$, the sub-category obtained by restricting to the $\otimes$-fragment of $\mathcal{NP}(N)$, coincides with the symmetric category $\mathcal{P}(N)$ of deterministic processes [2,13], we can view arrows in $\mathcal{NP}(N)$ as lists of deterministic processes. This fact is deepened and formalised in the next section.

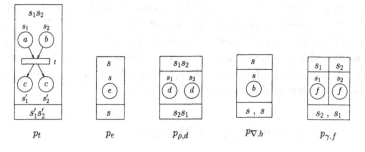

Fig. 8. Basic concatenable processes

3.3 Processes as Terms

Let us begin the section by recalling the main result concerning $\mathcal{DP}(N)$ and the category of concatenable (deterministic) processes.

For stating this result and its generalisation to the non-deterministic case we need the five basic processes represented in Fig. 8. In the discussion t represents a generic transition of a fixed net N and a, b, c, d, e, f are names for places. Any transition t can be seen as a concatenable (deterministic) process p_t. As an example, on the far left of the figure, we have a representation of the process p_t, for a transition t such that $\zeta_0(t) = a \otimes b$ and $\zeta_1(t) = c \otimes c$. Next, there is the representation of p_e, the unique (deterministic) process with no transitions from e to itself. Process $p_{\rho,d}$ is the deterministic process from $d \otimes d$ to itself, simply swapping the multiset ordering. Then $p_{\nabla,b}$ is the non-deterministic processes consisting of one place b only, with source b and as target twice the maximal cut $\{b\}$, i.e., $b \oplus b$. Finally, $p_{\gamma,f}$ represents the permutation for the two underlying identity processes: source and target are f, f.

Proposition 3 (deterministic correspondence [13]). *Let N be a net. The function $\mathcal{C}_N$ from the class of generating arrows of the category $\mathcal{DP}(N)$ to the class of basic processes of N, defined by*

$$\mathcal{C}_N(id_a) = p_a \text{ and } \mathcal{C}_N(\rho_{a,a}) = p_{\rho,a} \text{ for } a \in S_N$$

$$\mathcal{C}_N(t) = p_t \text{ for } t \in T_N$$

lifts to a full and faithful (symmetric monoidal) functor $\mathcal{P}_N : \mathcal{DP}(N) \to \mathbf{CP}(N)$.

Note that the functor induces a bijective correspondence between the arrows of the category $\mathcal{DP}(N)$ and the concatenable (deterministic) processes of the net N itself. Finally, our main result is now stated below.

Theorem 1 (non-deterministic correspondence). *Let N be a net. The function $\mathcal{CN}_N$ from the class of generating arrows of the category $\mathcal{NP}(N)$ to the class of basic processes of N, defined by extending $\mathcal{C}_N$ with*

$$\mathcal{CN}_N(\nabla_a) = p_{\nabla,a} \text{ and } \mathcal{CN}_N(\gamma_{a,a}) = p_{\gamma,a} \text{ for } a \in S_N$$

lifts to a full and faithful (diodal) functor $\mathcal{NP}_N : \mathcal{NP}(N) \to \mathbf{CNP}(N)$.

The theorem clearly exploits the decomposition result discussed in Proposition 2. For our purposes, it basically states that the arrows of $\mathcal{NP}(N)$ do capture the essence of the non-deterministic processes of a net. Note that the introduction of concatenable non-deterministic processes is indeed pivotal, since e.g. the encodings $\mathcal{CN}_N(\nabla_s; (t \oplus id_s))$ and $\mathcal{CN}_N(t)$ have the same underlying process, even if the decoration of their targets differ.

4   Conclusions and Further Works

Along the lines of the seminal paper [10], our work offered an algebraic presentation for non-deterministic processes of Petri nets.

A first contribution of our work is the introduction of the concatenable version of non-deterministic processes, building on the original proposal by Engelfriet [3]. To the best of our knowledge, also putting diodal categories into the limelight represents a small addition to the categorical lore. With respect to former proposals for the categorical characterization of non-determinism, our solution closely recalls *linear categories* [9]: our diodal categories lack a suitable terminal object, in order to be monoidal categories with finite products. It is precisely such a weaker structure that allows us to establish our main result: a functorial bijection between concatenable non-deterministic processes of a net N and the arrows of the free diodal category built out of N.

As for further refinements on the categorical model, as e.g. the self-dual category for modelling processes of contextual nets proposed in [4], let us just mention that we toyed with the idea of capturing the idempotency of $\oplus$ by making ∇ a natural isomorphism (hence, more in tune with the algebraic notion of dioids). The concrete description of concatenable non-deterministic processes does not allow it, since there would be no possible interpretation for the arrow $(\nabla_a)^{-1} : a \oplus a \to a$. However, this is not unfortunate, since the naturality of ∇ would actually make the diagram below commute

$$
\begin{array}{ccccc}
a \oplus a & \xrightarrow{(\nabla_a)^{-1}} & a & \xrightarrow{\nabla_a} & a \oplus a \\
{\scriptstyle \nabla_a \oplus \nabla_a} \downarrow & & & & \uparrow {\scriptstyle (\nabla_a)^{-1} \oplus (\nabla_a)^{-1}} \\
a \oplus a \oplus a \oplus a & & \xrightarrow{\quad a \oplus \gamma_{a,a} \oplus a \quad} & & a \oplus a \oplus a \oplus a
\end{array}
$$

We would e.g. infer that $(t_1 \oplus t_2); (t_3 \oplus t_4)$ is equated by functoriality to $(t_1; t_3) \oplus (t_2; t_4)$ and by naturality to $(t_1; t_3) \oplus (t_1; t_4) \oplus (t_2; t_3) \oplus (t_2; t_4)$, while those two expressions should intuitively represent different non-deterministic processes. Idempotency and functoriality do look like clashing properties for the $\oplus$ operator, and we were not ready to let the latter go.

References

1. Bruni, R., Gadducci, F., Montanari, U.: Normal forms for algebras of connections. Theor. Comp. Sci. 286(2), 247–292 (2002)

2. Degano, P., Meseguer, J., Montanari, U.: Axiomatizing the algebra of net computations and processes. Acta Informatica 33(7), 641–667 (1996)

3. Engelfriet, J.: Branching processes of Petri nets. Acta Informatica 28(6), 575–591 (1991)

4. Gadducci, F., Montanari, U.: Axioms for contextual net processes. In: Larsen, K.G., Skyum, S., Winskel, G. (eds.) ICALP 1998. LNCS, vol. 1443, pp. 296–308. Springer, Heidelberg (1998)

5. Goltz, U., Reisig, W.: The non-sequential behaviour of Petri nets. Information and Control 57(2/3), 125–147 (1983)

6. Green, A., Altenkirch, T.: From reversible to irreversible computations. In: Workshop on Quantum Programming Languages. Electronic Notes in Theoretical Compuer Science. Elsevier, Amsterdam (2006)

7. Laplaza, M.: Coherence for distributivity. In: Coherence in Categories. Lecture Notes in Mathematics, vol. 281, pp. 29–72. Springer, Heidelberg (1972)

8. Lane, S.M.: Categories for the Working Mathematician. Springer, Heidelberg (1971)

9. Martì-Oliet, N., Meseguer, J.: From Petri nets to linear logic through categories: A survey. Intl. Journal of Foundations of Computer Science 2(4), 297–399 (1991)

10. Meseguer, J., Montanari, U.: Petri nets are monoids. Information and Computation 88(2), 105–155 (1990)

11. Petri, C.A.: Kommunikation mit Automaten. PhD thesis, Institut für Instrumentelle Matematik, Bonn (1962)

12. Reisig, W.: Petri Nets: An Introduction. EACTS Monographs on Theoretical Computer Science. Springer, Heidelberg (1985)

13. Sassone, V.: An axiomatization of the algebra of Petri net concatenable processes. Theor. Comp. Sci. 170(1-2), 277–296 (1996)

14. Sassone, V.: An axiomatization of the category of Petri net computations. Mathematical Structures in Computer Science 8(2), 117–151 (1998)

Towards an Efficient Implementation of Tree Automata Completion*

Emilie Balland[1], Yohan Boichut[1], Thomas Genet[2], and Pierre-Etienne Moreau[1]

[1] Loria, INRIA Nancy – Grand Est, France
[2] Irisa, INRIA Rennes-Bretagne Atlantique, France

Abstract. Term Rewriting Systems (TRSs) are now commonly used as a modeling language for applications. In those rewriting based models, reachability analysis, i.e. proving or disproving that a given term is reachable from a set of input terms, provides an efficient verification technique. Using a tree automata completion technique, it has been shown that the non reachability of a term t can be verified by computing an over-approximation of the set of reachable terms and proving that t is not in the over-approximation. Since the verification of real programs gives rise to rewrite models of significant size, efficient implementations of completion are essential. We present in this paper a TRS transformation preserving the reachability analysis by tree automata completion. This transformation makes the completion implementation based on rewriting techniques possible. Thus, the reduction of a term to a state by a tree automaton is fully handled by rewriting. This approach has been prototyped in Tom, a language extension which adds rewriting primitives to Java. The first experiments are very promising relative to the state-of-the-art tool Timbuk.

1 Introduction

In the context of infinite state systems verification, a rising approach uses Term Rewriting Systems (TRSs) as a model and reachability analysis as a verification technique. In comparison with some other modeling techniques, TRSs have a great advantage: they can be both executed *and* verified. On one hand, comparing the execution of a TRS with the execution of a program gives a pragmatic way to check the coherence between the formal model and the program to be analyzed. On the other hand, most of the verification techniques have their Term Rewriting counterpart: model-checking [10], static analysis and abstract interpretation [13,12,19] or even interactive proofs [7]. Hence, it permits to use any of them on the TRS model. Furthermore, since all those techniques operate on a *common formal model*, i.e. TRS, this may lead to an elegant way to combine their verification power. However, like in the general verification setting, efficiency problems occur when trying to apply those rewriting techniques to real-size applications. This is the case when using model-checking on TRS

---

* This work was partially supported by ANR funding number ANR-06-SETI-14.

J. Meseguer and G. Roşu (Eds.): AMAST 2008, LNCS 5140, pp. 67–82, 2008.

models of Java programs [18,11] or when using TRS based static analysis on cryptographic protocols [14] or on Java Bytecode programs [5]. Thus, having efficient verification tools on TRS models is crucial to guarantee their success as a modeling technique.

In this paper, we aim at improving significantly the static analysis part. The state of the art implementation is called Timbuk [16] and has been used to prove properties on TRS models of cryptographic protocols [14,6] and Java Bytecode programs [5]. This tool constructs approximations of reachable terms using the so-called *tree automata completion* algorithm. Starting from a set of initial terms (representing respectively all possible function calls, initial configuration for parallel processes, etc.) it computes a regular super-set of all terms reachable by rewriting initial terms. This over-approximation, recognized by a tree automaton, represents either a super-set of all possible evaluations (partial or completed) for functions, or a super-set of all possible processes' behaviors for parallel processes. Then, it is possible to check some properties related to reachability (in particular safety and security properties) on this approximation. The work reported here improves by a factor 10 in general, and up to 100 on some Java examples, the efficiency of the tree automata completion. First, the proposed technique consists of decomposing each rewrite rule of the TRS in several simpler rules and to apply the completion on the transformed TRS. We show that the resulting automaton is also an approximation and thus the reachability is preserved by this TRS transformation. Second, an efficient implementation is obtained using compilation techniques, thanks to Tom [3,4], a Java extension that offers powerful pattern-matching features.

After presenting the classical approach in Section 2, we present the transformation and prove that the reachability analysis after completion is preserved. Then, we detail in Section 4 how it has been implemented in Tom and show especially how some of the Tom features make the development painless. To conclude, we present in Section 5 promising experimental results on the verification of cryptographic protocols and Java program analysis.

2   Preliminaries

2.1   Terms and TRSs

Comprehensive surveys can be found in [9,2] for term rewriting systems, and in [8,17] for tree automata and tree language theory.

Let $\mathcal{F}$ be a possibly infinite set of symbols, associated with an arity function $ar : \mathcal{F} \rightarrow \mathbb{N}$, and let $\mathcal{X}$ be a countable set of variables. Let $<_{\mathcal{X}}$ be a total order relation on variables. $\mathcal{T}(\mathcal{F}, \mathcal{X})$ denotes the set of terms, and $\mathcal{T}(\mathcal{F})$ denotes the set of ground terms (terms without variables). The set of variables of a term t is denoted by $\mathcal{V}ar(t)$. A substitution is a function σ from $\mathcal{X}$ into $\mathcal{T}(\mathcal{F}, \mathcal{X})$, which can be extended uniquely to an endomorphism of $\mathcal{T}(\mathcal{F}, \mathcal{X})$. A position p for a term t is a word over $\mathbb{N}$. The empty sequence ϵ denotes the top-most position. The set $\mathcal{P}os(t)$ of positions of a term t is inductively defined by $\mathcal{P}os(f(t_1, \ldots, t_n)) = \{\epsilon\} \cup \{i.p \mid 1 \leq i \leq n$ and $p \in \mathcal{P}os(t_i)\}$, and $\mathcal{P}os(t) = \{\epsilon\}$ when $t \in \mathcal{X}$. The depth of a term t, denoted by $depth(t)$ is the length of the maximal sequence in $Pos(t)$. If $p \in Pos(t)$, then $t|_p$ denotes the subterm of t at position p and $t[s]_p$ denotes the term obtained by replacement of the subterm $t|_p$ at position p by the term s. We also denote by $t(p)$ the symbol occurring in t at position p. Given a term $t \in \mathcal{T}(\mathcal{F}, \mathcal{X})$ and A a set of symbols, let $Pos_A(t) = \{p \in Pos(t) \mid t(p) \in A\}$. Thus $Pos_{\mathcal{F}}(t)$ is the set of positions of t, at each of which a function symbol appears.

A term t is said to be *flat* if t is either a simple constant or a term of the form $f(x_1, \ldots, x_n)$ where $x_1, \ldots, x_n \in \mathcal{X}$. We say a term t is *almost flat* if t is of the form $f(t_1, \ldots, t_n)$ and the t_i's are flat terms or variables.

A TRS $\mathcal{R}$ is a set of *rewrite rules* $l \to r$, where $l, r \in \mathcal{T}(\mathcal{F}, \mathcal{X})$ and $l \notin \mathcal{X}$. A rewrite rule $l \to r$ is *left-linear* (resp. right-linear) if each variable of l (resp. r) occurs only once within l (resp. r). A TRS $\mathcal{R}$ is left-linear (resp. right-linear) if every rewrite rule $l \to r$ of $\mathcal{R}$ is left-linear (resp. right-linear). A TRS $\mathcal{R}$ is linear if it is right and left-linear. The TRS $\mathcal{R}$ induces a rewriting relation $\to_{\mathcal{R}}$ on terms whose reflexive transitive closure is written $\to_{\mathcal{R}}^*$. The set of $\mathcal{R}$-descendants of a set of terms $E \subseteq \mathcal{T}(\mathcal{F}, \mathcal{X})$ is $\mathcal{R}^*(E) = \{t \in \mathcal{T}(\mathcal{F}, \mathcal{X}) \mid \exists s \in E \text{ s.t. } s \to_{\mathcal{R}}^* t\}$.

2.2 Tree Automata Completion

Note that $\mathcal{R}^*(E)$ is possibly infinite: $\mathcal{R}$ may not terminate and/or E may be infinite. The set $\mathcal{R}^*(E)$ is generally not computable [17]. However, it is possible to over-approximate it [12] using tree automata, i.e. a finite representation of infinite (regular) sets of terms. We next define tree automata that will be used to represent set E and over-approximation of $\mathcal{R}^*(E)$.

Let $\mathcal{Q}$ be an infinite set of symbols, with arity 0, called *states* such that $\mathcal{Q} \cap \mathcal{F} = \emptyset$. $\mathcal{T}(\mathcal{F} \cup \mathcal{Q})$ is called the set of *configurations*.

Definition 1 (Transition and normalized transition). *A transition is a rewrite rule $c \to q$, where c is a configuration i.e. $c \in \mathcal{T}(\mathcal{F} \cup \mathcal{Q})$ and $q \in \mathcal{Q}$. A normalized transition is a transition $c \to q$ where $c = f(q_1, \ldots, q_n)$, $f \in \mathcal{F}$ whose arity is n, and $q_1, \ldots, q_n \in \mathcal{Q}$.*

Definition 2 (Bottom-up non-deterministic finite tree automaton). *A bottom-up non-deterministic finite tree automaton (tree automaton for short) is a quadruple $\mathcal{A} = \langle \mathcal{F}, \mathcal{Q}, \mathcal{Q}_f, \Delta \rangle$, where the finite set of final states $\mathcal{Q}_f$ is such that $Q_f \subseteq \mathcal{Q}$ and Δ is a finite set of normalized transitions.*

The *rewriting relation* on $\mathcal{T}(\mathcal{F} \cup \mathcal{Q})$ induced by the transitions of $\mathcal{A}$ (the set Δ) is denoted by $\to_{\Delta}$. When Δ is clear from the context, $\to_{\Delta}$ is also denoted by $\to_{\mathcal{A}}$.

Definition 3 (Recognized language). *The tree language recognized by $\mathcal{A}$ in a state q is $\mathcal{L}(\mathcal{A}, q) = \{t \in \mathcal{T}(\mathcal{F}) \mid t \to_{\mathcal{A}}^* q\}$. The language recognized by $\mathcal{A}$ is $\mathcal{L}(\mathcal{A}) = \bigcup_{q \in \mathcal{Q}_f} \mathcal{L}(\mathcal{A}, q)$. A tree language is regular if and only if it can be recognized by a tree automaton.*

Example 1. Let $\mathcal{A}$ be the tree automaton such that $\mathcal{Q}_f = \{q_0\}$ and $\Delta = \{a \to q_4,$ $b \to q_5,\ c \to q_6,\ d \to q_7,\ f(q_4, q_5) \to q_1,\ h(q_6) \to q_2,\ h(q_7) \to q_3,\ g(q_1, q_2) \to q_0,\ g(q_1, q_3) \to q_0\}$. The language recognized by $\mathcal{A}$ is $\mathcal{L}(\mathcal{A}) = \{g(f(a,b), h(c)),$ $g(f(a,b), h(d))\}$. This example is used throughout this paper to explain the concepts and algorithms presented in the paper.

Given a tree automaton $\mathcal{A}$ and a TRS $\mathcal{R}$, the tree automata completion algorithm, proposed in [13,12], computes a tree automaton $\mathcal{A}_\mathcal{R}^k$ such that $\mathcal{L}(\mathcal{A}_\mathcal{R}^k) = \mathcal{R}^*(\mathcal{L}(\mathcal{A}))$ when it is possible (for the classes of TRSs where an exact computation is possible, see [12]) and such that $\mathcal{L}(\mathcal{A}_\mathcal{R}^k) \supseteq \mathcal{R}^*(\mathcal{L}(\mathcal{A}))$ otherwise.

The tree automata completion works as follows. From $\mathcal{A} = \mathcal{A}_\mathcal{R}^0$ completion builds a sequence $\mathcal{A}_\mathcal{R}^0 . \mathcal{A}_\mathcal{R}^1 \ldots \mathcal{A}_\mathcal{R}^k$ of automata such that if $s \in \mathcal{L}(\mathcal{A}_\mathcal{R}^i)$ and $s \to_\mathcal{R} t$ then $t \in \mathcal{L}(\mathcal{A}_\mathcal{R}^{i+1})$. If we find a fix-point automaton $\mathcal{A}_\mathcal{R}^k$ such that $\mathcal{R}^*(\mathcal{L}(\mathcal{A}_\mathcal{R}^k)) = \mathcal{L}(\mathcal{A}_\mathcal{R}^k)$, then we have $\mathcal{L}(\mathcal{A}_\mathcal{R}^k) = \mathcal{R}^*(\mathcal{L}(\mathcal{A}_\mathcal{R}^0))$ (or $\mathcal{L}(\mathcal{A}_\mathcal{R}^k) \supseteq \mathcal{R}^*(\mathcal{L}(\mathcal{A}))$ if $\mathcal{R}$ is not in the class of [12]). To build $\mathcal{A}_\mathcal{R}^{i+1}$ from $\mathcal{A}_\mathcal{R}^i$, we achieve a *completion step* which consists of finding *critical pairs* between $\to_\mathcal{R}$ and $\to_{\mathcal{A}_\mathcal{R}^i}$. To define the notion of critical pair, we extend the definition of substitutions to terms of $\mathcal{T}(\mathcal{F} \cup \mathcal{Q})$. If there exists a substitution $\sigma : \mathcal{X} \mapsto \mathcal{Q}$, a rule $l \to r \in \mathcal{R}$, and $q \in \mathcal{Q}$ satisfying $l\sigma \to_{\mathcal{A}_\mathcal{R}^i}^* q$ and $l\sigma \to_\mathcal{R} r\sigma$, we say that $\langle r\sigma, q \rangle$ is a critical pair. Note that since $\mathcal{R}$, $\mathcal{A}_\mathcal{R}^i$, and the set of states of $\mathcal{Q}$ used in $\mathcal{A}_\mathcal{R}^i$ are finite, there is only a finite number of critical pairs. Note also that, in our case, it is enough to consider only root overlap between rules of $\mathcal{R}$ and transitions of $\mathcal{A}_\mathcal{R}^i$. For every critical pair detected between $\mathcal{R}$ and $\mathcal{A}_\mathcal{R}^i$ such that $r\sigma \not\to_{\mathcal{A}_\mathcal{R}^i}^* q$, the tree automaton $\mathcal{A}_\mathcal{R}^{i+1}$ is constructed by adding a new transition $r\sigma \to q$ to $\mathcal{A}_\mathcal{R}^i$ such that $\mathcal{A}_\mathcal{R}^{i+1}$ recognizes $r\sigma$ in q, i.e. $r\sigma \to_{\mathcal{A}_\mathcal{R}^{i+1}} q$.

However, the transition $r\sigma \to q$ is not necessarily a normalized transition of the form $f(q_1, \ldots, q_n) \to q$ and so it has to be normalized first. Since normalization consists of associating state symbols to subterms of the left-hand side of the new transition, it always succeeds. Note that, when using new states to normalize the transitions, completion is as precise as possible. However, without approximation, completion is likely not to terminate (because of general undecidability results [17]). To enforce termination, and produce an over-approximation, the completion algorithm is parametrized by a set N of *approximation rules*. When the set N is used during completion to normalize transitions, the obtained tree automata are denoted by $\mathcal{A}_{N,\mathcal{R}}^1, \ldots, \mathcal{A}_{N,\mathcal{R}}^k$. Each such rule describes a context in which a list of rules can be used to normalize a term. For all $s, l_1, \ldots, l_n \in \mathcal{T}(\mathcal{F} \cup \mathcal{Q}, \mathcal{X})$ and for all $x, x_1, \ldots, x_n \in \mathcal{Q} \cup \mathcal{X}$, the general form for an approximation rule is:

$$[s \to x] \to [l_1 \to x_1, \ldots, l_n \to x_n].$$

The expression $[s \rightarrow x]$ is a pattern to be matched with the new transitions $t \rightarrow q'$ obtained by completion. The expression $[l_1 \rightarrow x_1, \ldots, l_n \rightarrow x_n]$ is a set of rules used to normalize t. To normalize a transition of the form $t \rightarrow q'$, we match s with t and x with q', obtain a substitution σ from the matching and then we normalize t with the rewrite system $\{l_1\sigma \rightarrow x_1\sigma, \ldots, l_n\sigma \rightarrow x_n\sigma\}$. Furthermore, if $\forall i \in [1..n]$, $x_i \in \mathcal{Q}$ or $x_i \in Var(l_i) \cup Var(s) \cup \{x\}$ then, since $\sigma : \mathcal{X} \mapsto \mathcal{Q}$, $x_1\sigma, \ldots, x_n\sigma$ are necessarily states. If a transition cannot be fully normalized using approximation rules N, normalization is finished using some new states, see Example 2. Such normalization rules can either be defined by hand, in order to prove precise properties on specific systems or can be automatically generated in more specific settings [5,6].

The main property of the tree automata completion algorithm is that, whatever the state labels used to normalize the new transitions are, if completion terminates then it produces an over-approximation of reachable terms [12].

Theorem 1 ([12]). *Let $\mathcal{R}$ be a left-linear TRS, $\mathcal{A}$ be a tree automaton, and N be a set of approximation rules. If completion terminates on $\mathcal{A}^k_{N,\mathcal{R}}$ then*

$$\mathcal{L}(\mathcal{A}^k_{N,\mathcal{R}}) \supseteq \mathcal{R}^*(\mathcal{L}(\mathcal{A})).$$

Here is a simple example illustrating completion and the use of approximation rules when the language $\mathcal{R}^*(E)$ is not regular.

Example 2. Let $\mathcal{A}$ be the tree automaton given in Example 1. In the following we illustrate the effect of approximation rules. First, we consider the TRS $\mathcal{R} = \{g(f(a, x), h(y)) \rightarrow g(f(a, f(a, x)), h(h(y)))\}$, composed of a single rule. The set of $\mathcal{R}$-descendants of $\mathcal{L}(\mathcal{A})$ is $\mathcal{R}^*(\mathcal{L}(\mathcal{A})) = \{g(f^n(a, b), h^n(\{c, d\})) \mid n \geq 0\}$.

Let N be the set of approximation rules such that $N = \{[g(f(a, f(a, x)), h(h(y))) \rightarrow z] \rightarrow [a \rightarrow q_4, f(q_4, x) \rightarrow q_5, f(q_4, q_5) \rightarrow q_5, h(y) \rightarrow q_6, h(q_6) \rightarrow q_6, g(q_5, q_6) \rightarrow z]\}$. Intuitively, the *approximated* set of descendants will be the following: $\mathcal{L}(\mathcal{A}^2_{N,\mathcal{R}}) = \{g(f^n(a, b), h^m(\{c, d\})) \mid n, m \geq 0\}$.

To get this result, we first compute the critical pairs. Let us consider $\sigma_1 = \{x \mapsto q_5, y \mapsto q_6\}$ and $\sigma_2 = \{x \mapsto q_5, y \mapsto q_7\}$, we have:

1. $g(f(a, q_5), h(q_6)) \rightarrow^*_{\mathcal{A}} q_0$ and $g(f(a, q_5), h(q_6)) \rightarrow_{\mathcal{R}} g(f(a, f(a, q_5)), h(h(q_6)))$,
2. $g(f(a, q_5), h(q_7)) \rightarrow^*_{\mathcal{A}} q_0$ and $g(f(a, q_5), h(q_7)) \rightarrow_{\mathcal{R}} g(f(a, f(a, q_5)), h(h(q_7)))$.

Let us call $l = g(f(a, x), h(y))$ and $r = g(f(a, f(a, x)), h(h(y)))$ the respective left-hand side and right-hand side of the rule of $\mathcal{R}$. The transitions (1) $r\sigma_1 \rightarrow q_0$ and (2) $r\sigma_2 \rightarrow q_0$ have to be normalised using N. To normalize the transition (1), we match the pattern of the approximation rule , i.e. $g(f(a, f(a, x)), h(h(y)))$, with $r\sigma_1$ and match z with q_0, and thus obtain a substitution $\sigma = \{x \mapsto q_5, y \mapsto q_6, z \mapsto q_0\}$. Applying σ to $[a \rightarrow q_4, f(q_4, x) \rightarrow q_5, f(q_4, q_5) \rightarrow q_5, h(y) \rightarrow q_6, h(q_6) \rightarrow q_6, g(q_5, q_6) \rightarrow z]$ gives $[a \rightarrow q_4, f(q_4, q_5) \rightarrow q_5, h(q_6) \rightarrow q_6, g(q_5, q_6) \rightarrow q_0]$. This last system is used to normalize the transition $r\sigma_1 \rightarrow q_0$ into the set $S_1 = \{a \rightarrow q_4, f(q_4, q_5) \rightarrow q_5, h(q_6) \rightarrow q_6, g(q_5, q_6) \rightarrow q_0\}$. At the same time, the same process is performed for the transition (2), resulting in $S_2 = \{a \rightarrow q_4,$

$f(q_4, q_5) \rightarrow q_5$, $h(q_7) \rightarrow q_6$, $h(q_6) \rightarrow q_6$, $g(q_5, q_6) \rightarrow q_0\}$. The tree automaton $\mathcal{A}_{N,\mathcal{R}}^1$ is then obtained by adding $S_1 \cup S_2$ to $\mathcal{A}$.

The completion process continues for another step. As there are no more critical pair, it ends on $\mathcal{A}_{N,\mathcal{R}}^2 = \mathcal{A}_{N,\mathcal{R}}^1$ whose set of transitions is $\{a \rightarrow q_4,$ $b \rightarrow q_5$, $c \rightarrow q_6$, $d \rightarrow q_7$, $f(q_4, q_5) \rightarrow q_1$, $h(q_6) \rightarrow q_2$, $h(q_7) \rightarrow q_3$, $g(q_1, q_2) \rightarrow q_0$, $g(q_1, q_3) \rightarrow q_0$, $f(q_4, q_5) \rightarrow q_5$, $h(q_6) \rightarrow q_6$, $g(q_5, q_6) \rightarrow q_0$, $h(q_7) \rightarrow q_6\}$. We have $\mathcal{L}(\mathcal{A}_{N,\mathcal{R}}^2) = \{g(f^n(a, b), h^m(\{c, d\})) \mid n, m \geq 0\}$ which is an over-approximation of $\mathcal{R}^*(\mathcal{L}(\mathcal{A})) = \{g(f^n(a, b), h^n(\{c, d\})) \mid n \geq 0\}$.

The tree automata completion algorithm and the approximation mechanism are implemented in the Timbuk [16] tool. In the previous example, once the fix-point automaton $\mathcal{A}_{N,\mathcal{R}}^k$ has been computed, it is possible to check whether some terms are reachable, i.e. recognized by $\mathcal{A}_{N,\mathcal{R}}^k$ or not. This can be done using tree automata intersections [12]. Another way to do that is to search for instances of a pattern t, where t is a linear term of $\mathcal{T}(\mathcal{F}, \mathcal{X})$, in the tree automaton. Given t it is possible to check if there exists a substitution $\sigma : \mathcal{X} \mapsto \mathcal{Q}$ and a state $q \in \mathcal{Q}$ such that $t\sigma \rightarrow_{\mathcal{A}_{N,\mathcal{R}}^k}^* q$. If such a solution exists then it proves that there exists a term $s \in \mathcal{T}(\mathcal{F})$, a position $p \in Pos(s)$ and a substitution $\sigma' : \mathcal{X} \mapsto \mathcal{T}(\mathcal{F})$ such that $s[t\sigma']_p \in \mathcal{L}(\mathcal{A}_{N,\mathcal{R}}^k) \supseteq \mathcal{R}^*(\mathcal{L}(\mathcal{A}))$, i.e. that $t\sigma'$ occurs as a subterm in the language recognized by $\mathcal{L}(\mathcal{A}_{N,\mathcal{R}}^k)$. On the other hand, if there is no solution then it proves that no such term is in the over-approximation, hence it is not in $\mathcal{R}^*(\mathcal{L}(\mathcal{A}))$, i.e. it is not reachable. For instance, the pattern $g(h(x), f(y, z))$ has no solution on $\mathcal{A}_{N,\mathcal{R}}^2$ of Example 2, meaning that no term containing any ground instance of this pattern is reachable from $g(f(a, b), h(c))$ and from $g(f(a, b), h(d))$.

3   TRS Transformation Preserving Reachability

In this section, we propose a TRS transformation preserving the reachability analysis of the original one. This transformation makes the completion implementation in Section 4 simpler because of the particular form of the resulting rules.

3.1   Definition of the TRS Transformation ϕ

We first propose in Definition 4 a function which associates to a term over $\mathcal{F}$ and $\mathcal{X}$ a term which we consider as its context.

Definition 4. *Let $\mathcal{F}'$ be the set of function symbols C_t with $t \in \mathcal{T}(\mathcal{F}, \mathcal{X})$ and $\mathcal{F} \cap \mathcal{F}' = \emptyset$. We define the function $\rho : \mathcal{T}(\mathcal{F}, \mathcal{X}) \rightarrow \mathcal{T}(\mathcal{F}', \mathcal{X})$ such that $\forall t \in \mathcal{T}(\mathcal{F}, \mathcal{X})$:*

$$\rho(t) = \begin{cases} C_t(x_1, \ldots, x_n) & where\ \mathcal{V}ar(t) = \{x_1, \ldots, x_n\}\ and\ x_i <_{\mathcal{X}} x_{i+1}\ if \\ & t = f(t_1, \ldots, t_n) \\ t & if\ t \in \mathcal{X} \end{cases}$$

Example 3. Consider $l = g(f(a, x), h(y))$ which is the left hand-side of the rule in Example 2. Then, $\rho(l)$ is equal to $C_{g(f(a,x),h(y))}(x, y)$. Note that for any ground term t, $\rho(t) = C_t$.

The following definition allows the construction of a set of rules from a given term. This TRS allows the rewriting of the given term t into its context C_t. This definition is central for the construction of the transformation $\phi(\mathcal{R})$ given in Definition 6.

Definition 5. *Given a term* $t \in T(\mathcal{F}, \mathcal{X})$ *and the function* $\rho : T(\mathcal{F}, \mathcal{X}) \to T(\mathcal{F}', \mathcal{X})$:

$$\text{TRS}_\rho(t) = \begin{cases} \{f(\rho(t_1), \ldots, \rho(t_n)) \to \rho(t)\} \cup \bigcup_{i=1}^n \text{TRS}_\rho(t_i) & \text{if } t = f(t_1, \ldots, t_n) \\ \emptyset & \text{if } t \in \mathcal{X}. \end{cases}$$

Example 4. Let $l = g(f(a, x), h(y))$ be the left hand-side of the rule in Example 2. Then, $\text{TRS}_\rho(l) = \{a \to C_a,\ f(C_a, x) \to C_{f(a,x)}(x),\ h(y) \to C_{h(y)}(y), g(C_{f(a,x)}(x), C_{h(y)}(y)) \to C_{g(f(a,x),h(y))}(x, y)\}$.

Now we define the transformed TRS $\phi(\mathcal{R})$.

Definition 6 (TRS Transformation). *Given a set of rewrite rules* $\mathcal{R}$:

$$\phi(\mathcal{R}) = \bigcup_{l \to r \in \mathcal{R}} \text{TRS}_\rho(l) \cup \{\rho(l) \to r\}$$

Example 5. Let $\mathcal{R}$ be the TRS defined in Example 2. As there is only one rule $l \to r$ with $l = g(f(a, x), h(y))$ and $r = g(f(a, f(a, x)), h(h(y)))$, we have $\phi(\mathcal{R}) = \text{TRS}_\rho(l) \cup \{C_l(x, y) \to r\}$ where $\text{TRS}_\rho(l)$ is defined as in Example 4.

Note that for any TRS $\mathcal{R}$, the TRS $\phi(\mathcal{R})$ has two properties. First, for each rule $l \to r$ of $\phi(\mathcal{R})$, l is almost flat (see the definition in Section 2.1). So $depth(l)$ is in the worst case equal to three. And second, for a rule $l \to r \in \mathcal{R}$, r is reachable by rewriting from l and using $\phi(\mathcal{R})$. The latter is emphasized in the following proposition.

Proposition 1. *Let* $\mathcal{R}$ *be a left-linear TRS, for any rule* $l \to r \in \mathcal{R}$:

$$r \in \phi(\mathcal{R})^*(l)$$

Proof. Direct consequence of Definition 6. $\square$

Another trivial property of $\phi(\mathcal{R})$ is about its linearity which is the same as $\mathcal{R}$.

Proposition 2. *If* $\mathcal{R}$ *is a left-linear TRS, then so is* $\phi(\mathcal{R})$.

Proof. Direct consequence of Definitions 6 and 4. $\square$

3.2 Preservation of Reachability

As claimed at the very beginning of this section, the reachability analysis performed on $\phi(\mathcal{R})$ can be propagated to the one performed on $\mathcal{R}$ itself. In other words, given a set of terms E, an over-approximation of the set of terms reachable from E and using $\phi(\mathcal{R})$ is also an over-approximation of the set of reachable terms which can be computed from E using $\mathcal{R}$.

Theorem 2. *Let $\mathcal{R}$ and $\mathcal{A}$ be respectively a left-linear TRS and a tree automaton such that $\mathcal{A} = \langle \mathcal{F}, \mathcal{Q}, \mathcal{Q}_f, \Delta \rangle$. Let $\mathcal{A}'$ be a tree automaton such that $\mathcal{A}' = \langle \mathcal{F} \cup \mathcal{F}', \mathcal{Q}, \mathcal{Q}_f, \Delta \rangle$ where $\mathcal{F}'$ is specified as in Definition 4. For any set of approximation rules N, if completion terminates on $\mathcal{A}'^k_{N,\phi(\mathcal{R})}$ then*

$$\mathcal{R}^*(\mathcal{L}(\mathcal{A})) \subseteq \mathcal{L}(\mathcal{A}'^k_{N,\phi(\mathcal{R})}).$$

Proof. Let t and u be two ground terms over $\mathcal{F}$ such that $t \rightarrow_{\mathcal{R}} u$. There exists a rule $l \rightarrow r$ in $\mathcal{R}$, a substitution $\mu : \mathcal{X} \rightarrow \mathcal{T}(\mathcal{F})$ and a position p of t such that $t|_p = l\mu$ and $u = t[r\mu]_p$. According to Proposition 1, for a rule $l \rightarrow r \in \mathcal{R}$, $r \in \phi(\mathcal{R})^*(l)$. Thus, $t \rightarrow^*_{\phi(\mathcal{R})} u$. Consequently, for $\mathcal{R}$ and $\mathcal{A}'$, $\mathcal{R}^*(\mathcal{L}(\mathcal{A}')) \subseteq \phi(\mathcal{R})^*(\mathcal{L}(\mathcal{A}'))$. Note that since $\mathcal{A}'$ differs from $\mathcal{A}$ only because of its set $\mathcal{F}'$ of symbols, we have $\mathcal{L}(\mathcal{A}) = \mathcal{L}(\mathcal{A}')$ and thus $\mathcal{R}^*(\mathcal{L}(\mathcal{A})) \subseteq \phi(\mathcal{R})^*(\mathcal{L}(\mathcal{A}'))$. According to Theorem 1 and Proposition 2, $\phi(\mathcal{R})^*(\mathcal{L}(\mathcal{A}')) \subseteq \mathcal{L}(\mathcal{A}'^k_{N,\phi(\mathcal{R})})$. So one can deduce that $\mathcal{R}^*(\mathcal{L}(\mathcal{A})) \subseteq \mathcal{L}(\mathcal{A}'^k_{N,\phi(\mathcal{R})})$. $\qquad\square$

Note that given $\mathcal{A}$, $\mathcal{R}$ and N, one can perform completion using $\phi(\mathcal{R})$ and N without modifying N. Moreover, for each r' of $l' \rightarrow r' \in \phi(\mathcal{R})$, either r' occurs in the right-hand side of a rule in $\mathcal{R}$, or r' is a flat term. The former is normalized by the set of approximation rules if it is necessary. For the latter, any transition resulting from the application of such a rule is already normalised. For example, given an automaton $\mathcal{A}$ and the rule $g(C_{f(a,x)}(x), C_{h(y)}(y)) \rightarrow C_{g(f(a,x),h(y))}(x,y)$ introduced in Example 4, if there exists $\sigma : \mathcal{X} \rightarrow \mathcal{Q}$ and q a state of $\mathcal{A}$ such that $g(C_{f(a,x)}(\sigma(x)), C_{h(y)}(\sigma(y))) \rightarrow^*_{\mathcal{A}} q$, then $C_{g(f(a,x),h(y))}(\sigma(x), \sigma(y)) \rightarrow q$ is added to $\mathcal{A}$. And this transition is already normalised. Consequently, N does not act for this kind of rule.

We have shown in this section that the TRS transformation is sound from a reachability point of view: each term actually reachable by $\mathcal{R}$ can be computed using $\phi(\mathcal{R})$. Indeed, for an over-approximation *App* computed using $\phi(\mathcal{R})$ from a set of terms E ($\mathcal{R}^*(E) \subseteq App$), if a term $t \notin App$ then t is actually unreachable from E using either $\phi(\mathcal{R})$ or $\mathcal{R}$.

4   Implementation in Tom

In this section, we show how the completion with $\phi(\mathcal{R})$ has been implemented in the Tom language. The main principle of Tom is to integrate rewriting statements into Java. After the compilation, every Tom statement is translated into Java and we obtain a standalone Java program. In this section, we show how Tom pattern-matching features have been the key of the completion implementation with $\phi(\mathcal{R})$. See [3] for more details about the Tom language features.

4.1   General Process

In Figure 1, we present the general process which leads to the implementation of the completion. In order to compare easily our implementation with Timbuk, we use a similar input format.

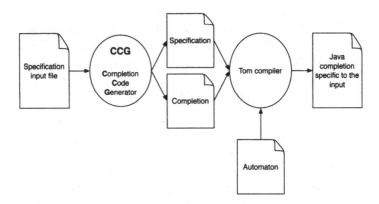

Fig. 1. CCG application: from a Specification to its dedicated Completion Program

For a given Timbuk specification, the application CCG generates a Tom program of the completion algorithm dedicated to this specification. Actually, this program is composed of three files. The file `Specification` defines the algebraic signature and the file `Completion` describes the completion implementation. These two files are specific to the input specification file. The last file `Automaton` is generic and corresponds to a Tom program in which all data structures handling tree automata can be found. These Tom files are finally compiled into Java files providing an efficient application dedicated to the completion on the given Timbuk specification.

To present how completion is encoded in Tom, we consider again the Example 2 in the following sections.

4.2 The `Specification` File

Tom provides several constructs to manipulate algebraic structures. In particular, it is possible to directly define an algebraic signature and from this signature, Tom generates a typed term structure that can be directly used by a Java programmer.

For the Example 2, the signature generated by CCG in the file `Specification` contains the set of symbols $\mathcal{F}$, a new constructor denoted `q(int)`, for specifying states. The transitions are represented using the constructor `transition` of arity 2. Each context symbol C_t of the set $\mathcal{F}'$ introduced by $\phi(\mathcal{R})$ is denoted `C_i`. The signature also contains a variadic operator called `sons` which is used to represent *expanded states*. The expanded states of a state `q` corresponds to the list, built using the variadic operator `sons`, of all `t_i` such that `transition(t_i,q)` is a transition of the current automaton. For example, for the tree automaton given in Example 2, the expanded state of q_0, denoted `q(0)` in the implementation, is `sons(g(q(1),q(2)), g(q(1),q(3)))`.

Below, we give the signature generated by our compiler CCG, for the automaton $\mathcal{A}$ and the set of rules $\mathcal{R}$ given in Example 2. The constructors C_a, $C_{f(a,x)}$, $C_{h(y)}$ and $C_{g(f(a,x),h(y))}$ have been respectively renamed into C1, C2, C3 and C4.

```
Term = f(Term,Term)
     | g(Term,Term)
     | h(Term)
     | a() | b() | c() | d()
     | q(int)
     | sons(Term*)
     | C1() | C2(Term) | C3(Term)| C4(Term,Term)
     | transition(config:Term,state:Term)
```

4.3 The Automaton File

A tree automaton is an object of the class Automaton. This class is mainly composed of two fields: transitionsByFunctionSymbol and expandedForms, both of sort HashTable. The keys of the former are the function symbols of the generated signature and its values are the sets of transitions. Given a function symbol f (a key), the corresponding value is the set composed of transitions whose left-hand side is built from f. The latter stores the expanded form of states. Both hash-tables are updated during the completion process. Another field newTransitions stores the new transitions built by a completion step. Both data structures expandedForms and transitionsByFunctionSymbol are updated according to this field when the method update() implemented in this class is invoked. This method resets the set newTransitions to the empty set. There are also other fields specifying the final states, handling the new states introduced and so on.

4.4 The Completion File

The code of this class is automatically generated from the automaton $\mathcal{A}$ and the TRS $\mathcal{R}$ given in the input specification. This class contains one field currentA of sort Automaton representing the current automaton, as well as methods to implement the completion with $\phi(R)$.

In Example 2, the main method completeAllSteps iterates by applying every rule and updating currentA until reaching a fix-point (if it exists). The function hasNewTransitions() returns true if the set newTransitions is not empty. Note that for each rule of $\phi(\mathcal{R})$, a method completeStepWithRule[i] is generated. Such a method performs one completion step for a given rule.

```
public void completeAllSteps(){
  do {
    // Current automaton update
    currentA.update();
    // Completion step with a -> C1
    completeStepWithRule1();
    // Completion step with f(C1,x) -> C2(x)
    completeStepWithRule2();
    // Completion step with h(y) -> C3(y)
    completeStepWithRule3();
```

```
    // Completion step with g(C2(x),C3(y)) -> C4(x,y)
    completeStepWithRule4();
    // Completion step with C4(x,y) -> g(f(a,f(a,x)),h(h(y)))
    completeStepWithRule5();
  } while(currentA.hasNewTransitions());
}
```

We recall that, to perform a completion step, we need to find, for each rule $l \to r \in \phi(\mathcal{R})$, all substitutions $\sigma : \mathcal{X} \to \mathcal{Q}$ such that $l\sigma \to_{\mathcal{A}}^* q$ and $r\sigma \not\to_{\mathcal{A}}^* q$. Here, we use uttermost Tom matching on variadic operators to implement efficiently this operation. This is possible because in $\phi(\mathcal{R})$, the left-hand sides are almost flat (see the definition in Section 2.1).

In particular, according to Definition 6, l can be only of the form

(1) $f(t_1, \ldots, t_n)$ with $t_i \in \mathcal{X}$ or $t_i = C_k(x_1, \ldots, x_m)$, for $i \in [1, n]$, $C_k \in \mathcal{F}'$, and $x_1, \ldots, x_m \in \mathcal{X}$, or

(2) $C_{k'}(x_1, \ldots, x_n)$, $C_{k'} \in \mathcal{F}'$ and $x_1, \ldots, x_n \in \mathcal{X}$.

When l is of the form (2), finding a substitution σ such that $l\sigma \to_{\mathcal{A}}^* q$ consists of looking for every transition of $\mathcal{A}$ of the form $C_{k'}(q_1, \ldots, q_n) \to q$ and matching their left-hand side with $C_{k'}(x_1, \ldots, x_n)$.

When l is of the form (1), every substitution σ satisfying $l\sigma \to_{\mathcal{A}}^* q$ is such that $\exists q_1, \ldots q_n$, n states of $\mathcal{A}$, for which $\forall t_i$, either $t_i\sigma = q_i$, or $t_i\sigma \to q_i$ is a transition of $\mathcal{A}$, and $f(q_1, \ldots, q_n) \to q$ is a transition of $\mathcal{A}$. In the following we show how this operation can be realized using list matching on variadic operators.

Let l' be $l = f(t_1, \ldots, t_n)$ where every t_i of the form $C_k(x_1, \ldots, x_m)$ has been replaced by the Tom pattern sons(_*,C_k(x_1,...,x_m),_*). Let us consider a transition $f(q_1, \ldots, q_n) \to q \in \mathcal{A}$. Remember that we look for σ such that $f(t_1, \ldots, t_n)\sigma \to_{\mathcal{A}}^* q$. Such a σ exists if $t_1\sigma \to_{\mathcal{A}}^* q_1, \ldots, t_n\sigma \to_{\mathcal{A}}^* q_n$. Thanks to our encoding using sons, we can expand every q_i such that the corresponding t_i in l is not a variable. Finding σ simply consists of matching l' against the expanded form of $f(q_1, \ldots, q_n)$. Moreover, when the right-hand side r is of the form $C_k(x_1, \ldots, x_m)$, verifying that $r\sigma \not\to_{\mathcal{A}}^* q$ consists just of checking that $r\sigma$ is in the expanded form of q.

Let us consider the following rule $g(C_{f(a,x)}(x), C_{h(y)}(y)) \to C_{g(f(a,x),h(y))}(x, y)$. Its completion method is completeStepWithRule4 and it is implemented in Tom as follows.

```
public void completeStepWithRule4() {
  for (Term tr: currentA.getExpectedTransitions("g")) {
    Term t = tr.getconfig();
    Term te = t.expandForRule4(currentA);
    Term q = tr.getstate();
    Term qe = q.expand(currentA);
    %match(te) {
      g(sons(_*,C2(x),_*),sons(_*,C3(y),_*)) -> {
        if (! qe.contains('C4(x,y)) {
          currentA.addNewTransitions('transition(C4(x,y),q));
```

```
          }
        }
      }
    }
}
```

The method `getExpectedTransitions("g")` returns a set of transitions whose topmost function symbol of its left-hand side is g. The function symbol g is the symbol occurring at the root of the left-hand side of the considered rule i.e. $g(C_{f(a,x)}(x), C_{h(y)}(y)) \rightarrow C_{g(f(a,x),h(y))}(x,y)$. The instruction `tr.getconfig()` (resp. `tr.getstate()`) returns the value stored in the first (resp. second) subterm of `tr` (see the signature in Section 4.2). According to the current tree automaton, the function `expand` returns the expanded form of a state and the function `expandForRule4` builds the expanded form of t required for this rule. As in this rule, each child of the left-hand side is of the form `C_k(...)`, this form corresponds to t where each child (state) has been replaced by its expanded form.

In this function, two new Tom constructs are used. The first one is the ' (back-quote), whose action is to build a term in memory from the algebraic signature described in Section 4.3. For instance, the last instruction of the method `completeStepWithRule4` builds the ground term `'transition(C4(x,y),q)` (with the variables x and y at this program point) and stores it into the set `newTransitions` of `currentA`.

The second construct provided by Tom is the `%match`, which executes an action associated to a pattern, when this one matches the subject. In the example above, the first part of the pattern `sons(_*,C2(x),_*)` means that we try to find each element of the list, placed under the symbol sons, which is of the form `C2(x)`. The second part `sons(_*,C3(y),_*))` is interpreted similarly. The complete pattern `g(sons(_*,C2(x),_*),sons(_*,C3(y),_*))` matches for every couple of elements of the form `C2(x)` and `C3(y)` and computes the corresponding substitution for x and y. At the right-hand side of this pattern, there is a Java action that calls the method `addNewTransitions` on `currentA`. `addNewTransitions` takes as parameter either a transition or a collection of transitions and adds it (or them) into the set `newTransitions`. This action is executed as many times as the pattern matches.

Note that the methods `completeStepWithRule1`, `completeStepWithRule2` and `completeStepWithRule3` can be defined similarly.

Below, we consider the method `completeStepWithRule5` corresponding to the rule `C4(x,y) -> g(f(a,f(a,x)),h(h(y)))`. This method differs from the other ones mainly because the right-hand side is neither flat, nor almost flat. So to test if $r\sigma \not\rightarrow_A^* q$, we use the function `reduceIn(t,q)` that returns `true` if t can be reduced to q by the current automata `currentA`. Moreover, the resulting transition must be normalized using the approximation rules N. Note that this normalization is not necessary for the other rules because the resulting transitions are already normalized.

```
public void completeStepWithRule5() {
  for (Term tr: currentA.getExpectedTransitions("C4")) {
    Term t = tr.getconfig();
    Term te = t.expandForRule5();
    Term q = tr.getstate();
    %match(te) {
      C4(x,y) -> {
        if (! currentA.reduceIn('g(f(a,f(a,x)),h(h(y))),q)) {
          currentA.addANewTransitions(Norm(N,
              'transition(g(f(a,f(a,x)),h(h(y))),q)));
        }
      }
    }
  }
}
```

In this example, as no child of the rule left-hand side is of the form C_k(...),
expandForRule5 returns simply t.

Thus, the files Completion, Specification and Automaton are generated
and compiled with Tom. The resulting Java files are then compiled and the file
Completion.class can be executed using the command java.

5   Experiments

We give in this section significant examples to demonstrate the efficiency of
this technique. In the table below, the automaton size is given as (nb of transitions / nb of states). The benchmarks were done on a intel based platform
($2\times$Pentium 3GHz, running under FreeBSD), using Tom 2.5, Timbuk 2.2 and
Java 1.5.

	Combinatory	NSPK	View-Only	Java prog. 1	Java prog. 2
TRS size (nb of rules)	1	13	15	279	303
Initial Automaton size	43 / 23	14 / 4	21 / 18	26 / 49	33 / 33
Tom:					
Final Automaton size	8043 / 23	171 / 21	938 / 89	1974 / 637	1611 / 672
Time (secs)	5.9	5.9	150	360	303
Timbuk:					
Final Automaton size	8043 / 23	151 / 16	730 / 74	1127 / 334	751 / 335
Time (secs)	51.1	19.7	6420	25266	37387

Combinatory Example: This tiny example emphasizes that our prototype
is better than Timbuk in particular when a large number of substitutions is
computed during the completion. Let $\mathcal{R} = \{g(f(x_1), h(h(h(x_2, x_3), x_4), x_5)) \rightarrow$
$u(x_1, x_2, x_3, x_4, x_5)\}$ and $\mathcal{A}$ be the tree automaton whose transition set is the
following: $\{nil \rightarrow q_h, f(q_{a_1}) \rightarrow q_f, g(q_f, q_h) \rightarrow q_g\} \cup \{t \rightarrow q_t, h(q_h, q_t) \rightarrow q_h \mid t \in$
$\{a_i, b_i, c_i, d_i \mid i = 1, \ldots, 5\}\}$. For the variables x_1, x_3, x_4 and x_5 there are twenty
possible instantiations during the completion. The variables x_1 and x_2 take only

and respectively the values q_{a_1} and q_h. So, there are 20^3 transitions to compute by completion.

Needham-Schröeder Public Key Protocol: NSPK is a security protocol whose goal is to ensure the mutual authentication of two participants. The first version established in 1976 has been corrected by G. Lowe in 1995. Indeed, in this first version, a man-in-the-middle attack was possible. The second version of NSPK was already verified using Timbuk in [14]. Using the same approximation rules, our prototype leads also to an over-approximation allowing us to verify this protocol. The computation time of our prototype is better than Timbuk was.

The View-Only protocol: Let us now focus on the *View-Only* protocol. This protocol is a component of the *Smartright* system [20] designed by Thomson. In the context of home digital network, this system prevents users from unlawfully copying movie broadcasts on the network. The *view-only* devices are a decoder (DC) and a digital TV set (TVS). They share a secret key Kab securely sealed in both of them. The goal of this protocol is to periodically change a secret control word (CW) enabling to decode the current broadcast program. The Timbuk specification of this protocol is described in [15]. The same properties have been successfully verified with our encoding i.e. secrecy of CW, authentication of CW (no control word sent by the intruder has been accepted) and no replay attack on CW. The fix-point automaton has been obtained within a couple of minutes, while Timbuk terminates within 107 minutes.

Java programs: In [5], Java program analysis is performed using approximations, i.e. tree automata completion. Starting from a Java byte code program P, a TRS encoding the Java Virtual Machine and the semantics of P is automatically produced. The Java program 1 is the one detailed in [5]. For this program, a fix-point automaton is obtained with Tom within 360 seconds whereas it takes several hours for Timbuk to obtain the result. On this fix-point, the same analysis as in [5] have been successfully performed.

The Java program 2 represents the construction of two linear chained lists of integers. One is supposed to contain only positive integers, and the other only negative ones. Integers are entered and stored in the corresponding list while their value is different from 0. For verifying this program, we define approximation rules in such a way that all integers are abstracted into three equivalence classes (equal to 0, strictly positive and strictly negative), the input stream is specified as an infinite stack of integers and abstractions are performed on the memory in order to handle an infinite number of object creations. On both fix-point automaton, we can conclude that there are: no positive integer in the list of negative ones and no negative integer in the list of positive ones.

Our experiments show that the new implementation is faster than the last version of Timbuk. And this is the case for examples dealing with numerous combinations and computations. It is often the case when we are dealing with approximations. We have also applied the transformation ϕ on the input TRS of the Timbuk tool. Thanks to these experiments, we are convinced that ϕ is not the only reason for our better performance. In Timbuk, the most time consuming operation is the computation of critical pairs. Indeed, for every rule $l \to r$, we need to find every ground instance of l which can be reduced to a state q of the current automaton. In [12], a solution based on tree automata intersections is proposed but it remains inefficient when the number of rules and the size of their left-hand side are huge. In our case, as CCG generates a completion algorithm dedicated to a given specification, we do not need to implement a general matching algorithm as in Timbuk. Moreover, since the left-hand sides of $\phi(\mathcal{R})$ rules are almost flat, we use only the Tom pattern-matching features to compute critical pairs.

6 Conclusion

In this paper, we have developed an original and efficient implementation of tree automata completion. The first contribution is to have shown that decomposing the TRS into smaller rules preserves the over-approximation property. The second contribution is to have shown that, because of the special form of the decomposed rules, it is possible to define completion in a non-standard way. Instead of sophisticated and heavy algorithms over tree automata, our completion is built using simple rewriting techniques. Finally, another contribution of this paper is to propose an implementation taking advantage of the list-matching compilation feature of Tom to greatly improve the efficiency. On Java programs, which are now our main concerns, the obtained results are up to 100 times faster than the current state of the art implementation, i.e. Timbuk. The implementation proposed in this paper is a first promising step towards efficient verification tools for infinite state systems. We plan to apply this tool to the static analysis of industrial Java applications in the context of the RAVAJ project [1]. Since Tom generates *thread-safe code* – code supporting simultaneous execution by multiple threads – we are currently studying a multi-threaded implementation of the completion. This could also be a way to greatly improve the overall performance of our tree automata completion tool.

References

1. RAVAJ project (ANR-06-SETI-014)– Rewriting and Approximations for Java Applications Verification, http://www.irisa.fr/lande/genet/RAVAJ/index.html
2. Baader, F., Nipkow, T.: Term Rewriting and All That. Cambridge University Press, Cambridge (1998)
3. Balland, E., Brauner, P., Kopetz, R., Moreau, P.-E., Reilles, A.: Tom: Piggybacking rewriting on java. In: Baader, F. (ed.) RTA 2007. LNCS, vol. 4533, pp. 36–47. Springer, Heidelberg (2007)
4. Balland, E., Moreau, P.-E.: Optimizing pattern matching compilation by program transformation. In: 3rd Workshop on Software Evolution through Transformations (SeTra 2006). Electronic Communications of EASST (2006) ISSN 1863-2122
5. Boichut, Y., Genet, T., Jensen, T., Le Roux, L.: Rewriting Approximations for Fast Prototyping of Static Analyzers. In: Baader, F. (ed.) RTA 2007. LNCS, vol. 4533, pp. 48–62. Springer, Heidelberg (2007)

6. Boichut, Y., Héam, P.-C., Kouchnarenko, O.: Automatic Verification of Security Protocols Using Approximations. Research Report RR-5727, INRIA-Lorraine - CASSIS Project (October 2005)
7. Clavel, M., Palomino, M., Riesco, A.: Introducing the ITP tool: a tutorial. J. UCS 12(11), 1618–1650 (2006)
8. Comon, H., Dauchet, M., Gilleron, R., Jacquemard, F., Lugiez, D., Tison, S., Tommasi, M.: Tree automata techniques and applications (2002),
   http://www.grappa.univ-lille3.fr/tata/
9. Dershowitz, N., Jouannaud, J.-P.: Rewrite Systems. In: Handbook of Theoretical Computer Science, ch.6, vol. B. Elsevier Science Publishers B. V (North-Holland) (1990) Also as: Research report 478, LRI
10. Eker, S., Meseguer, J., Sridharanarayanan, A.: The Maude LTL Model Checker and its Implementation. In: Ball, T., Rajamani, S.K. (eds.) SPIN 2003. LNCS, vol. 2648, pp. 230–234. Springer, Heidelberg (2003)
11. Farzan, A., Chen, C., Meseguer, J., Rosu, G.: Formal analysis of java programs in javafan. In: Alur, R., Peled, D.A. (eds.) CAV 2004. LNCS, vol. 3114, pp. 501–505. Springer, Heidelberg (2004)
12. Feuillade, G., Genet, T., Tong, V.V.T.: Reachability Analysis over Term Rewriting Systems. JAR 33(3-4), 341–383 (2004)
13. Genet, T.: Decidable approximations of sets of descendants and sets of normal forms. In: Nipkow, T. (ed.) RTA 1998. LNCS, vol. 1379, pp. 151–165. Springer, Heidelberg (1998)
14. Genet, T., Klay, F.: Rewriting for Cryptographic Protocol Verification. In: Proc. 17th CADE Conf. LNCS (LNAI), vol. 1831. Springer, Heidelberg (2000)
15. Genet, T., Tang-Talpin, Y.-M., Tong, V.V.T.: Verification of Copy Protection Cryptographic Protocol using Approximations of Term Rewriting Systems. In: Proceedings of Workshop on Issues in the Theory of Security (2003)
16. Genet, T., Tong, V.V.T.: Timbuk 2.0 – a Tree Automata Library. IRISA / Université de Rennes 1 (2000), http://www.irisa.fr/lande/genet/timbuk/
17. Gilleron, R., Tison, S.: Regular tree languages and rewrite systems. Fundamenta Informaticae 24, 157–175 (1995)
18. Meseguer, J., Rosu, G.: Rewriting logic semantics: From language specifications to formal analysis tools. In: Basin, D., Rusinowitch, M. (eds.) IJCAR 2004. LNCS (LNAI), vol. 3097, pp. 1–44. Springer, Heidelberg (2004)
19. Takai, T.: A Verification Technique Using Term Rewriting Systems and Abstract Interpretation. In: Proc. 15th RTA Conf., Aachen, Germany. LNCS, vol. 3091, pp. 119–133. Springer, Heidelberg (2004)
20. Thomson. Smartright technical white paper v1.0. Technical report, (October 2001),
   http://www.smartright.org

Calculating Invariants as Coreflexive Bisimulations

Luís S. Barbosa[1], José N. Oliveira[1], and Alexandra Silva[2,*]

[1] CCTC, Universidade do Minho, 4700-320 Braga, Portugal
[2] Centrum voor Wiskunde en Informatica (CWI), Kruislaan 413, NL-1098 SJ Amsterdam

Abstract. Invariants, bisimulations and assertions are the main ingredients of coalgebra theory applied to software systems. In this paper we reduce the first to a particular case of the second and show how both together pave the way to a theory of coalgebras which regards invariant predicates as types. An outcome of such a theory is a calculus of invariants' proof obligation discharge, a fragment of which is presented in the paper.

The approach has two main ingredients: one is that of adopting relations as "first class citizens" in a pointfree reasoning style; the other lies on a synergy found between a relational construct, Reynolds' *relation on functions* involved in the *abstraction theorem* on parametric polymorphism and the coalgebraic account of bisimulations and invariants. This leads to an elegant proof of the equivalence between two different definitions of bisimulation found in coalgebra literature (due to B. Jacobs and Aczel & Mendler, respectively) and to their instantiation to the classical Park-Milner definition popular in process algebra.

Keywords: coalgebraic reasoning; proof obligations; pointfree transform; program calculation.

1 Introduction

The most widespread application of computer systems today is to support business operations. For this reason, the onus is on the software developer to ensure that business rules are properly taken into account. Computer scientists regard such rules as examples of invariant properties. The word "invariant" captures the idea that such desirable properties are to be maintained *invariant*, that is, unharmed across all transactions which are embodied in the system's functionality.

Changing business rules (ie. invariants) has a price: the code needs to be upgraded so as to ensure that changes are properly taken into account. This calls for a general theory of invariant preservation upon which one could base such an extended static checking mechanism. And this theory requires a broad view of computer systems able to take into account data persistence and continued interaction.

Coalgebra theory, widely acknowledged as the *mathematics of state-based systems* [22], provides an adequate modeling framework for such systems. The basic insight in coalgebraic modelling is that of representing state-based systems by functions of type

$$p : X \longrightarrow \mathsf{F} X \qquad (1)$$

* Partially supported by the Fundação para a Ciência e a Tecnologia, Portugal, under grant number SFRH/BD/27482/2006.

J. Meseguer and G. Roşu (Eds.): AMAST 2008, LNCS 5140, pp. 83–99, 2008.

which, for every state $x \in X$, describe the observable effects of an elementary step in the evolution of the system (*i.e.*, a state transition). The possible outcomes of such steps are captured by notation F X, where functor F acts as a *shape* for the system's interface.

Jacobs [11] identifies three cornerstones in the theory of coalgebras: *invariants*, *bisimilarity* and *assertions*. The latter are modal properties of states. About the first he writes: *an important aspect of formally establishing the safety of systems is to prove that certain crucial predicates are actually invariants.*

In this paper we develop a theory of invariant preservation whose novelty resides in explicitly expressing invariants as *bisimulations*. (See section 3 and its follow up.) The third cornerstone, assertions, is addressed in section 6. Altogether, we adopt a calculational style which stems from the explicit use of relational techniques, a body of knowledge often referred to as the *algebra of programming* [7].

Our starting point is Jacobs definition of an invariant for a given coalgebra [11]:

Definition 1. *Let* F $: Sets \rightarrow Sets$ *be a polynomial functor. An **invariant** for a coalgebra* $c : X \rightarrow$ F(X) *is a predicate* $P \subseteq X$ *satisfying for all* $x \in X$,

$$x \in P \Rightarrow c(x) \in Pred(\mathsf{F})(P). \tag{2}$$

$Pred(\mathsf{F})(P)$ stands for the *lifting* of predicate P via functor F. (We will spell out the meaning of this construct very soon.)

Our approach will be to reason about (2) via the PF-transform [2,7,17] — a transformation of first order predicate formulæ into *pointfree* binary relation formulæ which will enable us to blend the concept of invariant with that of bisimulation in a handy way. (In fact, we will show the former is a particular case of the latter.) By *pointfree* we mean formulæ which are free of quantifiers and variables (points) such as x above [1].

Structure of the paper. The paper starts by PF-transforming definition (2), in section 2, to conclude that invariants are a special case of bisimulations (section 3). Section 4 recasts bisimulations in terms of Reynolds' arrow combinator and resorts to its calculational power to provide elegant proofs of equivalence between three most common definitions of bisimulation. The development of (a fragment of) the theory of invariants is pursued in section 5, upon a category of "predicates as types". Moving on, section 6 illustrates how the approach proposed in this paper can be also of use to reason about modal assertions over coalgebras. Finally, section 7 concludes and gives pointers to related and future work.

2 Invariants PF-Transformed

Our first step is to convert definition (2) into a binary relational formula. The principle is that of PF-transforming universally quantified formulæ by applying, from right to

---

[1] The idea of encoding predicates in terms of relations was initiated by De Morgan in the 1860s and followed by Peirce who, in the 1870s, found interesting equational laws of the calculus of binary relations [19]. The pointfree nature of the notation which emerged from this embryonic work was later further exploited by Tarski and his students [23]. In the 1980's, Freyd and Ščedrov [9] developed the notion of an *allegory* (a category whose morphisms are partially ordered) which finally accommodates the binary relation calculus [7] as special case.

left, the definition of relational inclusion which follows,

$$R \subseteq S \;\equiv\; \langle \forall\, y, x \;::\; y\, R\, x \Rightarrow y\, S\, x \rangle \tag{3}$$

for R, S two binary relations [2]. In the case of (2), this means that R will have to capture set (predicate) P and S will have to do the same for set $Pred(\mathsf{F})(P)$. One of the standard ways of encoding a set X as a binary relation is as follows: one defines a relation Φ_X such that

$$y\, \Phi_X\, x \;\equiv\; y = x \wedge x \in X \tag{4}$$

Relations of this kind are referred to as *coreflexives* because they are fragments of the identity relation id: $\Phi_X \subseteq id$. For instance, set $\{1, 2, 3\}$ is captured by relation $\Phi_{\{1,2,3\}} = \{(1,1),(2,2),(3,3)\}$. We also need the binary relation composition operator

$$b(R \cdot S)c \;\equiv\; \langle \exists\, a \;::\; b\, R\, a \wedge a\, S\, c \rangle \tag{5}$$

(read $R \cdot S$ as "R after S") and to assert a rule which will prove convenient,

$$(f\, b)R(g\, a) \;\equiv\; b(f^\circ \cdot R \cdot g)a \tag{6}$$

where f and g are functions and $\_^\circ$ denotes the relational converse operator defined by:

$$a(R^\circ)b \;\equiv\; b\, R\, a \tag{7}$$

In this context, we reason:

$$\langle \forall\, x \;::\; x \in P \Rightarrow c(x) \in Pred(\mathsf{F})(P) \rangle$$

$\equiv \qquad \{\ \forall\text{-one point rule }\}$

$$\langle \forall\, y, x \;:\; y = x \;:\; x \in P \Rightarrow c(y) = c(x) \wedge c(x) \in Pred(\mathsf{F})(P) \rangle$$

$\equiv \qquad \{\ \forall\text{-trading }\}$

$$\langle \forall\, y, x \;::\; y = x \wedge x \in P \Rightarrow c(y) = c(x) \wedge c(x) \in Pred(\mathsf{F})(P) \rangle$$

$\equiv \qquad \{\ (4)\ \text{twice }\}$

$$\langle \forall\, y, x \;::\; y\, \Phi_P\, x \Rightarrow c(y)\, \Phi_{Pred(\mathsf{F})(P)}\, c(x) \rangle$$

$\equiv \qquad \{\ \text{rule (6) }\}$

$$\langle \forall\, y, x \;::\; y\, \Phi_P\, x \Rightarrow y(c^\circ \cdot \Phi_{Pred(\mathsf{F})(P)} \cdot c)x \rangle$$

$\equiv \qquad \{\ \text{rule (3) }\}$

$$\Phi_P \subseteq c^\circ \cdot \Phi_{Pred(\mathsf{F})(P)} \cdot c \tag{8}$$

Predicate $Pred(\mathsf{F})(P)$ is defined in [11] (Def. 4.1.1) by induction on the structure of polynomial F. This can be abbreviated by regarding F as a relator [5] and representing

---

[2] By $y\, R\, x$ we mean the fact that pair (y, x) belongs to R. (Similarly for $y\, S\, x$.)

P by its coreflexive Φ_P. The concept of a *relator* F extends that of *functor* to relations: $F\,A$ describes a parametric type while $F\,R$ is a relation from $F\,A$ to $F\,B$ provided R is a relation from A to B. Relators are monotone and commute with composition, converse and the identity. In this context, $Pred(\mathsf{F})(P)$ coincides with relation $F\,\Phi_P$. Thus we resume to (8) and calculate further:

$$\Phi_P \subseteq c^\circ \cdot F\,\Phi_P \cdot c$$

$$\equiv \qquad \{ \text{ see (10) below } \}$$

$$c \cdot \Phi_P \subseteq F\,\Phi_P \cdot c \tag{9}$$

where the last step is justified by the first of the following laws of the relational calculus,

$$f \cdot R \subseteq S \ \equiv \ R \subseteq f^\circ \cdot S \tag{10}$$

$$R \cdot f^\circ \subseteq S \ \equiv \ R \subseteq S \cdot f \tag{11}$$

known as the *shunting rules* [7] [3].

Altogether, we arrive at (9), a quite compact version of (2). It tells that wherever c runs on states satisfying P, any of its successor states will do so. The sections which follow will give evidence of the advantages of such a transformation.

3   Invariants Are Bisimulations

We move on to the second cornerstone of coalgebra theory — bisimilarity. This is based on the concept of *bisimulation* which is given by Jacobs [11] as follows:

Definition 2. *A bisimulation for coalgebras $c : X \to \mathsf{F}(X)$ and $d : Y \to \mathsf{F}(Y)$ is a relation $R \subseteq X \times Y$ which is* closed under c and d:

$$(x, y) \in R \Rightarrow (c(x), d(y)) \in Rel(\mathsf{F})(R). \tag{12}$$

for all $x \in X$ and $y \in Y$.

(a)   (b)

This time $Rel(\mathsf{F})(R)$ stands for the relational *lifting* of R via functor F which, in our relational setting, is captured by notation $F\,R$.

An exercise at all similar to the one carried out in the previous section will show (12) PF-transformed into

$$c \cdot R \subseteq F\,R \cdot d \tag{13}$$

as depicted in diagram (a) above, where X and Y are the carriers of coalgebras c and d, respectively. Since (9) instantiates (13) we have that invariants are *special* cases of bisimulations: exactly those which are coreflexive relations, cf. diagram (b).

---

[3] Functions are denoted by lowercase characters (eg. f, g, ϕ) and function application will be abbreviated by juxtaposition, eg. $f\,a$ instead of $f(a)$. Coalgebras qualify for these rules because they are functions.

We shall see briefly that this conclusion brings about its benefits, as much of the theory of coalgebraic invariants stems directly from that of bisimulations [4]. We will address this one first.

4   Calculating Bisimulations

Let us first show how the classical definition of bisimulation used in process algebra (due to Milner and Park [18]) can be retrieved from (13) simply by instantiating F to the powerset relator $\mathcal{P}X = \{S \mid S \subseteq X\}$. We need the universal property of the *power-transpose* isomorphism Λ

$$f = \Lambda R \ \equiv \ R = \in \cdot f \tag{14}$$

which converts binary relations to set-valued functions [7], where $A \xleftarrow{\in} \mathcal{P}A$ is the membership relation. In [7] the powerset relator is defined by

$$\mathcal{P}R = (\in \setminus (R \cdot \in)) \cap (\in \setminus (R^\circ \cdot \in))^\circ \tag{15}$$

where $\cap$ denotes relation intersection and $R \setminus S$ denotes relational division,

$$a(R \setminus S)c \ \equiv \ \langle \forall b : b R a : b S c \rangle$$

a relational operator whose semantics is captured by universal property

$$R \cdot X \subseteq S \ \equiv \ X \subseteq R \setminus S \tag{16}$$

The main ingredient of the calculation below is (14), which ensures that every powerset coalgebra uniquely determines a binary relation (Λ is a bijection). In this context, let R be a bisimulation between two powerset coalgebras ΛS and ΛU. We reason:

$(\Lambda S) \cdot R \subseteq (\mathcal{P}R) \cdot (\Lambda U)$

$\equiv \qquad \{$ unfolding $\mathcal{P}R$ (15) $\}$

$(\Lambda S) \cdot R \subseteq (\in \setminus (R \cdot \in)) \cap (\in \setminus (R^\circ \cdot \in))^\circ \cdot (\Lambda U)$

$\equiv \qquad \{$ distribution (since ΛU is a function) thanks to (11) $\}$

$(\Lambda S) \cdot R \subseteq (\in \setminus (R \cdot \in)) \cdot (\Lambda U) \ \wedge \ (\Lambda S) \cdot R \subseteq (\in \setminus (R^\circ \cdot \in))^\circ \cdot (\Lambda U)$

$\equiv \qquad \{$ property $R \setminus (S \cdot f) = (R \setminus S) \cdot f$; converses $\}$

$(\Lambda S) \cdot R \subseteq \in \setminus (R \cdot \in \cdot \Lambda U) \ \wedge \ R^\circ \cdot (\Lambda S)^\circ \subseteq (\Lambda U)^\circ \cdot (\in \setminus (R^\circ \cdot \in))$

$\equiv \qquad \{$ shunting rules (10,11) and property above $\}$

$(\Lambda S) \cdot R \subseteq \in \setminus (R \cdot \in \cdot \Lambda U) \ \wedge \ (\Lambda U) \cdot R^\circ \subseteq \in \setminus (R^\circ \cdot \in \cdot \Lambda S)$

$\equiv \qquad \{$ (16) twice $\}$

---

[4] It is interesting to note that Lemma 4.2.2 in [11] proves that relation $\{(x, x) \mid x \in P\}$ is a bisimulation yielded by invariant P, but no further advantage is taken from this fact.

$$\in \cdot (\Lambda S) \cdot R \subseteq R \cdot \in \cdot \Lambda U \ \wedge \ \in \cdot (\Lambda U) \cdot R^\circ \subseteq R^\circ \cdot \in \cdot \Lambda S$$

$$\equiv \quad \{ \text{ cancellation } \in \cdot (\Lambda R) = R \text{ four times } \}$$

$$S \cdot R \subseteq R \cdot U \ \wedge \ U \cdot R^\circ \subseteq R^\circ \cdot S$$

The two conjuncts state that R and its converse are *simulations* between state transition relations S and U, which corresponds to the Park-Milner definition [5]: *a bisimulation is a simulation between two LTS such that its converse is also a simulation, where a simulation between two LTS S and U is a relation R such that, if $(p,q) \in R$, then for all p' such that $(p',p) \in S$, then there is a q' such that $(p',q') \in R$ and $(q',q) \in U$ — see diagram on the right [6].*

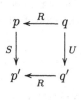

We furthermore want to check (13) against another (also coalgebraic) definition of bisimulation due to Aczel & Mendler [1]: *given two coalgebras $c : X \to F(X)$ and $d : Y \to F(Y)$ an F-bisimulation is a relation $R \subseteq X \times Y$ which can be extended to a coalgebra ρ such that projections π_1 and π_2 lift to F-coalgebra morphisms.* (See diagram aside.)

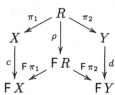

Jacobs [11] spends some time in proving the equivalence between the two definitions. Our proof will be much shorter and calculational thanks to a small trick: we identify (13) as instance

$$c(F R \leftarrow R)d \tag{17}$$

of Reynolds "arrow combinator" $R \leftarrow S$ which, given R and S, relates two functions f and g as follows [2]:

$$f(R \leftarrow S)g \ \equiv \ f \cdot S \subseteq R \cdot g \tag{18}$$

With points, $f(R \leftarrow S)g$ means $\langle \forall \, y, x \ :: \ y \, S \, x \Rightarrow (f \, y) R(g \, x) \rangle$. For instance, for f and g the same function and S and R two partial orders, (18) means that such a function is monotonic.

The fact that we can write (17) instead of $c \cdot R \ \subseteq F R \cdot d$ (13) to mean that R is a bisimulation between F coalgebras c and d is of great notational, conceptual and calculational advantage. As far as notation is concerned, (17) is very appropriate for telling that c and d produce F R-related outputs $c \, y$ and $d \, x$ provided their inputs are R-related ($y \, R \, x$). Conceptually, $F R \leftarrow R$ may be regarded as a relation involving all coalgebras which are R-bisimilar. But it is the calculational power implicit in (17) which really justifies the recasting of (13) in terms of Reynolds' arrow combinator.

In another context, this combinator is studied in some detail in [2], where the following PF-properties can be found:

$$id \leftarrow id = id \tag{19}$$

---

[5] The pointwise definition of simulation is better perceived once $S \cdot R \subseteq R \cdot U$ is re-written into $R \subseteq S \backslash (R \cdot U)$, recall (16) — similarly for the other conjunct. Matteo Vaccari [24] performs a calculation similar to the above starting directly from this pointwise definition.

[6] A popular presentation of the classical definition of bisimulation uses LTS defined by the labelled powerset relator $\mathcal{P}(A \times X)$, for A a given set of actions. The reasoning for this functor is the same: only $\mathcal{P}(id \times R)$ should replace $\mathcal{P}R$ in the calculation.

$$(R \leftarrow S)^{\circ} = R^{\circ} \leftarrow S^{\circ} \tag{20}$$
$$R \leftarrow S \subseteq V \leftarrow U \Leftarrow R \subseteq V \wedge U \subseteq S \tag{21}$$
$$k(f \leftarrow g)h \equiv k \cdot g = f \cdot h \tag{22}$$

From property (21) we learn that the combinator is monotonic on the left hand side — and thus facts

$$S \leftarrow R \subseteq (S \cup V) \leftarrow R \tag{23}$$
$$\top \leftarrow S = \top \tag{24}$$

hold [7] — and anti-monotonic on the right hand side — and thus property

$$R \leftarrow \bot = \top \tag{25}$$

and the two distributive laws which follow:

$$S \leftarrow (R_1 \cup R_2) = (S \leftarrow R_1) \cap (S \leftarrow R_2) \tag{26}$$
$$(S_1 \cap S_2) \leftarrow R = (S_1 \leftarrow R) \cap (S_2 \leftarrow R) \tag{27}$$

Let us see how the properties above explain those of bisimulation by themselves. Property (20) ensures that the converse of a bisimulation is also a bisimulation. This turns out to be an equivalence:

R is a bisimulation

$\equiv \qquad \{ (17) \} \qquad\qquad\qquad d((\mathsf{F}\,R)^{\circ} \leftarrow R^{\circ})c$

$\quad c(\mathsf{F}\,R \leftarrow R)d \qquad\qquad \equiv \qquad \{ \text{ relator F } \}$

$\equiv \qquad \{ \text{ converse } \} \qquad\qquad d(\mathsf{F}(R^{\circ}) \leftarrow R^{\circ})c$

$\quad d(\mathsf{F}\,R \leftarrow R)^{\circ}c \qquad\qquad \equiv \qquad \{ (17) \}$

$\equiv \qquad \{ (20) \} \qquad\qquad\qquad R^{\circ} \text{ is a bisimulation}$

Next, we recall the definition of a coalgebra morphism:

Definition 3. *Let* $(X, p : X \longrightarrow \mathsf{F}X)$ *and* $(Y, q : Y \longrightarrow \mathsf{F}Y)$ *be coalgebras for functor* F. *A morphism* connecting p and q *is a function* h *between their carriers such that* $q \cdot h = \mathsf{F}h \cdot p$.

Clearly, property (22) tells immediately that coalgebra morphisms are bisimulations.

The easy calculation of $\mathsf{F}\,id \leftarrow id = id$ (19) ensures id is a bisimulation between a given coalgebra and itself. On the other side of the spectrum, (25) tells us that $\bot$ is a bisimulation for *any* pair of coalgebras c and d. (Just introduce points in $\mathsf{F}\bot \leftarrow \bot$ and simplify.)

Let us now see how the fact that bisimulations are closed under union,

$$c(\mathsf{F}\,R_1 \leftarrow R_1)d \wedge c(\mathsf{F}\,R_2 \leftarrow R_2)d \Rightarrow c(\mathsf{F}(R_1 \cup R_2) \leftarrow (R_1 \cup R_2))d \tag{28}$$

---

[7] Cf. $f \cdot S \cdot g^{\circ} \subseteq \top \equiv \text{TRUE}$ concerning (24).

stems from properties (21,23) and (26). First we PF-transform (28) to

$$(\mathsf{F}\,R_1 \leftarrow R_1) \cap (\mathsf{F}\,R_2 \leftarrow R_2) \subseteq \mathsf{F}(R_1 \cup R_2) \leftarrow (R_1 \cup R_2)$$

and reason:

$$(\mathsf{F}\,R_1 \leftarrow R_1) \cap (\mathsf{F}\,R_2 \leftarrow R_2)$$

$\subseteq$ { (23) (twice) ; monotonicity of $\cap$ }

$$((\mathsf{F}\,R_1 \cup \mathsf{F}\,R_2) \leftarrow R_1) \cap ((\mathsf{F}\,R_1 \cup \mathsf{F}\,R_2) \leftarrow R_2)$$

$=$ { (26) }

$$(\mathsf{F}\,R_1 \cup \mathsf{F}\,R_2) \leftarrow (R_1 \cup R_2)$$

$\subseteq$ { F is monotonic; (21) }

$$\mathsf{F}(R_1 \cup R_2) \leftarrow (R_1 \cup R_2)$$

Eventually, we are in position to address the equivalence between Jacobs' and Aczel-Mendler's definitions of bisimulation. To the set of known rules about (18) we add the following law

$$(r \cdot s^\circ) \leftarrow (f \cdot g^\circ) = (r \leftarrow f) \cdot (s \leftarrow g)^\circ \;\Leftarrow\; \text{pair } r, s \text{ is a tabulation} \qquad (29)$$

where a pair of functions $A \xleftarrow{\;r\;} C \xrightarrow{\;s\;} B$ form a tabulation iff split function $\langle r, s \rangle$ is injective, that is, iff $r^\circ \cdot r \cap s^\circ \cdot s = id$ holds [8].

Below we show that (29) is what matters in proving the equivalence between Jacobs' definition of bisimulation (once PF-transformed) and that of Aczel & Mendler:

$c(\mathsf{F}\,R \leftarrow R)d$

$\equiv$ { tabulate $R = \pi_1 \cdot \pi_2^\circ$ }

$c(\mathsf{F}(\pi_1 \cdot \pi_2^\circ) \leftarrow (\pi_1 \cdot \pi_2^\circ))d$

$\equiv$ { relator commutes with composition and converse }

$c(((\mathsf{F}\,\pi_1) \cdot (\mathsf{F}\,\pi_2)^\circ) \leftarrow (\pi_1 \cdot \pi_2^\circ))d$

$\equiv$ { new rule (29) }

$c((\mathsf{F}\,\pi_1 \leftarrow \pi_1) \cdot ((\mathsf{F}\,\pi_2)^\circ \leftarrow \pi_2^\circ))d$

$\equiv$ { converse rule (20) }

$c((\mathsf{F}\,\pi_1 \leftarrow \pi_1) \cdot (\mathsf{F}\,\pi_2 \leftarrow \pi_2)^\circ)d$

$\equiv$ { (5) }

$\langle \exists\, a \;::\; c(\mathsf{F}\,\pi_1 \leftarrow \pi_1)a \,\wedge\, d(\mathsf{F}\,\pi_2 \leftarrow \pi_2)a \rangle$

cf.

$$\begin{array}{ccc} X & \xleftarrow{\;R\;} & Y \\ {\scriptstyle c}\downarrow\;\; {\scriptstyle \pi_1}\searrow & \;\;Z\;{\scriptstyle \pi_2}\nearrow & \;\;\downarrow {\scriptstyle d} \\ & \downarrow {\scriptstyle a} & \\ & \mathsf{F}\,Z & \\ \mathsf{F}\,X & \xleftarrow{\;\mathsf{F}\,R\;} & \mathsf{F}\,Y \end{array}$$

Clearly, the meaning of the last line above is exactly Aczel-Mendler's definition (cf. diagram): it states that *there exists a coalgebra a whose carrier is the "graph" of bisimulation R and which is such that projections π_1 and π_2 lift to the corresponding coalgebra morphisms.*

---

[8] The proof of (29) can be found in [14]. It is a standard result that every R can be factored in a tabulation $R = r \cdot s^\circ$ [7]. An obvious and easy to check tabulation is $r, s := \pi_1, \pi_2$ [14], which boils down to pairwise equality: $(b, a) = (d, c)$ equivalent to $b = d \wedge a = c$.

Note how simple the proof is. The elegance of the calculation lies in the synergy with Reynolds' arrow combinator. To the best of our knowledge, such a synergy is new in the literature [9].

5 Calculating Invariants

Let us write $F\Phi_P \xleftarrow{c} \Phi_P$ to denote the fact that P is an invariant (9), which we abbreviate to $F\Phi \xleftarrow{c} \Phi$ since predicates and coreflexives are in one to one correspondence. (We will use uppercase Greek letters to denote such coreflexives and will refer to them as "invariants" with no further explanation.)

This notation suggests a category Pred of "predicates as objects" as a suitable universe for describing coalgebraic systems subject to invariants. Pred's objects are predicates, represented by coreflexives. An arrow $\Psi \xleftarrow{f} \Phi$ in Pred means a function which ensures property Ψ on its output whenever property Φ holds on its input. Arrows in Pred can therefore be seen as *proof-obligations* for the corresponding functions [10]. Formally:

$$\Psi \xleftarrow{f} \Phi \equiv f(\Psi \leftarrow \Phi)f \equiv f \cdot \Phi \subseteq \Psi \cdot f \qquad (30)$$

Clearly, any relator (in Rel) restricts to a functor in Pred. In particular, the functorial image of an arrow $\Psi \xleftarrow{f} \Phi$ is well-typed, cf.

$$F\Psi \xleftarrow{Ff} F\Phi$$

$$\equiv \quad \{ (30) \}$$

$$Ff \cdot F\Phi \subseteq F\Psi \cdot Ff$$

$$\equiv \quad \{ \text{functors} \}$$

$$F(f \cdot \Phi) \subseteq F(\Psi \cdot f)$$

$$\Leftarrow \quad \{ F \text{ is monotone; (30)} \}$$

$$\Psi \xleftarrow{f} \Phi$$

Such a "predicates as types" view carries over universal constructs. As Pred's hom sets are included in Set, in order to verify whether a particular universal property in

---

[9] For a longer bi-implication proof of this equivalence see Backhouse and Hoogendijk's work on final *dialgebras* [6]. A proof of the same result is implicit in Corollary 3.1 of [21] which invokes a result by Carboni *et al* [8] on extending functors to relators.

[10] See [16], where this view of proof obligations is actually extended to arbitrary binary relations. This is suitable for specification languages such as eg. VDM, where *the inclusion of a subtyping mechanism which allows truth-valued functions forces the type checking here to rely on proofs* [12].

the latter lifts to a universal in Pred it is enough to check whether the corresponding diagram exists and the universal arrow in Set is still an arrow in Pred. The fact that composition satisfies constraints,

$$\Psi \xleftarrow{\;g\cdot f\;} \Phi \;\Leftarrow\; \Psi \xleftarrow{\;g\;} \Upsilon \;\wedge\; \Upsilon \xleftarrow{\;f\;} \Phi \tag{31}$$

stems directly from (30), as does the obvious rule concerning identity:

$$\Psi \xleftarrow{\;id\;} \Phi \;\equiv\; \Phi \subseteq \Psi \tag{32}$$

(From (31) we infer also that exponential $g^{\Phi} f = g \cdot f$ is well-typed.) For a slightly more elaborate example consider, for instance, functional *products* in the new setting:

$$\Psi \xleftarrow{\;\pi_1\;} \Psi \times \Upsilon \xrightarrow{\;\pi_2\;} \Upsilon \tag{33}$$

with f, $\langle f,g\rangle$, g and Φ below.

Clearly, the proof-obligations associated to the two projections

$$\pi_1 \cdot (\Psi \times \Upsilon) \subseteq \Psi \cdot \pi_1 \quad , \quad \pi_2 \cdot (\Psi \times \Upsilon) \subseteq \Upsilon \cdot \pi_2$$

are instances of Reynolds abstraction theorem [20,25,2]:

$$G\,A \xleftarrow{\;f\;} F\,A \;\text{ is polymorphic} \equiv \langle \forall\, R \;::\; f(G\,R \leftarrow F\,R)f\rangle \tag{34}$$

So there is nothing to prove. To show that $\langle f, g \rangle$ is indeed an arrow in Pred we need to recall the universal property of relational splits [7]

$$X \subseteq \langle R, S \rangle \;\equiv\; \pi_1 \cdot X \subseteq R \wedge \pi_2 \cdot X \subseteq S \tag{35}$$

and that $\times$-absorption holds. We reason [11]:

$$\Psi \times \Upsilon \xleftarrow{\;\langle f,g\rangle\;} \Phi$$

$\equiv$ { definition (30) }

$$\langle f, g \rangle \cdot \Phi \subseteq (\Psi \times \Upsilon) \cdot \langle f, g \rangle$$

$\equiv$ { absorption law for relational product }

$$\langle f, g \rangle \cdot \Phi \subseteq \langle \Psi \cdot f, \Upsilon \cdot g \rangle$$

$\equiv$ { universal law for relational product (35) }

$$\pi_1 \cdot \langle f, g \rangle \cdot \Phi \subseteq \Psi \cdot f \;\wedge\; \pi_2 \cdot \langle f, g \rangle \cdot \Phi \subseteq \Upsilon \cdot g$$

---

[11] Note that the $\Leftarrow$ part of this equivalence is also ensured by the abstraction theorem (34) of the *split* combinator (on functions).

$$\equiv \quad \{\text{ cancellation law for functional product }\}$$

$$f \cdot \Phi \subseteq \Psi \cdot f \;\wedge\; g \cdot \Phi \subseteq \Upsilon \cdot g$$

$$\equiv \quad \{\text{ definition (30) twice }\}$$

$$\Psi \xleftarrow{\;f\;} \Phi \;\wedge\; \Upsilon \xleftarrow{\;g\;} \Phi$$

As expected, a coalgebra $F\Phi \xleftarrow{\;c\;} \Phi$ in Pred maintains property Φ invariant. Final coalgebras (and initial algebras) exist and coincide with the ones in Set. Let us check, in this respect, the diagram of *unfold* (aside), where νF denotes the final coalgebra and $[\![c]\!]$ is the coinductive extension, or *unfold*, of coalgebra c. We reason:

$$\begin{array}{ccc} F(\nu F) & \xleftarrow{\;out\;} & \nu F \\ {\scriptstyle F[\![c]\!]}\big\uparrow & & \big\uparrow{\scriptstyle [\![c]\!]} \\ F\Phi & \xleftarrow{\;c\;} & \Phi \end{array}$$

$$\nu F \xleftarrow{\;[\![c]\!]\;} \Phi$$

$$\equiv \quad \{\text{ definition (30) }\}$$

$$[\![c]\!] \cdot \Phi \subseteq [\![c]\!]$$

$$\Leftarrow \quad \{\text{ fusion: } [\![T]\!] \cdot S \subseteq [\![R]\!] \;\Leftarrow\; T \cdot S \subseteq F S \cdot R \}$$

$$c \cdot \Phi \subseteq F\Phi \cdot c$$

$$\equiv \quad \{\text{ definition (30) }\}$$

$$F\Phi \xleftarrow{\;c\;} \Phi$$

We close this section by showing how the "invariants as bisimulations" approach helps in developing of a number of simple, yet powerful rules to reason about "invariant-typed" coalgebras. Our calculations below address three such rules.

Separation rule:

$$F(\Phi \cdot \Psi) \xleftarrow{\;c\;} \Phi \cdot \Psi \;\Leftarrow\; F\Phi \xleftarrow{\;c\;} \Phi \;\wedge\; F\Psi \xleftarrow{\;c\;} \Psi \qquad (36)$$

This rule enables the decomposition of the proof obligation of a compound invariant into two separate proof obligations, one per conjunct. Its calculation is as follows:

$$F\Phi \xleftarrow{\;c\;} \Phi \;\wedge\; F\Psi \xleftarrow{\;c\;} \Psi$$

$$\equiv \quad \{\text{ (30) twice }\}$$

$$c \cdot \Phi \subseteq F\Phi \cdot c \;\wedge\; c \cdot \Psi \subseteq F\Psi \cdot c$$

$$\Rightarrow \quad \{\text{ monotonicity of composition (twice) }\}$$

$$c \cdot \Phi \cdot \Psi \subseteq F\Phi \cdot c \cdot \Psi \;\wedge\; F\Phi \cdot c \cdot \Psi \subseteq F\Phi \cdot F\Psi \cdot c$$

$$\Rightarrow \quad \{ \text{ transitivity } \}$$

$$c \cdot \Phi \cdot \Psi \subseteq F\Phi \cdot (F\Psi \cdot c)$$

$$\equiv \quad \{ \text{ relator F and (30) } \}$$

$$F(\Phi \cdot \Psi) \xleftarrow{\;c\;} \Phi \cdot \Psi$$

Interleaving rule:

$$F(\Phi \times \Psi) \xleftarrow{\;c|||d\;} \Phi \times \Psi \;\Leftarrow\; F\Phi \xleftarrow{\;c\;} \Phi \;\wedge\; F\Psi \xleftarrow{\;d\;} \Psi \qquad (37)$$

where $|||$ is an interleaving operator defined by $c ||| d \stackrel{\text{def}}{=} \delta \cdot (c \times d)$ whenever F has a distributive law $\delta : F\Phi \times F\Psi \longrightarrow F(\Phi \times \Psi)$ corresponding to the Kleisli composition of F's left and right strength (see [13] for details). The calculation of (37) follows:

$$F\Phi \xleftarrow{\;c\;} \Phi \;\wedge\; F\Psi \xleftarrow{\;d\;} \Psi$$

$$\equiv \quad \{ \text{ (30) twice } \}$$

$$c \cdot \Phi \subseteq F\Phi \cdot c \;\wedge\; d \cdot \Psi \subseteq F\Psi \cdot d$$

$$\Rightarrow \quad \{ \text{ monotonicity of product and composition } \}$$

$$\delta \cdot (c \cdot \Phi \times d \cdot \Psi) \subseteq \delta \cdot (F\Phi \cdot c \times F\Psi \cdot d)$$

$$\Rightarrow \quad \{ \times \text{ relator } \}$$

$$\delta \cdot (c \times d) \cdot (\Phi \times \Psi) \subseteq \delta \cdot (F\Phi \times F\Psi) \cdot (c \times d)$$

$$\Rightarrow \quad \{ \delta\text{'s free theorem (34) } \}$$

$$\delta \cdot (c \times d) \cdot (\Phi \times \Psi) \subseteq F(\Phi \times \Psi) \cdot \delta \cdot (c \times d)$$

$$\equiv \quad \{ \text{ definition of } c ||| d \text{ and (30) } \}$$

$$F(\Phi \times \Psi) \xleftarrow{\;c|||d\;} \Phi \times \Psi$$

Pipeline. For F a monad,

$$F\Phi \xleftarrow{\;c\bullet d\;} \Phi \;\Leftarrow\; F\Phi \xleftarrow{\;c\;} \Phi \;\wedge\; F\Phi \xleftarrow{\;d\;} \Phi \qquad (38)$$

where $c \bullet d$ corresponds to the Kleisli composition of c and d. We calculate:

$$(c \bullet d) \cdot \Phi$$

$$= \quad \{ \text{ definition of Kleisli composition } \}$$

$$\mu \cdot Fc \cdot d \cdot \Phi$$

$$\subseteq \quad \{ \; F\Phi \xleftarrow{\;d\;} \Phi \text{ and monotonicity } \}$$

$$\mu \cdot \mathsf{F} c \cdot \mathsf{F} \Phi \cdot d$$

$$= \quad \{ \mathsf{F} \text{ relator} \}$$

$$\mu \cdot \mathsf{F} (c \cdot \Phi) \cdot d$$

$$\subseteq \quad \{ \mathsf{F}\Phi \xleftarrow{c} \Phi \text{ and monotonicity} \}$$

$$\mu \cdot \mathsf{F} (\mathsf{F}\Phi \cdot c) \cdot d$$

$$= \quad \{ \mathsf{F} \text{ relator and } \mu \text{'s free theorem (34)} \}$$

$$\mathsf{F}\Phi \cdot \mu \cdot \mathsf{F} c \cdot d$$

$$= \quad \{ \text{ definition of Kleisli composition} \}$$

$$\mathsf{F}\Phi \cdot (c \bullet d)$$

6   Calculating Assertions

As mentioned in the introduction to this paper, the third main ingredient of coalgebraic reasoning identified in [11] is a language of modal *assertions* in which specifications of the behaviour of systems can be expressed. Clearly, invariants bring about a *"next time"* modal operator,

$$c(\mathsf{F}\Phi \leftarrow \Phi)c \;\equiv\; c \cdot \Phi \subseteq \mathsf{F}\Phi \cdot c$$

$$\equiv \quad \{ \text{ shunting (10)} \}$$

$$\Phi \subseteq \underbrace{c^\circ \cdot (\mathsf{F}\Phi) \cdot c}_{\bigcirc_c \Phi} \tag{39}$$

which holds for those states whose all immediate successors, if any, satisfy Φ. From this a PF-definition of the *"next time Φ holds"* modal operator emerges

$$\bigcirc_c \Phi \stackrel{\text{def}}{=} c^\circ \cdot (\mathsf{F}\Phi) \cdot c \tag{40}$$

which PF-transforms Def. 4.3.1 of [11]. So, assertion $\Phi \subseteq \bigcirc_c \Phi$ is an alternative statement of "Φ in an invariant" for coalgebra c.

This modal operator is easily shown to be the upper adjoint of Galois connection

$$\pi_c \Phi \subseteq \Psi \equiv \Phi \subseteq \bigcirc_c \Psi \tag{41}$$

whose lower adjoint is the *projection* operator $\pi_c \Phi \stackrel{\text{def}}{=} c \cdot \Phi \cdot c^\circ$ which is central to [15] in studying the PF-refactoring of data dependency theory (a part of database theory). From this, one immediately infers that $\bigcirc_c$ is monotonic and distributes over conjunction: $\bigcirc_c(\Phi \cdot \Psi) = (\bigcirc_c \Phi) \cdot (\bigcirc_c \Psi)$. Note that we express conjunction by composition because these two operators coincide on coreflexives:

$$\Phi \cap \Psi = \Phi \cdot \Psi \tag{42}$$

Such properties can then be used to reason about operator $\bigcirc_c$, as in, for example,

$$\Phi \text{ is an invariant}$$

$$\equiv \quad \{ \ (39) \ \}$$

$$\Phi \subseteq \bigcirc_c \Phi$$

$$\Rightarrow \quad \{ \text{ monotonicity of } \bigcirc_c \text{ stemming from (41) } \}$$

$$\bigcirc_c \Phi \subseteq \bigcirc_c(\bigcirc_c \Phi)$$

$$\equiv \quad \{ \ (39) \ \}$$

$$\bigcirc_c \Phi \text{ is an invariant}$$

The whole construction of a modal logic relative to a coalgebra c, which is the basis of *assertion* reasoning in coalgebra theory, can be pursued along similar lines. Consider, for example, the definition of $\Box P$, the *henceforth P* operator of [11, Def. 4.2.8]:

$$(\Box P)x \stackrel{\text{def}}{=} \langle \exists\, Q \ : \ Q \text{ is invariant} : \ Q \subseteq P \wedge (Q\, x) \rangle$$

Converting predicates P and Q to coreflexives Φ and Ψ, respectively, and making explicit the *supremum* implicit in the existential quantification one gets,

$$\Box\Phi = \langle \bigcup \Psi \ : \ \Psi \subseteq \bigcirc_c \Psi : \ \Psi \subseteq \Phi \rangle$$

$$= \quad \{ \text{ trading [4] } \}$$

$$\langle \bigcup \Psi \ :: \ \Psi \subseteq \bigcirc_c \Psi \wedge \Psi \subseteq \Phi \rangle$$

$$= \quad \{ \ \cap\text{-universal } \}$$

$$\langle \bigcup \Psi \ :: \ \Psi \subseteq \bigcirc_c \Psi \cap \Phi \rangle$$

$$= \quad \{ \ \cap \text{ of coreflexives is composition (42) } \}$$

$$\langle \bigcup \Psi \ :: \ \Psi \subseteq \Phi \cdot \bigcirc_c \Psi \rangle$$

which leads to a greatest (post)fixpoint definition:

$$\Box\Phi = \langle \nu\, \Psi \ :: \ \Phi \cdot \bigcirc_c \Psi \rangle \tag{43}$$

We end this section by showing how the PF-transform (and in particular the replacement of intersection of coreflexives by composition (42)) together with the fixpoint calculus [3] speed up derivation of laws in such a logic. The law we have chosen to calculate is Lemma 4.2.9(ii) of [11]: $\Box\Phi \ \subseteq \ \Box\Box\Phi$. We drop subscript c of $\bigcirc_c$ (for economy of notation) and calculate:

$$\Box\Phi \subseteq \Box\Box\Phi$$

$$\equiv \quad \{ \ (43) \ \}$$

$$\Box\varPhi \subseteq \langle \nu\,\varPsi \,::\, (\Box\varPhi)\cdot\bigcirc\varPsi\rangle$$

$\Leftarrow$ { greatest fixed point induction: $x \leq fx \Rightarrow x \leq \nu f$ [3] }

$$\Box\varPhi \subseteq \Box\varPhi \cdot \bigcirc(\Box\varPhi)$$

$\equiv$ { $\Box\varPhi\cdot\varPhi = \Box\varPhi$ thanks to (42), since $\Box\varPhi \subseteq \varPhi$ }

$$\Box\varPhi \subseteq \Box\varPhi \cdot \varPhi \cdot \bigcirc(\Box\varPhi)$$

$\equiv$ { property (for $\varPhi$ coreflexive) $\varPhi\cdot R \subseteq S \equiv \varPhi\cdot R \subseteq \varPhi\cdot S$ }

$$\Box\varPhi \subseteq \varPhi \cdot \bigcirc(\Box\varPhi)$$

$\equiv$ { (43) and fixpoint calculus ($\nu_f \subseteq f\nu_f$) }

$true$

7 Epilogue

Invariants are constraints on the carrier of coalgebras which restrict their behavior in some desirable way but whose maintenance entails some kind of proof obligation discharge. An approach is put forward in this paper for reasoning about coalgebraic invariants which is both *compositional* and *calculational*: compositional because it is based on rules which break the complexity of such proof obligations across the structures involved; calculational because such rules are derived thanks to an algebra of invariants regarded as coreflexive bisimulations, which is what invariants are once encoded in the language of binary relations. Such calculational capabilities arise, in turn, from encoding bisimulations as instances of Reynolds *relation on functions*. In this process, functors which capture coalgebras' dynamics are generalized to relators and the objects of the underlying category are generalized to predicates.

The main contribution of the paper is the explicit adoption of such a constructive, calculational style in approaching the problem. Both [21,6] already suggest a relational/relator-based approach to bisimulation, [6] actually generalizing from coalgebras to dialgebras. However, no relationship is established with the algebra of Reynolds *relation on functions* which, in close association with Reynolds abstraction theorem, naturally leads to a category (Pred) whose objects are predicates (invariants).

In a wider context, the explicit adoption of such a category has potential to support a constructive discipline of extended static checking (ESC) in a coalgebraic view of computer systems, but surely there is much work to be done before this becomes of practical use. On the theory side, the authors would like to investigate a possible connection between the "predicates as objects" approach and *Frege structures* [10] [12]. Quoting this reference:

> *A Frege structure is a lambda structure $\mathcal{F}$ on the set A together with a designated subset of A whose elements are called propositions (...) the propositional connectives are required to yield propositions as values only when they operate on propositions as arguments.*

This is regarded as an interesting topic for future research.

---

[12] We thank Peter Dybjer for pointing out this possibility.

References

1. Aczel, P., Mendler, N.: A final coalgebra theorem. In: Category Theory and Computer Science, London, UK, pp. 357–365. Springer, Heidelberg (1989)
2. Backhouse, K., Backhouse, R.C.: Safety of abstract interpretations for free, via logical relations and Galois connections. SCP 15(1–2), 153–196 (2004)
3. Backhouse, R.: Galois connections and fixed point calculus. In: Crole, R., Backhouse, R., Gibbons, J. (eds.) Algebraic and Coalgebraic Methods in the Mathematics of Program Construction. LNCS, vol. 2297, pp. 89–148. Springer, Heidelberg (2002)
4. Backhouse, R., Michaelis, D.: Exercises in quantifier manipulation. In: Uustalu, T. (ed.) MPC 2006. LNCS, vol. 4014, pp. 70–81. Springer, Heidelberg (2006)
5. Backhouse, R.C., de Bruin, P., Hoogendijk, P., Malcolm, G., Voermans, T.S., van der Woude, J.: Polynomial relators. In: AMAST 1991, pp. 303–362. Springer, Heidelberg (1992)
6. Backhouse, R.C., Hoogendijk, P.F.: Final dialgebras: From categories to allegories. Informatique Theorique et Applications 33(4/5), 401–426 (1999)
7. Bird, R., de Moor, O.: Algebra of Programming. Hoare, C.A.R.(series ed.). Series in Computer Science. Prentice-Hall International, Englewood Cliffs (1997), http://www.phptr.com/ptrbooks/ptr_013507245x.html
8. Carboni, A., Kelly, G., Wood, R.: A 2-categorical approach to change of base and geometric morphisms I. Technical Report 90-1, Dept. of Pure Maths, Univ. Sydney (1990)
9. Freyd, P.J., Ščedrov, A.: Categories, Allegories. Mathematical Library, vol. 39. North-Holland, Amsterdam (1990)
10. Hatcher, W.S.: Review: Peter Aczel. Frege structures and the notions of proposition, truth and set. The Journal of Symbolic Logic 51(1), 244–246 (1986)
11. Jacobs, B.: Introduction to Coalgebra. Towards Mathematics of States and Observations. Draft Copy. Institute for Computing and Information Sciences, Radboud University Nijmegen, P.O. Box 9010, 6500 GL Nijmegen, The Netherlands
12. Jones, C.B.: Systematic Software Development Using VDM. Prentice-Hall Int., Englewood Cliffs (1986)
13. Kock, A.: Strong functors and monoidal monads. Archiv für Mathematik 23, 113–120 (1972)
14. Oliveira, J.N.: Invariants as coreflexive bisimulations — in a coalgebraic setting, Presentation at the IFIP WG 2.1 #62 Meeting Namur (December 2006)
15. Oliveira, J.N.: Pointfree foundations for (generic) lossless decomposition (submitted, 2007)
16. Oliveira, J.N.: Theory and applications of the PF-transform, Tutorial at LerNET 2008, Piriàpolis, Uruguay (slides available from the author's website) (February 2008)
17. Oliveira, J.N., Rodrigues, C.J.: Pointfree factorization of operation refinement. In: Misra, J., Nipkow, T., Sekerinski, E. (eds.) FM 2006. LNCS, vol. 4085, pp. 236–251. Springer, Heidelberg (2006)
18. Park, D.: Concurrency and automata on infinite sequences. LNCS, vol. 104, pp. 561–572. Springer, Heidelberg (1981)
19. Pratt, V.: Origins of the calculus of binary relations. In: Proc. of the 7th Annual IEEE Symp. on Logic in Computer Science, Santa Cruz, CA, pp. 248–254. IEEE Computer Society Press, Los Alamitos (1992)
20. Reynolds, J.C.: Types, abstraction and parametric polymorphism. Information Processing 83, 513–523 (1983)
21. Rutten, J.J.M.M.: Relators and metric bisimulations. ENTCS 11, 1–7 (1998)
22. Rutten, J.J.M.M.: Coalgebraic foundations of linear systems. In: Mossakowski, T., Montanari, U., Haveraaen, M. (eds.) CALCO 2007. LNCS, vol. 4624, pp. 425–446. Springer, Heidelberg (2007)

23. Tarski, A., Givant, S.: A Formalization of Set Theory without Variables. American Mathematical Society, vol. 41. AMS Colloquium Publications, Providence (1987)
24. Vaccari, M.: Calculational derivation of circuits. PhD thesis, Univ. S. Milano (1998)
25. Wadler, P.L.: Theorems for free! In: 4th Int. Symp. on FPLCA, London, September 1989. ACM Press, New York (1989)

Types and Deadlock Freedom in a Calculus of Services, Sessions and Pipelines[*]

Roberto Bruni[1] and Leonardo Gaetano Mezzina[2]

[1] Computer Science Department, University of Pisa, Italy
bruni@di.unipi.it
[2] IMT Lucca, Institute for Advanced Studies, Italy
leonardo.mezzina@imtlucca.it

Abstract. The notion of a session is fundamental in service-oriented applications, as it serves to separate interactions between clients and different instances of the same service, and to group together logical units of work. Recently, the Service Centered Calculus (SCC) has been proposed as a process calculus designed around the concept of a dyadic session between a service side and an invoker side, where interaction protocols and service orchestration can be conveniently expressed. In this paper we propose a generic type system to collect services' behaviours and then we fix a class of well-typed processes that are guaranteed to be deadlock free, in the sense that they either diverge by invoking new service instances or reach a normal form. The type system is based on previous research on traditional mobile calculi, here conveniently extended and simplified thanks to the neat discipline imposed by the linguistic primitives of SCC.

1 Introduction

The success of service orientation is attracting the interest of both industry and academy. On the one hand, important standardisation bodies and industrial consortia are developing the WS-* stack, targeting the engineering of web services technologies from a pragmatic perspective. The related documentation is often centred around common programming patterns: it is more focused on technical details of some case-studies, than on the overall methodology, leaving many ambiguities open. On the other hand, several efforts are posed on mathematical foundations, by developing formal languages and models tailored to service-oriented architectures. The main aim is to provide current standards with unambiguous semantics, but hopefully, tackling the scenarios from a more abstract perspective, the formalisation can lay the basis for sound service orchestration methodologies. Within this research thread, many process calculi have emerged ([6,5,17,4,2,16], to cite a few), that are enhanced with service-specific primitives.

The aim of this paper is to study a type system for one of the above proposals, called Service Centered Calculus (SCC) [2]. More precisely, we study a calculus derived from SCC and from its refined variant CaSPiS [3] in which service invocation encompasses

---

[*] Research supported by the EU within the FET-GC II Integrated Project IST-2005-016004 SEN-SORIA and by the Italian FIRB Project TOCAI.IT.

J. Meseguer and G. Roşu (Eds.): AMAST 2008, LNCS 5140, pp. 100–115, 2008.

one-way and *request-response* protocols available in current WS-technology and allows for more sophisticated message exchanges, according to the protocol exposed by the service. The key feature is considering the messages exchanged between caller and callee as correlated, enclosed in special units of work, called *sessions*, and isolated from messages belonging to different invocations to the same service. Differently from other session languages inspired by pi-calculus [11,12,19,9], object-orientation [8,7] and correlation sets [17], here the programmers should not bother with the manipulation of sessions: they are created automatically, in a transparent manner, upon service invocation. In particular, in SCC the communication media for exchanging messages is always implicit and determined by the context surrounding active abstractions and concretions. For this reason, we allow service name mobility, but not session name mobility.

The automatic teller machine example in [12] can serve well to illustrate our approach to the typing of SCC. The ATM offers three options to choose from: deposit, withdraw and balance. Once the user chooses one option the ATM establishes a new direct connection with the bank to account for the operation. Afterwards, the result is returned by the ATM to the user who can choose another option. At the type system level, even if the connection with the bank is reiterated each time the user chooses an option, it is only necessary to check a single instance to guarantee safety of the communication, because each interaction belongs to a distinct session. For SCC we show that, by constraining the communication activities, well-typedness not only guarantees safety but a much stronger property such as deadlock freedom.

Since sessions can be nested but cannot be addressed explicitly in communication primitives, the language is endowed with children-to-parent communications and with in-session communications. These two communication patterns not only are expressive enough to encode lazy λ-calculus [2] but also makes it possible that typing a single instance of a session suffices to guarantee deadlock freedom of recursive processes such as the factorial service (see Example 2). Another feature of SCC is the presence of a pipe construct, inspired by Orc [6], an elegant language for structured orchestration. Pipelines offer a basic mechanism for composing processes: it is more general and better suited w.r.t. concurrency than sequential composition and it does not require the improper use of channels for a task that pertains to orchestration. As far as we know, our type system is the first one to address the direct typing of such a pipe primitive.

The resulting language is somehow too permissive to be dealt with using session types [11,19,12] directly, as they would require, e.g., each input in a session to be matched by only an output. This condition is violated (and consequently subject reduction does not hold) if, for example, in the presence of an input we introduce parallel outputs of different types. Our type system extends ordinary session types to work correctly with our language. Differently from [13], this permits each variable to be statically assigned a basic type or a service type (in the case of service name mobility).

The type system characterises a subclass of SCC processes typical of the service-oriented scenarios (e.g., service declarations are top level and replicated) for which we show the main theorem of this paper: we prove that these processes are deadlock free in the sense that they either diverge by invoking service instances and opening new sessions or reach a normal form in which only service declarations remain; that is, every client terminates its computation unless someone diverges, but the entire system cannot block on pending communications. The proof technique makes an extensive use of types to limit the number of possible cases, resulting less error prone.

A similar type system exists for SSCC (a variant of SCC based on named streams instead of pipelines) [16] that guarantees session safety. Streams introduce some sort of global buffers for extra-session communication and permit only a single type of values for each stream. Likewise, the type system described in [1] resembles ours but it deals asymmetrically with services and clients, by guaranteeing only client progress. Concerning deadlock freedom we use definitions in [14,15] as main references for our definition, which is slightly different because tailored to the service-oriented scenario.

Synopsis. Section 2 introduces our SCC-like calculus. Section 3 presents the type system and the subject reduction result. Section 4 defines the class of initial processes and proves the main theorem: every well-typed initial process is deadlock free. Section 5 summarises the results and points out directions for further work. Due to space limitation proofs are just sketched or omitted.

2   Session Centered Calculus

2.1   SCC Overview: Room Reservation Example

Consider the following reservation service *reserve* for hotel rooms:

$$R \ = \ reserve.\big(\ \text{(double)}.(x,y).\langle code(x,y)\rangle \ + \ \text{(single)}.(x).\langle code(x,"")\rangle \ \big)$$

reserve offers two kinds of rooms, double or single, depending on the client choice. If the client after an invocation $\overline{reserve}$ sends the label double to the service then the service waits for a pair of names x and y (both of type *str*), and after receiving them, generate a numeric reservation code (type *int*) derived from x and y that is sent back to the client. Here code : $str \times str \rightarrow int$ is a function only available on service side.

$$C \ = \ \overline{reserve}.\text{if}(test) \ \text{then} \ \langle single\rangle.\langle"Bob"\rangle.(x).\text{return } x$$
$$\text{else} \ \langle double\rangle.\langle"Bob","Leo"\rangle.(y).\text{return } y$$

The above client, after invoking $\overline{reserve}$ and depending on some condition *test*, chooses between the two available options. The situation of the freshly established session r after the client's choice of double is the following:

$$(\nu\ r) \ \Big(\ r^- \triangleright \langle"Bob","Leo"\rangle.(y).\text{return } y \ \mid \ r^+ \triangleright (x,y).\langle code(x,y)\rangle \ \mid \ R \ \Big)$$

where the client protocol is running on the left (the session side r^- with negative polarity) and the service protocol on the right (the session side r^+ with positive polarity). Abstractions (e.g., (x,y)) and concretions (e.g., $\langle"Bob","Leo"\rangle$) running on opposite sides (r^+ and r^-) of the same session (bound name r) can exchange data, leading to

$$(\nu\ r) \ \Big(\ r^- \triangleright (y).\text{return } y \ \mid \ r^+ \triangleright \langle code("Bob","Leo")\rangle \ \mid \ R \ \Big)$$

Say code("Bob", "Leo") evaluates to 556047. Then, after another interaction, the client side ($r^- \triangleright$ return 556047) can return the result outside of r (to the parent session,

$$
\begin{array}{lll}
P, Q, R ::= \mathbf{0} & \text{(nil)} \\
\quad | \quad s.P & \text{(service definition)} \\
\quad | \quad \bar{v}.P & \text{(invocation)} \\
\quad | \quad \text{if } v = v_1 \text{ then } P \text{ else } Q & \text{(if-then-else)} \\
\quad | \quad (\tilde{x}).P & \text{(tuple input)} \\
\quad | \quad \langle \tilde{v} \rangle.P & \text{(values output)} \\
\quad | \quad \Sigma_{i=1}^{n}(l_i).P_i & \text{(label-guarded sum)} \\
\quad | \quad \langle l \rangle.P & \text{(label choice)} \\
\quad | \quad \text{return } \tilde{v}.P & \text{(return)} \\
\quad | \quad (vm)P & \text{(restriction)} \\
\quad | \quad r^p \rhd P & \text{(session)} \\
\quad | \quad P > \tilde{x} > Q & \text{(pipe)} \\
\quad | \quad P|Q & \text{(parallel)}
\end{array}
$$

$$
\begin{array}{lll}
v ::= \mathsf{f}(\tilde{v}) & \text{(function call)} \\
\quad | \quad x & \text{(variable)} \\
\quad | \quad m & \text{(service/session)} \\
\quad | \quad b & \text{(basic data value)} \\
\\
p, q ::= + \,|\, - & \text{(polarities)}
\end{array}
$$

Fig. 1. Syntax of our service calculus

if any). For example $\overline{reserve}.\langle\mathsf{single}\rangle.\langle"\mathrm{Bob}"\rangle.(x).\mathtt{return}\ x > y > Q$ invokes *reserve* and delivers the result in y to Q. As many instances of Q are spawn as the number of values that are issued. Since the execution of an invocation prefix opens a nested session, the conjunct use of return and pipe is the easiest way to continue the computation within the pre-existing session.

2.2 Syntax

The set of processes is defined by the grammar in Fig. 1. We let P, Q, R range over processes, s over service names, r over session names, m over both session and service names, l over labels, x over variables (for service names and data), and v over values, which include an elsewhere specified set of basic data and expressions (possibly with names, variables and functions). Tuples are denoted by $\tilde{\cdot}$. Operators are listed in Fig. 1 in decreasing order of precedence, e.g., $r^- \rhd P > \tilde{x} > Q|R$ reads $((r^- \rhd P) > \tilde{x} > Q)|R$.

As usual, $\mathbf{0}$ is the nil process, the trailing of $\mathbf{0}$ is often omitted, parallel composition is denoted by $P|Q$ and restriction by $(vm)P$. The construct $r^p \rhd P$ indicates a generic session side with polarity p (taking values in $\{+, -\}$). Sessions are mostly intended as run-time syntax. In fact, differently from other languages that provide primitives for explicit session naming and creation, here all sessions could be built automatically, resulting in a more elegant and disciplined style of writing processes. A fresh session name r and two polarised session ends $r^- \rhd P$ and $r^+ \rhd Q$ are generated (on client and service sides, respectively) upon each service invocation $\bar{s}.P$ of the service $s.Q$. We say $r^- \rhd P$ is the dual session side of $r^+ \rhd Q$ and vice versa. As P and Q share a session, their I/O communications are directed toward the dual session side. We let p, q range over polarities and $\bar{p}, \bar{q}$ are the opposite polarities of p and q, where $\overline{+} = -$ and $\overline{-} = +$.

Labels l allow for expressing a choice on one side among a set of available options at the other side. The primitive `return` is used to output values to the parent session and the pipe $P > \tilde{x} > Q$ is a construct for on-side communications, i.e., for propagating

$$P|0 \equiv P \qquad P|Q \equiv Q|P \qquad (P|Q)|R \equiv P|(Q|R)$$
$$(vm_1)(vm)P \equiv (vm)(vm_1)P \qquad ((vm)P)|Q \equiv (vm)(P|Q) \text{ if } m \notin \text{fn}(Q)$$
$$((vm)P) > \tilde{x} > Q \equiv (vm)(P > \tilde{x} > Q) \text{ if } m \notin \text{fn}(Q) \qquad r^p \triangleright (vm)P \equiv (vm)(r^p \triangleright P) \text{ if } r \neq m$$
$$0 > \tilde{x} > P \equiv 0 \qquad (P|Q) > \tilde{x} > R \equiv (P > \tilde{x} > R)|(Q > \tilde{x} > R)$$
$$(r^p \triangleright 0) > \tilde{x} > R \equiv r^p \triangleright 0 \qquad r_1^p \triangleright (Q|r_2^q \triangleright 0) \equiv r_1^p \triangleright Q|r_2^q \triangleright 0 \qquad (vr)(r^+ \triangleright 0|r^- \triangleright 0) \equiv 0$$

Fig. 2. Structural congruence

values in the same side of a session. Pipe is inspired by Orc [6] to activate a fresh instance of Q on any value produced by P.

Processes are taken up to α-equivalence considering $(\tilde{x}).Q$ and $P > \tilde{x} > Q$ as binders for variables $\tilde{x}$ in Q and $(vm)P$ as the binder for m in P. The set $\text{fn}(P)$ of free names of P is defined as expected. It is worth noting that the standard capture avoiding substitution $P[^{\tilde{v}}/_{\tilde{x}}]$, which replaces a tuple of variables with a tuple of values, assumes that variables cannot appear in certain positions (i.e., $x \triangleright P$ and $x.P$ are forbidden by the syntax).

Each service definition is persistent (i.e., not consumed after an invocation) and available at top level (see Definition 4). For this reason, in the type system we shall give in Section 3, their protocols are not supposed to return any value to the parent.

2.3   Operational Semantics

We describe the semantics of our language by means of an LTS that exploits the structural congruence $\equiv$, which is the least one defined by the equations in Fig. 2. They include ordinary axioms about parallel and restriction, together with distributivity of parallel over pipes, and a few axioms for garbage collecting terminated session ends $r^p \triangleright 0$. We say that Q is at the *top level* in P if $P \equiv (v\tilde{m})Q|R$ for some $\tilde{m}$ and R.

Our transition system exploits the labels λ in Fig. 3. We write $\leftrightarrow$ to mean either $\leftarrow$ or $\rightarrow$. We write $(\tilde{m})\lambda$ to mean the label λ where the names $\tilde{m}$ become bound. The notions of bound names $\text{bn}(\lambda)$, free names $\text{fn}(\lambda)$ and names $\text{n}(\lambda)$ of a label λ are defined as expected. We remark that α-conversion is not applicable to labels.

The semantics is given in the early style, which guesses the values and labels in the rules (IN) and (BRANCH), respectively. Rule (DEF) shows the replicated nature of the service and together with (INV) creates two processes which are ready to communicate after that (SCOM) creates a new shared common session. (SESSIONOUT) accounts for the return of a value, which is converted in an output out of the current session when the session construct is traversed. (SESSION) marks with the name of the exchanging session each operation in that session. (COMM) permits both communication of basic values and service names. Extrusion is handled by (OPEN) and (PAR), but thanks to (EQUIV) restricted names can be moved to the top before communication and a closure rule is not necessary. On the other hand, side condition of rule (PAR) is useful for session floating since r is bound in labels for the service invocation. Rule (PIPE) creates a new concurrent copy of process Q together with the residual $P' > \tilde{x} > Q$ in the case that P outputs a value. Rule (PIPEPASS) makes a move in P if the action is not an output.

We shall write $P \xrightarrow{\lambda}$ if there is a Q such that $P \xrightarrow{\lambda} Q$.

$$
\begin{aligned}
\lambda ::= \quad & s \Rightarrow r \mid \quad s \Leftarrow r & \text{(service invocation / definition)} \\
& \mid \quad \rightarrow \tilde{v} \mid \quad \leftarrow \tilde{v} & \text{(value production / consumption)} \\
& \mid \quad r^p :\rightarrow \tilde{v} \mid r^p :\leftarrow \tilde{v} & \text{(value production / consumption within } r) \\
& \mid \quad \rightarrow l \mid \quad \leftarrow l & \text{(choice selection / branching)} \\
& \mid \quad r^p :\rightarrow l \mid r^p :\leftarrow l & \text{(choice selection / branching within } r) \\
& \mid \quad \tau \mid \quad r\tau & \text{(silent steps)} \\
& \mid \quad \uparrow \tilde{v} \mid \quad (m)\lambda & \text{(value return / extrusion)}
\end{aligned}
$$

Fig. 3. Labels of the transition system

(IN)
$$(\tilde{x}).P \xrightarrow{\leftarrow \tilde{v}} P[^{\tilde{v}}/_{\tilde{x}}]$$

(OUT)
$$\langle \tilde{v} \rangle.P \xrightarrow{\rightarrow \tilde{v}} P$$

(SESSION)
$$\frac{P \xrightarrow{\lambda} P' \quad \lambda \in \{\leftrightarrow \tilde{v}, \leftrightarrow l,\}}{r^p \triangleright P \xrightarrow{r^p:\lambda} r^p \triangleright P'}$$

(COMM)
$$\frac{P \xrightarrow{r^p:\leftarrow \tilde{v}} P' \quad Q \xrightarrow{r:\overline{p}:\rightarrow \tilde{v}} Q'}{P|Q \xrightarrow{r\tau} (P'|Q')}$$

(BRANCH)
$$\Sigma_{i=0}^{n}(l_i).P_i \xrightarrow{\leftarrow l_i} P_i$$

(CHOICE)
$$\langle l \rangle.P \xrightarrow{\rightarrow l} P$$

(SELECT)
$$\frac{P \xrightarrow{r^p:\rightarrow l} P' \quad Q \xrightarrow{\overline{p}:\leftarrow l} Q'}{P|Q \xrightarrow{r\tau} (P'|Q')}$$

(DEF)
$$\frac{r \notin \mathsf{fn}(s.P)}{s.P \xrightarrow{(r)s \Leftarrow r} r^+ \triangleright P|s.P}$$

(INV)
$$\frac{r \notin \mathsf{fn}(\overline{s}.P)}{\overline{s}.P \xrightarrow{(r)s \Rightarrow r} r^- \triangleright P}$$

(SCOM)
$$\frac{P \xrightarrow{(r)s \Rightarrow r} P' \quad Q \xrightarrow{(r)s \Leftarrow r} Q'}{(P|Q) \xrightarrow{\tau} (vr)(P'|Q')}$$

(RET)
$$\mathtt{return}\ \tilde{v}.P \xrightarrow{\uparrow \tilde{v}} P$$

(SESSIONOUT)
$$\frac{P \xrightarrow{\uparrow \tilde{v}} P'}{r^p \triangleright P \xrightarrow{\rightarrow \tilde{v}} r^p \triangleright P'}$$

(NESTINV)
$$\frac{P \xrightarrow{(r')s \Rightarrow r'} P' \quad r \neq r'}{r^p \triangleright P \xrightarrow{(r')s \Rightarrow r'} r^p \triangleright P'}$$

(RES)
$$\frac{P \xrightarrow{\lambda} P' \quad s \notin \mathsf{n}(\lambda)}{(vs)P \xrightarrow{\lambda} (vs)P'}$$

(OPEN)
$$\frac{P \xrightarrow{\lambda} P' \quad \lambda \in \{\rightarrow \tilde{v}, r^p :\rightarrow \tilde{v}\} \wedge s \in \mathsf{n}(\tilde{v})}{(vs)P \xrightarrow{(s)\lambda} P'}$$

(SESSRES)
$$\frac{P \xrightarrow{r\tau} P'}{(vr)P \xrightarrow{\tau} (vr)P'}$$

(PIPE)
$$\frac{P \xrightarrow{\rightarrow \tilde{v}} P'}{P > \tilde{x} > Q \xrightarrow{\tau} Q[^{\tilde{v}}/_{\tilde{x}}]|(P' > \tilde{x} > Q)}$$

(PIPEPASS)
$$\frac{P \xrightarrow{\lambda} P' \quad \lambda \neq \rightarrow \tilde{v}}{P > \tilde{x} > Q \xrightarrow{\lambda} P' > \tilde{x} > Q}$$

(IFL)
$$\frac{P \xrightarrow{\lambda} P'}{\mathtt{if}\ v = v\ \mathtt{then}\ P\ \mathtt{else}\ Q \xrightarrow{\lambda} P'}$$

(IFR)
$$\frac{v_1 \neq v \quad Q \xrightarrow{\lambda} Q'}{\mathtt{if}\ v = v_1\ \mathtt{then}\ P\ \mathtt{else}\ Q \xrightarrow{\lambda} Q'}$$

(PAR)
$$\frac{P \xrightarrow{\lambda} P' \quad \mathsf{bn}(\lambda) \cap \mathsf{fn}(Q) = \emptyset}{P|Q \xrightarrow{\lambda} P'|Q}$$

(EQUIV)
$$\frac{P \equiv Q \quad Q \xrightarrow{\lambda} Q' \quad Q' \equiv P'}{P \xrightarrow{\lambda} P'}$$

Fig. 4. Operational semantics

3 Typing

The set of session types, $U, T, \ldots$, is defined by the grammar in Fig. 5. Session types express sequences of typed tuples of input and output. Internal choice $\oplus$ records all the choices at a certain point of a session, requested in the branches of a conditional process. External choice & records the types of all offered options.

Sorts S can be either $[T]$ which represents a session with session type T or an elements of a given set of basic data types $\mathcal{B}$. By convention we denote $\tau_b \in \mathcal{B}$ the type of the basic value b. We shall assume that $int, str \in \mathcal{B}$.

Our set of typing rules is in Fig. 6. Type judgements for values take the form $\Gamma \vdash v : S$ where S is the sort of v. Type judgements for processes take the form $\Gamma \vdash P : U[T]$, where the type U represents the outputs of P to the parent session, while T is the type of admissible interactions for the current session. We shall refer to such types as *usages*. Sometimes we write $[T]$ as a shorthand for $\mathbf{end}[T]$. The *type environment* Γ is a finite partial mapping from variables and services to sorts and function types. The empty environment is annotated $\emptyset$. When $x \notin dom(\Gamma)$ we write $\Gamma, x : S$ for the environment obtained by extending Γ with the binding of x to S (the same holds for $m \notin dom(\Gamma)$).

The first four rules for values are standard and the signature of each used external function must be inserted in the environment as a functional type (rule (FuncV)) because they are not bound by processes.

The type of $\mathbf{0}$ in (Tzero) is $\mathbf{end}[\mathbf{end}]$ since no action is performed neither in the current session nor towards the parent session. Rule (Tdef) constrains the protocol of the service to be the same as that of the body process P and rule (Tinv) checks that the invoked service behaves in the dual manner with respect to the client. Here the dual of T, written $\overline{T}$ is inductively defined as:

$$\overline{\mathbf{end}} = \mathbf{end} \qquad \frac{\overline{?(\tilde{S}).T} = !(\tilde{S}).\overline{T}}{\overline{!(\tilde{S}).T'} = ?(\tilde{S}).\overline{T'}} \qquad \frac{\overline{\&\{l_1 : T_1, \ldots, l_n : T_n\}} = \oplus\{l_1 : \overline{T_1}, \ldots, l_n : \overline{T_n}\}}{\overline{\oplus\{l_1 : T_1, \ldots, l_n : T_n\}} = \&\{l_1 : \overline{T_1}, \ldots, l_n : \overline{T_n}\}}$$

It can be readily observed that duality exchanges the role of ! with ? and of & with $\oplus$.

Rules (Tin), (Tout) and (Tret) insert the usage type in the correct place. The type for the input variable $\tilde{x}$ in rule (Tin) is not declared in the syntax, but it can be inferred with the help of the algorithm described in [18]. Rule (Tbranch) allows for considering a subset of possible branches; this subset can be chosen in a minimal way by letting it include the branches used by the dual sessions in the rule (Tchoice). In fact, the $\mathtt{if}$ construct allows to choose between many branches at the same time and also different clients can invoke the same service making their own choices, and rule (Tif) force all of them to agree on the least common set of choices that must be available at the other side.

$$
\begin{aligned}
T, U ::= \ &\mathbf{end} && \text{(no action)} \\
| \ &?(S_1, \ldots, S_n).T && \text{(input of a tuple)} \\
| \ &!(S_1, \ldots, S_n).T && \text{(output of a tuple)} \\
| \ &\&\{l_1 : T_1, \ldots, l_n : T_n\} && \text{(external choice)} \\
| \ &\oplus\{l_1 : T_1, \ldots, l_n : T_n\} && \text{(internal choice)}
\end{aligned}
$$

$$
\begin{aligned}
S ::= \ &[T] && \text{(session)} \\
| \ &\mathcal{B} && \text{(basic data types)}
\end{aligned}
$$

Fig. 5. Syntax of types

(SERVICE)   (VAR)   (BASV)   (FUNC)
$\Gamma, s : S \vdash s : S$ $\Gamma, x : S \vdash x : S$ $\dfrac{\tau_b \in \mathcal{B}}{\Gamma \vdash b : \tau_b}$ $\dfrac{\Gamma \vdash v_1 : S_1 \dots \Gamma \vdash v_n : S_n \quad \tau_b \in \mathcal{B}}{\Gamma, f : S_1 \times \dots \times S_n \to \tau_b \vdash f(v_1, \dots, v_n) : \tau_b}$

(TZERO)   (TDEF)   (TINV)
$\dfrac{}{\Gamma \vdash 0 : end[end]}$ $\dfrac{\Gamma \vdash P : end[T] \quad \Gamma \vdash s : [T]}{\Gamma \vdash s.P : end[end]}$ $\dfrac{\Gamma \vdash P : U[T] \quad \Gamma \vdash v : [\overline{T}]}{\Gamma \vdash \bar{v}.P : end[U]}$

(TIN)   (TOUT)   (TRET)
$\dfrac{\Gamma, \tilde{x} : \tilde{S} \vdash P : U[T]}{\Gamma \vdash (\tilde{x}).P : U[?(\tilde{S}).T]}$ $\dfrac{\Gamma \vdash P : U[T] \quad \Gamma \vdash \tilde{v} : \tilde{S}}{\Gamma \vdash \langle \tilde{v} \rangle.P : U[!(\tilde{S}).T]}$ $\dfrac{\Gamma \vdash P : U[T] \quad \Gamma \vdash \tilde{v} : \tilde{S}}{\Gamma \vdash return \; \tilde{v}.P : !(\tilde{S}).U[T]}$

(TBRANCH)   (TPARL)
$\dfrac{I \subseteq \{1, \dots, n\} \quad \forall i \in I \quad \Gamma \vdash P_i : U[T_i]}{\Gamma \vdash \Sigma_{i=0}^{n}(l_i).P_i : U[\&\{l_i : T_i\}]_{i \in I}}$ $\dfrac{\Gamma \vdash P : U[T] \quad \Gamma \vdash Q : U'[end] \quad U'' = U \circ U'}{\Gamma \vdash P|Q : U''[T]}$

(TCHOICE)   (TPARR)
$\dfrac{l = l_i \in \{l_1, \dots, l_n\} \quad \Gamma \vdash P : U[T_i]}{\Gamma \vdash \langle l \rangle.P : U[\oplus\{l_1 : T_1, \dots, l_n : T_n\}]}$ $\dfrac{\Gamma \vdash P : U[end] \quad \Gamma \vdash Q : U'[T] \quad U'' = U \circ U'}{\Gamma \vdash P|Q : U''[T]}$

(TPIPE)
$\dfrac{\Gamma \vdash P : U[T] \quad \Gamma, \tilde{x} : \tilde{S} \vdash Q : U'[T'] \quad pipe(U[T], U'[T'], \tilde{S}) = U''[T'']}{\Gamma \vdash P > \tilde{x} > Q : U''[T'']}$

(TSES)   (TSESI)
$\dfrac{\Gamma \vdash P : U[T]}{\Gamma, r : [T] \vdash r^+ \triangleright P : end[U]}$ $\dfrac{\Gamma \vdash P : U[T]}{\Gamma, r : [\overline{T}] \vdash r^- \triangleright P : end[U]}$

(TNEW)   (TIF)
$\dfrac{\Gamma, m : S \vdash P : U[T] \quad exists(m, P)}{\Gamma \vdash (vm)P : U[T]}$ $\dfrac{\Gamma \vdash v_i : S_i \quad i = 1, 2 \quad \Gamma \vdash P : U[T] \quad \Gamma \vdash Q : U[T]}{\Gamma \vdash if \; v_1 = v_2 \; then \; P \; else \; Q : U[T]}$

Fig. 6. Typing rules

The two rules for parallel composition (TPARL) and (TPARR) allow parallel composition of two processes only if at least one does not have any action in the current session, i.e. if it has type $U[end]$. Note instead that both P and Q are allowed to produce values upwards, in which case the operation $U \circ U'$ is defined only if all the atomic parts in U and U' are of the same kind, say $!(\tilde{S})$, and in that case $U \circ U' = U.U' = U' \circ U$. This operation is sound because tail outputs of parallel values of the same type are not observable at the type system level. Rule (TPIPE) uses the function defined as

$$
\begin{aligned}
&pipe(U[end], U'[T'], \tilde{S}) &&= U[end] &&\text{(no pipe activation)}\\
&pipe(U[!(\tilde{S})], U'[T], \tilde{S}) &&= U \circ U'[T] &&\text{(pipe activated once)}\\
&pipe(U[!(\tilde{S})^k], U'[end], \tilde{S}) = U \circ U'^k[end] &&\quad k > 1 &&\text{(multiple pipe activation)}
\end{aligned}
$$

where U'^k is a sequence of $k > 1$ output usages of the same type. If no value is passed to the pipe, then it is inessential. If it can be activated once, then its instance will act as a continuation for the current session. If multiple activations are considered, which will run in parallel, then each instance usage in the session must be end. Intuitively pipe constrains $P > \tilde{x} > Q$ in the current session to allow a single output P whenever the type of Q is different from a single input or vice versa Q to be a single input whenever the type of P is $!(\tilde{S})^k$ *a sequence of k-times* $!(\tilde{S})$. In this case the result is visible upward, repeating U' for k times. The first case of **pipe** is necessary to guarantee the subject reduction. (TSES) and (TSESI) are similar to service definition and invocation rules but r is removed from the environment to forbid the nesting of the same session name.

With respect to the two type systems presented in [19] ours is more similar to the one with balanced typing. In case the bound name m is a service, rule (TNEW) checks the existence of a corresponding service definition by means of exists(m, P). Function **exists** ensures that the process P declares the announced service (its inductive definition is as expected). Finally, rule (TIF) handles conditionals in the usual way.

Typing rules allow a deduction for processes like $r : !(int) \vdash r^+ \triangleright \langle 1 \rangle | r^+ \triangleright \langle 2 \rangle$ which do not preserve session linearity. We will exclude such processes by inroducing the notions of balanced and initial processes (see Definitions 1 and 4, and Theorem 1).

Example 1. Let us take the reservation example. The type $!(int)[!(str, str).?(int)]$ expresses the following client usage: the output of two strings is followed by the reading of the result and an integer is returned outside the session (the first output out of the square brackets indicates a return action, that is an output out of the current session). Previous usage is compared with the session usage $?(str, str).!(int)$ to ensure that the invocation is sound. Below we report the typing proof for the client, where we let $\Gamma = reserve :$ [&{double :?$(str, str).!(int)$, single :?$(str).!(int)$}], $P = \langle$"Bob"$\rangle.(x).$return x, $Q = \langle$"Bob","Leo"$\rangle.(x).$return x and $T = \oplus$\{double :!$(str, str).?(int)$, single :!$(str).?(int)$\}:

$$
\frac{
\dfrac{
\text{(TOUT)} \dfrac{\vdots}{\Gamma \vdash P : !(int)[!(str).?(int)]}
}{
\text{(TCHOICE)} \;\; \Gamma \vdash \langle single \rangle.P : !(int)[T]
}
\qquad
\dfrac{
\dfrac{\vdots}{\Gamma \vdash Q : !(int)[!(str, str).?(int)]} \text{(TOUT)}
}{
\Gamma \vdash \langle double \rangle.Q : !(int)[T] \;\; \text{(TCHOICE)}
}
}{
\Gamma \vdash \text{if } (test) \text{ then } \langle single \rangle.P \text{ else } \langle double \rangle.Q : !(int)[T]
} \text{(TIF)}
$$

Moreover, we could safely replace the service definition with

$$reserve.\Big((double).(x,y).\langle code(x,y)\rangle \; + \; (single).(x).\langle code(x,"")\rangle \; + \; (suite).R \Big)$$

(which extends the previous version of the service with additional behaviours) and still we correctly type check the client. In fact, our type system can statically exclude the new branch **suite** when the client is typed.

Example 2. Let us consider the factorial service $fatt$, defined by:

$$fatt.(n). \text{ if } (n=0) \text{ then } \langle 1 \rangle$$
$$\text{else } \overline{fatt}.\langle n-1 \rangle.(x).\text{return } x > x > \langle mul(x,n) \rangle$$

Notice that in this case we are able to express the factorial thanks to service persistence, which guarantees a separation between each invocation. The entire program is well-typed by type checking only a single session instance. As the Theorem 2 will show, this check suffices to ensure that $fatt$ is deadlock free. The typing proof is below, where we recall that end$[!(int)] = [!(int)]$ and let $P' = \langle n-1 \rangle.(x).$return x, $P = \overline{fatt}.P'$, $Q' = \langle mul(x,n) \rangle$, $Q = P > x > Q'$ and $\Gamma = fatt : [?(int).!(int)], n : int, mul : int \times int \rightarrow int$.

$$\frac{\begin{array}{c} \vdots \\ \Gamma \vdash P' : !(int)[!(int).?(int)] \\ \hline \Gamma \vdash P : [!(int)] \end{array} \qquad \begin{array}{c} \vdots \\ \Gamma, x : int \vdash Q' : [!(int)] \end{array}}{\dfrac{\dfrac{\begin{array}{c} \vdots \\ \emptyset \vdash \langle 1 \rangle : [!(int)] \end{array} \qquad \Gamma \vdash P > x > Q' : [!(int)]}{\Gamma \vdash \text{if } (n = 0) \text{ then } \langle 1 \rangle \text{ else } Q : \text{end}[!(int)]}}{\dfrac{fatt : [?(int).!(int)], \text{mul} : \ldots \vdash (n).\text{if } (n = 0) \text{ then } \langle 1 \rangle \text{ else } Q : \text{end}[?(int).!(int)]}{fatt : [?(int).!(int)], \text{mul} : \ldots \vdash fatt.(n).\text{if } (n = 0) \text{ then } \langle 1 \rangle \text{ else } Q : \text{end}[\text{end}]}}}$$

Example 3. Beyond basic types, expressions may take the name of a service as a parameter. Take a load balancing service that is called to discover, at each invocation, which service between a and b is more reliable for executing P.

$$(\nu \ a \ b) \left(loadbalance.\text{if choose}(a, b) = 1 \text{ then } \langle a \rangle \text{ else } \langle b \rangle \ | \ a.P \ | \ b.P \right)$$
$$| \ \overline{loadbalance}.(x).\text{return } x > x > \overline{x}.Q$$

Here the function choose is a basic expression of type $[T] \times [T] \rightarrow int$ and uses the names of the two services as parameters. The client after receiving the name of the reliable service can substitute it for x for all future invocations of the service. It is a nice exercise to verify that the ensemble of the above processes is well-typed under the assumption that P and Q have types $[T]$ and $[\overline{T}]$ respectively.

The type system enjoys subject congruence and subject reduction. In their proofs we need some auxiliary lemmas that are proved by straightforward induction on the derivation of typing judgements.

Lemma 1 (Weakening). *If $\Gamma \vdash P : U[T]$ and $m \notin \text{fn}(P)$ then $\Gamma, m : S \vdash P : U[T]$.*

Lemma 2 (Strengthening). *If $\Gamma, m : S \vdash P : U[T]$ and $m \notin \text{fn}(P)$ then $\Gamma \vdash P : U[T]$.*

Proposition 1 (Subject Congruence). *If $\Gamma \vdash P : U[T]$ and $P \equiv Q$ then $\Gamma \vdash Q : U[T]$*

The following substitution lemma is needed in the proof of subject reduction for dealing with rules (IN) and (PIPE).

Lemma 3 (Substitution). *Let $\Gamma, x : S \vdash P : U[T]$. If $\Gamma \vdash v : S$ then $\Gamma \vdash P[^v/_x] : U[T]$.*

Definition 1 (Balanced Process). *A process P is* balanced *if $\Gamma \vdash P : U[T]$ for some Γ, U, T and for each session name r in P, each of r^+ and r^- appears exactly once in P.*

Theorem 1 (Subject Reduction). *Let P be a balanced process and $\sqsubseteq$ be the smallest relation such that: $T \sqsubseteq ?(\tilde{S}).T$, $T \sqsubseteq !(\tilde{S}).T$, $T_i \sqsubseteq \&\{l_i : T_i\}_{i \in I}$ and $T_i \sqsubseteq \oplus\{l_i : T_i\}_{i \in I}$.*

1. *If $P \xrightarrow{\lambda} Q$ with $\lambda \in \{\tau, r\tau\}$, then Q is balanced (session linearity).*
2. *If $\Gamma \vdash P : U[T]$ and $P \xrightarrow{\tau} Q$ then $\Gamma \vdash Q : U[T]$.*
3. *If $\Gamma, r : [T] \vdash P : U[T'']$ and $P \xrightarrow{r\tau} Q$ then $\Gamma, r : [T'] \vdash Q : U[T'']$ where $T' \sqsubseteq T$.*

The proof is by induction on the derivation of the transition. Lemmas 1 and 2 serve to insert in /remove from Γ assumptions about session names. Session linearity guarantees that only "safe" programs are produced starting from balanced processes, i.e., that situation like $r^+ \triangleright \langle 1 \rangle | r^+ \triangleright \langle 1 \rangle$ (where r^+ appears twice) cannot arise at run-time.

4   Deadlock Freedom and Normal Form

Hereafter, we let $\omega, \gamma \ldots$ range over possibly empty sequences of labels τ, $r\tau$ and $r\iota$, where $r\iota$ will be introduced later by the rule (SCom'). We let $\overset{\omega}{\longrightarrow}^*$ represents the reflexive and transitive closure of $\overset{\tau}{\longrightarrow} \cup \overset{r\tau}{\longrightarrow} \cup \overset{r\iota}{\longrightarrow}$ (for all session names r). We say that a process is deadlock free if it cannot be blocked waiting a synchronisation unless it reaches the *normal form*. Normal form means that all the possible communications are exhausted and only service definitions remain.

Definition 2 (Normal form). *A process P is in normal form if there exist service names $s_1, \ldots, s_n$ and processes $Q_1, \ldots, Q_n$ such that $P \equiv (\nu s_1) \ldots (\nu s_n)(s_1.Q_1 | \ldots | s_n.Q_n)$.*

Definition 3 (Deadlock free). *A process P is deadlock free if for each Q s.t. $P \overset{\omega}{\longrightarrow}^* Q$ then either Q reaches a normal form or $Q \overset{\tau}{\longrightarrow}$.*

Since deadlock freedom is a strong property we need to focus on a specific set of processes, called initial processes.

Definition 4 (Initial process). *A process P is initial if it does not contain session constructs, all service definitions are at the top level and $\emptyset \vdash P :$ end[end].*

Note that initial processes are also balanced. Our main theorem shows that all initial processes are deadlock free (see Theorem 2). Proving deadlock freedom involves the possibility of exhibiting a τ reduction after an arbitrary number of evaluation steps. However, to characterise the next admissible reduction in a constructive way, we need to argue about some specific session. To observe the name of the session in which a synchronisation is taking place we need a mild modification to the rule (SCom) of the transition system. The basic idea is to remove the binders for session names, i.e., to consider P' instead of P, for $P \equiv (\nu \tilde{r})P'$ where P' has no binder on session names. The revised rule (SCom') does not restrict the fresh session with a binder and uses the already mentioned label $r\iota$ to identify the created session.

(SCom')
$$\frac{P \overset{(r)s \Rightarrow r}{\longrightarrow} P' \quad Q \overset{(r)s \Leftarrow r}{\longrightarrow} Q'}{(P|Q) \overset{r\iota}{\longrightarrow} (P'|Q')}$$

Another subtle aspect is that now session r is bound in the label $r\iota$, because it must be fresh w.r.t. all the other pre-existing session names: we omit parentheses in favour of a lighter syntax. On the other hand, the type environment Γ for closed processes can now contain assumptions about session names. The modification of the rule is sound since we are considering only processes that are reachable from initial processes. In fact, any initial process will produce for each new session a corresponding binder to restrict the session. For this reason the LTS with rule (SCom') has essentially the same behaviour of the previous LTS with rule (SCom) (just read both labels $r\iota$ and $r\tau$ as τ).

Lemma 4. *If P is initial and $P \overset{\omega}{\longrightarrow}^* Q$, then there exists a typing environment Γ for session names in ω such that $\Gamma \vdash Q :$ end[end].*

To reason inductively on the way sessions are nested we introduce some convenient notation for contexts $\mathbb{C}[\![\cdot]\!]$ and $\mathbb{C}_{r^p}[\![\cdot]\!]$, parent/children sessions relation $\prec_P$ and session ancestors relation $<_P$. The set of contexts is defined by the grammar:

$$\mathbb{C} ::= [\![\cdot]\!] \mid \mathbb{C}|P \mid r^p \blacktriangleright \mathbb{C} \mid (\nu s)\mathbb{C} \mid \mathbb{C} > \tilde{x} > P \qquad \mathbb{C}_{r^p} ::= r^p \blacktriangleright ([\![\cdot]\!]|P)$$

As usual $\mathbb{C}[\![P]\!]$ and $\mathbb{C}_{r^p}[\![P]\!]$ are the processes obtained by filling the holes with P.

Definition 5 (Session nesting relation). *Let* $r_1 \prec_P r_2$ *iff* $P \equiv \mathbb{C}[\![\mathbb{C}_{r_1^p}[\![r_2^q \blacktriangleright Q]\!]]\!]$ *for some contexts* $\mathbb{C}, \mathbb{C}_{r_1^p}$, *session* r_2^q, *and process* Q. *We let* $<_P$ *be the transitive closure of* $\prec_P$.

The relation $<_P$ for initial processes is also acyclic ($<_P$ is irreflexive), it is preserved by τ reductions and it holds that if $P \xrightarrow{\tau} Q$ then $<_Q = <_P \cup\{(x,r) \mid \exists r_1.r_1 \prec_P r \wedge x <_P r_1\}$.

The next proposition is a sort of progress property valid for the outermost (in terms of $\prec$-relation) active sessions. In fact, if one of such sessions has a pending action enabled then it is either guaranteed that after a finite number of steps a suitable synchronisation is accomplished or a service invocation can open a new nested session.

Proposition 2. *Let* P *be an initial process. If* $P \xrightarrow{\omega}{}^* Q$, *then for any session name* r *in* Q *if* $\nexists \mathbb{C}, \mathbb{C}_{r^p}, \nu'$ *and* R *such that* $Q \equiv \mathbb{C}[\![\mathbb{C}_{r^p}[\![\text{return } \tilde{\nu}'.R]\!]]\!]$ *all of the following hold:*

1. *if* $Q \xrightarrow{r^p:\leftarrow\tilde{\nu}}$ *then* $Q \xrightarrow{\gamma}{}^* \xrightarrow{r^{\bar{p}}:\to\tilde{\nu}} \vee Q \xrightarrow{\gamma}{}^* \xrightarrow{r_1\iota} Q_1$ *and* $r <_{Q_1} r_1$
2. *if* $Q \xrightarrow{r^p:\to\tilde{\nu}}$ *then* $Q \xrightarrow{\gamma}{}^* \xrightarrow{r^{\bar{p}}:\leftarrow\tilde{\nu}} \vee Q \xrightarrow{\gamma}{}^* \xrightarrow{r_1\iota} Q_1$ *and* $r <_{Q_1} r_1$
3. *if* $Q \xrightarrow{r^p:\leftarrow l}$ *then* $Q \xrightarrow{\gamma}{}^* \xrightarrow{r^{\bar{p}}:\to l} \vee Q \xrightarrow{\gamma}{}^* \xrightarrow{r_1\iota} Q_1$ *and* $r <_{Q_1} r_1$
4. *if* $Q \xrightarrow{r^p:\to l}$ *then* $Q \xrightarrow{\gamma}{}^* \xrightarrow{r^{\bar{p}}:\leftarrow l} \vee Q \xrightarrow{\gamma}{}^* \xrightarrow{r_1\iota} Q_1$ *and* $r <_{Q_1} r_1$
5. *if* $Q \equiv \mathbb{C}[\![\mathbb{C}_{r^p}[\![P' > \tilde{x} > Q']\!]]\!]$ *and* $\Gamma_1 \vdash P' : U[!(\tilde{S}).T]$ *then*
   $$\mathbb{C}[\![\mathbb{C}_{r^p}[\![P']\!]]\!] \xrightarrow{\gamma}{}^* \xrightarrow{r^p:\to\tilde{\nu}} \vee \mathbb{C}[\![\mathbb{C}_{r^p}[\![P']\!]]\!] \xrightarrow{\gamma}{}^* \xrightarrow{r_1\iota} Q_1 \text{ and } r <_{Q_1} r_1$$

Proof. Take any pair (r^p, Q) satisfying the premise. The proof is by induction on the well-founded order over pairs (r^p, Q) defined as the least transitive relation such that $(r_1^{p_1}, Q_1) < (r_2^{p_2}, Q_2)$ if one of the following holds:

- $llns(r_1, Q_1) < llns(r_2, Q_2)$,
- or $llns(r_1, Q_1) = llns(r_2, Q_2)$, $Q_1 \equiv \mathbb{C}[\![\mathbb{C}_{r^p}[\![Q_1'[{}^{\tilde{\nu}}/\tilde{x}]]\!]]\!]$ and $Q_2 \equiv \mathbb{C}[\![\mathbb{C}_{r^p}[\![Q_2']\!]]\!]$ and Q_1' is a sub-term of Q_2' with $fn(Q_2') = \tilde{x}$ (the substitution $[{}^{\tilde{\nu}}/\tilde{x}]$ is possibly empty),

where we let $llns(r, Q)$ denote the length of the longest nesting sequence induced by $\prec_Q$ and starting with r, that is of the form $r \prec_Q r_1 \prec_Q r_2 \ldots r_{n-1} \prec_Q r_n$.

We sketch the proof for case (1). By Lemma 4, we know that there is a suitable Γ such that $\Gamma \vdash Q : \text{end}[\text{end}]$. Depending on p, we need to prove one of cases below:

1.a if $Q \xrightarrow{r:\leftarrow\tilde{\nu}}$ and $\Gamma = \Gamma_1, r : [!(\tilde{S}).T]$ then $Q \xrightarrow{\gamma}{}^* \xrightarrow{r^+:\to\tilde{\nu}} \vee Q \xrightarrow{\gamma}{}^* \xrightarrow{r_1\iota} Q_1$ and $r <_{Q_1} r_1$

1.b if $Q \xrightarrow{r^+:\leftarrow\tilde{\nu}}$ and $\Gamma = \Gamma_1, r : [?(\tilde{S}).T]$ then $Q \xrightarrow{\gamma}{}^* \xrightarrow{r:\to\tilde{\nu}} \vee Q \xrightarrow{\gamma}{}^* \xrightarrow{r_1\iota} Q_1$ and $r <_{Q_1} r_1$

$$\text{(Tout)} \qquad \qquad \qquad \qquad \text{(Tinv)}$$

$$\frac{\Delta, \tilde{v} : \tilde{S} \vdash W : U[T]}{\Gamma' \vdash \langle \tilde{v} \rangle.W : U[!(\tilde{S}).T]} \qquad \qquad \frac{\Delta, s : [\overline{T'}] \vdash W :!(\tilde{S}).T[T']}{\Delta, s : [\overline{T'}] \vdash \overline{s}.W : [!(\tilde{S}).T]}$$

(a) Some rule instances considered in base cases: output and invoke

$$\text{(TparL)} \qquad \qquad \qquad \qquad \qquad \text{(Tpipe)}$$

$$\frac{\Gamma' \vdash W : U_W[!(\tilde{S}).T] \quad \Gamma' \vdash R : U_R[end]}{\Gamma' \vdash W|R : U_W \circ U_R[!(\tilde{S}).T]} \qquad \frac{\Gamma' \vdash W : U_W[!(\tilde{S}')] \quad \Gamma', \tilde{x} : \tilde{S}' \vdash R : U_R[!(\tilde{S}).T]}{\Gamma' \vdash W > \tilde{x} > R : U_W \circ U_R[!(\tilde{S}).T]}$$

(b) Some rule instances considered in inductive cases: parallel and pipe

$$\text{(TsesI)} \qquad \qquad \qquad \qquad \qquad \text{(TsesI + Tin)}$$

$$\frac{\Delta \vdash W :!(\tilde{S}).T[T']}{\Delta, r_1 : [\overline{T'}] \vdash r_1^- \triangleright W : end[!(\tilde{S}).T]} \qquad \frac{\Delta \vdash W :!(\tilde{S}).T[T'']}{\Delta, r_1 : [\overline{T'}] \vdash r_1^- \triangleright (\tilde{x}).W : end[!(\tilde{S}).T]}$$

(c) Some rule instances considered in inductive cases: nested session

Fig. 7. Deduction rules

We can read the above statements as "a session side must respect, after a finite number of steps γ, the obligation imposed by its type unless it postpones the obligation with a new service call". The fact that the type of r reflects the enabled action is a direct consequence of the subject reduction.

Case 1.a: If $r : [!(\tilde{S}).T]$ it means that $Q \equiv \mathbb{C}[\![r^+ \triangleright Q']\!]$ with $\Gamma' \vdash Q' : U[!(\tilde{S}).T]$ for suitable Q, Γ' and U. The entire proof is completely type-driven, the key idea is that we consider only instances of rules able to yield $Q' : U[!(\tilde{S}).T]$ in the conclusion. To ease readability, in the rules we use W to range over processes and Δ over environments.

Base cases: The base cases are when $llns(r, Q)$ has length 0, i.e., there is no nested session in r^+ and r^-. Since $\Gamma' \vdash Q' : U[!(\tilde{S}).T]$ we consider the instances of rules compatible with an r^+ output action. Some of them are in Fig. 7(a). If (Tout) is used, then it means that $Q' \equiv \langle \tilde{v} \rangle.W$. Then $Q \xrightarrow{r:\rightarrow\tilde{v}}$ and we are done by taking γ empty. Similarly, if (Tinv) is used, then $Q' \equiv \overline{s}.W$. Then $Q \xrightarrow{r_1 t} Q_1$ with $r <_{Q_1} r_1$ (by invoking s) and we are done by taking γ empty.

Inductive cases: When (TparL) is used the thesis follows by inductive hypothesis on $\mathbb{C}[\![r^+ \triangleright W]\!]$ (see Fig. 7(b)) and similarly when (TparR) is used. For (Tpipe) we apply the inductive hypothesis on $\mathbb{C}[\![r^+ \triangleright W]\!]$. By case (5), either $\mathbb{C}[\![r^+ \triangleright W]\!] \xrightarrow{\gamma}{}^* \xrightarrow{r^+ \rightarrow \tilde{v}} \mathbb{C}[\![r^+ \triangleright W']\!]$ and then $\mathbb{C}[\![r^+ \triangleright (W > \tilde{x} > R)]\!] \xrightarrow{\gamma}{}^* \xrightarrow{\tau} \mathbb{C}[\![r^+ \triangleright ((W' > \tilde{x} > R)|R[\tilde{v}/\tilde{x}])]\!]$, and then the thesis follows by inductive hypothesis on $\mathbb{C}[\![r^+ \triangleright R[\tilde{v}/\tilde{x}]]\!]$, or instead $\mathbb{C}[\![r^+ \triangleright W]\!] \xrightarrow{\gamma}{}^* \xrightarrow{r_2 t}$ and therefore $\mathbb{C}[\![r^+ \triangleright (W > \tilde{x} > R)]\!] \xrightarrow{\gamma}{}^* \xrightarrow{r_2 t} Q_1$ and $r <_{Q_1} r_2$. If (TsesI) is used, then a nested session r_1 is present, with $r <_Q r_1$ (see Fig. 7(c)), and we have various cases all similar. For example, if $Q' \equiv r_1^- \triangleright (\tilde{x}).W'$ then $Q \xrightarrow{r_1:\leftarrow\tilde{v}'}$ and by inductive hypothesis either $Q \xrightarrow{\gamma}{}^* \xrightarrow{r_1^+:\rightarrow\tilde{v}'}$ and then the thesis follows adding $r_1\tau$ at the begin of the resulting sequence generated by another application of the inductive hypothesis on $\mathbb{C}[\![r^+ \triangleright (r_1^- \triangleright W)]\!]$, or $Q \xrightarrow{\gamma}{}^* \xrightarrow{r_2 t} Q_1$ with $r_1 <_{Q_1} r_2$ and then the thesis follows since $r <_Q r_1$ and $r_1 <_{Q_1} r_2$.

Case 1.b is similar (we might also have $Q \equiv \mathbb{C}[\![r^- \triangleright \mathtt{return}\ \tilde{v}.W]\!]$, but this case can be discarded because it contradicts the assumptions).   □

We are now ready to prove the main result.

Theorem 2 (Deadlock freedom). *Let P an initial process. Then for each Q s.t. $P \xrightarrow{\omega}{}^* Q$ then either $Q \xrightarrow{\tau}$ or Q is in normal form.*

Proof. If Q is in normal form we are done. If not, by contradiction, if Proposition 2 holds then it cannot be the case Q blocked on a pending action in the middle of a session. In fact, it is always possible to accomplish the synchronisation choosing the right session that fits the proposition hypothesis since Q has type end[end]. Such a session cannot have a `return` enabled because it would be seen as an output of the parent session. Since the process is closed the type system ensures that every service call is successful (rule (T$_{\text{NEW}}$)).   □

Remark 1. The result can be extended to processes P that can output some values. In fact, if $\Gamma \vdash P : \text{end}[!(\tilde{S})^k]$ then we can take any suitable Q (designed to work on the resulting values) such that $\Gamma \vdash P > \tilde{x} > Q : \text{end}[\text{end}]$, thus fitting the requirements of Proposition 2. (The simplest case is $Q \equiv \mathbf{0}$.)

Example 4. The process $P = s.(x).\bar{s}.\langle x\rangle.(y).\mathtt{return}\ y \mid \bar{s}.\langle 5\rangle.(y)$ is well-typed in the environment $s : ?(int).!(int)$ and hence is deadlock free. Notice that the input of y never succeeds but the process is deadlock free since it keeps invoking new instances of s (all nested within the first established top session).

Even if simple, our framework also correctly type-checks non-tail recursive processes. For example, the initial process $s.\bar{s}.\mathtt{return}\ 1.(x)|\bar{s}.(y)$ is well-formed and well-typed in $\Gamma = s :!(int)$ and thus it is deadlock free (in our sense). An equivalent π-calculus process is $*s(r).(vr')(\bar{s}(r').\bar{r}(1).r'(x))|(vr)\bar{s}(r).r(y)$ and in Kobayashi's type system [14] the action $\bar{r}(1)$ cannot of course be ensured to succeed (check the tool available at http://www.kb.ecei.tohoku.ac.jp/~koba/typical/). In fact, r and r' have the same type and hence the capability level of r equal to the obligation level of r' but rule A'[14] is not applicable since r is created less recently than r'.

5   Conclusion

We have studied a service language with sessions and pipelines. Differently from [11,12,19,8,9,7] our language build sessions automatically on each service invocation and disallows session name mobility (but not service name mobility). To some extent, the simple type system we have devised is similar to that of simply typed π-calculus because it only tracks the exchanged values in each session. In fact, since sessions are developed as low level run-time primitives, the type system does not need to check session linearity. Instead we track active session usages w.r.t. the current session and the parent session. Subsequently, we restrict on the class of initial processes for which well-typedness implies a suitable notion of deadlock freedom. Together with the type interference algorithm, reported in [18], we have a simple tool to check deadlock freedom. Among the main novelties we emphasise the typing rules for pipelines and the particular well-founded order used for the induction in the proof of Proposition 2.

The full version of this work will address the enhancement of the type system with a notion of sub-typing so that different usages of the same service can be typed consistently. Moreover, recursion and regular μ-types [10] will be accounted for in the type system, even if Proposition 2 will no longer hold in the present form. To see this, think of a process making the same unbounded number of inputs and returns: if we type the process as $\mu\alpha.!(\tilde{S}).\alpha[\mu\alpha.?(\tilde{S}).\alpha]$ then different numbers of inputs and returns are allowed. As future work, we want to relax some requirements on parallel usages, admit session passing and extend the result to multiparty sessions.

Acknowledgements. We would like to thank Mariangiola Dezani-Ciancaglini, Marija Kolundzija and the anonymous referees for their helpful and detailed comments.

References

1. Acciai, L., Boreale, M.: A type system for client progress in a service-oriented calculus. In: Festschrift in Honour of Ugo Montanari, on the Occasion of His 65th Birthday. LNCS, vol. 5065. Springer, Heidelberg (to appear, 2008)
2. Boreale, M., Bruni, R., Caires, L., De Nicola, R., Lanese, I., Loreti, M., Martins, F., Montanari, U., Ravara, A., Sangiorgi, D., Vasconcelos, V., Zavattaro, G.: SCC: A service centered calculus. In: Bravetti, M., Núñez, M., Zavattaro, G. (eds.) WS-FM 2006. LNCS, vol. 4184, pp. 38–57. Springer, Heidelberg (2006)
3. Boreale, M., Bruni, R., De Nicola, R., Loreti, M.: Sessions and pipelines for structured service programming. In: Barthe, G., de Boer, F. (eds.) FMOODS 2008. LNCS, vol. 5051, pp. 19–38. Springer, Heidelberg (2008)
4. Busi, N., Gorrieri, R., Guidi, C., Lucchi, R., Zavattaro, G.: Sock: a calculus for service oriented computing. In: Dan, A., Lamersdorf, W. (eds.) ICSOC 2006. LNCS, vol. 4294, pp. 327–338. Springer, Heidelberg (2006)
5. Carbone, M., Honda, K., Yoshida, N.: Structured communication-centred programming for web services. In: De Nicola, R. (ed.) ESOP 2007. LNCS, vol. 4421, pp. 2–17. Springer, Heidelberg (2007)
6. Cook, W., Kitchin, D., Misra, J.: A language for task orchestration and its semantic properties. In: Baier, C., Hermanns, H. (eds.) CONCUR 2006. LNCS, vol. 4137, pp. 477–491. Springer, Heidelberg (2006)
7. Coppo, M., Dezani-Ciancaglini, M., Yoshida, N.: Asynchronous session types and progress for object oriented languages. In: Bonsangue, M.M., Johnsen, E.B. (eds.) FMOODS 2007. LNCS, vol. 4468, pp. 1–31. Springer, Heidelberg (2007)
8. Dezani-Ciancaglini, M., Mostrous, D., Yoshida, N., Drossopoulou, S.: Session types for object-oriented languages. In: Thomas, D. (ed.) ECOOP 2006. LNCS, vol. 4067, pp. 328–352. Springer, Heidelberg (2006)
9. Dezani-Ciancaglini, M., de Liguoro, U., Yoshida, N.: On progress for structured communications. In: Barthe, G., Fournet, C. (eds.) TGC 2007. LNCS, vol. 4912, pp. 257–275. Springer, Heidelberg (2008)

10. Gapeyev, V., Levin, M., Pierce, B.: Recursive subtyping revealed. J. Funct. Program. 12(6), 511–548 (2002)
11. Gay, S., Hole, M.: Subtyping for session types in the pi calculus. Acta Inform. 42(2), 191–225 (2005)
12. Honda, K., Vasconcelos, V., Kubo, M.: Language primitives and type discipline for structured communication-based programming. In: Hankin, C. (ed.) ESOP 1998. LNCS, vol. 1381, pp. 122–138. Springer, Heidelberg (1998)
13. Igarashi, A., Kobayashi, N.: A generic type system for the pi-calculus. ACM SIGPLAN Notices 36(3), 128–141 (2001)
14. Kobayashi, N.: New type system for deadlock-free processes. In: Baier, C., Hermanns, H. (eds.) CONCUR 2006. LNCS, vol. 4137, pp. 233–247. Springer, Heidelberg (2006)
15. Kobayashi, N., Sangiorgi, D.: A hybrid type system for lock-freedom of mobile processes. In: CAV 2008. LNCS. Springer, Heidelberg (to appear, 2008)
16. Lanese, I., Vasconcelos, V., Martins, F., Ravara, A.: Disciplining orchestration and conversation in service-oriented computing. In: Proceedings of SEFM 2007, pp. 305–314. IEEE Computer Society Press, Los Alamitos (2007)
17. Lapadula, A., Pugliese, R., Tiezzi, F.: A calculus for orchestration of web services. In: De Nicola, R. (ed.) ESOP 2007. LNCS, vol. 4421, pp. 33–47. Springer, Heidelberg (2007)
18. Mezzina, L.G.: How to infer finite session types in a calculus of services and sessions. In: Lea, D., Zavattaro, G. (eds.) COORDINATION 2008. LNCS, vol. 5052, pp. 216–231. Springer, Heidelberg (2008)
19. Yoshida, N., Vasconcelos, V.: Language primitives and type discipline for structured communication-based programming revisited: Two systems for higher-order session communication. Elect. Notes in Th. Comput. Sci. 171(4), 73–93 (2007)

A Declarative Debugger for Maude[*]

Adrian Riesco, Alberto Verdejo, Narciso Martí-Oliet, and Rafael Caballero

Facultad de Informática, Universidad Complutense de Madrid, Spain

Abstract. Declarative debugging has been applied to many declarative programming paradigms; in this paper, a declarative debugger for rewriting logic specifications, embodied in the Maude language, is presented. Starting from an incorrect computation (a reduction, a type inference, or a rewrite), the debugger builds a tree representing this computation and guides the user through it to find a wrong statement. We present the debugger's main features, such as support for functional and system modules, two possible constructions of the debugging tree, two different strategies to traverse it, use of a correct module to reduce the number of questions asked to the user, selection of trusted vs. suspicious statements, and trusting of statements "on the fly".

1 Introduction

Declarative debugging, introduced by E. Y. Shapiro [8], is a semi-automatic technique that starts from a computation considered incorrect by the user (error symptom) and locates a program fragment responsible for the error. It has been widely employed in the logic [6], functional [7], and multiparadigm [3] programming languages. The declarative debugging scheme uses a *debugging tree* as a logical representation of the computation. Each node in the tree represents the result of a computation step, which must follow from the results of its child nodes by some logical inference. Diagnosis proceeds by traversing the debugging tree, asking questions to an external oracle (generally the user) until a so-called *buggy node* is found. Any buggy node represents a wrong computation step, and the debugger can display the program fragment responsible for it.

Maude [4] is a declarative language based on both equational and rewriting logic for the specification and implementation of a whole range of models and systems. Here we present a declarative debugger for *Maude functional and system modules*. Functional modules define data types and operations on them by means of *membership equational logic* theories that support multiple sorts, subsort relations, equations, and assertions of membership in a sort. Declarative debugging of functional modules has been presented in [2,1]. System modules specify rewrite theories that also support *rules*, defining local concurrent transitions that can take place in a system.

The debugging process starts with an incorrect computation from an initial term. Our debugger, after building a proof tree for that inference, will present to the user questions about the computation. Moreover, since the questions are located in the proof tree, the

---

[*] Research supported by MEC Spanish projects *DESAFIOS* (TIN2006-15660-C02-01) and *MERIT-FORMS* (TIN2005-09027-C03-03), and Comunidad de Madrid program *PROMESAS* (S-0505/TIC/0407).

J. Meseguer and G. Roşu (Eds.): AMAST 2008, LNCS 5140, pp. 116–121, 2008.

answer allows the debugger to discard a subset of the questions, leading and shortening the debugging process. The current version of the tool supports all kinds of modules (except for the attribute `strat`), different ways of trusting statements, two possible constructions of the debugging tree for rewritings, and two strategies for traversing it. The debugger is implemented on top of Full Maude [4, Chap. 18]—allowing to debug the different modules provided by it, such as object-oriented and parameterized ones— and exploiting the reflective capabilities of Maude. Complete explanations about the fundamentals and novelties of our debugging approach can be found in the technical report [10], which, together with the source files for the debugger, examples, and related papers, is available from the webpage `http://maude.sip.ucm.es/debugging`.

2   Using the Debugger

We make explicit first what is assumed about the modules introduced by the user; then we present the available commands.

Assumptions. A rewrite theory has an underlying equational theory, containing equations and memberships, which is expected to satisfy the appropriate executability requirements, namely, it has to be terminating, confluent, and sort decreasing. Rules are assumed to be coherent with respect to the equations; for details, see [4].

In our debugger, unlabeled statements are assumed to be correct. Moreover, the user can trust more statements or introduce a correct module to check the inferences. In order to obtain a nonempty abbreviated proof tree, at least the buggy statement must be suspicious; the user is responsible for the correctness of these decisions.

Commands. The debugger is initiated in Maude by loading the file `dd.maude`, which starts an input/output loop that allows the user to interact with the tool. Since the debugger is implemented on top of Full Maude, all modules must be introduced enclosed in parentheses. If a module with correct definitions is used to reduce the number of questions, it must be indicated before starting the debugging with the command `(correct module MODULE-NAME .)`. Since rewriting with rules is not assumed to terminate, a bound, which is 42 by default although can be unbounded, is used when searching in the correct module and can be set with the command `(set bound BOUND .)`. The user can debug with only a subset of the labeled statements by using the command `(set debug select on .)`. Once this mode is activated, the user can select and deselect statements by using `(debug [de]select LABELS .)`. Moreover, all the labeled statements of a flattened module can be selected or deselected with the commands `(debug include/exclude MODULES .)`. When debugging rewrites, two different trees can be built: one whose questions are related to one-step rewrites and another one whose questions are related to several steps. The user can switch between these trees with the commands `(one-step tree .)`, which is the default one, and `(many-steps tree .)`, taking into account that the many-steps debugging tree usually leads to shorter debugging sessions (in terms of the number of questions) but with likely more complicated questions. The proof tree can be navigated by using two different strategies: the more intuitive *top-down* strategy, that traverses the tree from the root asking each time for the correctness of all the children of the current node, and then continues with one of the incorrect children; and the more efficient *divide and query* strategy, that each time selects the node whose subtree's size is the closest one to half the size of the whole tree, the latter being the default one. The user can switch between them with the commands (top-down strategy .) and (divide-query strategy .). Debugging is started with the following commands for wrong reductions, memberships, and rewrites.[1]

```
(debug [in MODULE-NAME :] INITIAL-TERM -> WRONG-TERM .)
(debug [in MODULE-NAME :] INITIAL-TERM : WRONG-SORT .)
(debug [in MODULE-NAME :] INITIAL-TERM =>* WRONG-TERM .)
```

How the process continues depends on the selected strategy. In case the top-down strategy is selected, several nodes will be displayed in each question. If there is an invalid node, we must select one of them with the command (node N .). If all the nodes are correct, we answer (all valid .). In the divide and query strategy, each question refers to one inference that can be either correct or wrong. The different answers are transmitted with the commands (yes .) and (no .). Instead of just answering yes, we can also *trust* some statements on the fly if, once the process has started, we decide the bug is not there. To trust the current statement we type the command (trust .). Finally, we can return to the previous state by using the command (undo .).

We show in the next sections how to use these commands to debug several examples.

3   Functional Module Example: Multisets

We use sets and multisets to illustrate how to debug functional modules. We describe sets by means of a membership that asserts that a set is a multiset without repetitions. However, the equation mt2 is wrong, because it should add 1 to mult(N, S):

```
cmb [set] : N S : Set if S : Set /\ mult(N, S) = 0 .
eq [mt2] : mult(N, N S) = mult(N, S) .
```

If we check now the type of 1 1 2 3 we obtain it is Set! We debug this wrong behavior with the command

```
Maude> (debug 1 1 2 3 : Set .)
```

that builds the associated debugging tree, and selects a node using divide and query:

```
Is this membership (associated with the membership set) correct?
1 2 3  : Set
Maude> (yes .)
```

The debugger continues asking the questions below, now associated to equations:

```
Is this reduction (associated with the equation mt3) correct?
mult(1, 2 3) -> 0
Maude> (yes .)
Is this reduction (associated with the equation mt2) correct?
mult(1, 1 2 3) -> 0
Maude> (no .)
```

---

[1] If no module name is given, the current module is used by default.

With this information, the debugger finds the wrong statement:

```
The buggy node is: mult(1, 1 2 3) -> 0
With the associated equation: mt2
```

4 System Module Example: Operational Semantics

We illustrate in this section how to debug system modules by means of the semantics of the WhileL language, a simple imperative language described in [5] and represented in Maude in [9]. The syntax of the language includes skip, assignment, composition, conditional statement, and while loop. The state of the execution is kept in the *store*, a set of pairs of variables and values.

Evaluation semantics. The evaluation semantics takes a pair consisting of a command and a store and returns a store.[2] However, we have committed an error in the while loop:

```
crl [WhileR2] : < While be Do C, st > => < skip, st' >
                if < be, st > => T /\ < C, st > => < skip, st' > .
```

That is, if the condition is true, the body is evaluated only once. Thus, if we execute the program below to multiply x and y and keep the result in z

```
Maude> (rew < z := 0 ; (While Not Equal(x, 0) Do
                        z := z +. y ; x := x -. 1), x = 2 y = 3 z = 1 > .)
result Statement : < skip, y = 3 z = 3 x = 1 >
```

we obtain z = 3, while we expected to obtain z = 6. We debug this behavior with the top-down strategy and the default one-step tree by typing the commands

```
Maude> (top-down strategy .)
Maude> (debug < z := 0 ; (While Not Equal(x, 0) Do
                          z := z +. y ; x := x -. 1), x = 2 y = 3 z = 1 >
        =>* < skip, y = 3 z = 3 x = 1 > .)
```

The debugger computes the tree and asks about the validity of the root's children:

```
Please, choose a wrong node:
Node 0 : < z := 0, x = 2 y = 3 z = 1 > =>1 < skip, x = 2 y = 3 z = 0 >
Node 1 : < While Not Equal(x,0) Do z := z +. y ; x := x -. 1, x = 2 y = 3 z = 0 >
         =>1 < skip, y = 3 z = 3 x = 1 >
Maude> (node 1 .)
```

The second node is erroneous, because x has not reached 0, so the user selects this node to continue the debugging, and the following question is related to its children:

```
Please, choose a wrong node:
Node 0 : < Not Equal(x,0), x = 2 y = 3 z = 0 > =>1 T
Node 1 : < z := z +. y ; x := x -. 1, x = 2 y = 3 z = 0 >
         =>1 < skip, y = 3 z = 3 x = 1 >
Maude> (all valid .)
```

---

[2] In order to reuse this module later, the returned result is a pair < skip, st >.

Since both nodes are right, the debugger determines that the current node is buggy:

```
The buggy node is:
< While Not Equal(x,0) Do z := z +. y ; x := x -. 1, x = 2 y = 3 z = 0 >
=>1 < skip, y = 3 z = 3 x = 1 >
With the associated rule: WhileR2
```

Computation semantics. In contrast to the evaluation semantics, the computation semantics describes the behavior of programs in terms of small steps. In order to illustrate this, we make a mistake in the rule describing the semantics of the composition, keeping the initial state instead of the new one computed in the condition:

```
crl [ComRc1] : < C ; C', st > => < C'' ; C', st >
            if < C, st > => < C'', st' > /\ C =/= C'' .
```

If we rewrite now a program to swap the values of two variables, their values are not exchanged. We use the many-steps tree to debug this wrong behavior:

```
Maude> (many-steps tree .)
Maude> (debug < x := x -. y ; y := x +. y ; x := y -. x, x = 5 y = 2 >
            =>* < skip, y = 2 x = 0 > .)
Is this rewrite correct?
< y := x +. y ; x := y -. x, x = 5 y = 2 > =>+ < skip, y = 2 x = 0 >
Maude> (no .)
```

The transition is wrong because the variables have not been properly updated.

```
Is this rewrite (associated with the rule ComRc1) correct?
< y := x +. y ; x := y -. x,x = 5 y = 2 > =>1 < x := y -. x,x = 5 y = 2 >
Maude> (no .)
Is this rewrite (associated with the rule OpR) correct?
< x +. y, x = 5 y = 2 > =>1 7
Maude> (trust .)
```

We consider that the application of a primitive operation is simple enough to be trusted. The next question is related to the application of an equation to update the store

```
Is this reduction (associated with the equation st1) correct?
x = 5 y = 2[7 / y] -> x = 5 y = 7
Maude> (yes .)
```

Finally, a question about assignment is posed:

```
Is this rewrite (associated with the rule AsRc) correct?
< y := x +. y, x = 5 y = 2 > =>1 < skip, x = 5 y = 7 >
Maude> (yes .)
```

With this information, the debugger is able to find the bug. However, since we have the evaluation semantics of the language already specified and debugged, we can use that module as correct module to reduce the number of questions to only one.

```
Maude> (correct module EVALUATION-WHILE .)
Maude> (debug ... .)
Is this rewrite correct?
< y := x +. y ; x := y -. x, x = 5 y = 2 > =>+ < skip, y = 2 x = 0 >
Maude> (no .)
```

5 Conclusions

We have implemented a declarative debugger for Maude modules that allows to debug wrong reductions, type inferences, and rewrites. Although the complexity of the
debugging process increases with the size of the proof tree, it does not depend on the
total number of statements but on the number of applications of suspicious statements
involved in the wrong inference. Moreover, bugs found when reducing complex initial
terms can, in general, be reproduced with simpler terms which give rise to smaller proof
trees. We plan to improve the interaction with the user by providing a complementary
graphical interface that allows the user to navigate the tree with more freedom. This interaction could also be improved by allowing the user to give the answer "don't know,"
that would postpone the answer to the question by asking alternative questions. We are
also studying how to handle the strat operator attribute, that allows the specifier to
define an evaluation strategy. This can be used to represent some kind of laziness.

References

1. Caballero, R., Martí-Oliet, N., Riesco, A., Verdejo, A.: A declarative debugger for Maude
   functional modules. In: Proceedings Seventh International Workshop on Rewriting Logic
   and its Applications, WRLA 2008. Elsevier, Amsterdam (to appear, 2008)
2. Caballero, R., Martí-Oliet, N., Riesco, A., Verdejo, A.: Declarative debugging of membership
   equational logic specifications. In: Degano, P., Nicola, R.D., Meseguer, J. (eds.) Concurrency,
   Graphs and Models. LNCS, vol. 5065, pp. 174–193. Springer, Heidelberg (2008)
3. Caballero, R., Rodríguez-Artalejo, M.: DDT: A declarative debugging tool for functional-
   logic languages. In: Proc. 7th International Symposium on Functional and Logic Programming (FLOPS 2004). LNCS, vol. 2998, pp. 70–84. Springer, Heidelberg (2004)
4. Clavel, M., Durán, F., Eker, S., Lincoln, P., Martí-Oliet, N., Meseguer, J., Talcott, C.: All
   About Maude: A High-Performance Logical Framework. LNCS, vol. 4350. Springer, Heidelberg (2007)
5. Hennessy, M.: The Semantics of Programming Languages: An Elementary Introduction Using Structural Operational Semantics. John Wiley & Sons, Chichester (1990)
6. Lloyd, J.W.: Declarative error diagnosis. New Generation Computing 5(2), 133–154 (1987)
7. Nilsson, H., Fritzson, P.: Algorithmic debugging of lazy functional languages. Journal of
   Functional Programming 4(3), 337–370 (1994)
8. Shapiro, E.Y.: Algorithmic Program Debugging. ACM Distinguished Dissertation. MIT
   Press, Cambridge (1983)
9. Verdejo, A., Martí-Oliet, N.: Executable structural operational semantics in Maude. Journal
   of Logic and Algebraic Programming 67, 226–293 (2006)
10. Riesco, A., Verdejo, A., Caballero, R., Martí-Oliet, N.: Declarative debugging of Maude
    modules. Technical Report SIC-6/08, Dpto. Sistemas Informáticos y Computación, Univer-
    sidad Complutense de Madrid (2008), http://maude.sip.ucm.es/debugging

Long-Run Cost Analysis by Approximation of Linear Operators over Dioids

David Cachera[1], Thomas Jensen[2], Arnaud Jobin[3], and Pascal Sotin[4]

[1] ENS Cachan (Bretagne)
[2] CNRS
[3] INRIA
[4] CNRS/DGA
Irisa, Campus de Beaulieu, 35042 Rennes, France

Abstract. We present a static analysis technique for modeling and approximating the long-run resource usage of programs. The approach is based on a quantitative semantic framework where programs are represented as linear operators over dioids. We provide abstraction techniques for such linear operators which make it feasible to compute safe overapproximations of the long-run cost of a program. A theorem is proved stating that such abstractions yield correct approximations of the program's long-run cost. These approximations are effectively computed as the eigenvalue of the matrix representation of the abstract semantics. The theoretical developments are illustrated on a concrete example taken from the analysis of the cache behaviour of a simple bytecode language.

1 Introduction

This article is concerned with the semantics-based program analysis of quantitative properties pertaining to the use of resources (time, memory, ...). Analysis of such non-functional properties relies on an operational model of program execution where the cost of each computational step is made explicit. We take as starting point a standard small-step operational semantics expressed as a transition relation $\sigma \rightarrow^q \sigma'$ between states $\sigma, \sigma' \in \Sigma$ extended with *costs* $q \in Q$ associated to each transition. The set Q of costs is supposed to have two operations for composing costs: a "product" operator that combines the costs along an execution path, and a "sum" operator that combines costs coming from different paths. These operators will give Q a structure of dioid. The sum operator induces a partial order on costs that will serve as a basis for approximating costs. From such a rule-based semantics, there is a straightforward way to obtain a transition matrix, which entries represent the cost of passing from one state of the program to another. This expresses the semantics of a program as a linear operator on $Q(\Sigma)$, the moduloid of vectors of elements of Q indexed over Σ.

In this paper, we are interested in analysing programs with cyclic behaviour (such as reactive systems) in which the asymptotic average cost along cycles, rather than the global cost of the entire execution, is of interest. We define the notion of *long-run cost* for a program which provides an over-approximation of

J. Meseguer and G. Roşu (Eds.): AMAST 2008, LNCS 5140, pp. 122–138, 2008.
© Springer-Verlag Berlin Heidelberg 2008

the average cost per transition of long traces. This notion corresponds to the maximum average of costs accumulated along a cycle of the program semantics and is computed from the traces of the successive iterates of the cost matrix. The quantitative operational semantics operates on state spaces that may be large or even infinite so the computation of quantitative semantic models, like their qualitative counterparts, is usually not tractable. Hence, it is necessary to develop techniques for abstracting this semantics, in order to return an approximation of the program costs that is feasible to compute.

In line with the semantic machinery used to model programs, abstractions are also defined as linear operators from the moduloid over the concrete state space into the moduloid over the abstract one. Given such an abstraction over the semantic domains, we then have to abstract the transition matrix of the program itself into a matrix of reduced size. We give a sufficient condition for an abstraction of the semantics to be correct, *i.e.* to give an over-approximation of the real cost, and show how an abstract semantics that is correct by construction can be derived from the concrete one. The long-run cost of a program is thus safely approximated by an abstract long-run cost, with respect to the order relation induced by the summation operator of the dioid.

The framework proposed here covers a number of different costs related to resource usage (time and memory) of programs. To demonstrate the generality of the framework, our running example considers the less common (compared to time and space) analysis of cache behaviour and the number of cache misses in programs. We illustrate the notions of quantitative semantics, abstraction and long-run cost on a program written in a simple, intermediate bytecode language (inspired by Java Card) onto which we impose a particular cache model.

The paper is structured as follows. Section 2 defines the quantitative semantics as a linear operator over a moduloid. We give the general form of this semantics, and precisely define the notion of cost dioid we use throughout the paper. Section 3 defines the notion of abstraction together with its correctness, and shows how we can derive an abstract semantics that is correct by construction. Section 4 defines the notion of long-run cost, relating it to the asymptotic behaviour of the trace semantics, and shows how a correct abstraction yields an over-approximation of the concrete long-run cost of a program. Section 5 lists related work and Section 6 concludes and discusses future research directions.

2   Linear Operator Semantics

We give a general framework for expressing quantitative operational semantics. Transitions of these semantics will be equipped with *quantities* (or *costs*) depending on the accessed states. Let P be a program; its semantic domain is the countable set of states Σ. The quantitative operational semantics of P is given as a transition relation, defined by inference rules of the following form: $\sigma \rightarrow^q \sigma'$ where σ, σ' are states of Σ, and q is the cost attached to the transition from σ to σ' (q is function of σ and σ'). We associate to P the transition system $T = \langle \rightarrow, I \rangle$, where I is the set of initial states of P. The trace semantics of P is defined as the trace semantics of T.

$$[\![P]\!]_{tr} = [\![T]\!]_{tr} = \{\sigma_0 \to^{q_0} \ldots \sigma_{n-1} \to^{q_{n-1}} \sigma_n \mid \sigma_0 \in I, \sigma_i \to^{q_i} \sigma_{i+1}\}$$

2.1   Cost Dioid

The small-step, quantitative operational semantics induces a labelled transition system over Σ with labels in Q and a transition relation $\to \cdot \subseteq \Sigma \times \Sigma \to Q$, written $\sigma \to^q \sigma'$. Such a transition states that a direct (one-step) transition from σ to σ' costs q. These unitary transitions can be combined into big-step transitions, using two operators: $\otimes$ for accumulating costs and $\oplus$ to get a maximum of different costs. These operators will form a dioid on Q, as explained below. Costs can be defined in more general ways (for instance, one could use a more general algebra of costs as in [4]) but the present definition covers a number of different costs and has interesting computational properties, since it can be used within a linear operator semantic framework, as presented in the next subsection.

The operator $\otimes$ on Q defines the global cost of a sequence of transitions, $\sigma \to^{q_1} \ldots \to^{q_n} \sigma'$ simply as $q = q_1 \otimes \ldots \otimes q_n$. This is written $\sigma \overset{\pi}{\Rightarrow}^q \sigma'$ where π is a sequence of states that has σ (resp. σ') as first (resp. last) state.

There may be several ways to reach a state σ' from a state σ, due to the presence of loops and non-determinism in the semantics. Let the corresponding set of possible paths be $\Pi_{\sigma,\sigma'} = \{\pi \mid \sigma \overset{\pi}{\Rightarrow}^{q_\pi} \sigma'\}$. The global cost between σ and σ' will be defined, using the operator $\oplus$ on Q, to be $q = \bigoplus_{\pi \in \Pi_{\sigma,\sigma'}} q_\pi$. Formally, the two operators have to fulfill the conditions of a (commutative) dioid.

Definition 1. *A commutative dioid is a structure $(Q, \oplus, \otimes)$ such that*

1. *Operator $\otimes$ is associative, commutative and has a neutral element e. Quantity e represents a transition that costs nothing.*
2. *Operator $\oplus$ is associative, commutative and has $\perp$ as neutral element. Quantity $\perp$ represents the impossibility of a transition.*
3. *$\otimes$ is distributive over $\oplus$, and $\perp$ is absorbing element for $\otimes$ $(\forall x.x \otimes \perp = \perp \otimes x = \perp)$.*
4. *The preorder defined by $\oplus$ $(a \leq b \Leftrightarrow \exists c : a \oplus c = b)$ is an order relation (i.e. it satisfies $a \leq b$ and $b \leq a \Rightarrow a = b$).*

By nature, a dioid cannot be a ring, since there is an inherent contradiction between the fact that $\oplus$ induces an order relation and the fact that every element has an inverse for $\oplus$. The following lemma is a classical result of dioid theory [17].

Lemma 1. *$\oplus$ and $\otimes$ preserve the order $\leq$, i.e., for all $a, b, c \in Q$ with $a \leq b$, $a \otimes c \leq b \otimes c$ and $a \oplus c \leq b \oplus c$.*

If several paths go from some state σ to a state σ' at the same cost q, we will require that the global cost is also q, *i.e.* we work with idempotent dioids.

Definition 2. *A dioid* $(Q, \oplus, \otimes)$ *is* idempotent *if* $q \oplus q = q$ *for all* q *in* Q.

For instance, $(\overline{\mathbb{R}}, \max, +)$ and $(\overline{\mathbb{R}}, \min, +)$ are idempotent dioids, where $\overline{\mathbb{R}}$ stands for $\mathbb{R} \cup \{-\infty, +\infty\}$. The induced orders are, respectively, the orders $\leq$ and $\geq$ over real numbers, extended to $\overline{\mathbb{R}}$ in the usual way. Note that in an idempotent dioid $a \leq b \Leftrightarrow a \oplus b = b$. Idempotent dioids are also called tropical semirings in the literature. The fact that sets of states may be infinite, together with the use of residuation theory in Section 3 impose that our dioids are complete [7].

Definition 3. *An idempotent dioid is* complete *if it is closed with respect to infinite sums (operator $\oplus$) and the distributivity law holds also for an infinite number of summands.*

A complete dioid is naturally equipped with a top element, that we shall write $\top$, which is the sum of all its elements. Remark that a complete dioid is always a complete lattice, thus equipped with a meet operator $\wedge$ [6]. The notion of long-run cost we will define in Section 4 relies on the computation of an average cost along the transitions of a cycle. This requires the existence of a nth root function.

Definition 4. *A dioid* $(Q, \oplus, \otimes)$ *is equipped with a* nth root function *if for all* q *in* Q, *equation* $X^n = q$ *has a* unique *solution in* Q, *denoted by* $\sqrt[n]{q}$.

A sequence containing n transitions, each costing, on the average, $\sqrt[n]{q}$, will thus cost q. Some examples of nth root can be found in Figure 1. To be able to easily deal with the nth root, we make the assumption that the nth power is $\oplus$-lower-semicontinuous ($\oplus$-lsc for short).

Definition 5. *In a complete dioid* Q, *the* nth power *is said to be* $\oplus$-lsc *if for all* $X \subseteq Q$, $(\bigoplus_{x \in X} x)^n = \bigoplus_{x \in X} x^n$.

This assumption and its consequences will be very useful for the theorems relating long-run cost and trace semantics in Section 4. Note that this equality remains true for finite X (in that case the nth power is said a $\oplus$-*morphism*).

The following definition summarizes the required conditions for our structure.

Definition 6 (Cost dioid). *A* cost dioid *is a complete* and *idempotent commutative dioid, equipped with an nth root operation, where the nth power is $\oplus$-lsc.*

Proposition 1. *In a cost dioid* Q, *we have:*

(i) The nth root is $\oplus$-lsc: $\forall X \subseteq Q, \forall n > 0$, $\sqrt[n]{\bigoplus_{x \in X} x} = \bigoplus_{x \in X} \sqrt[n]{x}$,

(ii) For all $a, b \in Q$ *and* $n, m > 0$, $\sqrt[n]{a} \oplus \sqrt[m]{b} \geq \sqrt[n+m]{a \otimes b}$.

These properties follow from the fact that the nth power is $\oplus$-lsc [10].

Although the definition of cost dioids may seem rather restrictive, we now show that many classes of dioids found in the literature are indeed cost dioids. We first recall some standard definitions.

Definition 7. *A dioid* $(Q, \oplus, \otimes)$ *is:*

- selective *if for all* a, b *in* Q, $a \oplus b =$ *either* a *or* b.
- double-idempotent *if both* $\oplus$ *and* $\otimes$ *are idempotent.*
- cancellative *if for all* a, b, c *in* Q, $a \otimes b = a \otimes c$ *and* $a \neq \perp$ *imply* $b = c$.

Note that in a double-idempotent dioid, $x^n = x$. Thus, a double-idempotent dioid is naturally equipped with a nth root, which is the identity function.

Proposition 2. *The following dioids are cost dioids.*

(1) Complete and selective commutative dioids with an nth root operation.
(2) Complete and double-idempotent commutative dioids.
(3) Complete idempotent commutative dioids satisfying the cancellation condition, and for which for all q in Q, equation $X^n = q$ has always a solution.

For dioids of kind (1) and (2) we only have to prove that the nth power is $\oplus$-lsc. For dioids of type (3) we also have to prove that if equation $X^n = q$ has a solution, this solution is unique [10].

For instance, $(\overline{\mathbb{R}}, \max, +)$ is a cost dioid that may be used for the definition of the Worst Case Execution Time: when two states can be joined by several sequences of transitions which

	carrier set	$\oplus$	$\otimes$	$\sqrt[n]{q}$
Double-idempotent	$\mathbb{Q} \cup \{+\infty, -\infty\}$	min	max	q
	$\mathbb{R} \cup \{+\infty, -\infty\}$	max	min	q
	$\mathcal{P}(S)$	$\cap$	$\cup$	q
	$\mathcal{P}(S)$	$\cup$	$\cap$	q
Cancellative	$(\mathbb{R}_+ \cup \{+\infty\})^m$	min	$+$	$\frac{q}{n}$
Selective	$\mathbb{R}_+ \cup \{+\infty\}$	max	$\times$	$q^{\frac{1}{n}}$
	$\mathbb{Q} \cup \{+\infty, -\infty\}$	max	$+$	$\frac{q}{n}$
	$\mathbb{R} \cup \{+\infty, -\infty\}$	min	$+$	$\frac{q}{n}$

Fig. 1. Examples of cost dioids

cost different times, the worst time is taken. To compute the cost of a sequence of transitions, we sum the costs of each transition. Figure 1 lists some cost dioids.

2.2 Semantics as Linear Operators over Dioids

The upshot of using the adequate cost dioid is that the cost computation can be defined in terms of matrix operations in this dioid. The set of one-step transitions can be equivalently represented by a *transition matrix* $M \in \mathcal{M}_{\Sigma \times \Sigma}(Q)$ with

$$M_{\sigma, \sigma'} = \begin{cases} q \; \textit{if } \sigma \rightarrow^q \sigma' \\ \perp \; \textit{otherwise} \end{cases}$$

Here, $\mathcal{M}_{\Sigma \times \Sigma}(Q)$ stands for the set of matrices with rows and columns indexed over Σ, and values in Q. This set of matrices is naturally equipped with two operators $\oplus$ and $\otimes$ in the classical way: operator $\oplus$ is extended pointwise, and operator $\otimes$ corresponds to the matrix product (note that the iterate M^n embed the costs for paths of length n). The resulting structure is also an idempotent and complete dioid. The order induced by $\oplus$ corresponds to the pointwise extension of the order over Q: $M \leq M' \Leftrightarrow \forall i, j. M_{i,j} \leq M'_{i,j}$. A transition matrix may also be seen as a linear operator on the moduloid $Q(\Sigma)$, as defined below.

Definition 8. *Let $(E, \oplus, \otimes)$ be a commutative dioid. A moduloid over E is a set V with an internal operation $\oplus$ and an external operation $\odot$ such that*

1. *$(V, \oplus)$ is a commutative monoid, with 0 as neutral element;*
2. *the $\odot$ operator ranges from $E \times V$ to V, and verifies*
   - *(a) $\forall \lambda \in E, \forall (x, y) \in V^2, \lambda \odot (x \oplus y) = (\lambda \odot x) \oplus (\lambda \odot y)$,*
   - *(b) $\forall (\lambda, \mu) \in E^2, \forall x \in V, (\lambda \oplus \mu) \odot x = (\lambda \odot x) \oplus (\mu \odot x)$,*
   - *(c) $\forall (\lambda, \mu) \in E^2, \forall x \in V, \lambda \odot (\mu \odot x) = (\lambda \otimes \mu) \odot x$,*
   - *(d) $\forall x \in V, e \odot x = x$ and $\perp \odot x = 0$,*
   - *(e) $\forall \lambda \in E, \lambda \odot 0 = 0$.*

If E is an idempotent dioid, then any moduloid V over E is also equipped with a canonical order defined from the pointwise $\oplus$ operation. As for vector spaces, if n is a given integer, E^n, set of vectors with n components in E, is a moduloid. More generally, a vector $u \in E(\Sigma)$, with Σ finite, $|\Sigma| = n$ can be seen as a function $\delta_u : [1, n] \rightarrow E$. Since Q is complete, we can generalize to the infinite (countable) case: δ_u becomes a mapping from $\mathbb{N}$ to E, and the same technique applies for matrices. The matrix-vector product is defined by: $(Mu)_i = \bigoplus_{j=1}^{+\infty} \delta_M(i, j) \otimes \delta_u(j)$. In this paper, we will keep the matrix notation for the sake of simplicity, even for an infinite set of indices.

2.3 Running Example: Quantitative Semantics

We illustrate the notions of cost and quantitative semantics on a simple bytecode language, inspired by the Java Card language. Figure 2 shows part of the factorial program written in this language. The quantity we are interested in is the number of cache misses related to read accesses (read miss behaviour). In order to describe the read miss behaviour of programs, we extend the semantics of a simple bytecode language [19,16] with a cache model and with quantities expressing the number of read misses.

Source	Bytecode
x=1;	1: push 1
	2: store x
for (i=2;...	3: push 2
	4: store i
...i<=n;...	5: load i
	6: load n
	7: if ≤goto 14
x=x*i;	8: load x
	9: load i
	10: numop mul
	11: store x
...i++)	12: inc i
	13: goto 5
return x;	14: load x
	15: return

Fig. 2. Factorial program

The cost dioid considered here is $(\mathbb{R}, \mathbf{max}, +)$. A state contains a heap, a call stack of frames, and within each frame an instruction pointer for the current method, an array of local variables and an operand stack. In addition to these standard elements, a state contains a set of *logical addresses*, representing which values are present in the cache at this point of the execution. This set is managed similarly to the cache. For example, the maximum size of this set will correspond to the size of the physical cache, and the replacement policy will model the one it provides (*e.g.* LRU, FIFO). The cache description is hidden in a function $C' = update(C, [access])$ where C and C' denote the cache before and after a transition, respectively, and where [*access*] is a list of memory accesses. Due to the lack of space, full descriptions of possible *update* functions are not given.

Memory is accessed with two primitives (a read or write access) which take two parameters, specifying what volume of data is to be accessed, and where these data are stored. For example, $read_\tau(\textbf{heap}.3.x)$ means that data of type τ is read at the address $\textbf{heap}.3.x$, *i.e.* field x of the third object in the heap. In the same way, $\textbf{stack}.frameId.n$ points to the n-nth element in the operand stack of a given frame, and $\textbf{local}.frameId.local$ points to a local variable in a certain frame. We give an example of a semantic rule: the load instruction, which loads a typed local variable, indexed by i, on the top of the operand stack. The first two premises of the rule correspond to the standard semantics. The third and fourth premises define how the cache evolves when executing a load. The fifth premise computes the cost. Some other rule examples can be found in [10].

$$
\frac{
\begin{array}{c}
InstrAt(m, ip) = \text{load } \tau \ i \land L[i] = d \\
S' = d :: S \land size(S) = t \\
access = [read_\tau(\textbf{local}.f.i); write_\tau(\textbf{stack}.f.t{+}1)] \\
C' = update(C, access) \\
q = nbRmiss(C, access)
\end{array}
}{
\langle H, \ll f, m, ip, L, S \gg :: fr, C \rangle \rightarrow^q \langle H, \ll f, m, ip + 1, L, S' \gg :: fr, C' \rangle
}
$$

The number of read misses depends on the current state of the cache and the way it is accessed. This is defined precisely by the function $nbRmiss(C, access)$ that computes the number of read misses generated by the list of memory accesses *access* if the cache at the beginning of the instruction is C. Here is the pseudocode of function $nbRmiss$.

$$nbRmiss(c, []) = 0$$

$$nbRmiss(c, [a|r]) = nbRmiss(update(c, [a]), r) + \begin{cases} 1 & \text{if } a = read \ m \text{ and } m \notin c \\ 0 & \text{otherwise} \end{cases}$$

3   Abstraction

The transition matrix representing a program is in general of infinite dimension, so neither transitive closure nor traces can be computed in finite time. To overcome this problem, we define an abstract matrix that can be used to approximate the computations of the original matrix. For example, if we compute the minimum memory needed to run a program, a correct approximation of this quantity must be greater than the effective minimum. In this section, we give a sufficient condition for this approximation to be correct with respect to the ordering induced by the dioid. To prove the correctness of an abstraction, we restate the classical abstract interpretation theory [12] in terms of linear operators over moduloids.

3.1   Galois Connections and Pseudo-Inverses

We first briefly recall the definition of Galois connections that are used in the classical abstract interpretation theory.

Definition 9. *Let $(C, \leq_C)$ and $(D, \leq_D)$ be two partially ordered sets (posets). Two mappings $\alpha : C \mapsto D$ (called abstraction function) and $\gamma : D \mapsto C$ (called concretization function) form a Galois connection (C, α, γ, D) iff:*

- *$\forall c \in C, \forall d \in D, c \leq_C \gamma(d) \iff \alpha(c) \leq_D d$, or equivalently*
- *α and γ are monotonic and $\alpha \circ \gamma \leq Id_D$ and $Id_C \leq \gamma \circ \alpha$*

In our setting, the partial orders will be the orders induced by the $\oplus$ operators over vectors in a moduloid. The question that naturally arises is that of the existence of a concretization function, given an abstraction α. In [15], Di Pierro and Wiklicky describe the framework of Probabilistic Abstract Interpretation, where the abstraction function is a linear operator over the semiring of probabilities. They obtain a concretization function through the Moore-Penrose pseudo-inverse. As we will not be able to define an exact inverse in the general case, nor to apply the Moore-Penrose pseudo-inverse since we do not work in a field, we will use the theory of *residuation* to get a kind of inverse for α.

Proposition 3. *Let E and F be two complete posets, f a monotone mapping from E to F. We call subsolution of equation $f(x) = b$ an element y such that $f(y) \leq b$. The following properties are equivalent.*

1. *For all $b \in E$, there exists a greatest subsolution to the equation $f(x) = b$.*
2. *$f(\perp_E) = \perp_F$, and f is $\oplus$-lsc.*
3. *There exists a monotone mapping from F into E which is upper[1] semi-continuous such that $f \circ f^\dagger \leq Id_F$ and $Id_E \leq f^\dagger \circ f$.*

As a consequence, $f^\dagger$ is unique. When f satisfies these properties, it is said to be residuated, and $f^\dagger$ is called its residual.

3.2   Abstraction over Cost Dioids

We now show how the notions of abstraction and concretization can be recast in our setting. In the following, Σ will denote a set of *concrete* states and $\Sigma^\sharp$ a set of *abstract* states. An abstraction function maps concrete states in Σ to their abstraction in $\Sigma^\sharp$. Given an abstraction function α, we can lift it to a linear abstraction operator $\alpha^\uparrow \in \mathcal{M}_{\Sigma^\sharp \times \Sigma}(Q)$ by setting

$$\alpha^\uparrow_{\sigma^\sharp, \sigma} = \begin{cases} e \text{ if } \alpha(\sigma) = \sigma^\sharp \\ \perp \text{ otherwise} \end{cases}$$

In what follows, $\alpha^\uparrow$ will be denoted by α when no confusion can arise and $\leq$ will stand for the order defined on $\mathcal{M}_{\Sigma^\sharp \times \Sigma^\sharp}(Q)$ in Section 2.2.

As the abstraction function is linear, it trivially fulfills requirements 2 of Proposition 3 and we get the following result.

---

[1] Upper semi-continuity is the analog of lower semi-continuity for the $\wedge$ operator.

Theorem 1. *Let Σ and $\Sigma^\sharp$ be the domains of concrete and abstract states, α a mapping from Σ to $\Sigma^\sharp$, and $\alpha^\uparrow \in \mathcal{M}_{\Sigma^\sharp \times \Sigma}(Q)$ the linear mapping obtained by lifting α. There exists a unique monotonic $\alpha^\uparrow$ such that $\alpha^\uparrow \circ \alpha^\uparrow \leq Id_{\Sigma^\sharp}$ and $Id_\Sigma \leq \alpha^\uparrow \circ \alpha^\uparrow$.*

3.3 Induced Abstract Semantics

Let T be a transition system in the concrete domain Σ, over the cost dioid $(Q, \oplus, \otimes)$. We now want to define an abstract transition system over the abstract domain $\Sigma^\sharp$ that is "compatible" with T, both from the point of view of its traces and from the costs it will lead to compute. The following definition of a correct abstraction will ensure that the long-run cost of a program, as defined in the next section, will be correctly over-approximated during the abstraction process.

Definition 10 (Correct abstraction). *Let $T = \langle M, I \rangle$ a transition system over the concrete domain, with $M \in \mathcal{M}_{\Sigma \times \Sigma}(Q)$ and $I \subseteq \Sigma$. Let $T^\sharp = \langle M^\sharp, I^\sharp \rangle$ be a transition system over the abstract domain, with $M^\sharp \in \mathcal{M}_{\Sigma^\sharp \times \Sigma^\sharp}(Q)$ and $I^\sharp \subseteq \Sigma^\sharp$. Let α be an abstraction from Σ to $\Sigma^\sharp$. The triple $(T, T^\sharp, \alpha)$ is a correct abstraction from Σ to $\Sigma^\sharp$ if $\alpha^\uparrow \circ M \leq M^\sharp \circ \alpha^\uparrow$ and $\{\alpha(\sigma) \mid \sigma \in I\} \subseteq I^\sharp$.*

The classical framework of abstract interpretation gives a way to define a best correct abstraction for a given concrete semantic operator. In the same way, given an abstraction α and a concrete semantics linear operator, we can define an abstract semantics operator that is correct by construction, as expressed by the following proposition.

Proposition 4. *Let α be an abstraction from Σ to $\Sigma^\sharp$, and $T = \langle M, I \rangle$ be a transition system with $M \in \mathcal{M}_{\Sigma \times \Sigma}(Q)$ a linear operator over the concrete moduloid and I the subset of initial states. We set $T^\sharp = \langle M^\sharp, I^\sharp \rangle$ with*

$$M^\sharp = \alpha^\uparrow \circ M \circ \alpha^\uparrow \quad and \quad I^\sharp = \{\alpha(\sigma) \mid \sigma \in I\}$$

Then $(T, T^\sharp, \alpha)$ is a correct abstraction from Σ to $\Sigma^\sharp$. Moreover, given T and α, $T^\sharp$ provides the best possible abstraction in the sense that if $(T, \langle M', I' \rangle, \alpha)$ is another correct abstraction, then $M^\sharp \leq M'$ and $I^\sharp \subseteq I'$.

Proof. The proof follows from the facts that $Id \leq \alpha^\uparrow \circ \alpha$ and $\alpha \circ \alpha^\uparrow \leq Id$.

The above definitions and properties deal with the matrix view of the semantics, but what can be said about traces? The following proposition states that for each program trace, there exists an "abstract" trace of same length which costs are given by the induced abstract matrix. This property will be useful for ensuring the correctness of abstractions in Section 4.

Proposition 5. *Let consider the transition system $T = \langle q, I \rangle$ with $I \subseteq \Sigma$ its set of initial states and $q : \Sigma \times \Sigma \rightarrow Q$ its quantitative transition system in the cost dioid Q. Let α be an abstraction function from Σ to $\Sigma^\sharp$. Let $T^\sharp = \langle q^\sharp, I^\sharp \rangle$ an abstract transition system defined by:*

- $I^\sharp = \{\alpha(\sigma) \mid \sigma \in I\}$
- $\alpha^{-1} : \Sigma^\sharp \to \mathcal{P}(\Sigma)$ with $\alpha^{-1}(\sigma^\sharp) = \{\sigma \mid \alpha(\sigma) = \sigma^\sharp\}$
- $q^*(\Sigma_1, \Sigma_2) = \displaystyle\bigoplus_{(\sigma_1,\sigma_2) \in \Sigma_1 \times \Sigma_2} q(\sigma_1, \sigma_2)$
- $q^\sharp(\sigma_1^\sharp, \sigma_2^\sharp) = q^*(\alpha^{-1}(\sigma_1^\sharp), \alpha^{-1}(\sigma_2^\sharp))$

then forall $t = \sigma_0 \to^{q_0} \ldots \sigma_n \in [\![T]\!]_{tr}, |t| = n$, there exists $t^\sharp = \sigma_0^\sharp \to^{q_0'} \ldots \sigma_n^\sharp \in$ $[\![T^\sharp]\!]_{tr}, |t| = n$ such that $q_i \leq q_i'$ $\forall i \in [0, n-1]$ and $\sigma_i^\sharp = \alpha(\sigma_i)$ $\forall i \in [0, n]$. In addition, $M^\sharp = \alpha^\uparrow \circ M \circ \alpha^\uparrow$ is the transition matrix for $q^\sharp$.

3.4   Running Example: Abstraction

In 2.3, we introduced a quantitative semantics describing the number of cache misses in read access. M is the matrix describing this quantitative semantics for the factorial program (see Figure 2 for the code). The exact computation of the semantics would be too costly, even if we work with bounded numerical domains. In this subsection, we are using the abstractions techniques in order to compute an abstract semantics $M^\sharp$ from the matrix M.

We abstract a concrete state by the instruction pointer and the k last data accessed. Within this abstract domain, the loss of information lies in three points:

- Values (*i.e.* locals, stack and heap) are forgotten. This prevents us from determining the value of branching condition.
- The cache size is reduced to k elements. When k grows, precision increase, and so do the cost of the analysis.
- The method call stack is forgotten. We turn the analysis into an intra-procedural one, not for efficiency but for clearer notation, as our factorial function involves only one non-recursive function.

We write the abstract state as $(ip, [v_1, \ldots, v_k])$ where ip is the instruction pointer and $[v_1, \ldots, v_k]$ is a list of logical addresses of the last data accessed, v_k being the most recent. s.0 refers to the bottom element of the local stack, 1.x refers to the local variable called x in the source code. We recall that we use the dioid $Q = (\overline{\mathbb{R}}, \mathtt{max}, +)$.

$$M^\sharp = \begin{pmatrix} & | \ldots 9, [1.x, \mathbf{s}.0] \ldots 9, [1.i, 1.x, \mathbf{s}.0] \ldots \\ \vdots & & \\ 8, [] & 1 & \bot \\ 8, [1.x] & 0 & \bot \\ 8, [\mathbf{s}.0] & 1 & \bot \\ 8, [\mathbf{s}.0, 1.x] & 0 & \bot \\ 8, [1.x, \mathbf{s}.0] & 0 & \bot \\ 8, [1.i, 1.x] & \bot & 0 \\ 8, [1.i] & \bot & 1 \\ \vdots & & \end{pmatrix}$$

Fig. 3. Transition matrix

We construct the abstract matrix associated to our abstract system. Its size is bounded in terms of the cardinality of $\mathcal{I}$, the set of all instruction pointers appearing in program P, and the number of up-to-k-combinations of the different logical data used in this function (which form a finite set $\mathcal{L}$). A value $q^\sharp$ of this matrix, standing at row $a^\sharp$ and column $b^\sharp$ ($a^\sharp$ and $b^\sharp$ are two abstract states), is computed in this way: let A and B be the set of concrete states abstracted by $a^\sharp$ and $b^\sharp$. Then $q^\sharp = \bigoplus\{q \mid a \to^q b, a \in A, b \in B\}$. For example

- $\sigma = (8, [1.x]) \to^0 (9, [1.x, \mathbf{s}.0]) = \sigma'$,
  Whatever the concrete state and its precise values, if it is abstracted by σ, then it can turn into a state abstracted by σ' for a cost of 0 read miss.
- $\sigma = (8, [\mathbf{s}.0]) \to^1 (9, [1.x, \mathbf{s}.0]) = \sigma'$,
  In the same way, all states abtracted by σ can generate up to one read miss on their next instruction, turning into states abstracted by σ'.

Recall that the load x instruction at line 8 accesses these memory locations: $[read_\tau(\texttt{local}.f.i); write_\tau(\texttt{stack}.f.t+1)]$ with i the local variable, t the current stack height and f the current frame.

A $\perp$-transition denotes an incompatibility between the two abstract states, either in its control flow or its the cache evolution. Most of the matrix will be filled by $\perp$. This kind of matrix is called sparse matrix, and permits the use of particularly small representations together with efficient algorithms. Figure 3 gives a submatrix of the abstract matrix $M^\sharp \in \mathcal{M}_{(\mathcal{I} \times \{\emptyset \cup \mathcal{L} \cup \mathcal{L}^2\})^2}(Q)$.

4   Long-Run Cost

So far, we have seen that all single-transition costs can be summarized in a transition matrix. We now use this matrix and the mathematical results of dioid algebra to define a notion of long run cost for a whole program. In [20] we proposed a notion of *global cost* of a program, representing its cost from initial to final states. It correctly deals with programs which are meant to terminate, but in some cases this global cost turns out to be $\top$, in particular when it is evaluated on a coarse abstraction of the initial system. Getting $\top$ as a result for the global cost is rather unsatisfactory as it does not tell anything about the concrete cost. For this case and for the case of programs which are not meant to terminate (as reactive systems), we propose the notion of *long-run cost*, that represents a maximal average cost over cycles of transitions. This terminology is taken from [2,9], in the context of probabilistic processes modelled by Markov decision processes. Behaviour patterns of interest (described by labelled graphs) are associated to real numbers representing the success or the duration of the pattern, and extensions of branching time temporal logics are proposed in order to measure their long-run average outcome.

The average cost of a finite path is defined as the arithmetical mean (w.r.t. the $\otimes$ operator) of the costs labelling its transitions. In other words, it is the nth root of the global cost of the path, where n is its length. We write $\tilde{q}(\pi) = \sqrt[|\pi|]{q(\pi)}$ for the average cost of path π, where $q(\pi)$ is the global cost of π, and $|\pi|$ its length. The "maximum" average cost of all cycles in the graph will be the quantity we are interested in: this quantity will be called *long-run cost*. The following example illustrates these notions on a simple graph.

Average cost of path abc $= (8+3)/2 = 5.5$
Cycle bcdb average cost $= (3+4+5)/3 = 4$
Cycle cc average cost $= 2/1 = 2$
Long-run cost $= \max(4,2) = 4$

By the properties of the dioids we consider, matrix M^k sums up the transition costs of all paths of length k. The diagonal of this matrix thus contains the costs of all cycles of length k. If we add up all the elements on this diagonal, we get the trace of the matrix. This observation gives rise to the following definition.

Definition 11. *Let P be a program having $T = \langle M, I \rangle$ for transition system. Let R be M restricted to the set of states, Σ, reachable from I. The long-run cost of program P is defined as the long-run cost of T*

$$\rho(P) = \rho(T) = \bigoplus_{k=1}^{|\Sigma|} \sqrt[k]{tr\, R^k} \quad \text{where} \quad tr\, R = \bigoplus_{1}^{|\Sigma|} R_{i,i}.$$

Note that this definition is valid even for an infinite number of states, since we work with complete dioids. As an example, if we work in the dioid $(Time, \max, +)$, where $Time$ is isomorphic to $\overline{\mathbb{R}}$, $\rho(P)$ is the maximal average of time spent per instruction, where the average is computed on any cycle by dividing the total time spent in the cycle by the number of instructions in this cycle. In the case of a finite set of states, the long-run cost is computable, and we note in the passing that its definition coincides with the definition of the maximum of eigenvalues of the matrix, in the case of an irreducible matrix in an idempotent semiring [11].

4.1   Semantics of the Long Run Cost

The following proposition establishes in a more formal manner the link between this definition of long-run cost and the cycles of the semantics.

Proposition 6. *Let Γ be the set of cycles in T. Then $\rho(T) = \bigoplus_{c \in \Gamma} \tilde{q}(c)$.*

The idea of the proof is to show that the cycles of length less than $|\Sigma|$ are enough to know average costs, and that a partition of these cycles is related with the different iterates of the matrix appearing in Definition 11. The proof becomes straightforward in the case of an infinite set of states.

As we aim at giving a characterisation of the asymptotic behaviour of a program, an alternative definition for long-run cost could have been:

$$lrc(T) = \limsup_{n \to \infty} \bigoplus_{\substack{t \in [\![T]\!]_{tr} \\ |t|=n}} \tilde{q}(t)$$

Instead of defining the long-run cost w.r.t. the cycles, this definition considers arbitrarily long traces. Unlike $\rho(P)$, $lrc(P)$ is not suitable for computation, even if the set of states is finite. We will see in Subsection 4.3 that those two notions coincide in a restricted class of cost dioids and when the set of states is finite.

4.2 Ensuring Correctness

The question that naturally arises is to know if the notion of long-run cost is preserved by abstraction. The following theorem states that a correct abstraction gives an over-approximation of the concrete long-run cost.

Theorem 2. *If $(T, T^\sharp, \alpha)$ is a correct abstraction, then $\rho(T) \leq_Q \rho(T^\sharp)$.*

The proof of theorem relies on the fact that the correctness is preserved when the concrete and abstract matrices are iterated simultaneously [10].

Recall that Proposition 5 states that for any concrete trace, there exists an abstract trace which cost is over the concrete one. It follows that the alternative definition of long-run cost given in Section 4.1 is also preserved by abstraction:

Proposition 7. *If $(T, T^\sharp, \alpha)$ is a correct abstraction, then*

$$\limsup_{n \to \infty} \bigoplus_{\substack{t \in \llbracket T \rrbracket_{tr} \\ |t| = n}} \tilde{q}(t) \leq \limsup_{n \to \infty} \bigoplus_{\substack{t^\sharp \in \llbracket T^\sharp \rrbracket_{tr} \\ |t^\sharp| = n}} \tilde{q}^\sharp(t^\sharp)$$

4.3 Traces Meet Cycles

We now show that, if Σ is finite, and for dioids where the carrier set is $\mathbb{R}$ and operator $\otimes$ is the arithmetical $+$ (so that the nth root operator corresponds to division by n), the notion of long-run cost defined w.r.t. accessible cycles coincides with the notion of long-run cost defined as the limit of the maximum average cost of traces which length tends to infinity. To establish this result, we have to show that the cost of a prefix of a trace becomes negligible when this trace becomes arbitrarily long. We thus impose the following hypothesis:

Hypothesis 1 *All transitions δ which are not in a cycle verify $q(\delta) \neq +\infty$.*

Hypothesis 1 excludes certain pathological matrices with atomic operations that have infinite costs. If a cycle contains a $+\infty$ transition, the ρ value indicates it.

Theorem 3. *Let $T = \langle M, I \rangle$ be a transition system with $M \in \Sigma \times \Sigma \to Q$. If Σ is finite and Q is a cost dioid where the carrier set is $\mathbb{R}$ and operation $\otimes$ is the arithmetical $+$, then with Hypothesis 1, we have*

$$\rho(T) = \lim_{n \to \infty} \bigoplus_{\substack{t \in \llbracket T \rrbracket_{tr} \\ |t| = n}} \tilde{q}(t)$$

This theorem establishes a link between the semantics and a computable definition of the long-run cost. The key points of the proof are to ensure that this limit exist, and to show that a small part of a trace can be neglected for very long traces. This is proved by bounding $\bigoplus \tilde{q}(t)$ [10].

4.4   Running Example: Long-Run Cost

To illustrate the use of the long-run cost (ρ), we will consider a cache which can contain 4 integers. Such a small size could seem weird to the reader and unrealistic for a cache size, but the term cache can be interpreted here as some kind of registers. The semantics of the factorial program is abstracted as described in Section 3.4, with $k = 4$. Using Definition 11, we compute $\rho(M^\sharp) = 2/9$, meaning that in an execution long enough, we observe on average 2 cache misses each 9 instructions. A prototype is under developement for the standard Java bytecode, that already handles this kind of example. It implements the analysis technique presented in this paper with the help of an existing Scilab library for max-plus algebra, that offers an efficient ways to compute the long-run cost (sparse matrices and Howard's algorithm for eigenvalues [11]).

If we now consider a FIFO replacement policy for the same 4 integer registers, we obtain a different long-run cost. The FIFO policy implementation is cheaper in electronic components than the LRU one, but the analysis of the factorial function says that $\rho = 4/9$, $i.e.$, that we now have on average 4 cache misses for 9 instruction executed. Such a slowdown is coherent with the observations that small cache memory requires more advanced cache policies.

5   Related Work

The present work is inspired by the quantitative abstract interpretation framework developed by Di Pierro and Wiklicky [15]. We have followed their approach in modeling programs as linear operators over a vector space, with the notable technical difference that their operators act over a semiring of probabilities whereas ours work with idempotent dioids. Working with idempotent dioids means that we have been able to exploit known results from Discrete Event Systems theory which makes intensive use of such structures. Another difference with respect to [15] lies in the kind of program being analyzed: we have been considering an intermediate bytecode language rather than declarative languages (probablistic concurrent constraint programming and the lambda calculus [14]).

In Di Pierro and Wiklicky's work, the relation with abstract interpretation is justified by the use of the pseudo-inverse of a linear operator, similar to a Galois connection mechanism, enforcing the soundness of abstractions. Our approach can be seen as intermediate between their and classical abstract interpretation: on one hand, we use residuation theory in order to get a pseudo-inverse for linear abstraction functions; on the other hand, we benefit from the partially ordered structure of dioids to give guarantees of soundness under the assumption $\alpha \circ M \leq_D M^\sharp \circ \alpha$, which is a classical requirement in abstract interpretation.

Several other works make use of idempotent semiring for describing quantitative aspects of computations, namely under the form of constraint semirings [8]. Recently, these have been used in the field of Quality of Services [13], in particular with systems modelled by graph rewriting mechanisms [18]. In all these approaches, the $\oplus$ and $\otimes$ operators of the constraint semiring are used for combining constraints. In [5], Aziz makes use of semirings in a mobile process calculus derived from the π-calculus, in order to model the cost of communicating actions. He also defines a static analysis framework, by abstracting "concrete" semirings into abstract semirings of reduced cardinality, and defining abstract semiring operators accordingly. For instance, the $(\mathbb{R}_+ \cup \{+\infty\}, \min, +)$ semiring can be abstracted by a $(\{low, medium, high\}, \min, \max)$ one. Even if dealing with dioids as we do, none of these approaches make use of a notion of long-run cost to express an average quantitative behaviour of a system.

In the specific context of Java bytecode, Albert and al. [1] defined a cost analysis based on the generation of cost relations and recurrence equations. Approximation of costs is done in two steps: first, a classical abstract interpretation is used to approximate size relations between variables. Secondly, combining size relations then gives recurrence equations whose solutions are approximated by using intervals when no closed form solution has been found. This gives interesting results for a class of simple programs, in particular when arithmetic operations are restricted to linear ones.

Our running example of estimating cache usage is meant for illustrative purposes and is based on a rather abstract view of cache analysis, compared e.g. to the detailed modeling and cache abstraction of Wilhelm and al. [3] who propose in the AbsInt tool a cache behaviour prediction by abstract interpretation. Three points of their work could be almost directly used in our framework: the various models of cache (e.g. direct-mapped, A-way) to implement our update function, their abstract domain, in order to design our quantitative abstractions, and their observations about caches and writing, in order to develop an accurate model. Their approach however is not directed toward long-run cost computation.

6   Conclusion

We have shown how to abstract the long-run cost of programs whose operational semantics is defined as transition systems labelled by costs taken from a particular kind of dioids. In such cases, we have shown that the semantics is a linear operator over the moduloid associated to this dioid. We have used a well-known characterization of the asymptotic behaviour of a discrete event system to define the notion of long-run cost of such a semantics, and proposed a novel way of analyzing the long-run behaviour of the program. We have characterized this long-run cost as being a maximal average cost per transition on very long traces of the semantics. Computing the exact long-run cost of a program is in general too expensive, so we have extended the linear operator framework with a notion of abstraction of the semantics which is also expressed as a linear operator. A correctness relation between concrete and abstract semantic matrices ensures that the cost computed from the abstract semantics is an over-approximation of the concrete one. The notions of dioids, quantitative semantics, abstraction and long-run cost have been illustrated all along the paper through a cache miss analysis on a program written in a simple bytecode language.

Future work. The examples in the paper have been computed both by hand (for the abstraction part) and by a prototype analyzer for the computation of long-run costs themselves. Future work includes improvement of the prototype and developement of a framework for validating experimental results.

An interesting avenue for further work would be to relax the correctness criterion so that the abstract estimate is "close" to (but not necessarily greater than) the exact quantity. For certain quantitative measures, a notion of "closeness" might be of interest, as opposed to the qualitative case where static analyses must err on the safe side.

References

1. Albert, E., Arenas, P., Genaim, S., Puebla, G., Zanardini, D.: Cost Analysis of Java Bytecode. In: De Nicola, R. (ed.) ESOP 2007. LNCS, vol. 4421, pp. 157–172. Springer, Heidelberg (2007)
2. Alfaro, L.D.: How to Specify and Verify the Long-Run Average Behavior of Probabilistic Systems. In: 13th Symposium on Logic in Computer Science (LICS 1998), pp. 174–183. IEEE Computer Society Press, Los Alamitos (1998)
3. Alt, M., Ferdinand, C., Martin, F., Wilhelm, R.: Cache Behavior Prediction by Abstract Interpretation. In: Cousot, R., Schmidt, D.A. (eds.) SAS 1996. LNCS, vol. 1145, pp. 51–66. Springer, Heidelberg (1996)
4. Aspinall, D., Beringer, L., Hofmann, M., Loidl, H.-W., Momigliano, A.: A program logic for resources. Theor. Comput. Sci. 389(3), 411–445 (2007)
5. Aziz, B.: A Semiring-based Quantitative Analysis of Mobile Systems. Electronic Notes in Theoretical Computer Science 157(1), 3–21 (2006)
6. Baccelli, F., Cohen, G., Olsder, G.J., Quadrat, J.-P.: Synchronization and Linearity. Wiley, Chichester (1992)
7. Bistarelli, S., Gadducci, F.: Enhancing Constraints Manipulation in Semiring-Based Formalisms. In: European Conf. on Artificial Intelligence, pp. 63–67 (2006)
8. Bistarelli, S., Montanari, U., Rossi, F.: Semiring-Based Constraint Satisfaction and Optimization. Journal of the ACM 44(2), 201–236 (1997)
9. Brazdil, T., Esparza, J., Kucera, A.: Analysis and Prediction of the Long-Run Behavior of Probabilistic Sequential Programs with Recursion. In: FOCS 2005: Proceedings of the 46th Annual IEEE Symposium on Foundations of Computer Science, Washington, DC, USA, pp. 521–530. IEEE Computer Society, Los Alamitos (2005)
10. Cachera, D., Jensen, T., Jobin, A., Sotin, P.: Long-run cost analysis by approximation of linear operators over dioids. Research Report 6338, INRIA (2007)
11. Cochet-Terrasson, J., Cohen, G., Gaubert, S., Mc Gettrick, M., Quadrat, J.-P.: Numerical Computation of Spectral Elements in Max-Plus Algebra. In: Proceedings of the IFAC Conference on System Structure and Control (1998)
12. Cousot, P., Cousot, R.: Abstract Interpretation: A Unified Lattice Model for Static Analysis of Programs by Construction or Approximation of Fixpoints. In: 4th Symposium on Principles of Programming Languages (POPL 1977) (1977)
13. De Nicola, R., Ferrari, G., Montanari, U., Pugliese, R., Tuosto, E.: A Basic Calculus for Modelling Service Level Agreements. In: Jacquet, J.-M., Picco, G.P. (eds.) COORDINATION 2005. LNCS, vol. 3454. Springer, Heidelberg (2005)
14. Di Pierro, A., Hankin, C., Wiklicky, H.: Probabilistic λ-calculus and Quantitative Program Analysis. J. Logic and Computation 15(2), 159–179 (2005)

15. Di Pierro, A., Wiklicky, H.: Concurrent Constraint Programming: Towards Probabilistic Abstract Interpretation. In: PPDP (2000)
16. Freund, S.N., Mitchell, J.C.: A Formal Framework for the Java Bytecode Language and Verifier. ACM SIGPLAN Notices 34(10), 147–166 (1999)
17. Gondran, M., Minoux, M.: Graphes, dioïdes et semi-anneaux. Tec & Doc (2001)
18. Hirsch, D., Tuosto, E.: SHReQ: Coordinating Application Level QoS. In: SEFM 2005: Proceedings of the Third IEEE International Conference on Software Engineering and Formal Methods, Washington, DC, USA, pp. 425–434 (2005)
19. Siveroni, I.: Operational Semantics of the Java Card Virtual Machine. J. Logic and Automated Reasoning (2004)
20. Sotin, P., Cachera, D., Jensen, T.: Quantitative Static Analysis over Semirings: Analysing Cache Behaviour for Java Card. In: Di Pierro, A., Wiklicky, H. (eds.) QAPL 2006, Quantitative Aspects of Programming Languages (2006)

Towards Validating a Platoon of Cristal Vehicles Using CSP‖B*

Samuel Colin[1], Arnaud Lanoix[1],
Olga Kouchnarenko[2], and Jeanine Souquières[1]

[1] LORIA – DEDALE Team – Campus scientifique
F-54506 Vandoeuvre-Lès-Nancy
`firstname.lastname@loria.fr`
[2] LIFC – TFC Team – 16 route de Gray
F-25030 Besançon
`firstname.lastname@lifc.univ-fcomte.fr`

Abstract. The so-called platooning problem consists in making autonomous vehicles move in a convoy. It crosses several domains: distributed systems, embedded systems, multi-agent systems and critical systems. We thus propose to use the combination named CSP‖B of two well-known formal methods to assess and verify properties of this complex system. To that end we make use of previous theoretical results on CSP‖B. We also illustrate how this methodology spans the multiple composition levels of the resulting model.

Keywords: formal methods, CSP‖B, distributed systems, case study, platooning.

1 Introduction

This paper is dedicated to the validation of land transportation systems. These systems, which are both distributed and embedded, require the expression of functional as well as non functional-properties, for example time-constrained response and availability of required services. Their dual nature is problematic: distributedness may exhibit behaviours hard to understand while embeddedness imposes the satisfaction of safety/security/confidence requirements.

To address this problem we use the CSP‖B combination [1] of well-established formal methods, CSP [2] and B [3]. Our case study is a convoy of so-called Cristal vehicles seen as a multi-agent system which evolves following the Influence/Reaction model (I/R) [4] in which agents are described separately from the environment.

This convoy, called a *platoon*, is a set of autonomous vehicles which have to move following the path of the leader in a row. Its control concerns both a longitudinal control, i.e. maintaining an *ideal* distance between each vehicle, and a lateral control, i.e. each vehicle should follow the track of its predecessor. As both controls can be studied independently [5] we will only focus on the longitudinal one. The Cristal driving

* This work is supported by the French National Research Agency ANR-06-SETI-017 TACOS project, (`http://tacos.loria.fr`), and the pôle de compétitivité Alsace/Franche-Comté/CRISTAL project (`http://www.projet-cristal.net`).

J. Meseguer and G. Roşu (Eds.): AMAST 2008, LNCS 5140, pp. 139–144, 2008.

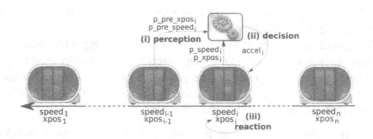

Fig. 1. A platoon of Cristals

system perceives information about its environment before producing an instantaneous acceleration passed to its engine. As we consider only longitudinal control, we represent the position of the ith Cristal by a single variable $xpos_i$ and its velocity by $speed_i$. The behaviour of the Cristal controllers can be summarised as follows, see Fig. 1:

(i) perception step: each Cristal driving system receives its velocity p_speed_i and its position p_xpos_i, from the physical part of the Cristal. Furthermore, it receives by network communication the velocity $p\_pre\_speed_i$ and the position $p\_pre\_xpos_i$ of its leading Cristal;

(ii) decision step: each Cristal driving system can influence its speed and position by computing and sending to its engine an instantaneous acceleration $accel_i$. The acceleration can be negative, corresponding to the braking of the Cristal;

(iii) reaction step: $xpos_i$ and $speed_i$ are updated, depending on the current speed $speed_i$ of the Cristal and a decided instantaneous acceleration $accel_i$ of the engine.

Our approach is "bottom-up"-oriented: B machines describe the various components of a Cristal vehicle while CSP expresses their assembly at the level of a single vehicle and at the level of the whole convoy[1]. Our experience shows that writing and checking CSP‖B specifications can help eliminate errors and ambiguities in an assembly and its communication protocols.

2   Theoretical Background on CSP‖B

CSP‖B is a combination of formal methods aimed at exploiting the best features of CSP and B, which happen to complement each other. Indeed, basic components are B machines interacting with the rest of the world through operation calls. The assembly is provided by CSP whose processes describe how B machines are scheduled and communicate with each other. We don't explain here the B and CSP semantics though for lack of space.

The main problem with combined specifications is *consistency*: CSP and B parts should not be contradictory. The consistency is obtained through a verification

---

[1] CSP‖B specifications are available at http://tacos.loria.fr/platoon.zip.

technique [6] consisting of verifying the *divergence-freedom* of a B machine-CSP process coupling, and its *deadlock-freedom*.

The divergence-freedom of (P‖M) can be deduced by using a technique based on *Control Loop Invariants* (CLI) [1]. Divergence-freedom is verified by exhibiting a predicate that holds for each possible path the process P can take. Let $BBODY_{S(p)}$ be the rewriting of the pth path S(p) of P into B using the translation rules of [1]. Here are the most important theorems we will use throughout this paper:

Theorem 1 ([7, Theorem 1]). *If there exists a predicate CLI such that for each $BBODY_{S(p)}$ in P, CLI $\wedge$ I $\Rightarrow$ [$BBODY_{S(p)}$] CLI, then (P‖M) is divergence-free.*

The deadlock-freedom of (P‖M) can be deduced by establishing the deadlock-freedom of the P part.

Theorem 2 ([6, Theorem 5.9]). *If P is a CSP controller for M with no blocking assertion on any machine channels of M, and P is deadlock-free in the stable failures model, then (P‖M) is deadlock-free in the stable failures model.*

The following result is useful for establishing safety properties of controlled components. It means that the trace refinement established purely for the CSP part of a controlled component suffices to ensure the trace refinement for the overall component.

Corollary 1 ([6, Corollary 7.2]). *For any controller P and any B machine M, one has if S $\sqsubseteq_T$ P then S $\sqsubseteq_T$ (P‖M).*

The given results are also generalised in [6] to a collection of B machine-CSP process couples.

3 Specifying a Single Cristal

A Cristal vehicle is composed of two parts: its engine and a driving system, as depicted in Fig. 2. Each part is built upon a B machine controlled by an associated CSP process.

The properties we want to be ensured by the model are deadlock-freedom of communications between components of the vehicle and accuracy of the information about position and speed. The former property is motivated by the fact that a vehicle could become stuck because two components wait for each other. The latter property can be interpreted as the fact that a decided acceleration should match as closely as possible the perceptions. A solution then can be to force the Cristal to alternate between "perception mode" and "reaction mode". This is what we strive for as a safety property.

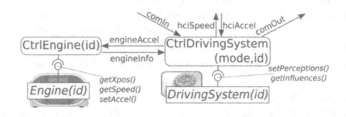

Fig. 2. Architectural view of a Cristal

3.1 The Engine

```
MODEL Engine(Id)
VARIABLES
  speed, xpos
OPERATIONS
  speed0 ⟵ getSpeed = ...
  xpos0 ⟵ getXpos = ...
  setAccel(accel) =
    PRE
      accel ∈ MIN_ACCEL..MAX_ACCEL
    THEN
      ANY new_speed
      WHERE new_speed = speed + accel
      THEN
        IF (new_speed > MAX_SPEED)
        THEN
          xpos := xpos + MAX_SPEED
          ‖ speed := MAX_SPEED
        ELSE
          IF (new_speed < 0)
          THEN
            xpos := xpos − (speed × speed) / (2 × accel)
            ‖ speed := 0
          ELSE
            xpos := xpos + speed + accel / 2
            ‖ speed := new_speed
          END
        END
      END
    END
END
```

The engine is built upon a B machine that describes its knowledge about its current speed and position, and its reaction when passed a new instantaneous acceleration.

The CtrlEngine CSP controller alternates PerEngine and ActEngine. In PerEngine, we call through getSpeed?speed and getXpos?xpos the homonymous B methods to retrieve the speed and the position of the Cristal which are then passed on to engineInfo.id!xpos!speed. In ActEngine, a new instantaneous acceleration is received through engineAccel.id?accel and passed on through setAccel!accel to the B machine which calculates the vehicle position and speed updates w.r.t. this new acceleration.

The whole engine component is then defined as the composition, for a given id, of the Engine(id) machine and its CtrlEngine(id) controller.

```
PerEngine(id) =
    getXpos ? xpos → getSpeed ? speed → engineInfo.id ! xpos ! speed → ActEngine(id)
    □
    getSpeed ? speed → getXpos ? xpos → engineInfo.id ! xpos ! speed → ActEngine(id)
ActEngine(id) =
    engineAccel.id ? accel → setAccel ! accel → PerEngine(id)
CtrlEngine(id) = PerEngine(id)
```

Verification. The Engine(Id) B machine consistency is successfully checked using B4Free. The CtrlEngine(id) controller *deadlock-freedom* (in the stable failures model) and its *divergence-freedom* are successfully checked with FDR2.

The composition of the B machine and the controller is verified for *divergence-freedom* by applying Theorem 1: it is specific to CSP‖B and is not supported by tools hence the translation to B is done by hand. The chosen CLI is actually as simple as the ⊤ predicate modulo the mandatory typing predicates. Then, by way of Theorem 1, we deduce that (CtrlEngine(id) ‖ Engine(id)) is divergence-free. *Deadlock-freedom* of (CtrlEngine(id) ‖ Engine(id)) is obtained from the deadlock-freedom of CtrlEngine(id) and the application of Theorem 2 as well.

3.2 The Driving System

The (CtrlDrivingSystem‖DrivingSystem) controller‖B machine construction is built in a similar way. This driving system can update its perceptions and decide of an acceleration passed to the engine later on. hciSpeed, hciAccel correspond to the interaction with a human driver (if the vehicle is in SINGLE or LEADER mode). comIn and comOut correspond to the interaction with the leading and following vehicle (**PLATOON** mode). engineInfo and engineAccel are used to exchange with the engine.

Using the same techniques and theorems as for the engine, the driving system is shown divergence-free and deadlock-free.

3.3   The Cristal(mode,id) Assembly

A Cristal is defined as the composition of the engine and the driving system:

$$Cristal(mode,id) = (CtrlDrivingSystem(mode,id) \parallel DrivingSystem(id))$$
$$\parallel_{\{lengineInfo,\ engineAccell\}} (CtrlEngine(id) \parallel Engine(id))$$

Divergence-freedom is obtained by applying the generalised version of Theorem 1 to the divergence-freedom of both components (CtrlEngine(id) ∥ Engine(id)) and (CtrlDri vingSystem(mode,id)∥DrivingSystem(id)). Deadlock-freedom of the Cristal stems from deadlock-freedom of (CtrlEngine(id) ∥ CtrlDrivingSystem(mode,id)) and by applying the generalised version of Theorem 2.

Let us note that earlier versions of the models had deadlocks exhibited by the FDR2 tool: having access to the faulty traces helped us understand the errors and modify the driving system controller with a tighter scheduling leading to deadlock-freedom.

Safety Property. The property stating that perception and reaction should always alternate can be re-expressed as a CSP process:

$$Property(id) = engineInfo.id?xpos?speed \rightarrow engineAccel.id?accel \rightarrow Property(id)$$

Checking that the Cristal meets this property is akin to checking that there is a trace refinement between it and the Cristal. This is achieved by checking that Property(id) $\sqsubseteq_T$ CtrlEngine(id) ∥ CtrlDrivingSystem2(mode,id), from which it can be deduced by Corollary 1 that Property(id) $\sqsubseteq_T$ Cristal (mode,id): the property is refined hence satisfied.

4   Specifying a Platoon of Cristals

Once we have a correct model for a single Cristal, we can focus on the specification of a platoon, as shown Fig. 3. We want the Cristals to avoid going stale when they are in the **PLATOON** mode. This might happen because one Cristal waits for information from its leading Cristal, for instance, i.e. the communications are deadlocked.

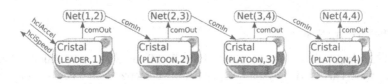

Fig. 3. A Platoon of four Cristals

The first Cristal of the platoon runs in the LEADER mode, while the others run in the PLATOON mode. A process Net(id,id2) is associated with each Cristal for managing communication: it receives information from id before sending these data to id2. Finally, the platoon is defined by the parallel composition of all the Cristals and all the Nets, synchronised on the communication channels:

$$Platoon(n) = (Cristal(LEADER,1) \ ||| \ (|||_{d:\{2..n\}} \ Cristal(PLATOON,id)))$$
$$||_{\{comIn,comOut\}} \ ((|||_{d:\{1..n-1\}} \ Net(id,id+1)) \ ||| \ Net(n,n))$$

Verification. Using FDR2, we successfully check that Net(id,id2) is deadlock-free and divergence-free. As each Cristal and each Net have been proved divergence-free, the platoon is divergence-free. To achieve consistency checking, the parallel composition of the CSP parts of each Cristal and Net is shown deadlock-free, thanks to FDR2. Consequently, by Theorem 2 the platoon is deadlock-free too. This verification validates that the communications (expressed through the Nets components) do not deadlock.

5   Conclusion

The development of a new type of urban vehicle and the need for its certification necessitate their formal specification and validation. We propose a formal CSP∥B specification development of an autonomous vehicle's components, and an architecture for assembling vehicles in a convoy to follow the path of the leader vehicle in a row. Application of known results to the composition in the CSP∥B framework and verification using existing tools – the FDR2 model-checker and the B4Free prover – allow us to ensure the consistency of the whole multi-agent system, in a compositional manner. Having formal CSP∥B specifications helps – by establishing refinement relations – in preventing incompatibility among various implementations. Moreover, writing formal specifications helps in designing a way to manage the multiple architectural levels.

References

1. Treharne, H., Schneider, S.: Using a process algebra to control B OPERATIONS. In: 1st International Conference on Integrated Formal Methods, pp. 437–457. Springer, Heidelberg (1999)
2. Hoare, C.A.R.: Communicating Sequential Processes. Prentice-Hall, Englewood Cliffs (1985)
3. Abrial, J.R.: The B Book. Cambridge University Press, Cambridge (1996)
4. Ferber, J., Muller, J.P.: Influences and reaction: a model of situated multiagent systems. In: 2nd Int. Conf. on Multi-agent Systems, pp. 72–79 (1996)
5. Daviet, P., Parent, M.: Longitudinal and lateral servoing of vehicles in a platoon. In: Proceeding of the IEEE Intelligent Vehicles Symposium, pp. 41–46 (1996)
6. Schneider, S.A., Treharne, H.E.: CSP theorems for communicating B machines. Formal Aspects of Computing, Special issue of IFM 2004 (2005)
7. Schneider, S., Treharne, H.: Communicating B machines. In: Bert, D., Bowen, J.P., Henson, M.C., Robinson, K. (eds.) B 2002 and ZB 2002. LNCS, vol. 2272, pp. 416–435. Springer, Heidelberg (2002)

Explaining Verification Conditions

Ewen Denney[1] and Bernd Fischer[2]

[1] USRA/RIACS, NASA Ames Research Center, Moffett Field, CA 94035, USA
Ewen.W.Denney@nasa.gov
[2] DSSE Group, School of Electronics and Computer Science, University of Southampton, UK
B.Fischer@ecs.soton.ac.uk

Abstract. Hoare-style program verification relies on the construction and discharge of verification conditions (VCs) but offers no support to trace, analyze, and understand the VCs themselves. We describe a systematic extension of the Hoare rules by labels so that the calculus itself can be used to build up *explanations* of the VCs. The labels are maintained through the different processing steps and rendered as natural language explanations. The generated explanations are based only on an analysis of the labels rather than directly on the logical meaning of the underlying VCs or their proofs. The explanations can be customized to capture different aspects of the VCs; here, we focus on labelings that explain their structure and purpose.

1 Introduction

Program verification is easy when automated tools do all the work: a verification condition generator (VCG) takes a program that is "marked-up" with logical annotations (i.e., pre-/post-conditions and invariants) and produces a number of verification conditions (VCs) that are simplified, completed by a domain theory, and finally discharged by an automated theorem prover (ATP). In practice, however, many things can, and typically do, go wrong: the program may be incorrect or unsafe, the annotations may be incorrect or incomplete, the simplifier may be too weak, the domain theory may be incomplete, or the ATP may run out of resources. In each of these cases, users are typically confronted only with failed VCs (i.e., the failure to prove them automatically) but receive no additional information about the causes of the failure. They must thus analyze the VCs, interpret their constituent parts, and relate them through the applied Hoare rules and simplifications to the corresponding source code fragments. Even if all VCs can be proven automatically, there is often still a need to understand their intent, for example if the formal verification is being used to support a code review. Unfortunately, VCs are a detailed, low-level representation of both the underlying information and the process used to derive it, so understanding them is often difficult.

Here we describe an technique that helps users to trace and understand VCs. Our idea is to systematically extend the Hoare rules by "semantic mark-up" so that we can use the calculus itself to build up *explanations* of the VCs. This mark-up takes the form of structured *labels* that are attached to the meta-variables used in the Hoare rules (or to the annotations in the program), so that the VCG produces labeled versions of the VCs. The labels are maintained through the different processing steps, and are then extracted from the final VCs and rendered as natural language explanations.

Most verification systems based on Hoare logic offer some basic tracing support by emitting the current line number whenever a VC is constructed. However, these line numbers on their own are insufficient to understand a VC since they do not provide any information as to which other parts of the program have contributed to the VC, how it has been constructed, or what its purpose is, and are thus insufficient as a basis for informative explanations. Some systems produce short captions for each VC (e.g., JACK [1] or Perfect Developer [2]). Other techniques focus on a detailed linking between source locations and VCs to support program debugging [11,12]. Our approach, in contrast, serves as a customizable basis to explain different aspects of VCs. Here, we focus on explaining the *structure* and *purpose* of VCs, helping users to understand what a VC means and how it contributes to the overall certification of a program.

In our approach we only explain what has been explicitly declared to be significant using labels. The generated explanations are based on an analysis of the labels and not of the structure or logical meaning of the underlying VCs. For example, we do not try to infer that two formulas are the base and step case of an induction and hence would not generate an explanation to that end unless the formulas are specifically marked up with this information. Finally, we restrict ourselves to explaining the construction of VCs (which is the essence of the Hoare approach) rather than their proof. Hence, we maintain, and can also introduce, labels during simplification, but strip them off before proving the VCs. Techniques for explaining proofs (e.g., [9]) provide no additional insight, and are in fact less useful for our purposes since the key information is expressed in the annotations and VCs.

We developed our technique as part of an autocode certification system [4,6], and we will use the safety verification of automatically generated code as an application example. Here, human-readable explanations of the VCs are particularly important to gain confidence into the generated code. However, our technique is not tied to either code generation or safety certification and can be used in any Hoare-style verification context. We first briefly describe the core calculus, and then its labeled extension. We also describe several refinements to the labels, which give rise to richer explanations. Some of these refinements are specific to our application domain (i.e., safety verification) while others are specific to our verification method (i.e., automated annotation).

2   Logical Background

Hoare Logic and Program Verification. We follow the usual Hoare-style program verification approach: first, a VCG applies the rules of the underlying Hoare calculus to the annotated program to produce a number of VCs, then an ATP discharges the VCs. This splits the decidable construction of the VCs from their undecidable discharge, but in return the VCs become removed from the program context, which exacerbates the understanding problem.

Here, we restrict our attention to an imperative core language which is sufficient for the programs generated by NASA's certifiable code generators, AUTOBAYES [10] and AUTOFILTER [15], and by Real-Time Workshop (RTW), a commercial code generator for Matlab. Extensions to other language constructs are straightforward, as long as the appropriate (unlabeled) Hoare rules have been formulated.

$$\text{(assign)} \quad \frac{}{Q[e/x, \text{INIT}/x_{\text{init}}] \wedge safe_{\text{init}}(e) \{x := e\} Q}$$

$$\text{(update)} \quad \frac{}{\left(\begin{array}{c} Q[upd(x, e_1, e_2)/x, upd(x_{\text{init}}, e_1, \text{INIT})/x_{\text{init}}] \\ \wedge\, safe_{\text{init}}(e_1) \wedge safe_{\text{init}}(e_2) \end{array} \right) \{x[e_1] := e_2\} Q}$$

$$\text{(if)} \quad \frac{P_1 \{c_1\} Q \quad P_2 \{c_2\} Q}{(b \Rightarrow P_1) \wedge (\neg b \Rightarrow P_2) \wedge safe_{\text{init}}(b) \{\textbf{if } b \textbf{ then } c_1 \textbf{ else } c_2\} Q}$$

$$\text{(while)} \quad \frac{P \{c\} I \quad I \wedge b \Rightarrow P \quad I \wedge \neg b \Rightarrow Q}{I \wedge safe_{\text{init}}(b) \{\textbf{while } b \textbf{ inv } I \textbf{ do } c\} Q}$$

$$\text{(for)} \quad \frac{P \{c\} I[i + 1/i] \quad I[\text{INIT}/i_{\text{init}}] \wedge e_1 \leq i \leq e_2 \Rightarrow P \quad I[e_2 + 1/i, \text{INIT}/i_{\text{init}}] \Rightarrow Q}{e_1 \leq e2 \wedge I[e_1/i] \wedge safe_{\text{init}}(e_1) \wedge safe_{\text{init}}(e_2) \{\textbf{for } i := e_1 \textbf{ to } e_2 \textbf{ inv } I \textbf{ do } c\} Q}$$

$$\text{(skip)} \frac{}{Q \{\textbf{skip}\} Q} \qquad \text{(comp)} \frac{P \{c_1\} R \quad R \{c_2\} Q}{P \{c_1 ; c_2\} Q} \qquad \text{(assert)} \frac{P' \Rightarrow P \quad P \{c\} Q' \quad Q' \Rightarrow Q}{P' \{\textbf{pre } P' \ c \textbf{ post } Q'\} Q}$$

Fig. 1. Core Hoare rules for initialization safety

Source-Level Safety Certification. Safety certification demonstrates that the execution of a program does not violate certain conditions, which are formalized as a *safety property*. A *safety policy* is a set of Hoare rules designed to show that safe programs satisfy the safety property of interest [3]. Here, the important aspect of safety certification is that the formulas in the rules have more internal structure. This can be exploited by our approach to produce more detailed explanations.

Figure 1 shows the initialization safety policy, which we will use as our main example here; we omit the rules for functions and procedures. The rules use the usual Hoare triples $P \{c\} Q$, i.e., if the condition P holds and the command c terminates, then Q holds afterwards. For example, the *assert* rule says that we must first prove that the asserted postcondition Q' implies the arbitrary incoming postcondition Q. We then compute the P as *weakest precondition* (WPC) of c for Q' and show that the asserted precondition P' implies P. The asserted precondition P' is then passed on as WPC; note that P is only WPC of the "plain" statement c, but not of the annotated statement.

Initialization safety ensures that each variable or individual array element has been explicitly assigned a value before it is used. It uses a "shadow" environment where each shadow variable x_{init} contains the value INIT after the corresponding variable x has been assigned a value; shadow arrays capture the status of the individual array elements. All statements accessing lvars affect the value of a shadow variable, and each corresponding rule (the *assign-*, *update-*, and *for* rules) is responsible for updating the shadow environment accordingly. The rules also add the appropriate *safety predicates* $safe_{\text{init}}(e)$ for all immediate subexpressions e of the statements. Since an expression is defined to be safe if all corresponding shadow variables have the value INIT, $safe_{\text{init}}(x[i])$ for example translates to $i_{\text{init}} = \text{INIT} \wedge x_{\text{init}}[i] = \text{INIT}$. Safety certification then computes the WPC for the safety requirements on the output variables. The WPC contains all applied safety predicates and safety substitutions. If the program is safe then the WPC will follow from the assumptions, and all VCs will be provable. Rules for other policies can be given by modifying the shadow variables and safety predicate.

Annotation Construction. Hoare-style program verification requires logical annotations, in particular loop invariants. In our application, we use the code generator to provide them together with the code [4,6]. The generator first produces core annotations that focus on on locally relevant aspects, without describing all the global information that may later be necessary for the proofs. A propagation step then pushes the core annotations along the edges of the control flow graph. This ensures that all loops have the required invariant; typically, however, they consist mainly of assertions propagated from elsewhere in the program. Figure 2 shows an example code fragment with annotations. The VCG then processes the code after propagation.

Human-readable explanations provide insight into the VCs. For us, this is particularly important because the underlying annotations have been derived automatically: the explanations help us to gain confidence into the (large and complex) generator and the certifier, and thus into the generated code. However, our approach is not tied to code generation; we only use the generator as a convenient source of the annotations that allow the construction of the VCs and thus the Hoare-style proofs.

3   Explaining the Purpose and Structure of VCs

After simplification, the VCs usually have a form that is reminiscent of Horn clauses (i.e., $H_1 \wedge \ldots \wedge H_n \Rightarrow C$). Here, the unique conclusion C of the VC can be considered its *purpose*. However, for a meaningful explanation of the *structure*, we need a more detailed characterization of the sub-formulas. This information cannot be recovered from the VCs or the code but must be specified explicitly. The key insight of our approach is that the different sub-formulas stem from specific positions in the Hoare rules, and that the VCG can thus add the appropriate labels to the VCs. Here we first show generated example explanations, and then explain the underlying machinery. Section 4 shows more refined explanations for our running example.

3.1   Simple Structural Explanations

Figure 2 shows a fragment of a Kalman filter algorithm with Bierman updates that has been generated by AUTOFILTER from a simplified model of the Crew Exploration Vehicle (CEV) dynamics; the entire program comprises about 800 lines of code. The program initializes some of the vectors and matrices (such as h and r) with model-specific values before they are used and potentially updated in the main while-loop. It also uses two additional matrices u and d that are repeatedly zeroed out and then partially recomputed before they are used in each iteration of the main loop (lines 728–731). We will focus on these nested for-loops.

For initialization safety the annotations need to formalize that each of the vectors and matrices is fully initialized after the respective code blocks. For the loops initializing u and d, invariants formalizing their partial initialization are required to prove that the postcondition holds. However, since these loops precede the use of vectors and matrices initialized outside the main loop, the invariants become cluttered with propagated annotations that are required to discharge the safety conditions from the later uses.

```
  ...
5 const M=6,  N=12;
  ...
  <init h>
183 post ∀ 0≤i<M,0≤j<N· h_init[i,j]=INIT
  ...
  <init r>
525 post ∀ 0≤i,j<M· r_init[i,j]=INIT
  ...
683 while t<Tmax
     inv ∀0≤i<M,0≤j<N· h_init[i,j]=INIT ∧...∧∀0≤i,j<M· r_init[i,j]=INIT ∧... do
  ...
728   for k:=0 to N-1
       inv ∀0≤i<M,0≤j<N· h_init[i,j]=INIT ∧...∧∀0≤i,j<M· r_init[i,j]=INIT ∧...
        ∧∀0≤i,j<N· i<k ⇒ u_init[i,j]=INIT ∧ d_init[i,j]=INIT do
729     for l:=0 to N-1
         inv ∀0≤i<M,0≤j<N· h_init[i,j]=INIT ∧...∧∀0≤i,j<M· r_init[i,j]=INIT ∧...
          ∧∀0≤i,j<N· (i<k ∨ i=k ∧ j<l) ⇒ u_init[i,j]=INIT ∧ d_init[i,j]=INIT do
730       u[k,l]:=0;
731       d[k,l]:=0;
         post ∀0≤i<M,0≤j<N· h_init[i,j]=INIT ∧...∧∀0≤i,j<M· r_init[i,j]=INIT ∧...
          ∧∀0≤i,j<N· i≤k ⇒ u_init[i,j]=INIT ∧ d_init[i,j]=INIT
       post ∀0≤i<M,0≤j<N· h_init[i,j]=INIT ∧...∧∀0≤i,j<M· r_init[i,j]=INIT ∧...
        ∧∀0≤i,j<N· u_init[i,j]=INIT ∧ d_init[i,j]=INIT
  ...
  <use u, d>
  ...
  <use h,..., r>
  ...
end;
```

Fig. 2. Example code fragment and annotations generated by AutoFilter

The certification of the program generates 71 VCs; 12 of these are related to the loop at lines 728–731. This shows that location information alone is insufficient as a basis for explaining VCs. Here, we focus on one VC

$$0 \leq k \leq 11 \wedge 0 \leq l \leq 11 \wedge \forall 0 \leq i,j < 12 \cdot h_{init}[i,j] = \text{INIT}$$
$$\wedge \ldots \wedge$$
$$\forall 0 \leq i < 6, 0 \leq j < 12 \cdot r_{init}[i,j] = \text{INIT} \wedge$$
$$\forall 0 \leq i,j < 12 \cdot i < k \Rightarrow d_{init}[i,j] = \text{INIT} \wedge \forall 0 \leq i,j < 12 \cdot i = k \wedge j < l \Rightarrow d_{init}[i,j] = \text{INIT} \wedge$$
$$\forall 0 \leq i,j < 12 \cdot i < k \Rightarrow u_{init}[i,j] = \text{INIT} \wedge \forall 0 \leq i,j < 12 \cdot i = k \wedge j < l \Rightarrow u_{init}[i,j] = \text{INIT}$$
$$\Rightarrow \forall 0 \leq i,j < 12 \cdot (i = k \wedge j \leq l \wedge j \neq l) \Rightarrow u_{init}[i,j] = \text{INIT}$$

that emerges from showing that the invariant is preserved through one iteration of the inner loop. The full VC is substantially larger (approx. 180 lines) and contains many irrelevant hypotheses, which make it hard for a human to grasp. In fact, the sheer amount of irrelevant information is often the biggest hurdle to understand automatically generated VCs. However, if we (manually) interpret the formula, we can see that the hypotheses are either constraints that originate from the loop bounds ($0 \leq k, l \leq 11$), post-conditions that have originally been established before the loop and then been propagated into the invariant (e.g., $\forall 0 \leq i,j < 12 \cdot h_{init}[i,j] = \text{INIT}$), or the actual "local" invariant as hypotheses. The conclusion comprises parts of the invariant (where l has been replaced by $l + 1$), but due to simplification this is difficult to see. In addition, all constants have been replaced by their values. This post hoc analysis of the VC, however, is not possible automatically. Simplification can change the VC structure arbitrarily, and even without simplification two subformulas can look the same but have different meaning (cf. the different occurrences of the loop invariant in the *while* rule.) In our approach, the VC is marked up with labels that represent this information in order to generate the explanation shown below; multiple annotations at the same source line are marked with #-signs. Note that the generated explanation also spells out the verification context, which is the VCs "secondary" purpose.

> The purpose of this VC is to show that the loop invariant at line 729 (#1) under the substitutions originating in line 5 and line 730 is still true after each iteration to line 731; it is also used to show the preservation of the loop invariants at line 728, which in turn is used to show the preservation of the loop invariants at line 683. Hence, given
> - the loop bounds at line 728 under the substitution originating in line 5,
> - the invariant at line 729 (#1) under the substitution originating in line 5,
> - the invariant at line 729 (#2) under the substitution originating in line 5,
>   ...
> - the invariant at line 729 (#15) under the substitution originating in line 5,
> - the loop bounds at line 729 under the substitution originating in line 5,
> show that the loop invariant at line 729 (#1) under the substitutions originating in line 5 and line 730 is still true after each iteration to line 731.

3.2   Mark-Up Structure

Concepts. The basic information for explanation generation is a set of underlying concepts, which depends of course on the particular aspect of the VCs to be explained. In the case of the structural explanations, most concepts characterize a proposition either as hypotheses or conclusions, reflecting their eventual position in the VC. Other concepts capture information about origin and secondary purpose of the propositions.

Hypotheses consist of assertions and control flow predicates. *Assertions* refer to subformulas that occur as annotations in the program, either originally or after propagation. They include asserted pre- and post-conditions (labels ass_pre and ass_post), function pre- and post-conditions (ass_fpre and ass_fpost), and loop invariants. Since the loop rules use the loop invariant as hypothesis in two different positions and instantiations, we distinguish ass_inv and ass_inv_exit (Figure 3). *Control flow predicates* refer to subformulas that reflect the program's control flow. For both *if*-statements and *while*-loops, the control flow predicates occur in positive and negated forms, giving four different concepts: if_tt, if_ff, while_tt, and while_ff. For *for*-loops, the control flow predicate does not directly occur in the program but is derived from the given loop bounds.

Conclusions capture the primary purpose of a VC, which includes establishing (i.e., showing to hold at the given location) the different types of assertions. As in the case of the hypotheses, invariants are used in two different forms, the *entry form* (or base case) est_inv and the *step form* est_inv_iter. Note that an assertion can be used both as hypothesis and as conclusion, even in the same VC. The explanations distinguish these two bits of information from the same source. For safety verification, we additionally have the safety conditions safety that have to be demonstrated.

Qualifiers further characterize both hypotheses and conclusions by recording the origin of a sub-formula. The different *substitution* concepts reflect the substitutions of the underlying Hoare calculus. The concepts sub and upd capture the origin and effect of assignments and array updates on the form of the resulting VCs; for the shadow environment (Section 2), we additionally get *safety substitutions* sub_safety and upd_safety.

Contributors capture the secondary purpose of a VC; this arises when a recursive call to the VCG produces VCs that are conceptually connected to the purpose of the larger structure. In general, contributors arise for nested program structures which result in "nested" VCs (e.g., loops within loops). For example, all VCs emerging from the premise $P\ \{c\}\ I$ of the *while* rule (cf. Figure 1) contribute to showing the preservation of the invariant I over the loop body c, independent of their primary purpose, and are thus labeled with pres_inv.

Label Structure and Labeled Terms. We use labeled terms $\ulcorner t \urcorner^l$, where each term t can be adorned with a label l, or, by abuse of notation, a list of labels. Labels have the form $c(o, n)$. Here c is one of the concepts introduced above; it describes the role the labeled term plays and thus determines how it is rendered. The location o records where it originated; it refers either to an individual position or to a range. We use file names and line numbers for locations. n is a list of labels that contains further qualifying information. Initially, n is empty; after normalization, it holds labels that have been "bubbled-up" from subterms. In our running example, the loop bounds are originally represented as $\ulcorner 0 \leq k \leq \ulcorner 11 \urcorner^{\text{sub}(5,\langle\rangle)} \urcorner^{\text{bounds}(728,\langle\rangle)}$, i.e., with the label on the upper bound reflecting the source of the substitution, and the label on the sub-formula reflecting its role. After simplification, the sub-label is nested inside the bounds-label, reflecting the original nesting in the term: $\ulcorner 0 \leq k \leq 11 \urcorner^{\text{bounds}(728,\langle\text{sub}(5,\langle\rangle)\rangle)}$.

3.3 Modified Hoare Rules

In general, it is not sufficient to just output explanations as the VCs are constructed. Instead, the VCG must add the right labels at the right positions; it must also pass mark-up back through the program by attaching it to the WPC, so that information from one point in the program can be used at any other point. Modified Hoare rules concisely capture the semantic mark-up (i.e., label types and positions) required for any given explanation aspect. Labels are added in three places: to the "incoming" postcondition of a recursive VCG call in the premise of an inference rule, to the WPC, or to a generated VC. Figure 3 shows the core rules of the initialization safety policy marked-up for explaining the structural aspect of VCs. The rules derive the usual triples, $P\ \{c\}\ Q$, but now all elements can be labeled. For clarity, we omit the location information in the rule formulation but assume that the VCG obtains it from the statements and annotations and appropriately incorporates it into the labels.

The *assign* and *update* rules only require mark-up in the WPC. The safety predicate can be a complex sub-formula, depending on the property to be certified and the structure of the expression(s), but the mark-up is not dependent on the specific safety property—all we need to know for an explanation is that this is in fact the safety predicate. The substitutions need mark-up to record their type and the origin of the substituted expressions. By labeling only the expressions and not the variables we can use the normal substitution mechanisms.

$(assign)$ $\dfrac{}{Q[\ulcorner e\urcorner^{\mathsf{sub}}/x,\ulcorner\mathrm{INIT}\urcorner^{\mathsf{sub\_safety}}/x_{\mathrm{init}}]\wedge\ulcorner safe_{\mathrm{init}}(e)\urcorner^{\mathsf{safety}}\ \{x := e\}\ Q}$

$(update)$ $\dfrac{}{\left(\begin{array}{l}Q[\ulcorner upd(x,e_1,e_2)\urcorner^{\mathsf{upd}}/x,\ulcorner upd(x_{\mathrm{init}},e_1,\mathrm{INIT})\urcorner^{\mathsf{upd\_safety}}/x_{\mathrm{init}}]\wedge\\ \ulcorner safe_{\mathrm{init}}(e_1)\urcorner^{\mathsf{safety}}\wedge\ulcorner safe_{\mathrm{init}}(e_2)\urcorner^{\mathsf{safety}}\end{array}\right)\ \{x[e_1] := e_2\}\ Q}$

(if) $\dfrac{P_1\ \{c_1\}\ Q\quad P_2\ \{c_2\}\ Q}{(\ulcorner b\urcorner^{\mathsf{if\_tt}}\Rightarrow P_1)\wedge(\ulcorner\neg b\urcorner^{\mathsf{if\_ff}}\Rightarrow P_2)\wedge\ulcorner safe_{\mathrm{init}}(b)\urcorner^{\mathsf{safety}}\ \{\mathbf{if}\ b\ \mathbf{then}\ c_1\ \mathbf{else}\ c_2\}\ Q}$

$(while)$ $\dfrac{\ulcorner P\ \{c\}\ \ulcorner I\urcorner^{\mathsf{est\_inv\_iter}}\urcorner^{\mathsf{pres\_inv}}\quad\begin{array}{c}\ulcorner\ulcorner I\urcorner^{\mathsf{ass\_inv}}\wedge\ulcorner b\urcorner^{\mathsf{while\_tt}}\Rightarrow P\urcorner^{\mathsf{pres\_inv}}\\ \ulcorner I\urcorner^{\mathsf{ass\_inv\_exit}}\wedge\ulcorner\neg b\urcorner^{\mathsf{while\_ff}}\Rightarrow Q\end{array}}{\ulcorner I\urcorner^{\mathsf{est\_inv}}\wedge\ulcorner safe_{\mathrm{init}}(b)\urcorner^{\mathsf{safety}}\ \{\mathbf{while}\ b\ \mathbf{inv}\ I\ \mathbf{do}\ c\}\ Q}$

(for) $\dfrac{\ulcorner P\ \{c\}\ \ulcorner I[i+1/i]\urcorner^{\mathsf{est\_inv\_iter}}\urcorner^{\mathsf{pres\_inv}}\quad\begin{array}{c}\ulcorner\ulcorner I\urcorner^{\mathsf{ass\_inv}}\wedge\ulcorner e_1\le i\le e_2\urcorner^{\mathsf{bounds}}\Rightarrow P\urcorner^{\mathsf{pres\_inv}}\\ \ulcorner I[e_2+1/i,\mathrm{INIT}/i_{\mathrm{init}}]\urcorner^{\mathsf{ass\_inv\_exit}}\Rightarrow Q\end{array}}{\left(\begin{array}{l}e_1\le e_2\wedge\ulcorner I[e_1/i]\urcorner^{\mathsf{est\_inv}}\wedge\\ \ulcorner safe_{\mathrm{init}}(e_1)\urcorner^{\mathsf{safety}}\wedge\ulcorner safe_{\mathrm{init}}(e_2)\urcorner^{\mathsf{safety}}\end{array}\right)\ \{\mathbf{for}\ i := e_1\ \mathbf{to}\ e_2\ \mathbf{inv}\ I\ \mathbf{do}\ c\}\ Q}$

$(assert)$ $\dfrac{\ulcorner P'\urcorner^{\mathsf{ass\_pre}}\Rightarrow P\quad P\ \{c\}\ \ulcorner Q'\urcorner^{\mathsf{est\_post}}\quad\ulcorner Q'\urcorner^{\mathsf{ass\_post}}\Rightarrow Q}{\ulcorner P'\urcorner^{\mathsf{est\_pre}}\ \{\mathbf{pre}\ P'\ c\ \mathbf{post}\ Q'\}\ Q}$

Fig. 3. Hoare rules for initialization safety with semantic markup

While labeling the *if* rule is straightforward, the loop rules are more complicated; we focus on the *while* rule but the *for* rule has a similar structure. The WPC comprises the safety predicate, which is labeled as before, and the invariant, which has to be established for loop entry and is thus labeled with est_inv. In the premise, individual sub-formulas of both the exit-condition $I\wedge\neg b\Rightarrow Q$ and the step-condition $I\wedge b\Rightarrow P$ are labeled appropriately; in addition, the entire step-condition is labeled with its secondary purpose, namely to contribute to showing the preservation of the invariant. In the triple $P\ \{c\}\ I$, the incoming postcondition I must be labeled with its purpose (i.e., re-establish the invariant after one loop iteration) for the recursive call; moreover, all emerging VCs must be marked up with the secondary purpose pres_inv. We indicate this by labeling the entire triple. Note how the same formula I is used in four different roles and consequently labeled in four different ways. This contextual knowledge is only available at the point of rule application and can not be easily recovered by a post hoc analysis of the generated VCs.

Finally, the *assert* rule is straightforward to mark up. The asserted pre- and post-conditions are labeled according to their use either as hypotheses (in the VCs) or as conclusions (in the WPC and recursion).

3.4   Labeled Rewriting

The VCs (whether labeled or unlabeled) become quite complex and need to be simplified aggressively before they can be proven by an ATP. Unfortunately, unlabeled simplification rules cannot be reused "as is" for the labeled case because (i) the labeling changes the term structure and thus the applicability of the rules and (ii) the labels need careful handling—on the one hand, they cannot simply be distributed over all operators because this can destroy their proper scope, while on the other, they cannot just be pushed to the top of the VC because this would result in redundant and imprecise explanations. The purpose of the labeled simplification rules is thus (i) to remove redundant labels, (ii) to minimize the scope of the remaining labels, and (iii) to keep enough labels to explain any unexpected failures, based on the assumption that the majority of the VCs can be rewritten to *true*.

The rules themselves fall into five different groups. The first group contains rules such as $\ulcorner true \urcorner^l \rightarrow true$ or $P \Rightarrow P' \rightarrow true$ if $| P | = | P' |$ that remove labels from trivially true (sub-) formulas because these require no explanations;[1] The next group consists of rules such as $\ulcorner false \urcorner^l \vee P \rightarrow P$ that *selectively* remove trivially false labeled sub-formulas. The remaining context then provides the information for the explanations. However, the labels obviously need to be retained if the underlying unlabeled rule version rewrite the *entire* formula into *false*, since there is no remaining context to explain the failure, e.g., $\ulcorner false \urcorner^l \wedge P \rightarrow \ulcorner false \urcorner^l$. The rules $\ulcorner P \wedge Q \urcorner^l \rightarrow \ulcorner P \urcorner^l \wedge \ulcorner Q \urcorner^l$ and $P \Rightarrow \ulcorner Q \Rightarrow R \urcorner^l \rightarrow P \wedge \ulcorner Q \urcorner^l \Rightarrow \ulcorner R \urcorner^l$ comprise the fourth group; they distribute labels over conjunction and (nested) implication, respectively, so that the label scopes are minimized in the final simplified VCs. The last group encodes knowledge about how the labels will be interpreted in the underlying domain. For example, the rule $sel(\ulcorner upd(x, i_1, t) \urcorner^l, i_2) \rightarrow \ulcorner i_1 = i_2 \urcorner^l ? \ulcorner t \urcorner^l : sel(x, i_2)$ specifies the effect of selecting into an updated array: in order to explain the resulting term we need to know that the disappearing *upd*-functor is conceptually reflected in the guard and the success-branch of the conditional, but not in the failure-branch, and that the label must thus be attached to these two only. This group also contains an unnesting rule $\ulcorner \ulcorner t \urcorner^m \urcorner^n \rightarrow \ulcorner t \urcorner^{n \otimes m}$ that "bubbles" nested labels to the top term, and so enables other labeled and unlabeled rules to apply, but keeps the nesting structure on the labels itself. This ensures that qualifiers remain nested properly, and apply to the originally qualified term.

3.5 Rendering

The final stage is generation of the actual explanations, i.e., turning the (labeled) VCs into human-readable text, is called *rendering*. The underlying structure and actual textual representation of the explanations can be specified as a grammar (omitted here), where the right-hand side of each rule is an *explanation template* that is similar to a format string in C. These templates allow an easy customization and fine-grained control of the textual explanations. The renderer contains code to interpret the templates as well as some glue code (e.g., sorting label lists by line numbers) that is spliced in to support the text generation. It also provides default templates for concepts that are useful for different explanation aspects, for example substitutions and the sim- and nested-labels. Rendering comprises four steps: (i) VC normalization, using the labeled rewrite system; (ii) label extraction, using the unnesting rule; (iii) label normalization,

---

[1] We use an auxiliary function $| \cdot |$ to remove labels from terms and the label composition operator $\otimes$ to append a list of inner labels to the list of labels nested in the outer label, i.e., $c(o, l) \otimes m = c(o, l \bullet m)$, where $\bullet$ is list concatenation.

to fit the labels to the explanation templates; (*iv*) text generation, using the explanation templates. The third step flattens nested qualifiers, so that for example the label sub(p, sub(q, sub(r))) is rewritten into the list $\langle$sub(p), sub(q), sub(r)$\rangle$. It also merges back together conclusions from the same line which have been split over different literals during the first step.

3.6 Putting It All Together

Our example VC emerges from the first hypothesis (i.e., $I \wedge e_1 \leq i \leq e_2 \Rightarrow P$) of the *for* rule. P is computed as the WPC of the two assignments in lines 730 and 731 with respect to the appropriately labeled step form of the invariant at line 729:

$$\ulcorner (\forall 0 \leq i,j < N \cdot i = k \wedge j \leq l+1 \Rightarrow (\ulcorner upd(u_{\text{init}}, [k, l], \text{INIT})\urcorner^{\text{upd\_safety}(728)})[i,j] = \text{INIT})$$
$$\wedge \dots \urcorner^{\text{est\_inv\_iter}(729-731)}$$

Here, the *update* rule added the upd_safety-label, while the substitution of N by 12 will eventually introduce a sub-label. Since all this happens as part of handling the enclosing for- and while-loops, P will be wrapped into two corresponding pres_inv-labels.

Simplification splits the implication into several independent VCs, including the example, and "bubbles" all labels to the top. The renderer then strips away the enclosing contributors (i.e., the pres_inv-labels) and uses the user-defined templates to convert them into the text shown in Section 3.1. It will then search the remaining label list for the unique conclusion (here est_inv_iter) to produce a caption from the corresponding template and the contributor text, before it renders the assumptions.

3.7 Local Assumptions and Simultaneous Conclusions

All VCs generated in the example above have a unique conclusion that denotes their primary purpose. However, for VCs that contain existential quantifiers (introduced by the annotations or by the rule for procedure calls), this is not necessarily the case any longer. Hence, we must explicitly represent and render multiple conclusions that have to be satisfied simultaneously for an existentially quantified witness, and conclusions from local assumptions. Consider, for example, the following VC, that arises in certifying frame safety (i.e., consistent use of coordinate frames [14]) in navigation software generated by Real-Time Workshop from a Simulink model:

$$\dots \wedge \text{lo}(T) = 0 \wedge \text{hi}(T) = 8 \wedge T[0] + T[4] + T[8] > 0 \wedge \text{frame}(T, \text{dcm}(\text{eci}, \text{ned}))$$
$$\Rightarrow \forall q_0 : \text{real}, v : \text{vec} \cdot \exists d : \text{DCM} \cdot$$
$$\text{tr}(d) = T[0] + T[4] + T[8] \wedge \text{tr}(d) > 0 \wedge \text{rep\_dcm}(d, T[5], T[7], T[2], T[6], T[1], T[3])$$
$$\wedge (\exists q : \text{quat} \cdot \text{eq\_dcm\_quat}(d, q) \wedge \text{rep\_quat}(q, q_0, v[0], v[1], v[2])$$
$$\Rightarrow \text{frame}(\text{vupd}(\text{upd}(M, 0, q_0), 1, 3, v), \text{quat}(\text{eci}, \text{ned})))$$

The purpose of this VC is to show the correctness of a procedure call. Hence, we need to show for each argument (i.e., q_0 and v) the existence of a direction cosine matrix d such that the function's three preconditions are satisfied and that the function postcondition implies the required postcondition. Our system explains this as follows:

... Hence, given
- the precondition at line 794 (#1),
- the condition at line 798 under the substitution originating in line 794,

show that there exists a DCM that will simultaneously
- establish the function precondition for the call at line 799 (#1),
- establish the function precondition for the call at line 799 (#2),
- establish the function precondition for the call at line 799 (#3) under the substitution originating in line 794,
- establish the postcondition at line 815 (#1) assuming the function postcondition for the call at line 799 (#1).

Note that the structure of the explanation reflects the VC's logical structure, and shows which goals have to be established simultaneously, and that the function postcondition can only be used as assumption to establish the call-time postcondition, but of course not the function's preconditions. These labels do not give a detailed explanation of the VC's individual parts (e.g., the function postcondition); for that, we would need to mark up the annotations with additional policy-specific details (see Section 4.3).

We only need to introduce two additional conclusion labels local and sim to represent local assumptions and simultaneous conclusions, as outlined above. In addition, we need simplification rules that introduce these labels to properly maintain the VC structure in the explanations, e.g., $\exists x : t \cdot \ulcorner P \urcorner^{\mathsf{l}} \Rightarrow \ulcorner Q \urcorner^{\mathsf{m}} \rightarrow \ulcorner \exists x : t \cdot P \Rightarrow Q \urcorner^{\mathsf{local}(\langle \mathsf{l}, \mathsf{m} \rangle)}$.

4   Refined Explanations

Even though the explanations constructed so far relate primarily to the structure of the VCs, they already provide some "semantic flavor", since they distinguish the multiple roles a single annotation can take. However, for structurally complex programs, the labels do not yet convey enough information to allow users to understand the VCs in detail. For example, a double-nested for-loop can produce a variety of VCs that will all refer to "the invariant", without further explaining whether it is the invariant of the inner or the outer loop, leaving the user to trace through the exact program locations to resolve this ambiguity. We can produce refined explanations that verbalize such conceptual distinctions by introducing additional qualification labels that are wrapped inside the existing structural labels. We chose this solution over extending the structural labels because it allows us to handle orthogonal aspects independently, and makes it easier to treat the extensions uniformly in different contexts.

4.1   Adding Index Information to Loop Explanations

Explanations of VCs emerging from for-loops are easier to understand if they are tied closer to the program by adding more detailed information about the index variables and bounds; our running example then becomes (cf. Section 3.1; emphasis added manually):

> The purpose of this VC is to show that the loop invariant at line 729 (#1) under the substitutions originating in line 5 and line 730 is still true after each iteration to line 731 (*i.e., in the form with l+1 replacing l*); it is also used to show the preservation of the loop invariants at line 728, which in turn ...

Note that the way the qualifier is rendered depends on the particular loop concept that it qualifies, to properly reflect the different substitutions that are applied to the invariant in the different cases (see Figure 3); for example, in the step case (i.e., for the est_inv_iter-label), the variable is used, while in the base case, the lower bound is used; the qualifier is ignored when the invariant is used as asserted hypothesis (i.e., for the ass_inv-label).

The information required for all different cases (i.e., variable name, lower and upper bounds) is almost impossible to recreate with a post hoc analysis of the formula. The VCG can easily extract this from the index of the for-loop itself and add it as qualifier to the different labels used in the *for*-rule, changing for example the label added to the invariant in the base case to est_inv($\langle i := e_1$ **to** $e_2 \rangle$) (cf. Figure 3). Since the labeled simplification rules ensure that the qualifiers are never moved outside their base label, the explanation templates for the qualifiers simply need to take the base label as an additional argument to produce the right text, for example render(est_inv_iter, $i := e_1$ **to** e_2) = "in the form with " • i • "+1 replacing " • i.

4.2 Adding Relative Positions to Loop Explanations

VCs emerging from nested loops refer to the underlying loops via their absolute source locations but since these are often very close to each other, they can easily be confused. We can thus further improve the explanations by adding information about the relative loop ordering, distinguishing, for example, the inner from the outer invariant. In conjunction with the the syntactic index information described above, our running example then becomes (emphasis added manually):

> The purpose of this VC is to show that the loop invariant at line 729 (#1) *(i.e., the inner invariant)* under the substitutions originating in line 5 and line 730 is still true after each iteration to line 731 (i.e., in the form with $l+1$ replacing l); it is also used to show the preservation of the loop invariants at line 728, which in turn ...

Since the VCG has no built-in notion of "outer" and "inner" loops, it cannot add the respective qualifiers automatically. Instead, the annotations in the program must be labeled accordingly, either by the programmer, or, in our case, the annotation generator. No further changes are required to the machinery: the VCG simply processes the labeled annotations, and the outer- and inner-qualifiers are rendered by parameterized templates as before.

4.3 Adding Domain-Specific Semantic Explanations

We can construct semantically "richer" explanations if we further expand the idea outlined in the previous section, and add more *semantic labels* to the annotations, which represent domain-specific interpretations of the labeled sub-formulae. For example, in initialization safety the VCs usually contain sub-formulae of the form $\forall 0 \leq i, j < N \cdot A_{\text{init}}[i, j] = \text{INIT}$, which expresses the fact that the array A is fully initialized (e.g, most postconditions in Figure 2). By labeling this formula, or more precisely, the annotation from which it is taken, we can produce an appropriate explanation without any need to analyze the formula structure: [2]

---

[2] Note that the formulae expressing the domain-specific concepts can become arbitrarily complex, and make any post hoc analysis practically infeasible. For example, to express the row-major, partial initialization of an array up to position (k, l), we would already need to identify a formula equivalent to $\forall 0 \leq i, j < N \cdot (i < k \lor i = k \land j < l) \Rightarrow A_{\text{init}}[i, j] = \text{INIT}$.

... Hence, given
  - the loop bounds at line 728 under the substitution originating in line 5,
  - the invariant at line 729 (#1) (i.e., the array h is fully initialized, which is established at line 183) under the substitution originating in line 5,

...

  - the invariant at line 729 (#11) (i.e., the array r is fully initialized, which is established at line 525) under the substitution originating in line 5,

...

  - the invariant at line 729 (#15) under the substitution originating in line 5,
  - the loop bounds at line 729 under the substitution originating in line 5,

show that the loop invariant at line 729 (#1) under the substitutions originating in line 5 and line 730 is still true after each iteration to line 731 (i.e., the array u is initialized up to position (k,l)).

For this extension, we need two different qualifiers, init(a, o) which states that the array a is fully initialized after line o, and init_upto(a, k, l) which states that a is initialized in a row-major fashion up to position (k, l). Again, the annotation generator can add these labels to the annotations in the program.

We can use the domain-specific information to give a semantic explanation of the hierarchical relations between the VCs which complements the purely structural view provided by the pres_inv labels. We thus generalize the *assert* rule to use the domain-specific labels as contributors:

$$(label) \frac{\ulcorner P \urcorner \text{ass\_pre(l)} \Rightarrow \ulcorner P \urcorner \text{contrib(l)} \quad \ulcorner P \{c\} \ulcorner Q \urcorner \text{est\_post(l)} \urcorner \text{contrib(l)} \quad \ulcorner Q \urcorner \text{ass\_post(l)} \Rightarrow Q}{\ulcorner P \urcorner \text{est\_pre(l)} \{\mathbf{pre}\ P'\ c\ \mathbf{post}\ \ulcorner Q'^{l} \urcorner\}\ Q}$$

The *label* rule "plucks" the label off the post-condition and passes it into the appropriate positions. The labels need to be modified to take the domain-specific labels as an additional argument. For example, ass_post(init(183, h)) refers to the postcondition asserted after the statements that initialize the array h. In addition, we also introduce a new contribution label (e.g., contrib(init(183, h)), similar to the invariant preservation in the structural concept hierarchy. This is added to the WPC that is recursively computed for the annotated statement, and to all VCs emerging during that process (e.g., if the initialization uses a nested loop and thus generates multiple VCs). These more refined labels let the renderer determine whether a VC actually establishes the asserted post-condition of a domain-specific block, or whether it is just an individual contributor to this.

5 Related Work

Most VCGs link VCs to source locations, i.e., the actual position in the code where the respective rule was applied and hence where the VC originated. Usually, the systems only deal with line numbers but Fraer [11] describes a system that supports a "deep linking" to detailed term positions. JACK [1] and Perfect Developer [2] classify the VCs on the top-level and produce short captions like "precondition satisfied", "return value satisfies specification", etc. In general, however, none of these approaches maintain more non-local information (e.g., substitution applications) or secondary purpose.

Our work grew out of the earlier work by Denney and Venkatesan [8] which used information from a particular subset of VCs (in the current terminology: where the purpose is to establish a safety condition) in order to give a textual account for why the code is safe. It soon became clear, however, that a full understanding of the certification process requires the VCs themselves to be explained (as does any debugging of failed VCs). The current work extends the explanations to arbitrarily constructed formulas, that is, VCs where the labels on constituent parts come from different sources. This allows formulas to be interpreted in different ways.

Leino et al. [12] use explanations for traces to safety conditions. This is sufficient for debugging programs, which is their main motivation. Like our work, Leino's approach is based on extending an underlying logic with labels to represent explanatory semantic information. Both approaches use essentially the same types of structural labels, and Leino's use of two different polarities (lblpos and lblneg) corresponds to our distinction between asserting and establishing an annotation. However, their system does not represent the origin of substitutions nor the secondary purpose of the VCs. Similarly, it does not incorporate refined explanations with additional information. Moreover, the approaches differ in how these labels are used by the verification architectures. Leino's system introduces the labels by first desugaring the language into a lower-level form. Labels are treated as uninterpreted predicate symbols and labeled formulas are therefore just ordinary formulas. This labeled language is then processed by a standard VCG which is "label-blind". In contrast, we do not have a desugaring stage, and mainly use the VCG to insert the labels, which allows us to take advantage of domain-specific labels. While our simplifier needs to be label-aware, we strip labels off the final VCs after the explanation has been constructed, and thus do not place special requirements on the ATP like they do. This allows us to use off-the-shelf high-performance ATPs.

6   Conclusions and Future Work

The explanation mechanism which we have described here has been successfully implemented and incorporated into our certification browser [5,7]. This tool is used to navigate the artifacts produced during certifiable code generation, and it uses the system described in this paper to successfully explain all the VCs produced by AUTOFILTER, AUTOBAYES, and Real-Time Workshop for a range of safety policies. Complexity of VCs is largely independent of the size of the program, but we have applied our tool up to the subsystem level (around 1000 lines of code), where the largest VCs are typically around 200 lines of formula.

In addition to its use in debugging, the explainer can also be used as a means of gaining assurance that the verification is itself trustworthy. This complements our previous work on proof checking [13]: there a machine checks one formal artifact (the proof), here we support human checking of another (the VCs). With this role in mind, we are currently extending the tool to be useful for code reviews.

Much more work can be done to improve and extend the actual explanations themselves. Our approach can, for example, also be used to explain the *provenance* of a VC (i.e., the tools and people involved in its construction) or to link it together with supporting information such as code reviews, test suites, or off-line proofs. More generally, we would like to allow explanations to be based on entirely different explanation structures or *ontologies*.

Finally, there are also interesting theoretical issues. The renderer relies on the existence of an *Explanation Normal Form*, which states intuitively that each VC is labeled with a unique conclusion. This is essentially a rudimentary soundness result, which can be shown in two steps, first by induction over the marked-up Hoare rules in Figure 3 and then by induction over the labeled rewrite rules. We are currently developing a theoretical basis for the explanation of VCs that is generic in the aspect that is explained, with appropriate notions of soundness and completeness.

Acknowledgments. This material is based upon work supported by NASA under awards NCC2-1426 and NNA07BB97C.

References

1. Barthe, G., et al.: JACK – a tool for validation of security and behaviour of Java applications. In: Formal Methods for Components and Objects. LNCS, vol. 4709, pp. 152–174. Springer, Heidelberg (2007)
2. Crocker, D.: Perfect Developer: a tool for object-oriented formal specification and refinement. In: Tool Exhibition Notes, FM 2003, pp. 37–41 (2003)
3. Denney, E., Fischer, B.: Correctness of source-level safety policies. In: Araki, K., Gnesi, S., Mandrioli, D. (eds.) FME 2003. LNCS, vol. 2805, pp. 894–913. Springer, Heidelberg (2003)
4. Denney, E., Fischer, B.: Certifiable program generation. In: Glück, R., Lowry, M. (eds.) GPCE 2005. LNCS, vol. 3676, pp. 17–28. Springer, Heidelberg (2005)
5. Denney, E., Fischer, B.: A program certification assistant based on fully automated theorem provers. In: Proc. Intl. Workshop on User Interfaces for Theorem Provers (UITP 2005), Edinburgh, pp. 98–116 (2005)
6. Denney, E., Fischer, B.: A generic annotation inference algorithm for the safety certification of automatically generated code. In: GPCE 2006, pp. 121–130. ACM Press, New York (2006)
7. Denney, E., Trac, S.: A software safety certification tool for automatically generated guidance, navigation and control code. In: IEEE Aerospace Conference Electronic Proceedings, IEEE, Big Sky (2008)
8. Denney, E., Venkatesan, R.P.: A generic software safety document generator. In: Basin, D., Rusinowitch, M. (eds.) IJCAR 2004. LNCS (LNAI), vol. 3097, pp. 102–116. Springer, Heidelberg (2004)
9. Fiedler, A.: Natural language proof explanation. In: Hutter, D., Stephan, W. (eds.) Mechanizing Mathematical Reasoning. LNCS (LNAI), vol. 2605, pp. 342–363. Springer, Heidelberg (2005)
10. Fischer, B., Schumann, J.: AutoBayes: A system for generating data analysis programs from statistical models. J. Functional Programming 13(3), 483–508 (2003)
11. Fraer, R.: Tracing the origins of verification conditions. In: Nivat, M., Wirsing, M. (eds.) AMAST 1996. LNCS, vol. 1101, pp. 241–255. Springer, Heidelberg (1996)
12. Leino, K.R.M., Millstein, T., Saxe, J.B.: Generating error traces from verification-condition counterexamples. Science of Computer Programming 55(1–3), 209–226 (2005)
13. Sutcliffe, G., Denney, E., Fischer, B.: Practical proof checking for program certification. In: Proc. CADE-20 Workshop on Empirically Successful Classical Automated Reasoning (ESCAR 2005), Tallinn (July 2005)
14. Vallado, D.A.: Fundamentals of Astrodynamics and Applications, 2nd edn. Space Technology Library. Microcosm Press and Kluwer Academic Publishers (2001)
15. Whittle, J., Schumann, J.: Automating the implementation of Kalman filter algorithms. ACM Trans. Mathematical Software 30(4), 434–453 (2004)

Towards Formal Verification of TOOLBUS Scripts

Wan Fokkink[1,2], Paul Klint[1,3], Bert Lisser[1], and Yaroslav S. Usenko[1,4]

[1] Software Engineering Cluster,
Centrum voor Wiskunde en Informatica,
Amsterdam, The Netherlands
[2] Theoretical Computer Science Section,
Vrije Universiteit Amsterdam, The Netherlands
[3] Programming Research Group,
Universiteit van Amsterdam, The Netherlands
[4] Laboratory for Quality Software (LaQuSo),
Technische Universiteit Eindhoven, The Netherlands

Abstract. TOOLBUS allows one to connect tools via a software bus. Programming is done using the scripting language TSCRIPT, which is based on the process algebra ACP. TSCRIPT was originally designed to enable formal verification, but this option has so far not been explored in any detail. We present a method for analyzing a TSCRIPT by translating it to the process algebraic language mCRL2, and then applying model checking to verify behavioral properties.

1 Introduction

TOOLBUS [1,2] provides a simple, service-oriented view on organizing software systems by separating the *coordination* of software components from the actual *computation* that they perform. It organizes a system along the lines of a programmable software bus. Programming is done using the scripting language TSCRIPT that is based on the process algebra ACP (Algebra of Communicating Processes) [3] and abstract data types. The tools connected to the TOOLBUS can be written in any language and can run on different machines.

A TSCRIPT can be tested, like any other software system, to observe whether it exhibits the desired behavior. An alternative approach for analyzing communication protocols is model checking, which constitutes an automated check of whether some behavioral property is satisfied. This can be, roughly, a safety property, which must be satisfied throughout any run of the system, or a liveness property, which should eventually be satisfied in any run of the system. To perform model checking, the communication protocol must be specified in some formal language, and the behavioral properties in some temporal logic. Strong points of model checking are that it attempts to performs an exhaustive exploration of the state space of a system, and that it can often be fully automated.

As one of the main aims of TSCRIPT, Bergstra and Klint [2] mention that it should have "a formal basis and can be formally analyzed". The formal basis is

J. Meseguer and G. Roşu (Eds.): AMAST 2008, LNCS 5140, pp. 160–166, 2008.

offered by the process algebra ACP, but ways to formally analyze TSCRIPTs were lacking so far. This is partly due to a number of obstructions for an automatic translation from TSCRIPT to ACP, which are explained below. This work was initiated by the developers of the TOOLBUS, who are keen to integrate model checking into the design process. This paper constitutes an important step in this direction. We have charted the most important distinctions between ACP and TSCRIPT, and investigated how TSCRIPT can be translated into the formal modeling language mCRL2 [4]. This language is also based on the process algebra ACP, extended with equational abstract data types [5].

Since both TSCRIPT and mCRL2 are based on data terms and ACP, an automated translation is in principle feasible. And as a result, TSCRIPT can then be model checked using the mCRL2 or CADP toolset [6]. This method has been applied on a standard example from the TOOLBUS distribution: a distributed auction. An implementation of an automatic translator from TOOLBUS to mCRL2 is under development. However, we did have to circumvent several obstructions in the translation from TSCRIPT to mCRL2. Firstly, each TSCRIPT process has a built-in queue to store incoming messages, which is left implicit in the process description; in mCRL2, all of these queues are specified explicitly as a separate process. Secondly, TSCRIPT supports dynamic process creation; in mCRL2, we chose to start with a fixed number of TOOLBUS processes, and let a master process divide connecting tools over these processes. Thirdly, we expressed the iterative star operator of TSCRIPT as a recursive equation in mCRL2. And fourthly, we developed some guidelines on how to deal with so-called result variables in TSCRIPT.

Our work has its origins in the formal verification of interface languages [7,8]. The aim is to get a separation of concerns, in which the (in our case TSCRIPT) interfaces that connect software components can be analyzed separately from the components themselves. Our work is closest in spirit to Pipa [9], an interface specification language for an aspect-oriented extension of Java called AspectJ [10]. In [9] it is discussed how one could transform an AspectJ program together with its Pipa specification into a Java program and JML specification, in order to apply existing JML-based tools for verifying AspectJ programs, see also [11]. Diertens [12,13] uses the TOOLBUS to implement a platform for simulation and animation of process algebra specifications in the language PSF. In this approach TSCRIPT is automatically generated from a PSF specification.

2   ToolBus and Tscript

The behavior of the TOOLBUS consists of the parallel composition of a variable number of processes. In addition to these processes, a variable number of external tools may be connected to the TOOLBUS. All interactions between processes and connected tools are controlled by TSCRIPTs, which are based on predefined communication primitives. The classical procedure interface (a named procedure with typed arguments and a typed result) is thus replaced by a more general behavior description.

A TSCRIPT process is built from the standard process algebraic constructs: atomic actions (including the deadlock delta and the internal action tau), alternative composition +, sequential composition · and parallel composition ‖. The binary star operation $p * q$ represents zero or more repetitions of p, followed by q. Atomic actions are parametrized with data parameters (see below), and can be provided with a relative or absolute time stamp. A process definition is of the form $Pname(x_1, \ldots, x_n)$ is P, with P a TSCRIPT process expression and $x_1, \ldots, x_n$ a list of data parameters. Process instances may be created dynamically using the create statement.

The following communication primitives are available. A process can send a message (using snd-msg), which should be received, synchronously, by another process (using rec-msg). Furthermore, a process can send a note (using snd-note), which is broadcast to other, interested, processes. A process may subscribe and unsubscribe to certain notes. The receiving processes read notes asynchronously (using rec-note) at a low priority. Processes only receive notes to which they have subscribed. Communication between TOOLBUS and tools is based on handshaking communication. A process may send messages in several formats to a tool (snd-eval, snd-do, snd-ack-event), and can receive values (rec-value) and events (rec-event) from a tool.

The only values that can be exchanged between the TOOLBUS and connected tools are terms of some sort (basic data types booleans, integers, strings and lists). In these terms, two types of variables are distinguished: *value* variables whose value is used in expressions, and *result* variables (written with a question mark) that get a value assigned to them as a result of an action or a process call. Manipulation of data is completely transparent, i.e., data can be received from and sent to tools, but inside TOOLBUS there are hardly any operations on them. ATERMS [14] are used to represent data terms; ATERMS support maximal subterm sharing, and use a very concise, binary format. In general, an adapter is needed for each connected tool, to adapt it to the common data representation and message protocols imposed by TOOLBUS.

The TOOLBUS was introduced for the implementation of the ASF+SDF Meta-Environment [15,16] but has been used for the implementation of various other systems as well. The source code and binaries of the TOOLBUS and related documentation can be found at www.meta-environment.org.

3   mCRL2 and CADP

An mCRL2 [4] specification is built from the standard process algebraic constructs: atomic actions (including the deadlock δ and the internal action τ), alternative composition +, sequential composition · and parallel composition ‖. One can define synchronous communication between actions. The following two operators combine data with processes. The sum operator $\sum_{d:D} p(d)$ describes the process that can execute the process $p(d)$ for some value d selected from the sort D. The conditional operator $\_ \rightarrow \_ \diamond \_$ describes the *if-then-else*.

The process $b \rightarrow x \diamond y$ (where b is a boolean) has the behavior of x if b is true and the behavior of y if b is false.

Data elements are terms of some sort. In addition to equational abstract data types, mCRL2 also supports built-in functional data types. Atomic actions are parametrized with data parameters, and can be provided with an absolute time stamp. A process definition is of the form $\mathsf{Pname}(x_1, \ldots, x_n) = P$, with P an mCRL2 process and $x_1, \ldots, x_n$ a list of parameters.

The mCRL2 toolset (`www.mcrl2.org`) supports formal reasoning about systems specified in mCRL2. It is based on term rewriting techniques and on formal transformation of process algebraic and data terms. mCRL2 specifications are first transformed to a linear form [4, Section 5], in a *condition-action-effect* style. The resulting specification can be simulated interactively or automatically, there are a number of symbolic optimization tools, and the corresponding Labeled Transition System (LTS) can be generated. This LTS can, in turn, be minimized modulo a range of behavioral semantics and model checked with the mCRL2 toolset or the CADP toolset [6].

4   From Tscript to mCRL2

Both TSCRIPT and mCRL2 are based on the process algebra ACP [3]. In spite of this common origin, the languages have some important differences, presented later in this section.

Note queues. According to the semantics of the TOOLBUS, each process created by TSCRIPT has a queue for incoming notes. A `rec-note` will inspect the note queue of the current process, and if the queue contains a note of a given form, it will remove the note and assign values to variables appearing in its argument list; these can be used later on in the process expression in which the `rec-note` occurs.

mCRL2 contains no built-in primitives for asynchronous communications. Therefore in mCRL2, note queues are handled by a separate AsyncComm process. It also takes care of subscriptions/unsubscriptions and lets any process send any note at any time. Any process can inspect its queue for incoming notes by synchronously communicating with AsyncComm.

Dynamic process creation. Process instances may be created dynamically in TSCRIPT using the `create` statement. Although not part of the language, such a process creation mechanism can, in principle, be modeled in mCRL2 using *recursive parallelism*. The latter, however, is not currently supported by the tools in the mCRL2 toolset.

Here, we present a simple solution to this problem, by statically fixing the *maximal* number of process instances that can be active simultaneously. These process instances are present from the start, and the master process divides connecting tools over these processes. To be more precise, for a given TSCRIPT process definition `Pname`, we assume the maximal number of its simultaneously

active instances to be some m. For a translation of **Pname** to an mCRL2 process
Pname, we define the following process Pname_inactive,

proc Pname_inactive($pid:Pid$) = r_create($Pname, pid$) · Pname(pid)

which after synchronizing with an action s_create proceeds as the process Pname.
We instantiate m instances of Pname_inactive in parallel by Pname_inactive(1) ∥
... ∥ Pname_inactive(m).

Successful termination of (dynamically) created processes in TSCRIPT is denoted by a **delta** statement. In our approach, the mCRL2 processes do not
terminate, but become inactive instead. Therefore, the terminating **delta** statements of **Pname** are translated to Pname_inactive(pid) recursive calls.

A process willing to create an instance of **Pname** has to execute the mCRL2
expression $\sum_{pid:Pid}$ s_create($Pname, pid$) (instead of a **create** command). As a
result of the synchronization with r_create, the creating process gets the pid of
the "created" process.

Binary star versus recursion. TSCRIPT makes use of the binary star operation
$p * q$, representing zero or more repetitions of p followed by q. Assuming that the
TSCRIPT expression p is translated to an mCRL2 process expression P, and q to
Q, the whole TSCRIPT expression $p * q$ is represented in mCRL2 by the recursion
variable PQ defined as $PQ = P \cdot PQ + Q$.

Local variables. TSCRIPT process definitions may make use of local variables and
assignments to them. They can be directly translated to process parameters in
mCRL2, provided all of them are (made) unique.

Special care has to be taken with the result variables of TSCRIPT, which
get a value assigned depending on the context in which they occur. In case they
occur in input communication statements like **rec-msg**, **rec-note** or **rec-value**,
they can be represented as summations in mCRL2. For example, the TSCRIPT
expression **let** V:Type **in** rec-msg(msg(V?))...**endlet** can be represented as
the mCRL2 expression $\sum_{V:Type}$ rec_msg(V) · ....

In case the result variables occur in process calls, the only way we see to translate them to mCRL2, is to (at least partially) *unfold* the process call instance,
so that we get to a situation where the input variable occurs in a communicating
statement.

Discrete time. One simple option to implement discrete time in mCRL2, is to
make use of the **tick** action synchronization (cf. [17,18,19]). First, we identify the
places where waiting makes sense. These are places where input communication
statements are possible. In case no delays are present in these statements, we
introduce a possibility to perform the **tick** action and remain in the current state.
In case a TSCRIPT statement is specified with a certain delay, we prepend the
resulting mCRL2 translation with the appropriate number of ticks. All TSCRIPT
process translations have to synchronize on their **tick** actions.

Another option is to use the real-time operations built into mCRL2. The
current version of the mCRL2 toolset, however, has only limited support for the
analysis of such timed specifications. An interesting possibility is to use clocks
to specify timed primitives of TSCRIPTs, and to use well-known techniques for

analyzing Timed Automata [20] like regions and zones [21] in the context of mCRL2 (cf. [22]).

Unbounded data types. A TSCRIPT can use variables of unbounded data types, like integers, in communications with the tools. These can be modeled in mCRL2, but the analysis with *explicit-state* model checking techniques will not work. An alternative approach could be in the use of abstract interpretation techniques in the context of mCRL2 (cf. [23]).

5   Conclusion and Future Work

Our general aim is to have a process algebra-based software development environment where both formal verification and production of an executable system is possible. In this paper we looked at a possibility to bring formal verification with mCRL2 to TOOLBUS scripts.

We presented a translation scheme from TSCRIPT to mCRL2. This translation makes it possible to apply formal verification techniques to TSCRIPT. We aim at an automated translation tool from TSCRIPT to mCRL2, which will make it possible to verify TSCRIPT in a fully automated fashion, and to explore behavioral properties of large software systems that have been built with the TOOLBUS.

The following issues remain as future work.

- Although the translated mCRL2 model is similar in size to the original TOOLBUS script, its underlying state space may be too large for formal verification. The issues with unbounded data types, timing, and growing note queues due to asynchronous communication, mentioned in Section 4, have to be further addressed.
- The mCRL2 model generated from a particular TOOLBUS script can be checked for deadlocks, livelocks and some other standard properties. For the analysis of more specific behavioral details one would need properties formulated by the developer of this particular script. Alternatively, a reference mCRL2 model of the tools that communicate with the original script can be considered as an environment for the generated mCRL2 model. Putting this environment model in parallel with the generated mCRL2 model could lead to a more detailed analysis of the external behavior of the original TOOLBUS script.

References

1. Bergstra, J., Klint, P.: The ToolBus coordination architecture. In: Hankin, C., Ciancarini, P. (eds.) COORDINATION 1996. LNCS, vol. 1061, pp. 75–88. Springer, Heidelberg (1996)
2. Bergstra, J., Klint, P.: The discrete time ToolBus - a software coordination architecture. Sci. Comput. Program. 31(2-3), 205–229 (1998)
3. Bergstra, J., Klop, J.W.: Process algebra for synchronous communication. Information and Control 60(1-3), 109–137 (1984)

4. Groote, J.F., Mathijssen, A., Reniers, M., Usenko, Y., van Weerdenburg, M.: The formal specification language mCRL2. In: Proc. Methods for Modelling Software Systems. Number 06351 in Dagstuhl Seminar Proceedings (2007)
5. Bergstra, J., Heering, J., Klint, P.: Module algebra. J. ACM 37(2), 335–372 (1990)
6. Garavel, H., Mateescu, R., Lang, F., Serwe, W.: CADP 2006: A toolbox for the construction and analysis of distributed processes. In: Damm, W., Hermanns, H. (eds.) CAV 2007. LNCS, vol. 4590, pp. 158–163. Springer, Heidelberg (2007)
7. Wing, J.: Writing Larch interface language specifications. ACM TOPLAS 9(1), 1–24 (1987)
8. Guaspari, D., Marceau, C., Polak, W.: Formal verification of Ada programs. IEEE Trans. Software Eng. 16(9), 1058–1075 (1990)
9. Zhao, J., Rinard, M.: Pipa: A behavioral interface specification language for AspectJ. In: Pezzé, M. (ed.) ETAPS 2003 and FASE 2003. LNCS, vol. 2621, pp. 150–165. Springer, Heidelberg (2003)
10. Kiczales, G., Hilsdale, E., Hugunin, J., Kersten, M., Palm, J., Griswold, W.: An overview of AspectJ. In: Knudsen, J.L. (ed.) ECOOP 2001. LNCS, vol. 2072, pp. 327–353. Springer, Heidelberg (2001)
11. Larsson, D., Alexandersson, R.: Formal verification of fault tolerance aspects. In: Proc. ISSRE 2005, pp. 279–280. IEEE, Los Alamitos (2005)
12. Diertens, B.: Simulation and animation of process algebra specifications. Technical Report P9713, University of Amsterdam (1997)
13. Diertens, B.: Software (re-)engineering with PSF III: An IDE for PSF. Technical Report PRG0708, University of Amsterdam (2007)
14. van den Brand, M., de Jong, H., Klint, P., Olivier, P.: Efficient annotated terms. Softw. Pract. Exper. 30(3), 259–291 (2000)
15. Klint, P.: A meta-environment for generating programming environments. ACM TOSEM 2(2), 176–201 (1993)
16. van den Brand, M., van Deursen, A., Heering, J., de Jong, H., de Jonge, M., Kuipers, T., Klint, P., Moonen, L., Olivier, P., Scheerder, J., Vinju, J., Visser, E., Visser, J.: The ASF+SDF Meta-Environment: a Component-Based Language Development Environment. In: Wilhelm, R. (ed.) CC 2001 and ETAPS 2001. LNCS, vol. 2027, pp. 365–370. Springer, Heidelberg (2001)
17. Fokkink, W., Ioustinova, N., Kesseler, E., van de Pol, J., Usenko, Y., Yushtein, Y.: Refinement and verification applied to an in-flight data acquisition unit. In: Brim, L., Jančar, P., Křetínský, M., Kucera, A. (eds.) CONCUR 2002. LNCS, vol. 2421, pp. 1–23. Springer, Heidelberg (2002)
18. Blom, S., Ioustinova, N., Sidorova, N.: Timed verification with μCRL. In: Broy, M., Zamulin, A.V. (eds.) PSI 2003. LNCS, vol. 2890, pp. 178–192. Springer, Heidelberg (2004)
19. Wijs, A.: Achieving discrete relative timing with untimed process algebra. In: Proc. ICECCS 2007, pp. 35–46. IEEE, Los Alamitos (2007)
20. Alur, R., Dill, D.: A theory of timed automata. Theor. Comput. Sci. 126, 183–235 (1994)
21. Alur, R.: Timed automata. In: Halbwachs, N., Peled, D.A. (eds.) CAV 1999. LNCS, vol. 1633, pp. 8–22. Springer, Heidelberg (1999)
22. Groote, J.F., Reniers, M., Usenko, Y.: Time abstraction in timed μCRL a la regions. In: Proc. IPDPS 2006. IEEE, Los Alamitos (2006)
23. Valero Espada, M., van de Pol, J.: An abstract interpretation toolkit for μCRL. Formal Methods in System Design 30(3), 249–273 (2007)

A Formal Analysis of Complex Type Flaw Attacks on Security Protocols[*]

Han Gao[1], Chiara Bodei[2], and Pierpaolo Degano[2]

[1] Informatics and Mathematical Modelling, Technical University of Denmark,
Richard Petersens Plads bldg 322, DK-2800 Kongens Lyngby, Denmark
hg@imm.dtu.dk
[2] Dipartimento di Informatica, Università di Pisa,
Largo B. Pontecorvo, 3, I-56127, Pisa, Italy
{chiara,degano}@di.unipi.it

Abstract. A simple type confusion attack occurs in a security protocol, when a principal interprets data of one type as data of another. These attacks can be successfully prevented by "tagging" types of each field of a message. Complex type confusions occur instead when tags can be confused with data and when fields or sub-segments of fields may be confused with concatenations of fields of other types. Capturing these kinds of confusions is not easy in a process calculus setting, where it is generally assumed that messages are correctly interpreted. In this paper, we model in the process calculus LySA only the misinterpretation due to the confusion of a concatenation of fields with a single field, by extending the notation of one-to-one variable binding to many-to-one binding. We further present a formal way of detecting these possible misinterpretations, based on a Control Flow Analysis for this version of the calculus. The analysis over-approximates all the possible behaviour of a protocol, including those effected by these type confusions. As an example, we considered the amended Needham-Schroeder symmetric protocol, where we succeed in detecting the type confusion that lead to a complex type flaw attacks it is subject to. Therefore, the analysis can capture potential type confusions of this kind on security protocols, besides other security properties such as confidentiality, freshness and message authentication.

1 Introduction

In the last decades, formal analyses of cryptographic protocols have been widely studied and many formal methods have been put forward. Usually, protocol specification is given at a very high level of abstraction and several implementation aspects, such as the cryptographic ones, are abstracted away. Despite the abstract working hypotheses, many attacks have been found that are independent of these aspects. Sometimes, this abstract view is not completely adequate, though. At a high level, a message in a protocol consists of fields: each represents some value, such as the name of a principal, a nonce or a key. This structure can

---

[*] This work has been partially supported by the project SENSORIA.

J. Meseguer and G. Roşu (Eds.): AMAST 2008, LNCS 5140, pp. 167–183, 2008.
© Springer-Verlag Berlin Heidelberg 2008

be easily modelled by a process calculus. Nevertheless, at a more concrete level, a message is nothing but a raw sequence of bits. In this view, the recipient of a message has to decide the interpretation of the bit string, i.e. how to decompose the string into substrings to be associated to the expected fields (of the expected length) of the message. The message comes with no indication on its arity and on the types of its components. This source of ambiguity can be exploited by an intruder that can fool the recipient into accepting as valid a message different from the expected one. A *type confusion attack* arises in this case.

A *simple* type confusion occurs when a field is confused with another [16]. The current preventing techniques [13] consists in systematically associating message fields with tags representing their intended type. On message reception, honest participants check tags so that fields with different types cannot be mixed up. As stated by Meadows [17], though, simple tags could not suffice for more complex type confusion cases: "in which tags may be confused with data, and terms of pieces of terms of one type may be confused with concatenations of terms of several other types." Tags should also provide the length of tagged fields.

Here, we are interested in semantically capturing attacks that occur when a concatenation of fields is confused with a single field [24]. Suppose, e.g. that the message pair (A, N), where A is a principal identity and N is a fresh nonce, is interpreted as a key K, from the receiver of the message. For simplicity, we call them *complex type confusion attacks*. This level of granularity is difficult to capture with a standard process calculus. An alternative could be separating control from data, as in [1], and using equational theories on data; this however makes mechanical analysis more expensive. In a standard process algebraic framework, there is no way to confuse a term (A, N) with a term K. The term is assumed to abstractly model a message, plugging in the model the hypothesis that the message is correctly interpreted. In concrete implementation this confusion is instead possible, provided that the two strings have the same length.

As a concrete example, consider the Amended Needham Schroeder symmetric key protocol [9]. It aims at distributing a new session key K between two agents, Alice (A) and Bob (B), via a trusted server S. Initially each agent is assumed to

1. $A \to B : A$	1. $A \to B :$ A
2. $B \to A : \{A, N_B\}_{K_B}$	2. $B \to A :$ $\{A, N_B\}_{K_B}$
3. $A \to S : A, B, N_A, \{A, N_B\}_{K_B}$	3. $A \to S :$ $A, B, N_A, \{A, N_B\}_{K_B}$
4. $S \to A : \{N_A, B, K, \{K, N_B, A\}_{K_B}\}_{K_A}$	1'. $M \to A :$ N_A, B, K'
5. $A \to B : \{K, N_B, A\}_{K_B}$	2'. $A \to M :$ $\{N_A, B, K', N'_A\}_{K_A}$
6. $B \to A : \{N\}_K$	4. $M(S) \to A :$ $\{N_A, B, K', N'_A\}_{K_A}$
7. $A \to B : \{N - 1\}_K$	5. $A \to M(B) : N'_A$
(a)	6. $M(B) \to A : \{N\}_{K'}$
	7. $A \to M :$ $\{N - 1\}_{K'}$
	(b)

Fig. 1. Amended Needham-Schroeder Symmetric Protocol: Protocol Narration (a) and Type Flaw Attack (b)

share a long term key, K_A and K_B resp., with the server. The protocol narration is reported in Fig. 1 (a). In messages 1 and 2, A initiates the protocol with B. In message 3 S generates a new session key K, that is distributed in messages 4 and 5. Nonces created by A and B are used to check freshness of the new key. Finally, messages 6 and 7 are for mutual authentication of A and B: B generates a new nonce N and exchanges it with A, encrypted with the new session key K.

The protocol is vulnerable to a complex type flaw attack, discovered by Long [14] and shown in Fig. 1 (b). It requires two instances of the protocol, running in parallel. In one, A plays the roles of initiator and in the other that of responder. In the first instance, A initiates the protocol with B. In the meantime, the attacker, M, initiates the second instance with A and sends the triple N_A, B, K' to A (in step $1'$). The nonce N_A is a copy from step 3 in the first instance and K' is a faked key generated by the attacker. A will generate and send out the encryption of the received fields, N_A, B, K', and a nonce N'_A. The attacker $M(S)$ impersonates S and replays this message to A in the first instance. A decrypts this message, checks the nonce N_A and the identity B, and accepts K' as the session key, which is actually generated by the attacker. After the challenge and response steps (6 and 7), A will communicate with M using the faked key K'.

Our idea is to explore complex type confusion attacks, by getting closer to the implementation, without crossing the comfortable borders of process calculi. To this aim, we formally model the possible misinterpretations between terms and concatenations of terms. More precisely, we extend the notation of one-to-one variable binding to many-to-one binding in the process calculus LySa [5], that we use to model security protocols. The Control Flow Analysis soundly over-approximates the behaviour of protocols, by collecting the set of messages that can be sent over the network, and by recording which values variables may be bound to. Moreover, at each binding occurrence of a variable, the analysis checks whether there is any many-to-one binding possible and records it as a binding violation. The approach is able to detect complex type confusions possibly leading to attacks in cryptographic protocols. Other security properties can be addressed in the same framework, by just changing the values of interest of the Control Flow Analysis, while its core does not change.

The paper is organized as follows. In Section 2, we present the syntax and semantics of the LySa calculus. In Section 3, we introduce the Control Flow Analysis and we describe the Dolev-Yao attacker used in our setting. Moreover, we conduct an experiment to analyse the amended Needham-Schoreder symmetric key protocol. Section 4 concludes the paper.

2   The LySa Calculus

The LySa calculus [5] is a process calculus, designed especially for modelling cryptographic protocols in the tradition of the π- [20] and Spi- [2] calculi. It differs from these essentially in two aspects: (1) the absence of channels: all processes have only access to a single global communication channel, the network; (2) the inclusion of pattern matching *into* the language constructs where values can become bound to values, i.e. into input and into decryption (while usually there is a separate construct).

Syntax. In LYSA, the basic building blocks are values, $V \in Val$, which correspond to *closed* terms, i.e. terms without free variables. Values are used to represent keys, nonces, encrypted messages, etc. Syntactically, they are described by expressions $E \in Expr$ (or terms) that may either be variables, names, or encryptions. Variables and names come from two disjoint sets Var, ranged over by x, and $Name$, ranged over by n, respectively. Finally, expressions may be encryptions of a k-tuple of other expressions, in which case, E_0 is the key used to perform the encryption. LYSA expressions are, in turn, used to construct LYSA processes $P \in Proc$ as shown below. Here, we assume perfect cryptography.

$$E ::= n \mid x \mid \{E_1, \ldots, E_k\}_{E_0}$$
$$P ::= \langle E_1, \ldots, E_k \rangle.P \mid (E_1, \ldots, E_j; x_{j+1}, \ldots, x_k)^l.P$$
$$\text{decrypt } E \text{ as } \{E_1, \ldots, E_j; x_{j+1}, \ldots, x_k\}^l_{E_0} \text{ in } P \mid$$
$$(\nu\, n)P \mid P_1 | P_2 \mid !P \mid 0$$

The set of free variables, resp. free names, of a term or a process is defined in the standard way. As usual we omit the trailing 0 of processes. The label l from a denumerable set Lab ($l \in Lab$) in the input and in the decryption constructs uniquely identifies each input and decryption point, resp., and is mechanically attached.

In addition to the classical constructs for composing processes, LYSA contains an input and a decryption construct with pattern matching. Patterns are in the form $(E_1, \cdots, E_j; x_{j+1}, \cdots, x_k)$ and are matched against k-tuples of values $\langle E'_1, \cdots, E'_k \rangle$. The intuition is that the matching succeeds when the first $1 \leq i \leq j$ values E'_i pairwise correspond to the values E_i, and the effect is to bind the remaining $k - j$ values to the variables $x_{j+1}, \cdots, x_k$. Syntactically, this is indicated by a semi-colon that separates the components where matching is performed from those where only binding takes place. For example, let $P = \text{decrypt } \{y\}_K$ as $\{x; \}^l_K$ in P' and $Q = \text{decrypt } \{y\}_K$ as $\{; x\}^l_K$ in Q'. While the decryption in P succeeds only if x matches y, the one in Q always does, binding x to y.

Extended LYSA. As seen above, in LYSA, values are passed around among processes through pattern matching and variable binding. This is the way to model how principals acquire knowledge from the network, by reading messages (or performing decryptions), provided they have certain format forms. A requirement for pattern matching is that patterns and expressions are of the same length: processes only receive (or decrypt) messages, whose length is exactly as expected and each variable is binding to one single value, later on as *one-to-one* binding. We shall relax this constraint, because it implicitly prevents us from modelling complex type confusions, i.e. the possibility to accept a concatenation of fields as a single one. Consider the complex type flaw attack on the amended Needham-Schroder protocol, shown in the Introduction. The principal A, in the role of responder, is fooled by accepting N_A, B, K' as the identity of the initiator and generates the encryption $\{N_A, B, K', N'_A\}_{K_A}$, which will be replayed by the attacker later on in the first instance. In LYSA, A's input can be roughly expressed as $(; x_b)$, as she is expecting a single field representing the identity of the initiator of the protocol. Because of the length requirement, though, x_b can only be binding to a single value and not to a concatenation of values, such as the (N_A, B, K') object of the output of the attacker.

To model complex type confusions, we need to allow a pattern matching to succeed also in the cases in which the length of lists is different. The extension of the notation of pattern matching and variable binding will be referred as *many-to-one* binding. Patterns are then allowed to be matched against expressions with *at least* the same number of elements. A single variable can then be bound also to a concatenation of values. Since there may be more values than variables, we partition the values into groups (or lists) such that there are the same number of value groups and variables. Now, each group of values is bound to the corresponding variable. In this new setting, the pattern in A's input $(; x_b)$ can instead successfully match the expression in the faked output of the attacker $\langle N_A, B, K' \rangle$ and result in the binding of x_b to the value (N_A, B, K').

We need some auxiliary definitions first. The domain of *single values* is built from the following grammar and represents closed expressions (i.e. without free variables), where each value is a singleton, i.e. it is not a list of values. In other words, no many-to-one binding has affected the expression. These are the values used in the original LYSA semantics.

$val \ni v ::= n \mid \{v_1, \ldots, v_k\}_{v_0}.$

General values are closed expressions, where each value V can be a list of values $(V_1, .., V_n)$. These values are used to represent expressions closed after at least one many-to-one-binding and are the values our semantics handles.

$Val \ni V ::= v \mid (V_1, .., V_n) \mid \{V_1, .., V_n\}_{V_0}$

To perform meaningful matching operations between lists of general values, we first flatten them, thus obtaining *flattened values* that can be either single values v or encryptions of general values.

$Flat \ni T := v \mid \{V_1, .., V_n\}_{V_0}$

Flattening is obtained by using the following *Flatten* function $Fl : Val \to Flat$

- $Fl(v) = v;$
- $Fl((V_1, .., V_n)) = Fl(V_1), \ldots, Fl(V_n);$ • $Fl(\{V_1, .., V_n\}_{V_0}) = \{V_1, .., V_n\}_{V_0}.$

Example 1. $Fl(((n_1, n_2), (\{m_1, (m_2, m_3)\}_{m_0}))) = n_1, n_2, \{m_1, (m_2, m_3)\}_{m_0}$

The idea is that encryptions cannot be directly flattened when belonging to a list of general values. Their contents are instead flattened when received and analysed in the decryption phase.

To perform many-to-one bindings, we resort to a partition operator $\prod_k$ that, given a list of flattened values $(T_1, \ldots, T_n)$, returns all the possible partitions composed by k *non-empty* groups (or lists) of flattened values. For simplicity, we use $\widetilde{T}$ to represent a list of flattened values $(T_1, \ldots, T_j)$

$$\prod_k (T_1, \ldots, T_n) = \{(\widetilde{T_1}, ..., \widetilde{T_k}) \mid \forall i : \widetilde{T_i} \neq \emptyset \wedge Fl((\widetilde{T_1}, ..., \widetilde{T_k})) = (T_1, \ldots, T_n)\} \text{ if } n \geq k$$

Note that the function is only defined if $n \geq k$, in which case it returns a set of lists satisfying the condition. Now binding k variables $x_1, ..., x_k$ to n flattened values amounts to partitioning the values into k (the number of variables) non-empty lists of flattened values, $(\widetilde{T_1}, ..., \widetilde{T_k}) \in \prod_k(T_1, ..., T_n)$, and binding variables x_i to the corresponding list $\widetilde{T_i}$.

Example 2. Consider the successful matching of $(m; x_1, x_2)$ against (m, n_1, n_2, n_3). Since $\prod_2(n_1, n_2, n_3) = \{((n_1), (n_2, n_3)), ((n_1, n_2), (n_3))\}$, it results in two possible effects (recall that for each i, $\widetilde{T_i}$ must be non-empty), i.e.

- binding variable x_1 to (n_1) and binding variable x_2 to (n_2, n_3), or
- binding variable x_1 to (n_1, n_2) and binding variable x_2 to (n_3).

Finally, we define the relation $=^F$ as the least equivalence over Val and (by overloading the symbol) and over $Flat$ that includes:
- $v =^F v'$ iff $v = v'$;
- $(V_1, ..., V_k) =^F (V_1', ..., V_n')$ iff $Fl(V_1, ..., V_k) = Fl(V_1', ..., V_n')$;
- $\{V_1, ..., V_k\}_{V_0} =^F \{V_1', ..., V_n'\}_{V_0'}$ iff $Fl(V_1, ..., V_k) = Fl(V_1', ..., V_n')$ and $Fl(V_0) = Fl(V_0')$;

Semantics. LYSA has a reduction semantics, based on a standard structural equivalence. The *reduction relation* $\rightarrow_\mathcal{R}$ is the least relation on closed processes that satisfies the rules in Tab. 1. It uses a standard notion of structural congruence $\equiv$.

At run time, the complex type confusions are checked by a reference monitor, which aborts when there is a possibility that a concatenation of values is bound to a single variable. We consider two variants of the *reduction relation* $\rightarrow_\mathcal{R}$, graphically identified by a different instantiation of the relation $\mathcal{R}$, which decorates the transition relation. The first variant takes advantage of checks on type confusions, while the other one discards them: essentially, the first semantics checks for the presence of complex type confusions. More precisely, the reference monitor performs its checks at each binding occurrence, i.e. when the pattern $V_1, ..., V_k$ is matched against $V_1', ..., V_k'; x_j, ..., x_t$. Both the lists of values are flattened and result in s values $T_1, ..., T_s$, len values $T_1', ..., T_{len}'$, resp. The reference monitor checks whether the length of the list $len + (t - j)$ of the flattened values of the pattern, corresponds to the length s of the list of the general values to match against it. If $(len + t - j) = s$ then there is a one-to-one correspondence between variables and flattened values. Otherwise, then there exists at least a variable x_i, which may bind to a list of more than one value. Formally:

- the reference monitor semantics, $P \rightarrow_{\mathsf{RM}} P'$, takes $\mathcal{R} = \mathsf{RM}(s, len + t - j)$ true when $s = len + t - j$, where s and $len + t - j$ are defined as above;
- the standard semantics, $P \rightarrow P'$ takes $\mathcal{R}$ to be universally true.

The rule (Com) in the Tab. 1 states when an output $\langle V_1, ..., V_k \rangle.P$ is matched by an input $(V_1', ..., V_j'; x_{j+1}, ..., x_t)^l.P'$. It requires that: (i) the first j general values of the input pattern $V_1', ..., V_j'$ are flattened into len flattened values $T_1', ..., T_{len}'$; (ii) the general values $V_1, ..., V_k$ in the output tuple are flattened into s flattened values $T_1, ..., T_s$; (iii) if $s \geq (len + t - j)$ and the first len values of $T_1, ..., T_s$ pairwise match with $T_1', ..., T_{len}'$ then the matching succeeds; (iv) in

Table 1. Operational Semantics; $P \to_{\mathcal{R}} P'$, parameterised on $\mathcal{R}$

(Com)
$$\frac{\wedge_{i=1}^{len} T_i =^F T_i' \ \wedge \ \mathcal{R}(s, len + t - j)}{\langle V_1, \ldots, V_k \rangle.P \mid (V_1', \ldots, V_j'; x_{j+1}, \ldots, x_t)^l.P' \to_{\mathcal{R}} P \mid P'[\widetilde{T}_{j+1}/x_{j+1}, \ldots, \widetilde{T}_t/x_t]}$$
where (A) holds

(Dec)
$$\frac{V_0 =^F V_0' \ \wedge \ \wedge_{i=1}^{len} T_i =^F T_i' \ \wedge \ \mathcal{R}(s, len + t - j)}{\text{decrypt } \{V_1, \ldots, V_k\}_{V_0} \text{ as } \{V_1', \ldots, V_j'; x_{j+1}, \ldots, x_t\}_{V_0'}^l \text{ in } P \to_{\mathcal{R}} P[\widetilde{T}_{j+1}/x_{j+1}, \ldots, \widetilde{T}_t/x_t]}$$
where (A) holds

(New)
$$\frac{P \to_{\mathcal{R}} P'}{(\nu\, n)P \to_{\mathcal{R}} (\nu\, n)P'}$$

(Par)
$$\frac{P_1 \to_{\mathcal{R}} P_1'}{P_1 \mid P_2 \to_{\mathcal{R}} P_1' \mid P_2}$$

(Congr)
$$\frac{P \equiv P' \ \wedge \ P' \to_{\mathcal{R}} P'' \wedge P'' \equiv P'''}{P \to_{\mathcal{R}} P'''}$$

$$A = \left\{ \begin{array}{l} Fl((V_1, \ldots, V_k)) = T_1, \ldots, T_{len}, T_{len+1}, \ldots, T_s \\ Fl(V_1', \ldots, V_j')) = T_1', \ldots, T_{len}' \\ (\widetilde{T}_{j+1}, \ldots, \widetilde{T}_t) \ \in \ \prod_{t-j}(T_{len+1}, \ldots, T_s) \end{array} \right\}$$

this case, the remaining values $T_{len+1}, \ldots, T_s$ are partitioned into a sequence of non-empty lists $\widetilde{T}_i$, whose number is equal to the one of the variables (i.e. $t - j$), computed by the operator $\prod_{t-j}$. Furthermore, the reference monitor checks for the possibility of many-to-one binding, i.e. checks whether $s \geq (len + t - j)$. If this is the case, it aborts the execution. Note that, if instead $s = (len + t - j)$, then $Fl(V_1, \ldots, V_k) = V_1, \ldots, V_k$, $Fl(V_1', \ldots, V_j') = V_1', \ldots, V_j'$, $k = s$, and $j = len$.

The rule (Dec) performs pattern matching and variable binding in the same way as in (Com), with the following additional requirement: the keys for encryption and decryption have to be equal, i.e. $V_0 =^F V_0'$. Similarly, the reference monitor aborts the execution if many-to-one binding occurs.

The rules (New), (Par) and (Congr) are standard, where the (Congr) rule also makes use of structural equivalence $\equiv$.

As for the dynamic property of the process, we say that a process is *complex type coherent*, when there is no complex type confusions, i.e. there is no many-to-one binding in any of its executions. Consequently, the reference monitor will never stop any execution step.

Definition 1 (Complex Type Coherence). *A process P is complex type coherent if for all the executions $P \to^* P' \to P''$ whenever $P' \to P''$ is derived using either axiom*
- *(Com) on $\langle V_1, \ldots, V_k \rangle.Q \mid (V_1', \ldots, V_j'; x_{j+1}, \ldots, x_t)^l.Q'$ or*
- *(Dec) on decrypt $\{V_1, \ldots, V_k\}_{V_0}$ as $\{V_1', \ldots, V_j'; x_{j+1}, \ldots, x_t\}_{V_0'}^l$ in Q*

it is always the case that $s = len + t - j$, where $Fl(V_p, \ldots, V_k) = T_p, \ldots, T_s$ and $Fl(V_p', \ldots, V_j') = T_p, \ldots, T_{len}$ with $p = 1$ ($p = 0$) in the case of (Com), (Dec), respectively.

3 The Control Flow Analysis

Our analysis aims at safely over-approximating how a protocol behaves and when the reference monitor may abort the computation.

The Control Flow Analysis describes a protocol behaviour by collecting all the communications that a process may participate in. In particular, the analysis records which value tuples may flow over the network (see the analysis component κ below) and which value variables may be bound to (component ρ). This gives information on bindings due to pattern matching. Moreover, at each binding occurrence, the Control Flow Analysis checks whether there is any many-to-one binding possible, and records it as a binding violation (component ψ). Formally, the approximation, or *estimate*, is a triple (ρ, κ, ψ) (respectively, a pair (ρ, θ) when analysing an expression E) that satisfies the judgements defined by the axioms and rules in Tab. 2.

Analysis of Expressions. For each expression E, our analysis will determine a superset of the possible values it may evaluate to. For this, the analysis keeps track of the potential values of variables, by recording them into the global *abstract environment*:
- $\rho : \mathcal{X} \to \mathcal{P}(Val)$ that maps the variables to the sets of general values that they may be bound to, i.e. if $a \in \rho(x)$ then x may take the value a.

The judgement for expressions takes the form $\rho \models E : \vartheta$ where $\vartheta \subseteq Val^*$ is an acceptable *estimate* (i.e. a sound over-approximation) of the set of general value lists that E may evaluate to in the environment ρ. The judgement is defined by the axioms and rules in the upper part of Tab. 2. Basically, the rules demand that ϑ contains all the value lists associated with the components of a term, e.g. a name n evaluates to the set ϑ, provided that n belongs to ϑ; similarly for a variable x, provided that ϑ includes the set of value lists $\rho(x)$ to which x is associated with.

The rule (Enc) (i) checks the validity of estimates θ_i for each expression E_i; (ii) requires that all the values $T_1, ..., T_s$ obtained by flattening the k-tuples $V_1, ..., V_k$, such that $V_i \in \theta_i$, are collected into values of the form $(\{T_1, \cdots, T_s\}_{V_0}^l)$, (iii) requires these values to belong to ϑ.

Analysis of Processes. In the analysis of processes, we focus on which tuples of values can flow on the network:
- $\kappa \subseteq \mathcal{P}(Val^*)$, the *abstract network environment*, includes all the tuples forming a message that may flow on the network, e.g. if the tuple $\langle a, b \rangle$ belongs to κ then it can be sent on the network.

The judgement for processes has the form: $(\rho, \kappa) \models P : \psi$, where ψ is the possibly empty set of "error messages" of the form l, indicating a binding violation at the point labelled l. We prove in Theorem 2 below that when $\psi = \emptyset$ we may do without the reference monitor. The judgement is defined by the axioms and rules in the lower part of Tab. 2 (where $A \Rightarrow B$ means that B is analysed only when A is evaluated to be *true*) and are explained below.

CFA Rules Explanation. The rule for *output* (Out), computes all the messages that can be obtained by flattening all the general values to which

Table 2. Analysis of terms; $\rho \models E : \vartheta$, and processes: $(\rho, \kappa) \models P : \psi$

$$\text{(Name)} \quad \frac{(n) \in \vartheta}{\rho \models n : \vartheta} \qquad \text{(Var)} \quad \frac{\rho(x) \subseteq \vartheta}{\rho \models x : \vartheta}$$

$$\text{(Enc)} \quad \frac{\begin{array}{c} \wedge_{i=0}^{k} \rho \models E_i : \vartheta_i \ \wedge \\ \forall V_0, \ldots, V_k : \wedge_{i=0}^{k} V_i \in \vartheta_i \ \wedge \ Fl(V_1, \ldots, V_k) = T_1, \ldots, T_s \Rightarrow \\ (\{T_1, \ldots, T_s\}_{V_0}) \in \vartheta \end{array}}{\rho \models \{E_1, \ldots, E_k\}_{E_0} : \vartheta}$$

$$\text{(Out)} \quad \frac{\begin{array}{c} \wedge_{i=1}^{k} \rho \models E_i : \vartheta_i \ \wedge \\ \forall V_1, \ldots, V_k : \wedge_{i=1}^{k} V_i \in \vartheta_i \ \wedge \ Fl(V_1, \ldots, V_k) = T_1, \ldots, T_s \Rightarrow \\ \langle T_1, \ldots, T_s \rangle \in \kappa \ \wedge \ (\rho, \kappa) \models P : \psi \end{array}}{(\rho, \kappa) \models \langle E_1, \ldots, E_k \rangle . P : \psi}$$

$$\text{(In)} \quad \frac{\begin{array}{c} \wedge_{i=1}^{j} \rho \models E_i : \vartheta_1 \ \wedge \\ \forall V'_1, \ldots, V'_j : \wedge_{i=1}^{j} V'_i \in \vartheta_i \ \wedge \ Fl(V'_1, \ldots, V'_j) = T'_1, \ldots, T'_{len} \Rightarrow \\ \forall \langle T_1, \ldots, T_s \rangle \in \kappa : T_1, \ldots, T_{len} =^F T'_1, \ldots, T'_{len} \Rightarrow \\ \forall (\widetilde{T}_{j+1}, \ldots, \widetilde{T}_t) \in \prod_{t-j}(T_{len+1}, \ldots, T_k) \Rightarrow \\ (\wedge_{i=j+1}^{t} \widetilde{T}_i \in \rho(x_i) \ \wedge \ (s > len + t - j) \Rightarrow l \in \psi \ \wedge \ (\rho, \kappa) \models P : \psi) \end{array}}{(\rho, \kappa) \models (E_1, \ldots, E_j; x_{j+1}, \ldots, x_t)^l . P : \psi}$$
$$\text{where } s \geq len + t - j$$

$$\text{(Dec)} \quad \frac{\begin{array}{c} \rho \models E : \vartheta \ \wedge \ \wedge_{i=0}^{j} \rho \models E_i : \vartheta_i \ \wedge \\ \forall V'_0, \ldots, V'_j : \wedge_{i=0}^{j} V'_i \in \vartheta_i \ \wedge \ Fl(V'_1, \ldots, V'_j) = T'_1, \ldots, T'_{len} \Rightarrow \\ \forall \{T_1, \ldots, T_s\}_{V_0} \in \vartheta : T_1, \ldots, T_{len} =^F T'_1, \ldots, T'_{len} \Rightarrow \\ \forall (\widetilde{T}'_{j+1}, \ldots, \widetilde{T}'_t) \in \prod_{t-j}(T_{len+1}, \ldots, T_k) \Rightarrow \\ (\wedge_{i=j+1}^{t} \widetilde{T}'_i \in \rho(x_i) \ \wedge \ (s > len + t - j) \Rightarrow l \in \psi \ \wedge \ (\rho, \kappa) \models P : \psi) \end{array}}{(\rho, \kappa) \models \mathsf{decrypt} \ E \ \mathsf{as} \ \{E_1, \ldots, E_j; x_{j+1}, \ldots, x_t\}_{E_0}^l \ \mathsf{in} \ P : \psi}$$
$$\text{where } s \geq len + t - j$$

$$\text{(New)} \quad \frac{(\rho, \kappa) \models P : \psi}{(\rho, \kappa) \models (\nu \, n) P : \psi} \qquad \text{(Par)} \quad \frac{(\rho, \kappa) \models P_1 : \psi \ \wedge \ (\rho, \kappa) \models P_2 : \psi}{(\rho, \kappa) \models P_1 | P_2 : \psi}$$

$$\text{(Rep)} \quad \frac{(\rho, \kappa) \models P : \psi}{(\rho, \kappa) \models \, ! P : \psi} \qquad \text{(Nil)} \quad (\rho, \kappa) \models 0 : \psi$$

sub-expressions may be evaluated. The use of the flatten function makes sure that each message is plain-structured, i.e. redundant parentheses are dropped.

More precisely, it (i) checks the validity of estimates θ_i for each expression E_i; (ii) requires that all the values obtained by flattening the k-tuples $V_1, \ldots, V_k$, such that $V_i \in \theta_i$, can flow on the network, i.e. that they are in the component ρ; (iii) requires that the estimate (ρ, κ, ψ) is valid also for the continuation process P. Suppose e.g. to analyse $\langle A, N_A \rangle . 0$. In this case, we have that $\rho \models A : \{(A)\}$, $\rho \models N_A : \{(N_A)\}$, $Fl((A), (N_A)) = A, N_A$ and $\langle A, N_A \rangle \in \kappa$. Suppose instead to have $\langle A, x_A \rangle . P$ and $\rho(x_A) = \{(N_A), (N'_A)\}$. In this case we have $Fl((A), (N_A)) = A, N_A$, $Fl((A), (N'_A)) = A, N'_A$, $\langle A, N_A \rangle \in \kappa$ and also $\langle A, N'_A \rangle \in \kappa$.

The rule for *input* (In) basically looks up in κ for matched tuples and performs variable binding before analysing the continuation process. This is done in the following steps: the rule (i) evaluates the first j expressions, whose results are general values, V_i'. These are flattened into a list of values $T_1', ..., T_{len}'$ in order to perform the pattern matching. Then, the rule (ii) checks whether the first len values of any message $\langle T_1, ..., T_s \rangle$ in κ (i.e. any message predicted to flow on the network) matches the values from previous step, i.e. $T_1', ..., T_{len}'$. Also, the rule (iii) partitions the remaining $T_{len+1}, ..., T_s$ values of the tuple $\langle T_1, ..., T_s \rangle$ in all the possible ways to obtain $t - j$ lists of flattened values $\widetilde{T}_i$ and requires each list is bound to the corresponding variable $\widetilde{T}_i \in \rho(x_i)$. The rule (iv) checks whether the flattened pattern and the flattened value are of the same length. If this is not the case, the final step should be in putting l in the error component ψ. Finally, the rule (v) analyses the continuation process. Suppose to analyse the process $(A, x_A; x, x_B).0$, where $\langle A, N_A, B, N_B \rangle \in \kappa$ and $(N_A) \in \rho(x_A)$. Concretising the rule (Inp) gives $j = 2, t = 2$ and the followings,

$$
\frac{
\begin{array}{ll}
\rho \models A : \vartheta_1 \wedge \rho \models x_A : \vartheta_2 & \text{yielding } \vartheta_1 \ni (A) \text{ and } \vartheta_2 \ni (N_A) \\
\forall V_1', V_2' : V_1' \in \vartheta_1 \wedge V_2' \in \vartheta_2 \wedge & \text{taking } V_1' = (A) \text{ and } V_2' = (N_A) \wedge \\
Fl(V_1', V_2') = T_1', ..., T_{len}' & len = 2 \text{ and } T_1', ..., T_{len}' = A, N_A \\
\forall \langle T_1, ..., T_s \rangle \in \kappa : & \text{if } \langle A, N_A, B, N_B \rangle \in \kappa \text{ and } s = 4 \\
& \text{i.e. } T_1 = A, T_2 = N_A, T_3 = B, T_4 = N_B \\
T_1, ..., T_{len} =^F T_1', ..., T_{len}' \Rightarrow & T_1, T_2 =^F T_1', T_2' = A, N_A \\
\forall (\widetilde{T_3}, \widetilde{T_4}) \in \prod_2 (T_3, T_4) \Rightarrow & \prod_2 (T_3, T_4) = \prod_2 (B, N_B) = \{((B), (N_B))\} \\
(\widetilde{T_3} \in \rho(x) \wedge \widetilde{T_4} \in \rho(x_A) \wedge & \text{gives } (B) \in \rho(x) \wedge (N_B) \in \rho(x_B) \\
(s > len + t - j) \Rightarrow l \in \psi \wedge & \text{and } 4 = 4 \text{ does not require } l \notin \psi \\
(\rho, \kappa) \models 0 : \psi & true
\end{array}
}{
(\rho, \kappa) \models (A, x_A; x, x_B)^l.0 : \psi
}
$$

In particular, $((B), (N_B)) \in \prod_2 (B, N_B)$ implies that $(B) \in \rho(x)$ and $(N_B) \in \rho(x_B)$. Suppose to have also that $\langle A, N_A, B, N_B, K \rangle \in \kappa$. In this case, $((B), (N_B, K)) \in \prod_2 (B, N_B, K)$ and therefore $(B) \in \rho(x)$ and $(N_B, K) \in \rho(x_B)$ and also $((B, N_B), K) \in \prod_2 (B, N_B, K)$ and therefore $(B, N_B) \in \rho(x)$ and $(K) \in \rho(x_B)$. More precisely:

$$
\frac{
\begin{array}{ll}
\rho \models A : \vartheta_1 \wedge \rho \models x_A : \vartheta_2 & \text{yielding } \vartheta_1 \ni (A) \text{ and } \vartheta_2 \ni (N_A) \\
\forall V_1', V_2' : V_1' \in \vartheta_1 \wedge V_2' \in \vartheta_2 \wedge & \text{taking } V_1' = (A) \text{ and } V_2' = (N_A) \wedge \\
Fl(V_1', V_2') = T_1', ..., T_{len}' & len = 2 \text{ and } T_1', ..., T_{len}' = A, N_A \\
\forall \langle T_1, ..., T_s \rangle \in \kappa : & \text{if } \langle A, N_A, B, N_B, K \rangle \in \kappa \text{ and } s = 5 \\
& \text{i.e. } T_1 = A, T_2 = N_A, T_3 = B, T_4 = N_B, T_5 = K \\
T_1, ..., T_{len} =^F T_1', ..., T_{len}' \Rightarrow & T_1, T_2 =^F T_1', T_2' = A, N_A \\
\forall (\widetilde{T_3}, \widetilde{T_4}) \in \prod_2 (T_3, T_4, T_5) \Rightarrow & \prod_2 (T_3, T_4, T_5) = \prod_2 (B, N_B, K) = \\
& \{((B), (N_B, K)), ((B, N_B), (K))\} \\
(\widetilde{T_3} \in \rho(x) \wedge \widetilde{T_4} \in \rho(x_A) & \text{gives } (B), (B, N_B) \in \rho(x) \text{ and } (K), (N_B, K) \in \rho(x_B) \\
(s > len + t - j) \Rightarrow l \in \psi \wedge & 5 > 2 + 4 - 2 \text{ requires } l \in \psi \\
(\rho, \kappa) \models 0 : \psi & true
\end{array}
}{
(\rho, \kappa) \models (A, x_A; x, x_B)^l.0 : \psi
}
$$

The rule for *decryption* (Dec) is similar to (In): the values to be matched are those obtained by evaluating the expression E; while the matching ones are the terms inside decryption. If the check succeeds then variables are bound and the continuation process P is analysed. Moreover, the rule checks the possibility of many-to-one binding: the component ψ must contain the label l corresponding to the decryption. Suppose e.g. to have decrypt E as $\{E_1, \ldots, E_2; x_3, \ldots, x_4\}_{E_0}^l$ in P, with $E = \{A, N_A, B, N_B\}_K$, $E_0 = K$, $E_1 = A$, $E_2 = x_A$ and $\rho(x_A) = \{(N_A)\}$. Then we have that $\rho \models A : \{(A)\}$, $\rho \models x_A : \{(N_A)\}$ and $Fl((A), (N_A)) = A, N_A$. Then $((B), (N_B)) \in \prod_2(B, N_B)$ implies that $(B) \in \rho(x_3)$ and $(N_B) \in \rho(x_4)$. Suppose to have instead $E = \{A, N_A, B, N_B, K_0\}_K$, then $((B), (N_B, K_0)) \in \prod_2(B, N_B, K_0)$ and therefore $(B) \in \rho(x_3)$ and $(N_B, K_0) \in \rho(x_4)$ and also $((B, N_B), (K_0)) \in \prod_2(B, N_B, K_0)$ and therefore $(B, N_B) \in \rho(x_3)$ and $(K_0) \in \rho(x_4)$. Furthermore $l \in \psi$.

The rule (Nil) does not restrict the estimate, while the rules (New), (Par) and (Rep) ensure that the estimate also holds for the immediate sub-processes.

Semantics Properties. Our analysis is correct with respect to the operational semantics of LySa. The detailed proofs are omitted due to space limitations and can be found in [4].

We have the following results. The first states that estimates are resistant to substitution of closed terms for variables, and it holds for both extended terms and processes. The second one says that estimates respect $\equiv$.

Lemma 1.   *1.* (a) $\rho \models E : \vartheta \wedge (T_1, \ldots, T_k) \in \rho(x)$ *imply* $\rho \models E[T_1, \ldots, T_k/x] : \vartheta$
  (b) $(\rho, \kappa) \models P : \psi \wedge (T_1, \ldots, T_k) \in \rho(x)$ *imply* $(\rho, \kappa) \models P[T_1, \ldots, T_k/x] : \psi$
2. If $P \equiv Q$ *and* $(\rho, \kappa) \models P$ *then* $(\rho, \kappa) \models Q$

Our analysis is semantically correct regardless of the way the semantics is parameterised, furthermore the reference monitor semantics cannot stop the execution of P when ψ is empty. The proof is by induction on the inference of $P \rightarrow Q$.

Theorem 1. *(Subject reduction) If* $P \rightarrow Q$ *and* $(\rho, \kappa) \models P : \psi$ *then* $(\rho, \kappa) \models Q : \psi$. *Additionally, if* $\psi = \emptyset$ *then* $P \rightarrow_{RM} Q$.

The next theorem shows that our analysis correctly predicts when we can safely do without the reference monitor. We shall say that the reference monitor RM *cannot abort* a process P when there exist no Q, Q' such that $P \rightarrow^* Q \rightarrow Q'$ and $P \rightarrow^*_{RM} Q \nrightarrow_{RM}$. (As usual, * stands for the transitive and reflexive closure of the relation in question, and we omit the string of labels in this case; while $Q \nrightarrow_{RM}$ stands for $\nexists Q' : Q \rightarrow_{RM} Q'$.) We then have:

Theorem 2. *(Static check for reference monitor)*

If $(\rho, \kappa) \models P : \psi$ *and* $\psi = \emptyset$ *then* RM *cannot abort* P.

Modelling the Attackers. In a protocol execution, several principals exchange messages over an open network, which is therefore vulnerable to a malicious attacker. We assume it is an active Dolev-Yao attacker [10]: it can eavesdrop, and replay, encrypt, decrypt, generate messages providing that the necessary information is within his knowledge, that it increases while interacting with the network. This attacker can be modelled in LYSA as a process running in parallel with the protocol process. Formally, we shall have $P_{sys} \mid P_\bullet$, where P_{sys} represents the protocol process and $P_\bullet$ is some *arbitrary* attacker. To get an account of the infinitely many attackers, the overall idea is to find a formula $\mathcal{F}$ (for a similar treatment see [5]) that characterizes $P_\bullet$: this means that whenever a triple (ρ, κ, ψ) satisfies it, then $(\rho, \kappa) \models P_\bullet : \psi$ and this holds for all attackers, in particular for the hardest one [21]. Intuitively, the formula $\mathcal{F}$ has to mimic how $P_\bullet$ is analysed. The attacker process is parameterised on some attributes of P_{sys}, e.g. the length of all the encryptions that occurred and all the messages sent over the network. In the formula, the names and variables the attacker uses are apart from the ones used by P_{sys}. We can then postulate a new distinguished name $n_\bullet$ (variable $z_\bullet$) in which the names (variables, resp.) of the attacker are coalesced; therefore $n_\bullet$ may represent any name generated by the attacker, while $\rho(z_\bullet)$ represents the attacker knowledge. It is possible to prove that if an estimate of a process P with $\psi = \emptyset$ satisfies the attacker formula than RM does not abort the execution of $P \mid Q$, regardless of the choice of the attacker Q. Further details are in [4,5].

Implementation. Following [5], the implementation can be obtained along the lines that first transform the analysis into a logically equivalent formulation written in Alternation free Least Fixed Point logic (ALFP) [22], and then followed by using the Succinct Solver [22], which computes the least interpretation of the predicate symbols in a given ALFP formula.

3.1   Validation of the Amended Needham-Schroeder Protocol

Here, we will show that the analysis applied to the Amended Needham-Schroeder protocol, successfully captures the complex type confusion leading to the attack, presented in the Introduction.

In LYSA, each instance of the protocol is modelled as three processes, A, B and S, running in parallel within the scope of the shared keys. To allow the complex type confusion to arise, we put two instances together, and add indices to names and variables used in each instance in order to tell them apart, namely

$$P_{NS} = (\nu K_A)(\nu K_B)(A_1 \mid A_2 \mid B_1 \mid B_2 \mid S)$$

To save space, processes without indices are shown in Tab. 3. For clarity, each message begins with the pair of principals involved in the exchange. In LYSA we do not have other data constructors than encryption, but the predecessor operation can be modelled by an encryption with the key PRED that is also known to the attacker. For the sake of readability, we directly use $N - 1$. We can apply our analysis and check that $(\rho, \kappa) \models P_{NS} : \psi$, where ρ, κ and ψ have the non-empty entries (only the interesting ones) listed in Tab. 3.

The message exchanges of the regular run (the first instance) performed by A and B are correctly reflected by the analysis. In step 1, B receives the tuple

Table 3. Amended Needham-Schroeder protocol: specification (above); some analysis results (below)

Initiator A :	Responder B :
$/*1*/$ $\langle A, B, A \rangle$.	$/*1*/$ $(A, B; y_a)^{l_6}$.
$/*2*/$ $(B, A; x_{enc})^{l_1}$.	$/*2*/$ (νN_B) $\langle B, A, \{y_a, N_B\}_{K_B} \rangle$.
$/*3*/$ $(\nu N_A)\langle A, S, A, B, N_A, x_{enc} \rangle$.	
$/*4*/$ $(S, A; x_z)^{l_2}$.	
$\quad$ decrypt x_z as $\{N_A, B; x_k, x_y\}^{l_3}_{K_A}$ in	$/*5*/$ $(A, B; y_{enc})^{l_7}$.
$/*5*/$ $\langle A, B, x_y \rangle$.	$\quad$ decrypt y_{enc} as $\{N_B, A; y_k\}^{l_8}_{K_B}$ in
$/*6*/$ $(B, A; x_{no})^{l_4}$.	$/*6*/$ $(\nu N_0)\langle B, A, \{N_0\}_{y_k} \rangle$.
$\quad$ decrypt x_{no} as $\{; x_n\}^{l_5}_{x_k}$ in	$/*7*/$ $(A, B; y_{no})^{l_9}$.
$/*7*/$ $\langle A, B, \{x_n - 1\}_{x_k} \rangle$.0	$\quad$ decrypt y_{no} as $\{N_0 - 1\}^{l_{10}}_{y_k}$ in 0

Server S :
$/*3*/$ $(A, S, A, B; z_{na}, z_{enc})^{l_{11}}$.
$\quad$ decrypt z_{enc} as $\{A; z_{nb}\}^{l_{12}}_{K_B}$ in
$/*4*/$ (νK)
$\quad\quad$ $\langle S, A, \{z_{na}, B, K, \{z_{nb}, A, K\}_{K_B}\}_{K_A} \rangle$.0

$(A) \in \rho(y^1_a)$	$(B) \in \rho(z_\bullet)$	$(n_\bullet) \in \rho(x^1_k)$
$(\{A, N^1_B\}_{K_B}) \in \rho(x^1_{enc})$	$(N^1_A) \in \rho(z_\bullet)$	$\langle A, B, N^1_A, B, n_\bullet, N^2_A \rangle \in \kappa$
$(N^2_A) \in \rho(x^1_y)$	$\langle A, B, N^1_A, B, n_\bullet \rangle \in \kappa$	$(N^1_A, B, n_\bullet, N^2_A) \in \rho(x^1_z)$
$\langle A, B, N^1_A, \{A, N^1_B\}_{K_B} \rangle \in \kappa$	$(N^1_A, B, n_\bullet) \in \rho(y^2_a)$	$l_6 \in \psi$

sent by A and binds variable y^1_a to the value (A), as predicted by $(A) \in \rho(y^1_a)$. In step 2, B generates a nonce N^1_B, encrypts it together to the value of y^1_a and sends it out to the network. A reads this message, binds the variable x^1_{enc} to the value $(\{A, N^1_B\}_{K_B})$, as reflected by $(\{A, N^1_B\}_{K_B}) \in \rho(x^1_{enc})$; then, in step 3, it generates N^1_A and sends it to S as a plain-text, together with x^1_{enc} as predicted by $\langle A, S, N^1_A, \{A, N^1_B\}_{K_B} \rangle \in \kappa$, and so on.

Moreover, the non-empty error component ψ shows that a many-to-one binding may happen in the decryption with label l_6 and therefore suggests a possible complex type confusion leading to a complex type flaw attack.

By studying the contents of the analysis components ρ and κ, we can rebuild the attack sequence. Since $\langle A, S, N^1_A, \{A, N^1_B\}_{K_B} \rangle \in \kappa$, then $(N^1_A) \in \rho(z_\bullet)$. This corresponds to the fact that the attacker, able to intercept messages on the net, can learn N^1_A. The entry $\langle A, B, N^1_A, B, n_\bullet \rangle \in \kappa$ reflects that the attacker is able to constructs and sends to A a new message $(N^1_A, B, n_\bullet)$ to initiate the second instance, where $(n_\bullet)$ is within its knowledge. The entry $(N^1_A, B, n_\bullet)$ in $\rho(y^2_a)$ corresponds to the fact A receives this message, by binding y^2_a to the value $(N^1_A, B, n_\bullet)$. This is a many-to-one binding, detected by the analysis, as reported by the error component: $l_6 \in \psi$. Afterwards, A encrypts what she has received with a new nonce N^2_A and sends it out, as indicated by $\langle A, B, N^1_A, B, n_\bullet, N^2_A \rangle \in \kappa$. The attacker replays this to A, who takes it as the message from S in the step 4 of the first instance $((N^1_A, B, n_\bullet, N^2_A) \in \rho(x^1_z))$. The entry $(n_\bullet) \in \rho(x^1_k)$ reflects that in decrypting message 4, A binds x^1_k to the concatenation of values $(n_\bullet)$ to be used as the session key. After completing the challenge and response in step

6 and 7, A then believes she is talking to B using the session key K, but indeed she is talking to the attacker using $(n_\bullet)$ as the new key. This exactly corresponds to the complex type flaw attack shown before.

The protocol can be modified such that each principal use different keys for different roles, i.e. all the principals taking the initiator's role A_i share a master key K_A^i with the server and all the principals taking the responder's role B_j share K_B^j with the server. In this case, the analysis holds for $\psi = \emptyset$ and thereby it guarantees the absence of complex type confusions attacks.

Here, only two sessions are taken into account. However, as in [5], the protocol can be modelled in a way that multiple principals are participating in the protocol at the same time and therefore mimic the scenario that several sessions are running together. Due to space limitation, further details are skipped here.

4   Conclusion

We say that a complex type confusion attack happens when a concatenation of fields in a message is interpreted as a single field. This kind of attack is not easy to deal with in a process algebraic setting, because message specifications are given at a high level: the focus is on their contents and not on their structure. In this paper, we extended the notation of variable binding in the process calculus LySA from one-to-one to many-to-one binding, thus making it easier to model the scenario where a list of fields is confused with a single field. The semantics of the extended LySA makes use of a reference monitor to capture the possible many-to-one bindings at run time. We mechanise the search for complex type confusions by defining a Control Flow Analysis for the extended LySA calculus. It checks at each input and decryption place whether a many-to-one binding may happen. The analysis ensures that, if no such binding is possible, then the process is not subject to complex type flaw attacks at run time. As far as the attacker is concerned, we adopted the standard notion from Dolev-Yao threat model [10], and we enriched it to deal with the new kind of variable binding.

We applied our Control Flow Analysis to the Amended Needham-Schroeder Protocol (as shown in Section 3), to Otway-Rees [23], Yahalom [8] (not reported, because of lack of space). It has confirmed that we can successfully detect the complex type confusions leading to type flaw attacks on those protocols. This detection is done in a purely mechanical and static way. The analysis also confirms the complex type flaw attacks on a version of the Neuman-Stubblebine protocol, found in [27].

The technique presented here is for detecting *complex* type flaw attacks only. *Simple* type flaw attacks, i.e. two single fields of different types are confused with each other, not considered here, have been addressed instead in [6], under a framework similar to the present one. Besides the type tags, several kinds of annotations for LySA has been developed for validating various security properties, e.g. confidentiality [12], freshness [11] and message authentication [5]. They can be easily combined with the annotations introduced here, thus giving more comprehensive results.

Usual formal frameworks for the verification of security protocols need to be suitably extended for modelling complex type flaw confusions. Extensions include the possibility to decompose and rebuild message components, that we obtain by playing with single, general and flattened values. In [7], for instance, the author uses a concatenation operator to glue together different components in messages. The approach is based on linear logic and it is capable of finding the complex type flaw attack on the Otway-Rees protocol. Meadows [17,18] approach is more general and can address also even more complex type confusions, e.g. those due to the confusion between pieces of fields of one type with pieces of another. The author, using the GDOI protocol as running example, develops a model of types that assumes differing capacities for checking types by principals. Moreover, Meadows presents a procedure to determine whether the types of two messages can be confused, then also evaluating the probability of possible misinterpretations. In [15], using the AVISPA [3] model checking tool, type flaw attacks of the GDOI protocol are captured. Furthermore, by using the Object-Z schema calculus [28,14] the authors verify the attacks at a lower level and find which are the low-level assumptions that lead to the attacks and which are the requirements that prevent them. Type confusions are captured also in [19], by using an efficient Prolog based constraint solver. The above settings, especially the ones in [17,18,15], are more general than our, e.g. they capture more involved kinds of type confusions in a complex setting, like the one of the GDOI protocol. Our work represents a first step in modelling lower level features of protocol specifications in a process algebraic setting, like the ones that lead to type confusions. The idea is to only perform the refinement of the high-level specifications necessary to capture the low-level feature of interest. Our control flow analysis procedure always guarantees termination, even though it only offers an approximation of protocols behaviour and of their dynamic properties. Due to the nature of the over-approximation, false positives may happen, as some of the many-to-one bindings are not necessary leading to a complex type flaw attack. By taking the bit length of each field into account, i.e. using them as thresholds like in [25,26], may greatly reduce the number of false positives. For example, assuming that a nonce, N, is always represented by 8 bits, an agent's name, A, by 8 bits, and a key, K, by 12 bits, the concatenation of A and N will be never confused with K and therefore it can be ruled out. In this paper we focussed on a particular kind of confusions, leaving other kind of type confusions for future work. We could use one-to-many bindings to deal with the case in which pieces of fields are confused with each other. We also would like to move to the multi-protocol setting, where the assumptions adopted in each protocol could be different, but messages could be easily confused, typically, because of the re-use of keys.

References

1. Abadi, M., Fournet, C.: Mobile values, new names, and secure communication. In: POPL, pp. 104–115 (2001)
2. Abadi, M., Gordon, A.D.: A Calculus for Cryptographic Protocols: The Spi Calculus. Information and Computation 148(1), 1–70 (1999)

3. Armando, A., et al.: The AVISPA tool for the automated validation of internet security protocols and applications. In: Etessami, K., Rajamani, S.K. (eds.) CAV 2005. LNCS, vol. 3576, pp. 281–285. Springer, Heidelberg (2005)
4. Bodei, C., Gao, H., Degano, P.: A Formal Analysis of Complex Type Flaw Attacks on Security Protocols. TR-08-03, Pisa University
5. Bodei, C., Buchholtz, M., Degano, P., Nielson, F., Riis Nielson, H.: Static Validation of Security Protocols. Journal of Computer Security 13(3), 347–390 (2005)
6. Bodei, C., Degano, P., Gao, H., Brodo, L.: Detecting and Preventing Type Flaws: a Control Flow Analysis with tags. In: Proc. of 5th International Workshop on Security Issues in Concurrency (SecCO). ENTCS (2007)
7. Bozzano, M.: A Logic-Based Approach to Model Checking of Parameterized and Infinite-State Systems. PhD Thesis, DISI, University of Genova (2002)
8. Burrows, M., Abadi, M., Needham, R.: A Logic of Authentication. TR 39, Digital Systems Research Center (February 1989)
9. Clark, J., Jacob, J.: A survey of authentication protocol literature: Version 1.0 (1997), http://www.cs.york.ac.uk/~jac/papers/drareviewps.ps
10. Dolev, D., Yao, A.C.: On the Security of Public Key Protocols. IEEE TIT IT-29(12), 198–208 (1983)
11. Gao, H., Bodei, C., Degano, P., Riis Nielson, H.: A Formal Analysis for Capturing Replay Attacks in Cryptographic Protocols. In: Cervesato, I. (ed.) ASIAN 2007. LNCS, vol. 4846, pp. 150–165. Springer, Heidelberg (2007)
12. Gao, H., Riis Nielson, H.: Analysis of LySa calculus with explicit confidentiality annotations. In: Proc. of Advanced Information Networking and Applications (AINA). IEEE Computer Society, Los Alamitos (2005)
13. Heather, J., Lowe, G., Schneider, S.: How to prevent type flaw attacks on security protocols. In: Proc. of the 13th Computer Security Foundations Workshop (CSFW). IEEE Computer Society Press, Los Alamitos (2000)
14. Long, B.W.: Formal verification of a type flaw attack on a security protocol using Object-Z. In: Treharne, H., King, S., C. Henson, M., Schneider, S. (eds.) ZB 2005. LNCS, vol. 3455, pp. 319–333. Springer, Heidelberg (2005)
15. Long, B.W., Fidge, C.J., Carrington, D.A.: Cross-layer verification of type flaw attacks on security protocols. In: Proc. of the 30th Australasian conference on Computer science, vol. 62 (2007)
16. Meadows, C.: Analyzing the Needham-Schroeder public key protocol: A comparison of two approaches. In: Proc. of European Symposium on Research in Computer Security. Springer, Heidelberg (2006)
17. Meadows, C.: Identifying potential type confusion in authenticated messages. In: Proc. of Workshop on Foundation of Computer Security (FCS), Copenhagen, Denmark, DIKU TR 02/12, pp. 75–84 (2002)
18. Meadows, C.: A procedure for verifying security against type confusion attacks. In: Proc. of the 16th Workshop on Foundation of Computer Security (CSFW) (2003)
19. Millen, J., Shmatikov, V.: Constraint Solving for Bounded-Process Cryptographic Protocol Analysis. In: ACM Conference on Computer and Communications Security, pp. 166–175 (2001)
20. Milner, R.: Communicating and mobile systems: the π-calculus. Cambridge University Press, Cambridge (1999)
21. Nielson, F., Riis Nielson, H., Hansen, R.R.: Validating firewalls using flow logics. Theor. Comput. Sci. 283(2), 381–418 (2002)
22. Nielson, F., Seidl, H., Nielson, H.R.: A Succinct Solver for ALFP. Nordic Journal of Computing 9, 335–372 (2002)

23. Otway, D., Rees, O.: Efficient and timely mutual authentication. ACM Operating Systems Review 21(1), 8–10 (1987)
24. Snekkenes, E.: Roles in cryptographic protocols. In: Proc. of the Computer Security Symposium on Research in Security and Privacy, pp. 105–119. IEEE Computer Society Press, Los Alamitos (1992)
25. Stubblebine, S., Gligor, V.: On Message Integrity in Cryptographic Protocols. In: IEEE Computer Society Symposium on Research in Security and Privacy, pp. 85–104 (1992)
26. Stubblebine, S., Gligor, V.: Protocol Design for Integrity Protection. In: IEEE Computer Society Symposium on Research in Security and Privacy, pp. 41–53 (1993)
27. Syverson, P., Meadows, C.: Formal requirements for key distribution protocols. In: Advances in Cryptology - EUROCRYPT. LNCS, vol. 950, pp. 320–331. Springer, Heidelberg (1994)
28. Wordsworth, J.B.: Software development with Z - A practical approach to formal methods in software engineering. International Computer Science Series. Addison-Wesley Publishers Ltd., London (1992)

Abstract Interpretation Plugins for Type Systems

Tobias Gedell and Daniel Hedin

Chalmers University of Technology

Abstract. The precision of many type based analyses can be significantly increased given additional information about the programs' execution. For this reason it is not uncommon for such analyses to integrate supporting analyses computing, for instance, nil-pointer or alias information. Such integration is problematic for a number of reasons: 1) it obscures the original intention of the type system especially if multiple additional analyses are added, 2) it makes use of already available analyses difficult, since they have to be rephrased as type systems, and 3) it is non-modular: changing the supporting analyses implies changing the entire type system.

Using ideas from abstract interpretation we present a method for parameterizing type systems over the results of abstract analyses in such a way that one modular correctness proof can be obtained. This is achieved by defining a general format for information transferal and use of the information provided by the abstract analyses. The key gain from this method is a clear separation between the correctness of the analyses and the type system, both in the implementation and correctness proof, which leads to a comparatively easy way of changing the parameterized analysis, and making use of precise, and hence complicated analyses.

In addition, we exemplify the use of the framework by presenting a parameterized type system that uses additional information to improve the precision of exception types in a small imperative language with arrays.

1 Introduction

In the book Types and Programming Languages [14] Pierce defines a type system in the following way: "A type system is a tractable syntactic method for proving the absence of certain program behaviors by classifying phrases according to the kinds of values they compute".

Pierce limits his definition to the absence of *certain* program behaviors, since many interesting (bad) behaviors cannot be ruled out statically. Well-known examples of this include division by zero, nil-pointer dereference and class cast errors. The standard solution to this is to lift the semantics and include these errors into the valid results of the execution, often in the form of exceptions, and to have the type system rule out all errors not modeled in the semantics, typically in addition to tracking what errors a program may result in.

For a standard type system this solution is adequate; the types of programs are not affected in any other way than the addition of a set of possible exceptions. In particular, any inaccuracies in the set of possible exceptions are unproblematic to the type system itself (albeit inconvenient to the programmer), and, thus, in standard programming

J. Meseguer and G. Roşu (Eds.): AMAST 2008, LNCS 5140, pp. 184–198, 2008.

languages not much effort is made to rule out syntactically present but semantically impossible exceptions.

For type based program analyses, however, the situation is different. Not only are we not able to change the semantics to fit the capabilities of the type system, since we are, in effect, retrofitting a type system onto an existing language, but for some analyses — notably, for *information flow security* type systems [15] — inaccuracies propagate from e.g. the exception types via *implicit flows* to the other types lowering the precision of the type system and possibly rendering more semantically secure programs to be classified as insecure. Consider the following example:

```
try c1; c2; ... catch (Exception e) ch
```

If the command c_1 may fail this affects whether the succeeding commands $c_2, \ldots$ are run or not, and thus any side effects — e.g. output on a public network — will encode information about the data manipulated by c_1. If this information must be protected, this put serious limits on the succeeding commands $c_2, \ldots$ and on the exception handler ch.

This is problematic, since dynamic error handling introduces many possible branches — every partial instruction becomes a possible branch to the error handler *if it cannot be guaranteed not to crash*, and, thus, a source of implicit flows. Hence, from a practical standpoint, there is a need to increase the accuracy of type based information flow analyses as demonstrated by some recent attempts [2,12,1]. Noting that the majority of the information flow analyses are formulated in terms of type systems, we focus on how to strengthen a type system with additional information to increase its accuracy.

Even though our main motivation for this work comes from information flow type systems, we investigate the problem in terms of a standard type system; this both generalizes the method and simplifies the presentation. All our results are immediately applicable to information flow type systems.

We see two major different methods of solving the problem of strengthening type systems: 1) by *integration*, and 2) by *parameterization*. Briefly, 1) relies on extending the type system to compute the additional needed information, and 2) relies on using information about the programs' execution provided by other analyses. Integration is problematic for a number of reasons: 1) it obscures the original intention of the type system especially if multiple additional analyses are added, 2) it makes use of already available analyses difficult, since they have to be rephrased as type systems, and 3) it is non-modular: changing the supporting analysis implies changing the entire type system.

Contribution. We present a modular approach for parameterizing type systems with information about the program execution; the method is modular not only at the type system level, but also at the proof level.

The novelty of the approach lies not in the idea of parameterizing information in itself, rather, the novelty is the setting — the parameterization of *type systems* with information from *abstract analyses* — together with the identification of a general, widely applicable format for information passing and inspection, which allows for modularity with only small modifications to the type system and its correctness proof, and no modifications to the abstract analyses. This modularity makes instancing parameterized type systems with the results of different abstract analyses relatively cheap, which can be leveraged to create staged type systems, where increasingly precise analyses are chosen based on previous typing errors.

Finally, we exemplify the use of the method in terms of a parameterized type system for a small imperative language with arrays, and explore how the parameterization can be used to rule out nil-pointer exceptions, and exceptions stemming from array indices outside the bounds of the corresponding arrays.

Outline. Section 2 presents a small imperative language with arrays, used to explain the method more concretely. Section 3 presents the parameterization: the abstract environment maps, the plugins properties and the plugins, and describes the process of parameterizing a type system. Section 4 is a concrete example of applying the method to get a parameterized type system of the language of Section 2. Section 5 discusses related work, and finally Section 6 concludes and discusses future work.

2 Language

To be concrete we use a small imperative language with arrays to illustrate our method.

Syntax. The language is a standard while language with arrays. For simplicity we consider all binary operators to be total; the same techniques described to handling the partiality of array indexing apply to partial operators. The syntax of the language is found in Table 1, where the allocation type $\tau[i]$ indicates that an array of size i with elements of type τ should be allocated; the primitive types ranged over by τ are defined in Section 4.1 below.

Table 1. Syntax

Expressions $e ::= nil \mid i \mid x \mid e \star e \mid x[e] \mid len(x)$
Commands $c ::= x := e \mid x[e] := x \mid if\ e\ c\ c \mid while\ e\ c \mid c; c \mid x := new(\tau[i]) \mid skip$

Semantics. The semantics of the expressions is given in terms of a big step semantics with transitions of the form $\langle E, e \rangle \Downarrow v_\perp$, where $v_\perp$ ranges over error lifted values v ($\perp$ indicates errors), and E ranges over the set of environments Env, i.e. pairs (s, h) of a store, and a heap. The values consist of the integers i and the pointers p. The arrays a are pairs (i, d) of the size of the array and a map from integers to values with a continuous domain starting from 0. Formally, d ranges over $\bigcup_{n \in \mathbb{N}}\{[0 \mapsto v_1, \ldots, n \mapsto v_n]\}$. The stores s are maps from variables x to values, and the heaps h are maps from pointers to arrays.

In the definition of the semantics, if $a = (i_1, d)$ then let $a(i_2)$ denote $d(i_2)$. Further, for $E = (s, h)$, let $E(x)$ denote $s(x)$, $E[x \mapsto v]$ denote $(s[x \mapsto v], h)$, $E(p)$ denote $h(p)$, and similarly for other operations on environments including variables or pointers.

The semantics of commands is given in terms of a small step semantics between configurations C with transitions of the form $\langle E, c \rangle \rightarrow C$, where C is either one of the terminal configurations $\perp_E$ and $\langle E, skip \rangle$ indicating abnormal and normal termination

Table 2. Selected Semantic Rules for Expressions and Commands

$$\frac{E(x) = p \quad E(p) = (i, d)}{\langle E, len(x)\rangle \Downarrow i} \qquad \frac{E(x) = nil}{\langle E, len(x)\rangle \Downarrow \bot} \qquad \frac{E(x_1) = nil}{\langle E, x_1[i] := x_2\rangle \to \bot_E}$$

$$\frac{E(x_1) = p \quad E(p) = (i_2, d) \quad E(x_2) = v \quad i_1 \notin [0..(i_2 - 1)]}{\langle E, x_1[i_1] := x_2\rangle \to \bot_E}$$

$$\frac{E(x_1) = p \quad E(p) = (i_2, d) \quad E(x_2) = v \quad i_1 \in [0..(i_2 - 1)]}{\langle E, x_1[i_1] := x_2\rangle \to \langle E[p \mapsto (i_2, d[i_1 \mapsto v])], skip\rangle}$$

$$\frac{}{\langle E, while\ e\ c\rangle \to \langle E, if\ e\ (c; while\ e\ c)\ skip\rangle}$$

$$\frac{\langle E, e\rangle \Downarrow v}{\langle E, R[e]\rangle \to \langle E, R[v]\rangle} \qquad \frac{\langle E, e\rangle \Downarrow \bot}{\langle E, R[e]\rangle \to \bot_E} \qquad \frac{E(x) = p \quad E(p) = (i_1, d)}{\langle E, e\rangle \Downarrow i_2 \quad i_2 \notin [0..i_1 - 1]}{\langle E, x[e]\rangle \Downarrow \bot}$$

$$\frac{\langle E_1, c_1\rangle \to \langle E_2, c_2\rangle}{\langle E_1, R[c_1]\rangle \to \langle E_2, R[c_2]\rangle} \qquad \frac{\langle E, c\rangle \to \bot_E}{\langle E, R[c]\rangle \to \bot_E}$$

in the environment E, respectively, or a non-terminal configuration $\langle E, c\rangle$ where $c \neq skip$. A selection of the semantic rules for expressions and commands are presented in Table 2; the omitted rules are found in the extended version of this paper [9].

As is common for small step semantics we use evaluation contexts R.

$$R ::= \cdot \mid x := R \mid x[R] := x \mid if\ R\ c\ c \mid R; c$$

The accompanying standard reduction rules allow for leftmost reduction of sequences, error propagation and reduction of expressions inside commands.

3 Parameterization

With this we are ready to detail the method of parameterization. First, let us recapture our goal: we want to describe a modular way of parameterizing a type system with information about the programs' execution in such a way that a modular correctness proof can be formed for the resulting system, with the property that an instantiated system satisfies a correspondingly instantiated correctness proof.

To achieve this, we define a general format of parameterized information and a general method to access this information. Using the ideas of abstract interpretation, we let the parameterized information be a map from program points to abstract environments, intuitively representing the set of environments that can reach each program point. Such a map is semantically sound — a *solution* in our terminology — w.r.t. a set of initial concrete environments and a program, if every possible execution trace the initial environments can give rise to is modeled by the map.

For modularity we do not want to assume anything about the structure of the abstract environments, but treat them as completely opaque. Noting that each type system uses a finite number of forms of questions, we parameterize the type system not only over the abstract environment map, but also over a set of *plugins* — sound approximations of the semantic properties of the questions used by the type system.

Labeled Commands. Following the elegant approach of Sands and Hunt [13] we extend the command language with label annotations, which allow for a particularly direct way of recording the environments that enter and leave the labeled commands. Let l range over labels drawn from the set of labels $\mathcal{L}$. A command c can be annotated with an entry label $(c)^l$, an exit label $(c)_l$, or both.

We extend the reduction contexts with $(R)_l$, which allows for reduction under exit labels, and the semantics with the following transitions.

$$\frac{}{\langle E, (c)^l \rangle \rightarrow \langle E, c \rangle} \qquad \frac{}{\langle E, (skip)_l \rangle \rightarrow \langle E, skip \rangle}$$

The idea is that a transition of the form $\langle E, (c)^l \rangle \rightarrow \langle E, c \rangle$ leaves a marker in the execution sequence that the command labeled with the entry label l was executed in E, and a transition of the form $\langle E, (skip)_l \rangle \rightarrow \langle E, skip \rangle$ indicates that the environment E was produced by the command labeled with the exit label l, which is why allowing reduction under exit labels but not under entry labels is important.

3.1   Abstract Environment Maps

Using the ideas of abstract interpretation [4,5], let $\mathbb{Env}$ be the set of abstract environments ranged over by $\mathbb{E}$, equipped with a concretization function $\gamma : \mathbb{Env} \rightarrow \mathcal{P}(Env)$, and let an abstract environment map $\mathbb{M} : \mathcal{L} \rightarrow \mathbb{Env}$ be a map from program points to abstract environments, associating each program point with an abstract environment representing all concrete environments that may reach the program point.

We define two soundness properties for abstract environment maps that relate the maps to the execution of a program when started in environments drawn from a set of initial environments $\mathcal{C}$.

An abstract environment map $\mathbb{M}$ is an *entry solution* written $entrysol_{c_1}^{E_1}(\mathbb{M})$ w.r.t. an initial concrete environment E_1, and a program c_1 if all $\langle E_2, (c_2)^l \rangle \rightarrow \langle E_2, c_2 \rangle$ transitions in the trace originating in $\langle E_1, c_1 \rangle$ are captured by $\mathbb{M}$. The notion of *exit solution* written $exitsol_c^{E_1}(\mathbb{M})$ is defined similarly but w.r.t. all transitions of the form $\langle E_2, (skip)_l \rangle \rightarrow \langle E_2, skip \rangle$.

$$entrysol_{c_1}^{E_1}(\mathbb{M}) \equiv \forall E_2, c_2, l \,.\, \langle E_1, c_1 \rangle \rightarrow^* \langle E_2, R[(c_2)^l] \rangle \implies E_2 \in \gamma(\mathbb{M}(l))$$
$$exitsol_c^{E_1}(\mathbb{M}) \equiv \forall E_2, l \,.\, \langle E_1, c \rangle \rightarrow^* \langle E_2, R[(skip)_l] \rangle \implies E_2 \in \gamma(\mathbb{M}(l))$$

The definitions are lifted to sets of initial environments $\mathcal{C}$ in the obvious way.

Both the entry and exit solution properties are preserved under execution as defined below.

Lemma 1 (Preservation of Entry and Exit Solutions under Execution). *In the following, let C_1 be the set of initial concrete environments and C_2 the set of environments that reach c_2, i.e. $C_2 = \{E_2 \mid E_1 \in C_1, \langle E_1, c_1 \rangle \rightarrow \langle E_2, c_2 \rangle\}$.*

$$entrysol_{c_1}^{C_1}(\mathbb{M}) \implies entrysol_{c_2}^{C_2}(\mathbb{M}) \text{ and } exitsol_{c_1}^{C_1}(\mathbb{M}) \implies exitsol_{c_2}^{C_2}(\mathbb{M})$$

These properties immediately extend to any finite sequence of execution steps by inductions over the length of the sequence.

Further, solutions can freely be paired to form new solutions similarly to the independent attribute method for abstract interpretation [5]. This is important since it shows that no generality is lost by parameterizing a type system over only one abstract environment map.

3.2 Plugins

To the parameterized type systems, the structure of the abstract environments is opaque and cannot be accessed directly. This allows for the decoupling of the parameterized type system and the external analysis computing the abstract environments. However, the parameterized type systems need a way to extract the desired information. To this end we introduce the concept of *plugins*. Intuitively, a plugin provides information about a specific property of an environment; for instance, a nil-pointer plugin provides information about which parts of the environment are nil.

The plugins are defined to be sound approximations of *plugin properties*, defined as families of relations on expressions.

Plugin Properties. Let R be an n-ary relation on values; R induces a *plugin property*, written $R^\diamond$, which is a family of n-ary relations on expressions indexed by environments in the following way.

$$(e_1, \ldots, e_n) \in R_E^\diamond \iff \langle E, e_1 \rangle \Downarrow v_1 \wedge \ldots \wedge \langle E, e_n \rangle \Downarrow v_n \implies (v_1, \ldots, v_n) \in R$$

We can use the expression language to define semantic properties about environments, since the expression language is simple, in particular, since it does not contain iteration, and is free from side effects. A major advantage of the approach is that it allows for a relatively simple treatment of expressions in programs.

The choice of using the expression language as the plugin language is merely out of convenience — languages with richer expression language would mandate a separate language for the plugins and treat the exceptions similarly to the statement, i.e. extend the labeling and the solutions to the expressions. In our case, however, a separate plugin language would be identical to the expressions.

Example 1 (Non-nil and Less-than Plugin Properties). The non-nil plugin property $nn^\diamond$ can be defined by a family of predicates indexed over concrete environments induced by the value property nn defined such that $nn(v)$ holds only if the value v is not equal to *nil*. Similarly, the less-than plugin property $lt^\diamond$ can be defined by lt such that $lt(v_1, v_2)$ holds only if the value v_1 is less than the value v_2. □

Plugins. A plugin is a family of relations on expressions indexed by abstract environments. Given a plugin property $R^\diamond$ we define *plugins*, $R^\sharp$ as follows.

$$(e_1, \ldots, e_n) \in R_{\mathbb{E}}^\sharp \implies \forall E \in \gamma(\mathbb{E}). \, (e_1, \ldots, e_n) \in R_E^\diamond$$

It is important to note that for each plugin property there are many possible plugins, since the above formulation allows for approximative plugins. This means that regardless of the abstract environment, and the decidability of the plugin property $R^\diamond$, there exist decidable plugins, which guarantees the possibility of preservation of decidability for parameterized type systems.

Example 2 (Use of Plugins). Assume a type system computing a set of possibly thrown exceptions. When typing, for example, the array length operator $len(x)$ we are interested in the plugin property given by the non-nil predicate *nn*. Let $\mathbb{E}$ be a sound representation of all environments reaching $len(x)$. Given $nn^{\sharp}_{\mathbb{E}}(x)$, we know that x will not be nil in any of the concrete environments represented by $\mathbb{E}$, and, since $\mathbb{E}$ is a sound representation of all environments that can reach the array length operator, we know that a nil-pointer exception will not be thrown.   □

Despite the relative simplicity of the plugin format it is surprisingly powerful; in addition to the obvious information, such as is x ever nil, it turns out that plugins can be used to explore the structure of the heap as we show in [10] where we use the parameterization to provide flow sensitive heap types.

3.3   Overview of a Parameterized Type System

Assume an arbitrary flow insensitive type system[1] of the form $\Gamma \vdash_A c$ expressing that c is well-typed in the type signature Γ, under the additional assumption A. We let the exact forms of Γ and A be abstract; however, typical examples are that Γ is a store type, and, for information flow type systems, that A is the security level of the context, known as the pc [15].

The first step in parameterizing the type system is to identify the plugin properties $R^{\diamond}_1, \ldots, R^{\diamond}_m$ that are to be used in the parameterized type rules. For instance the non-nil plugin property can be used to increase the precision of the type rule for the array length operator as discussed in Example 2 above, cf. the corresponding type rules in Section 4 below. Each type rule is then parameterized with an abstract environment map M, and a number of plugins $R^{\sharp}_1, \ldots R^{\sharp}_m$, one for each of the plugin properties, forming a parameterized system of the following form.

$$\Gamma \vdash^{\mathsf{M}, R^{\sharp}_1, \ldots, R^{\sharp}_m}_A c$$

A typical correctness argument for type systems is *preservation* [14], i.e. the preservation of a type induced invariant, well-formedness, (see Section 4.3 below) under execution. Well-formedness defines when an environment conforms to an environment type, e.g. that all variables of integer type contain integers. Let $wf_\Gamma(E)$ denote that E is well-formed in the environment type Γ; a typical preservation statement has the following form:

$$\Gamma \vdash_A c \Longrightarrow wf_\Gamma(E_1) \wedge \langle E_1, c \rangle \to E_2 \Longrightarrow wf_\Gamma(E_2)$$

More generally, a class of correctness arguments for type systems have the form of preservation of an arbitrary type indexed relation $\mathcal{R}_\Gamma$ under execution:

---

[1] Our method works equally well for flow sensitive type systems, but for brevity of explanation this section is done in terms of a flow insensitive system.

$$\Gamma \vdash_A c \implies \mathcal{R}_\Gamma(E_{11}, \ldots, E_{1n}) \wedge$$
$$\langle E_{11}, c \rangle \to E_{21} \wedge \cdots \wedge \langle E_{1n}, c \rangle \to E_{2n} \implies \mathcal{R}_\Gamma(E_{21}, \ldots, E_{2n})$$

This generalization is needed to capture invariants that are not *safety properties*, for instance noninterference or live variable analysis.

For *conservative* parameterizations, i.e. where we add type rules with increased precision, the proofs of correctness are essentially identical to the old proofs, where certain execution cases have been ruled out using the semantic interpretation of the plugins. To see this consider that a typical proof of the above lemma proceeds with a case analysis on the possible ways c can execute in the different environments E_{11} to E_{1n} and proves the property for each case. See the proof of Theorem 1 in Section 4.3 for an example of this. The correctness statement for the parameterized types system becomes:

$$entrysol_c^{\mathcal{C}}(\mathsf{M}) \wedge E_{11} \in \mathcal{C} \wedge \cdots \wedge E_{1n} \in \mathcal{C} \wedge \Gamma \vdash_A^{\mathsf{M}, R_1^{\flat}, \ldots, R_m^{\flat}} c \implies$$
$$\mathcal{R}_\Gamma(E_{11}, \ldots, E_{1n}) \wedge \langle E_{11}, c \rangle \to E_{21} \wedge \cdots \wedge \langle E_{1n}, c \rangle \to E_{2n} \implies \mathcal{R}_\Gamma(E_{21}, \ldots, E_{2n})$$

The interpretation of this statement is that execution started in any of the environments in the set of possible initial environments is $\mathcal{R}_\Gamma$-preserving, i.e. it narrows the validity of the original lemma to the set of initial environments.

Proof of Correctness. It is important to note that we do not need to redo any parts of the correctness proof when instantiating a parameterized type system.

The assumption that the extracted abstract environment maps are sound for the program and set of initial environments under consideration, i.e. that they are solutions, is established once per family of external analysis. This is established by, e.g., formulating the family as a family of abstract interpretations and proving that all environment maps extracted from an abstract analysis belonging to the family are sound for the program and set of initial environments that the analysis was started with.

What is left per instantiation is to show that the used plugins are valid. In most cases, this is trivial since the structure of the abstract environments have been chosen with this in mind. Furthermore, many type systems can be improved with similar information; thus, it should be possible to build a library with plugins for different plugin properties that can be used when instantiating implementations of parameterized type systems. This is important because it shows that creating new correct instantiations is a comparatively cheap operation, which leads to interesting implementation possibilities.

4 A Parameterized Type System

In this section we exemplify the ideas described in the previous section by presenting a parameterized type system for the language introduced in Section 2. The type system improves over the typical type system for such a language by using the parameterized information to rule out exceptions that cannot occur.

A larger example of a parameterized type system, showing how plugins can be used to perform structural weakening and strong updates for a flow-sensitive type system, can be found in [10].

4.1 Type Language

The primitive types ranged over by τ are the type of integers int, and array types, $\tau[]$, indicating an array with elements of type τ. The store types ranged over by Σ are maps from variables to primitive types. The exception types ranged over by ξ are $\bot_\Sigma$, indicating the possibility that an exception is thrown, and $\top$, indicating that no exception is thrown. This is a simplification from typical models of exceptions, where multiple types are used to indicate the reason for the exception. However, for the purpose of exemplifying the parameterization this model suffices; the results are easily extended to a richer model. In addition we use a standard subtype relation $<:$ (omitted for space reasons) with invariant array types.

4.2 Type Rules

The judgments for expressions, $\Sigma \vdash^{\mathbb{E},nn^\sharp,lt^\sharp} e : \tau, \xi$, is read as the expression e is well-typed w.r.t. the abstract environment $\mathbb{E}$, the non-nil plugin $nn^\sharp$, and the less-than plugin $lt^\sharp$, in the environment type Σ, with return type τ possibly resulting in exceptions as indicated by ξ. The type system for commands is flow-sensitive; the judgment, $\Sigma_1 \vdash^{\mathbb{M},nn^\sharp,lt^\sharp} c \Rightarrow \Sigma_2, \xi$ is read as the command c is well-typed w.r.t. the abstract environment map $\mathbb{M}$, the non-nil plugin $nn^\sharp$, and the less-than plugin $lt^\sharp$, in the environment type Σ_1 resulting in the environment type Σ_2, possibly resulting in an exception as indicated by ξ. The relevant type rules for expressions and commands are found in Table 3 where we use $\vdash^\dagger$ as short notation for $\vdash^{\mathbb{M},nn^\sharp,lt^\sharp}$ and $\vdash^\ddagger$ as short notation for $\vdash^{\mathbb{E},nn^\sharp,lt^\sharp}$; the omitted rules are found in the extended version of this paper [9].

Apart from the parts related to the parameterization, the expression and command type rules are entirely standard. With respect to the parameterization specifics, the type rules for array size, and array indexing make use of the parameterized information and

Table 3. Selected Type Rules for Expressions and Commands

$$\frac{\Sigma \vdash^{\mathbb{M}(l),nn^\sharp,lt^\sharp} e : int, \xi \quad \Sigma(x_1) = \tau_1[] \quad \Sigma(x_2) = \tau_2 \quad \tau_2 <: \tau_1}{\neg(nn^\sharp_{\mathbb{M}(l)}(x_1) \wedge -1\ lt^\sharp_{\mathbb{M}(l)}\ e \wedge e\ lt^\sharp_{\mathbb{M}(l)}\ len(x_1))}{\Sigma \vdash^\dagger (x_1[e] := x_2)^l \Rightarrow \Sigma, \bot_\Sigma}$$

$$\frac{\Sigma \vdash^{\mathbb{M}(l),nn^\sharp,lt^\sharp} e : int, \xi \quad \Sigma(x_1) = \tau_1[] \quad \Sigma(x_2) = \tau_2 \quad \tau_2 <: \tau_1}{nn^\sharp_{\mathbb{M}(l)}(x_1) \quad -1\ lt^\sharp_{\mathbb{M}(l)}\ e \quad e\ lt^\sharp_{\mathbb{M}(l)}\ len(x_1)}{\Sigma \vdash^\dagger (x_1[e] := x_2)^l \Rightarrow \Sigma, \xi}$$

$$\frac{\Sigma(x) = \tau[] \quad \neg nn^\sharp_{\mathbb{E}}(x)}{\Sigma \vdash^\ddagger len(x) : int, \bot_\Sigma} \qquad \frac{\Sigma(x) = \tau[] \quad nn^\sharp_{\mathbb{E}}(x)}{\Sigma \vdash^\ddagger len(x) : int, \top}$$

occur in two forms: one that is able to exclude the possibility of exceptions, and one that is not.

For the array size operator it suffices to rule out that the variable x ever contains nil to rule out the possibility of exceptions, for array indexing (for both the expression and the command) we must demand that the index is greater or equal to zero, and that the index is smaller than the size of the array in addition to the demand that the variable is non-nil. For an example detailing the type derivation of a small program with different parameterized information see the example in the extended version of this paper [9].

4.3   Correctness

With this we are ready to formulate correctness for the parameterized type system. As is standard we split the correctness argument into two theorems, *progress* — intuitively, that well-typed commands and expressions are able to execute in all environments that conform to the entry environment type of the command or expression — and *preservation* — intuitively, that the result of running the command or expression conforms to the exit type of the same. In contrast to the preservation proof, the progress proof is independent of the parameterized information. For space reasons we omit the progress proof.

Well-formedness. The well-formedness relation in Table 4 defines when a context is well-formed w.r.t. a type. It is the extension of a standard well-formedness relation to exception types. Most of the standard well-formedness relation has been omitted for space reasons and is found in the extended version of this paper [9].

Table 4. Well-formedness

$$
\frac{\delta \vdash v : \tau}{\delta \vdash v : \tau, \xi} \qquad \frac{}{\delta \vdash \bot : \tau, \bot_{\Sigma}}
$$

$$
\frac{\delta \vdash E : \Sigma_2 \qquad}{\delta \vdash^{M,nn^{\sharp},lt^{\sharp}} \bot_E : \Sigma_1, \bot_{\Sigma_2}} \qquad \frac{\delta \vdash E : \Sigma}{\delta \vdash^{M,nn^{\sharp},lt^{\sharp}} E : \Sigma, \xi}
$$

$$
\frac{\Sigma_1 \vdash^{M,nn^{\sharp},lt^{\sharp}} c \Rightarrow \Sigma_2, \xi \qquad \delta \vdash E : \Sigma_1}{\delta \vdash^{M,nn^{\sharp},lt^{\sharp}} \langle E, c \rangle : \Sigma_2, \xi} \qquad \frac{\forall i \in dom(a) . \delta \vdash a[i] : \tau}{\delta \vdash a : \tau[]}
$$

In short, a value is well-formed w.r.t. any exception type, whereas an error is only well-formed w.r.t. an exception type that indicates the possibility of the error, and similarly for well-formed environments, with the addition of the demand that the exception environment is well-formed in the exception environment type. A configuration is well-formed in the type Σ_2, ξ if there exists an environment type Σ_1 in which the environment E is well-formed such that the command is well-typed with Σ_1 as entry type and the Σ_2, ξ as exit type.

Preservation of Types of Expressions and Commands. Preservation of types of expressions expresses that well-typed expressions preserve well-formedness under execution, i.e. for an expression e s.t. $\Sigma \vdash^{E,nn^{\sharp},lt^{\sharp}} e : \tau, \xi$ running e in Σ-well-formed environments that are modeled by the abstract environment $\mathbb{E}$ will result in τ, ξ-well-formed values.

Theorem 1 (Preservation of Types of Expressions)

$$\Sigma \vdash^{\mathbb{E},nn^{\sharp},lt^{\sharp}} e : \tau, \xi \implies \forall E \in \gamma(\mathbb{E}) \,.\, \delta \vdash E : \Sigma \wedge \langle E, e \rangle \Downarrow v \implies \delta \vdash v : \tau, \xi$$

Proof By induction on the derivation of $\Sigma \vdash^{\mathbb{E},nn^{\sharp},lt^{\sharp}} e : \tau, \xi$. Intuitively, in each case, the proof proceeds by an inversion of $\langle E, e \rangle \Downarrow v$, which results in a number of sub-cases — one for each semantic rule for the expression, including the ones resulting in exceptions. However, in the cases where the type system can rule out exception it contains enough information about the execution from the use of the plugins on the abstract environment to disprove the possibility of an exception.

We exemplify the difference between a standard proof and a parameterized proof by proving the correctness for the array indexing cases, corresponding to the two type rules for array indexing — for space reasons, in the cases the antecedents of the expression type rules and semantics rules are subsets of their command counterparts the expression rules have been omitted in this version of the paper, and we refer the reader to the command type rules in order to follow the proof below.

Assume $\Sigma \vdash^{\mathbb{E},nn^{\sharp},lt^{\sharp}} e : \tau, \xi$, (2) $E \in \gamma(\mathbb{E})$, (3) $\delta \vdash E : \Sigma$ and (4) $\langle E, e \rangle \Downarrow v$. We must show $\delta \vdash v : \tau, \xi$.

array indexing with exceptions. In this case the last applied type rule in the derivation is the rule that cannot rule out exceptions, which gives (5) $\Sigma(x) = \tau[]$, $\Sigma \vdash^{\mathbb{E},nn^{\sharp},lt^{\sharp}} e' : int, \xi'$, $\neg(nn_{\mathbb{E}}^{\sharp}(x) \wedge -1 \, lt_{\mathbb{E}}^{\sharp} \, e' \wedge e' \, lt_{\mathbb{E}}^{\sharp} \, len(x))$, $\xi = \perp_{\Sigma}$ and that $e = x[e']$. Inversion of (4) gives us the following four cases.

1) **nil-pointer exception** This case gives $v = \perp$ from which the result $\delta \vdash \perp : \tau, \perp_{\Sigma}$ is immediate.

2) *e* **leads to an exception** Same as the case above.

3) **index out of bounds** Same as the case above.

4) **successful execution** Let $E = (s, h)$; this case gives (6) $s(x) = p$, $h(p) = (i_1, d)$, $\langle E, e' \rangle \Downarrow i_2$, (7) $i_2 \in [0..(i_1 - 1)]$ and $v = d(i_2)$. From (3, 5, 6) we get $\delta \vdash p : \tau[]$, which in turn gives $\delta(p) <: \tau[]$, which means (8) $\delta(p) = \tau[]$, since array subtyping is invariant. Further, (3) and (8) give $\delta \vdash h(p) : \tau[]$, which gives $\forall i \in dom((i_1, d)) \,.\, \delta \vdash (i_1, d)(i) : \tau$. Thus, (7) gives us that $i_2 \in dom((i_1, d))$, from which we get the result $\delta \vdash d(i_2) : \tau$.

array indexing without exceptions In this case the last applied type rule in the derivation is the rule that rules out exceptions, which gives $\Sigma(x) = \tau[]$, $\Sigma \vdash^{\mathbb{E},nn^{\sharp},lt^{\sharp}} e' : int, \xi$, (5) $nn_{\mathbb{E}}^{\sharp}(x)$, (6) $-1 \, lt_{\mathbb{E}}^{\sharp} \, e'$, (7) $e' \, lt_{\mathbb{E}}^{\sharp} \, len(x)$, and that $e = x[e']$. Again, inversion of (4) gives us the following four cases.

1) **nil-pointer exception** This case gives (8) $s(x) = nil$. (1) and (5) give $\forall E \in \gamma(\mathbb{E})$. $x \in nn_E^{\circ}$, which together with (2) gives (9) $\langle E, x \rangle \Downarrow nil \implies nil \in nn$. (8) gives $\langle E, x \rangle \Downarrow nil$, which together with (9) gives $nil \in nn$ which is a contradiction.

2) *e* **leads to an exception** This case gives $\langle E, e' \rangle \Downarrow \perp$ which together with the induction hypothesis gives $\xi = \perp_{\Sigma}$ from which the result is immediate.

3) **index out of bounds** This case gives $s(x) = p$, $h(p) = (i_1, d)$, $\langle E, e' \rangle \Downarrow i_2$ and (8) $i_2 \notin [0..(i_1 - 1)]$. In a way similar to 1) above, we use (6) to disprove

that i_2 is less than 0 and (7) to disprove that i_2 is greater than or equal to i_1. Together this contradicts (8) and we have reached a contradiction.

4) successful execution This case is proven in the same way as case 4) in array indexing with exceptions.

Thus, as the proof of preservation of types for array indexing shows, we achieve higher precision in the exception type by using the parameterized information to disprove some cases as described in Section 3.3. As discussed, the proof for the parameterized type system is essentially identical to the original proof where there is no parameterized information, with the difference that two cases are disproved.

Given the well-formedness formulation for configurations above, preservation of types of commands can be formulated in the same way as preservation of types of expressions.

Theorem 2 (Preservation of Types of Commands)

$$\Sigma_1 \vdash^{M,nn^\sharp,lt^\sharp} c \Rightarrow \Sigma_2, \xi \wedge entrysol_c^C(M) \Longrightarrow$$

$$\forall E \in C \,.\, \delta_1 \vdash E : \Sigma_1 \wedge \langle E, c \rangle \to C \Longrightarrow \exists \delta_2 \,.\, \delta_2 \vdash^{M,nn^\sharp,lt^\sharp} C : \Sigma_2, \xi$$

Proof For space reasons the proof is found in the extended version of this paper [9].

Top-level Correctness of Commands. Let $\langle E, c \rangle \to^n C$ be the obvious lifting of the small step evaluation to evaluation of n consecutive steps. With this we are ready to formulate the top-level correctness of commands, that well-typed commands terminate in a well-formed environment or result in well-formed configurations regardless of the number of execution steps. For convenience we let T range over terminal configurations.

Theorem 3 (Top-level Correctness of Commands)

$$\Sigma_1 \vdash^{M,nn^\sharp,lt^\sharp} c_1 \Rightarrow \Sigma_2, \xi \wedge entrysol_{c_1}^C(M) \Longrightarrow \forall E_1 \in C \,.\, \delta_1 \vdash E_1 : \Sigma_1 \Longrightarrow$$

$$\forall n. \, (\exists n' \le n, T, \delta_2. \, \langle E_1, c_1 \rangle \to^{n'} T \wedge \delta_2 \vdash T : \Sigma_2, \xi) \vee$$

$$(\exists E_2, c_2, \delta_2. \, \langle E_1, c_1 \rangle \to^n \langle E_2, c_2 \rangle \wedge \delta_2 \vdash^{M,nn^\sharp,lt^\sharp} \langle E_2, c_2 \rangle : \Sigma_2, \xi)$$

Proof For space reasons the proof is found in an extended version of this paper [9].

5 Related Work

The method presented in this paper combines an analysis, formulated as a type system, with a number of external analyses, computing information useful to the type system, by parameterizing the type system over the computed information.

Similar in spirit is the work by Foster, Fähndrich and Aiken [8] in which they present a framework for augmenting existing type systems with type qualifiers, e.g. `const` and `nonnil`. Our work differs from theirs in that they provide a framework to compute the qualifiers, rather than making use of them.

In [3] Chin, Markstrum and Millstein investigate a method for supporting user-defined semantic type qualifiers that are closely related to unary plugins. As above, their work is aimed at computing an analysis result, rather than modularly making use of it. In addition to reason about soundness they propose a method to automatically verify the soundness of the extension using an automatic theorem prover.

Among the type systems making use of additional information are type systems that eliminate array bound checks, e.g. [16], using a decidable formulation of dependent types. It should be pointed out that even though the type checking is decidable the inference is not; nothing in our approach rules out inference. In [12] Hedin and Sands use a simplistic type based inference of nil-pointers needed to allow the use of non-secret fields in objects pointed to by pointers with secret pointer values. We believe that the clarity, correctness proof and power of their system could benefit greatly by being reformulated in our framework.

In [6] Crary and Weirich present a type system for resource bound verification, e.g. memory usage and execution time. Their type system goes beyond the capacity of the plugins framework — time and memory usage are not values in a standard semantics. It could potentially be interesting to see to what extent the plugins model can be modified to encompass such extensions.

While this work suggests resolving type errors by using more and more elaborate parameterized analyses, Flanagan [7] suggests pushing checks that cannot be statically resolved to runtime checks, cf. type cast checks in Java. For many uses of the plugins framework, uniting the two approaches could prove beneficial — if the program cannot be statically proven correct using a different external analysis, Flanagan's method could be applied to insert a dynamic check.

With respect to other work on combining static analyses, if the analyses we want to combine are formulated as abstract interpretations, a number of techniques from the large body of work on abstract interpretation [4,5,11] becomes applicable. An example of such a combination is the reduced product method. Similar to our method, the combination can be done in a systematic way and correctness of the resulting analysis follows from correctness of the combined analyses.

An advantage of the abstract interpretation framework is that for partially overlapping analyses and a combination like the reduced product, the analyses will benefit from each other. Each analysis can make use of the information computed by the other analyses, which stands in contrast to our method where the external analyses cannot make direct use of the derivation of the parameterized type system.

However, an obvious restriction of the abstract interpretation framework is that all analyses must be formulated as abstract interpretations, which is not always the case. Reformulating, for example, a type based analysis into an abstract interpretation is not always easily done nor desirable, as for example indicated by the field of security where the analyses tend to be type based [15]. Our approach does not have that restriction. A type system can be combined with any external analyses that compute valid solutions. If the external analyses are formulated as abstract interpretations our method can be combined with the abstract interpretation framework to make use of, for example, reduced products.

6   Conclusions and Future Work

We have presented a method for parameterizing program analyses for imperative small step languages with information about the programs' execution. The appeal of the method compared to approaches where additional information about the programs' execution is provided by extending the type system with capabilities of computing the additional information, i.e. fusing the type system with another analysis, lies in that:

- The parameterization does not impose heavy changes to the type system. The rules remain relatively close to the original rules; only the use of the additional information is added to the rules where the information is used — other rules remain essentially unaffected. Comparatively, fusing an analysis modifies all rules to compute the information, in addition to the uses of the information in certain rules.
- The parameterization gives the possibility of changing the parameterized analysis with relative ease — proofs for the family of analyses[2], and decision procedures with corresponding soundness proofs have to be done. Comparatively, changing the analysis for a fused type system means creating a new fused type system and correctness proof from scratch.

The method is based on the identification of a generic format for information exchange between the program analysis and the parameterized results, together with methods — the plugins — for asking specific questions about the each program parts execution environment.

To exemplify the method we have given an overview of the steps involved in parameterizing an existing type system, including the changes to the type system itself, but also the changes to the correctness proof of the type system. A corner stone in this work is the attempt to make the correctness proof a natural part of the parameterization process so that the proof burden for each parameterization is relatively low.

A drawback is that the resulting system may no longer be compositional; e.g. a compositional type system becomes non-compositional if the parameterized information is not compositional. Another restriction is that the parameterization is one-way only; there is no back propagation of type information that could have been used by the parameterized analysis.

Future Work. The motivation for this work grew out of a perceived need to increase the precision of type based analyses of secure information flow. For this reason a natural continuation of this work is to apply the method to an information flow type system.

In addition to this, an implementation of the parameterized type system of this paper would be valuable to asses the practicality of the approach. Of particular interest would be to implement a staged type system, where the reason for a type failure is analyzed and given as feedback to the next stage. The benefit of doing this is apparent in cases where the abstract environment map is a combination of the result of a number of external analyses. One way to view a set of increasingly precise external analyses is as a matrix with one dimension for each type of analysis and plugin property. In the general setting where a parameterized type system uses multiple external analyses the external analyses build up a multi-dimensional matrix where each point corresponds to a particular instantiation of the type system.

---

[2] The proof only has to be done once for each family, and typically includes a way of converting the analysis information provided by the family to the format of the parameterization.

Acknowledgements. This work was partly supported by the Swedish research agencies SSF, VR and Vinnova, and by the Information Society Technologies programme of the European Commission, Future and Emerging Technologies under the IST-2005-015905 MOBIUS project.

References

1. Amtoft, T., Bandhakavi, S., Banerjee, A.: A logic for information flow in object-oriented programs. In: POPL 2006: Conference record of the 33rd ACM SIGPLAN-SIGACT symposium on Principles of programming languages, pp. 91–102. ACM Press, New York (2006)
2. Barthe, G., Pichardie, D., Rezk, T.: A certified lightweight non-interference java bytecode verifier. In: De Niccola, R. (ed.) European Symposium on Programming. LNCS. Springer, Heidelberg (to appear, 2007)
3. Chin, B., Markstrum, S., Millstein, T.: Semantic type qualifiers. SIGPLAN Not. 40(6), 85–95 (2005)
4. Cousot, P., Cousot, R.: Abstract interpretation: a unified lattice model for static analysis of programs by construction or approximation of fixpoints. In: Conference Record of the Fourth Annual ACM SIGPLAN-SIGACT Symposium on Principles of Programming Languages, Los Angeles, California, pp. 238–252. ACM Press, New York (1977)
5. Cousot, P., Cousot, R.: Systematic design of program analysis frameworks. In: Conference Record of the Sixth Annual ACM SIGPLAN-SIGACT Symposium on Principles of Programming Languages, San Antonio, Texas, pp. 269–282. ACM Press, New York (1979)
6. Crary, K., Weirich, S.: Resource bound certification. In: POPL 2000: Proceedings of the 27th ACM SIGPLAN-SIGACT symposium on Principles of programming languages, pp. 184–198. ACM, New York (2000)
7. Flanagan, C.: Hybrid type checking. In: POPL 2006: Conference record of the 33rd ACM SIGPLAN-SIGACT symposium on Principles of programming languages, pp. 245–256. ACM, New York (2006)
8. Foster, J.S., Fähndrich, M., Aiken, A.: A theory of type qualifiers. SIGPLAN Not. 34(5), 192–203 (1999)
9. Gedell, T., Hedin, D.: Abstract interpretation plugins for type systems. Technical Report 2008:10, Computing Science Department, Chalmers
10. Gedell, T., Hedin, D.: Plugins for structural weakening and strong updates (unpublished)
11. Gulwani, S., Tiwari, A.: Combining abstract interpreters. In: PLDI 2006: Proceedings of the 2006 ACM SIGPLAN conference on Programming language design and implementation, pp. 376–386. ACM Press, New York (2006)
12. Hedin, D., Sands, D.: Noninterference in the presence of non-opaque pointers. In: Proceedings of the 19th IEEE Computer Security Foundations Workshop. IEEE Computer Society Press, Los Alamitos (2006)
13. Hunt, S., Sands, D.: Just forget it – the semantics and enforcement of information erasure. In: Programming Languages and Systems. 17th European Symposium on Programming, ESOP 2008. LNCS, vol. 4960, pp. 239–253. Springer, Heidelberg (2008)
14. Pierce, B.C. (ed.): Types and Programming Languages. MIT Press, Cambridge (2002)
15. Sabelfeld, A., Myers, A.C.: Language-based information-flow security. IEEE J. Selected Areas in Communications 21(1), 5–19 (2003)
16. Xi, H., Pfenning, F.: Eliminating array bound checking through dependent types. SIGPLAN Not. 33(5), 249–257 (1998)

Separation Logic Contracts for a Java-Like Language with Fork/Join

Christian Haack[1,*] and Clément Hurlin[2,**]

[1] Radboud Universiteit Nijmegen, The Netherlands
[2] INRIA Sophia Antipolis - Méditerranée, France

Abstract. We adapt a variant of permission-accounting separation logic to a concurrent Java-like language with fork/join. To support both concurrent reads and information hiding, we combine fractional permissions with abstract predicates. As an example, we present a separation logic contract for iterators that prevents data races and concurrent modifications. Our program logic is presented in an algorithmic style: we avoid structural rules for Hoare triples and formalize logical reasoning about typed heaps by natural deduction rules and a set of sound axioms. We show that verified programs satisfy the following properties: data race freedom, absence of null-dereferences and partial correctness.

1 Introduction

1.1 Context

Over the past ten years or so, substructural logics and type systems have proven to be very valuable formalisms for reasoning about pointer-manipulating programs. Examples include static capabilities [10,11], alias types [29] and separation logic [18,28]. In these systems, the underlying specification language contains linear formulas for specifying memory access policies. Whereas traditional program logics control memory access via frame conditions, separation logic tightly integrates access policy specifications into the formula language itself. Formulas represent access tickets to heap space, and possession of access tickets gets verified statically. Access policies are tightly coupled with assertions about memory content, so that separation logic's Hoare rules make it impossible to maintain assertions that can be invalidated by thread interference or memory updates through unknown aliases. This is achieved without annoying side conditions like non-interference tests or frame conditions.

While initially separation logic mostly focused on low level programs, researchers have more recently started to adapt it to object-oriented features for use in contract languages for OO [25,26], and very recently [9,27].

1.2 Contributions

We present the careful design of a small Java-like model language with separation logic contracts, including the definition of a program logic and its soundness proof. Our

---

* Supported in part by IST-FET-2005-015905 Mobius project.
** Supported in part by ANR-06-SETIN-010 ParSec and IST-FET-2005-015905 Mobius.

J. Meseguer and G. Roşu (Eds.): AMAST 2008, LNCS 5140, pp. 199–215, 2008.

language has simple threads, with fork/join as concurrency primitives. In order to facilitate concurrent reads we employ fractional permissions [5]. Our rules allow multiple
threads to join on the same thread, in order to read-share the dead thread's resources.
This is not possible with a lexically scoped parallel composition operator or with Posix
threads, and is thus not supported by recent work that adapts separation logic to Posix
threads [14]. To support data abstraction and recursive data types, we use abstract
predicates [26]. *Class axioms* complement abstract predicates to export relations between predicates without revealing their full definitions. Abstract predicates satisfying
a split/merge axiom generalize datagroups [21], which are common in specification languages for OO. In order to support concurrent read access to whole datagroups (rather
than single fields), access permission to datagroups can be split by splitting their permission parameters. In order to allow fine-grained permission-splitting for overlapping
datagroups, we support datagroups with multiple permission parameters. To achieve
modular soundness in the presence of subclassing, we axiomatize the "stack of class
frames" [12,1] in separation logic. We support *value-parametrized classes*, where class
parameters have the same purpose as f i n a l ghost fields in specification languages like
JML [20]. In particular, class parameters can represent static ownership relations.

1.3   Background on Separation Logic and Fractional Permissions

Separation logic combines the usual logical operators with the points-to predicate $x.f \mapsto v$, the resource conjunction $F * G$, and the resource implication $F -\!\!* G$.

The predicate $x.f \mapsto v$ has a *dual purpose*: firstly, it asserts that the object field $x.f$
contains data value v and, secondly, it represents a *ticket* that grants permission to access
the field $x.f$. This is formalized by separation logic's Hoare rules for reading and writing
fields:

$$\{x.f \mapsto \_ * F\}x.f = v\{x.f \mapsto v * F\} \qquad \{x.f \mapsto v * F\}y = x.f\{x.f \mapsto v * v == y * F\}$$

The crucial difference to standard Hoare logic is that both these rules have a precondition of the form $x.f \mapsto \_.$[1] This formula functions as an *access ticket* for $x.f$.

It is important that tickets are not forgeable. One ticket is not the same as two tickets!
For this reason, the resource conjunction $*$ is not idempotent: F is not equivalent to
$F * F$. The resource implication $-\!\!*$ matches the resource conjunction $*$, in the sense
that the modus ponens law is satisfied: $F * (F -\!\!* G)$ implies G. However, $F * (F -\!\!* G)$
does not imply $F * G$. In English, $F -\!\!* G$ is pronounced as "consume F yielding G". In
terms of tickets, $F -\!\!* G$ permits to trade ticket F and receive ticket G in return.

Separation logic is particularly useful for concurrent programs: two concurrent
threads simply split the resources that they may access, as formalized by the rule for the
parallel composition $t \mid t'$ of threads t and t' [22].

$$\frac{\{F\}t\{G\} \quad \{F'\}t'\{G'\}}{\{F * F'\}t \mid t'\{G * G'\}}$$

---

[1] $x.f \mapsto \_$ is short for $(\exists v)(x.f \mapsto v)$.

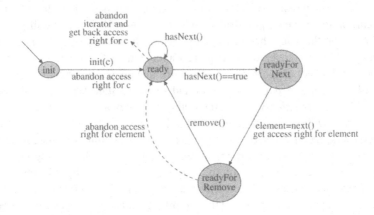

Fig. 1. Usage Protocol for Iterators

With this concurrency rule, separation logic prevents data races. There is a caveat, though. The rule does not allow concurrent reads. Boyland [5] solved this problem with a very intuitive idea, which was later adapted to separation logic [4]. The idea is that (1) *access tickets are splittable*, (2) *a split of an access ticket still grants read access* and (3) *only a whole access ticket grants write access*. To account for multiple splits, Boyland uses fractions, hence the name *fractional permissions*. In permission-accounting separation logic [4], access tickets $x.f \mapsto v$ are superscripted by fractions π. $x.f \overset{\pi}{\longmapsto} v$ is equivalent to $x.f \overset{\pi/2}{\longmapsto} v * x.f \overset{\pi/2}{\longmapsto} v$. In the Hoare rules, writing requires the full fraction 1, whereas reading just requires *some* fraction π:

$$\{x.f \overset{1}{\longmapsto} \_ * F\}x.f = v\{x.f \overset{1}{\longmapsto} v * F\} \qquad \{x.f \overset{\pi}{\longmapsto} v * F\}y = x.f\{x.f \overset{\pi}{\longmapsto} v * v == y * F\}$$

Permission-accounting separation logic maintains the global invariant that the sum of all fractional permissions to the same cell is always at most 1. This prevents read-write and write-write conflicts, but permits concurrent reads.

In our Java-like language, we use ASCII and write $\texttt{Perm}(x.f, \pi)$ for $x.f \overset{\pi}{\longmapsto} \_$, and $\texttt{PointsTo}(x.f, \pi, v)$ for $x.f \overset{\pi}{\longmapsto} v$.

1.4 Example: A Usage Protocol for Iterators

Often one wants to constrain object clients to adhere to certain usage protocols. Object usage protocols can, for instance, be specified in typestate systems [12] or, using ghost fields, in general purpose specification languages. A limitation of these techniques is that state transitions must always be associated with method calls. This is sometimes not sufficient. Consider for instance a variant of Java's `Iterator` interface (enriched with an `init` method to avoid constructor contracts):

```
interface Iterator {
    void init(Collection c);
    boolean hasNext();
    Object next();
    void remove();
}
```

If iterators are used in an undisciplined way, there is the danger of unwanted concurrent modification of the underlying collection (both of the collection elements and the collection itself). Moreover, in concurrent programs bad iterator usage can result in data races. It is therefore important that Iterator clients adhere to a usage discipline.

Figure 1 shows a state machine that defines a safe iterator usage discipline. Unfortunately, the dashed transitions are not supported by existing typestate systems, because they are not associated with method calls. Specifying this protocol with classical program logics would be clumsy. In [13] (Section 1.1.4), Girard explains how *linear implications can be used to logically represent state transitions*. Applying this idea to the iterator protocol, we obtain the following formalization where the dashed transitions are represented by resource implications:

```
interface Iterator<perm p, Collection iteratee> {
    pred ready;                               // prestate for iteration cycle
    pred readyForNext;                        // prestate for next()
    pred readyForRemove<Object element>;      // prestate for remove()

    axiom ready -* iteratee.state<p>;                  // stop iterating
    axiom readyForRemove<e> * e.state<p> -* ready;  // back to ready

    req init * c.state<p> * c==iteratee; ens ready;
    void init(Collection c);

    req ready; ens ready & (result -* readyForNext);
    boolean hasNext();

    req readyForNext; ens result.state<p> * readyForRemove<result>;
    Object next();

    req readyForRemove<_> * p==1; ens ready;
    void remove();
}
```

The interface has two parameters: firstly, a permission p and, secondly, the iteratee. If the permission parameter is instantiated by a fraction $p < 1$, one obtains a read-only iterator, otherwise a read-write iterator. The states of our our state diagram are represented by three abstract predicates: ready, readyForNext and readyForRemove.

Class axioms express relations between abstract predicates, without revealing the complete predicate definitions. Implementations must define the abstract predicates by separation logic formulas such that the class axioms are tautologically true. In the example, the two class axioms represent the dashed transitions of the state machine. We represent the heap space associated with an object by a generic datagroup state, which has a default definition in the Object class and needs to be overridden by each class. The definition of this state predicate should describe the heap space associated with the object. Often this heap space will consist of the object's fields only, but sometimes it will also include other objects and change dynamically, as in the case of Collection objects. The state predicate is parametrized by a fraction so that it can be read-shared.

The precondition of `init()` consumes a fraction p of the access right for the iteratee and puts the iterator in the `ready` state. The crux is that, by linearity, the iterator client temporarily looses a p-fraction of the access right on the collection, which he can only gain back by "invoking" the first class axiom. The `init` predicate in `init()`'s precondition is a special abstract predicate that every object enters right after object creation and that grants access to all of the object's fields.

The postcondition of `hasNext()` uses a resource implication whose antecedent is a boolean expression. We treat boolean expressions as *copyable resources* that satisfy $e -\!* (e * e)$.[2] Furthermore, `hasNext()`'s postcondition uses *additive conjunction* &. A resource satisfies F & G, if it satisfies both F and G.[3] Operationally, & represents *choice*. If F & G holds, then F and G are available, but are interdependent: using either one of them destroys the other one, too. Additive conjunction can conveniently represent non-deterministic state transitions, as exhibited in `hasNext()`'s postcondition. Note that this postcondition allows clients to stay in the `ready`-state, even if `hasNext()==true`. This can, for instance, be useful for removing the 10th element of an ordered collection.

In our companion report [16], we have implemented the `Iterator` interface for a doubly linked list implementation of the `Collection` interface. In [15], we refine the protocol to support unrestricted access to immutable collection elements, and to support shallow collections that do not govern access to their elements.

1.5   Example: Representing Datagroups

We represent *datagroups* [21] as abstract predicates satisfying a datagroup axiom that says *split/merging datagroup parameters split/merges datagroups*:

$$\text{group } P<\bar{T}\,\bar{x}>; \quad \overset{\Delta}{=} \quad \begin{array}{l} \text{pred } P<\bar{T}\,\bar{x}>;\ \text{axiom } P<\bar{x}> *\!-\!* (P<\bar{e}> * P<\bar{e}>);\\ \text{where } e_i \overset{\Delta}{=} x_i/2,\ \text{if } T_i = \text{perm, and } e_i \overset{\Delta}{=} x_i,\ \text{otherwise} \end{array}$$

The formula $F *\!-\!* G$ is short for $(F -\!* G)$ & $(G -\!* F)$. Here are simple examples of a legal and an illegal datagroup definition (where | is disjunction):

```
group P<perm p> = Perm(this.f,p) * Perm(this.g,p);
   legal because the datagroup axiom holds
group P<perm p> = Perm(this.f,p) | Perm(this.g,p);
   illegal because the datagroup axiom's right-to-left direction does not hold
```

---

[2] We could equivalently use classical implication: `result` $\Rightarrow$ `readyForNext`. Even the two class axioms could equivalently use classical implication, because they are tautologies, and in intuitionistic separation logic $F -\!* G$ is a tautology if and only if $F \Rightarrow G$ is. However, in our implementations of the `Iterator` interface, we use true resource implications that cannot be replaced by classical implications. In this paper, we avoid classical implication because having just one implication simplifies the natural deduction rules for reasoning about resources.

[3] In contrast, a resource satisfies $F * G$ if it can be split into separate resources, one of which satisfies F and the other satisfies G.

On the right, you see a fractional permission version of Leino's running example [21]. The datagroups `position` and `color` are nested in `state`, as expressed by the two class axioms. The formula "F ispartof G" is a derived form for $G -\!\!* (F * (F -\!\!* G))$. Intuitively, this formula says that F is a physical part of G: one can take G apart into F and its complement $F -\!\!* G$, and one can put the two parts back together to obtain G back.

```
interface Sprite {
    group position<perm p>;
    group color<perm p>;

    axiom position<p> ispartof state<p>;
    axiom color<p> ispartof state<p>;

    req position<1>; ens position<1>;
    void updatePosition();

    req color<1>; ens color<1>;
    void updateColor();

    req state<1>; ens state<1>;
    void update();

    req state<p>; ens state<p>;
    void display();
}
```

1.6 Example: Recursive and Overlapping Datagroups

Our next example illustrates that multiple threads can concurrently access overlapping datagroups, as long as they only read-access their intersection. Consider a linked list that implements a simple class roster. Each node stores a student identifier and a grade. We design the roster interface so that multiple threads can concurrently read the roster. Moreover, when a thread updates the grades we allow other threads to concurrently read the student identifiers. To this end, the interface defines two datagroups `ids_and_links<p,q>` and `grades_and_links<p,q>` that overlap in the links of the list. The permission parameter p is associated with the student id fields and grade fields, respectively. The permission parameter q is associated with the links.

```
interface Roster {
    group ids_and_links<perm p, perm q>;
    group grades_and_links<perm p, perm q>;

    axiom state<p> *-* (ids_and_links<p,p/2> * grades_and_links<p,p/2>);

    req grades_and_links<1,p> * ids_and_links<q,r>;
    ens grades_and_links<1,p> * ids_and_links<q,r>;
    void updateGrade(int id, int grade);

    req ids_and_links<p,q>; ens ids_and_links<p,q>;
    bool contains(int id);
}
```

The `updateGrade()` method requires write access (permission 1) for the grades and read access for the links and ids. The `contains()` method requires read permission for the ids and the links. The axiom exposes that the `state` datagroup is the union of the datagroups `ids_and_links` and `grades_and_links` and that these datagroups overlap on the links. In our companion report [16], we have implemented this interface.

2 A Model Language with Separation Logic Contacts

2.1 Syntax

We distinguish between read-only variables ι, read-write variables ℓ, and logic variables α. Method parameters (including this) are read-only. Logic variables can only occur in specifications and types. They range over both fractional permissions and values (like integers, object identifiers and null).

$$C, D \in \mathsf{ClassId} \quad I \in \mathsf{InterId} \quad s, t \in \mathsf{TyId} = \mathsf{ClassId} \cup \mathsf{InterId} \quad o, p, q \in \mathsf{ObjId} \quad f \in \mathsf{FieldId}$$
$$m \in \mathsf{MethId} \quad P \in \mathsf{PredId} \quad \iota \in \mathsf{RdVar} \quad \ell \in \mathsf{RdWrVar} \quad \alpha \in \mathsf{LogVar} = \mathsf{PermVar} \cup \mathsf{ValVar}$$
$$x, y, z \in \mathsf{Var} = \mathsf{RdVar} \cup \mathsf{RdWrVar} \cup \mathsf{LogVar}$$

We include read-only variables (but not read-write variables) in the syntax domain of *values*. This is convenient for our substitution-based operational semantics. *Fractional permissions* are represented symbolically: $\mathtt{split}^n(1)$ represents the concrete fraction $\frac{1}{2^n}$. In examples, we sometimes write $\frac{1}{2^n}$ as syntax sugar for $\mathtt{split}^n(1)$. *Specification values* union values and fractional permissions. Interfaces and classes are parametrized by specification values. Correspondingly, object types $t<\bar{\pi}>$ instantiate the parameters.

$$n \in \mathsf{Int} \qquad \text{integers} \qquad b \in \mathsf{Bool} = \{\mathtt{true}, \mathtt{false}\} \qquad \text{booleans}$$
$$u, v, w \in \mathsf{Val} ::= \mathtt{null} \mid n \mid b \mid o \mid \iota \qquad \text{values}$$
$$\pi \in \mathsf{SpecVal} ::= v \mid 1 \mid \mathtt{split}(\pi) \qquad \text{specification values}$$
$$T, U, V, W \in \mathsf{Ty} ::= \mathtt{void} \mid \mathtt{int} \mid \mathtt{bool} \mid t<\bar{\pi}> \mid \mathtt{perm} \qquad \text{types}$$

Interface Declarations:

$F \in \mathsf{Formula} ::= \ldots$	specification formulas (defined in Section 2.3)
$spec ::= \mathtt{req}\, F;\, \mathtt{ens}\, F;$	pre- and postconditions
$mt ::= <\bar{T}\,\bar{\alpha}>\, spec\; U\; m(\bar{V}\,\bar{\iota})$	method types (scope of $\bar{\alpha}, \bar{\iota}$ is $\bar{T}, spec, U, \bar{V}$)
$pt ::= \mathtt{pred}\, P<\bar{T}\,\bar{\alpha}>$	predicate types
$ax ::= \mathtt{axiom}\, F$	class axioms
$int \in \mathsf{Interface} ::= \mathtt{interface}\, I<\bar{T}\,\bar{\alpha}>\, \mathtt{ext}\, \bar{U}\, \{pt^*\; ax^*\; mt^*\}$	
	interfaces (scope of $\bar{\alpha}$ is $\bar{T}, \bar{U}, pt^*, ax^*, mt^*$)

Syntactic restriction: The type "perm" may only occur inside angle brackets or formulas.

Method types include pre- and postconditions and are parametrized by logic variables. In examples, we often leave these quantifiers over logic variables implicit. Interfaces may declare *abstract predicates* and classes must implement them by providing concrete definitions as separation logic formulas. Like [26], we allow abstract predicates to have parameters in addition to the implicit self-parameter (as listed in the typed formal parameter lists $\bar{T}\,\bar{\alpha}$). The types $\bar{T}$ for predicate parameters range over all Java types and the distinguished type perm for fractional permissions.

We assume that the Object class declares a distinguished datagroup called state:

```
class Object { group state<perm p> = true; }
```

This datagroup represents the access permissions for the *object state*. Every class must extend it and thereby define what the object states of its instances are. Our syntax for predicate extensions is as follows:

$$\text{class } C \text{ ext } D \;\{\; \ldots \; \text{ext pred } P{<}\bar{T}\,\bar{x}{>} \text{ by } F; \quad \ldots \;\}$$

Semantically, the extension F of abstract predicate P gets *-conjoined* with P's definition in C's superclass D. We do not allow arbitrary predicate redefinitions in subclasses in order to facilitate modular verification, avoiding re-verification of inherited methods.

Class Declarations:

$fd ::= T\,f$	field declarations
$pd ::=$	predicate definitions
$\quad$ final? pred $P{<}\bar{T}\,\bar{\alpha}{>}{=}F$	root definition (scope of $\bar{\alpha}$ is F)
$\quad$ final? ext pred $P{<}\bar{T}\,\bar{\alpha}{>}$ by F	extension (scope of $\bar{\alpha}$ is F)
$md ::=$ final? $<\bar{T}\,\bar{\alpha}>\,spec\; U\; m(\bar{V}\,\bar{\imath})\,\{c\}$	method (scope of $\bar{\alpha},\bar{\imath}$ is $\bar{T},spec,U,\bar{V},c$)
$cl \in$ Class $::=$ final? class $C{<}\bar{T}\,\bar{\alpha}{>}$ ext U impl $\bar{V}$ $\{fd^*\,pd^*\,ax^*\,md^*\}$	
	class (scope of $\bar{\alpha}$ is $\bar{T},U,\bar{V},fd^*,pd^*,ax^*,md^*$)
$ct \subseteq$ Interface $\cup$ Class	class tables

Syntactic restrictions:
- The type "perm" may only occur inside angle brackets or specification formulas.
- Cyclic predicate definitions in ct must be positive.

The *first syntactic restriction* ensures that fractional permissions do not spill into the executable part of the language. The *second syntactic restriction* ensures that predicate implementations (which can be recursive) are well-founded. We allow negative dependencies of predicate P on predicate Q as long as Q does not also depend on P.

We use the symbol $\preceq_{ct}$ for the partial order on type identifiers induced by class table ct, usually leaving the subscript ct implicit. We write $s \prec_1 t$ when s and t are neighbours with respect to $\preceq$. *Subtyping* is inductively defined by the following rules:

$$T <: T \qquad T <: U, U <: V \;\Rightarrow\; T <: V \qquad s{<}\bar{T}\,\bar{\alpha}{>} \text{ ext } t{<}\bar{\pi}'{>} \;\Rightarrow\; s{<}\bar{\pi}{>} <: t{<}\bar{\pi}'[\bar{\pi}/\bar{\alpha}]{>}$$

$$t{<}\bar{\pi}{>} <: \text{Object} \qquad t{<}\bar{T}\,\bar{\alpha}{>} \text{ impl } I{<}\pi'{>} \;\Rightarrow\; t{<}\bar{\pi}{>} <: I{<}\bar{\pi}'[\bar{\pi}/\bar{\alpha}]{>}$$

We assume that class tables always contain the following class declaration:

```
class Thread ext Object {
    final void fork(); final void join();
    req false; ens true; void run() { null }
}
```

The run-method is meant to be overridden. The contracts for fork and join are omitted, because our verification system ignores them anyway. Instead, it uses the precondition for run as the precondition for fork and the postcondition for run as the postcondition for join. The methods fork and join do not have implementations, but the operational semantics treats them in a special way[4]: o.fork() creates a new thread,

---
[4] In reality, they would be implemented natively.

whose thread identifier is o, and executes o.run() in this thread. The o.fork-method should not be called more than once (on the same receiver o). A second call results in blocking. o.join() blocks until thread o has terminated.

Commands:

$op \in \mathsf{Op} \supseteq \{==, !, \&, |\} \cup \{C \text{ isclassof} \mid C \in \mathsf{ClassId}\}$

$c \in \mathsf{Cmd} ::=$ commands

v	return value (or null in case of type void)
$T\,\ell; c$	local variable declaration (scope of ℓ is c)
final $T\,\iota = \ell; c$	local read-only variable declaration (scope of ι is c)
unpack (ex $T\,\alpha$)(F); c	unpacking an existential (scope of α is F, c)
$hc; c$	first do hc, then do c

$hc \in \mathsf{HeadCmd} ::= \ell = v \mid \ell = op(\bar{v}) \mid \ell = v.f \mid v.f = v \mid \ell = (T)v \mid \ell = \mathsf{new}\,C{<}\bar{\pi}{>} \mid$
$\qquad\qquad\qquad \mathsf{if}\,(v)\{c\}\mathsf{else}\{c'\} \mid \ell = v.m{<}\bar{\pi}{>}(\bar{v}) \mid \mathsf{assert}(F)$

Synt. Restr.: Logic variables that occur in $\ell = \mathsf{new}\,C{<}\bar{\pi}{>}$ must be bound by class parameters.

Our command language assumes that Java-like commands have been transformed so that intermediate values are always assigned to local variables. Following [17], we assume that methods only return at the end of their body. We omit the return-command. Values are included in the syntax domain of commands, so that a terminating, non-blocking execution of a command results in the return value. Methods of type void return null, which is the only member of type void. We usually omit terminating occurrences of null. The operator for *existential unpacking* has no effect at runtime. It makes the existential variable α available in the continuation c for instantiation of logic method parameters. In examples, we often omit explicit existential unpacking and instantiation of logic method parameters. Making these explicit helps with the theory.

2.2 Operational Semantics

Runtime Structures:

$\mathsf{ClVal} = \mathsf{Val} \setminus \mathsf{RdVar}$	closed values
$s \in \mathsf{Stack} = \mathsf{RdWrVar} \rightharpoonup \mathsf{ClVal}$	stacks
$t \in \mathsf{Thread} = \mathsf{Stack} \times \mathsf{Cmd} ::= s \text{ in } c$	threads
$ts \in \mathsf{ThreadPool} = \mathsf{ObjId} \rightharpoonup \mathsf{Thread} ::= o_1 \text{ is } t_1 \mid \cdots \mid o_n \text{ is } t_n$	thread pools
$os \in \mathsf{ObjStore} = \mathsf{FieldId} \rightharpoonup \mathsf{ClVal}$	object stores
$obj \in \mathsf{Obj} = \mathsf{Ty} \times \mathsf{ObjStore} ::= (T, os)$	objects
$h \in \mathsf{Heap} = \mathsf{ObjId} \rightharpoonup \mathsf{Obj}$	heaps
$st \in \mathsf{State} = \mathsf{Heap} \times \mathsf{ThreadPool} ::= \langle h, ts \rangle$	states
$prog \in \mathsf{Program} = \mathsf{ClassTable} \times \mathsf{Cmd} ::= (ct, c)$	programs

Each thread "s in c" consists of a thread-local stack s and a process continuation c. In thread pools, each thread t is associated with a unique object identifier, which serves as a thread identifier. The dynamic semantics of our language is a small-step operational semantics $st \rightarrow_{ct} st'$ and can be found in [16].

There is one (and only one) reduction rule where our operational semantics depends on class parameters, namely the reduction rule for type casts. Downcasts to parametrized types require a runtime check that looks at the type parameters, which the standard JVM does not keep track of. There are at least three ways how one could deal with that in practice: Firstly (and most pragmatically), one could simply forbid downcasts to reference types that have a non-empty parameter list. Secondly, one could develop an enhanced virtual machine that keeps track of class parameters. Thirdly, one could devise a syntactic translation that erases class parameters such that the target of this translation throws a `ClassCastException` whenever the source does.

2.3 Specification Formulas and Their Semantics

Specification Formulas:

$e \in \mathsf{Exp} ::= \pi \mid \ell \mid op(\bar{e})$		$lop \in \{*, -*, \&, \mid\}$	$qt \in \{\mathtt{ex}, \mathtt{fa}\}$

$\kappa \in \mathsf{Pred} ::=$ predicates

   P P at receiver's dynamic class

   $P@C$ P at class C

$E, F, G, H \in \mathsf{Formula} ::=$ specification formulas

   e boolean expression

   $\mathsf{PointsTo}(e.f, \pi, e')$ $e.f$ points to e' and the access permission for $e.f$ is π

   $\mathsf{Perm}(e.\mathtt{join}, \pi)$ permission to use a split of `join`'s postcondition

   $\pi.\kappa\langle\bar{\pi}'\rangle$ predicate $\pi.\kappa$ applied to $\bar{\pi}'$

   $F\ lop\ G$ binary logical operator

   $(qt\ T\ \alpha)\,(F)$ quantifier

Derived forms: $F *-* G \stackrel{\Delta}{=} (F -\!* G) \,\&\, (G -\!* F)$ F **assures** $G \stackrel{\Delta}{=} F -\!* (F * G)$

F **ispartof** $G \stackrel{\Delta}{=} G -\!* (F * (F -\!* G))$

The formula semantics is defined by a Kripke resource interpretation [23] of the form $\Gamma \vdash \mathscr{E}; \mathscr{R}; s \models F$, where Γ is a type environment, $\mathscr{E}$ is a predicate environment that maps predicate names to predicates, $\mathscr{R}$ is a resource, and s is a stack. Resources are triples $\mathscr{R} = (h, \mathscr{P}, \mathscr{Q})$ of heaps h and two permission tables $\mathscr{P}$ and $\mathscr{Q}$. Permission tables are functions of type $\mathsf{ObjId} \times (\mathsf{FieldId} \times \{\mathtt{join}\}) \to [0,1]$ that map fields and `join` to fractional permissions. The resource components h and $\mathscr{P}$ are local resources, whereas $\mathscr{Q}$ is a global resource. We denote the projections to the resource components by $\mathscr{R}_{\mathsf{hp}}$, $\mathscr{R}_{\mathsf{loc}}$ and $\mathscr{R}_{\mathsf{glo}}$. The definition of the forcing relation $\models$ is pretty standard, and we refer to [16] for details.

2.4 Soundness Theorems

Below, we define a verification system whose top level judgment is $prog : \diamond$ (read: "*prog* is verified"). We have proven a *preservation theorem* from which we can draw several corollaries, namely, *data race freedom, null error freedom* and *partial correctness*.

A pair (hc, hc') of head commands is called a *data race* iff $hc = (o.f = v)$ and either $hc' = (o.f = v')$ or $hc' = (\ell = o.f)$ for some o, f, v, v', ℓ. A head command hc is called a *null error* iff $hc = (\ell = \mathtt{null}.f)$ or $hc = (\mathtt{null}.f = v)$ or $hc = (\ell = \mathtt{null}.m\langle\bar{\pi}\rangle(\bar{v}))$. We define *initial states*: $\mathsf{init}(c) = \langle\{\mathsf{main} \mapsto (\mathtt{Thread}, \emptyset)\}, \mathsf{main\ is}\ (\emptyset\ \mathsf{in}\ c)\rangle$, where main is some distinguished object id for the main thread. The main thread has an empty set of fields (hence the first $\emptyset$), and its stack is initially empty (hence the second $\emptyset$).

Theorem 1 (Verified Programs are Data Race Free). *If* $(ct,c) : \diamond$ *and* $\mathsf{init}(c) \to^*_{ct}$ $\langle h, ts \mid o_1 \text{ is } (s_1 \text{ in } hc_1;c_1) \mid o_2 \text{ is } (s_2 \text{ in } hc_2;c_2)\rangle$, *then* (hc_1, hc_2) *is not a data race.*

Theorem 2 (Verified Programs are Null Error Free). *If* $(ct,c) : \diamond$ *and* $\mathsf{init}(c) \to^*_{ct}$ $\langle h, ts \mid o \text{ is } (s \text{ in } hc;c)\rangle$, *then* hc *is not a null error.*

Theorem 3 (Partial Correctness).
If $(ct,c) : \diamond$ *and* $\mathsf{init}(c) \to^*_{ct} \langle h, ts \mid o \text{ is } (s \text{ in } \mathsf{assert}(F);c)\rangle$, *then* $(\Gamma \vdash \mathcal{E};\mathcal{R};s \models F[\sigma])$
for some $\Gamma, \mathcal{E}, \mathcal{R}$ *such that* $\mathcal{R}_{\mathsf{hp}} = h$, *and* $\sigma \in \mathsf{LogVar} \rightharpoonup \mathsf{SpecVal}$.

3 The Verification System

3.1 Proof Theory

Many presentations of separation logic are based on a model-theoretic logical consequence. We, instead, define logical consequence proof-theoretically. This gives our system an algorithmic flavour, similar to recent static assertion checkers for fragments of separation logic [2,9] that are built upon proof-theoretic decision procedures[5].

$\Gamma;v;\bar{F} \vdash G$	from v's point of view, G is a logical consequence of the $*$-conjunction of $\bar{F}$
$\Gamma;v \vdash F$	from v's point of view, F is an axiom

In the former judgment, $\bar{F}$ is a *multiset* of formulas. The parameter v represents the *current receiver*, which is needed to determine the scope of predicate definitions.

The logical consequence judgment is driven by standard natural deduction rules that are common to the logic of bunched implications [23] and linear logic [30]. These rules are detailed in [16]. We admit weakening, because Java is a garbage-collected language. The link between $\Gamma;v;\bar{F} \vdash G$ and the axiom judgment $\Gamma;v \vdash F$ is established by the following rule. (We omit the definitions of typing judgments $\Gamma \vdash v : T$ and $\Gamma \vdash F : \diamond$.)

$$\frac{\Gamma;v \vdash G \quad \Gamma \vdash v : \texttt{Object} \quad \Gamma \vdash \bar{F}, G : \diamond}{\Gamma;v;\bar{F} \vdash G}$$

We now define the complete set of axioms. First, we repeat the split/merge law:

$$\Gamma;v \vdash \texttt{PointsTo}(e.f,\pi,e') *\!\!-\!\!* (\texttt{PointsTo}(e.f,\tfrac{\pi}{2},e') * \texttt{PointsTo}(e.f,\tfrac{\pi}{2},e'))$$
$$\Gamma;v \vdash \texttt{Perm}(e.\texttt{join},\pi) *\!\!-\!\!* (\texttt{Perm}(e.\texttt{join},\tfrac{\pi}{2}) * \texttt{Perm}(e.\texttt{join},\tfrac{\pi}{2}))$$

For the following axioms, recall that "F assures G" abbreviates "$F -\!\!* (F * G)$".

$$\Gamma;v \vdash \texttt{true} \quad \Gamma;v \vdash \texttt{false} -\!\!* F \quad \Gamma;v \vdash (e \,\&\, F) -\!\!* (e * F)$$
$$\Gamma;v \vdash (\texttt{PointsTo}(e.f,\pi,e') \,\&\, \texttt{PointsTo}(e.f,\pi',e'')) \text{ assures } e' == e''$$
$$(\Gamma \vdash e,e' : T \,\wedge\, \Gamma,x:T \vdash F : \diamond) \Rightarrow \Gamma;v \vdash (F[e/x] * e == e') -\!\!* F[e'/x]$$

The third of these axioms implies that boolean expressions are copyable: $e -\!\!* (e * e)$.

---

[5] Unfortunately, these fragments do not include $-\!\!*$, as needed for our iterator implementation.

The following axiom lifts semantic validity of boolean expressions (which we do not axiomatize) to our proof theory:

$$(\Gamma \models !e_1 \mid !e_2 \mid e') \Rightarrow \Gamma;v \vdash (e_1 * e_2) \mathrel{-\!\!*} e'$$

The next axiom allows to apply class axioms. Here, $\mathrm{axiom}(t<\bar{\pi}'>)$ is the $*$-conjunction of all class axioms in $t<\bar{\pi}'>$ and its supertypes.

$$(\Gamma \vdash \pi : t<\bar{\pi}'> \wedge \mathrm{axiom}(t<\bar{\pi}'>) = F) \Rightarrow \Gamma;v \vdash F[\pi/\texttt{this}]$$

The *open/close axiom* allows predicate receivers to replace abstract predicates by their definitions. It uses a function $\mathrm{pbody}(v.P<\bar{\pi}>,C<\bar{\pi}'>)$ that returns the extension F of predicate $v.P<\bar{\pi}>$ in class $C<\bar{\pi}'>$.

$$(\Gamma \vdash v : C<\bar{\pi}''> \wedge \mathrm{pbody}(v.P<\bar{\pi},\bar{\pi}'>,C<\bar{\pi}''>) = F \wedge C \prec_1 D)$$
$$\Rightarrow \Gamma;v \vdash v.P@C<\bar{\pi},\bar{\pi}'> \mathrel{*\!\!-\!\!*} (F * v.P@D<\bar{\pi}>)$$

Note that the current receiver, as represented on the left of $\vdash$, has to match the predicate receiver on the right. This rule is the only reason why our logical consequence judgment tracks the current receiver. Note also that $P@C$ may have a higher arity than $P@D$: following [26] we allow subclasses to extend predicate arities.

The following axiom deals with unqualified predicates with missing parameters:

$$\Gamma;v \vdash \pi.P<\bar{\pi}> \mathrel{*\!\!-\!\!*} (\mathrm{ex}\ \bar{T}\ \bar{\alpha})\,(\pi.P<\bar{\pi},\bar{\alpha}>)$$

The following axioms capture additional facts about abstract predicates. Recall that "F ispartof G" is defined as $G \mathrel{-\!\!*} (F * (F \mathrel{-\!\!*} G))$.

$$\Gamma;v \vdash \mathtt{null}.\kappa<\bar{\pi}> \qquad \Gamma;v \vdash \pi.P@\mathtt{Object} \qquad \Gamma;v \vdash \pi.P@C<\bar{\pi}> \text{ ispartof } \pi.P<\bar{\pi}>$$
$$C \preceq D \Rightarrow \Gamma;v \vdash \pi.P@D<\bar{\pi}> \text{ ispartof } \pi.P@C<\bar{\pi},\bar{\pi}'>$$

The next axioms allow to drop the class modifier C from $\pi.P@C$, if we know that C is π's dynamic class:

$$\Gamma;v \vdash (\pi.P@C<\bar{\pi}> * C \text{ isclassof } \pi) \mathrel{-\!\!*} \pi.P<\bar{\pi}>$$
$$(C \text{ is final or } P \text{ is final in } C) \Rightarrow \Gamma;v \vdash \pi.P@C<\bar{\pi}> \mathrel{-\!\!*} \pi.P<\bar{\pi}>$$

Here, the expression "π isclassof C" evaluates to true whenever C is π's dynamic class. "C isclassof π" surely holds right after object π of class C has been created. Consequently, our Hoare rules introduce it as a postcondition of object creation commands. The second axiom makes use of final classes (resp. predicates), which are classes (resp. predicates) that are prohibited to be extended.

3.2 Method Subtyping

Method types are of the following form:

$$<\bar{T}\ \bar{\alpha}> \texttt{req}\ F; \texttt{ens}\ G; U\,m\,(V_0\,\iota_0;\bar{V}\,\bar{\iota})$$

In method types, we make the self-parameter explicit, separated from the other formal parameters by a semicolon. In the scheme above, ι_0 is the self-parameter.

Before presenting the method subtyping rule in full generality, we present its instance for method types without logic parameters:

$$\frac{U, V_0, \bar{V}' <: U', V_0', \bar{V} \quad \Gamma, \iota_0 : V_0, \bar{\iota} : \bar{V}'; \iota_0; \text{true} \vdash F' -\!\!* (F * (\text{fa } U \text{ result}) (G -\!\!* G'))}{\Gamma \vdash \text{req } F; \text{ens } G; U \, m (V_0 \iota_0; \bar{V} \bar{\iota}) <: \text{req } F'; \text{ens } G'; U' m (V_0' \iota_0; \bar{V}' \bar{\iota})}$$

This rule has the following two derived rules (where types are elided):

$$\frac{\vdash F' -\!\!* F \quad \vdash G' -\!\!* G}{\vdash \text{req } F; \text{ens } G <: \text{req } F'; \text{ens } G'} \qquad \frac{}{\vdash \text{req } F; \text{ens } G <: \text{req } F * H; \text{ens } G * H}$$

The first of these derived rules is standard behavioural subtyping, the second one abstracts separation logic's frame rule. In order to see that these two rules follow from the above rule, note that the following two formulas are tautologies (as can be easily proven by natural deduction):

$$(F' -\!\!* F) * H -\!\!* F' -\!\!* F * H \qquad F * H -\!\!* F * (\text{fa } U x) (G -\!\!* G * H)$$

The general method subtyping rule also accounts for logic parameters:[6]

$$\frac{m \neq \text{run} \quad \bar{T}', U, V_0, \bar{V}' <: \bar{T}, U', V_0', \bar{V}}{\Gamma, \iota_0 : V_0; \iota_0; \text{true} \vdash (\text{fa } \bar{T}' \bar{\alpha}) (\text{fa } \bar{V}' \bar{\iota}) (F' -\!\!* (\text{ex } \bar{W} \bar{\alpha}') (F * (\text{fa } U \text{ result}) (G -\!\!* G')))}{\Gamma \vdash <\bar{T} \bar{\alpha}, \bar{W} \bar{\alpha}'> \text{req } F; \text{ens } G; U \, m (V_0 \iota_0; \bar{V} \bar{\iota}) <: <\bar{T}' \bar{\alpha}> \text{req } F'; \text{ens } G'; U' m (V_0' \iota_0; \bar{V}' \bar{\iota})}$$

Note that the subtype may have more logic parameters than the supertype. For instance, we obtain the following derived rule:

$$\frac{}{\vdash <T \alpha> \text{req } F; \text{ens } G <: \text{req } (\text{ex } T \alpha) (F); \text{ens } (\text{ex } T \alpha) (G)}$$

This derived rule is an abstraction of separation logic's auxiliary variable rule. It follows from the method subtyping rule by the following tautology:

$$(\text{ex } T \alpha) (F) -\!\!* (\text{ex } T \alpha) (F * (\text{fa } U x) (G -\!\!* (\text{ex } T \alpha) (G)))$$

3.3 Hoare Triples

Our Hoare rules are syntax-directed, omitting structural rules. Separation logic's frame rule is admissible. Separation logic's auxiliary variable rule is subsumed by our syntax for existential unpacking. We omit the rules of conjunction and disjunction, and did not need them in the examples we considered. We could soundly add the rule of disjunction. To add the rule of conjunction, we would need to assume that preconditions of run() are *supported* [14].[7]

---

[6] The subtyping rule for run is restricted to avoid dependencies between pre- and postcondition.

[7] Supported formulas are formulas that have the property that, for any resource, the set of sub-resources that satisfy it is either empty or has a least element. They play a similar role for intuitionistic predicates, as *precise* formulas for non-intuitionistic predicates [24]. In our variant of separation logic, all predicates are intuitionistic, as we admit weakening.

Hoare triples have the forms $(\Gamma; v \vdash \{F\}c : T\{G\})$ and $(\Gamma; v \vdash \{F\}hc\{G\})$, where v is the receiver parameter. We present a few selected rules and refer to [16] for the complete rule system.

The rules for reading and writing fields are standard:

$$\frac{\Gamma; v; F \vdash \texttt{PointsTo}(w.f, \pi, u) \quad \Gamma \vdash w : U \quad Tf \in \mathsf{fld}(U) \quad T[w/\texttt{this}] <: \Gamma(\ell) \quad \ell \notin F}{\Gamma; v \vdash \{F\}\ell = w.f\{F * \ell == u\}}$$

$$\frac{\Gamma \vdash v, F : \texttt{Object}, \diamond \quad \Gamma \vdash u : U \quad Tf \in \mathsf{fld}(U) \quad \Gamma \vdash w : T[u/\texttt{this}]}{\Gamma; v \vdash \{F * \texttt{PointsTo}(u.f, 1, T)\}u.f = w\{F * \texttt{PointsTo}(u.f, 1, w)\}}$$

The rule for forking a thread consumes run's precondition. The postcondition of fork() is empty.[8] The rule makes use of the function $\mathsf{mtype}(m, T)$, which looks up m's type in the smallest supertype of T that declares m:

$$\frac{\mathsf{mtype}(\texttt{run}, T) = \texttt{req } G; \texttt{ens } G'; \texttt{void run}(T \, \iota_0;)}{\ell \notin F \quad \Gamma(\ell) = \texttt{void} \quad \Gamma \vdash u : T <: \texttt{Thread} \quad \Gamma; v; F \vdash u \texttt{!=null}}{\Gamma; v \vdash \{F * G[u/\iota_0]\}\ell = u.\texttt{fork}()\{F\}}$$

The most interesting rule is the one for joining threads. It allows the caller to exchange a fraction fr of the join-permission $\texttt{Perm}(u.\texttt{join}, 1)$ for a fraction fr of u's run's postcondition:[9]

$$\frac{\mathsf{mtype}(\texttt{run}, T) = \texttt{req } G; \texttt{ens } G'; \texttt{void run}(T \, \iota_0;) \quad fr = \texttt{all or } G' \text{ is supported}}{\ell \notin F \quad \Gamma(\ell) = \texttt{void} \quad \Gamma \vdash u : T <: \texttt{Thread} \quad \Gamma; v; F \vdash u \texttt{!=null}}{\Gamma; v \vdash \{F * fr \cdot \texttt{Perm}(u.\texttt{join}, 1)\}\ell = u.\texttt{join}()\{F * fr \cdot G'[u/\iota_0]\}}$$

Here, fr ranges over *linear combinations*. These represent numbers of the forms 1 or $\sum_{i=1}^{n} bit_i \cdot \frac{1}{2^i}$:

$$bit \in \{0, 1\} \qquad bits ::= 1 \mid bit, bits \qquad fr \in \mathsf{BinFrac} ::= \texttt{all} \mid \mathsf{fr}() \mid \mathsf{fr}(bits)$$

To define the scalar multiplication $fr \cdot F$, we first extend the split-operation from permissions to formulas:

$$\mathsf{split}(e) \triangleq e \qquad \mathsf{split}(\pi.\kappa{<}\bar{\pi}'{>}) \triangleq \pi.\kappa{<}\mathsf{split}(\bar{\pi}'){>}$$
$$\mathsf{split}(\texttt{PointsTo}(e.f, \pi, e')) \triangleq \texttt{PointsTo}(e.f, \mathsf{split}(\pi), e')$$
$$\mathsf{split}(\texttt{Perm}(e.\texttt{join}, \pi)) \triangleq \texttt{Perm}(e.\texttt{join}, \mathsf{split}(\pi))$$
$$\mathsf{split}(F \, lop \, G) \triangleq \mathsf{split}(F) \, lop \, \mathsf{split}(G) \qquad \mathsf{split}((qt \, T \, \alpha)(F)) \triangleq (qt \, T \, \alpha)(\mathsf{split}(F))$$

Now, the scalar multiplication $fr \cdot F$ is defined as follows: $\texttt{all} \cdot F = F$, $\mathsf{fr}() \cdot F = \texttt{true}$, $\mathsf{fr}(1) \cdot F = \mathsf{split}(F)$, $\mathsf{fr}(0, bits) \cdot F = \mathsf{fr}(bits) \cdot \mathsf{split}(F)$, and $\mathsf{fr}(1, bits) \cdot F = \mathsf{split}(F) * \mathsf{fr}(bits) \cdot \mathsf{split}(F)$. For instance, $\mathsf{fr}(1, 0, 1) \cdot F \, \text{*-*} \, (\mathsf{split}(F) * \mathsf{split}^3(F))$.

Via the bijection $\mathsf{fr}(bits) \mapsto \sum_{i=1}^{n} bit_i \cdot \frac{1}{2^i}$, we can define an addition on linear combinations that reflects the addition on concrete binary fractions. For proving soundness of the join()-rule, it is crucial that join()'s postcondition satisfies the following distributivity law, which holds if G' is supported:

$$(fr_1 + fr_2) \cdot G' \, \text{*-*} \, (fr_1 \cdot G' * fr_2 \cdot G')$$

---

[8] The permission $\texttt{Perm}(u.\texttt{join}, 1)$ gets introduced when the thread object u is created.

[9] We assume that postconditions of methods with return type void do not mention the result-variable.

4   Comparison to Related Work and Conclusion

Parkinson/Bierman are the first to adapt separation logic to a Java-like language [25,26]. We build on their work, using abstract predicates, but extend it to a concurrent language and combine abstract predicates with fractional permissions.

Boyland and Retert [7] explain the relation between write-effects, uniqueness and datagroups in terms of a linear type-and-effect system. Their system features a nesting operation and recursive definitions, which serve as an abstraction mechanism similar to abstract predicates, but in addition promote linear formulas to non-linear ones. Recently, Boyland presented a semantics for formulas that combine nesting and fractional permissions [6]. His semantics is quite different from ours. Generally speaking, our semantics is closer to standard semantics of BI [23]. Boyland facilitates permission splitting for datagroups through an operation that scales formulas by fractions, whereas we require datagroups to be fully permission-parametrized and scale the parameters. Because we allow multiple parameters, our approach permits more fine-grained scaling for overlapping datagroups (see Section 1.6 for an example).

Bierhoff and Aldrich [3] combine typestates and fractional permissions to specify object usage protocols. They use iterators as an example, but they do not allow linear implications in method contracts. As a result, their usage protocol regulates access to the collection itself, but not access to the elements of the collection, and their protocol would not prevent data races in concurrent programs. Krishnaswami [19] (in higher-order separation logic) and Boyland et al [8] (in their linear type-and-effect system) present iterator contracts that use linear implication and are related to ours.

Gotsman et al [14] recently adapted concurrent separation logic to Posix threads, treating storable locks. They do not support read-sharing of join's postcondition like us.

Regarding the interplay between abstract predicates and subclassing, we axiomatize the "stack of class frames" [12,1] to control predicate extensions in subclasses. The stack of class frames supports the use of subclassing for specialization and is well-suited for dealing with extended object state. Furthermore, the stack of class frames facilitates fully modular verification, avoiding the need to re-verify inherited methods, which is required in [25,26] where unrestricted predicate re-definitions in subclasses are allowed. In recent work, Parkinson and Bierman argue that a verification systems should support subclassing for code reuse in addition to subclassing for specialization, and present a system that supports both uses of subclassing while avoiding re-verification of inherited methods [27]. To this end, they associate with each method *two* contracts: a concrete "static" contract, and an abstract "dynamic" contract. Their system checks that predicate re-definitions in subclasses are compatible with concrete static contracts of inherited methods, thereby avoiding re-verification of implementations of inherited methods. The advantage over the stack of class frames is increased flexibility, the disadvantage is heavier specification machinery, although much of this can be hidden behind good defaults. Chin et al [9] make a similar proposal.

Conclusion. We have presented a variant of concurrent separation logic with fractional permissions for a Java-like language with fork/join and proved it sound. Future work includes algorithmic checking and extension to handle lock synchronization.

Acknowledgments. We thank John Boyland, Marieke Huisman, Erik Poll and anonymous reviewers for their very useful comments that helped to improve this paper.

References

1. Barnett, M., DeLine, R., Fähndrich, M., Leino, K.R.M., Schulte, W.: Verification of object-oriented programs with invariants. Journal of Object Technology 3(6) (2004)
2. Berdine, J., Calcagno, C., O'Hearn, P.W.: Smallfoot: Modular automatic assertion checking with separation logic. In: Formal Methods for Components and Objects (2005)
3. Bierhoff, K., Aldrich, J.: Modular typestate verification of aliased objects. In: ACM Conference on Object-Oriented Programming Systems, Languages, and Applications (2007)
4. Bornat, R., O'Hearn, P., Calcagno, C., Parkinson, M.: Permission accounting in separation logic. In: Principles of Programming Languages. ACM Press, New York (2005)
5. Boyland, J.: Checking interference with fractional permissions. In: Cousot, R. (ed.) SAS 2003. LNCS, vol. 2694. Springer, Heidelberg (2003)
6. Boyland, J.: Semantics of fractional permissions with nesting. Technical report, University of Wisconsin at Milwaukee (2007)
7. Boyland, J., Retert, W.: Connecting effects and uniqueness with adoption. In: Principles of Programming Languages (2005)
8. Boyland, J., Retert, W., Zhao, Y.: Iterators can be independent "from" their collections. In: International Workshop on Aliasing, Confinement and Ownership in object-oriented programming (2007)
9. Chin, W., David, C., Nguyen, H., Qin, S.: Enhancing modular OO verification with separation logic. In: Principles of Programming Languages (2008)
10. Crary, K., Walker, D., Morrisett, G.: Typed memory management in a calculus of capabilities. In: Principles of Programming Languages (1999)
11. DeLine, R., Fähndrich, M.: Enforcing high-level protocols in low-level software. In: Programming Languages Design and Implementation (2001)
12. DeLine, R., Fähndrich, M.: Typestates for objects. In: European Conference on Object-Oriented Programming (2004)
13. Girard, J.-Y.: Linear logic: Its syntax and semantics. In: Girard, J.-Y., Lafont, Y., Regnier, L. (eds.) Advances in Linear Logic. Cambridge University Press, Cambridge (1995)
14. Gotsman, A., Berdine, J., Cook, B., Rinetzky, N., Sagiv, M.: Local reasoning for storable locks and threads. In: Asian Programming Languages and Systems Symposium (2007)
15. Haack, C., Hurlin, C.: Resource usage protocols for iterators, http://www.cs.ru.nl/~chaack/papers/iterators.pdf
16. Haack, C., Hurlin, C.: Separation logic contracts for a Java-like language with fork/join. Technical Report 6430, INRIA (2008)
17. Igarashi, A., Pierce, B., Wadler, P.: Featherweight Java: a minimal core calculus for Java and GJ. ACM Trans. Program. Lang. Syst. 23(3) (2001)
18. Ishtiaq, S., O'Hearn, P.: BI as an assertion language for mutable data structures. In: Principles of Programming Languages (2001)
19. Krishnaswami, G.: Reasoning about iterators with separation logic. In: Specification and Verification of Component-Based Systems (2006)
20. Leavens, G.T., Baker, A.L., Ruby, C.: Preliminary design of JML: a behavioral interface specification language for Java. SIGSOFT Software Engineering Notes 31(3) (2006)
21. Leino, K.R.M.: Data groups: Specifying the modification of extended state. In: ACM Conference on Object-Oriented Programming Systems, Languages, and Applications (1998)
22. O'Hearn, P.: Resources, concurrency and local reasoning. Theor. Comp. Science 375(1–3) (2007)
23. O'Hearn, P.W., Pym, D.J.: The logic of bunched implications. Bulletin of Symbolic Logic 5(2) (1999)

24. O'Hearn, P.W., Yang, H., Reynolds, J.C.: Separation and information hiding. In: Principles of Programming Languages, Venice, Italy. ACM Press, New York (2004)
25. Parkinson, M.: Local reasoning for Java. Technical Report UCAM-CL-TR-654, University of Cambridge (2005)
26. Parkinson, M., Bierman, G.: Separation logic and abstraction. In: Principles of Programming Languages (2005)
27. Parkinson, M., Bierman, G.: Separation logic, abstraction and inheritance. In: Principles of Programming Languages (2008)
28. Reynolds, J.C.: Separation logic: A logic for shared mutable data structures. In: Logic in Computer Science, Copenhagen, Denmark. IEEE Press, Los Alamitos (2002)
29. Smith, F., Walker, D., Morrisett, G.: Alias types. In: Smolka, G. (ed.) ESOP 2000 and ETAPS 2000. LNCS, vol. 1782. Springer, Heidelberg (2000)
30. Wadler, P.: A taste of linear logic. In: Mathematical Foundations of Computer Science (1993)

An Algebraic Semantics for Contract-Based Software Components*

Michel Bidoit[1] and Rolf Hennicker[2]

[1] Centre de recherche INRIA Saclay - Île-de-France, France
[2] Institut für Informatik, Ludwig-Maximilians-Universität München, Germany

Abstract. We propose a semantic foundation for the contract-based design of software components. Our approach focuses on the characteristic principles of component-oriented development, like provided and required interface specifications and strong encapsulation. Semantically, we adopt classical concepts of mathematical logic using models, in our framework given by labelled transition systems with "states as algebras", sentences, and a satisfaction relation which characterizes those properties of a component which are observable by the user in the "strongly reachable" states. We distinguish between models of interfaces and models of component bodies. The latter are equipped with semantic encapsulation constraints which guarantee, that if the component body is a correct user of the required interface operations, then it can safely rely on all properties of the required interface specification. Our model-theoretic semantics of interfaces and component bodies suggests two semantic views on a component, its external and its internal semantics which must be properly related to ensure the correctness of a component. We also study a refinement relation between required and provided interface specifications of different components used for component composition.

1 Introduction

In this study we propose a semantic foundation for contract-based component systems in a state-based, sequential environment. Having its roots in the Hoare calculus for imperative programs, contracts are often formulated in terms of assertions describing invariants and pre/postconditions of operations. While for object-oriented programs quite a number of assertion-based techniques have been developed (see e.g. [8,2]), fewer proposals exist supporting the contract-based development of components with provided *and* required interfaces. In particular, some of those approaches lack a formal semantics (e.g. [6]) or are tailored to an object-oriented setting (e.g. [9,12]).

Our goal is to provide a general semantic component model which reflects the crucial ideas behind contract-based component design. A crucial aspect of components concerns encapsulation via provided and required interfaces. The

---

* This research has been partially supported by the GLOWA-Danube project 01LW0602A2 sponsored by the German Federal Ministry of Education and Research.

practical problem with this approach is that, to our knowledge, no established programming language exists which supports strongly encapsulated component development and thus most of so-called component-based systems are implemented by common object-oriented implementation techniques which are known to be not safe w.r.t. encapsulation. In this paper we propose a rigorous approach to the semantics of components based on states as algebras and transition systems. Our component model allows us to characterize, on the semantic level, the concept of encapsulation which has the benefit to be abstract and thus to be usable as a reference model that exposes the semantic requirements for any concrete component-based implementation language. More precisely, we claim that (the sequential part of) a well-designed component language should lead to programs which can be interpreted as models of our semantic domain and thus our conditions for models of component bodies can be seen as a catalogue of requirements. Hence, we do deliberately not study techniques that overcome the problem of encapsulation and modular verification by investigating concrete features, like ownership types etc. for object-oriented systems (see e.g. [2,10]) but we focus on the semantic principles of models for component-oriented design.

It is another goal of our approach to study the meaning of contracts that are used in provided and required interfaces. As pointed out in [4] there is a variety of possibilities to understand invariants and pre/postconditions of operations. In our aproach we follow the idea of [11] to consider application requirements for operations which we will formalize as domain constraints for interface operations. Since, according to the contract principle, the domain constraint must be satisfied whenever an operation is called we can identify the so-called strongly reachable states as the relevant states that have to be taken into account when defining a satisfaction relation for invariants and operation specifications. Thus we show how our ideas for object-oriented specifications in [4] can be lifted to the level of components which leads to a model-theoretic interpretation of interface specifications. Let us stress that the concept of interface specifications as defined here is generic and can be used to give semantics to any interface specification language which deals with invariants and operation specifications.

By considering both, the semantics of interfaces and of component bodies, we can distinguish the external and the internal semantics of a component. In particular the internal semantics of a component is given by a function which maps each model of the required interface of the component to an internal model determined by the component's body. A component is semantically correct, if those models can be restricted by an abstraction function to a model of the provided interface of the component. Since the semantics of interface specifications is given by model classes we can easily define a formal refinement relation between required and provided interface specifications of different components which can be used to construct the composition of components. In the sequel of this paper we will use as a running example the following Bank component.

component Bank is
provided interface spec BankI =
observers isAccount: int -> boolean; balAccount: int -> int;

```
operations   transfer(input from, to, amount: int)
   ..."further operations for opening, closing accounts etc. are omitted"
domain transfer :
      isAccount(from) and isAccount(to) and amount >= 0 and
      balAccount(from) >= amount;
init ∀no:int. not(isAccount(no));
inv  ∀no:int. isAccount(no) implies balAccount(no) >=0;
effect   transfer :
      balAccount(from) = balAccount(from)@pre - amount and
      balAccount(to) = balAccount(to)@pre + amount;
```

required interface spec AccountI =
```
observer bal: -> int;
operations
   getBal(output amount: int); credit(input i: int); withdraw(input i: int);
domains   getBal : true; credit : i >= 0; withdraw : i >=0 and bal >= i;
init bal = 0;
inv   bal >= 0;
effects getBal : amount = bal and bal = bal@pre;
        credit : bal = bal@pre + i;
        withdraw : bal = bal@pre - i;
```
body
```
let Account:AccountI;
private Map<Integer,Account> accounts = new HashMap<Integer,Account>();
public boolean isAccount(int no) {return accounts.containsKey(no);}
public int balAccount(int no) {return accounts.get(no).getBal();}
public void transfer(int from, to, amount)
   {Account source = accounts.get(from); source.withdraw(amount);
    Account target = accounts.get(to); target.credit(amount);}
```

2   Preliminaries

We assume that the reader is familiar with the basic notions of algebraic specifications, like the notions of (many-sorted) *algebraic signature* $\Sigma = (S, F)$ (where S is a set of *sorts*, also called *types*, and F is a set of *function symbols* $f : s_1, \ldots, s_n \to s$), *(partial)* Σ-*algebra* $A = ((A_s)_{s \in S}, (f^A)_{f \in F})$, class $\text{Alg}(\Sigma)$ of all (partial) Σ-algebras, *valuation* $\rho : X \to A$ (where X is an S-sorted set of variables), *signature morphism* $\gamma : \Sigma \to \Sigma'$ and *reduct* $A'|_\gamma$ of a Σ'-algebra A' along γ. Throughout this paper we fix a primitive signature Σ_P for predefined types and function symbols (e.g. for booleans, integers, collections, etc.) and a fixed interpretation of Σ_P by a given Σ_P-algebra $\mathscr{P}$. In the context of component bodies we also consider user defined types. Given a (user-defined) type t, the fixed signature Σ_P is extended in a canonical way to a signature $\Sigma_P(t)$ which contains generic predefined types applied to the new type t, e.g. *List<t>*, etc. Then, given any carrier set t^A for t, the fixed Σ_P-algebra $\mathscr{P}$ is assumed to be extended in a canonical way to a $\Sigma_P(t)$-algebra $\mathscr{P}(t^A)$.

3   Interface Specifications

3.1   Observer Signatures and Abstract States

As shown in our examples of interface specifications (BankI and AccountI above), the application domain and the effect of an operation are specified by using so-called (state) observers. An *observer signature* Σ_{Obs} is a pair $(\Sigma_{\mathrm{P}}, Obs)$ consisting of the primitive signature Σ_{P} (see Section 2) and a set Obs of *(state) observers*. An observer in Obs is a function symbol $obs : t_1 \times \cdots \times t_n \to t$ with primitive types $t_1, \ldots, t_n, t$ resp. (which can be considered as a higher-order state variable). Hence an observer signature Σ_{Obs} provides an algebraic signature which extends the primitive signature Σ_{P} by the observers Obs. A state is uniquely determined by an interpretation of the observers. Thus a state is formally represented by a Σ_{Obs}-algebra $\sigma \in \mathrm{Alg}(\Sigma_{\mathrm{Obs}})$ (following the ideas of the "state as algebra" approach; see e.g. [5]). Examples of observers are given in the two interface specifications BankI and AccountI of Sect. 1. Considering the AccountI interface, the underlying observer signature $\Sigma_{\mathrm{Obs}}^{\mathrm{AccountI}}$ consists of the predefined signature Σ_{P} together with the observer `bal: -> int`. An actual state of an account with balance zero would be given by the $\Sigma_{\mathrm{Obs}}^{\mathrm{AccountI}}$-algebra σ with $\mathtt{bal}^{\sigma} = 0$. For any observer signature Σ_{Obs} we assume given a set of Σ_{Obs}-*sentences* which are:

1. either *mono-state* Σ_{Obs}-sentences φ with associated set $\mathrm{var}(\varphi)$ of sorted variables of predefined types;
2. or *bi-state* Σ_{Obs}-sentences π with associated (disjoint) sets $\mathrm{var}_{\mathrm{in}}(\pi)$ of sorted *input variables* and $\mathrm{var}_{\mathrm{out}}(\pi)$ of sorted *output variables* of predefined types.

The Σ_{Obs}-sentences are assumed to be equipped with a *satisfaction relation* $\models_{\Sigma_{\mathrm{Obs}}}$ for Σ_{Obs}-states (i.e. for Σ_{Obs}-algebras):

1. $\sigma, \rho \models_{\Sigma_{\mathrm{Obs}}} \varphi$ for a mono-state Σ_{Obs}-sentence φ, a Σ_{Obs}-state σ, and a valuation $\rho : \mathrm{var}(\varphi) \to \mathscr{P}$;
2. $\sigma, \rho; \sigma', \rho' \models_{\Sigma_{\mathrm{Obs}}} \pi$ for a bi-state Σ_{Obs}-sentence π, Σ_{Obs}-states σ, σ', and valuations $\rho : \mathrm{var}_{\mathrm{in}}(\pi) \to \mathscr{P}$, $\rho' : \mathrm{var}_{\mathrm{out}}(\pi) \to \mathscr{P}$.

In order to be generic and to focus on the essential ideas of our semantic framework later on we do neither assume any particular syntax for Σ_{Obs}-sentences nor any particular satisfaction relation for states. Intuitively, mono-state Σ_{Obs}-sentences can be seen as state predicates and bi-state Σ_{Obs}-sentences as transition predicates. In the example in Sect. 1 we use an OCL-like syntax where the `@pre` construct is used in bi-state sentences to refer to previous states.

3.2   Interface Signatures and Their Models

Interface signatures extend observer signatures by introducing operations which may change states. An *operation* op has the form $opname(X_{\mathrm{in}}, X_{\mathrm{out}})$ where X_{in}, in the following denoted by $\mathrm{var}_{\mathrm{in}}(op)$, is a (possibly empty) sequence of input variables and X_{out}, in the following denoted by $\mathrm{var}_{\mathrm{out}}(op)$, is a disjoint (possibly empty) sequence of output variables, in each case of primitive types.

For each operation we assume given a so-called domain constraint (which can be considered as an application requirement in the sense of [11] or as a UML stereotyped «pre» constraint). A domain constraint imposes obligations on both the user and the implementor of an operation: The user of the interface should only call an operation in a state where the domain constraint of the operation is satisfied. The implementor guarantees that then the operation will be executed. Given an observer signature Σ_{Obs}, a domain constraint dom_{op} of an interface operation op is a mono-state Σ_{Obs}-sentence with $\mathrm{var}(dom_{op}) \subseteq \mathrm{var_{in}}(op)$.

Definition 1. *An interface signature $\Sigma_I = (\Sigma_{\mathrm{Obs}}, Op, dom)$ consists of an observer signature Σ_{Obs}, a set Op of operations and a family $dom = (dom_{op})_{op \in Op}$ of domain constraints (w.r.t. Σ_{Obs}).*

Considering the interface specifications BankI and AccountI of Sect. 1, the underlying interface signatures Σ_I^{BanI} and $\Sigma_I^{\mathrm{AccountI}}$ extend the respective observer signatures by the declared operations and their domain constraints.

We will now provide a model-theoretic interpretation of interface signatures. The crucial idea is that for a given interface signature Σ_I, a Σ_I-model provides an abstract representation of a program which realizes the interface operations Op. For this purpose we use as an underlying formalism labelled transition systems. More precisely, given an interface signature $\Sigma_I = (\Sigma_{\mathrm{Obs}}, Op, dom)$, we consider structures (Q, α, q_0, Δ) where Q is a set of states which is equipped with an abstraction function $\alpha : Q \to \mathrm{Alg}(\Sigma_{\mathrm{Obs}})$ mapping "concrete" states in Q to (fully) abstract states in $\mathrm{Alg}(\Sigma_{\mathrm{Obs}})$, $q_0 \in Q$ is the initial state and

$$\Delta \subseteq Q \times Label_{\Sigma_I} \times (Q \times Output_{\Sigma_I})$$

is a transition relation. The labels in $Label_{\Sigma_I}$ express operation calls, formally represented by pairs (op, ρ) consisting of the called operation op together with actual input parameters provided by a valuation $\rho : \mathrm{var_{in}}(op) \to \mathscr{P}$. Similarly, the outputs in $Output_{\Sigma_I}$ represent results of operations, formally represented by valuations $\rho' : \mathrm{var_{out}}(op) \to \mathscr{P}$ with $op \in Op$. A transition $(q, (op, \rho), q', \rho') \in \Delta$ models the fact that if in state q the operation op is called with actual input parameters determined by the valuation ρ, then the operation can be executed with successor state q' and output values determined by ρ'.

Obviously, in the transition systems described above the non-reachable states are of no interest. According to the contract principle one can even go further and assume that a user calls an interface operation only in a state where its domain constraint is satisfied (after abstraction w.r.t. α). Hence, in the context of contract-based interfaces the only relevant states are those states reachable from the initial state by admissible operation calls which will be called *strongly reachable states*. Given an interface signature Σ_I and a transition system $M = (Q, \alpha, q_0, \Delta)$ as above the subset $SRS(Q) \subseteq Q$ of the strongly reachable states of M is inductively defined as follows:

(0) $q_0 \in SRS(Q)$.
(1) If $q \in SRS(Q)$ and $(q, (op, \rho), q', \rho') \in \Delta$ such that $\alpha(q), \rho \models_{\Sigma_{\mathrm{Obs}}} dom_{op}$, then $q' \in SRS(Q)$.

The concept of the strongly reachable states reflects the obligations of the user of the interface operations. However, the domain constraints do also impose an obligation on the implementor of the interface operations who must guaranhtee that an operation op is executable if it is called in a state where the domain constraint dom_{op} is satisfied (w.r.t. the given input parameters). Thus we obtain the following constraint for the transition relation Δ:

(dom). For all $q \in SRS(Q)$, $op \in Op$, and $\rho : \mathrm{var}_{in}(op) \to \mathscr{P}$, if $\alpha(q), \rho \models_{\Sigma_{Obs}}$ dom_{op} then there exist $q' \in Q$ and $\rho' : \mathrm{var}_{out}(op) \to \mathscr{P}$ such that $(q, (op, \rho), q', \rho') \in \Delta$.

Definition 2. *Let $\Sigma_I = (\Sigma_{Obs}, Op, dom)$ be an interface signature. A Σ_I-model is a transition system (Q, α, q_0, Δ) as described above such that the condition (dom) is satisfied. The class of all Σ_I-models is denoted by $\mathrm{Mod}(\Sigma_I)$.*

3.3 Σ_I-Sentences, Satisfaction Relation and Interface Specifications

We will now associate a set of Σ_I-sentences to any interface signature Σ_I which allow to express three kinds of properties that are commonly considered in state-based systems: initialization conditions, invariants and sentences describing the (observable) effects of operations. Given an interface signature $\Sigma_I = (\Sigma_{Obs}, Op, dom)$, the set of Σ_I-*sentences* is defined as follows:

For each mono-state Σ_{Obs}-sentence φ with $\mathrm{var}(\varphi) = \emptyset$,
1. *init* φ is a Σ_I-sentence, called *initialization sentence* and
2. *inv* φ is a Σ_I-sentence, called *invariant sentence*.
3. For each $op \in Op$ and for each bi-state Σ_{Obs}-sentence π with $\mathrm{var}_{in}(\pi) \subseteq \mathrm{var}_{in}(op)$ and $\mathrm{var}_{out}(\pi) \subseteq \mathrm{var}_{out}(op)$, $op : \pi$ is a Σ_I-sentence, called *operation effect sentence*.

The satisfaction relation $\models_{\Sigma_I}$ between Σ_I-models and Σ_I-sentences is defined by:

1. $M \models_{\Sigma_I} init\ \varphi$ if $\alpha(q_0), \rho \models_{\Sigma_{Obs}} \varphi$.[1]
2. $M \models_{\Sigma_I} inv\ \varphi$ if for all $q \in SRS(Q)$ it holds $\alpha(q), \rho \models_{\Sigma_{Obs}} \varphi$.
3. $M \models_{\Sigma_I} op : \pi$ if for all $(q, (op, \rho), q', \rho') \in \Delta$ with $q \in SRS(Q)$ it holds: If $\alpha(q), \rho \models_{\Sigma_{Obs}} dom_{op}$ then $\alpha(q), \rho; \alpha(q'), \rho' \models_{\Sigma_{Obs}} \pi$.

The satisfaction relation abstracts from concrete states by the abstraction function α (which comes with each Σ_I-model) and it is based on the satisfaction relation $\models_{\Sigma_{Obs}}$ for Σ_{Obs}-algebras; cf. Sect. 3.1. Moreover, it takes only into account strongly reachable states because, according to the user's obligations, these are the only relevant states. The satisfaction relation for operation effect sentences together with the (dom) condition for Σ_I-models express the implementor's obligations of the contract: For any admissible operation call the operation must be executable (according to (dom)) and in this case the operation must have the desired effect.

---

[1] In 1. and 2. the valuation ρ is irrelevant because the sentences have no variables.

Definition 3. *An* interface specification $SP_I = (\Sigma_I, Ax)$ *consists of an interface signature* Σ_I *and a set Ax of* Σ_I*-sentences, called the* axioms *of the specification. The* semantics *of* SP_I *is given by* $[\![SP_I]\!] = \{M \in Mod(\Sigma_I) \mid M \models_{\Sigma_I} Ax\}$. *Any* $M \in [\![SP_I]\!]$ *is called a* model *of* SP_I.

The semantics of an interface specification describes all Σ_I-models which can be considered as (abstract representations of) *correct realizations* of the interface specification. The interface specifications BankI and AccountI displayed in Sect. 1 consist of the respective interface signatures Σ_I^{BankI} and $\Sigma_I^{AccountI}$ together with the given initialization, invariant and operation effect sentences. It may be interesting to note that the explicit invariants are even redundant because they are logical consequences of the specifications which can be proved by induction on the *strongly* reachable states. This statement examplifies the power of our satisfaction relation based on the strongly reachable states. It would not be true for the reachable states which are usually considered because, e.g. the AccountI invariant could be easily violated by a call to withdraw if the domain constraint of withdraw is not respected.

4   Component Bodies

In this section we focus on the second essential ingredient of components which are component bodies.

4.1   Attribute Signatures and Concrete States

The provided interface of a component must be implemented by a component body. For this purpose it is first necessary to define an appropriate concrete state space over which the interface operations are implemented. In the following we assume that the state space of a component body is provided by a set of attributes (often called instance variables). Since the component body relies on the required interface specification, the attributes may involve required types. For the sake of simplicity we assume that a component refers to a single required interface specification SP_{req}. To actually use the required interface, the body must include a declaration $rt:SP_{req}$ of a required type rt which then can be used (additionally to the predefined types) for typing attributes. The state space of a component body is (syntactically) described by an attribute signature.

An *attribute signature* Σ_{Att} (w.r.t. a given required interface specification SP_{req}) is a triple $(rt:SP_{req}, \Sigma_P(rt), Att)$ where $rt:SP_{req}$ is a type declaration introducing a new type rt associated to SP_{req}, $\Sigma_P(rt)$ is the extension of the primitive signature Σ_P w.r.t. the new type rt (see Section 2), and Att is a set of *attributes* which is used to define (concrete) states. An attribute in Att is a (nullary) function symbol $a :\rightarrow t$ with a result type in $\Sigma_P(rt)$. Hence, the pair $(\Sigma_P(rt), Att)$ provides an algebraic signature. Considering the Bank component of Sect. 1 the attribute signature Σ_{Att}^{Bank} of the body of the component introduces (in the *let* construct) a new (local) type `Account` and one attribute, algebraically represented by the constant `accounts: -> Map<Integer,Account>`.

Let us now discuss how to associate a state space to a given attribute signature. As for observer signatures the main idea is again to use algebras for the representation of states. Given an attribute signature $\Sigma_{\text{Att}} = (rt{:}\text{SP}_{\text{req}}, \Sigma_{\text{P}}(rt), Att)$, any $(\Sigma_{\text{P}}(rt), Att)$-algebra σ provides indeed an interpretation for all attributes and therefore can be considered as a state. In particular, σ includes a carrier set rt^σ for the type rt. Intuitively, according to the type declaration $rt{:}\text{SP}_{\text{req}}$, the new type rt denotes a set of instances of (some implementation of) SP_{req}. In contrast to the interpretations of the primitive types, the interpretation of rt is not fixed but can change from one state σ to another σ' according to the actually existing instances of type rt. Moreover, it is important that the actual state of a component body depends also on the current state of each of the instances of rt which in turn depends on the chosen implementation of the required interface specification SP_{req}. Since an implementation of SP_{req} is formally given by a model of SP_{req}, states according to an attribute signature Σ_{Att} can be represented by so-called "indexed-algebras" which depend on a given model $M_{\text{req}} \in [\![\text{SP}_{\text{req}}]\!]$ and which are indexed in the sense that to each instance of rt there is assigned a state in the state space of M_{req}. Examples of indexed algebras are shown in Fig. 1.

Definition 4. *Let* $\Sigma_{\text{Att}} = (rt{:}\text{SP}_{\text{req}}, \Sigma_{\text{P}}(rt), Att)$ *be an attribute signature. For a model* $M_{\text{req}} \in [\![\text{SP}_{\text{req}}]\!]$ *with state space* Q_{req}, *an* M_{req}-Σ_{Att}-*indexed algebra is a pair* (σ, μ) *where* $\sigma \in \text{Alg}(\Sigma_{\text{P}}(rt), Att)$ *and* $\mu : rt^\sigma \to Q_{\text{req}}$ *is a function.* $\text{Alg}(\Sigma_{\text{Att}})_{M_{\text{req}}}$ *denotes the class of* M_{req}-Σ_{Att}-*indexed algebras. The family* $\text{Alg}(\Sigma_{\text{Att}}) = (\text{Alg}(\Sigma_{\text{Att}})_{M_{\text{req}}})_{M_{\text{req}} \in [\![\text{SP}_{\text{req}}]\!]}$ *is the class of* Σ_{Att}-*indexed algebras.*

4.2 Body Signatures and Their Models

Body signatures extend attribute signatures by introducing operations. For instance, the body signature $\Sigma_{\text{Body}}^{\text{Bank}}$ of the body of the component Bank extends its attribute signature $\Sigma_{\text{Att}}^{\text{Bank}}$ by the operations isAccount, balAccount and transfer.

Definition 5. *A* body signature $\Sigma_{\text{Body}} = (\Sigma_{\text{Att}}, Op)$ *consists of an attribute signature* $\Sigma_{\text{Att}} = (rt{:}\text{SP}_{\text{req}}, \Sigma_{\text{P}}(rt), Att)$ *and a set* Op *of operations.*

Given a body signature $\Sigma_{\text{Body}} = (\Sigma_{\text{Att}}, Op)$, a Σ_{Body}-model should represent an implementation of the operations Op and hence will be again a labelled transition system. Since such an implementation obviously depends on an actually used realization of SP_{req} we will consider families $\text{Mod}(\Sigma_{\text{Body}}) = (\text{Mod}(\Sigma_{\text{Body}})_{M_{\text{req}}})_{M_{\text{req}} \in [\![\text{SP}_{\text{req}}]\!]}$ where each $\text{Mod}(\Sigma_{\text{Body}})_{M_{\text{req}}}$ is a class of labelled transition systems, called M_{req}-Σ_{Body}-*models*, which are supposed to provide an implementation of the operations Op by *using* a given realization M_{req} of SP_{req}.

Let us discuss which transition systems are appropriate for M_{req}-Σ_{Body}-models. First we notice that since we work already on concrete states there is, in contrast to models of interface signatures, no need for an abstraction function. Hence an M_{req}-Σ_{Body}-model $M = (Q, q_0, \Delta)$ will be a triple with a set Q of states, an initial state q_0 and a transition relation

$$\Delta \subseteq Q \times Label_{\Sigma_{\text{Body}}} \times (Q \times Output_{\Sigma_{\text{Body}}})$$

To be more precise about the states, the labels and the transitions, we assume given an arbitrary model $M_{req} = (Q_{req}, \alpha_{req}, q_{0,req}, \Delta_{req})$ of SP_{req}. According to the considerations on states in Section 4.1, the state space Q should obviously be a subset of the class $Alg(\Sigma_{Att})_{M_{req}}$, i.e. states are indexed algebras over M_{req}.

The set $Label_{\Sigma_{Body}} = Label_{Op} \cup Label_{req} \cup Label_{int}$ is the union of three different kinds of labels. The labels in $Label_{Op}$ express calls to operations $op \in Op$ represented, as before for interface operations, by pairs (op, ρ). The labels in $Label_{req}$ express calls to required operations of SP_{req} represented by pairs $(o.op_{req}, \rho)$ where o is an instance of the required type rt, op_{req} is an operation of the required interface specification SP_{req}, and ρ is a valuation of the input variables of op_{req}. Finally, we assume given a set $Label_{int}$ of internal labels which model internal actions that can be performed in the body implementation. The outputs in $Output_{\Sigma_{Body}}$ are again defined as valuations of the output variables of operations.

There are several constraints concerning the admissibility of transitions of an M_{req}-Σ_{Body}-model. First, since such a model is supposed to represent an abstract program which implements each operation in Op by an appropriate "operation body" we require the following condition:

(impl). Any transition $(q, (op, \rho), q', \rho') \in \Delta$ with $op \in Op$ has a *realization* by a sequence of transitions $(q_i, (l_i, \rho_i), q_{i+1}, \rho_{i+1}) \in \Delta$, $i = 1, \ldots, n-1, n \geq 2$ such that $q_1 = q, q_n = q'$ and $l_i \in Label_{req} \cup Label_{int}$ for $i = 1, \ldots, n-1$.

Transitions of the form $(q, (op, \rho), q', \rho')$ with $op \in Op$ are often called "big step" transitions while the transitions occurring in their realization are called "small step" transitions. Small step transitions involve internal actions as well as calls $(o.op_{req}, \rho)$ to required interface operations. To guarantee that those calls are really performed in accordance with the given model M_{req} of SP_{req} (i.e. that M_{req} is really used when a call to a required interface operation occurs) we need the following second condition.

(use). For any transition $(q, (o.op_{req}, \rho), q', \rho') \in \Delta$ with $(o.op_{req}, \rho) \in Label_{req}$ and indexed algebras $q = (\sigma, \mu), q' = (\sigma', \mu')$ it holds $o \in rt^\sigma \cap rt^{\sigma'}$ and $(\mu(o), (op_{req}, \rho), \mu'(o), \rho') \in \Delta_{req}$, i.e. the latter is a transition in M_{req}.

The next condition requires that an M_{req}-Σ_{Body}-model $M = (Q, q_0, \Delta)$ should respect the initial state of M_{req}.

(init). For the indexed algebra $q_0 = (\sigma_0, \mu_0)$ it holds that for all $o \in rt^{\sigma_0}$, $\mu_0(o) = q_{0,req}$.

A crucial requirement in any framework for modular system design concerns encapsulation. In our context this means that in any realization of an operation $op \in Op$ the state of each instance o of the required type rt can only be modified by calling a required interface operation on o. Since a realization consists of (small step) transitions with labels in $Label_{req} \cup Label_{int}$, we can formalize the encapsulation requirement by two conditions according to the two kinds of labels.

The first condition says that calling a required operation on an instance o of the required type rt cannot modify the set of the existing instances of rt and can also not change states of instances different from o.

(enc$_{\text{req}}$). For each transition $(q, (o.op_{\text{req}}, \rho), q', \rho') \in \Delta$ with label $(o.op_{\text{req}}, \rho) \in$
  $Label_{\text{req}}$, indexed algebras $q = (\sigma, \mu), q' = (\sigma', \mu')$ and instance $o \in rt^{\sigma}$ it
  holds $rt^{\sigma} = rt^{\sigma'}$ and for all $p \in rt^{\sigma} \setminus \{o\}, \mu(p) = \mu'(p)$.

The second encapsulation condition says (1) that transitions with internal labels cannot modify the state of instances of the required type, and (2) that any new instance generated by an internal action must be in the initial state according to M_{req}.

(enc$_{\text{int}}$). For each transition $(q, l, q', \rho') \in \Delta$ with internal label $l \in Label_{\text{int}}$ and
  indexed algebras $q = (\sigma, \mu), q' = (\sigma', \mu')$ the following holds:
  (1) For all $o \in rt^{\sigma} \cap rt^{\sigma'}, \mu(o) = \mu'(o)$.
  (2) For all $o \in rt^{\sigma'} \setminus rt^{\sigma}, \mu'(o) = q_{0,\text{req}}$.

Definition 6. *Let $\Sigma_{\text{Body}} = (\Sigma_{\text{Att}}, Op)$ be a body signature with attribute signature $\Sigma_{\text{Att}} = (rt{:}\text{SP}_{\text{req}}, \Sigma_{\text{P}}(rt), Att)$. The class of Σ_{Body}-models is given by the family $\text{Mod}(\Sigma_{\text{Body}}) = (\text{Mod}(\Sigma_{\text{Body}})_{M_{\text{req}}})_{M_{\text{req}} \in [\![\text{SP}_{\text{req}}]\!]}$ where $\text{Mod}(\Sigma_{\text{Body}})_{M_{\text{req}}}$ is the class of M_{req}-Σ_{Body}-models $M = (Q, q_0, \Delta)$ described above such that the conditions* (impl), (use), (init), (enc$_{\text{req}}$) *and* (enc$_{\text{int}}$) *are satisfied.*

We claim that $\text{Mod}(\Sigma_{\text{Body}})$ provides an appropriate semantic domain for the interpretation of component-oriented (sequential) programs. Indeed the first three conditions (impl), (use) and (init) are well supported already by object-oriented programming languages: (impl) means that the operations of Op are not abstract, (use) means that a client cannot override imported (required) operations and (init), as well as part (2) of (enc$_{\text{int}}$), mean that newly created objects are in the initial state according to a particular object constructor. To ensure the other encapsulation constraints in concrete programs is however still a significant issue.

On the other hand encapsulation is the crucial prerequisite to support modular verification. Indeed we can show that the conditions required for Σ_{Body}-models ensure that for each model M_{req} of SP_{req} with signature Σ_{req} all properties expressed by Σ_{req}-sentences, which are valid in M_{req}, can be propagated to the level of any M_{req}-Σ_{Body}-model M under the assumption that M is a correct user of M_{req}, i.e. calls to a required interface operation op_{req} occur only in states where the domain constraint of op_{req} is satisfied. This is expressed by the following definition and theorem.

Definition 7. *Let $M_{\text{req}} = (Q_{\text{req}}, \alpha_{\text{req}}, q_{0,\text{req}}, \Delta_{\text{req}}) \in [\![\text{SP}_{\text{req}}]\!]$.*
An M_{req}-Σ_{Body}-model $M = (Q, q_0, \Delta)$ is a correct user of M_{req} if for each transition $(q, (o.op_{\text{req}}, \rho), q', \rho') \in \Delta$ with $(o.op_{\text{req}}, \rho) \in Label_{\text{req}}$ and with indexed algebra $q = (\sigma, \mu)$ it holds $\alpha_{\text{req}}(\mu(o)), \rho \models_{\Sigma_{Obs_{\text{req}}}} dom_{op_{\text{req}}}$

Theorem 1. *Let $\Sigma_{\text{Body}} = (\Sigma_{\text{Att}}, Op)$ be a body signature with attribute signature $\Sigma_{\text{Att}} = (rt{:}\text{SP}_{\text{req}}, \Sigma_{\text{P}}(rt), Att)$ and required interface specification SP_{req} with signature $\Sigma_{\text{req}} = (\Sigma_{Obs_{\text{req}}}, Op_{\text{req}}, dom_{\text{req}})$.*

Let $M_{req} = (Q_{req}, \alpha_{req}, q_{0,req}, \Delta_{req}) \in [\![SP_{req}]\!]$ and $M = (Q, q_0, \Delta)$ be an M_{req}-Σ_{Body}-model which is a correct user of M_{req}. Then the following holds for all Σ_{req}-sentences init φ, inv φ and $op_{req} : \pi$:

1. If $M_{req} \models_{\Sigma_{req}} init \varphi$ then
   1.a. for $q_0 = (\sigma_0, \mu_0)$ and for all $o \in rt^{\sigma_0}$ it holds $\alpha_{req}(\mu_0(o)), \rho \models_{\Sigma_{Obs_{req}}} \varphi$.
   1.b. for all transitions $(q, l, q', \rho') \in \Delta$ with internal label $l \in Label_{int}$ with $q = (\sigma, \mu), q' = (\sigma', \mu')$ and for all $o \in rt^{\sigma'} \setminus rt^{\sigma}$ it holds $\alpha_{req}(\mu_0(o)), \rho \models_{\Sigma_{Obs_{req}}} \varphi$.
2. If $M_{req} \models_{\Sigma_{req}} inv \varphi$ then for all reachable states $q = (\sigma, \mu)$ of M and for all $o \in rt^{\sigma}$ it holds $\alpha_{req}(\mu(o)), \rho \models_{\Sigma_{Obs_{req}}} \varphi$.
3. If $M_{req} \models_{\Sigma_{req}} op_{req} : \pi$ then for all reachable states q of M and for all transitions $(q, (o.op_{req}, \rho), q', \rho') \in \Delta$ with $q = (\sigma, \mu), q' = (\sigma', \mu')$ and $o \in rt^{\sigma}(= rt^{\sigma'})$ it holds $\alpha_{req}(\mu(o)), \rho; \alpha_{req}(\mu'(o)), \rho' \models_{\Sigma_{Obs_{req}}} \pi$.

Proof. (1.a): According to the constraint (init), $\mu_0(o) = q_{0,req}$. Since $M_{req} \models_{\Sigma_{req}} init \varphi$, $\alpha_{req}(q_{0,req}), \rho \models_{\Sigma_{Obs_{req}}} \varphi$. Hence, $\alpha_{req}(\mu_0(o)), \rho \models_{\Sigma_{Obs_{req}}} \varphi$. (1.b) is proved similarly. (2) and (3) are straightforward consequences of a lemma which says that under the given assumptions:

(*) For all reachable states $q = (\sigma, \mu)$ of M and for all $o \in rt^{\sigma}$, it holds $\mu(o) \in SRS(Q_{req})$, i.e. $\mu(o)$ is a strongly reachable state of M_{req}.

The proof of (*) is performed by induction on the number of transitions that are used to reach q. The induction base is obvious due to the constraint (init). For the induction step it is enough, because of the constraint (impl), to consider transitions with labels in $Label_{req} \cup Label_{int}$.

Let us first consider a transition of the form $(q_{pre}, (p.op_{req}, \rho), q, \rho) \in \Delta$ with $q_{pre} = (\sigma_{pre}, \mu_{pre})$ and $q = (\sigma, \mu)$. Let $o \in rt^{\sigma} = rt^{\sigma_{pre}}$, by constraint (enc$_{req}$). By induction hypothesis, $\mu_{pre}(o) \in SRS(Q_{req})$. Case 1: $o \neq p$. Then, by (enc$_{req}$), $\mu_{pre}(o) = \mu(o)$ and hence $\mu(o) \in SRS(Q_{req})$. Case 2: $o = p$. Then, according to (use), $(\mu_{pre}(o), (op_{req}, \rho), \mu(o), \rho)$ is a transition in M_{req}. Since $\mu_{pre}(o) \in SRS(Q_{req})$ and since, by assumption, M is a *correct* user of M_{req}, $\mu(o) \in SRS(Q_{req})$. Now, consider a transition $(q_{pre}, l, q, \rho) \in \Delta$ with $l \in Label_{int}$, $q_{pre} = (\sigma_{pre}, \mu_{pre})$ and $q = (\sigma, \mu)$. Case 1: $o \in rt^{\sigma}$ and $o \in rt^{\sigma_{pre}}$. Then, by part (1) of (enc$_{int}$), $\mu_{pre}(o) = \mu(o)$ and hence, by using the induction hypothesis, $\mu(o) \in SRS(Q_{req})$. Case 2: $o \in rt^{\sigma}$ but $o \notin rt^{\sigma_{pre}}$. Then, by part (2) of (enc$_{int}$), $\mu(o) = q_{0,req} \in SRS(Q_{req})$.   □

Example 1. Let us assume given a model $M_{req} \in [\![AccountI]\!]$ and an M_{req}-Σ_{Body}^{Bank}-model M, part of which contains transitions as shown in Fig. 1. $q1, q2, q3$ visualize M_{req}-indexed algebras as states of M. $qa1, qa2, qb1, qb2$ are states of M_{req} and their abstractions w.r.t. **bal** are shown below the respective lines.

Assume that M is a correct user of M_{req} and that $q1$ is a reachable state of M. Then, according to Theorem 1, in all account states $qa1, qa2, qb1, qb2$ the AccountI invariant **bal >= 0** must be valid and, similarly, the effects specified for the operations **withdraw** and **credit** must be valid in the respective states of

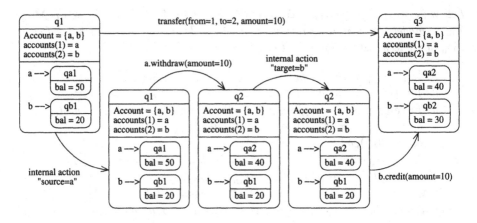

Fig. 1. Transitions in a body model of Bank

the accounts. So the user, i.e. the model M, can rely on these properties when checking its correctness (cf. Section 5.1), i.e. Theorem 1 provides a semantic foundation for modular verification.

4.3   Semantics of Component Bodies

A component body is a pair Body $= (\Sigma_{\text{Body}}, Prog)$ consisting of a body signature $\Sigma_{\text{Body}} = (\Sigma_{\text{Att}}, Op)$ and a program $Prog$ which implements the operations Op. Since the aim of this paper is merely to provide an abstract framework for components, a concrete syntax and detailed semantics for $Prog$ is clearly out of scope (in Sect. 1 we rely on a Java-like syntax). The idea, however, is that for any concrete realization M_{req} of SP_{req}, $Prog$ determines a particular implementation of the operations Op by using M_{req}, i.e. $Prog$ determines a particular model of the class $\text{Mod}(\Sigma_{\text{Body}})_{M_{\text{req}}}$. Hence, we propose that the semantics of a component body is given by a function $[\![\text{Body}]\!] : [\![SP_{\text{req}}]\!] \rightarrow \text{Mod}(\Sigma_{\text{Body}})$ such that $[\![\text{Body}]\!](M_{\text{req}}) \in \text{Mod}(\Sigma_{\text{Body}})_{M_{\text{req}}}$ for each $M_{\text{req}} \in [\![SP_{\text{req}}]\!]$. Let us remark that this definition also subsumes the case where the attribute signature of Σ_{Body} has no required type declaration, i.e. $\Sigma_{\text{Att}} = (\Sigma_P, Att)$. Then the transition systems of $\text{Mod}(\Sigma_{\text{Body}})$ simply work on states which are standard (non-indexed) algebras $\sigma \in \text{Alg}(\Sigma_{\text{Att}})$ and thus $[\![\text{Body}]\!]$ simply determines exactly one model in $\text{Mod}(\Sigma_{\text{Body}})$.

5   Components

A *component* C $= (SP_{\text{prov}}, SP_{\text{req}}, \text{Body}, \text{abs})$ consists of a provided interface specification SP_{prov}, a required interface specification SP_{req}, a component body which implements the provided interface operations by using SP_{req}, and a presentation, denoted by abs, of an abstraction function which relates concrete states of the body with abstract states of the provided interface.

5.1 Semantics and Correctness of Components

A component is syntactically well-formed if the component body provides implementations for all operations of the provided interface. The semantics of a component $C = (SP_{prov}, SP_{req}, Body, abs)$ consists of three parts,

1. its *external* semantics, seen by the user of the component, which is formally given by the class $[\![SP_{prov}]\!]$ of all models of SP_{prov},
2. its *internal* semantics which is given by the semantics of the component's body, i.e. by the function $[\![Body]\!] : [\![SP_{req}]\!] \to Mod(\Sigma_{Body})$, and by
3. the semantics of abs which is given by a function $[\![abs]\!] : Alg(\Sigma_{Att}) \to Alg(\Sigma_{Obs_{prov}})$ (where Σ_{Att} is the attribute signature underlying the component body and $\Sigma_{Obs_{prov}}$ is the observer signature underlying the provided interface specification).

Again we stay abstract and do not define a concrete syntax and semantics for abstraction functions. If, for instance, the observers of the provided signature are directly implemented in the component's body (as done in the example), then a correponding abstraction function can be derived automatically. If the observers are model variables, used e.g. in [9,12], an explicit abstraction function has to be defined.

To study the semantic correctness of a component we have to consider the relationship between its external and its internal semantics. The idea is that for any (used) model M_{req} of the required interface specification the resulting Σ_{Body}-model $[\![Body]\!](M_{req})$ is a model of the provided interface specification (taking into account the given abstraction function). For the formalization of this idea we still have to construct the restriction of Σ_{Body}-models to those transitions labelled with provided interface operations only.

Definition 8. *Let Op_{prov} be the set of operations of SP_{prov} and Op be the set of operations of Σ_{Body} such that $Op_{prov} \subseteq Op$. The restriction $\mathcal{R} : Mod(\Sigma_{Body}) \to Mod(\Sigma_{prov})$ of the Σ_{Body}-models to the operations Op_{prov} yields, for each $M = (Q, q_0, \Delta) \in Mod(\Sigma_{Body})$, the transition system $\mathcal{R}(M) = (Q, \alpha, q_0, \mathcal{R}(\Delta))$ where α is the restriction of $[\![abs]\!]$ to Q and $\mathcal{R}(\Delta) = \{(q, (op_{prov}, \rho), q', \rho') \in \Delta \mid (op_{prov}, \rho) \in Label_{Op}, op_{prov} \in Op_{prov}\}$.*

Definition 9. *Let $C = (SP_{prov}, SP_{req}, Body)$ be a (syntactically) well-formed component. C is correct, if for each $M_{req} \in [\![SP_{req}]\!]$, $\mathcal{R}([\![Body]\!](M_{req})) \in [\![SP_{prov}]\!]$.*

Hence, for proving the correctness of a component with provided interface specification $SP_{prov} = (\Sigma_{prov}, Ax_{prov})$ and required interface specification $SP_{req} = (\Sigma_{req}, Ax_{req})$ we have to verify that for any arbitrary model $M_{req} \in [\![SP_{req}]\!]$, first, $\mathcal{R}([\![Body]\!](M_{req}))$ is a Σ_{prov}-model, i.e. satisfies the condition (dom) for Σ_{prov}-models, and, secondly, $\mathcal{R}([\![Body]\!](M_{req})) \models_{\Sigma_{Obs_{prov}}} Ax_{prov}$, i.e. satisfies the initialization, invariant and operation effect sentences of SP_{prov}.

Of course, formal verification techniques to prove the correctness of a component are an important issue. For that purpose one would need a concrete, component-oriented specification and implementation language which is beyond the scope of this paper. However, the direction how to perform correctness proofs can be summarized by the following two steps:

(1) In a first step we construct the proof obligations. For this purpose we define a general mapping m that maps the axioms Ax_{prov} to appropriate formulas formulated in terms of the attribute signature of the component body. In particular, domain constraints and specifications of the provided interface operations would be mapped to pre- and postconditions for the body's operation implementations. Such a mapping depends, of course, on the concrete form of the abstraction function.

(2) In the second step we have to verify that the operation implementations in the component's body satisfy the generated proof obligations. For this purpose the idea is to adjust exisiting proof techniques (e.g. Hoare style proof rules or dynamic logic [1]) that work on the small step transitions of the operation implementations. Here it becomes crucial that, according to Theorem 1, one can indeed rely in each state of a small step transition on the properties described by the axioms Ax_{req} of the required interface specification SP_{req}; cf. Example 1.

5.2 Composition of Components

Up to now, we have considered *basic components* where the component body $(\Sigma_{Body}, Prog)$ consists of a body signature and a program. In this section we construct larger components from smaller ones by connecting required and provided interfaces of given components. To do the connection properly we need the notion of interface refinement. In the following we use, for lack of space, the simplified assumption that interface specifications, which are related by refinement, have the same underlying observer signature and the same set of operations (but possibly with different domain constraints).

Definition 10. *Let* $SP_{req} = (\Sigma_{req}, Ax_{req})$ *and* $SP'_{prov} = (\Sigma'_{prov}, Ax'_{prov})$ *be two interface specifications with signatures* $\Sigma_{req} = (\Sigma_{Obs}, Op, dom)$, $\Sigma'_{prov} = (\Sigma_{Obs}, Op, dom')$ *resp.* SP'_{prov} *is a refinement of* SP_{req} *if* $[\![SP'_{prov}]\!] \subseteq [\![SP_{req}]\!]$.

Definition 11. *Let two components* $C = (SP_{prov}, SP_{req}, Body, abs)$ *and* $C' = (SP'_{prov}, SP'_{req}, Body', abs')$ *be given which both are well-formed and correct and let* Σ_{Body} *be the signature of* Body. *Let* SP'_{prov} *be a refinement of* SP_{req}. *Then the* composition *of* C *and* C' *yields the* composite *component*

$$CC = (SP_{prov}, SP'_{req}, Body_{CC}, abs).$$

The external semantics of CC *is given by the external semantics of* C *(which is* $[\![SP_{prov}]\!]$), *the semantics of* abs *is the semantic abstraction function* $[\![abs]\!]$ *of* C *and the semantics of* $Body_{CC}$ *is given by the function* $[\![Body_{CC}]\!] : [\![SP'_{req}]\!] \to Mod(\Sigma_{Body})$ *such that for each* $M'_{req} \in [\![SP'_{req}]\!]$,

$$[\![Body_{CC}]\!](M'_{req}) = [\![Body]\!](\mathcal{R}'([\![Body']\!](M'_{req}))).$$

This means that $[\![\text{Body}_{\text{CC}}]\!]$ is the composition of the functions $[\![\text{Body}']\!] : [\![\text{SP}'_{\text{req}}]\!] \rightarrow \text{Mod}(\Sigma'_{\text{Body}})$, $\mathcal{R}' : \text{Mod}(\Sigma'_{\text{Body}}) \rightarrow \text{Mod}(\Sigma'_{\text{prov}})$ and $[\![\text{Body}]\!] : [\![\text{SP}_{\text{req}}]\!] \rightarrow \text{Mod}(\Sigma_{\text{Body}})$. The composition of these functions is well-defined since C' is correct, i.e. $\mathcal{R}' : \text{Mod}(\Sigma'_{\text{Body}}) \rightarrow [\![\text{SP}'_{\text{prov}}]\!]$, and since SP'$_{\text{prov}}$ is a refinement of SP$_{\text{req}}$, and hence $\mathcal{R}' : \text{Mod}(\Sigma'_{\text{Body}}) \rightarrow [\![\text{SP}_{\text{req}}]\!]$. Due to the correctness of C, the composite component CC is again correct. Obviously, the composition operator for components is associative (w.r.t. the given semantics).

6   Conclusion

We have shown how algebra and model theory can be adapted to provide a formal foundation of contract-based component systems. A key principle was strong encapsulation which has been formalized by semantic constraints which guarantee the preservation of the properties of required interface specifications. Of course, one may discuss whether the given semantic constraints are flexible enough in practice. However, it should be clear that whenever the constraints are violated encapsulation cannot be ensured anymore. On the other hand, models of component bodies as considered here can still contain arbitrary aggregates of instances of required type (even of different required types if our approach is extended in a straightforward way to arbitrary many required (and provided) interfaces). The difference to object-oriented programs is that in our approach these aggregates must be administered by instances of components on the next hierarchy level which makes reconfigurations specifiable and controllable. Since our approach implies a restricted communication structure that does not allow callbacks we still have to investigate to what extent practical examples can be reorganized to communication patterns that conform with our semantic model. Our approach is merely oriented towards the data of states and not to control states and interaction protocols. The integration of our approach with formalisms for dynamic systems and concurrent components (see e.g. [3]) is, of course, an important topic of future research.

The main differences of our approach to the literature on modular design and verification are: We do not focus on concrete techniques how to overcome the problem with modular verification in object-oriented systems like, e.g., [2,10] because we are interested in the basic semantic principles of encapsulation which should provide requirements for a good design of modular component-oriented languages. Modular verification should then be a direct consequence of the language design. Also our satisfaction relation for interface models and sentences is more powerful than the usual treatment of invariants and pre/postconditions due to the consideration of the strongly reachable states. Moreover, the purely model-theoretic approach pursued here allows us to reuse for free classical concepts of mathematical logic. This is also the idea of model-theoretic approaches to modular system design that have been studied in the context of institutions; see e.g. [7]. In contrast to the abstract ideas on encapsulation expressed by the satisfaction condition of institutions, we focus here on a particular setting concerning encapsulation in a state-based environment with explicit required and provided interfaces specified by contracts. In this setting we try to be as abstract as possible but also as concrete as necessary. But, indeed, Theorem 1 has been inspired by the abstract ideas of institutions. A more concrete approach considering modular specification of object-oriented components has been proposed in [12]. The concept of boxes found in [12] looks similar to our notion of indexed algebra and it would be interesting to work out in what extent [12] could be considered as a special case of our framework adapted to an object-oriented environment.

References

1. Ahrendt, W., Beckert, B., Hähnle, R., Schmitt, P.H.: KeY: A formal method for object-oriented systems. In: Bonsangue, M.M., Johnsen, E.B. (eds.) FMOODS 2007. LNCS, vol. 4468, pp. 32–43. Springer, Heidelberg (2007)
2. Barnett, M., Leino, K.R.M., Schulte, W.: The Spec# Programming System: An Overview. In: Barthe, G., Burdy, L., Huisman, M., Lanet, J.-L., Muntean, T. (eds.) CASSIS 2004. LNCS, vol. 3362, pp. 49–69. Springer, Heidelberg (2005)
3. Berger, K., Rausch, A., Sihling, M., Vilbig, A., Broy, M.: A Formal Model for Componentware. In: Leavens, G.T., Sitaraman, M. (eds.) Foundations of Component-Based Systems, pp. 189–210. Cambridge Univ. Press, Cambridge (2000)
4. Bidoit, M., Hennicker, R., Knapp, A., Baumeister, H.: Glass-box and black-box views on object-oriented specifications. In: Proc. SEFM 2004, Beijing, China. IEEE Comp. Society Press, Los Alamitos (2004)
5. Börger, E., Stärk, R.: Abstract State Machines: A Method for High-Level System Design and Analysis. Springer, Heidelberg (2003)
6. Cheesman, J., Daniels, J.: UML Components. Addison Wesley, Boston (2000)
7. Goguen, J.A., Tracz, W.: An Implementation-Oriented Semantics for Module Composition. In: Foundations of Component-Based Systems, pp. 231–263. Cambridge Univ. Press, Cambridge (2000)
8. Leavens, G.T., Baker, A.L., Ruby, C.: JML: A Notation for Detailed Design. In: Behavioral Specifications of Businesses and Systems, ch. 12, pp. 175–188. Kluwer, Dordrecht (1999)
9. Leavens, G.T., Dhara, K.K.: Concepts of Behavioral Subtyping and a Sketch of Their Extension to Component-Based Systems. In: Foundations of Component-Based Systems, pp. 113–136. Cambridge Univ. Press, Cambridge (2000)
10. Lu, Y., Potter, J., Xue, J.: Validity invariants and effects. In: Ernst, E. (ed.) ECOOP 2007. LNCS, vol. 4609, pp. 202–226. Springer, Heidelberg (2007)
11. Poetzsch-Heffter, A.: Specification and Verification of Object-Oriented Programs. Habilitationsschrift, Technische Universität München (1997)
12. Poetzsch-Heffter, A., Schäfer, J.: Modular Specification of Encapsulated Object-Oriented Components. In: de Boer, F.S., Bonsangue, M.M., Graf, S., de Roever, W.-P. (eds.) FMCO 2005. LNCS, vol. 4111, pp. 313–341. Springer, Heidelberg (2006)

Implementing a Categorical Information System⋆

Michael Johnson[1] and Robert Rosebrugh[2]

[1] Department of Computer Science
Macquarie University
mike@ics.mq.edu.au
[2] Department of Mathematics and Computer Science
Mount Allison University
rrosebrugh@mta.ca

Abstract. The authors have proposed using category-theoretic sketches to enhance database design and integration methodologies. The algebraic context is called the Sketch Data Model (SkDM) and mathematically describes databases, views and their updates, and other database concepts. The system described here is a freely available graphical Java environment with a module that compiles a design incorporating algebraically specified constraints into database schemas that interface directly with modern database management systems. It therefore supports, inter alia, rapid prototyping.

Keywords: Semantic data model, category theory, graphical database design.

1 Introduction

Although the database management systems (DBMS) in wide use for the past dozen years have all been "relational", the most popular design method remains the Entity-Relationship-Attribute (ERA) diagram. That this is so is not surprising given that the latter is a natural and simply understood graphical paradigm. Despite this design-implementation disconnect, there are straightforward procedures and a variety of both commercial and freely available software applications that allow creation and manipulation of ERA diagrams and then translate these designs into relational database schemas. See [8] for some examples.

The system described here similarly implements the database design concepts of the *Sketch Data Model (SkDM)* [4] which is based on categorical universal algebra. The SkDM extends both the entity-relationship model [1] and the functional data model of Shipman [6]. Entities and attributes are modeled using a simple graphical language. Relationships among entities are expressed, and may also be constrained, using concepts from category theory. SkDM constraints can express, among other things, the selection, projection, join and (disjoint) union operations of relational algebra. Formally, these ideas are expressed using a special case of

⋆ Research partially supported by grants from the Australian Research Council and NSERC Canada.

J. Meseguer and G. Roşu (Eds.): AMAST 2008, LNCS 5140, pp. 232–237, 2008.

the class of categorical theories called *sketches*. The particular sketches we use are called Entity-Attribute (EA) sketches and are described below.

For the Sketch Data Model, our EASIK system supports graphical definition and manipulation of EA-sketches and automatic compilation into SQL database schemas. It is capable of graphically specifying EA sketches, storing their description in XML documents and generating relational (SQL) database schemas that implement the SkDM designs, including constraints.

EASIK is the first system that supports SkDM modelling. It produces an SQL database schema which can be loaded into a DBMS. Furthermore the resulting database will enforce the SkDM constraints. Having such a system is crucial to validating the SkDM project. The current system has two main modules. The first module is a graphical engine that allows point-and-click construction and manipulation of an EA sketch. From the graphically presented EA sketch the system generates an XML document that encodes the sketch, including constraints. The second module compiles a design stored as an XML document to an SQL database schema that implements the design. The SkDM has been the subject of extensive theoretical studies by the authors and collaborators, for example [3,4,5]. M. Johnson and C. N. G. Dampney have been engaged for several industrial consultancies using the SkDM [2].

2   An Example

Before describing the EASIK implementation, we provide a short tour of the sketch data model with the aid of an EASIK screen. Many other examples can be found in [4] and papers cited there, including the case-studies and consultancies. We assume familiarity with standard data modeling concepts such as ERA diagrams and relational database schemas and algebra. Some familiarity with the basic language of categories applied to Computer Science (for example in [7]) will be helpful.

A conference program committee might use a database with information on its own members, authors, articles submitted, and their status. Among the rules we assume are the following: a person in the database is an author or committee member (not both); there is an assignment of a single committee member as first reader for each paper; papers may have several authors and vice versa; for accepted papers one or more of the authors is recorded as a presenter.

An EA sketch has four components which we outline for a database schema to support the program committee example. For a formal definition of EA sketch see [5].

The first component is a directed graph G, like that in Figure 1. We note some similarities with an Entity-Relationship diagram that might describe the same application domain, and some important differences.

Nodes of G represent entities, but there are no "relationship" nodes. The **authorship** entity allows several authors to be among the "authorship" of a paper and one author to have authorship of several papers. In an ER diagram **authorship** might be a relationship from **author** to **paper**. Here that is expressed by the

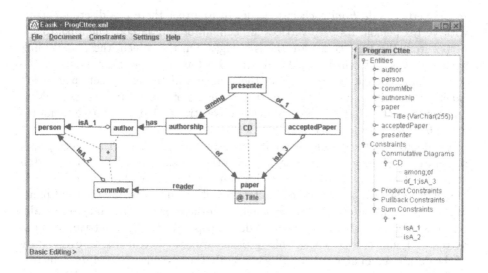

Fig. 1. EASIK screen for part of a Program Committee database

directed edges from **authorship**. Instead of being modeled as a relationship set in the ER fashion, **authorship** is also modeled as an entity set. Thus, the directed edges from **authorship** are modeled by functions specifying for each authorship who is the author and which paper they wrote. The is_a relationships are denoted here by edges indicated ◦—→ . The other directed edges in G, for example that from **paper** to **commMbr**, are modeled by functions (and can be thought of as methods or, from the database perspective, as integrity constraints). Given an instance of their source type they return an instance of their target type.

The other three components of an EA sketch do not appear in ER diagrams and they express database constraints. In EASIK they are indicated graphically.

The second component is a set of *commutative diagrams*. A commutative diagram is a pair of paths in G with common source and target. They are used to specify equality of function constraints. In our example, the two paths from **presenter** to **paper** are a commuting diagram. This represents a real-world constraint: Each **presenter** instance has an **authorship** of a **paper** and each **presenter** instance has an **acceptedPaper** which is *the same* **paper**. On the screen, this diamond of edges encloses a CD icon for which the details are also found among constraints in the right panel of the screen. In contrast, the two paths from **authorship** to **person** (around the parallelogram) do *not* form a commutative diagram.

The last two components of an EA sketch express database constraints graphically. They require a node of G to have a value in a database state that depends on values of other nodes in the state.

The third component of an EA sketch is a set of *finite cones* in G. For details of their syntax and semantics we refer the reader to [4] or [5], but we do note here that is_a edges are expressible using finite cones.

The fourth component of an EA sketch is a set of *finite discrete (or sum) cocones*. A discrete cocone has a single *vertex* node, a set of *base* nodes a path *to* the vertex node *from* each base node. In Figure 1 there is a discrete cocone with vertex **person**. Its base vertices are **commMbr** and **author**. The links to the vertex from the base nodes are the is_a edges. On the screen, these nodes link with a + icon for which the details are also found in the right panel of the screen. This cocone expresses that (the elements of the entity set) **person** are exactly the disjoint union (sum) of (the elements of the entity sets) **commMbr**, and **author**. Note that we thus enforce the constraint that committee members are not allowed to be authors.

We do not show most of the attributes—the "A" in EA—in the screen graph of Figure 1, but they are definitely a part of the EA sketch. Attributes are (often large) fixed value sets. Examples in this case are the name of a person, the title of a paper, the year-joined of a committee member, and so on. On the right panel attributes and their data-types are listed with their entity. They may optionally be shown on screen UML style, as we do for **paper**. Formally an attribute is the vertex of a sum cocone whose linking paths are called *elements*. In every state of the database, an attribute's value is exactly the disjoint union of its elements.

The theory of the sketch data model considers categories of *models* of EA sketches. A model is prescribed by value sets for entities and attributes and functions among them prescribed by the edges of G which satisfy the constraints. Our interest is instead to translate the sketch into an SQL database schema which maintains the constraints on entity sets prescribed by the sketch.

3 Implementation of the SkDM with EASIK

We begin the description of our implementation with some of the design desiderata for EASIK:

The graphical front end is written in Java for portability. All user input is gathered through the GUI environment. Saved files are XML documents. EASIK supports the database design and then handles the generation of an SQL database schema. Access to the database schema and data manipulation (input and queries) is via a user selected database management system. (Thus, database implementation requires an ambient DBMS; export of the SQL schema as text is also available.) Entities have a system-generated primary key. Keys are definable within the sketch and are in the exported SQL schema. Attributes must be based on data types for the platform specified by the user and are specified in an understandable format without adding clutter. Commutative diagrams and other constraints are representable graphically and exported as triggers and procedures to the SQL schema. The user may select a path of edges of any length to create constraints. The user may add, delete, edit and rename all sketch elements. Database schema export is accomplished automatically and includes all information about constraints, primary and foreign keys. Drivers for interactions with database platforms are included.

These design criteria are met by the application which is available for download from http://mathcs.mta.ca/research/rosebrugh/Easik/. EASIK uses the graph display package JGraph and translates between XML and Java via

SAX. The Java source code and a Java archive (jar) file (including a Help system) are available, as is extensive documentation and several examples.

EASIK opens with a graphical canvas with functionality for the creation of entities (nodes), attributes and edges joining entities. EA sketch constraints from several classes may be specified using the graphical interface. The components of the sketch are accessible from a text panel. A stored EA sketch may be loaded. The EA sketch information (entities, edges, attributes and constraints) in the graphical display can be edited on screen.

The displayed sketch may be saved to an XML document that encodes entities, attributes, edges and all of the constraints plus the current graphical display. The XML code follows a schema written in XSD. Fragments of XML code for the above example follow:

```
<entities>
<entity name="paper" x="365" y="228">
<attribute attributeType="VarChar(255)" name="Title"/> ...
<edges>
<edge id="of" inj="false" source="authorship" target="paper"/> ...
<commutativediagram isVisible="true" x="373" y="126">
<pathref id="among;of"/>
<pathref id="of_1;isA_3"/>...
```

Generation of data description language (SQL code) for a database schema from an EA sketch uses its stored XML document. The generation procedure begins by creating a table for each entity with keys derived from the graph of the EA sketch. A column of its entity table is created for each attribute. Each edge is encoded as a foreign key created for its source entity table on the primary key of its target entity table. The point is that, for any tuple in a source table (entity set) its value under the function implementing the edge is specified in the target table (entity set). The is_a (injective) edges also use UNIQUE. An example of generated SQL code follows. Note the attribute Title and the foreign key for reader.

```
CREATE TABLE paper (paper_id INTEGER AUTO_INCREMENT ,
Title VARCHAR(255), commMbr_id INTEGER NOT NULL ,
FOREIGN KEY (commMbr_id ) REFERENCES commMbr (commMbr_id ) ,
ON UPDATE CASCADE ON DELETE CASCADE ,
PRIMARY KEY (paper_id ));
```

Cascading updates and deletes for the foreign key is a design decision entailed by automatic generation.

The constraints of the EA sketch are coded as triggers and stored procedures. For example, inserting a tuple in the domain table of a commutative diagram invokes a trigger to enforce the requirement that the values the foreign keys used to express the participating edges do match after following the two paths in the commutative diagram. In the example following, the stored procedure ProgCttee_commDiag0 is called to traverse the paths involved.

```
CREATE TRIGGER presenterAInsertTrig AFTER INSERT ON presenter
FOR EACH ROW BEGIN call ProgCttee_commDiag0(NEW.presenter_id ); END
```

The stored procedure is fairly routine imperative code.

4 Conclusions

The challenging problem solved by this early version of EASIK is automatic compilation into SQL data definition language in a way that enforces the constraints of an EA sketch. Thus its powerful constraint definition facility is available to users via a simply understood graphical data model design tool. EASIK is the first system to do this. Furthermore EASIK will support the development of large systems using the SkDM approach. Such software support is vital with the large applications common in industrial practice. The system described has some limitations. Only a single EA sketch window may be opened. Limit cones are currently required to be one of two (very common) types. Testing with commercial DBMS has been limited. Future versions will address these issues.

Database theory has worked within its own Relational Algebra for many years, but enhancing the theory with categorical universal algebra is a more recent development. The system described here provides a positive link between theory (the algebraic methodology, SkDM) and practice (the software technology of database management systems).

References

1. Chen, P.P.S.: The Entity-Relationship Model—Toward a Unified View of Data. ACM Trans. Database Syst. 2, 9–36 (1976)
2. Dampney, C.N.G., Johnson, M.: Experience in developing interoperations among legacy information systems using partial reverse engineering. In: Proceedings of the IEEE International Conference on Software Maintenance, pp. 269–272 (2003)
3. Johnson, M., Rosebrugh, R.: Sketch data models, relational schema and data specifications. In: Proceedings of CATS 2002. Electronic Notes in Theoretical Computer Science, vol. 61(6), pp. 1–13 (2002)
4. Johnson, M., Rosebrugh, R.: Fibrations and universal view updatability. Theoretical Computer Science 388, 109–129 (2007)
5. Johnson, M., Rosebrugh, R.: Constant complements, reversibility and universal view updates. In: AMAST (to appear, 2008)
6. Shipman, D.: The functional data model and the data language DAPLEX. ACM Trans. Database Syst. 6, 140–173 (1981)
7. Walters, R.F.C.: Categories and Computer Science. Cambridge University Press, Cambridge (1991)
8. http://en.wikipedia.org/wiki/Entity-relationship (accessed on May 6, 2008)

Constant Complements, Reversibility and Universal View Updates*

Michael Johnson[1] and Robert Rosebrugh[2]

[1] Department of Computer Science
Macquarie University
mike@ics.mq.edu.au
[2] Department of Mathematics and Computer Science
Mount Allison University
rrosebrugh@mta.ca

Abstract. The algebraic specification of information systems (including databases) has been advanced by the introduction of category theoretic sketches and in particular by the authors' Sketch Data Model (SkDM). The SkDM led to a new treatment of view updating using universal properties already studied in category theory. We call the new treatment succinctly "universal updating". This paper outlines the theory of universal updating and studies the relationships between it and recent theoretical results of Hegner and Lechtenbörger which in turn studied the classical "constant complement" approach to view updates. The main results demonstrate that constant complement updates are universal, that on the other hand there are sometimes universal updates even in the absence of constant complements, and that in the SkDM constant complement updates are reversible. We show further that there may be universal updates which are reversible even for views which have no complement. In short, the universal updates provide an attractive option including reversibility, even when constant complements are not available. The paper is predominantly theoretical studying different algebraic approaches to information system software but it also has important practical implications since it shows that universal updates have important properties in common with classical updates but they may be available even when classical approaches fail.

Keywords: View update, semantic data model, category theory.

1 Introduction

To provide usability, security, access limitation, and even interoperability for database systems, the designer of a database schema may specify a subschema or "view". Any database state instantiating the database schema determines a view state instantiating the view schema by substitution. A user with access to the view state may perform an update to the view state. The question arising

* Research partially supported by grants from the Australian Research Council and NSERC Canada.

J. Meseguer and G. Roşu (Eds.): AMAST 2008, LNCS 5140, pp. 238–252, 2008.
© Springer-Verlag Berlin Heidelberg 2008

is how to determine an appropriate update to the state of the total database. This problem, known as the "view update problem" has been widely studied. There is a variety of "solutions", referred to as "translations", but many of these are either narrow in their application or not apparently close to actual database models. The implementation of view updates, especially within standards such as SQL, has been largely based on ad hoc and very limiting requirements.

Much of the literature on the view update problem is over 15 years old, but in recent years there have been several new contributions. In 2002, Hegner [6] introduced an order based theory of database views and their updates which generalized the constant complement approach to view updating originally developed by Bancilhon and Spyratos [1]. In 2003 Lechtenbörger [10] explored the relationship between the reversibility of updates and constant complements. More recently Bohannon, Pierce and Vaughan [4] introduced *lenses*, a structure providing a lifted state for a given state and the updated version of its view state. Lenses guarantee translations for the constant complement views and they noted that view updating in the style of Bancilhon and Spyratos allows only a "relatively small number of updates on a view to be translated". Dayal and Bernstein [5] were more permissive in the view update translations that they proposed and also considered a criterion that in modern terms would be described as a *universal property*: They discuss (p 401) the desire for view update translations to be *unique* and *minimal*. In a similar vein, Hegner finds that "within the constant complement order-based framework, the reflection of an order based update of a view to the base schema is unique, without qualification." The present authors have investigated an approach to database schemas, states and views based on categorical algebra [7]. This data model prescribes a solution to the view update problem using precisely universal properties (unique minimal translations).

The problem addressed by this paper is to understand better the relationship between universal updates and constant complement updates in the context of our data model. Hegner's order-based context models database states more accurately than considering them to be abstract sets, and his results are suggestive of what we will find. Lechtenbörger showed that, in a suitable sense, constant complement updates were always reversible, and conversely if all updates to a view are reversible then it is possible to find a constant complement for it. The main contributions of the present article are

1. To develop the framework in which universal updates properly reflect ambient database structure
2. To show that in that framework constant complement updates are, in harmony with Hegner's results, necessarily universal
3. To show that in that framework constant complement updates are, in harmony with Lechtenbörger's results, reversible
4. To provide examples to demonstrate that universal updates are more general than both constant complement updates and reversible updates

We note particularly that view updates can have very attractive properties including universality and even reversibility without necessarily having any constant complement (without contradicting Lechtenbörger's results, see below).

As mentioned above, the work presented here uses the *sketch data model (SkDM)* [8], [9] which is based on categorical algebra. This data model is related to both the popular and widely used entity-relationship model and to the functional data model of Shipman [12]. Entities and attributes are modelled using a simple graphical language. Relationships among them are constrained using concepts from category theory that express selection, projection, join and union constraints. The syntactic formalism derived from these ideas is expressed by the concept of "sketch". The sketches we use are called Entity-Attribute (EA)-sketches and are described in detail below.

Straightforward procedures and a variety of software applications translate entity-relationship diagrams into relational database schemas, whose semantics are database states. For the sketch data model, a similar implementation is in progress (see for example [11], an EA-sketch compiler which supports graphical manipulation of EA-sketches and automatic conversion into Oracle and MySQL database schemas).

The structure of the paper is as follows. In Section 2 we present a small motivating example of a sketch data model followed by the formal definitions of EA sketches, views, and propagatable (universal) updates. Section 3 is devoted to developing the main results relating propagatable updates to constant complements and reversibility respectively. Finally, Section 4 relates those main results to the work of others.

2   An Example and the Sketch Data Model

The results presented in Section 3 need the technical details of the sketch data model which are given below. First we work through a motivating example. Other examples can be found in [9] and in case-studies and consultancies, cited there.

We assume some familiarity with Entity-Relationship (ER) notation and the basic language of categories and functors applied to Computer Science as found, for example, in [2].

Example 1. When aircraft land at an airport in restricted visibility conditions they use an "instrument approach". We describe part of a database schema for instrument approaches. The main entities involved are airports, runways, waypoints (fixes) and the instrument approaches themselves. For example, there is a VOR (VHF Omni-Range) approach to Runway 18 at Willard Airport near Champaign. An approach also involves a specified waypoint of one of several types which defines its final approach fix (faf). The main types of waypoints are VOR, NDB (another kind of navigation aid) and GPS waypoints (GPSWP). Also required is a waypoint to fly to in case of a missed approach (overshoot).

An EA sketch has four components which we will now prescribe for our example. The first component (as for ER diagrams) is a directed graph G. Figure 1 shows (the main elements of) the directed graph for an EA sketch.

Entities are nodes of G, but there are no "relationship" nodes. In an ER diagram Approach might be a relationship from Runway to Waypoint. Here that

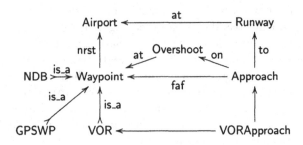

Fig. 1. Graph for part of an instrument approach database schema

is expressed by the directed edges to and faf. In a database state an entity node is modelled by an entity set just as for an ER diagram. Instead of being modelled as a relationship set in the ER fashion, Approach is also modelled as an entity set. However, the directed edges from Approach are modelled by functions. The is_a relationships are denoted here by edges indicated $\rightarrowtail$. As for an ER diagram, they are modelled by injective mappings. The other directed edges in G are modelled by functions (and can be thought of as methods or, from the database perspective, as integrity constraints). Given an instance of their source type they return an instance of their target type.

The other three components of an EA sketch do not appear in ER diagrams and they express database constraints. The second component is a set of *commutative diagrams*. Here a commutative diagram is a pair of paths in G with common source and target. They specify equality functional constraints. In our example, the right-then-top and bottom-then-left paths around the upper rectangle is a commuting diagram. It represents a real-world constraint: Each (instrument) Approach to a particular Runway at a particular Airport uses as faf a Waypoint located at that same airport. In contrast, the two paths from Approach to Waypoint (the triangle) is *not* a commutative diagram—the rules for a particular approach require that on overshooting, an aircraft holds at a particular Waypoint which will not usually be the final approach fix Waypoint. In this example, the bottom rectangle is also a commutative diagram as noted below.

The last two components of an EA sketch also express database constraints. They will require a node of G to have an entity set in a database state that depends on those of other nodes for the state. The third component of an EA sketch is a set of *finite cones* in G. A cone in G has a vertex, a base diagram, and projection edges from the vertex to base nodes. An example from Figure 1 follows. This cone has *vertex* VORApproach (the vertex is a node of G). The *base diagram* of the cone is the pair of edges VOR $\longrightarrow$ Waypoint $\longleftarrow$ Approach. The base is a diagram in the graph, given formally by a graph morphism to G. The *projections* from the vertex to the base nodes are the edges in G from VORApproach to Approach, VOR and Waypoint—the last edge is not shown in Figure 1, but it is the common value of the right-then-top and bottom-then-left paths (since the bottom rectangle is commutative!) The constraint this cone expresses is that in models VORApproach is the pullback of the base cospan. In fact this is precisely how join database constraints are specified. Selection, is_a and projection constraints can also be expressed with finite cones. We mention a further point about the cones. An EA sketch is required to have a special cone whose vertex is called 1 (and usually not depicted) and whose base diagram is empty so that in models its value is 1.

The fourth component of an EA sketch is a set of *finite discrete cocones*. A discrete cocone has a vertex, a base diagram and links *to* the vertex *from* base nodes. Being *discrete* means no edges are permitted in the base diagram. In Figure 1 there is a discrete cocone with vertex Waypoint. Its base nodes are NDB, VOR, and GPSWP. The links to the vertex from the base nodes are the is_a edges. For discrete cocones the links are called *injections*; they are necessarily injective functions in database states. This cocone expresses the constraint that the elements of (the entity set) Waypoint are exactly the disjoint union of (the elements of the entity sets) NDB, VOR, and GPSWP. The formal requirement is that the vertex be the *sum*, or coproduct, of the base nodes.

As is usual practice, we did not draw the attributes—the "A" in EA—in Figure 1, but they are definitely a part of the EA sketch. Attributes are (often large) fixed value sets. Examples in this case are the radio frequency of a navigation aid, the surface type of a runway, the length of a runway, the four character identifying code of an airport, etc. An attribute is the vertex of a cocone whose finite discrete base has all of its nodes specified by the special node 1 and whose injection edges are called *elements*. In every state, an attribute's value is exactly the sum of its elements. Formally, the cocones that define attributes are part of the underlying graph. (In practice, attributes are usually listed separately in a data dictionary.)

We now proceed with the formalism required for EA sketches and their model categories. The first three definitions are general [2] and are included to establish notation before we specialize to our EA sketches and their models.

Definition 1. *A sketch* $\mathbb{E} = (G, \mathbf{D}, \mathcal{L}, \mathcal{C})$ *consists of a directed graph* G, *a set* $\mathbf{D}$ *of pairs of directed paths in* G *with common source and target (called the commutative diagrams) and sets of cones* $\mathcal{L}$ *and cocones* $\mathcal{C}$ *in* G. *The category generated by the graph* G *with commutative diagrams* $\mathbf{D}$ *is denoted* $C(\mathbb{E})$.

Definition 2. *Let* $\mathbb{E} = (G, \mathbf{D}, \mathcal{L}, \mathcal{C})$ *and* $\mathbb{E}' = (G', \mathbf{D}', \mathcal{L}', \mathcal{C}')$ *be sketches. A sketch morphism* $h : \mathbb{E} \to \mathbb{E}'$ *is a graph morphism* $G \to G'$ *which carries, commutative diagrams in* $\mathbf{D}$, *cones in* $\mathcal{L}$ *and cocones in* $\mathcal{C}$ *to respectively commutative diagrams in* $\mathbf{D}'$, *cones in* $\mathcal{L}'$ *and cocones in* $\mathcal{C}'$.

Definition 3. *Denote the category of finite sets by* $\mathbf{set}_f$. *A model* M *of a sketch* $\mathbb{E}$ *is a functor* $M : C(\mathbb{E}) \to \mathbf{set}_f$ *such that the cones in* $\mathcal{L}$ *and cocones in* $\mathcal{C}$ *are sent to limit cones and colimit cocones in* $\mathbf{set}_f$. *If* M *and* M' *are models of* $\mathbb{E}$ *a morphism* $\phi : M \to M'$ *is a natural transformation from* M *to* M'. *The category* $\mathrm{Mod}(\mathbb{E})$ *has objects the models of* $\mathbb{E}$ *and arrows the morphisms of models.*

EA sketches as described in Example 1 have some limitations on their cones and cocones and they are adequate for describing the needed database constraints, but restrictive enough to permit definition of the query language.

Definition 4. *An EA sketch* $\mathbb{E} = (G, \mathbf{D}, \mathcal{L}, \mathcal{C})$ *is a sketch with only finite cones and finite discrete cocones and with a specified cone with empty base whose vertex is called* 1. *Edges with domain* 1 *are called* elements. *Nodes which are vertices of cocones all of whose injections are elements are called* attributes. *Nodes which are neither attributes, nor* 1, *are called* entities.

The next definitions are fundamental: the semantics i.e. database states, for an EA sketch are specified by a set for each node of the graph and a function for each edge subject to: equality of composition constraints (from the commutative diagrams); select, project and join constraints (from the cones); and (disjoint) union constraints (from the discrete cocones).

Definition 5. *A* database state D *for an EA sketch* $\mathbb{E}$ *is a model of* $\mathbb{E}$. *The category of database states of* $\mathbb{E}$ *is* $\mathrm{Mod}(\mathbb{E})$. *An* insert update *(respectively* delete update*) for a database state* D *is a monomorphism* $D \rightarrowtail D'$ *(respectively* $D' \rightarrowtail D$*) in* $\mathrm{Mod}(\mathbb{E})$.

A morphism of database states is a monomorphism when each component morphism is monic. Thus our definition of a delete (resp. insert) update means that some elements are deleted (resp. inserted) in in the set specified for each node. The following definition encodes the requirement of the relational model for *entity integrity*, since it means that there is a chosen primary key for each entity.

Definition 6. *The EA sketch* $\mathbb{E}$ *is* keyed *if for each entity* E *there is a specified attribute* A_E *called its* key attribute *and a chosen monic specification* $E \rightarrowtail A_E$.

For a keyed EA sketch, it turns out that all morphisms between database states are monomorphisms ([8], Proposition 4.7) since all of the natural transformation component mappings are injective.

Example 2. We give a simple EA sketch $\mathbb{E}_1$ that we will consider in the sequel. It is a variant of an example in [6]. The database records people, their names and departments and their assignments to projects.

The graph is just that depicted below. There are no commutative diagrams

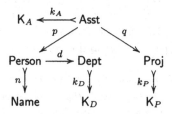

The attributes are K_A, Name, K_D and K_P (we do not show their cocone specifications in the diagram). Entities are Asst, Person, Dept and Proj. The edges k_A, n, k_D and k_P are keys, so there are also several cones not shown.   ◇

Before giving the definition of view, we briefly discuss the *query language* of an EA sketch. One of the advantages of the sketch data model is that an EA sketch comes equipped with a query language. For any EA sketch $\mathbb{E}$ there is a category called the *theory* of the sketch denoted $Q(\mathbb{E})$ (for details consult [3, Section 8.2]). This $Q(\mathbb{E})$ is constructed starting from $C(\mathbb{E})$ and then formally adding to it all finite limits and finite sums, subject to the (co)cones in $\mathcal{L}$ and $\mathcal{C}$. For example, $Q(\mathbb{E}_1)$ has objects like Pers $\times$ Proj and Dept $+$ Asst. From its construction, $Q(\mathbb{E})$ includes $\mathbb{E}$ and actually has *all* finite limits and finite sums. An essential point is that $\mathrm{Mod}(Q(\mathbb{E}))$ is equivalent as a category to $\mathrm{Mod}(\mathbb{E})$. This is because a $Q(\mathbb{E})$ model restricts to an $\mathbb{E}$ model and conversely an $\mathbb{E}$ model determines values on queries and so a $Q(\mathbb{E})$ model.

A *view* allows a user of an information system to manipulate data which are part of, or are derived from, an underlying database. As we are about to define it, a view of an EA sketch $\mathbb{E}$ has a new EA sketch $\mathbb{V}$ with the entities of $\mathbb{V}$ interpreted via a sketch morphism V as entities from the original EA sketch $\mathbb{E}$ or even query results (entities of $Q(\mathbb{E})$). Formally,

Definition 7. *A* view *of an EA sketch $\mathbb{E}$ is an EA sketch $\mathbb{V}$ together with a sketch morphism $V : \mathbb{V} \twoheadrightarrow Q(\mathbb{E})$.*

Example 3. A view $V_1 : \mathbb{V}_1 \longrightarrow Q(\mathbb{E}_1)$ of $\mathbb{E}_1$ is specified by the inclusion in $Q(\mathbb{E}_1)$ of the sketch whose graph is just the three edges k_A, np and k_{Pq} (the latter two being composites of edges in $\mathbb{E}_1$). Note that the composite edges np and k_{Pq} are not edges in $\mathbb{E}_1$ but they are present in $C(\mathbb{E}_1)$ and so in $Q(\mathbb{E}_1)$.   ◇

The equivalence of $\mathrm{Mod}(\mathbb{E})$ with $\mathrm{Mod}(Q(\mathbb{E}))$ means a database state $D : \mathbb{E} \to \mathrm{set}_f$ can also be considered as a model of $Q(\mathbb{E})$, also denoted D. Composing the model D with a view V gives a database state $DV : \mathbb{V} \twoheadrightarrow Q(\mathbb{E}) \to \mathrm{set}_f$ for $\mathbb{V}$, the *V-view of D*. This operation of *composing with V* is written V^* so $V^*D = DV$ and so we obtain a functor $V^* : \mathrm{Mod}(\mathbb{E}) \to \mathrm{Mod}(\mathbb{V})$ which sends a database state for $\mathbb{E}$ to one for $\mathbb{V}$.

We sometimes refer to a database state of the form V^*D as a "view". Context determines whether "view" refers to a database state, or to the sketch morphism V. To avoid ambiguity we also refer to V^*D as a *view state* and to $\mathbb{V}$ as the *view sketch*. Our framework implies an inessential difference from other work on views. When the database states are simply a set [1], [10] instead of a category like $\mathrm{Mod}(\mathbb{E})$ the analogue of V^* is a mapping called the *view definition mapping*. If the states are a partially ordered set [6] it is a monotone mapping. These mappings are usually required to be surjective so that every view state arises from a state of the underlying database. While V^* may be surjective on objects (view states), we do not require this, so we formally allow view states not derived from underlying database states. In examples V is usually one-one on objects making V^* surjective on objects.

Since a view state is itself a database state for its view sketch, we may (subject to the constraints of the view sketch) insert items in or delete items from a view state. An insertion in, or deletion from, the view state V^*D is translatable to the underlying database state D if there is an insertion in or deletion from the underlying database which, on application of V^*, becomes the given view insert/delete. We will say the insertion or deletion is *propagatable* if there is a unique "minimal" insert/delete in the following sense.

Definition 8. *Let $V : \mathbb{V} \to Q(\mathbb{E})$ be a view of $\mathbb{E}$. Suppose D is a database state for $\mathbb{E}$, T' a database state for $\mathbb{V}$, and $i : V^*D \rightarrowtail T'$ is an insert update of V^*D. The insertion i is propagatable if there exists an insert update $m : D \rightarrowtail D'$ in $\mathrm{Mod}(\mathbb{E})$ with the following property: $i = V^*m$ and for any database state D'' and insert update $m'' : D \rightarrowtail D''$ such that $V^*m'' = i'i$ for some $i' : T' \rightarrowtail V^*D''$, there is a unique insert $m' : D' \rightarrowtail D''$ such that $V^*m' = i'$ as in*

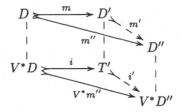

where the dashed vertical lines indicate, for example, that V^*D is the image of D under V^*. If every insert update on V^*D is propagatable, we say that the view state V^*D is insert updatable.

Definitions of *propagatable* for a deletion $d : T' \rightarrowtail V^*D$ and *delete updatable* for a view state are obtained by reversing some arrows. Note that the m whose existence is required is *essentially unique*. By this we mean that for any other $n : D \rightarrowtail E'$ that satisfies the requirements on m, there is an invertible morphism of database states $j : D' \to E'$ satisfying $jm = n$.

Example 4. Let D be a model of $\mathbb{E}_1$. We consider some updates for the view V_1 of Example 3.

First, any delete from the value $V_1^*D(\mathsf{Asst})$ is propagatable: the deleted assignment is simply deleted from $D(\mathsf{Asst})$. There are no other consequences. Since the other nodes of the graph of $\mathbb{V}_1$ are attributes and hence their values are the same in every database state, no other deletes are possible.

Next consider inserting an item a into the view state V_1^*D at $V_1^*D(\mathsf{Asst})$. That is, we wish to add an assignment in the view. Once again, there are no other possibilities for insertion in V_1^*D. This requires defining $V_1^*D \rightarrowtail T'$ and so defining K_A, Name and K_P values $T'(k_A)(a)$ and so on. If the proposed Name and K_P values, $T'(np)(a)$ and $T'(k_Pq)(a)$ are already in the images of $D(n)$ and $D(k_P)$ because the person and project exist already, and provided there is a free assignment key in $D(K_A)$ for the value of $T'(k_A)(a)$, then the insert is propagatable to a $D \rightarrowtail D'$ since values of $D'(p)(a)$ (and hence also $D'(d)(a)$) and $D'(q)(a)$ are determined. Even if the proposed K_P value is not an image of $D(k_P)$ this remains true since it is then possible to insert an item b into $D(\mathsf{Proj})$ and set $D'(q)(a) = b$ and $D'(k_P)(b) = T'(k_Pq)(a)$. However, if the proposed Name value is not an image of $D(n)$, there is no canonical choice of Dept value $D'(dp)(a)$ and consequently the update is not propagatable.   ◇

When all insert (respectively, delete) updates of a view are propagatable then V^* is called a *right (resp. left) fibration*. For criteria guaranteeing this property see [9]. For historical reasons, the arrow m in Definition 8 is called *op-cartesian*, while the analogous arrow for a delete is called *cartesian* and we will use these names below.

3   The Main Results

In this section we will study constant complements and reversibility.

A notion of *view complement* appeared in the influential article of Bancilhon and Spyratos [1], a study of the view update problem. They consider database states to be a *set* S, view states to be a set V and give a surjective view definition mapping $f : S \twoheadrightarrow V$ from the database states onto the view states. A *view update* is taken to be an endo-function u on the view states. A set U of view updates is specified and assumed to be *complete*, i.e. closed under composition and including the identity function. A *translation* T_u of a view update u is a database update (endo-function on S) such that the view of a translated database state is the update of the view of the state, i.e. $f(T_u(s)) = u(f(s))$ (and T_u acts as the identity on any s whenever u acts as the identity on $f(s)$). A translation T_u is a solution to the view update problem for the update u and a *translator* T for U is a set of translations $\{T_u \mid u \in U\}$. The diagram following is suggestive:

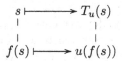

Bancilhon and Spyratos show that a translator T for a complete update set implies the existence of a "constant complement view" C. This is a second set C of view states with a second view definition mapping, say $g : S \twoheadrightarrow C$, such that the mapping $\langle f, g \rangle : S \longrightarrow V \times C$ is a bijection (C is a *complement* of V) and such that $g(T_u(s)) = g(s)$ holds for $T_u \in T, s \in S$ (any T_u in T is *constant* on C). They also showed a converse. This is the basis of the "constant complement" update strategy.

Lechtenbörger [10] has recently shown that constant complement translators exist when all of the view updates are reversible by other view updates.

In the description above the database states are taken to be an unstructured set and (subject to completeness) the updates are simply an abstract set of endo-functions. Hegner [6] suggests that the database states and the view states ought to be partially ordered sets. Then delete and insert updates should relate states that are comparable, i.e for a state s and update u, either $s \leq u(s)$ or $u(s) \leq s$. Our definition above suggests that updates should be arrows in a category of database states. We point out an important difference. In [1] and [6] an update u acts on every (view) state—it is a process mapping states to updated states—whereas for us, an update compares a single state to an updated state.

We start with the definition that begins to express these ideas in our context.

Definition 9. *Let* $\mathbb{E}$, $\mathbb{V}$ *and* $\mathbb{C}$ *be EA sketches and* $V : \mathbb{V} \longrightarrow Q(\mathbb{E})$ *and* $C : \mathbb{C} \longrightarrow Q(\mathbb{E})$ *be views. We say* C *is a complement of* V *if the functor*

$$\langle V^*, C^* \rangle : \mathrm{Mod}(\mathbb{E}) \longrightarrow \mathrm{Mod}(\mathbb{V}) \times \mathrm{Mod}(\mathbb{C})$$

is full, faithful and injective on objects.

Definition 10. *Let* $V : \mathbb{V} \longrightarrow Q(\mathbb{E})$ *and* $C : \mathbb{C} \longrightarrow Q(\mathbb{E})$ *be views with* C *a complement of* V *and* $\alpha : R \twoheadrightarrow V^*D$ *be an arrow in* $\mathrm{Mod}(\mathbb{V})$. *We say that* α *has a* C-*constant update if there is* $\hat{\alpha}$ *in* $\mathrm{Mod}(\mathbb{E})$ *with* $\alpha = V^*\hat{\alpha}$ *and* $C^*(\hat{\alpha})$ *an isomorphism. Dually,* α *has a* C-*opconstant update if* $\beta : V^*D \rightarrow S$ *is* $V^*\hat{\beta}$ *and* $C^*(\hat{\beta})$ *is an isomorphism.*

The definition does not require that α be propagatable, but only that it be the image under V^* of some $\hat{\alpha}$. More generally,

Definition 11. *Let* $V : \mathbb{V} \longrightarrow Q(\mathbb{E})$ *and* $C : \mathbb{C} \longrightarrow Q(\mathbb{E})$ *be views with* C *a complement of* V. *We say that* V *has* C-*constant updates if every* $\alpha : R \twoheadrightarrow V^*D$ *has a* C-*constant update.* V *has* C-*opconstant updates is defined dually.*

Example 5. Consider an EA sketch $\mathbb{E}$ that is specified completely (except for 1) by a sum diagram

$$\text{Support} \xrightarrow{i} \text{Dept} \xleftarrow{j} \text{Production}$$

That is, in any state the **Dept** entity set will be the disjoint union of the support departments and the production departments. Suppose that $\mathbb{V}$ and $\mathbb{C}$ are the EA sketches whose graphs have (in addition to 1) exactly one node each: **Support** and **Production** respectively and that $V : \mathbb{V} \longrightarrow Q(\mathbb{E})$ and $C : \mathbb{C} \longrightarrow Q(\mathbb{E})$ are the sketch morphisms providing the obvious inclusions of the two views. A state M of $\mathbb{E}$ is determined by a sum diagram:

$$M\text{Support} \xrightarrow{Mi} M\text{Dept} \xleftarrow{Mj} M\text{Production}$$

in $\mathbf{set}_f$ and a state of either $\mathbb{V}$ or $\mathbb{C}$ by any set. Thus

$$\langle V^*, C^* \rangle : \mathrm{Mod}(\mathbb{E}) \longrightarrow \mathrm{Mod}(\mathbb{V}) \times \mathrm{Mod}(\mathbb{C})$$

sends the sum diagram above to the pair $\langle M\text{Support}, M\text{Production} \rangle$ of sets. It is immediate that C is a complement of V. Indeed, here $\langle V^*, C^* \rangle$ is an equivalence.

Notice that any deletion $\alpha : R \twoheadrightarrow V^*M$ in $\mathrm{Mod}(\mathbb{V})$ is propagatable: simply delete appropriate elements from M**Support** and the corresponding elements from M**Dept**. If we denote the cartesian arrow by $\hat{\alpha} : \alpha M \longrightarrow M$, so $\alpha = V^*\hat{\alpha}$ we see that $C^*(\hat{\alpha})$ is the identity on M**Production**. Thus, α has a C-constant update, and indeed V has C-constant updates. Note further that $\hat{\alpha}$ is also opcartesian for the arrow $\alpha : V^*\alpha M \rightarrow M$**Support**. That is, α is 'reversible' in the sense of Definition 12.

Similarly, β has C-opconstant updates for any insertion $\beta : V^*M \rightarrowtail S$ in $\mathrm{Mod}(\mathbb{V})$, and β is reversible. $\diamond$

The next two theorems show that the constant complement updates are among the propagatable (universal) updates.

Theorem 1. *Let $V : \mathbb{V} \longrightarrow Q(\mathbb{E})$ be a view and let $C : \mathbb{C} \longrightarrow Q(\mathbb{E})$ be a complement and $\alpha : R \rightarrowtail V^*M$ be a deletion in $\mathrm{Mod}(\mathbb{V})$. If α has a C-constant update, then α is propagatable.*

Proof. Suppose that $\hat{\alpha} : N \twoheadrightarrow M$ satisfies $\alpha = V^*\hat{\alpha}$, $C^*\hat{\alpha}$ is invertible, $\hat{\beta} : P \longrightarrow M$ and $\gamma : V^*P \longrightarrow R$ satisfy $V^*\hat{\beta} = \alpha\gamma$. We need to construct a unique $\hat{\gamma} : P \twoheadrightarrow N$ satisfying $V^*\hat{\gamma} = \gamma$ as in:

$$
\begin{array}{ccccc}
P & \xrightarrow{\hspace{1.5em}\hat{\beta}\hspace{1.5em}} & N & \rightarrowtail & M \\
\downarrow & \xrightarrow{\hat{\gamma}} & \downarrow & \xrightarrow{\hat{\alpha}} & \downarrow \\
V^*P & \xrightarrow{\gamma} & R & \rightarrowtail & V^*M \\
& & & \alpha &
\end{array}
$$

Since C is α-constant, we have $\langle \gamma, (C^*\hat{\alpha})^{-1}C^*\hat{\beta}\rangle : \langle V^*P, C^*P\rangle \longrightarrow \langle V^*N, C^*N\rangle$. Now $\langle V^*, C^*\rangle$ is full by assumption, so there is an arrow $\hat{\gamma} : P \longrightarrow N$ with $V^*\hat{\gamma} = \gamma$ and $C^*\hat{\gamma} = (C^*\hat{\alpha})^{-1}C^*\hat{\beta}$.

To see that $\hat{\alpha}\hat{\gamma} = \hat{\beta}$, recall that $\langle V^*, C^*\rangle$ is faithful and note that:

$$
\begin{aligned}
\langle V^*, C^*\rangle\hat{\alpha}\hat{\gamma} &= \langle V^*\hat{\alpha}\hat{\gamma}, C^*\hat{\alpha}\hat{\gamma}\rangle \\
&= \langle \alpha\gamma, C^*\hat{\alpha}(C^*\alpha)^{-1}C^*\hat{\beta}\rangle \\
&= \langle V^*\hat{\beta}, C^*\hat{\beta}\rangle \\
&= \langle V^*, C^*\rangle\hat{\beta}
\end{aligned}
$$

To see that $\hat{\gamma}$ is unique, just note that $\hat{\alpha}$ is monic. $\square$

Theorem 2. *Let $V : \mathbb{V} \longrightarrow Q(\mathbb{E})$, let $C : \mathbb{C} \longrightarrow Q(\mathbb{E})$ be a complement and $\beta : V^*M \rightarrowtail S$ be an insertion in $\mathrm{Mod}(\mathbb{V})$. If β has a C-opconstant update, then β is propagatable.*

Proof. Suppose that $\hat{\beta} : M \rightarrowtail N$ satisfies $\beta = V^*\hat{\beta}$, $C^*\hat{\beta}$ is invertible, $\hat{\alpha} : P \longrightarrow M$ and $\gamma : V^*M \longrightarrow S$ satisfy $V^*\hat{\alpha} = \gamma\beta$. The construction of $\hat{\gamma} : N \twoheadrightarrow P$ satisfying $V^*\hat{\gamma} = \gamma$ is formally dual to that above, indeed $C^*\hat{\gamma} = C^*\hat{\alpha}(C^*\hat{\beta})^{-1}$. To see that $\hat{\gamma}$ is unique, suppose that $V^*\overline{\gamma} = \gamma$ and $\overline{\gamma}\hat{\beta} = \hat{\alpha}$. Then $C^*(\overline{\gamma}\hat{\beta}) = C^*\hat{\alpha}$ so $C^*\overline{\gamma} = C^*\overline{\gamma}C^*\hat{\beta}(C^*\hat{\beta})^{-1} = C^*\hat{\alpha}(C^*\hat{\beta})^{-1} = C^*\hat{\gamma}$. Now by faithfulness of $\langle V^*, C^*\rangle$ we conclude that $\overline{\gamma} = \hat{\gamma}$. $\square$

However, a view update may be propagatable for a view with a complement, but there may not be a constant complement.

Example 6. A complement C_1 for the view V_1 of the (keyed) assignments database from Example 3 is provided by the inclusion of the sketch $\mathbb{C}_1$ whose graph is:

$$
\begin{array}{ccccc}
\text{Person} & \xrightarrow{\;d\;} & \text{Dept} & & \text{Proj} \\
{\scriptstyle n}\downarrow & & {\scriptstyle k_D}\downarrow & & {\scriptstyle k_P}\downarrow \\
\text{Name} & & K_D & & K_P
\end{array}
$$

We saw in Example 4 that the insertion of an assignment with a new project value in a state of $\mathbb{V}_1$ can be propagatable. However, such an insertion α cannot have a C_1-constant update—its value at the entity Proj must change. Furthermore Proj must play a part in any complement, so this example shows not just that C_1 is not constant, but that no complement can be constant.   ◇

Even more, a view may have all of its updates propagatable, but have no constant complement updates at all.

Example 7. Suppose that an EA sketch $\mathbb{E}$ is specified completely by commutative square with P the vertex of a cone to the right side and bottom edges (a pullback diagram):

$$
\begin{array}{ccc}
P & \xrightarrow{\;b'\;} & \text{Suppliers} \\
\downarrow & & \downarrow {\scriptstyle \text{basedat}} \\
1 & \xrightarrow[\text{Pisa}]{} & \text{Locations}
\end{array}
$$

Suppose that $\mathbb{V}$ is the EA sketch with one node P, and that V is the obvious inclusion. No choice of view complement $C : \mathbb{C} \longrightarrow Q(\mathbb{E})$ whose image is contained in $\mathbb{E}$, but which does not contain P, can provide a complement for V. To see this notice first that P specifies an inverse image (it is really a simple selection of Suppliers where based at equals Pisa). Any complement of V must contain at least the nodes Suppliers and Locations and the edge based at. If any of these is not present in a view C then $\langle V^*, C^* \rangle$ fails to be injective on objects. On the other hand, if $\mathbb{C}$ contains all of them then $\langle V^*, C^* \rangle$ is injective on objects and faithful, but it fails to be full. Indeed, for states M and M', the only arrows $\langle h, k \rangle : \langle V^*M, C^*M \rangle \longrightarrow \langle V^*M', C^*M' \rangle$ in the image of $\langle V^*, C^* \rangle$ are those where h is the induced map between inverse image values at P.   ◇

This example is important since the view V has been shown [9] to be updatable universally. Indeed all inserts and deletes are propagatable for V. Even more, they are all reversible. We will show below in Theorem 3 that if a V has C-constant updates then it also has (even reversible) universal updatability, but this example shows that implication has no converse. If we modify the previous example by requiring that keys exist for P, Suppliers and Location, then the view which consists of P and its key does have a complement.

A desirable property of view updates is to be "reversible". For a view deletion this means that it is propagatable, and that the propagated deletion is also universal for the view insert which undoes the deletion. Formally,

Definition 12. *Let $V : \mathbb{V} \longrightarrow Q(\mathbb{E})$ be a view and $\alpha : R \twoheadrightarrow V^*M$ a propagatable deletion in $\mathrm{Mod}(\mathbb{V})$. We say that α is reversible if its cartesian arrow $\hat{\alpha} : \alpha M \longrightarrow M$ is also opcartesian. Similarly, a propagatable insertion is reversible if its opcartesian arrow is also cartesian.*

Note the requirement that a deletion must be propagatable to be considered reversible. This is because talking about reversibility depends upon having chosen an update strategy—we need to know how to propagate view updates in order to determine whether there is a view update whose propagation will undo a given update. Since we have already seen that the universal update strategy is more general than the constant complement update strategy, we base this definition on the former to provide the greatest generality. First we give an example showing that universal updatability does not guarantee reversibility.

Example 8. Consider the sketch $\mathbb{E}$ consisting of a single edge $\alpha : A \longrightarrow B$. For the two views V_A and V_B which respectively include the single node A and the single node B, it is the case that all deletes and inserts are propagatable. This is easy to see directly since V_A^* and V_B^* simply select the domain and codomain of a function (model), and it also follows from the well known fact that V_A^* and V_B^* are both left and right fibrations.

On the other hand, neither deletes nor inserts are reversible for V_A^*. Indeed, for a model, that is a function, say $f : X \longrightarrow Y$, let $V_A^* f$ be the insertion $X \rightarrowtail X + X'$. The propagated insertion is given by the model morphism from f to $f + X'$ while the propagated deletion for $X \rightarrowtail X + X' = V_A^*(f + X')$ is the (different) model morphism from jf to $f + X'$ where $j : Y \longrightarrow Y + X'$ is the injection. A similar argument shows that deletes are not reversible for V_A^*. For the case of V_B^* deletes may or may not be reversible, but it turns out that inserts are.   ◇

Next we show that deletions with updates that are constant in a complement are also reversible.

Theorem 3. *Let $V : \mathbb{V} \longrightarrow Q(\mathbb{E})$ and $C : \mathbb{C} \longrightarrow Q(\mathbb{E})$ be complementary views. If $\alpha : R \rightarrowtail V^*M$ is a deletion in $\mathrm{Mod}(\mathbb{V})$ with a C-constant update, then it is reversible. Furthermore, if V has C-constant updates , then any deletion $\alpha : R \rightarrowtail V^*M$ is reversible.*

The proof uses techniques very similar to those in Theorem 1. Lechtenbörger [10] showed that, in the context of [1] a constant complement translator implies reversibility of view updates. In that context reversibility for a set of updates means that there is an update that will undo any view update. Our definition of reversibility concerns a single propagatable update, but is similar to Lechtenbörger's.

4   Related Work and Conclusions

The article of Bancilhon and Spyratos [1] remains influential. They treat a database as an arbitrary set S, meant to specify its states, and consider a view to be an arbitrary surjective mapping $f : S \longrightarrow V$. They obtain a "translator under constant complement" i.e. a function $g : S \longrightarrow C$ so that $\langle f, g \rangle$ is bijective, corresponding to our *complement*, and a translation for which $gT_u = g$, corresponding to our *constant*. The approach of Bancilhon and Spyratos has been elucidated by Bohannon et al [4]. They show that the set of translators under constant complement (for a view) corresponds to the set of "very well behaved lenses". A lens is a (partial) view $f : C \longrightarrow A$ and a (partial) function $p : A \times C \longrightarrow C$ satisfying suitable axioms. On a database state and an *updated* view state the function p determines a database state—the updated database state for the updated view state. While it is easy to interpret a surjective mapping as a view substitution like the V^* above, the complements of [1] and [10] are projections to quotient sets. As Lechtenbörger [10] writes: "it is unexplored how such a view could be represented in SQL".

Closer to the spirit of the present work, Hegner [6] considers an ordered set D of database states. He defines a view to be a surjective monotone mapping $\gamma : D \twoheadrightarrow V$ to an ordered set V of view states such that γ reflects the order. For Hegner a "closed update family" is an order-compatible equivalence relation on the view poset. This means that related view states may be updated to one another, symmetry expressing reversibility of view updates and transitivity that they may be composed. Hegner defines an "update strategy" to be a function $V \times D \longrightarrow D$ satisfying certain axioms. It is very much like a lens, and an equivalence relation determined by the update strategy is the lifted closed update family.

We have seen that the existence of a constant complement view is sufficient to guarantee well-behaved view updatability (propagatability) and reversibility in the context of the sketch data model, but that it is by no means necessary. Either of these desirable properties may hold without complements being possible.

The work presented here has been driven by the need, motivated by industrial applications, to have definitions of view, complement, propagation, etc, which better integrate with the actual representations of databases. We have tried to move away from the idea of database states as an unstructured set, and to accurately capture the (mathematical) structures that database states bear. In addition, the theoretical operations which we develop on database states need to respect those structures.

The difference between the results presented here and those of Lechtenbörger is worth some reflection. At first sight they may appear contradictory: Lechtenbörger showed that reversibility implied the existence of a constant complement, a very appealing co-occurrence, while we showed that updates can be reversible even when no constant complement can exist. The difference of course lies in the definition of constant complement—when one requires views, and hence complements, to arise as databases with data derived from the original database (Definition 7), the extra structure limits the available views, eliminating some of the quotient views that provide some of Lechtenbörger's complements. We must emphasize that we see these limitations as positive, limiting us as they do to properly respect the actual structure of database states. Another noteworthy difference is that most earlier work studied complete sets of updates and single updates that could be applied to every possible database state (they were endofunctions on the set of database states). In contrast we have been studying the propagatability of individual insert or delete updates acting on a given state. This permits a more general treatment since we can study (universal) updates of particular states. We are currently exploring how individual universal updates can be collected into structures corresponding to complete sets of updates so that we can further compare the new results with earlier work.

References

1. Bancilhon, F., Spyratos, N.: Update semantics of relational views. ACM Trans. Database Syst. 6, 557–575 (1981)
2. Barr, M., Wells, C.: Category theory for computing science, 2nd edn. Prentice-Hall, Englewood Cliffs (1995)
3. Barr, M., Wells, C.: Toposes, Triples and Theories. Grundlehren Math. Wiss. 278 (1985)
4. Bohannon, A., Pierce, B., Vaughan, J.: Relational Lenses: A language for updatable views. In: Proceedings of ACM PODS 2006 (2006)
5. Dayal, U., Bernstein, P.A.: On the correct translation of update operations on relational views. ACM TODS 7, 381–416 (1982)
6. Hegner, S.J.: An order-based theory of updates for closed database views. Annals of Mathematics and Artificial Intelligence 40, 63–125 (2004)
7. Johnson, M., Rosebrugh, R.: View updatability based on the models of a formal specification. In: Oliveira, J.N., Zave, P. (eds.) FME 2001. LNCS, vol. 2021, pp. 534–549. Springer, Heidelberg (2001)
8. Johnson, M., Rosebrugh, R., Wood, R.J.: Entity-relationship-attribute designs and sketches. Theory and Applications of Categories 10, 94–112 (2002)
9. Johnson, M., Rosebrugh, R.: Fibrations and universal view updatability. Theoretical Computer Science (in press, 2007)
10. Lechtenbörger, J.: The impact of the constant complement approach towards view updating. In: Proceedings of ACM PODS 2003, pp. 49–55 (2003)
11. Rosebrugh, R., Fletcher, R., Ranieri, V., Green, K.: EASIK: An EA-Sketch Implementation Kit, http://www.mta.ca/~rrosebru
12. Shipman, D.: The functional data model and the data language DAPLEX. ACM Trans. Database Syst. 6, 140–173 (1981)

Coinductive Properties of Causal Maps

Jiho Kim

Department of Mathematics
Indiana University
Bloomington, IN 47405
jihokim@indiana.edu

Abstract. Variants of causal functions on streams are defined, and the interplay between them is studied from different perspectives with attention to coalgebraic considerations. We prove that the sets of causal and bicausal functions, respectively, are closed under a certain natural coinductive construction. This closure property paves the way to constructing new final stream coalgebras over finite alphabets. This result is used to show that the 2-adic version of the Collatz function yields a final bit-stream coalgebra.

1 Introduction

The notion of streams is a basic yet fruitful beginning to the theory of coalgebras. The ubiquity of sequences in computational and mathematical disciplines makes them natural objects to investigate, and streams of various types have already been extensively studied in coalgebraic terms. For example, Jan Rutten has developed a certain calculus on streams over real numbers and bits [7,8].

The coinductive nature of streams make them useful for the study of dynamical systems. As analytical calculus was created to observe and explain the continuous dynamics of planetary bodies, coinductive calculus has had some success in capturing discrete, state-based transition systems such as automata. The coalgebraic study of the rationality of the streams leads to applications in automata theory. Automata theory to a large extent is a study of certain sets (of languages) and operations defined on them. For example, the closure of regular languages under complementation, union, concatenation and the Kleene star is a celebrated result from automata theory. In the coalgebraic treatment of Mealy automata [3,7], the set of causal functions Γ plays an analogous role to that of the set of regular languages in classical automata theory in as much as it captures the long-term behavior of Mealy automata.

The set Γ is of particular interest because it is the state space of a final Mealy automata [8]. When a Mealy automaton M with input and output in sets A and B, respectively, is encoded as a $(B \times -)^A$-coalgebra, there exists a unique morphism from M into Γ. Building on variants of causal functions, this paper proves a certain coinductive closure property on Γ and a related subset Γ_{bi} of bicausal functions.

J. Meseguer and G. Roşu (Eds.): AMAST 2008, LNCS 5140, pp. 253–267, 2008.
© Springer-Verlag Berlin Heidelberg 2008

We apply this theory to see that a well-known phenomenon observed about the Collatz function extended to the 2-adic integers—which we will denote T— is essentially coinductive. In particular, map $\mathbb{Z}_2 \xrightarrow{\langle h, T \rangle} 2 \times \mathbb{Z}_2$ is a final stream coalgebra.

2   Streams

Let $\omega = \{0, 1, 2, 3, \ldots\}$ be the set of natural numbers, and let $\mathcal{A}$ be a fixed alphabet set. Then, $\mathcal{A}^\omega = \{\omega \xrightarrow{\sigma} \mathcal{A}\}$ is the set of all $\mathcal{A}$-streams (i.e. infinite $\mathcal{A}$-sequences). We will use variations of ρ, σ and τ to denote streams. For a stream σ, we call $\sigma(n)$ the nth *component of* σ.

We can define three basic stream functions of the following types:

$$\mathcal{A}^\omega \xrightarrow{h} \mathcal{A} \qquad\qquad \mathcal{A}^\omega \xrightarrow{t} \mathcal{A}^\omega \qquad\qquad \mathcal{A} \times \mathcal{A}^\omega \xrightarrow{c} \mathcal{A}^\omega$$

The functions h, t, and c are given by the following equations:

$$h(\sigma) = \sigma(0) \qquad t(\sigma)(n) = \sigma(n+1) \qquad c(\alpha, \sigma)(n) = \begin{cases} \alpha & \text{if } n = 0 \\ \sigma(n-1) & \text{if } n > 0 \end{cases}$$

for $\sigma \in \mathcal{A}^\omega$, $\alpha \in \mathcal{A}$, and $n \in \omega$. The head function h yields the first component in the stream, while the tail function t produces the stream where the first component has been removed. Conversely, given an element α in $\mathcal{A}$ and an $\mathcal{A}$-stream σ, the constructor function c creates a stream where α is the first component and σ is the tail. Note that the pair $\langle h, t \rangle \colon \mathcal{A}^\omega \to \mathcal{A} \times \mathcal{A}^\omega$ and $c \colon \mathcal{A} \times \mathcal{A}^\omega \to \mathcal{A}^\omega$ are inverses, i.e. $\sigma = c(h(\sigma), t(\sigma))$.

When it is necessary, these function names will be decorated with the alphabet (e.g. $h^{\mathcal{A}}$, $t^{\mathcal{A}}$, $c^{\mathcal{A}}$) to distinguish them from those derived from a different alphabet. Also, because it is visually useful to denote $c(\alpha, \sigma)$ as $\alpha{:}\sigma$, we will adhere to this infix convention throughout when referring to the application of the function c. Moreover, we extend the use of this notation to prepending any finite word to a stream. For a word $w \in \mathcal{A}^n$ and a stream $\sigma \in \mathcal{A}^\omega$, we let $w{:}\sigma$ be the obvious stream where the first n components form w, and the rest is σ. We also define particular restrictions of the constructor function c. For any fixed $\alpha \in \mathcal{A}$, let $c_\alpha \colon \mathcal{A}^\omega \to \mathcal{A}^\omega$ be given by $c_\alpha(\sigma) = \alpha{:}\sigma$.

Setting $\mathcal{A} = 2$ (where $2 = \{0, 1\}$) yields the simplest example of streams. The set 2^ω of so-called bit-streams appears in many contexts—computational complexity, algorithmic randomness, and number theory, to name a few. It also can appear as an idealization of physical models such as in cryptography, coding theory, data-compression, and telecommunication and networks.

In the realm of number theory, 2^ω appears as the underlying set of the commutative ring $\mathbb{Z}_2$ of *2-adic integers* [4]. Bit-streams encode a type of number which admits addition and multiplication operations, much like a (finite) two's complement representation of an integer. In fact, it is entirely appropriate to view $\mathbb{Z}_2$ as an infinite-precision implementation of two's complement arithmetic.

Indeed any nonnegative integer can be thought of as a 2-adic integer by padding its binary representation with 0's. For example, $5_2 = 101\bar{0}$ and $12_2 = 0011\bar{0}$. The 2-adic representation has the LSB (i.e. least significant bit) first, and when appropriate, $\bar{w}$ represents the infinite repetition of the word w for the rest of the stream. Negative integers can be represented as a 2-adic by using the heuristics of complementing each component and adding 1 (e.g. $-5_2 = 110\bar{1}$ and $-12_2 = 0010\bar{1}$). Addition and multiplication are performed with the usual two's complement algorithm including carry.

$$12_2 + (-5_2) = 0011\bar{0} + 1101\bar{1} = 1110\bar{0} = 7_2.$$

Of course, there are 2-adic integers such as $1\bar{1}\bar{0}$, which do not correspond to conventional integers. It is easy to check

$$3 \cdot 1\overline{10} = 1\overline{10} + 1\overline{10} + 1\overline{10} = 1\bar{0} = 1_2.$$

This computation illustrates the fact that $1\overline{10}$ is a 2-adic representation for $\frac{1}{3}$. In fact, any 2-adic integer with the least significant bit of 1 has a multiplicative inverse.

The four bit-stream operations—h, t, and c_0, and c_1—have natural 2-adic parallels. These will be useful for developing examples.

$$h(x) = \mathsf{LSB}(x) \qquad\qquad c_0(x) = 2x$$

$$t(x) = \begin{cases} \frac{x}{2} & \text{if } h(x) = 0 \\ \frac{x-1}{2} & \text{if } h(x) = 1 \end{cases} \qquad\qquad c_1(x) = 2x + 1$$

The tail function t is often known as the shift map in the dynamical systems literature.

Causal Maps

The results in this paper address properties of stream operators that preserve prefix equivalence to a certain extent. This section is devoted to defining and developing some intuition for these functions.

Definition 1 (Prefix Equivalence). *For a fixed set A and for any $\sigma, \tau \in A^\omega$ and $n \geq 1$, we say the two streams σ and τ are n-prefix-equivalent, denoted $\sigma \equiv \tau \pmod{A^n}$, if $\sigma(i) = \tau(i)$ for $0 \leq i < n$.[1]*

We will later make heavy use of the following obvious consequences of the definition of prefix equivalence.

Lemma 1. *For $\sigma, \tau \in A^\omega$,*

1. *$\sigma \equiv \tau \pmod{A}$ if and only if $h(\sigma) = h(\tau)$.*
2. *$\sigma = \tau$ if and only if $\sigma \equiv \tau \pmod{A^n}$ for all $n \geq 1$.*
3. *If $\sigma \equiv \tau \pmod{A^n}$, then $\sigma \equiv \tau \pmod{A^k}$ for any $k \leq n$.*

We can now introduce the main subjects of our study.

---

[1] Admittedly, the notation for prefix-equivalence is not the most economical. For the sake of harmony with existing literature—for the $3x + 1$ Problem (Section 4.2), in particular—we adopt this heavier, ring-theoretic idiom.

Definition 2. *Let A and B be sets, and let $f: A^\omega \to B^\omega$ be a function. The function f is* causal *if for all $n \geq 1$ and $\sigma, \tau \in A^\omega$,*

$$\sigma \equiv \tau \pmod{A^n} \quad \Longrightarrow \quad f(\sigma) \equiv f(\tau) \pmod{B^n}.$$

The function f is bicausal *if for all $n \geq 1$ and $\sigma, \tau \in A^\omega$,*

$$\sigma \equiv \tau \pmod{A^n} \quad \Longleftrightarrow \quad f(\sigma) \equiv f(\tau) \pmod{B^n}.$$

The function f is supercausal *if for all $n \geq 1$ and $\sigma, \tau \in A^\omega$,*

$$\sigma \equiv \tau \pmod{A^n} \quad \Longrightarrow \quad f(\sigma) \equiv f(\tau) \pmod{B^{n+1}}.$$

The function f is subcausal *if for all $n \geq 1$ and $\sigma, \tau \in A^\omega$,*

$$\sigma \equiv \tau \pmod{A^{n+1}} \quad \Longrightarrow \quad f(\sigma) \equiv f(\tau) \pmod{B^n}.$$

Intuitively, causal functions determine the n-prefix of the image given the n-prefix of a stream. The n-prefix of an image under a bicausal function also can determine the n-prefix of the preimage. Supercausal functions determine the $(n + 1)$-prefix of the image given only the n-prefix. Subcausal functions require the $(n+1)$-prefix to determine the n-prefix of the image. To gain some familiarity with these definitions, consider the following examples.

1. Bicausal maps and supercausal maps are causal. Causal maps are subcausal.
2. The identity function $\mathrm{id}_{A^\omega}: A^\omega \to A^\omega$ is certainly bicausal. Also, for any $\tau \in B^\omega$ the constant function $K_\tau: A^\omega \to B^\omega$, given by $K_\tau(\sigma) = \tau$ for all $\sigma \in A^\omega$, is causal.
3. The tail function $A^\omega \xrightarrow{t} A^\omega$ is subcausal but is not causal.
4. For any $\alpha \in A$, the map c_α is supercausal.
5. If a bicausal map is bijective, then its inverse is also bicausal.

In terms of arithmetic on 2-adics integers, we can see that addition by any constant is causal. It is easy to check that the first (i.e. least significant) n bits of the summands determine the first n bits of the sum. Further, for any two causal functions $S, T: \mathbb{Z}_2 \to \mathbb{Z}_2$, the function $U: \mathbb{Z}_2 \to \mathbb{Z}_2$ given by $U(x) = S(x) + T(x)$ is also causal.

Causal functions are exactly those which preserve prefix equivalence for every prefix length. First let us consider how to construct such maps. One way to produce a causal function is to map each symbol in the source alphabet to another in the target alphabet. In addition, for each component of the stream, one may have a different mapping between the alphabets. In fact, functions produced in this fashion are *more than* causal, since each component of the output stream is determined by a single component of the input. To be more precise, given a sequence of maps $\mathcal{E} = \{A \xrightarrow{e_n} B\}_{n \geq 0}$, let $\Pi_{\mathcal{E}}: A^\omega \to B^\omega$ be the map given by

$$\Pi_{\mathcal{E}}(\sigma)(i) = e_i(\sigma(i)). \tag{1}$$

$\Pi_{\mathcal{E}}$ is causal since it acts on each component of a stream independently. If e_n is also one-to-one for all $n \in \omega$, then $\Pi_{\mathcal{E}}$ is bicausal.

Another (more general) way to produce causal functions is the following. Given a sequence of maps $\mathcal{F} = \{A^{n+1} \xrightarrow{f_n} B\}_{n \geq 0}$, let $\Omega_{\mathcal{F}} \colon A^{\omega} \to B^{\omega}$ be a map given by

$$\Omega_{\mathcal{F}}(\sigma)(i) = f_i(\sigma(0), \ldots, \sigma(i)). \tag{2}$$

$\Omega_{\mathcal{F}}$ is causal since each f_n is a function. Another way to look at $\mathcal{F}$ is to think of it as a map f from finite non-empty A-strings to B (i.e. $f \colon A^+ \to B$). Any causal function can originate from this example, where for $n \geq 0$, each $(n+1)$-prefix in the source determines the nth component of the target stream.

Lemma 2. *Concerning the composition of causal functions.*

1. *If $S \colon A^{\omega} \to B^{\omega}$ and $T \colon B^{\omega} \to C^{\omega}$ are both (bi)causal, then $T \circ S$ is (bi)causal. Consequently, if $U \colon A^{\omega} \to A^{\omega}$ is (bi)causal, then U^n is also (bi)causal for $n \geq 1$.*
2. *If $S \colon A^{\omega} \to B^{\omega}$ is causal and $T \colon C^{\omega} \to D^{\omega}$ is supercausal (resp. subcausal), then $T \circ S$ and $S \circ T$ are supercausal (resp. subcausal), whenever the composition makes sense.*
3. *If $S \colon A^{\omega} \to B^{\omega}$ is supercausal and $T \colon B^{\omega} \to C^{\omega}$ is subcausal, then $T \circ S$ is causal.*

If the premise of last statement were altered so that S is subcausal and T is supercausal, then there is no guarantee that $T \circ S$ is causal. Consider the map $d \colon A^{\omega} \to A^{\omega}$, given by $d(\sigma) = h(\sigma){:}\sigma$. The map d prepends a duplicate of the first component of a stream onto itself. We can see that d is supercausal and t is subcausal, but the map $d \circ t$ is not causal. The function d does not recover from the loss of the first component caused by t. In spite of this counterexample, for any subcausal function $S \colon A^{\omega} \to B^{\omega}$ and $\beta \in B$, the composition $c_\beta \circ S$ is causal.

We can also observe that bicausal functions are not necessarily bijections. For example, consider the map $\Pi_{\mathcal{S}} \colon \mathbb{N}^{\omega} \to \mathbb{N}^{\omega}$ where $\mathcal{S} = \{\lambda x.(x+1)\}_{n \geq 1}$ is an $\mathbb{N}$-indexed set. Essentially, $\Pi_{\mathcal{S}}$ maps an $\mathbb{N}$-stream to a stream where each component has been incremented by 1. It is easy to see that $\Pi_{\mathcal{S}}$ is not onto though it is bicausal. Although bicausal functions are not surjective in general, bicausal functions are necessarily injective.

Conversely, one might consider the question of whether causal bijections are necessarily bicausal. Again, we can exhibit a counterexample. Let $\ell \colon \mathbb{N}^{\omega} \to \mathbb{N}^{\omega}$ be given by

$$\ell(\sigma) = \begin{cases} 0{:}[h(\sigma) + 2 \cdot h(t(\sigma))]{:}t^2(\sigma) & \text{if } h(\sigma) = 0 \text{ or } h(\sigma) = 1 \\ [h(\sigma) - 1]{:}t(\sigma) & \text{if } h(\sigma) \geq 2 \end{cases}$$

Here, ℓ is causal and bijective but not bicausal. The function ℓ uses the fact that the there is an injection from $2 \times \mathbb{N}$ into $\mathbb{N}$. The underlying alphabet A and B for the domain and codomain, respectively, are infinite in these examples. In the case where A and B have the same finite cardinality, a causal function is bicausal if and only if it is bijective, as shown later in Lemma 5.

3   Subcausal and Causal Functions

3.1   Subcausal Functions Are Woven from Causal Functions

Subcausal functions were defined in the previous section as functions which are almost causal. To be more precise, subcausal functions map streams with a common $(n+1)$-prefix to streams with a common n-prefix. The following lemma illustrates some simple properties of iterated subcausal functions.

Lemma 3. *Let* $T\colon A^\omega \to A^\omega$ *be a subcausal function. For all* n *and* k *such that* $1 \leq k \leq n$, *if* $\sigma \equiv \tau \pmod{A^{n+1}}$, *then* $T^k(\sigma) \equiv T^k(\tau) \pmod{A^{n+1-k}}$. *If we fix* $k = n$, *then for all* $n \geq 1$, *if* $\sigma \equiv \tau \pmod{A^{n+1}}$, *then* $T^n(\sigma) \equiv T^n(\tau) \pmod{A}$.

There is a somewhat more roundabout way to characterize subcausal functions, which we discuss presently.

Definition 3. *Let* $f\colon A \times A^\omega \to B^\omega$ *be any function. Let* $T_f\colon A^\omega \to B^\omega$ *be the map given by* $T_f = f \circ \langle h, t \rangle$. *We call* T_f *the* map woven from f.

From another perspective, we can think of $f\colon A \times A^\omega \to B^\omega$ as an A-indexed family of stream functions $\{A^\omega \xrightarrow{f_\alpha} B^\omega\}_{\alpha \in A}$ where each $f_\alpha(\sigma) = f(\alpha, \sigma)$. This correspondence is bijective and serves to illumine the choice of terminology. We could have alternatively defined T_f, the *map woven from* f, by cases:

$$T_f(\sigma) = f_{h(\sigma)}(t(\sigma)) \tag{3}$$

For an example, suppose $A = \{0, 1, 2\}$. Then this perspective yields the definition:

$$T_f(\sigma) = \begin{cases} f_0(t(\sigma)) & \text{if } h(\sigma) = 0 \\ f_1(t(\sigma)) & \text{if } h(\sigma) = 1 \\ f_2(t(\sigma)) & \text{if } h(\sigma) = 2 \end{cases}$$

This definition by cases incorporates several stream functions and creates a new one. In light of this perspective, we can re-characterize the notion of subcausal functions.

Theorem 1. *A function* $T\colon A^\omega \to B^\omega$ *is subcausal if and only if it is woven from a family of causal maps.*

Proof. First suppose that T is woven from an A-indexed family of causal maps $\{A^\omega \xrightarrow{f_\alpha} B^\omega\}$. Further suppose $\sigma \equiv \tau \pmod{A^{n+1}}$. In particular, $h(\sigma) = h(\tau)$, and consequently, $f_{h(\sigma)} = f_{h(\tau)}$. Also, $t(\sigma) \equiv t(\tau) \pmod{A^n}$ because t is subcausal. Since f_α is causal for each $\alpha \in A$, we have $f_{h(\sigma)}(t(\sigma)) \equiv f_{h(\tau)}(t(\tau))$ $\pmod{B^n}$, i.e. $T(\sigma) \equiv T(\tau) \pmod{B^n}$.

Conversely, suppose T is subcausal. Then for $\alpha \in A$, let $f_\alpha\colon A^\omega \to B^\omega$ be given by $f_\alpha(\sigma) = T(\alpha{:}\sigma) = T(c_\alpha(\sigma))$. Since each c_α is supercausal and T is subcausal, f_α is causal. Let $f\colon A \times A^\omega \to A^\omega$ be given by $f(\alpha, \sigma) = f_\alpha(\sigma)$. Then for all $\sigma \in A^\omega$,

$$T_f(\sigma) = f_{h(\sigma)}(t(\sigma)) = T(h(\sigma){:}t(\sigma)) = T(\sigma).$$

Therefore, $T = T_f$ is woven from a family of causal functions.

3.2   Causal Functions Are Inverse Limits of Solenoidal Systems

Generalizing some ideas from Bernstein and Lagarias [2], we arrive at an alternative characterization for causal functions. The property of stream functions, which has until now been expressed in terms of preserving prefixes, can be framed in category-theoretic language. The generality of the category-theoretic approach suggests ways to extend the notion of causal functions. In this section, however, we will use the new characterization to analyze when bicausal functions are bijective.

For each $n \geq 1$, let $\pi_n^A \colon A^n \to A^{n-1}$ given by $\pi_n^A(w)(i) = w(i)$ for $w \in A^n$ and $0 \leq i < n-1$. Given a finite string $w \in A^n$ of length n, the function π_n^A produces the (unique) $(n-1)$-prefix of w. For the sake of notational sanity, we will drop the superscripted A decoration on π_n^A and any similar notation whenever possible.

Definition 4. *A family of functions* $\{A^n \xrightarrow{U_n} B^n\}_{n=0}^{\infty}$ *is called a* solenoidal system *if* $U_{n-1} \circ \pi_n = \pi_n \circ U_n$ *for all* $n \geq 1$.

A solenoidal system $\{A^n \xrightarrow{U_n} B^n\}_{n=0}^{\infty}$ can be depicted in the following commuting diagram.

$$
\begin{array}{ccccccccccc}
A^0 & \xleftarrow{\pi_1} & A^1 & \xleftarrow{\pi_2} & A^2 & \xleftarrow{\pi_3} & \cdots & \xleftarrow{\pi_{n-1}} & A^{n-1} & \xleftarrow{\pi_n} & A^n & \longleftarrow & \cdots \\
\downarrow{\scriptstyle U_0} & & \downarrow{\scriptstyle U_1} & & \downarrow{\scriptstyle U_2} & & & & \downarrow{\scriptstyle U_{n-1}} & & \downarrow{\scriptstyle U_n} & & \\
B^0 & \xleftarrow{\pi_1} & B^1 & \xleftarrow{\pi_2} & B^2 & \xleftarrow{\pi_3} & \cdots & \xleftarrow{\pi_{n-1}} & B^{n-1} & \xleftarrow{\pi_n} & B^n & \longleftarrow & \cdots
\end{array}
\tag{4}
$$

Definition 5. *An* (inverse) limit *of such a solenoidal system is a function* $U \colon Z_A \to Z_B$ *along with functions* $p_i^A \colon Z_A \to A^i$ *and* $p_i^B \colon Z_B \to B^i$, *for each* i, *so that*

1. *The following diagram commutes for each* $n \geq 1$.

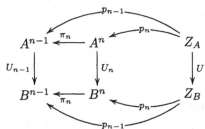

2. *If there is some other function* $V \colon Y_A \to Y_B$ *along with functions* $q_i^A \colon Y_A \to A^i$ *and* $q_i^B \colon Y_B \to B^i$, *for each* i, *so that the diagram*

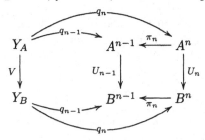

commutes for all $n \geq 1$, then there is a unique pair of functions $r^A \colon Y_A \to Z_A$ and $r^B \colon Y_B \to Z_B$ so that the following diagram commutes for all $n \geq 1$.

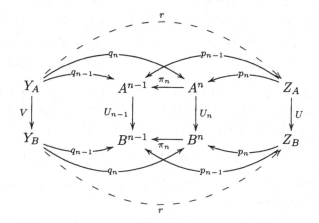

Technically, an inverse limit is only unique up to isomorphisms, but for the sake of clarity, given a solenoidal system, we fix *the* inverse limit to be the map $U \colon A^\omega \to B^\omega$ in the following way. First, fix $\delta_n^A \colon A^\omega \to A^n$ and $\delta_n^B \colon B^\omega \to B^n$ given by

$$\delta_n(\sigma)(i) = \sigma(i) \tag{5}$$

for $0 \leq i < n$. Intuitively, δ_n yields an n-prefix of a given stream. Note that the δ_n's are fixed independent of any solenoidal system. Let $\mathcal{U} = \{U_n\}$ be a solenoidal system. Then, let U be the function given by

$$U(\sigma)(n) = U_{n+1}(\delta_{n+1}(\sigma))(n). \tag{6}$$

Because $\mathcal{U}$ is a solenoidal system, the subscripted index of U_* and δ_* in (6) can be any integer greater than n. Consequently, U can then be shown to be the inverse limit of $\mathcal{U}$ (with $p_n = \delta_n$) via some diagram chasing that we omit. The important things to keep in mind are that for all $n \geq 1$,

1. $\delta_n \circ U = U_n \circ \delta_n$ and $\pi_n \circ \delta_n = \delta_{n-1}$
2. δ_n was chosen so that $\sigma \equiv \tau \pmod{A^n}$ if and only if $\delta_n(\sigma) = \delta_n(\tau)$.

Definition 6. *A function $U \colon A^\omega \to B^\omega$ is solenoidal if it is the inverse limit of a solenoidal system.*

Theorem 2. *A function $V \colon A^\omega \to B^\omega$ is causal if and only if it is solenoidal.*

Proof. Suppose $V \colon A^\omega \to B^\omega$ is causal. Then let $\mathcal{U} = \{U_n\}$ where

$$U_n(w) = \delta_n \circ V(w \colon \rho) \tag{7}$$

for $w \in A^n$ and $\rho \in A^\omega$. This definition is independent of the choice of $\rho \in A^\omega$, since V is causal. Let $U \colon A^\omega \to B^\omega$ be the inverse limit of $\mathcal{U}$. For any $\sigma \in A^\omega$ we need to show that $V(\sigma)(n) = U(\sigma)(n)$ for all n.

Observing that $\delta_k(\sigma){:}t^k(\sigma) = \sigma$ for all $k \geq 1$, we have

$$
\begin{aligned}
U(\sigma)(n) &= U_{n+1}(\delta_{n+1}(\sigma))(n) && \text{[def. of } U, \text{ (6)]}\\
&= \delta_{n+1}(V[\delta_{n+1}(\sigma){:}t^{n+1}(\sigma)])(n) && \text{[def. of } U_{n+1}, \text{ (7)]}\\
&= \delta_{n+1}(V(\sigma))(n) && [\delta_k(\sigma){:}t^k(\sigma) = \sigma \text{ for } k \geq 1]\\
&= V(\sigma)(n) && \text{[def. of } \delta_{n+1}, \text{ (5)]}
\end{aligned}
$$

This shows that $V(\sigma) = U(\sigma)$ for all $\sigma \in A^\omega$, and therefore that V is solenoidal.

Conversely, suppose V is solenoidal with a solenoidal system $\mathcal{V} = \{V_n\}$. Let $\sigma, \tau \in A^\omega$ be such that $\sigma \equiv \tau \pmod{A^n}$. Then, $\delta_n(\sigma) = \delta_n(\tau)$, and

$$
\delta_n(V(\sigma)) = V_n(\delta_n(\sigma)) = V_n(\delta_n(\tau)) = \delta_n(V(\tau))
$$

Therefore $V(\sigma) \equiv V(\tau) \pmod{B^n}$. Since σ and τ were arbitrarily chosen, this shows that V is indeed causal.

When the δ_n's were fixed previously, they essentially fixed the notion of the *unique* inverse limit of a solenoidal system. Conversely, the solenoidal system defined by (7) in this proof is then the unique solenoidal system that has U as the (unique) inverse limit. Therefore, there is a one-to-one correspondence between solenoidal (i.e. causal) functions and the solenoidal systems which yield them.

If we restrict to the case where the alphabet A is finite, we can say a little bit more.

Lemma 4. *Let A be a finite set. A casual function $U\colon A^\omega \to A^\omega$ is bijective if and only if its solenoidal system consists of bijections.*

Proof. Let $U\colon A^\omega \to A^\omega$ be a causal function and let $\mathcal{U} = \{U_n\}$ be its solenoidal system. First suppose each U_n is a bijection. Then $\mathcal{V} = \{U_n^{-1}\}$ is a solenoidal system and has an inverse limit $V\colon A^\omega \to A^\omega$. By appealing to the uniqueness of the inverse limit of $\{\mathrm{id}_{A^n} = U_n \circ U_n^{-1} = U_n^{-1} \circ U_n\}_{n\geq 0}$, we have $U \circ V = V \circ U = \mathrm{id}_{A^\omega}$, i.e. U is a bijection.

Conversely, assume that U is a causal bijection with a solenoidal system $\mathcal{U} = \{U_n\}$. Let $w \in A^n$ and $\tau \in A^\omega$. Then

$$
U_n(\delta_n(U^{-1}(w{:}\tau))) = \delta_n(U(U^{-1}(w{:}\tau))) = \delta_n(w{:}\tau) = w.
$$

Therefore $U_n\colon A^n \to A^n$ is a surjection. Since the domain and codomain of U_n are the same finite set, U_n is also injective.

Lemma 5. *Let A be a finite set, and let $U\colon A^\omega \to A^\omega$ be a causal function. Then, U is bijective if and only if U is bicausal.*

Proof. For this proof, let $U\colon A^\omega \to A^\omega$ be a causal function, and let $\mathcal{U} = \{U_n\colon A^n \to A^n\}$ be its solenoidal system.

First suppose U is a bijection. Then each U_n is a bijection. Take the solenoidal system $\mathcal{V} = \{U_n^{-1}\}$, consisting of the inverses. Since inverses of bijections are still bijections, there is a causal bijection V which has $\mathcal{V}$ as a solenoidal system. Moreover, $V = U^{-1}$. This proves that U is bicausal.

Conversely, suppose U is bicausal. Then for $v, w \in A^n$, if $U_n(v) = U_n(w)$, then $\delta_n(U(v{:}\rho)) = \delta_n(U(w{:}\rho))$ for any $\rho \in A^\omega$, i.e. $U(v{:}\rho) \equiv U(w{:}\rho) \pmod{A^n}$. Since U is bicausal, $v{:}\rho \equiv w{:}\rho \pmod{A^n}$, or equivalently, $v = w$. This shows that $U_n\colon A^n \to A^n$ is injective for each $n \geq 1$. Since A^n is finite, U_n is also surjective. By Lemma 4, U is bijective.

As an example, consider the following simple result.

Lemma 6. *The 2-adic map* $x \mapsto 3x + 2$ *is bicausal.*

Proof. Observe that $c_0\colon x \mapsto 2x$, id$\colon x \mapsto x$ and the constant map $x \mapsto 2$ are all causal. Therefore, $x \mapsto 3x + 2$ is causal since $3x + 2 = 2x + x + 2$. To see that it is a bijection, it suffices to note that $\mathbb{Z}_2$ is a ring and 3 (i.e. $11\bar{0}$) is invertible in $\mathbb{Z}_2$, which was verified earlier. Since $x \mapsto 3x + 2$ is a causal bijection on a stream over a finite alphabet, it is also bicausal by Lemma 5.

In this proof, we only used the fact that 3 is a unit in $\mathbb{Z}_2$. Any odd 2-adic integer (in $2\mathbb{Z}_2 + 1$) is invertible, so in fact the map $x \mapsto ax + b$ is bicausal for any $a \in 2\mathbb{Z}_2 + 1$ and $b \in \mathbb{Z}_2$.

4   Stream Coalgebra and Coinduction

There are many places where the theory of coalgebras (and stream coalgebras in particular) is presented in extensive detail [7,9], so we will omit most of the development. Suffice it to say that for a fixed set B, a *B-stream coalgebra* is simply a map of the type $X \to B \times X$, where X is some arbitrary set. A B-stream morphism from $(X \xrightarrow{\langle a,b \rangle} B \times X)$ to $(Y \xrightarrow{\langle a',b' \rangle} B \times Y)$ is a function $X \xrightarrow{f} Y$ so that

$$
\begin{array}{ccc}
X & \xrightarrow{\langle a,b \rangle} & B \times X \\
{\scriptstyle f}\downarrow & & \downarrow{\scriptstyle \mathrm{id}_B \times f} \\
Y & \xrightarrow{\langle a',b' \rangle} & B \times Y
\end{array}
$$

commutes, i.e. $(\mathrm{id}_B \times f) \circ \langle a, b \rangle = \langle a', b' \rangle \circ f$. The class of B-stream coalgebras forms a category with terminal objects which we call *final (B-stream) coalgebras*.

The canonical example of a final B-stream coalgebra is the map $B^\omega \xrightarrow{\langle h,t \rangle} B \times B^\omega$. Finality in this category can be stated in the following way. Given any B-stream coalgebra, $X \xrightarrow{\langle h',t' \rangle} B \times X$, there exists a unique map $\Phi\colon X \to B^\omega$ so that the diagram

$$
\begin{array}{ccc}
X & \xrightarrow{\langle h',t' \rangle} & B \times X \\
{\scriptstyle \Phi}\downarrow & & \downarrow{\scriptstyle \mathrm{id}_B \times \Phi} \\
B^\omega & \xrightarrow{\langle h,t \rangle} & B \times B^\omega
\end{array}
\qquad (8)
$$

commutes, i.e. $h' = h \circ \Phi$ and $t \circ \Phi = \Phi \circ t'$. Finality induces a map Φ into the final coalgebra. The map Φ here is the *coalgebra morphism coinductively induced by* $\langle h', t' \rangle$.

Note that even if $X = B^\omega$, a coinductively induced coalgebra morphism is not necessarily causal. To see this, consider a coalgebra morphism Ψ coinductively induced by $A^\omega \xrightarrow{\langle h, t^2 \rangle} A \times A^\omega$. It can be checked that $\Psi(\sigma)(n) = \sigma(2n)$ for all n. Ψ is not causal since a $2n$-prefix only determines n components of the output. The following are some results concerning some sufficient conditions for the coinductively induced coalgebra morphism to be causal.

Theorem 3. *Let* $T \colon A^\omega \to A^\omega$ *be woven from a family of causal functions, and let* $H \colon A^\omega \to B$ *be a function such that*

$$\sigma \equiv \tau \pmod{A} \qquad \Longleftrightarrow \qquad H(\sigma) = H(\tau), \tag{9}$$

for all $\sigma, \tau \in A^\omega$. *Let* $A^\omega \xrightarrow{\varphi} B^\omega$ *be the (unique) coalgebra homomorphism induced by the coalgebra* $A^\omega \xrightarrow{\langle H, T \rangle} B \times A^\omega$. *Then,* φ *is causal.*

Proof. Since φ is coinductively induced by $\langle H, T \rangle$, the commutative diagram (8) provides the equations $h \circ \varphi = H$ and $t \circ \varphi = \varphi \circ T$. More generally, $t^n \circ \varphi = \varphi \circ T^n$ for all $n \geq 1$.

The proof proceeds by induction. The base case is given as the hypothesis in (9).

$$
\begin{aligned}
\sigma \equiv \tau \pmod{A} \quad &\Leftrightarrow \quad H(\sigma) = H(\tau) && \text{[hyp., (9)]} \\
&\Leftrightarrow \quad h(\varphi(\sigma)) = h(\varphi(\tau)) && \text{[(8)]} \\
&\Leftrightarrow \quad \varphi(\sigma) \equiv \varphi(\tau) \pmod{B} && \text{[Lemma 1]}
\end{aligned}
$$

Now assume for some $n \geq 1$ that if $\hat{\sigma} \equiv \hat{\tau} \pmod{A^n}$, then $\varphi(\hat{\sigma}) \equiv \varphi(\hat{\tau})$ $\pmod{B^n}$. And suppose further that $\sigma \equiv \tau \pmod{A^{n+1}}$. This means in particular that $\sigma \equiv \tau \pmod{A^n}$, and by the induction hypothesis, $\varphi(\sigma) \equiv \varphi(\tau)$ $\pmod{B^n}$. Therefore, one only needs to show that $\varphi(\sigma)(n) = \varphi(\tau)(n)$.

The function T is subcausal by Theorem 1. Further, by Lemma 3, we see that $T^n(\sigma) \equiv T^n(\tau) \pmod{A}$, or equivalently, $H(T^n(\sigma)) = H(T^n(\tau))$ via the hypothesis given as (9).

We proceed:

$$
\begin{aligned}
\varphi(\sigma)(n) &= h(t^n(\varphi(\sigma))) && \text{[def.]} \\
&= h(\varphi(T^n(\sigma))) && [t^n \circ \varphi = \varphi \circ T^n] \\
&= H(T^n(\sigma)) && [h \circ \varphi = H] \\
&= H(T^n(\tau)) && \text{[Lemma 3, (9)]} \\
&= h(\varphi(T^n(\tau))) = h(t^n(\varphi(\tau))) = \varphi(\tau)(n)
\end{aligned}
$$

Therefore, $\varphi(\sigma) \equiv \varphi(\tau) \pmod{B^{n+1}}$, and this completes the induction.

By taking $B = A$ and $H = h^A$, we can immediately derive the following corollary.

Corollary 1. *Let* $T\colon A^\omega \to A^\omega$ *be a function. Let* $\varphi\colon A^\omega \to A^\omega$ *be the (unique) coalgebra homomorphism induced by the coalgebra* $A^\omega \xrightarrow{\langle h,T\rangle} A \times A^\omega$. *If* T *is woven from a family of causal functions, then* φ *is causal.*

Next, consider the similar situation where the induced homomorphism is bi-causal. In this case, we can also prove the converse.

Theorem 4. *Let* $T\colon A^\omega \to B^\omega$ *be a function, and let* $H\colon A^\omega \to B$ *be a map such that*

$$\sigma \equiv \tau \pmod{A} \quad \Longleftrightarrow \quad H(\sigma) = H(\tau), \tag{10}$$

for all $\sigma, \tau \in A^\omega$. *Let* $\varphi\colon A^\omega \to B^\omega$ *be the (unique) coalgebra homomorphism induced by the coalgebra* $A^\omega \xrightarrow{\langle H,T\rangle} B \times A^\omega$. *Then* φ *is a bicausal function if and only if* T *is woven from a family of bicausal functions.*

Proof. First we consider the "if" direction. Suppose T is woven from a family of bicausal functions $\{f_\alpha\}$. In light of Theorem 3, we only need to show that φ is "co-causal," i.e. for all $n \geq 1$, if $\varphi(\sigma) \equiv \varphi(\tau) \pmod{B^n}$, then $\sigma \equiv \tau \pmod{A^n}$. The proof proceeds by induction.

The base case is the same as the argument in Lemma 3 which relies on the given biconditional (10). Assume for some $n \geq 1$, for all $\hat{\sigma}, \hat{\tau} \in A^\omega$, that if $\varphi(\hat{\sigma}) \equiv \varphi(\hat{\tau}) \pmod{B^n}$, then $\hat{\sigma} \equiv \hat{\tau} \pmod{A^n}$. Also suppose for some $\sigma, \tau \in A^\omega$ that $\varphi(\sigma) \equiv \varphi(\tau) \pmod{B^{n+1}}$. In particular, $\varphi(\sigma) \equiv \varphi(\tau) \pmod{B}$, which implies that $\sigma \equiv \tau \pmod{A}$, via the base case. With Lemma 1, we conclude that the head of σ and τ coincide. Let $\alpha = h(\sigma) = h(\tau)$. Then,

$\varphi(\sigma) \equiv \varphi(\tau) \pmod{B^{n+1}}$

$\Rightarrow t(\varphi(\sigma)) \equiv t(\varphi(\tau)) \pmod{B^n}$ [t subcausal]

$\Leftrightarrow \varphi(T(\sigma)) \equiv \varphi(T(\tau)) \pmod{B^n}$ [$t \circ \varphi = \varphi \circ T$]

$\Rightarrow T(\sigma) \equiv T(\tau) \pmod{A^n}$ [induction hypothesis]

$\Leftrightarrow f_\alpha(t(\sigma)) \equiv f_\alpha(t(\tau)) \pmod{A^n}$ [def. of T]

$\Leftrightarrow t(\sigma) \equiv t(\tau) \pmod{A^n}$ [f_α is bicausal]

$\Leftrightarrow \alpha{:}t(\sigma) \equiv \alpha{:}t(\tau) \pmod{A^{n+1}}$ [c_α is supercausal]

$\Leftrightarrow \sigma \equiv \tau \pmod{A^{n+1}}$ [$\alpha = h(\sigma) = h(\tau)$; Lemma 1]

This concludes the induction.

Next consider the "only if" direction. Suppose that φ is bicausal. In addition, suppose that $\sigma \equiv \tau \pmod{A^{n+1}}$. Then,

$\sigma \equiv \tau \pmod{A^{n+1}}$ $\Leftrightarrow \varphi(\sigma) \equiv \varphi(\tau) \pmod{B^{n+1}}$ [φ is bicausal]

$\Rightarrow t(\varphi(\sigma)) \equiv t(\varphi(\tau)) \pmod{B^n}$ [t is subcausal]

$\Leftrightarrow \varphi \circ T(\sigma) \equiv \varphi \circ T(\tau) \pmod{B^n}$ [$t \circ \varphi = \varphi \circ T$]

$\Leftrightarrow T(\sigma) \equiv T(\tau) \pmod{A^n}$ [φ is bicausal]

This shows that T is subcausal, and therefore woven from a set Ξ of causal functions (via Theorem 1).

Recall from the proof of Theorem 1, that each causal function f_α in Ξ is given by $f_\alpha(\sigma) = T(\alpha{:}\sigma)$. Then,

$$f_\alpha(\sigma) \equiv f_\alpha(\tau) \pmod{A^n}$$
$$\begin{array}{llll}
\Leftrightarrow & T(\alpha{:}\sigma) \equiv T(\alpha{:}\tau) \pmod{A^n} & [\text{def. of } f_\alpha \in \Xi] \\
\Leftrightarrow & \varphi(T(\alpha{:}\sigma)) \equiv \varphi(T(\alpha{:}\tau)) \pmod{B^n} & [\varphi \text{ bicausal}] \\
\Leftrightarrow & t(\varphi(\alpha{:}\sigma)) \equiv t(\varphi(\alpha{:}\tau)) \pmod{B^n} & [t \circ \varphi = \varphi \circ T] \\
\Leftrightarrow & \varphi(\alpha{:}\sigma) \equiv \varphi(\alpha{:}\tau) \pmod{B^{n+1}} & [h(\varphi(\alpha{:}\sigma)) = h(\varphi(\alpha{:}\tau))] \\
\Leftrightarrow & \alpha{:}\sigma \equiv \alpha{:}\tau \pmod{A^{n+1}} & [\varphi \text{ bicausal}] \\
\Leftrightarrow & \sigma \equiv \tau \pmod{A^n} & [t \text{ subcausal}]
\end{array}$$

Therefore all the causal functions in Ξ are in fact bicausal.

Bernstein and Lagarias ([2], Appendix B) prove a variant of Theorem 4 for the case where $A = B = \{0, 1\}$, using the equivalence of bicausal functions and causal bijections. The result herein identifies the central role of bicausal functions and uses coinductive methods to handle the more general case.

As before, by taking $B = A$ and $H = h^A$, we can get the following corollary.

Corollary 2. *Let $T \colon A^\omega \to A^\omega$ be a function. Let $\varphi \colon A^\omega \to A^\omega$ be the (unique) coalgebra homomorphism induced by the coalgebra $A^\omega \xrightarrow{\langle h, T \rangle} A \times A^\omega$. Then φ is bicausal function if and only if T is woven from a family of bicausal functions.*

4.1   Coinductive Closure Property

Both Corollaries 1 and 2 can be viewed as a coinductive closure property on the set of (bi)causal functions. Let $\Gamma = \{f \colon A^\omega \to A^\omega \mid f \text{ is causal}\}$ and $\Gamma_{\mathrm{bi}} = \{f \colon A^\omega \to A^\omega \mid f \text{ is bicausal}\}$. Given an A-indexed subset $\{f_\alpha\}$ of Γ (or Γ_{bi}) we can construct a new (bi)causal function. Let $T \colon A^\omega \to A^\omega$ be woven from $\{f_\alpha\}$, i.e. $T(\sigma) = f_{h(\sigma)}(t(\sigma))$. The corollaries guarantee that the coalgebra morphism induced by $\langle h, T \rangle$ is (bi)causal. This construction gives a different way to specify causal functions in addition to the $\Pi_\mathcal{E}$ (1) and $\Omega_\mathcal{F}$ (2) constructions presented earlier.

The ability to construct new bicausal functions opens up an avenue toward producing stream coalgebra isomorphisms as long as the alphabet is finite. Fix A to be a finite set, and let $\{f_\alpha\} \subseteq \Gamma_{\mathrm{bi}}$ be an A-indexed family of bicausal functions. Let $S \colon A^\omega \to A^\omega$ be woven from $\{f_\alpha\}$. By Corollary 2, the coalgebra homomorphism ψ induced by $\langle h, S \rangle$ is bicausal.

$$\begin{array}{ccc}
A^\omega & \xrightarrow{\langle h, S \rangle} & A \times A^\omega \\
\psi \downarrow & & \downarrow \mathrm{id}_A \times \psi \\
A^\omega & \xrightarrow[\langle h, t \rangle]{} & A \times A^\omega
\end{array}$$

By Lemma 5, ψ is a bijection, and it can be checked that bijective coalgebra homomorphisms are isomorphisms [9]. Therefore, the coalgebra $A^\omega \xrightarrow{\langle h,S \rangle} A \times A^\omega$ is isomorphic to the canonical final coalgebra $A^\omega \xrightarrow{\langle h,t \rangle} A \times A^\omega$. In other words, $\langle h, S \rangle$ is itself a final stream coalgebra. Depending on the choice of bicausal functions in $\{f_\alpha\}$, one can produce many different final stream coalgebras using this construction.

4.2   3x + 1 Conjugacy Map

The inspiration of this paper came from a particular analysis of the $3x + 1$ Problem [2]. The unsettled conjecture is simply stated in terms of the Collatz function $C \colon \mathbb{N} \to \mathbb{N}$ given by

$$C(x) = \begin{cases} \frac{x}{2} & \text{if } x \equiv 0 \pmod 2 \\ \frac{3x+1}{2} & \text{if } x \equiv 1 \pmod 2 \end{cases} \tag{11}$$

The conjecture states that for all $n \geq 1$ there exists a k so that $C^k(n) = 1$. At this point, the $3x + 1$ Problem is still open [1,5,6].

The extension of the Collatz function to the 2-adic map $T \colon \mathbb{Z}_2 \to \mathbb{Z}_2$ is woven from two maps, $x \mapsto x$ and $x \mapsto 3x + 2$.

$$T(x) = \begin{cases} t(x) & \text{if } x \equiv 0 \pmod 2 \\ 3t(x) + 2 & \text{if } x \equiv 1 \pmod 2 \end{cases} \tag{12}$$

The observations that $t(x) = \frac{x}{2}$ and $3t(x) + 2 = \frac{3x+1}{2}$ shows that T is the 2-adic version of the Collatz function (11). Because T is woven from two bicausal maps, the coalgebra $\mathbb{Z}_2 \xrightarrow{\langle h,T \rangle} 2 \times \mathbb{Z}_2$ induces a coalgebra isomorphism $Q \colon \mathbb{Z}_2 \to 2^\omega$. Therefore, we can conclude:

Theorem 5. *Let $T \colon \mathbb{Z}_2 \to \mathbb{Z}_2$ be the extension of the Collatz function to the 2-adics. Then, the bit-stream coalgebra $\mathbb{Z}_2 \xrightarrow{\langle h,T \rangle} 2 \times \mathbb{Z}_2$ is (isomorphic to) a final bit-stream coalgebra.*

It is already well-known that T is topologically conjugate to the shift map, which in this paper is denoted t. That is to say, there exists a (homeomorphic) map $\Phi \colon \mathbb{Z}_2 \to \mathbb{Z}_2$ so that $t = \Phi^{-1} \circ T \circ \Phi$. Theorem 5 is very much related to topological conjugacy, but the coinductive approach in this paper is novel and gives a general way to produce such conjugacies without reference to the additional structures that the set of 2-adic integers often enjoys.

5   Discussion and Future Directions

Chronologically, this investigation began with the observation that the topological conjugacy of the 2-adic Collatz function T to the tail map t amounts to a stream coalgebra isomorphism. In particular, the finality of $\mathbb{Z}_2 \xrightarrow{\langle h,T \rangle} 2 \times \mathbb{Z}_2$ in the category of $(2 \times -)$-coalgebras (Theorem 5) is an interesting new fact in the field.

Looking to the future, the immediate question to raise is whether the new coinductive observation about the 2-adic Collatz function gives any insight into the conjecture itself. The principal difficulty has to do with the generality of this kind of approach [1]. The previous section shows that the conjugacy with the tail map is not a phenomenon limited to the Collatz function. Furthermore, the conjugacy comes from basic coinductive principles rather than algebraic, topological or measure-theoretic considerations. While the coinductive approach opens up another perspective into the $3x + 1$ Problem, whether it is ultimately useful in settling the conjecture remains to be seen.

In terms of the larger theory, other algebraic and coalgebraic properties of Γ and Γ_{bi} should be explored, especially in light of recent developments concerning Mealy automata [3,7]. We have shown that Γ and Γ_{bi} are both closed under composition and a certain coinductive construction. Moreover, Γ_{bi} is also closed under inverses when the alphabet is finite. It would be interesting to see whether the analogies between regular languages and causal functions can be made more explicit. In addition, given the category-theoretic perspective of causal functions as limits of a solenoidal systems, it may be possible to generalize the notion of causal functions to accommodate categories and endofunctors which encode more complicated infinite structures than streams.

Acknowledgment. I am very grateful for discussions with Jonathan Yazinski about the $3x + 1$ Problem which proved most inspirational.

References

1. Akin, E.: Why is the $3x + 1$ problem hard? In: Akin, E. (ed.) Chapel Hill Ergodic Theory Workshops, Contemp. Math. 356, Amer. Math. Soc., pp. 1–20 (2004)
2. Bernstein, D.J., Lagarias, J.C.: The $3x + 1$ Conjugacy Map. Can. J. Math. 48, 1154–1169 (1996)
3. Hansen, H.H., Costa, D., Rutten, J.J.M.M.: Synthesis of Mealy machines using derivatives. In: Proceedings of the 9th Workshop on Coalgebraic Methods in Computer Science (CMCS 2006), Vienna, Austria. ENTCS, vol. 164, pp. 27–45 (2006)
4. Koblitz, N.: p-adic Numbers, p-adic Analysis, and Zeta-Functions. Graduate Texts in Mathematics, vol. 58. Springer, Heidelberg (1977)
5. Lagarias, J.C., The 3x+1 problem: An annotated bibliography (1963–2000), http://www.arxiv.org/abs/math/0309224
6. Lagarias, J.C., The 3x+1 problem: An annotated bibliography (2000–), http://arxiv.org/abs/math/0608208
7. Rutten, J.J.M.M.: Algebraic specification and coalgebraic synthesis of Mealy automata. Electr. Notes Theor. Comput. Sci. 160, 305–319 (2006)
8. Rutten, J.J.M.M.: Behavioural differential equations: a coinductive calculus of streams, automata, and power series. Theor. Comput. Sci. 308, 1–53 (2003)
9. Rutten, J.J.M.M.: Universal Coalgebra: a Theory of Systems. Theor. Comput. Sci. 249, 3–80 (2000)

Extending Timed Process Algebra
with Discrete Stochastic Time

Jasen Markovski*,** and Erik P. de Vink

Formal Methods Group, Eindhoven University of Technology
Den Dolech 2, 5612 AZ Eindhoven, The Netherlands
j.markovski@tue.nl

Abstract. When extending timed process algebra with discrete stochastic time, typical standard notions like time additivity are hard to preserve in the presence of the race condition. We propose context-sensitive interpolation as a restricted form of time additivity to accommodate the extension with stochastic time. We also present a stochastic process algebra featuring an explicit account of two types of race conditions in terms of conditional random variables. The approach enables compositional modeling, a non-trivial expansion law, and explicit manipulation of maximal progress.

1   Introduction

Originally, process algebras focused on qualitative aspects of systems. Usually, the qualitative behavior is specified by using action prefix operators that give the dynamics of the system. The processes are combined using two basic operators: (1) alternative composition that provides the alternatives in a given situation/state and (2) parallel composition that enables the compositional modeling by allowing communication of action transitions.

Later, timed process algebras followed, which allowed for modeling and analysis of time features as well [1]. In this setting, action transitions are either immediate, i.e., they do not allow passage of time, or they are delayable, i.e., they allow arbitrary passage of time. Typically, time is introduced by means of a prefix for timed delay, which specifies the amount of time that passes before the remaining process is enabled or by means of time stamps, which record the time when the process starts. We focus on theories comprising timed delays, where the composition operators have to cater for the interaction between processes that allow and disallow passage of time.

To support the combined modeling of functionality and performance of a system in a compositional manner, stochastic process algebras emerged. First came the Markovian process algebras, like EMPA, PEPA, IMC, etc., which exploited the memoryless property of the exponential distribution. Later, prompted by the need for more accurate approximations, stochastic process algebras with general

---

* Corresponding author.
** This research has been funded by the Dutch BSIK/BRICKS project AFM 3.2.

J. Meseguer and G. Roşu (Eds.): AMAST 2008, LNCS 5140, pp. 268–283, 2008.

distribution were developed, like TIPP, GSMPA, SPADES, IGSMP, NMSPA, and MODEST [2,3,4,5,6,7]. They found their use, e.g., in modeling contemporary Internet protocols with real-time time-outs and communications governed by heavy-tail distributions of high variance. Stochastic time is commonly introduced by stochastic delay prefixes, often exploiting stochastic clocks. In this setting, the composition operators induce probabilistic choice, as passage of time imposes a race condition on the stochastic delays [8].

The transition from untimed process algebra to timed process algebras progressed by (conservatively) extending untimed theories with temporal capabilities. However, in turn, stochastic process theories did not simply replace timed delays by stochastic delays or clocks. It is argued that the main reason for this lies in the nature of the stochastic time and the underlying performance models. Stochastic time usually imposes a probabilistic choice in the form of a race condition on the stochastic delays, different from the typical merging of timed delays. The performance models are generally a type of Markov process, which does not conform to the semantics of the standard timed delays. It proved very difficult to support the characteristic features of the timed process theories, like time additivity and time determinism [1]. Therefore, stochastic process theories were developed from scratch, and afterwards, it was shown that timed process theories can be embedded in some form as well. For example, in the setting of SPADES, [9] gives a structural translation from stochastic automata to timed automata with deadlines that preserves timed traces and enables embedding of real-time. This approach has found its way into the MODEST formalism and associated toolset [7]. A translation from IGSMP into pure real-time models called interactive timed automata is reported in [5].

In this paper, we approach the above issue both from the timed and stochastic points of view. We investigate what needs to be in place to generalize timed delays to stochastic ones. Therefore, we analyze stochastic bisimulation as well as the fit of real-time features, like time determinism and time additivity, in a stochastic-time setting. This leads us to the notion of *context-sensitive interpolation* on the side of the timed theories and the notion of *dependent race condition* on the stochastic side. The former can be viewed as an interpretation of the race condition in the timed setting, whereas the latter allows merging of name-dependent stochastic delays with the same sample. We benefit from our findings in the development of a stochastic process algebra that retains many features of the timed process theories, but permits a restricted form of time additivity only.

The present work builds on earlier investigations. A preliminary effort to embed real-time in stochastic process algebras was given in [10]. A subsequent study led to the notion of dependent and independent race conditions that paved the way for the treatment of the expansion law and the maximal progress in the vein of timed process theories [11]. Equational theory that captures both real-time and stochastic-time aspects in the context of complete races was presented in [12]. There a decomposition of a race into disjoint events is exploited to explicitly state the winners and the losers of the race. The passage of time is stated in terms of (probabilistic) unit timed delays in a racing context. In this

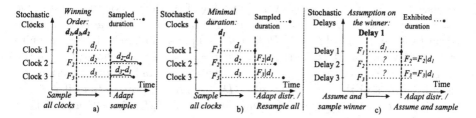

Fig. 1. a) Clocks with residual lifetimes, b) clocks with spent lifetimes, and c) stochastic delays with winning order. Aging of distribution F by time d is denoted by $F|d$.

setting, stochastic delays are expressed as (infinite) solutions of guarded recursive specifications.

The approach in the present paper is exactly the opposite and it reveals the other side of the same coin. Here, we treat timed and stochastic delays as 'atomic', rather than series of unit timed delays. This puts the timed delays on the same level with the stochastic ones as passage of time is studied in terms of discrete events, where the actual duration/sample of the delay plays a background role. We opt for discrete stochastic time to enable simultaneous expiration of multiple delays. The results should extend to continuous time for well-behaved measurable distributions [13]. The race condition remains the central notion in both settings. We only analyze process specifications that induce complete races with all possible outcomes. This simplifies matters of operational semantics and equational theory. Due to the substantial technical overhead, we focus here on the core issues and reduce technical detail to the bare minimum. The interested reader is referred to [14] for a more extensive explanation.

2 Race Conditions

In the absence of the memoryless property, stochastic delays are modeled using clocks. Clocks are set at the beginning of the delay, samples updated after each expiration. Clocks can keep track of the time that is left before expiration or the time that the clock has been active. The former technique [15] is depicted in Fig. 1a). It is argued to support discrete event simulation, but also considered unfair in the resolution of the race condition as the winners are known before the race is finished. The latter [2,3,5,6], depicted in Fig. 1b), has been advocated for its correspondence to standard time, as samples increase as time passes. An alternative, but equivalent approach, depicted in Fig. 1c), is to make a probabilistic assumption on the outcome of the race and, afterwards, to sample from the (joint) probability distribution of the winning clocks [16]. So, we do not keep track of clock lifetimes, but only the order in which they expire.

Preliminaries.   We use discrete random variables to represent durations of stochastic delays. The set of discrete distribution functions F such that $F(n)=0$ for $n \leq 0$ is denoted by $\mathcal{F}$; the set of the corresponding random variables by $\mathcal{V}$.

We use X, Y, and Z to range over $\mathcal{V}$ and F_X, F_Y and F_Z for their respective distribution functions. Also, W, L, V, and D range over $2^{\mathcal{V}}$. By assumption, the support set $\text{supp}(X) = \{ n > 0 \mid P(X = n) > 0 \}$ of a random variable X is finite or countably infinite. The domain of a function $f \colon A \to B$ is denoted by $\text{dom}(f)$. In case f is bijective, we write $f \colon A \leftrightarrow B$. We restrict and rename functions on disjoint subsets of the domain by $g\{f_1/D_1\} \ldots \{f_n/D_n\}(x) = f_i(x)$ if $x \in D_i$, and $g(x)$ if $x \in A \setminus (\bigcup_{i=1}^{n} D_i)$, for functions $g, f_1, \ldots, f_n \colon A \to B$ and disjoint subsets $D_1, \ldots, D_n \subseteq A$.

Racing delays.   A stochastic delay is a timed delay of a duration guided by a random variable. We use the random variable as the *name* of the stochastic delay. We observe simultaneous passage of time for a number of stochastic delays until one or some of them expire. This phenomenon is referred to as the *race condition* and the underlying process as the *race*. For multiple *racing stochastic delays*, different stochastic delays may be observed simultaneously as being the shortest. The ones that have the shortest sample are called *winners*, the others are referred to as *losers*. The *outcome* of a race is completely determined by the winners and the losers, and the set of all outcomes of a race forms a set of disjoint events. So, we can explicitly represent the outcome of the race by a pair of disjoint sets of stochastic delays $[^W_L]$, where W and L are the sets of winners and losers, respectively. We omit empty sets and set brackets when clear from the context. So, $[X]$ represents a stochastic delay guided by $X \in \mathcal{V}$.

Outcomes of races may be involved in other races. So, we refer to an outcome $[^W_L]$ as a (conditional) *stochastic delay* induced by the disjoint sets of winners W and losers L. The probability of the outcome $[^W_L]$ is

$$P(X_1 = X_2 \text{ for } X_1, X_2 \in W \text{ and } X_3 < Y \text{ for } X_3 \in W, Y \in L)$$

and the stochastic delay is guided by the conditional random variable

$$\langle X \mid X_1 = X_2 \text{ for } X_1, X_2 \in W \text{ and } X_3 < Y \text{ for } X_3 \in W, Y \in L \rangle$$

for any $X \in W$. Two stochastic delays $[^{W_1}_{L_1}]$ and $[^{W_2}_{L_2}]$ can form a joint outcome, if it is possible to consistently combine the winners and losers such that the resulting outcome has disjoint winners and losers. Therefore, we have to look at the relation between the winners and the losers. There are three possible combinations: (1) $L_1 \cap W_2 \neq \emptyset$, which means that the race is lost by $L_1 \cup W_2 \cup L_2$, (2) $W_1 \cap W_2 \neq \emptyset$, hence the race is won by $W_1 \cup W_2$, and (3) $W_1 \cap L_2 \neq \emptyset$, implying the race is lost by $W_1 \cup L_1 \cup L_2$. Obviously, these conditions are disjoint and cannot be applied together. For example, if (1) holds then the outcome is given by $[^{W_1}_{L_1 \cup W_2 \cup L_2}]$. If none of the restrictions hold, then there are three possible outcomes: $[^{W_1}_{L_1 \cup W_2 \cup L_2}]$, $[^{W_1 \cup W_2}_{L_1 \cup L_2}]$, and $[^{W_2}_{W_1 \cup L_1 \cup L_2}]$. If at least two restrictions apply, then the outcomes cannot be combined as they represent disjoint events. In this case we say for the delays $[^{W_1}_{L_1}]$ and $[^{W_2}_{L_2}]$, with $W_1 \cup L_1 = W_2 \cup L_2$, that the race is *resolved*. The extra condition ensures that the outcomes stem from the same race, i.e, they have the same racing delays. For example, $[^X_Y]$ and $[^Y_X{}^Z]$ cannot form a joint outcome, but they do not come from the same race, which renders their combination inconsistent.

Resolved races play an important role as they enumerate every possible outcome of the race. We define a predicate $\text{rr}([^{W_1}_{L_1}], [^{W_2}_{L_2}])$ that checks whether $[^{W_1}_{L_1}]$

and $\begin{bmatrix} W_2 \\ L_2 \end{bmatrix}$ are in a resolved race. It is satisfied if $W_1 \cup L_1 = W_2 \cup L_2$ and at least two of the following three conditions hold: (1) $L_1 \cap W_2 \neq \emptyset$, (2) $W_1 \cap W_2 \neq \emptyset$, and (3) $W_1 \cap L_2 \neq \emptyset$.

A discrete timed delay of duration n is denoted by σ^n. It expires after n units of time. Timed delays actually form a trivial race in which the shortest 'sample' is always exhibited by the same set of timed delays and always has a fixed duration. There are three possible disjoint outcomes of a race between timed delays, σ^m and σ^n, say: (1) if $m < n$ then σ^m wins, (2) if $m = n$ then they both win, and (3) if $m > n$ then σ^n wins. Now, it is clear that by replacing all timed delays with stochastic ones, instead of one outcome, one has potentially three possible outcomes of each race.

Timed and stochastic delay prefixes. By $\_.\_$ we denote the standard prefixing operation. To express a race, we use the alternative composition $\_ + \_$. So, the term $\sigma^m.p_1 + \sigma^n.p_2$ represents two processes in a race that are prefixed by timed delays of m and n time units, respectively. Suppose that $m < n$. Then this term is equivalent to $\sigma^m.(p_1 + \sigma^{n-m}.p_2)$, with p_1 and p_2 both prefixed by σ^m and, p_2 additionally prefixed by σ^{n-m}. The remaining two cases are $m = n$, with $\sigma^m.(p_1 + p_2)$, and $m > n$, with $\sigma^n.(\sigma^{m-n}.p_1 + p_2)$.

In the stochastic setting, we write $[X].p_1 + [Y].p_2$ for two processes in a race of the stochastic delays $[X]$ and $[Y]$. There are no restrictions in this race, so all outcomes are possible. There are three possible (disjoint) outcomes of this race yielding (1) $\begin{bmatrix} X \\ Y \end{bmatrix}$, (2) $\begin{bmatrix} X, Y \\ \emptyset \end{bmatrix}$, and (3) $\begin{bmatrix} Y \\ X \end{bmatrix}$. The probabilities for this outcomes are given by (1) $P(X < Y)$, (2) $P(X = Y)$, and (3) $P(Y < X)$, respectively. The passage of time is guided by the conditional random variables (1) $\langle X \mid X < Y \rangle$, (2) $\langle X \mid X = Y \rangle$, and (3) $\langle Y \mid Y < X \rangle$. In (1) the stochastic delay X expires, whereas Y becomes dependent on the amount of time that has passed for X. We represent this by the term $\begin{bmatrix} X \\ Y \end{bmatrix}.(p_1 + [Y].p_2)$, where both names Y refer to the same stochastic delay. The inner occurrence of Y, in $[Y]$, is bound by $\begin{bmatrix} X \\ Y \end{bmatrix}$ as time passes for both X and Y, according to the principle of time determinism [1,17]. In (2) the delays expire together as given by the term $\begin{bmatrix} X, Y \\ \emptyset \end{bmatrix}.(p_1 + p_2)$. In (3), symmetrical to (1), we have $\begin{bmatrix} Y \\ X \end{bmatrix}.([X].p_1 + p_2)$. We emphasize the similarity with standard-time semantics as discussed above.

Dependent and independent race condition. Consider the term $[X].p_1 \parallel [X].p_2$, where $\parallel$ denotes the parallel composition. We note that the alternative and the parallel composition impose the same race condition. Standardly, the race is performed on two stochastic delays with the same distribution $F_X \in \mathcal{F}$. However, both delays will not necessarily exhibit the same sample, unless F_X is Dirac. Intuitively, the above term is equivalent to $[X].p_1 \parallel [Y].p_2$ with $F_X = F_Y$ leading to the three possible outcomes.

However, in real-time semantics, timed delays with the same duration are merged together. For example, $\sigma^m.p_1 \parallel \sigma^m.p_2$ is equivalent to $\sigma^m.(p_1 \parallel p_2)$. This parallel composition represents components that should delay together. Note, this is not obtained above in the stochastic setting. Therefore, we introduced the notion of a *dependent race condition* in [11,12], in which stochastic delays with the same name exhibit the same sample. So, if a dependent race condition is imposed on the term $[X].p_1 \parallel [X].p_2$, it is equivalent to $[X].(p_1 \parallel p_2)$. However, the race may be independent as well (see Section 3 below).

We introduce a scope operator to specify dependent delay names, denoted by $|_{-}|_D$. The stochastic delays involved are those in D. They are treated as dependent. Thus, $| [{}^X_Y].p_1|_X$ denotes that X is a dependent stochastic delay and that Y is independent. By default, every delay is considered as dependent. Hence, $[{}^W_L].p$ is equivalent to $| [{}^W_L].p|_{W \cup L}$. Multiple scope operators intersect. E.g., $|| [{}^X_Y].p|_X|_Y$ denotes a process prefixed by the independent delay $[{}^X_Y]$ since $\{X\} \cap \{Y\} = \emptyset$. Coming back to our example, an independent race condition will be specified as $| [X].p_1|_\emptyset \parallel | [X].p_1|_\emptyset$; a dependent one as $[X].p_1 \parallel [X].p_2$. Additionally, (in)dependence on the winners can be specified as well. For example, in the term $[{}^X_Y].(| [Y].p_1|_\emptyset + [Y].p_2)$ the delay $[Y]$ in $| [Y].p_1|_\emptyset$ is not dependent on the passage of time for X, whereas the delay $[Y]$ occurring in $[Y].p_2$ is.

Bisimulation relations. Timed bisimulation requires that bisimilar processes delay the same amount of time. Typically, time additivity applies [1], i.e., merging of subsequent timed delays into a joint single delay with the same accumulative duration, to compare the delays. For example, $\sigma^3.\sigma^2.p$ and $\sigma^5.p$ are typically considered to be equivalent.

However, stochastic bisimulation is an atomic step bisimulation, i.e., it only considers one atomic stochastic delay transition at a time. To the best of our knowledge, with the exception of [18], all stochastic process theories consider stochastic bisimulation that is atomic in this sense: In [2], the actions are coupled with the stochastic clocks. In [4], there is an alternation between clocks and action transitions, whereas in [3,5] the merging is impeded by the combination of the pre-selection policy and start-termination semantics. Although originally introduced with atomic stochastic bisimulation [6], an effort is made in [18] to define a notion of weak stochastic bisimulation that merges subsequent stochastic delays. Unfortunately, such an approach is not compositional as the merging of stochastic delays does not support the race condition. A simple example illustrates this. Intuitively, the process $[X].[Y].p$ has the same stochastic properties as the process $[Z].p$ provided that $F_Z = F_{X+Y}$. However, standard compositions involving these processes may not be bisimilar. For example, $[X].[Y].p + [U].q$ is not bisimilar to $[Z].p + [U].q$, the latter not providing the interleaving point between $[X]$ and $[Y]$, which imposes different probabilistic behavior.

3   Context Sensitive Interpolation

Suppose we wish to extend the term $\sigma^2.\sigma^3.p$ with stochastic time. In view of time additivity, we may consider, e.g., the term $\sigma^5.p$ or even $\sigma^1.\sigma^3.\sigma^1.p$ as well. However, from the discussion in Section 2, it is clear that $[X_2].[X_3].p$ is different from $[X_5].p$ and $[X_1].[X_3].[X_1].p$, for any non-Dirac random variable $X_1, X_2, X_3, X_5 \in \mathcal{V}$, suitably chosen to represent the delays of duration 1, 2, 3, and 5, respectively. The race involving $[X_5]$ and $[X_2].[X_3]$ produces different probabilities and samples for the winning delays. A solution is to consider timed delays as atomic, i.e., to explicitly state the delay that we want model.

Extending timed delays with stochastic delays.   To manipulate atomic timed delays, a new, more restrictive notion of time additivity is required.

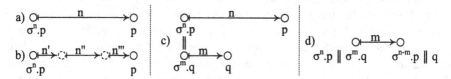

Fig. 2. a) A timed delay prefix $\sigma^n.p$, b) arbitrary interpolation of σ^n into $\sigma^{n'}, \sigma^{n''}$ and $\sigma^{n'''}$, c) parallel composition of $\sigma^n.p$ and $\sigma^m.q$, and d) context-sensitive interpolation of σ^n in the context of the parallel composition with $\sigma^m.q$

Fig. 2b) depicts arbitrary interpolation of the timed delay σ^n of the process $\sigma^n.p$ of Fig. 2a) to three timed delays $\sigma^{n'}, \sigma^{n''}$, and $\sigma^{n'''}$ satisfying $n' + n'' + n''' = n$. If interpreted as an atomic timed delay, the delay must be left intact, unless in a context of a composition that would induce a race. A race with another timed delay σ^m of the process $\sigma^m.q$ is depicted in Fig. 2c). Only then we can interpolate the longer delay (in this case $n > m$, as depicted in Fig. 2d), conforming to race condition semantics. We note that the resulting process $(\sigma^{n-m}.p) \parallel q$ performs the remaining delay σ^{n-m}.

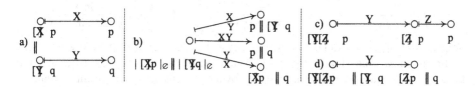

Fig. 3. a) Stochastic extension of the composition in Fig. 2c), b) independent race condition with every possible outcome, c) stochastic extension of $\sigma^n.p$ in accordance with Fig. 2d), and d) dependent race condition synchronizing the dependent delays

In stochastic time semantics, such behavior can be interpreted both for the independent or dependent race condition as depicted in Fig. 3. Suppose that the original timed delay σ^n is replaced by the stochastic delay $[X]$, obtaining $[X].p$ as depicted in Fig. 3a), and $\sigma^m.q$ is extended to $[Y].q$. In Fig. 3b), we consider an independent race given by the term $\mid [X].p\mid_\emptyset \parallel \mid [Y].q\mid_\emptyset$, which results in the three possible outcomes as discussed in Section 2. Here, we label the transitions with the winners on top and the losers below. This way independent components competing for the same resource can be modeled conveniently.

Now, suppose that the components are considered dependent regarding their timing aspects. For example, $\sigma^n.p$ is a controller that has a timeout greater than the response time of the process that it controls. This can be represented in the timed model as $\sigma^m.q$ and conditioned by the fact that $n > m$. In such a situation, the stochastic modeling using the independent race condition leads to undesirable behavior. For example, the premature expiration of the stochastic delay of the controller given by the outcome $[^X_Y]$ may introduce non-existent deadlock behavior as it did not wait for the result of the process that successfully finished its task. In this case, relying on the context-sensitive interpolation, the correct modeling of $\sigma^n.p$ would be $[Y].[Z].p$ as depicted in Fig. 3c). The idea is that both, the controller and the process, should synchronize on the dependent stochastic delay $[Y]$. The delay is followed by the short timeout $[Z]$ that models the extra timed delay σ^{n-m} in the context-sensitive interpolated representation $(\sigma^m.(\sigma^{n-m}.p) \parallel q)$ of $(\sigma^n.p) \parallel (\sigma^m.q)$. The situation is depicted in Fig. 3d).

Another way of modeling the above system is to explicitly state that the stochastic delay $[Y]$ should be the winner of the race between $[X]$ and $[Y]$. This is done by specifying $\sigma^m.q$ in stochastic time as $[^Y_X].q$. Such a specification expresses the result of the race between $[X]$ and $[Y]$. The parallel composition $[X].p \parallel [^Y_X].q$ is resolved as $[^Y_X].([X].p \parallel q)$. In this case, however, the race is incomplete, i.e., the other disjoint outcomes $[^{X}_{\emptyset}{}^{Y}]$ and $[^Y_X]$ are not present. A major consequence is that the equational theory of terms exhibiting incomplete races is more intricate as the alternative composition is no longer associative and one must rely on normal form representations [14].

Fingerprint of operational rules and axioms. From a process theoretical point of view, the fundamental properties of time are time determinism and time additivity [1,17]. They can be captured by the following operational rules.

$$(1) \; \frac{}{\sigma^n.p \stackrel{n}{\longmapsto} p} \qquad (2) \; \frac{p \stackrel{n}{\longmapsto} p'}{\sigma^m.p \stackrel{m+n}{\longmapsto} p'} \qquad (3) \; \frac{p_1 \stackrel{n}{\longmapsto} p_1', \; p_2 \stackrel{n}{\longmapsto} p_2'}{p_1 + p_2 \stackrel{n}{\longmapsto} p_1' + p_2'}.$$

When treating timed delays as atomic, rule 1 holds again, but rule 2 for time additivity now fails. Therefore, we add instead of rule 2, two new rules similar to rule 3 for time determinism that perform the context-sensitive interpolation when competing delays have different durations:

$$(4) \; \frac{p_1 \stackrel{m}{\longmapsto} p_1', \; p_2 \stackrel{n}{\longmapsto} p_2', m < n}{p_1 + p_2 \stackrel{m}{\longmapsto} p_1' + \sigma^{n-m}.p_2'} \qquad (5) \; \frac{p_1 \stackrel{m}{\longmapsto} p_1', \; p_2 \stackrel{n}{\longmapsto} p_2', m > n}{p_1 + p_2 \stackrel{n}{\longmapsto} \sigma^{m-n}.p_1' + p_2'}.$$

Note the emphasis on performing the shortest winning duration first. The rules 4 and 5 give rise to the following two axioms:

$$\sigma^m.p_1 + \sigma^m.p_2 = \sigma^m.(p_1 + p_2) \; \mathbf{A1} \qquad \sigma^m.p_1 + \sigma^{m+n}.p_2 = \sigma^m.(p_1 + \sigma^n.p_2) \; \mathbf{A2}.$$

Axiom A1 enables time determinism, whereas Axiom A2 replaces the standard axiom $\sigma^m.\sigma^n.p = \sigma^{m+n}.p$ for time additivity. Together with commutativity the latter allows for context-sensitive interpolation. If zero delays are allowed, then rule 3 and axiom A1 become obsolete. More details can be found in [19].

To summarize, at first sight context-sensitive interpolation may seem too restrictive, but it does exactly what time additivity is typically used for: merging of delays with the same duration by taking the shortest/minimal delay. Moreover, context-sensitive interpolation fits naturally in the expansion of the parallel composition, which makes it a suitable candidate for a finer notion of time additivity in real-time process algebras. We also note that the results can be directly extended to the continuous setting. Finally, the bisimulation relation remains unchanged as context-sensitive interpolation is handled in the operational semantics. However, it is noted that the resulting process equivalence is finer. For example, $\sigma^2.\sigma^3.p$ and $\sigma^5.p$ are no longer related, though $\sigma^2.\sigma^3.p$ and $\sigma^5.p+\sigma^2.\delta$ are, where δ represents the deadlock process constant obeying $p + \delta = p$.

We proceed by presenting a stochastic process theory that makes use of the concepts discussed above to deal with stochastic time as an extension of the real-time process theory. The gain lays in an expansion law that respects time determinism and the explicit treatment of the maximal progress.

4   The Stochastic Process Theory TCP^{dst}

We present the theory $\text{TCP}^{\text{dst}}(\mathcal{A}, \mathcal{V}, \gamma)$ of communicating processes with discrete stochastic time, where $\mathcal{A}$ denotes the set of actions, $\mathcal{V}$ is the set of stochastic delays, and γ is the action synchronization function extending ACP-style process algebras with discrete relative timing of [17]. The semantics is given in terms of *stochastic transition schemes* that, in essence, represent stochastic automata with symbolic explicit representation of the race condition. Here, we focus on the handling of the race condition, the expansion for the parallel composition and the maximal progress operator. We illustrate the process theory for *race-complete process specifications* that induce complete races only.

Environments and distributions of racing delays.   We use a construct, called an *environment*, to keep track of the dependencies of the racing delays. Recall, $\begin{bmatrix} W \\ L \end{bmatrix}$ denotes an outcome of a race that was won by W and lost by L, for $W, L \subseteq \mathcal{V}$. However, because of time determinism, time has passed equally for all racing delays in $W \cup L$. To denote that after a delay $\begin{bmatrix} W \\ L \end{bmatrix}$, the same time that passed for the winners W has also passed for the losers L, we use an environment $\alpha \colon \mathcal{V} \to 2^{\mathcal{V}}$. For each $X \in \mathcal{V}$, $\alpha(X)$ is a set that contains one representative of the winners of every race that X lost. One representative suffices, because all winners share the same sample in the winning race. If $\alpha(X) = \emptyset$, then X has never lost a race. We write $\mathcal{E}$ for the set of all environments.

For example, the process term $\begin{bmatrix} X \, Y \\ Z \end{bmatrix}.\begin{bmatrix} U \\ Z \end{bmatrix}.p$ has a stochastic delay transition in which X and Y are the winners and Z is the loser. In the resulting process $\begin{bmatrix} U \\ Z \end{bmatrix}.p$, the variable Z must be made dependent on the amount of time that has passed for X and Y before. This can be denoted either by $\alpha(Z) = \{X\}$ or $\alpha(Z) = \{Y\}$, assuming $\alpha(Z) = \emptyset$ initially. As Z again loses a race, this time to U, the transition induced by $\begin{bmatrix} U \\ Z \end{bmatrix}$ updates $\alpha(Z)$ to $\alpha(Z) = \{X, U\}$, provided X was chosen as a representative in the first race.

The environment does not affect the outgoing transitions. It is used to calculate the correct distribution of the racing delays. Suppose that $\text{s}(X)$ gives the exhibited sample for an expired delay X of a race. Then the racing delay Y in the environment α has participated in races that it lost with the total amount of time

$t(Y) = \sum_{X \in \alpha(Y)} (s(X) + t(X))$. By convention, $t(Y) = 0$ if $\alpha(Y) = \emptyset$. The distribution of Y, given $F_Y(t(Y)) < 1$, at that point in time is

$$F_Y(n) = \frac{F_Y(n + t(Y)) - F_Y(t(Y))}{1 - F_Y(t(Y))}.$$

Thus, in order to compute the updated distribution of a racing delay Y, one has to know its complete dependence history, i.e., the names of all delays that contribute in the derivation of $t(Y)$. The *dependence history* in an environment α of a set of racing delays R is defined by $H_\alpha(R) = R \cup \bigcup_{X \in R} (\alpha(X) \cup H_\alpha(\alpha(X)))$.

Stochastic transition schemes.   The semantics of process terms is given by stochastic transition schemes. A state s of the transition scheme in an environment α is given by the pair $\langle s, \alpha \rangle \in S \times \mathcal{E}$. The function $I(s)$ gives the set of independent delays of the state s. Every state may have a termination option, denoted by the predicate $\downarrow$. There are three types of transitions: (1) $\xrightarrow{a}$, immediate action transitions labeled by $a \in \mathcal{A}$, that do not allow passage of time and model undelayable action prefixes; (2) $\rightsquigarrow$, delay transitions that allow arbitrary passage of time; and (3) $\xrightarrow[L]{W}$, (resolved) stochastic delay transitions, driven by the winners W and the losers L, that model stochastic delay prefixes. The stochastic delay transitions must be well-defined: for every $u \xmapsto[L]{W} u'$, the set of winners W and the set of losers L are disjoint. Moreover, every two different transitions originating from the same state are in a resolved race. More precisely, if $u \xmapsto[L_1]{W_1} u_1 \neq u \xmapsto[L_2]{W_2} u_2$, then $rr([^{W_1}_{L_1}], [^{W_2}_{L_2}])$ holds, implying that $W_1 \cup L_1 = W_2 \cup L_2$. Thus, for every state s there exists a set of racing delays $R(s)$ satisfying $R(s) = W \cup L$ for every $\langle s, \alpha \rangle \xmapsto[L]{W} \langle s', \alpha' \rangle$. Then, the set of dependent delays is given by $D(s) = R(s) \setminus I(s)$.

Bisimulation.   We define a strong bisimulation relation on stochastic transition schemes. It requires stochastic delays to have the same dependence history modulo names of the independent delays. This ensures that the induced races have the same probabilistic behavior. As usual, bisimilar terms are required to have the same termination options, action and delay transitions [1,17].

A symmetric relation R on $S \times \mathcal{E}$ is a bisimulation if, for every two states u_1, u_2 such that $R(u_1, u_2)$, it holds that: (1) if $u_1 \downarrow$ then $u_2 \downarrow$; (2) if $u_1 \rightsquigarrow u_1'$ for some $u_1' \in S \times \mathcal{E}$, then $u_2 \rightsquigarrow u_2'$ for some $u_2' \in S \times \mathcal{E}$; (3) if $u_1 \xrightarrow{a} u_1'$ for some $u_1' \in S \times \mathcal{E}$, then $u_2 \xrightarrow{a} u_2'$ for some $u_2' \in S \times \mathcal{E}$; and (4) if $u_1 \xmapsto{W_1}_{L_1} u_1'$ for some $u_1' \in S \times \mathcal{E}$, then $u_2 \xmapsto{W_2}_{L_2} u_2'$ for some $u_2' \in S \times \mathcal{E}$. Moreover, u_1' and u_2' in (1)–(4) are again related by R. In (4) W_1 and L_1 differ from W_2 and L_2, respectively, only in the names of the independent racing delays, while comprising delays with the same distributions. Also, an additional condition is imposed to ensure that the dependence history of the losers of u_1 that are racing as dependent delays in u_1' is preserved in u_1' as well. Two states u_1 and u_2 are bisimilar if there exists a bisimulation relation R that relates them.

Signature.   The deadlocked process is denoted by δ; successful termination by ϵ. Undelayable and delayable action prefixes are unary operators $\underline{a}.\_$ and

Table 1. Some illustrative operational rules

(6) $\langle \underline{a}.p, \alpha \rangle \xrightarrow{a} \langle p, \alpha_{\emptyset} \rangle$ **(7)** $\langle a.p, \alpha \rangle \xrightarrow{a} \langle p, \alpha_{\emptyset} \rangle$ **(8)** $\langle a.p, \alpha \rangle \rightsquigarrow \langle a.p, \alpha \rangle$

(9) $\langle [{}^{W}_{L}].p, \alpha \rangle \xmapsto[L]{W} \langle |p|_{L}, \alpha_{\emptyset}\{\alpha'/H_{\alpha'}(L)\} \rangle,$
    with $\alpha' = \alpha\{(\alpha + W)/L\}$

(10) $\dfrac{\langle p, \alpha \rangle \xmapsto[L]{W} \langle p', \alpha' \rangle}{\langle |p|_{B}, \alpha \rangle \xmapsto[L]{W} \langle p', \alpha' \rangle}$

(11) $\dfrac{\langle p_1, \alpha \rangle \xmapsto[L_1]{W_1} \langle p'_1, \alpha_1 \rangle,\ \langle p_2, \alpha \rangle \nvdash, \nrightsquigarrow}{\langle p_1 + p_2, \alpha \rangle \xmapsto[L_1]{W_1} \langle p'_1, \alpha_1 \rangle}$

(12) $\dfrac{\langle p_1, \alpha \rangle \rightsquigarrow \langle p'_1, \alpha_1 \rangle,\ \langle p_2, \alpha \rangle \xmapsto[L_2]{W_2} \langle p'_2, \alpha_2 \rangle}{\langle p_1 + p_2, \alpha \rangle \xmapsto[L_2]{W_2} \langle p'_1 + p'_2, \alpha_2 \rangle}$

(13) $\dfrac{\langle p_1, \alpha \rangle \xmapsto[L_1]{W_1} \langle p'_1, \alpha_1 \rangle,\ \langle p_2, \alpha \rangle \xmapsto[L_2]{W_2} \langle p'_2, \alpha_2 \rangle,\ (W_1 \cup W_2) \cap (L_1 \cup L_2) = \emptyset}{\langle p_1 \parallel p_2, \alpha \rangle \xmapsto[L_1 \cup L_2]{W_1 \cup W_2} \langle p'_1 \parallel p'_2, \alpha_1\{\alpha_2/L_2\} \rangle}$

(14) $\dfrac{\langle p_1, \alpha \rangle \xmapsto[L_1]{W_1} \langle p'_1, \alpha_1 \rangle,\ \langle p_2, \alpha \rangle \xmapsto[L_2]{W_2} \langle p'_2, \alpha_2 \rangle,\ \mathrm{rr}([{}^{W_1}_{L_1}], [{}^{W_2}_{L_2}])}{\langle p_1 + p_2, \alpha \rangle \xmapsto[L_1]{W_1} \langle p'_1, \alpha_1 \rangle}$

$a._{\_}$, for every $a \in \mathcal{A}$. Similarly, a stochastic delay prefix is of the form $[{}^{W}_{L}]._{\_}$ for $W, L \subseteq \mathcal{V}$ disjoint, $W \neq \emptyset$. The dependence scope is given by $|_{\_}|_{D}$, for $D \subseteq \mathcal{V}$. The encapsulation operator $\partial_{H}(\_)$, for $H \subseteq \mathcal{A}$, suppresses the actions in H. The maximal progress operator $\theta_{H}(\_)$ gives priority to undelayable actions in H. The alternative composition is given by $\_ + \_$, at the same time representing a nondeterministic choice between actions and termination, a weak choice between action and passage of time, and imposing a race condition on the stochastic delays. The parallel composition is given by $\_ \parallel \_$. It allows passage of time only if both components do so. Recursion is introduced by guarded recursive specifications.

Structural operational semantics. The general idea of having both dependent and independent delays available is the following: For specification, one can use multiple instances of a component using independent delays. As the delays are independent, there is no need to worry about the actual samples. However, the racing delays in the stochastic transition schemes have unique names, whereas the process terms may exhibit naming conflicts. For example, the term $p = |[X].q|_{\emptyset} \parallel |[X].q|_{\emptyset}$ expresses a race between two components guided by independent delays with the same name. However, the stochastic delay transitions of $\langle p, \alpha \rangle$ comprise two racing delays with unique names, and equal distributions.

For p to have a proper semantics, the conflicting independent delays have to be detected and renamed, e.g., to $|[Y].q|_{\emptyset} \parallel |[X].q|_{\emptyset}$ where $F_{X} = F_{Y}$. For that purpose, we use $\mathrm{D}(p)$ and $\mathrm{I}(p)$ to extract dependent and independent racing delay names of the term p, respectively [14]. Then, the set of racing delay names is given by $\mathrm{R}(p) = \mathrm{D}(p) \cup \mathrm{I}(p)$. Now, p_1 and p_2 are not in conflict when composed, if $\mathrm{I}(p_1) \cap \mathrm{R}(p_2) = \mathrm{R}(p_1) \cap \mathrm{I}(p_2)$. We use α-conversion to enable dynamic renaming that resolves local conflicts in the vein of [15]. Intuitively, α-conversion enables renaming of independent delays without distorting the structure of the term, conforming to the bisimulation relation as stated below [14].

Table 2. Some illustrative axioms of the process theory TCP^{dst}

$$|\underline{a}.p|_{\emptyset} = \underline{a}.p \ \textbf{A3} \qquad \left[{}^W_L\right].p = \left[{}^W_L\right].|p|_L \ \textbf{A4} \qquad ||p|_{B_1}|_{B_2} = |p|_{B_1 \cap B_2} \ \textbf{A5}$$

$$|p_1 + p_2|_B = |p_1|_B + |p_2|_B \ \text{ if } \ \text{I}(|p_1|_B) \cap \text{R}(|p_2|_B) = \text{R}(|p_1|_B) \cap \text{I}(|p_2|_B) = \emptyset \ \textbf{A6}$$

$$a.p_1 + \left[{}^W_L\right].p_2 = a.p_1 + \left[{}^W_L\right].(a.p_1 + p_2) \ \textbf{A7}$$

$$\left[{}^{W_1}_{L_1}\right].p_1 + \left[{}^{W_2}_{L_2}\right].p_2 = \left[{}^{W_1}_{L_1 \cup W_2 \cup L_2}\right].(|p_1|_{L_1} + \left[{}^{W_2}_{L_2}\right].p_2) +$$
$$\left[{}^{W_1 \cup W_2}_{L_1 \cup L_2}\right].(|p_1|_{L_1} + |p_2|_{L_2}) + \left[{}_{W_1 \cup L_1^{W_2} \cup L_2}\right].(\left[{}^{W_1}_{L_1}\right].p_1 + |p_2|_{L_2})$$
$$\text{if } W_1 \cap W_2 = L_1 \cap W_2 = W_1 \cap L_2 = \emptyset \ \textbf{A8}$$

Theorem 1. *α-conversion is a congruence contained in bisimilarity.* $\qquad\square$

We illustrate the features of the operational semantics for some characteristic rules given in Table 1. We refer to [14] for the rest. Also, for compactness, we assume that terms do not exhibit naming conflicts. We define environments $\alpha_{\emptyset}$ by $\alpha_{\emptyset}(X) = \emptyset$, and $\alpha + W$ by $(\alpha + W)(X) = \alpha(X) \cup \{Y\}$ for $X \in \mathcal{V}$, $W \subseteq \mathcal{V}$ non-empty, and $Y \in W$ randomly chosen. The notation $\longmapsto$ and $\nrightarrow$ express that the term does not have a stochastic delay or a delay transition, respectively.

Let us comment on the rules. Rules 6 to 8 deal with undelayable and delayable actions. Rule 9 enables stochastic delay transitions. The environment is updated by first updating the dependence sets of the losers, obtaining the new environment α'. Afterward, only the relevant dependence history of the losers, given by $\text{H}_{\alpha'}(L)$, is retained. The losers in the resulting term $|p|_L$ are treated as dependent as their names must be protected. The dependence scope operator does not affect any transitions as illustrated by rule 10. It is only used to specify dependent and independent delay names. Rule 11 illustrates the default weak choice between action transitions and passage of time. Action transitions do not have priority, unless explicitly stated by the maximal progress operator. Delay transitions merge with other delay or stochastic delay transitions, illustrated by rule 12. Rule 13 gives the synchronization of stochastic delays in the parallel composition. Rule 14 illustrates handling of resolved races, if a probabilistic choice between stochastic delays transitions is enabled. Resolved races do not occur in the parallel composition, as they represent disjoint events that cannot occur concurrently.

The following result gives rise to a term model in the vein of [17].

Theorem 2. *Bisimilarity is a congruence in TCP^{dst}.* $\qquad\square$

Equational theory. We discuss a selection of axioms in Table 2. Axioms A3 and A4 illustrate how to deal with the dependence scope and prefix operators. Multiple scopes intersect as given by axiom A5. Axiom A6 allows the merging of scopes if there are no naming conflicts. Arbitrary passage of time of the delayable actions is expressed by axiom A7. Axiom A8 illustrates the resolution of a race without restrictions and all possible outcomes produced. Under restrictions, e.g., if $L_1 \cap W_2 \neq \emptyset$, only the first summand persists on the right.

Theorem 3. *The process theory* TCP^{dst} *is sound and ground-complete axiomatization for race-complete process specifications.* □

Head normal forms. To expand the parallel composition and the maximal progress operator, we want stochastic delays to be in a resolved race [11,14]. For that purpose, we rewrite terms in a head normal form that makes the race condition and the dependent delay names explicit.

Theorem 4. *Every term* p *can be rewritten in the following normal form:*

$$p = |\sum_{i=1}^{u} \underline{a}_i . p_i + \sum_{j=1}^{d} b_j . q_j + \sum_{k=1}^{s} [^{W_k}_{L_k}] . r_k \ (+\epsilon)(+\delta)|_D$$

with $W_k \cup L_k = \text{R}(p)$, $D \subseteq \text{R}(p)$, *and* $\text{rr}([^{W_k}_{L_k}], [^{W_{k'}}_{L_{k'}}])$ *holds for* $1 \le k, k' \le n$, $k \ne k'$, *and* $\underline{b}_j . q_j \in \{\underline{a}_i . p_i \mid 1 \le i \le u\}$ *for every* $1 \le j \le d$. □

The summand ϵ may or may not exist, $\sum_{i=1}^{n} p_i = p_1 + \ldots + p_n$ if $n > 0$ and otherwise it does not exist, δ exists if none of the other summands do.

The availability of head normal form is of technical importance. It is instrumental for proving ground-completeness and showing uniqueness of solutions of guarded recursive specifications in the term model [20]. Also, it enables an expansion of the parallel composition and resolution of the maximal progress.

Expansion law. First, we analyze the parallel composition of p, as above, and

$$p' = |\sum_{i'=1}^{u'} \underline{a}'_{i'} . p_{i'} + \sum_{j'=1}^{d'} b'_{j'} . q'_{j'} + \sum_{k'=1}^{s'} [^{W'_{k'}}_{L'_{k'}}] . r'_{k'} (+\epsilon)(+\delta)|_{D'}, \text{ separately for}$$

every type of prefix. By $\text{und}(p \parallel p')$ we denote the process

$$\sum_{i=1}^{u} \underline{a}_i . (|p_i|_\emptyset \parallel p') + \sum_{i'=1}^{u'} \underline{a}'_{i'} . (p \parallel |p'_{i'}|_\emptyset) + \sum_{\gamma(a_i, a'_{i'}) = aa_{ii'}} \underline{aa}_{ii'} . (|p_i|_\emptyset \parallel |p'_{i'}|_\emptyset)$$

that gives the expansion of the undelayable action prefixes. The stochastic delays that follow the leading prefix are independent as there is no race. Similarly, for delayable action prefixes, we put $\text{del}(p \parallel p') =$

$$\sum_{j=1}^{d} b_j . (|q_j|_\emptyset \parallel q') + \sum_{j'=1}^{d'} b'_{j'} . (q \parallel |q'_{j'}|_\emptyset) + \sum_{\gamma(b_j, b'_{j'}) = bb_{jj'}} bb_{jj'} . (|q_j|_\emptyset \parallel |q'_{j'}|_\emptyset).$$

The stochastic delay prefixes are merged according to the restrictions imposed on the races, as discussed above for axiom A8. We have $\text{std}(p \parallel p') =$

$$\sum_{W_k \cap W'_{k'} \ne \emptyset, W_k \cap L'_{k'} = L_k \cap W'_{k'} = \emptyset} [^{W_k \cup W'_{k'}}_{L_k \cup L'_{k'}}] . (|r_k|_{L_k} \parallel |r'_{k'}|_{L'_{k'}}) +$$

$$\sum_{L_k \cap W'_{k'} \ne \emptyset, W_k \cap W'_{k'} = W_k \cap L'_{k'} = \emptyset} [^{W_k}_{L_k \cup W'_{k'} \cup L'_{k'}}] . (|r_k|_{L_k} \parallel [^{W'_{k'}}_{L'_{k'}}] . r'_{k'}) +$$

$$\sum_{W_k \cap L'_{k'} \ne \emptyset, W_k \cap W'_{k'} = W'_{k'} \cap L_k = \emptyset} [^{W'_{k'}}_{W_k \cup L_k \cup L'_{k'}}] . ([^{W_k}_{L_k}] . r_k \parallel |r'_{k'}|_{L'_{k'}}) +$$

$$\sum_{W_k \cap W'_{k'} = W_k \cap L'_{k'} = L_k \cap W'_{k'} = \emptyset} \left([^{W_k}_{L_k \cup W'_{k'} \cup L'_{k'}}] . (|r_k|_{L_k} \parallel [^{W'_{k'}}_{L'_{k'}}] . r'_{k'}) + \right.$$

$$\left. [^{W_k \cup W'_{k'}}_{L_k \cup L'_{k'}}] . (|r_k|_{L_k} \parallel |r'_{k'}|_{L'_{k'}}) + [^{W'_{k'}}_{W_k \cup L_k \cup L'_{k'}}] . ([^{W_k}_{L_k}] . r_k \parallel |r'_{k'}|_{L'_{k'}}) \right).$$

The leading stochastic delay determines the set of losers in the term it prefixes.

Now, we have all the ingredients to state an expansion law.

Theorem 5. *The expansion of the parallel composition* $p \parallel p'$ *is given by*

$$p \parallel p' = |\text{und}(p \parallel p') + \text{del}(p \parallel p') + \text{std}(p \parallel p') \ (+\epsilon)(+\delta)|_{D \cup D'}$$

provided that there are no naming conflicts, i.e., $\text{R}(p) \cap D' = D \cap \text{R}(p') = \emptyset$. □

The summand ϵ exists if both p and p' contain it; δ exists if none of the other summands do.

For comparison, we give an abstract description of the expansion of the parallel composition in clock-based approaches [5,4,21,8] that employ start-termination semantics. There, the stochastic delay $[X]$ is split on a starting X^+ and an ending X^- activity. Intuitively

$$[X].p \parallel [Y].q = X^+.X^-.p \parallel Y^+.Y^-.q = X^+.Y^+.(X^-.p \parallel Y^-.q) + Y^+.X^+.(X^-.p \parallel Y^-.q).$$

This allows for a much more elegant expansion law, than Theorem 5. However, such treatment only involves the setting of the joint sets of clocks, i.e., the enabling of the starting activities. There is no relation between the passage of time of the components as in standard real-time semantics, where

$$t.p \parallel s.q = \min(t,s).\big((t - \min(t,s)).p \parallel (s - \min(t,s)).q\big) .$$

As a consequence, the maximal progress operator cannot be handled explicitly as there is no knowledge about the relationship between the winners and the losers. This leads to more complicated definitions of the bisimulation relations, which must account for the priority of the internal actions [4,5,6,7].

Maximal progress.   The advantage of the stochastic delays over clocks employing start-termination semantics is that by resolving the race condition explicitly, we can track how time advances. This gives a clear relation between the winning and the losing samples, so one can pinpoint the progress of time exactly. We are able to resolve the maximal progress operator θ_H using normal form representations as stated below.

Theorem 6. *For a normal form p, it holds that*

$$\theta_H(p) = |\textstyle\sum_{i=1}^{u} \underline{a}_i.\theta_H(p_i) + \sum_{j=1}^{d} b_j.\theta_H(q_j) + \sum_{k=1}^{s} [{}^{W_k}_{L_k}].\theta_H(r_k) \; (+\epsilon)(+\delta)|_D$$

if $(\bigcup_{i=1}^{u} a_i \cup \bigcup_{j=1}^{d} b_j) \cap H = \emptyset$, *or by*

$$\theta_H(p) = |\textstyle\sum_{i=1}^{u} \underline{a}_i.\theta_H(p_i) + \sum_{j=1}^{d} \underline{b}_j.\theta_H(q_j) \; (+\epsilon)(+\delta)|_D, \; otherwise. \qquad \square$$

As an aside, the explicit treatment of the race condition corresponds to the regional trees that are used in modelchecking of stochastic automata (in residual lifetime semantics) [22]. Originally, regional trees were obtained from stochastic automata [15] by explicitly ordering clock samples by their duration as symbolically represented by the stochastic delay prefix.

5   Conclusions and Future Work

We investigated the phenomenon of 'stochastifying' timed process theories, i.e., generalizing real-time process specifications to stochastic time. We approached the problem from both directions, aiming to apply the principles of timed process theories in stochastic time and adapting the real-time semantics to conform to the race condition. Regarding timed process algebra, we introduced the notion of context-sensitive interpolation, a restriction of time additivity that fits with race condition semantics. We built a stochastic process algebra featuring stochastic delay prefixes that come close to timed delay prefixes, as the relation between the winning and losing delays of the race is specifically modeled. This enabled an expansion of the parallel composition in the style of real-time process theories as well as explicit handling of the maximal progress.

As future work, we continue our axiomatization efforts to completely describe specifications that involve incomplete races as well. Current investigations point out that we need to work with normal forms, as the alternative composition is no longer associative. We also schedule further study of real-time process theories that implement context-sensitive interpolation and single-step-style timed bisimulation. At this point, we expect that such theories can accommodate for verification and analysis of processes with timed delays too. Our long-term goal is to analyze protocols, such as contemporary Internet protocols, involving both time-outs and generally distributed delays.

Acknowledgments.   Many thanks to Jos Baeten, Bas Luttik, Nikola Trčka, and Walter van Niftrik for fruitful discussions on the topic.

References

1. Nicollin, X., Sifakis, J.: An overview and synthesis of timed process algebras. In: Huizing, C., de Bakker, J.W., Rozenberg, G., de Roever, W.-P. (eds.) REX 1991. LNCS, vol. 600, pp. 526–548. Springer, Heidelberg (1992)
2. Hermanns, H., Mertsiotakis, V., Rettelbach, M.: Performance analysis of distributed systems using TIPP. In: Proc. UKPEW 1994, pp. 131–144 (1994)
3. Bravetti, M., Bernardo, M., Gorrieri, R.: From EMPA to GSMPA: Allowing for general distributions. In: Proc. PAPM 1997, pp. 17–33 (1997)
4. D'Argenio, P., Katoen, J.P.: A theory of stochastic systems, part II: Process algebra. Information and Computation 203(1), 39–74 (2005)
5. Bravetti, M.: Specification and Analysis of Stochastic Real-time Systems. PhD thesis, Universitá di Bologna (2002)
6. López, N., Núñez, M.: NMSPA: A non-Markovian model for stochastic processes. In: Proc. ICDS 2000, pp. 33–40. IEEE, Los Alamitos (2000)
7. Bohnenkamp, H., D'Argenio, P., Hermanns, H., Katoen, J.-P.: MODEST: A compositional modeling formalism for hard and softly timed systems. IEEE Transactions on Software Engineering 32, 812–830 (2006)
8. Katoen, J.P., D'Argenio, P.R.: General distributions in process algebra. In: Brinksma, E., Hermanns, H., Katoen, J.-P. (eds.) EEF School 2000 and FMPA 2000. LNCS, vol. 2090, pp. 375–429. Springer, Heidelberg (2001)
9. D'Argenio, P.: From stochastic automata to timed automata: Abstracting probability in a compositional manner. In: Proc. WAIT 2003(2003)
10. Markovski, J., de Vink, E.P.: Embedding real-time in stochastic process algebras. In: Horváth, A., Telek, M. (eds.) EPEW 2006. LNCS, vol. 4054, pp. 47–62. Springer, Heidelberg (2006)
11. Markovski, J., de Vink, E.-P.: Real-time process algebra with stochastic delays. In: Proc. ACSD 2007, pp. 177–186. IEEE Computer Society Press, Los Alamitos (2007)

12. Markovski, J., de Vink, E.: Discrete real-time and stochastic-time process algebra for performance analysis of distributed systems. In: Proc. ACSD 2008 (to be published, 2008)
13. Cattani, S., Segala, R., Kwiatkowska, M., Norman, G.: Stochastic transition systems for continuous state spaces and non-determinism. In: Sassone, V. (ed.) FOS-SACS 2005. LNCS, vol. 3441, pp. 125–139. Springer, Heidelberg (2005)
14. Markovski, J., de Vink, E.P.: Discrete real-time and stochastic-time process algebra for performance analysis of distributed systems. Technical Report CS 08/10, Eindhoven University of Technology (2008)
15. D'Argenio, P., Katoen, J.P.: A theory of stochastic systems, part I: Stochastic automata. Information and Computation 203(1), 1–38 (2005)
16. Howard, R.: Dynamic Probabilistic Systems. Wiley, Chichester (1971)
17. Baeten, J., Middelburg, C.: Process Algebra with Timing. Monographs in Theoretical Computer Science. Springer, Heidelberg (2002)
18. López, N., Núñez, M.: Weak stochastic bisimulation for non-Markovian processes. In: Van Hung, D., Wirsing, M. (eds.) ICTAC 2005. LNCS, vol. 3722, pp. 454–468. Springer, Heidelberg (2005)
19. van Niftrik, W.: Context sensitive interpolation. Master thesis, Eindhoven University of Technology (in progress, 2008)
20. Baeten, J.C.M., Bergstra, J.A., Klop, J.W.: On the consistency of Koomen's fair abstraction rule. Theoretical Computer Science 51(1), 129–176 (1987)
21. Bravetti, M., D'Argenio, P.: Tutte le algebre insieme – concepts, discussions and relations of stochastic process algebras with general distributions. In: Baier, C., Haverkort, B.R., Hermanns, H., Katoen, J.-P., Siegle, M. (eds.) Validation of Stochastic Systems. LNCS, vol. 2925, pp. 44–88. Springer, Heidelberg (2004)
22. Bryans, J., Bowman, H., Derrick, J.: Model checking stochastic automata. ACM Transactions on Computational Logic 4(4), 452–492 (2003)

Vx86: x86 Assembler Simulated in C Powered by Automated Theorem Proving

Stefan Maus[1], Michał Moskal[2], and Wolfram Schulte[3]

[1] Universität Freiburg, Freiburg, Germany
[2] European Microsoft Innovation Center, Aachen, Germany
[3] Microsoft Research, Redmond, WA, USA

Abstract. Vx86 is the first static analyzer for sequential Intel x86 assembler code using automated deductive verification. It proves the correctness of assembler code against function contracts, which are expressed in terms of pre-, post-, and frame conditions using first-order predicates. Vx86 takes the annotated assembler code, translates it into C code simulating the processor, and then uses an existing C verifier to either prove the correctness of the assembler program or find errors in it. First experiments on applying Vx86 on the Windows Hypervisor code base are encouraging. Vx86 verified the Windows Hypervisor's memory safety, arithmetic safety, call safety and interrupt safety.

1   Introduction

The correctness of operating systems is critical for the security and reliability of any computer system. However, debugging and testing operating systems is very difficult: kernel operations are hard to monitor, and algorithms are highly optimized and often concurrent. These factors suggest that one should verify operating systems. In fact, there are currently several projects that try to do just that [21,15,10,19]. However, such projects still leave us far from a practical methodology for verifying real systems.

One gap is in the verification targets. Existing verification projects often use idealistic sequential code written in clean programming languages. In contrast, modern system code is typically multithreaded, racy, written in C *and* assembler. Assembler is used (1) to access special instructions that are not available in C (like *CPUID*, which returns some important properties of the processor), and (2) to improve the performance of critical algorithms like interrupt dispatch, context switch, clearing pages, etc. While several verifiers for C exist [11,14,17], we think that it is imperative to verify the assembler portion of a verified operating system as well.

To address this gap, we developed an automatic static analysis tool, called Vx86, targeted towards the verification of the Windows Hypervisor [4,5]. Vx86 proves correctness of Intel x86 assembler code with AMD virtualization extensions against procedure contracts and loop invariants. It does so by building on top of other tools. First, Vx86 translates annotated assembler code to annotated C code. The C translation makes the machine model explicit and provides a meaning for the instructions by simulating the instructions on the machine

J. Meseguer and G. Roşu (Eds.): AMAST 2008, LNCS 5140, pp. 284–298, 2008.

state. The resulting C code is then passed to VCC, Microsoft's Verifying C Compiler [16]. VCC translates the annotated C programs into BoogiePL [9], an intermediate language for verification. Boogie [1] then generates logical verification conditions for the translated C code and passes them on to the automatic first-order theorem prover Z3 [8] to either prove the correctness of the translated assembler program or find errors in it.

We found that the simulation approach is a very good fit for our assembler verification effort. There are two reasons for that, one is technical and the other one is social. The technical reason is that C and assembler are in fact very closely related: both use arbitrary pointer arithmetic, both have a very weak type system (albeit a bit stronger in the case of C). So C verifiers, which are good enough for verifying low level OS code, should be good enough to deal with assembler code as well. Mapping assembler code to C thus obviates the need of implementing a full-blown assembler verifier. The social reason is that the users of the assembler verifier are likely to also use the C verifier for other parts of the code, therefore they can get familiar with only one tool instead of two.

This paper presents the design and use of Vx86. Our contributions are

- the development of a translator from annotated assembler code to C (see Subsection 3.1).
- the development of a semantics of x86 assembler with virtualization extensions by providing a simulator in C (see Subsection 3.2).
- the development of correctness criteria for assembler code (see Subsection 4.2).
- the application of the resulting verifier on the Windows Hypervisor code base (approximately 4,000 lines of assembler code) (see Subsection 4.3).

Section 2 introduces the challenges in assembler verification; furthermore it provides some background on VCC. Sections 5 and 6 discuss related work and conclude.

2 Background

2.1 Running Example: *SetZero*

We will explain the inner workings of Vx86 with the *SetZero* assembler code (see Figure 1 on the following page). It is literally taken from the Windows Hypervisor code base; it sets a memory block of 4096 bytes to zero.

This code is written in assembler, because it is optimized for branch prediction, cache lines and pipelines of the processor, something that the Microsoft C compiler cannot achieve.

2.2 Challenges in Assembler Verification

Verifying assembler code is challenging.

- Almost all assembler languages, including Microsoft's x86 assembler, are untyped; however, most of the automatic verification tools use type information to help with the problems of aliasing, framing, etc.

```
1        %LEAF_ENTRY SetZero, _TEXT$00
         db      066h, 066h, 066h, 090h
         db      066h, 066h, 066h, 090h
         db      090h
         ALTERNATE_ENTRY SetZero
6        xor     eax, eax
         mov     edx, X64_PAGE_SIZE / 64
  @@:
         mov     [rcx], rax
         mov     8[rcx], rax
11       mov     16[rcx], rax
         add     rcx, 64
         mov     (24 − 64)[rcx], rax
         mov     (32 − 64)[rcx], rax
         dec     edx
16       mov     (40 − 64)[rcx], rax
         mov     (48 − 64)[rcx], rax
         mov     (56 − 64)[rcx], rax
         jnz     short @b
         ret
21       LEAF_END SetZero, _TEXT$00
```

Fig. 1. Original *SetZero* assembler code

- Assembler control flow is unstructured, therefore we need to find a place where to put loop invariants.
- Many assembler instructions have side effects not only on the mentioned registers but on the whole processor state. For faithful verification all of these effects have to be captured, since program logic may later depend on them; conditional jumps, for instance, depend on a flag set in earlier instructions.
- Assembler code often uses bitfields and words interchangeably. For example, the flag register is typically used as a bitfield, but when saved and restored, it is used as a single unit.
- The use of general purpose registers is even more demanding; they are not only used as bitfields and as integers, but also as pointers. A register mask, for example, is used to select the page of a pointer address.

VCC, a verifier that is currently being developed for verifying the C part of the Windows Hypervisor, is designed so that it can support weak type systems, bitvectors, as well as arbitrary goto-systems. This allows us to build Vx86 on top of VCC because it meets all necessary requirements.

2.3   Microsoft's Verifying C Compiler

VCC is a static analysis tool that uses automatic first order theorem proving to show formally that a given sequential C program, compiled for the Intel or AMD x86-32 or x86-64 processors, does what is stated in its specification.

VCC's specification language includes first-order predicates expressed in pre–/postconditions, loop invariants, assertions and assumptions. For modular reasoning VCC introduces a "region-based" memory management using pure functions and abstract framing to guarantee that functions only write, read, allocate, and free certain locations. VCC also supports ghost state, that consists of specification-only variables that allow one to argue about values that were saved before.

VCC uses three formally related semantics. VCC's base memory model represents values as bit vectors and accesses memory in individual bytes, a simple abstraction represents values as mathematical integers and accesses memory in word sizes, the third model uses the C type system in addition to the second model to rule out many pointer aliases.

In this paper we show in detail how Vx86 uses VCC to verify the partial correctness of the *SetZero* function, as well discuss the results of verification of a sizable chunk of assembler code from the Windows Hypervisor.

3   Translating Annotated Assembler Code to C

Vx86 processes annotated x86 assembler code, written in the input language for Microsoft's Macro Assembler 8.0 (MASM). Vx86 works as follows:

1. the annotated assembler code is preprocessed by MASM, this inlines all needed assembler macros and definitions;
2. the expanded assembler file is translated to annotated C code;
3. the annotated C code is extended with definitions that (a) make the machine state explicit, and (b) provide a meaning for the assembler instructions in terms of the machine state;
4. the annotated and now self-contained C code is passed to VCC for verification.

3.1   Specification and Syntax Translation of the Assembler Language

To simplify our translation task and to make the verification of the Hypervisor's C code as well as assembler code as uniform as possible, we decided to simply adopt VCC's specification language for Vx86. Specification constructs in Vx86 are introduced using special comments, e.g. pre, post conditions, writes clauses and local ghost variables appear after the assembler header, invariants appear after labels, assumptions, assertions and assignments to ghost variables can appear anywhere in the running code. Figure 2 on the next page describes the fully annotated *SetZero* Code.

The *SetZero* assembler procedure requires (1) that $X64\_PAGE\_SIZE$ bytes in the main memory starting at the address pointed to by *rcx* are valid, i.e. allocated (let us call that region the *page*), and that $rcx + X64\_PAGE\_SIZE$ is not allowed to overflow. *SetZero* guarantees that it only writes the *page*, as well as the registers *rcx*, *edx*, *rax* and *rflags*. *SetZero* ensures that the *page* is zero. In the body, there is a loop between the label @@ and the jump *jnz* back to it. After the alignment a ghost variable *count* of type signed 64 bit integer is

```
 ;^          requires (valid ((U1*)rcx,X64_PAGE_SIZE))
 ;^          requires (rcx+X64_PAGE_SIZE < (U8)−1)
 ;^          writes (region ((U1*)(old(rcx)),X64_PAGE_SIZE), rcx, edx, rax, rflags)
 ;^          ensures ( forall (U4 i; (0 <= i && i < X64_PAGE_SIZE/8) ==>
 ;^                            *((U8*)(U1*)(old(rcx)) + i) == 0))
            LEAF_ENTRY SetZero, _TEXT$00


            db      066h, 066h, 066h, 090h  ;  fill  for  alignment
            db      066h, 066h, 066h, 090h  ;
            db      090h                    ;


 ;^            spec (I8 count = 0);
 ; a ghost  variable


            ALTERNATE_ENTRY SetZero
            xor     eax, eax
            mov     edx, X64_PAGE_SIZE / 64
@@:
 ;^          invariant  (valid ((U1*)(old(rcx)),X64_PAGE_SIZE))
 ;^          invariant   (8 * count == (U1*)rcx − (U1*)old(rcx))
 ;^          invariant  (0 < edx && edx <= (X64_PAGE_SIZE/64))
 ;^          invariant  ((U1*)(old(rcx))−64*edx+X64_PAGE_SIZE == (U1*)rcx)
 ;^          invariant  ((U1*)(old(rcx)) <= (U1*)rcx)
 ;^          invariant  ((U1*)rcx < (U1*)(old(rcx))+X64_PAGE_SIZE)
 ;^          invariant  (rax == 0)
 ;^          invariant  ( forall (U4 i; (0 <= i && i < count) ==>
 ;^                            *((U8*)(U1*)(old(rcx)) + i) == 0));
            mov     [rcx], rax
            mov     8[rcx], rax
            mov     16[rcx], rax
            add     rcx, 64
            mov     (24 − 64)[rcx], rax
            mov     (32 − 64)[rcx], rax
            dec     edx
            mov     (40 − 64)[rcx], rax
            mov     (48 − 64)[rcx], rax
            mov     (56 − 64)[rcx], rax
 ;^            spec ({ count += 8; })
            jnz     short @b
            ret


            LEAF_END SetZero, _TEXT$00
```

Fig. 2. With contracts annotated *SetZero* assembler code

introduced. This variable, which is updated as part of the loop body, is needed for describing the loop invariant.

Note that for verification purposes registers and the global memory are considered to be global variables, except that registers are treated specially; they are 64, 80 or 128 bit variables that lie outside the address range of global memory.

```
    typedef unsigned long long U8;
    typedef unsigned long U4;
3   typedef unsigned char U1;
    typedef struct Flags_t {
            unsigned cf : 1; unsigned res1 : 3;
            unsigned af :1; unsigned res2 :1;
            unsigned zf :1; unsigned sf :1;
8           unsigned res3 :3; unsigned of :1;
            unsigned res4 :20; U4 res6;
            } flags_t ;

    // registers
13  register U8 rax, rcx, rdx;
    //flags
    flags_t  rflags ;
    #define eax rax //casts are introduced automatically where needed
    #define edx rdx //casts are introduced automatically where needed
18  //eax and edx are the 32 bit versions of the 64 bit rax and rdx

    //flag computations
    #define zf_comp(a) rflags.zf = (unsigned)(a == 0)
    #define sf_comp(a) rflags.sf = (a < 0)
23  //instructions
    #define xor(a,b) a = (a^b); zf_comp(a); sf_comp(a); rflags.af=0; rflags.of=0
    #define mov_U4(a,b) unchecked(a = (U8)((U4)b))
    #define mov(a,b) unchecked(a = b)
    #define add(a,b) a = (U8)((U1*)a + (b)); zf_comp(a); sf_comp(a)
28  #define dec(a) a = a − 1; zf_comp(a); sf_comp(a)
    #define ret() return
    #define jnz(a) if (! rflags.zf) goto a
```

Fig. 3. Vx86's machine state and instruction definitions in C

A challenging part of the syntax translation is the introduction of casts. In x86 assembler every register and memory access can be 8, 16, 32, or 64 bit wide. The access modes do not only differ in the number of bits they read or write, but also in the side effects to the higher bits. 8 and 16 bit access modes are just writing the bits given, leaving the rest of the register unchanged. On the other hand, 32 bit access mode extends with zeroes to a 64 bit register. For Vx86 we decided to model general purpose registers as 64 bit unsigned integers; all access modes other than 64 bit are represented in terms of their effect on 64 bit quantities. Due to VCC's ability to switch between different memory models, registers can be viewed as bitvectors or integers.

In assembler, jumps often depend on the value of the status register, i.e. one instruction sets the status register and the following jump is depending on the flags. In our running example, *dec* may set the zero flag and *jnz* performs the jump if the zero flag was set. We translate goto systems from assembler directly into goto systems in C, we only have to resolve symbolic assembler labels, e.g. @b and @@ in our example are resolved to a unique label. While most verifiers do not support unstructured goto's, VCC does. It translates goto systems into unstructured control

```
    #include "vcc.h"
    #include "Assembler.h"

    //Page Size
 5  #define X64_PAGE_SIZE 0x01000ULL

    void SetZero()
     requires (...)  writes (...)  ensures  (...)
    {
10  spec  (...);
    SetZero:
            xor(eax, eax);
            mov_U4(edx, X64_PAGE_SIZE / 64);
    _l0:
15  invariant  (...)
            mov(*(U8*)((U1*)rcx), rax);
            mov(*(U8*)((U1*)rcx + 8), rax);
            mov(*(U8*)((U1*)rcx + 16), rax);
            add(rcx, 64);
20          mov(*(U8*)((U1*)rcx + (24 − 64)), rax);
    assert  (...);
            mov(*(U8*)((U1*)rcx + (32 − 64)), rax);
            dec(edx);
            mov(*(U8*)((U1*)rcx + (40 − 64)), rax);
25          mov(*(U8*)((U1*)rcx + (48 − 64)), rax);
            mov(*(U8*)((U1*)rcx + (56 − 64)), rax);
    spec  (...);
            jnz( _l0 );
            ret ();
30  }
```

Fig. 4. Vx86 generated C code for *SetZero*

flow in Boogie. Next, Boogie translates unstructured goto systems into a system of equations that represent the verification condition. Vx86 does not make the PC explicit. In x86 assembler it is quite difficult to compute addresses instead of using labels to jump, because instructions do not have fixed size.

3.2   Simulator for Assembler

Figure 3 on the preceding page provides an excerpt of the simulator for x86 assembler. The figure only provides the definitions which are needed to verify *SetZero*. The full file has approximately 8,000 bytes of definitions.

The general purpose registers of the x86 processor are defined as 64 bit global variables in our C model. Special registers, like the flag register, are represented using bitfields. Other registers like the floating point registers, which are 80 bit wide and the multimedia registers, which are 128 bit wide, are modelled with the help of structs that have the same form as they would have on the real processor.

The meaning of each assembler instruction is provided by a simulation on these newly introduced memory locations. For providing the instruction semantics we relied on the instruction manuals from AMD and Intel. For example, the instruction "*add rax,rbx*" is not only translated to the C construct "*rax=rax+rbx*" but also into several statements to report the proper flag changes like "*rflags.zf = (rax == 0)*" and "*rflags.sf = (rax < 0)*". Note that such flag changes are performed by most of the assembler instructions.

Unfortunately, the processor instruction manual is not very precise when it comes to the virtualization extensions. For those instructions, the processor state after executing certain operations is only partially defined (see also Subsection 4.1). On the other hand, the Windows Hypervisor does not contain code that operates on floating point and multimedia values; they are only used for saving and restoring the processor state, therefore we do not need to model these instructions in detail.

Figure 4 contains the translation of the annotated *SetZero* assembler code into C (note that we do not include the contracts here, because they are pasted literally from the assembler code into the C code). This code is then passed to VCC; it verifies in less than a second. Alternatively, the code can be passed to a normal C compiler, and then executed or debugged using a regular C debugger.

4   Evaluation

The goal of our verification effort is to verify the assembler portion of the Windows Hypervisor. This section provides some background on Windows Hypervisor, explains the properties that we have verified so far and gives performance data.

4.1   The Windows Hypervisor

The Windows Hypervisor is a thin layer of software written in C and assembler that sits directly on x64 hardware, turning a real multi-processor (MP) x64 machine into a number of MP x64 virtual machines (VMs). These VMs provide additional machine instructions (hypercalls) to create and manage VMs, hardware resources, and inter-VM communication. VMs are viewed as a key enabling technology for a variety of services, such as server consolidation, sandboxing of device drivers, testing, running multiple OSs on a hardware machine, live VM migration, snapshotting/recovery, and high availability. Moreover, it provides such functionality in an OS-neutral way, with a trusted computing base 2-3 orders of magnitude smaller than that of a typical commercial operating system.

The Windows Hypervisor code base is separated into source files written in C and x86 assembler. Assembler code is mainly used to achieve performance optimizations, which cannot be expressed in C, and to access processor instructions that do not have corresponding C instructions. For both reasons, it is obvious that the code should not be changed just to be able to verify it.

The assembler code of the Hypervisor is located in different files, which means there is no inline assembler in the C code. This allows for modular reasoning: the assembler code can be verified separately against its specification.

If C code calls assembler functions, a C prototype for the assembler function has to be provided that expresses the assembler specification not in terms of registers but in terms of C's parameters and memory. We assume that the C compiler translates calls to assembler code using a standard register transfer protocol, where the function's first parameter is passed in register *rcx*, the next in *rdx*, etc. We also assume that every variable of the calling C function is marked as volatile, which means that the compiler is not allowed to store variables temporarily in registers but variables are always read from and written to main memory.

Intel and AMD have developed hardware support for hypervisor systems. For example, they can switch to the hypervisor if hardware interrupts occur and provide multi-stage page tables so that the operating systems do not see that they are working in translated mode. Unfortunately, both companies have their own virtualization instructions. Since the AMD instruction set is older and the implementation in the hypervisor thus (hopefully) has less errors in it, we decided to first support AMD. In future work, there will also be an implementation of the Intel virtualization hardware. Both hardware types can be supported at the same time because they have different instruction names and different processor states. Compared to standard assembler instructions the virtualization instructions are very complex. They are used for context switches between the hypervisor (host system) and the operating systems (guest systems). A typical scenario for a context switch consists of the following sequence of operations: (1) save the host state, (2) load the guest state, (3) run the guest, (4) save the guest state, (5) load the host state. Properties about those virtualization instructions include facts like "the state of the host after the restoring process is the same as it was at the point of the saving". Such a property does not only include the values of registers but also the stack that is administrated by the processor. If the stack has changed (either the place or the content) then the host will have a completely different state. Properties involving virtualization typically range over many registers and memory locations. Additionally, the processor state is usually available twice: once for the host system and once for the guest system. The verification tool then has to scale well to handle such complex functions and specifications, and we have seen verification times for virtualization function degrade (see below).

On the other hand, several functions in the Windows Hypervisor are only used for optimization reasons. The specifications for those functions are not too complicated as we have seen before. However, looking at an optimized implementation is often scary; algorithms are optimized for filling the pipeline most efficiently, to exploit branch prediction and caching. Verifiers however are good at keeping track of detail and so these algorithms are a great target for modern verification technology.

4.2   Well-Formedness Properties

So far we verified only assembler code that is guaranteed to be executed sequentially; this amounts to approximately 4,000 lines. For these 4,000 lines we verified memory safety, arithmetic safety, call safety, and interrupt safety.

Memory safety means that all memory accesses are only performed on valid (i.e., previously allocated and not freed) memory. Therefore, the precondition of an assembler function needs to include validity of all memory locations that are accessed. If a function tries to access memory that cannot be proven valid, VCC reports an error. Similarly, we specify explicitly the set of memory locations being written to, and it is an error to write to a memory location not listed in the writes clause. These properties are enforced to be transitive, i.e., if function f calls g then the writes set of g needs to be contained within the writes set of f, and also the precondition of g needs to follow from the context at the call site (including preconditions of f).

Arithmetic safety means absence of overflows, unless otherwise stated. For operations that can overflow (like addition, multiplication or signed division) VCC automatically adds assertions that check if the result is in the proper range. When an overflow behavior is desired, the user can specify this explicitly.

Call safety means that the stack is cleaned up after every function call and registers are saved before every function call. If f calls g and the postcondition of g does not guarantee that it restores values of registers, then f needs to save itself the registers it cares about. The registers are saved on the stack, therefore it is important to know that g will not modify stack locations above the current stack pointer (stacks are growing down on x86 architecture), and that g does not change the stack pointer. This is expressed using the postcondition $ensures(rsp == old(rsp))$ and by not including region starting with rsp in the writes clause of g (or for that matter in its validity preconditions). On the other hand, all accesses of g to the stack (like push) need to be specified in the way we usually specify memory safety, that is by a precondition like $requires(valid(rsp-40, 40))$.

Interrupt safety means that the stack is cleaned up after processing the whole interrupt. We cannot verify interrupt handlers like regular functions, because some of their subroutines push some registers on the stack, while only other subroutines pop them.

For a few functions we also verified functional correctness, like in the *SetZero* example shown earlier.

4.3 Experimental Results

We analyzed all assembler files as given, i.e. without a single change except for adding contracts.

Sizes of Verification Task. Table 5 on the next page presents the size in bytes of different files in different processing stages. The column *Annotated ASM* denotes the size in bytes of the annotated assembler function, i.e. the files the user edits. The column *Preproc ASM* shows the file sizes after assembler macro expansion. The column *Translated C* shows the file size after the translation to C. At this point, we have the syntax translation but we do not have the simulator in the code, but only included as header file. Finally, column *Preproc C* presents the result of the C preprocessing phase. This is the file we finally give to *VCC* for

File	Annotated ASM	Preproc ASM	Translated C	Preproc C
zero	7,821	16,781	18,040	31,609
crashdump	5,625	17,791	20,217	31,028
GuestContext	1,422	16,673	18,136	29,297
Trap	82,316	420,854	444,865	486,510

Fig. 5. File sizes in bytes at different stage of the translation

Filename	Verification Time[s]
zero	1.45
crashdump	3.29
GuestContext	< 0.01
Trap	67.20

Fig. 6. Verification times for various files of the Windows Hypervisor

verification. Note that the translation is processing instruction by instruction. The time consumption is only mentionable for the largest file *Trap* and takes 2 seconds there.

Verification Times. Table 6 gives the verification time in seconds for different functions. We checked 17 files of the Windows Hypervisor for all previously mentioned properties, like memory safety, arithmetic safety, call safety, and interrupt safety. This corresponds to approximately 4,000 lines of assembler code, which is around 90% of the assembler code that is part of Windows Hypervisor. The remaining 10% might be executed concurrently, which we currently cannot handle.

The table shows only the functions of the four files we previously mentioned.

We observe that the time needed for verification increases linearly with size. This is due to the fact that our verification is modular, i.e. procedure by procedure. As long as the procedures do not grow too much in size and do not introduce too many control flow paths, we can verify substantial code. For instance, the procedure *ExceptionDispatch*, which is part of the *Trap* file, has approximately 300 instructions. These 300 instructions turn into several hundred C assignments. Nevertheless, it verifies in approximately 3 seconds. This shows that our approach cannot be used only for short toy functions but also for long and complex assembler implementations.

5 Related Work

The CLI stack project in the late 1980s [2] was the first project focussing on the pervasive verification of computer systems. In total the system consisted of four levels: starting from a verified FM 8502 microprocessor via a simple assembler language up to a verified operating system. Later Boyer and Yu [3] refined this approach and verified MC68020 assembler programs. They used the theorem prover Nqthm as their verification tool; they formalized the MC68020 as Nqthm theories, thus in effect giving an interpreter for the processor; assembler programs are then translated into expressions over this special logic. Vx86 differs in various dimensions from this early work, Vx86 works on the much more complex x86, Vx86 incorporates contracts (including framing) into the assembler, Vx86 uses an automatic theorem prover (ATP), Vx86 has been used to verify parts of a real industrial strength operating system.

There are various projects to verify micro-kernels. Verisoft [12] is in spirit similar to the CLI project. Verisoft developed machine-models for assembler, small step and big step semantics for more abstract programming languages, and programs for devices, kernels, operating systems and applications. However, the Verisoft project only dealt with idealistic processors, inline assembler, and OS. The L4.verifed project [13] aims at the formal verification of an industrial strength implementation of a L4 micro-kernel, which is highly optimized for the ARM platform. While the L4 project tries to do low level C verification, it has – to the best of our knowledge – not yet started verifying assembler code. Verisoft and the L4 project use the same verification technology. Both systems use the interactive theorem prover Isabelle and a Hoare calculus embedded in Isabelle [20] to verify properties of the micro-kernel. The automation was slightly improved with the integration of automatic tools that can verify parts of the proof obligations [7]. However the resulting system does not yet achieve the automatization we achieved.

Another approach to guarantee that assembler programs are safe are Typed Assembly Languages (TAL) [6]. TALs are low-level, statically typed target languages. TALs guarantee type safety, which typically implies memory safety. However, TALs do not guarantee arithmetic safety, call safety, interrupt safety or other functional properties. Furthermore, TALs are often idealistic assembler languages, they are only used as target languages for compilers; as such they do not deal with the whole instruction set of the processor. We, however, also have to deal with instructions like *HLT* or *CPUID* and the virtualization instruction set.

Proof carrying code (PCC) has a similar goal [18]. Instead of defining type safety for assembler code, PCC adds proofs to untrusted assembler files, which establish certain properties. The receiver of the untrusted code is then able to use a simple and fast proof validator to check that the proof is valid and hence the untrusted code is safe to execute. Like TAL, PCC has focuses on memory safety; it is not a general verification architecture. However, we think that translating contracts from source level into assembler and then using Vx86 to discharge those contracts could be an interesting alternative to extend the reach of PCC.

To our knowledge, there is no other project that tries to verify an existing code base for an optimized hypervisor or which verifies assembler code using contract annotations and an ATP.

6   Conclusion and Future Work

Vx86 is a verifier for proving the correctness of sequential Intel x86 assembler code with AMD virtualization extensions against their contracts. Our approach has been to (1) provide a C simulator for Intel x86, and (2) to translate the annotated assembler code into C code for this simulator. Despite the fact that providing a C simulator seems to be a detour for verifying assembler code, it has turned out that this still allows us to verify the assembler portion of a complex industrial program, like Windows Hypervisor, in reasonable time.

In the process of developing Vx86 we heave learnt the following characteristics of handwritten assembler programs: they might have complex control flow, but they operate only on a few registers and the memory; the operations on registers are often low-level, in addition operations have many side effects. Recursive data structures, which typically need transitivity to describe effects on them, are rarely used in hand-written assembler. As a consequence, changes to registers and the memory can often easily be described by enumeration and quantification.

We have also learned that assembler code is particularly well suited for automated verification:

- Providing an assembler verifier is overdue – except for assemblers there are no tools to help assembly writers.
- Verifying assembler code is beneficial – if assembler code fails systems typically crash.
- Writing assembler contracts is feasible – the contracts often only mention a limited amount of objects, furthermore the contracts are often easier than the highly optimized implementation.
- Discharging assembler contracts is a sweet spot for ATPs – ATPs can deal well with lots of low level detail, since they often have specialized decision procedures for them, they can also deal well with quantifiers; however they often cannot deal well with complex heap structures; luckily user written assembler programs do not use them.

Vx86's simulator semantics is currently based on our understanding of the Intel and AMD instruction manuals. To be more reliable we need a review by hardware developers. If changes are necessary we should be able to incorporate them easily, we just need to change the simulator, the rest of the translation is unaffected.

Vx86 is not yet concurrency aware. Certain parts of the assembler code base are often concurrent. If the Windows Hypervisor, for example, shuts down the physical machine, it does so by stopping all its processors, or in more detail: the last processor which is alive finally has to shut everything down. As soon as VCC will support concurrency, we will investigate how Vx86 can reuse that model.

Vx86 is of course not restricted to consume only Windows Hypervisor code, it can be used to verify other code bases as well. Furthermore, we think that the presented approach is a viable way to quickly provide verifiers for other processors. In fact, we were recently asked whether we could provide a verifier for an ARM assembler as well. We think that this should be possible in a couple of weeks.

Authors would like to thank Herman Venter for his help with getting Vx86 running and Peter Mueller for his very useful comments about this paper.

References

1. Barnett, M., Chang, B.-Y.E., DeLine, R., Jacobs, B., Leino, K.R.M.: Boogie: A modular reusable verifier for object-oriented programs. In: de Boer, F.S., Bonsangue, M.M., Graf, S., de Roever, W.-P. (eds.) FMCO 2005. LNCS, vol. 4111, pp. 364–387. Springer, Heidelberg (2006)
2. Bevier, W.R., Hunt Jr., W.A., Stroher Moore, J., Young, W.D.: An approach to systems verification. Journal of Automated Reasoning 5(4), 411–428 (1989)
3. Boyer, R.S., Yu, Y.: Automated correctness proofs of machine code programs for a commercial microprocessor. In: Kapur, D. (ed.) CADE 1992. LNCS, vol. 607, pp. 416–430. Springer, Heidelberg (1992)
4. Cohen, E.: Validating the Microsoft Hypervisor. In: Misra, J., Nipkow, T., Sekerinski, E. (eds.) FM 2006. LNCS, vol. 4085, p. 81. Springer, Heidelberg (2006)
5. Cohen, E., Hillebrand, M.A., Leinenbach, D., der Rieden, T.I., Moskal, M., Paul, W., Santen, T., Schirmer, N., Schulte, W., Tobies, S., Wolff, B.: The Microsoft Hypervisor verification project (to be published, 2008)
6. Crary, K., Gregory Morrisett, J.: Type structure for low-level programming languages. In: Wiedermann, J., Van Emde Boas, P., Nielsen, M. (eds.) ICALP 1999. LNCS, vol. 1644, pp. 40–54. Springer, Heidelberg (1999)
7. Daum, M., Maus, S., Schirmer, N., Seghir, M.N.: Integration of a software model checker into Isabelle. In: Sutcliff, G., Voronkov, A. (eds.) LPAR 2005. LNCS (LNAI), vol. 3835, pp. 381–395. Springer, Heidelberg (2005)
8. de Moura, L., Bjøner, N.: Z3: An efficient SMT solver. In: TACAS (2008)
9. De Line, R., Leino, K.R.M.: BoogiePL: A typed procedural language for checking object-oriented programs. Technical Report 70, Microsoft Research (May 2005)
10. Dörrenbächer, J.: Vamos microkernel: formal models and verification. In: International Workshop on System Verification (2006)
11. Filliâtre, J.-C., Marché, C.: Multi-prover verification of C programs. In: Davies, J., Schulte, W., Barnett, M. (eds.) ICFEM 2004. LNCS, vol. 3308, pp. 15–29. Springer, Heidelberg (2004)
12. Gargano, M., Hillebrand, M.A., Leinenbach, D., Paul, W.J.: On the correctness of operating system kernels. In: Hurd, J., Melham, T. (eds.) TPHOLs 2005. LNCS, vol. 3603, pp. 1–16. Springer, Heidelberg (2005)
13. Heiser, G., Elphinstone, K., Kuz, I., Klein, G., Petters, S.M.: Towards trustworthy computing systems: Taking microkernels to the next level (2007)
14. Leinenbach, D., Paul, W.J., Petrova, E.: Towards the formal verification of a C0 compiler: Code generation and implementation correctness. In: Aichernig, B.K., Beckert, B. (eds.) SEFM, pp. 2–12. IEEE Computer Society, Los Alamitos (2005)
15. Liedtke, J.: On microkernel construction. In: Proceedings of the 15th ACM Symposium on Operating System Principles (SOSP-15), Copper Mountain Resort, CO (December 1995)
16. Moskal, M., Schulte, W., Venter, H.: Bits, words and types: Memory models for a Verifying C Compiler (2008)

17. Mürk, O., Larsson, D., Hähnle, R.: KeY-C: A tool for verification of C programs. In: Pfenning, F. (ed.) CADE 2007. LNCS (LNAI), vol. 4603, pp. 385–390. Springer, Heidelberg (2007)
18. Necula, G.C.: Proof-carrying code. In: POPL, pp. 106–119 (1997)
19. Ni, Z., Yu, D., Shao, Z.: Using XCAP to certify realistic systems code: Machine context management. In: Schneider, K., Brandt, J. (eds.) TPHOLs 2007. LNCS, vol. 4732, pp. 189–206. Springer, Heidelberg (2007)
20. Schirmer, N.: Verification of Sequential Imperative Programs in Isabelle/HOL. PhD thesis, Technische Universität München (2006)
21. Tuch, H., Klein, G., Norrish, M.: Types, bytes, and separation logic. In: Hoffmann, M., Felleisen, M. (eds.) POPL, pp. 97–108. ACM, New York (2007)

Evolving Specification Engineering

Dusko Pavlovic, Peter Pepper, and Doug Smith

Kestrel Institute and Technische Universität Berlin
{dusko,smith}@kestrel.edu, pepper@cs.tu-berlin.de

Abstract. The motivation for this work is to support a natural separation of concerns during formal system development. In a development-by-refinement context, we would like to be able to first treat basic functionality and normal-case behavior, and then later add in complicating factors such as physical limitations (memory, time, bandwidth, hardware reliability, and so on) and security concerns. Handling these complicating factors often does not result in a refinement, since safety or liveness properties may not be preserved. We extend our earlier work on evolving specifications (1) to allow the preservation of both safety and liveness properties under refinement, and (2) to explore a more general notion of refinement morphism to express the introduction of complicating factors.

1 Introduction

It is natural for developers to initially focus on essential requirements, and to first consider only "normal" behaviors when writing specifications. Gradually, through refinement, the developer can then strengthen the initial optimistic assumptions, and handle the exceptional, unusual and abnormal cases, as well as introduce stronger requirements.

However, this approach presents a conceptual problem for a formal specification framework. Refining a specification by catching some exceptional behavior may not preserve the liveness properties of the system. Refining a specification by explicitly handling some exceptional behavior may not preserve its safety properties. So the question is: which properties should the useful refinement operations preserve?

In the present paper, this problem is formalized and solved in the framework of Evolving Specifications (especs) [11]. In order to express and characterize the conditions under which the relevant safety and liveness properties are preserved, we extend the framework by temporal modalities. In order to capture the specific preservation properties, combining safety and liveness in a way suitable for exception handling, we use *guard intervals* [9], spanned between the conditions under which an operation *may* fire, and the conditions under which it *must* fire. The capability to separate concerns for normal behavior from the exceptional cases opens an alley towards better understanding and implementing the mechanisms to introduce new safety and security policies in a system, and their semantic effects on a design.

J. Meseguer and G. Roşu (Eds.): AMAST 2008, LNCS 5140, pp. 299–314, 2008.

1.1 A Simple Real-World Example

We illustrate our approach with a running example that is taken from the automotive domain: A modern car contains numerous devices such as radio tuner, CD player, navigation system, mobile phone and so forth. We presume here that all these devices are connected through a MOST bus (a modern optical bus that is often used in European cars) such that the user interaction with all services can take place over a common microphone, amplifiers and graphical display. The MOST bus architecture [1] provides both synchronous and asynchronous channels (and also command channels) for the interconnection of devices. Throughout this paper we will use (admittedly oversimplified) features of the MOST architecture as illustrating examples. The basic concept is illustrated in Fig. 1: All devices – including the MOST bus itself – are considered as "components" (more or less like in UML).

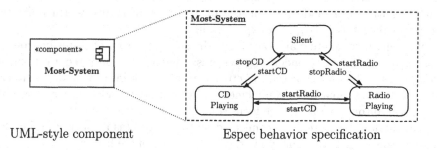

UML-style component   Espec behavior specification

Fig. 1. The modes and transitions of a trivial MOST system

The behavior of a component is described in the espec formalism. For the sake of illustration we consider an oversimplified two-device system consisting of a radio and a CD player. This leads to three general modes, namely *CD-Playing*, *Radio-Playing* and *Silent*. Therefore Fig. 1 essentially describes the system from the viewpoint of the MOST bus: At any given point in time either the radio is playing or the CD player or none of them. There are six transitions, for which we allow overloaded naming, as long as their source or target modes are different.

Each device requires four bus channels to connect with the amplifier. In a natural specification development process, we would like to be able to simply assume that four channels are available when transitioning, say, from *Silent* to *CD-Playing*. Only later would we deal with abnormal situations in which that is not the case, as illustrated in Section 5.

1.2 Background

In previous work we introduced Evolving Specifications (especs) as a framework for specifying, composing, and refining systems [11,12,10]. This framework extends our earlier work on the algebraic/categorical specification of software [8], which it still contains as a subframework. Especs add the dimension of stateful behavior, and thus leads into the realm of system specifications. This approach is in the tradition of many approaches in the literature to address issues of system design by utilizing category-theoretic mechanisms (e.g. [3].)

Modes and Transitions. Although formally our evolving specifications resemble state machines, we prefer to speak of *"modes (of operation)"*, rather than states. A specification usually describes how a system evolves from mode to mode: e.g., a CD player, may be in the mode *Playing*, performing the various activities within that mode, until a suitable event triggers a transition into another mode, say *Searching*. From an intuitive semantic point of view, a mode $\mathcal{M}$ can be viewed as a *set of (finite or infinite) traces of states*:

$$Beh(\mathcal{M}) = \{\ \mathcal{T} \mid \mathcal{T} = \langle \mathcal{S}_1, \mathcal{S}_2, \mathcal{S}_3, \dots \rangle,\ \mathcal{S}_i \models Theory(\mathcal{M})\ \} \qquad (1)$$

The modes $\mathcal{M}_1, \mathcal{M}_2, \dots$ are *specified* by logical theories[1] $M_1, M_2, \dots$. Therefore the semantics of a mode $\mathcal{M}_i$ consists of all traces of states, which fulfill the corresponding theory M_i, as is expressed in (1).

We remain completely abstract w.r.t. the specific nature of states in order to encompass all kinds of underlying systems; therefore we only require them to be models of the given theories. (Actually we also look into variants, where the state traces are replaced or complemented by continuous behaviors, comparable to hybrid automata.) Hence we focus solely on the modes from now on.

The modes of a system are connected by transitions (as illustrated in Fig. 2). These transitions t are usually guarded, which we denote here as $g \Rightarrow t$.

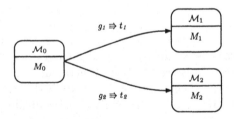

Fig. 2. Modes and transitions

Note: Each mode is assumed to have an *identity transition* with guard *true* and transition *id* (nothing changes). This transition – which we do not draw explicitly in our illustrations – corresponds to "stuttering", and is left to be specified in later refinements.

Semantically, a transition such as $g_1 \Rightarrow t_1$ in Fig. 2 usually means that, whenever the *guard* g_1 holds in some state $\mathcal{S}_j$ of $\mathcal{M}_0$, then the transition *may* be taken. But it can only be taken in states where the guard holds. For reasons to

---

[1] We essentially identify the modes with their theories; therefore we purposely distinguish them only by the font.

be seen in a moment we refer to these kinds of guards as *safety guards*. Safety guards represent very weak and liberal constraints: They may hold arbitrarily often during a mode without their transition being taken. In particular, guards g_1 and g_2 of competing transitions (such as in Fig. 2) need not be disjoint.

But there is a second view of guards, where a transition such as $g_1 \Rightarrow t_1$ in Fig. 2 means that, whenever the *guard* g_1 holds in some state S_j of $\mathcal{M}_0$, then the transition *must* be taken. Consequently, competing transitions must have disjoint guards g_1 and g_2. For reasons to become clear in a moment, we refer to guards of this kind as *liveness guards*.

These semantic intuitions have led to the formalism of evolving specifications [11]. Its main conceptual components are:

Transitions. The transition $\mathcal{M}_1 \xrightarrow{g \Rightarrow t} \mathcal{M}_2$ is captured as an interpretation $M_2 \xrightarrow{t} M_1$, which rewrites the theory M_2 in terms of the theory M_1:

$$M_2 \models q \quad \Longrightarrow \quad M_1 \models (g \Rightarrow t(q)) \tag{2}$$

Within the category of specifications, such guarded transitions are modeled as opspans of interpretations in the form

$$M_1 \longrightarrow (M_1 \wedge g) \xleftarrow{t} M_2 \tag{3}$$

The formal details of categorical semantics of evolving specifications can be found in [11,12]. Intuitively, the action t performed by a transition can be construed as a predicate transformer.

Within this formal and intuitive framework, the guards allow two semantically relevant interpretations:

Safety guards. An occurrence of the transition $\mathcal{M}_1 \xrightarrow{g \Rightarrow t} \mathcal{M}_2$ in an execution $\mathcal{Q}$ is *enabled*, when $M_1 \wedge g$ is satisfied for the variable assignments at that point of the execution.

Liveness guards. An occurrence of the transition $\mathcal{M}_1 \xrightarrow{g \Rightarrow t} \mathcal{M}_2$ in an execution $\mathcal{Q}$ is *forced*, when $M_1 \wedge g$ is satisfied for the variable assignments at that point of the execution.

While the framework of [12] left the choice between these two interpretations to the designer, deciding if the refinements should preserve safety or liveness, in Section 3 below, we shall present a unified semantical framework, subsuming both of the above interpretations.

Definition 1. *A* run *of a system is a sequence of modes* $\mathcal{M}_0 \rightarrow \mathcal{M}_1 \rightarrow \mathcal{M}_2 \rightarrow \ldots$ *for which there are transitions* $\mathcal{M}_i \xrightarrow{g \Rightarrow t} \mathcal{M}_{i+1}$. *The* behavior $Beh(Spec)$ *of a system specification is the set of all its runs.*

1.3   Refinement

The main point of especs is to provide a precise and convenient framework to specify the functions and behavior of software systems *incrementally*. The main point of their categorical semantics is to provide a formal underpinning for refinement and composition, in terms of morphisms and colimits.

The basic principle can be summarized as follows: As usual, a refinement adds details, but preserves certain properties. Hence, the theory increases and the set of models becomes smaller:

$$\left(Spec_a \xrightarrow{\;\varphi\;} Spec_c \right) \;\Longrightarrow\; \left(Beh\,(Spec_a) \supseteq Beh\,(Spec_c) \right) \tag{4}$$

Due to the added details, one often refers to the original specification $Spec_a$ as the *abstract model* and to the refined specification $Spec_c$ as the *concrete model*.

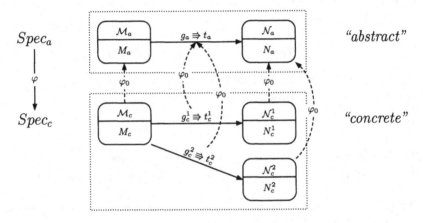

Fig. 3. Refinement of modes and transitions

As is illustrated in Fig. 3 it is possible that several modes of the concrete model correspond to ("refine") a single mode of the abstract model. And also several concrete transitions may correspond to ("refine") a single abstract transition (see [12]).

Definition 2. *A refinement $\varphi : Spec_a \longrightarrow Spec_c$ as depicted in Fig. 3 consists of two components:*

- *a graph morphism $\varphi_0 : Diag_c \longrightarrow Diag_a$, assigning to each concrete mode an abstract mode, and to each concrete transition an abstract transition, which it refines;*
- *a tuple of traditional specification morphisms $\varphi_1^N : \varphi_0(N) \longrightarrow N$, one for each concrete mode $N \in Diag_c$, telling how the specification of the mode N refines the specification of the mode $\varphi_0(N)$.*

Whereas this bipartite view of the structure preservation is rather familiar, e.g. from theory of institutions [5], the treatment of the *guards under refinement* is more intricate, since we need to distinguish *safety guards* and *liveness guards*.

Safety morphisms are required to preserve safety properties: the refinement
and the composition steps along the safety morphisms must not introduce
new runs — every run in the concrete system is a refinement of (or is simulated by) some run of the abstract system.

To preserve only the enabled executions, the specification components ς_1 of
a safety morphism $\varsigma : Spec_a \longrightarrow Spec_c$ must satisfy, for every concrete
transition $\mathcal{M}_c \xrightarrow{g_c \Rightarrow t_c} \mathcal{N}_c$,

$$M_c \models (g_c \Rightarrow \varsigma_1(g_a)) \tag{5}$$

where g_a is the guard of the φ_0-image of this transition.
This formalizes the fact that a concrete transition may only be taken if the
corresponding abstract transition may have been taken as well.

Liveness morphisms are required to preserve liveness properties: the refinement and the composition steps along the morphisms must not introduce
new deadlocks, but guarantee that every trace in the abstract system induces some refined trace in the concrete system.

To preserve all the forced executions, the specification components λ_1 of
a liveness morphism $\lambda : Spec_a \longrightarrow Spec_c$ must satisfy, for every concrete
transition $\mathcal{M}_c \xrightarrow{g_c \Rightarrow t_c} \mathcal{N}_c$,

$$M_c \models (\lambda_1(g_a) \Rightarrow g_c) \tag{6}$$

This formalizes the fact that whenever an abstract transition must be taken
then the corresponding concrete transition must be taken as well.

Every first order trace property can be expressed as a conjunction of a safety
property and a liveness property [2]. In order to specify refinements preserving
arbitrary first order properties of interest, it is therefore sufficient to assure that
both safety and liveness properties are preserved. A general method to realize this
by combining the two types of espec morphisms described above is presented in
Section 3. To motivate it, we first summarize a more special problem that drives
this paper.

1.4   The Problem to Be Solved

In rare cases, the process of system design can be subdivided into refinement
steps where only safety or only liveness is preserved. In most cases, however,
a property required from the system inextricably combines liveness and safety
aspects. See [6] or [7] for examples.

Related to this is another issue: In many situations it is natural to first specify the *normal* behaviors of the system, under some simplifying assumptions,
and to handle separately the *exceptional* behaviors, when these assumptions are
not satisfied. The refinement step where the exceptions are recognized does not
preserve liveness (since it blocks some runs), whereas the refinement step where
they are handled does not preserve safety (since it adds new runs).

This leaves us with two complementary tasks of refining the notion of espec
refinement, respectively capturing

1. general properties, which combine safety and liveness properties, and
2. exception recognition and handling.

The solutions of these two tasks will be outlined in Sections 3 and 4.2. As a preparatory step we formalize in Section 2 the above remarks about the safety guards and the liveness guards by defining an obvious interpretation of temporal logics of especs.

2   Temporal Evolving Specifications (tespecs)

The temporal statements in an espec are expressed in a global language, common to all modes. That is, the atomic formulas are given by the intersection of (the signatures of) all mode theories M_i. Over these we build temporal formulas using the usual connectors from propositional logic and the two tense operators

$$\bigcirc q \qquad \textbf{(next)}$$
$$q \, \mathcal{W} \, r \qquad \textbf{(waiting-for)}$$

We define the validity of a (temporal) formula q in a certain mode $\mathcal{M}_0$ based on its validity for all runs $\mathcal{M}_0 \rightarrow \mathcal{M}_1 \rightarrow \mathcal{M}_2 \rightarrow \ldots$ that begin with $\mathcal{M}_0$. Based on the standard notion of validity ($M_i \models q$) for non-temporal formulas q, we define the validity of the temporal formalas in the usual way:

$$M_0 \models \bigcirc q \quad \Longleftrightarrow \quad M_1 \models q \tag{7}$$
$$M_0 \models q \, \mathcal{W} \, r \quad \Longleftrightarrow \quad (\forall i. \, M_i \models q) \vee \exists k. \, (M_k \models r) \wedge (\forall j < k. \, M_j \models q) \tag{8}$$

Remark: Temporal formulas quantify over the coarse-grained modes (runs) and not over the fine-grained internal states (traces) inside the modes.

Together with the usual connectors of classical logic, we can introduce the well-known further temporal modalities

$$\begin{aligned} \Box q &= q \, \mathcal{W} \perp & \textbf{(henceforth)} \\ \Diamond q &= \neg \Box \neg q & \textbf{(eventually)} \\ q \, \mathcal{U} \, r &= q \, \mathcal{W} \, r \wedge \Diamond r & \textbf{(until)} \end{aligned} \tag{9}$$

Now we can formalize the statements from the Introduction. Actually, much stronger and more precise statements could be proved.

Definition 3. *A* safety property *has the form* $\Box q$. *A* liveness property *has the form* $\Diamond q$.

The following lemma points to the way in which the (global) safety and liveness properties are logically related to the (local) guards of transitions.

Lemma 1. *(i) A system described by an espec* **satisfies a safety property** $\Box q$, *if and only if in each run (i) the property q is satisfied at the initial mode $\mathcal{M}_0$, and (ii) it is invariant under every enabled transition, i.e.*

$$M_0 \models q$$
$$and \quad (M \models q \wedge g) \Longrightarrow (N \models q), \qquad for \; all \; M \xrightarrow{\; g \Rightarrow t \;} N \tag{10}$$

*(ii) A system **satisfies a liveness property** $\Diamond q$, if and only if in each run either the property q is satisfied at the initial mode, or there is an enabled transition, where q is established.*

$$M_0 \models q$$
$$or \quad (M \models \neg q \wedge g) \wedge (N \models q), \quad for\ some\ \mathcal{M} \xrightarrow{g \Rightarrow t} \mathcal{N} \quad (11)$$

Proposition 1. *An espec morphism preserves safety (resp. liveness) properties if and only if it preserves all safety (resp. liveness) guards.*

Note: The characterization of liveness in the definitions (8) and (9) and in Lemma 1(ii) reflects the liveness view of branching-time logic in the Manna-Pnueli style, where $\Diamond q$ essentially means that *in every run* there is at least one state where q holds. If we would instead internalize the quantification over all runs into the definition of the validity, we would obtain the view of the temporal logic CTL*. This view represents the very weak property that *there is at least one possible run containing at least one state, where q holds*. So our approach could be geared towards both variants without much effort.

3   Guard Intervals

In the previous sections we have been working with the *concepts* of safety and liveness guards, but *without notational means* to distinguish them. Since many specifications combine both safety *and* liveness aspects,it turns out to be useful to bring them together. This leads to the idea of *guard intervals*, originally implemented in the CommUnity system [9].

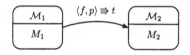

Definition 4. *A **guard interval** is given in the form $\langle f, p \rangle$, where as an additional constraint the implication $f \Rightarrow p$ must hold.*

- f is the **forcing guard**, i.e. the liveness guard that determines which (good) things must *happen*;
- p is the **permitting guard**, i.e. the safety guard that says which things are not bad *and* may *happen*.

Let S be some state in a run of $\mathcal{M}_1$. Then the transition $\mathcal{M}_1 \xrightarrow{\langle f,p \rangle \Rightarrow t} \mathcal{M}_2$ is

- *enabled if $S \models p$;*
- *forced if moreover $S \models f$.*

As we shall see next, under refinement the interval monotonically tightens, but not necessarily to a singleton.

Remark. The idea to capture the safety and the progress properties of executions by pairs of guards goes back to Fiadeiro's and Lopez' work on the CommUnity system [9]. Like especs, CommUnity belongs to the broad family of categorical specification systems [3,5], where the property preservation under refinements is enforced as the structure preservation, imposed on the morphisms. However, the differences between the tasks supported by CommUnity and the tasks set out in this paper lead to different treatments of guard intervals. In particular, while the superposition morphisms of CommUnity only allow strengthening of both safety and liveness guards [9, Def./Prop. 4.1], and their refinement morphisms add a further constraint [9, Def./Prop. 5.1], leading to the equivalence of each abstract liveness guard with the disjunction of its concretizations, a simpler preservation requirement will turn out to be more appropriate in our framework. This requirement is the subject of the next section.

Refinement with Guard Intervals

Let us consider a refinement of guard intervals as depicted in Fig. 4 below (where, as earlier, φ denotes the specification morphism and ψ the opposite morphism on the diagrams). When will it preserve both liveness and the safety? The answer is a direct consequence of equations (5) and (6) in Section 1.3:

- The forcing guard f has to be *weakened*;
- The permitting guard p has to be *strengthened*.

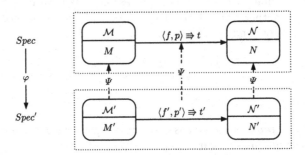

Fig. 4. Refinement of guard intervals

Gathering these implications, together with the constraint of Def. 4, in the form

$$\mathcal{M}' \models \varphi(f) \Rightarrow f' \wedge f' \Rightarrow p' \wedge p' \Rightarrow \varphi(p) \tag{12}$$

we see that the refinement actually *tightens* the guard interval, just like it does in real number computation, so that above implications can be construed as the interval inclusion $\langle f', p' \rangle \subseteq \langle \varphi(f), \varphi(p) \rangle$. For especs, this just captures the fact that the behaviors in which the refined transition is taken is strictly included, modulo the interpretations, among the behaviors where the abstract transition is taken. The effect of a nontrivial liveness guard (i.e. not always *false*) is to force the inclusion of the transition in *all* refinements.

If liveness properties are proved relative to the liveness guards (forced transitions) then since the liveness guards are only weakened under refinement, they will be preserved under any refinement. Similarly, if safety properties are proved relative to the safety guards (enabled transitions) then since the safety guards are only strengthened under refinement, they will be preserved under any refinement.

This extension of the espec formalism by the pairs of guards $\langle f, p \rangle$ is easily seen to be yet another instance of the abstract framework of [12]. The procedure of adjoining guards to the category **Spec** of specification, described in Section 3 of that paper, only needs to be modified by taking

$$\mathbb{G}(K, M) = \{\langle f, p \rangle \in \mathcal{L}_K^2 \mid K \wedge f \Rightarrow M \Rightarrow K \wedge p\} \tag{13}$$

Defining the espec morphisms as above then allows capturing the suitable combinations of safety and liveness properties, expressible by the guard intervals. The language of especs with guard intervals is more expressive than the ordinary guarded language, as it can express certain combinations of temporal modalities. The exact characterization of its expressiveness appears to be nontrivial.

The well-known topological analysis of liveness and safety properties [2] tells that every first order trace property can be expressed as an intersection of a safety and a liveness property, i.e. in the form $\Box q \wedge \Diamond r$.

Based on Lemma 1 we know that by representing a first order property in the form $\Box q \wedge \Diamond r$, and setting up the guard intervals in an abstract espec to realize this property, we can be sure that the espec morphisms preserving the guard intervals will preserve this property.

Proposition 2. *An espec morphism with guard intervals preserves all first order properties.*

4   "Normally" Modality

When they explain the functioning of a system (be it existing or planned), engineers usually begin in the style: *"Disregarding pathological borderline cases, the normal behavior is ... "*. In practice, there is a healthy distinction between the essential purpose of the system and all the nitty-gritty details of possible complications and unwanted effects. As soon as one tries to transfer this principle to the rigorous world of mathematical specifications, severe problems arise. Specifying the essential features without explicitly precluding the undesired exceptional situations often leads to inconsistencies. On the other hand, enumerating the undesired situations, and their interactions, is known to lead to "formal noise" that exceeds the specification proper by an order of magnitude.

We attempt to mitigate this situation by introducing a special operator *normally*, denoted by $\natural$. We could define this operator as some kind of modality, but our framework allows us to introduce it as a simple abbreviation.

Definition 5 (Normally). *The* normally *operator* ♮ *is an abbreviation for an uninterpreted guarding predicate n:*

| ♮ *property* | *abbreviates* | $nrml \Rightarrow property$ |
| ♮ *guard* $\Rrightarrow$ *transition* | *abbreviates* | $nrml \land guard \Rrightarrow transition$ |

Note that there is a fresh predicate symbol nrml for each occurrence of the operator ♮.

As a shorthand notation we may qualify a whole specification or a whole mode or transition with the normally operator. This means that every single axiom and transition is implicitly preceded by the operator ♮.

In the later course of the development of the model this variable *nrml* can be made explicit and then be more and more concretely interpreted by giving axioms for it. This way, one can successively add exception handling to an originally "purely optimistic" model.

Together with our concept of refinement, this operator stratifies specifications considerably. The following program illustrates our use of the normally operator.

   ESPEC *Player* IS

        ...

      MODE *Playing* IS

         ♮ *#(channels)* = 4

        ...

      END-ESPEC *Player*

This specification says that an active CD player "normally" has four channels available for streaming (thus enabling stereo). However, there may be situations in which the MOST bus does not have enough free channels. Then we have to take appropriate measures in order to build a workaround (e.g. changing to mono). But we do not want to clutter our specification of the essential behavior with that kind of exception handling in the early stages of our development. These kinds of complications need to be worked into the specification at some later stage – and it needs to be done in a systematic way; this is achieved in our approach by employing suitable refinement morphisms.

4.1 Refinement of "Normally"

Many of the occurrences of the normally operator ♮ can be refined by the standard mechanisms developed so far. Since the operator usually corresponds to the addition of uninterpreted predicate symbols, we simply need to define axioms that interpret these symbols in order to make the specification more concrete. This is a classical refinement morphism.

However, there is one additional activity that we need to add for purely pragmatic reasons, even though it partly conflicts with our notion of refinement morphisms: If in a specification **Syst** a whole transition is qualified as "normally", i.e. $♮(\mathcal{M} \xrightarrow{g \Rrightarrow t} \mathcal{N})$, then the designer often wants to express the fact that there may be further transitions out of $\mathcal{M}$, which are not yet relevant at this stage of the development.

A later refinement Syst' may then add another transition $\mathcal{M} \xrightarrow{g' \Rrightarrow t'} \mathcal{K}$ out of $\mathcal{M}$. The problem is that this need not correspond to any transition of the original specification Syst. Hence, the mapping φ_0 (see Section 1.3) is *not* a proper diagram morphism.

There are a number of ways out of this dilemma. In the next section we show a special instance of this paradigm in order to demonstrate how the principal mechanism works.

4.2 Especs of Exceptions

The normally operator $\natural$ allows a relatively fine-grained qualification of those aspects that are in the core of a system (as opposed to borderline cases such as errors or rare events). However, it does not really help to solve another unpleasant feature of real systems: *exceptions.*

Since exceptions can happen anywhere and anytime, the whole specification would have to be qualified by $\natural$, meaning that every single axiom, mode and transition is qualified as "normally". This would make the refinement effort to successively eliminate all occurrences of $\natural$ unbearable. Hence we need other means to systematically cope with this kind of global pathology.

Raising an exception interrupts some existing computation flow, and therefore may not preserve liveness properties. *Catching* an exception introduces some new computation flows, and therefore may not preserve safety properties. That is why imposing policies, to distinguish normal behaviors and to handle exceptional behaviors, is a challenge for systematic system design.

More precisely, we are given a basic system $\mathsf{Syst}_\natural$ satisfying a behavior B under "normal" circumstances, i.e. as long as there are no exceptions: $\mathsf{Syst}_\natural \models B$. From this system we want to derive a system Syst_E satisfying B whenever the norm $\neg E$ (no exceptions) is satisfied, otherwise satisfying the handling requirement H. Formally, we require:

$$\mathsf{Syst}_E \models (\neg E \Rightarrow B) \wedge (E \Rightarrow H) \tag{14}$$

This is realized by building system Syst_E with

$$\mathsf{Syst}_E \models (\neg E \wedge B) \; \mathcal{W} \; (E \wedge H) \tag{15}$$

The system Syst_E is systematically obtained from $\mathsf{Syst}_\natural$ as follows:

- the modes of Syst_E are:
  - the modes of $\mathsf{Syst}_\natural$,
  - an adjoined *handling* mode $\mathcal{H}$,
- the transitions of Syst_E are:
  - for each transition $\mathcal{M} \xrightarrow{\langle f,p \rangle \Rrightarrow t} \mathcal{N}$ in $\mathsf{Syst}_\natural$ a transition $\mathcal{M} \xrightarrow{\langle f, \neg E \wedge p \rangle \Rrightarrow t} \mathcal{N}$ in Syst_E, provided $f \Rightarrow \neg E$, and
  - for each mode $\mathcal{M}$ of $\mathsf{Syst}_\natural$ a new transition $\mathcal{M} \xrightarrow{E \Rrightarrow \hat{t}} \mathcal{H}$ in Syst_E, where $\hat{t}$ initializes the variables of H.

Proposition 3. Syst_E *satisfies (15) and hence (14).*

As can be seen here easily, this is a global treatment of a global normally operator: Such an operator implicitly qualifies all modes and transitions by $\natural$. And the above construction simply refines all the different predicate symbols (to which these $\natural$ operators correspond) by one single predicate $\neg E$.

The question is: *What kind of espec morphism supports refinements in the form* $\mathsf{Syst}_\natural \longrightarrow \mathsf{Syst}_E$? The problem is that the mode $\mathcal{H}$, adjoined in Syst_E does not arise from any mode present in $\mathsf{Syst}_\natural$.

One possible answer is to first extend $\mathsf{Syst}_\natural$ by an *unreachable* mode $\mathcal{H}$, with a transition from each mode $\mathcal{M}$, but guarded by $\bot$. Such an *unreachable abstraction* $\mathsf{Syst}_\natural \longleftarrow \mathsf{Syst}_\bot$ leads to an espec $\mathsf{Syst}_\bot$ semantically equivalent to $\mathsf{Syst}_\natural$; that is, both systems have the same traces. So $\mathsf{Syst}_\natural$ and $\mathsf{Syst}_\bot$ satisfy the same properties.

On the other hand, $\mathsf{Syst}_\bot$ can be refined to Syst_E. This refinement, of course, does not preserve safety, since $\mathcal{H}$ is not unreachable in Syst_E. However, it is not hard to prove that

Proposition 4. *The span* $\mathsf{Syst}_\natural \longleftarrow \mathsf{Syst}_\bot \longrightarrow \mathsf{Syst}_E$, *viewed as a generalized morphism, preserves liveness, and moreover it preserves all properties B of* $\mathsf{Syst}_\natural$, *relativized to* $\neg E$, *in the sense of (15).*

5 Parameterized Especs: Modeling the Environment

In system design, the need arises to specify the properties and behavior of a component's environment, including required behaviors, invariant properties, and required services. The correctness of the component's behavior follows from the assumption that the environment behaves as specified, together with the internal structure and behavior of the component. This is sometimes referred to as the "rely-guarantee" paradigm. Parameterized especs neatly satisfy this need.

A parameter to an espec is an espec that models the environment – what behavior and properties the component expects of the environment, and what services it requires. The binding of a parameter to the environment is given by an espec morphism π – the environment is expected to be a refinement of the parameter. The environment will typically have much more structure and behavior than is specified by the parameter, but it must have at least as much as is required for the correct operation of the component.

In our running example of the MOST bus this will typically lead to situations as depicted in Fig. 5. Each device has a *body specification* for the device proper and a *parameter specification* for its interface to the context; both are linked through a parameter morphism π. The interfaces are then linked to the overall system, i.e. the MOST bus, through refinement morphisms φ. This makes it relatively easy to add any number of components to some MOST system without running into an unmanageable combinatorial explosion of the size of the specifications and, above all, of the number of interconnections.

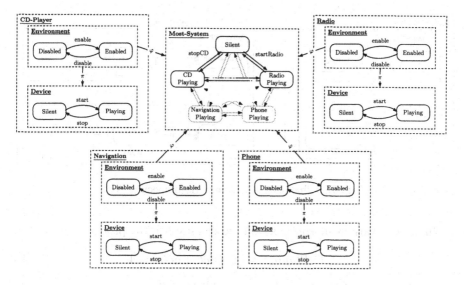

Fig. 5. Modularization through parameter morphisms

This raises the question of the refinement of parameterized specifications. Fig. 6 shows an example of such a refinement.

In the original abstract model an audio device is simply assumed to switch between the two modes *Silent* and *Playing*. Accordingly the environment is expected to consider the device as *Disabled* or *Enabled* (with the appropriate matchings).

However, in the MOST bus the enabling of a device is performed by a full-fledged *connection protocol*: In order to become playing, the device needs a number of channels to be allocated by the MOST bus. After having received them, the device still cannot play, since the channels also need to be allocated to the amplifiers. Therefore the device has to go into an intermediate mode *Ready*, while the environment is in the mode *Connecting*. (It is only by chance that the number of modes and transitions in the parameter and the body coincide in this example. In general they will be different.)

This refinement is realized by the morphism that is sketched in Fig. 6. However, this diagram only gives a rough idea of the construction, since it does not express the various compatibility constraints between the two parameter morphisms and the refinement morphism φ. Fortunately most of them are generated automatically by the category-theoretic principles underlying the construction.

Consider the situation of Fig. 5 and the little program in Section 4. Let us assume that the parameter specification establishes $\#(channels) = 4$ in the mode *Enabled*.

Now consider the mode *CD-Playing* of the MOST system in Fig. 5 and suppose that it only contains the assertion $\#(channels) \geq 2$. What does this mean in our overall design?

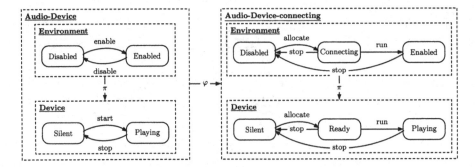

Fig. 6. Refinement of parameterized specifications

Due to our various morphisms we need to establish the property

$$CD\text{-}Playing \models \natural\ \#(channels) = 4 \qquad (16)$$

This leaves us with the problem of establishing the property (with an uninterpreted symbol *nrml*)

$$\#(channels) \geq 2 \models nrml \Rightarrow \#(channels) = 4 \qquad (17)$$

So the further refinements must add interpretations to *nrml* that allow us to complete this required proof. In practice this means that upon connection establishment the CD player needs to obtain the required number of channels from the MOST system, which is stored in a local variable *chNr*. Then *nrml* simply is refined to *chNr* = 4. The span construction of Proposition 4 adds a new transition to a handler mode for the case when *chNr* < 4.

6   Conclusion

The methodology that we have presented in this paper has a number of benefits. It allows the *systematic incremental development of models* as opposed to the predominant current practice of creating monolithic models in a more or less informally crafted process. Moreover, the resulting *models are formally specified*, which allows not only automatic code generation (at least of prototypes), but also supports all kinds of analyses, ranging from logical consistency or completeness checks to plain testing.

With respect to the underlying formalism, a lot of work still needs to be done. For example, we currently study different approaches to the role of the "normally" operator and its refinement. Also, the role of guard refinement in the context of automotive applications needs to be assessed in greater detail, in particular with respect to liveness vs. safety preservation. Moreover, the role of (dynamic) addition and deletion of components needs to be further investigated. Yet another challenge is to provide a more convenient notation that will be more readily accepted by engineers.

References

1. The MOST cooperation, http://www.mostcooperation.com/home/index.html
2. Alpern, B., Schneider, F.B.: Defining liveness. Information Processing Letters 21, 181–185 (1985)
3. Goguen, J.A.: Categorical foundations for general systems theory. In: Pichler, F., Trappl, R. (eds.) Advances in Cybernetics and Systems Research, pp. 121–130. Transcripta Books (1973)
4. Goguen, J.A., Burstall, R.M.: Institutions: Abstract model theory for computer science. Technical Report CSLI-85-30, Stanford University (1985)
5. Goguen, J.A., Burstall, R.M.: Institutions: Abstract model theory for computer science. Journal of the ACM 39(1), 95–146 (1992)
6. Huttel, Larsen: The use of static constructs in a modal process logic. In: LFCS: The 1st International Symposium on Logical Foundations of Computer Science (1989)
7. Fiadeiro, J., Lopes, A., Wermelinger, M.: A mathematical semantics for architectural connectors. In: FASE 2003. LNCS, vol. 2793, pp. 190–234 (2003)
8. Kestrel Institute. Specware System and documentation (2003), http://www.specware.org/
9. Lopes, A., Fiadeiro, J.L.: Using explicit state to describe architechtures. In: Finance, J.-P. (ed.) FASE 1999. LNCS, vol. 1577, pp. 144–160. Springer, Heidelberg (1999)
10. Pavlovic, D., Pepper, P., Smith, D.R.: Colimits for concurrent collectors. In: Dershowitz, N. (ed.) Verification: Theory and Practice. LNCS, vol. 2772, pp. 568–597. Springer, Heidelberg (2004)
11. Pavlovic, D., Smith, D.R.: Composition and refinement of behavioral specifications. In: Proceedings of Sixteenth International Conference on Automated Software Engineering, pp. 157–165. IEEE Computer Society Press, Los Alamitos (2001)
12. Pavlovic, D., Smith, D.R.: Guarded transitions in evolving specifications. In: Kirchner, H., Ringeissen, C. (eds.) AMAST 2002. LNCS, vol. 2422, pp. 411–425. Springer, Heidelberg (2002)

Verification of Java Programs with Generics

Kurt Stenzel, Holger Grandy, and Wolfgang Reif

Lehrstuhl für Softwaretechnik und Programmiersprachen
Institut für Informatik, Universität Augsburg
86135 Augsburg Germany
{stenzel,grandy,reif}@informatik.uni-augsburg.de

Abstract. Several proof systems allow the formal verification of Java programs, and a specification language was specifically designed for Java. However, none of these systems support generics that were introduced in Java 5. Generics are very important and useful when the collection framework (lists, sets, hash tables etc.) is used. Though they are mainly dealt with at compile time, they have some effect on the run-time behavior of a Java program. Most notably, *heap pollution* can cause exceptions. A verification system for Java must incorporate these effects. In this paper we describe what effects can occur at run time, and how they are handled in the KIV system [18] [2]. To the authors knowledge, this makes KIV the first verification system to support Java's generics.

1 Introduction

The Java programming language [9] was from the beginning very popular with respect to a formal treatment. Alves-Foss published early results (many of which dealt with Java's type system) in 1999 in [1]. Later work focused more on the specification and verification of Java programs. The *Java Modeling Language* JML [15] [19] allows the specification of Java programs in a language similar to Java itself and is supported by many tools [6]. Several tools support the formal verification of Java programs: the KeY tool [5], the LOOP compiler [14] using PVS, or Krakatoa [21], to name just three. ESC/Java2 [7] and Jack [4] are static checkers for Java that use underlying automated theorem prover(s) for their reasoning.

Impressive applications have been specified and verified. Many verification systems and case studies focus on Java Card [26] programs. This makes sense, because programs running on Smart Cards are typically security critical. They handle electronic cash (e.g. the Mondex card [22]), act as official documents, or contain important personal information like finger prints, or health records. A programming error could have serious consequences. And, from a verification point of view, the programs are small, and do not employ all features of the Java language. Examples are [13] [23] [11].

But there is a problem with 'normal' Java: The Java language evolves, and every few years new features are introduced that have a significant impact on a verification system. The same is true for C#. Java 1 [8] was released 1996,

J. Meseguer and G. Roşu (Eds.): AMAST 2008, LNCS 5140, pp. 315–329, 2008.

Java 2 [16] in 2000, and introduced inner classes. Java 5 [9] in 2005 added generics, annotations, enums, autoboxing, and other features (Java 6 added Scripting). Experience shows that it is very difficult for the developers of verification systems to keep up with the new features. (The same is true for formal API specifications.) They were designed without formal methods in mind, and it is very hard to estimate how difficult it is to include these features in a prover, and what their effects on actual proofs are without actually doing it. Furthermore, one may feel that these features are not really necessary. They simplify programming in Java, but if a program is to be formally proved anyway, this may not seem important.

We do not feel this way. We believe that there are programs worth verifying that use generics, and that it is important to analyze the effects of specific language features on formal proof systems. These and other results should be taken into account in the design of future programming languages.

Several groups are currently trying to support Java generics for formal specification or verification purposes. The JML developers are "working on Java 1.5 (generics)" [20]; "reason about Java 1.5 source" is "ongoing work" for ESC/-Java3 [17], and the KeY group has evaluated the consequences of supporting generics in the KeY prover [27]. Spec# [3] supports generics for C#, but this is easier because no heap pollution can occur.

This paper describes how generics are incorporated in the KIV prover. The results can probably be adapted to other proof systems with little effort. It turns out that generics have only a slight impact on run-time verification, mainly because of heap pollution. The rest of the paper is organized as follows: Section 2 gives a short introduction to generics from a user's (i.e. a programmer's) point of view, and section 3 describes the phenomenon of heap pollution. Section 4 gives a short introduction to the Java calculus in KIV, and the next two sections describe in detail the effects of generics on run-time behavior. Section 7 reports on results, and concludes.

2   Generics in Java

Generics were introduced in Java 5; they are described in the third edition of the Java Language Specification (JLS 3) [9]. This section provides only a very cursory overview that is focused on the run-time behavior of generics. Wildcards, or bounds are omitted since they are relevant only when their type erasure is computed (see Sect. 6).

Generic types are very useful for collections, e.g. lists. In Java 4, nothing is known about the elements of a list. When an element is retrieved with li.get(0) the result is of type Object. If a programmer uses a list of integers (i.e. he knows that all elements will be integers) the result must be cast anyway: (Integer)li.get(0). This can lead to an exception at run time if inadvertently a list of strings is supplied. The type system of Java without generics does not help in this case. With generics it is possible to declare a parameterized type List<Integer>. In this case the compiler will prevent the programmer from supplying a list of strings (of type List<String>) where a list of integers is expected, or to add a string to a list of integers. Additionally, no cast is necessary. Listing 1 shows a small example. The example includes two other features that were introduced in Java 5: *autoboxing* (automatic conversion of primitive types into their object counterpart and back) in lines 6, 11, 12, and the *enhanced* for *statement* in line 6.

```
1   import java.util.*;
2   public class Example1 {
3
4       public int sum(List<Integer> li) {
5       int res = 0;
6       for(int i : li) res += i;
7       return res;
8       }
9       public void example1() {
10      List<Integer> li = new ArrayList<Integer>();
11      li.add(5);
12      li.add(7);
13      System.out.println(sum(li));
14      }
15  }
```

Listing 1. An example with parameterized lists

Trying to call the sum method with a list of strings (of type List<String>) does not compile. The List interface is generic; it is declared as

public interface List<E> **extends** Collection<E> {

Here, E is a type variable that is instantiated with Integer in the example. The add method used in lines 11 and 12 is declared as **boolean** add(E e); and the get method (that is used implicitly in the loop) as E get(**int** index). This means the declared result type of the get method is the type variable E; if E is instantiated to Integer the compiler knows that the result will be of type Integer.

The most important aspect of generics with respect to formal verification is the fact that generics are "forgotten" at run time ("some type information is erased during compilation", JLS 3 p. 56). The reason is compatibility with existing code; see the discussion in JLS 3, p. 57. In fact, the byte code produced for the sum method in Listing 1 is identical to the byte code produced by the source code in listing 2.

This code does not use generics. Furthermore, the enhanced for loop has been replaced by a standard loop that uses an Iterator to access the list elements. Line 4 contains an explicit cast of the list element to Integer. Without it the code does not compile. However, the cast will produce a ClassCastException at run time if sum is called with a list of strings. The source code in Listing 2 compiles in Java 4, and also in Java 5. This may be unexpected because the parameterized interface List is used without an instance for the element type (A parameterized class or interface without its parameters is called a *raw* type).

```
1   public int sum(List li) {
2       int res = 0;
3       for(Iterator iter = li.iterator(); iter.hasNext(); ) {
4           int i = ((Integer)iter.next()).intValue();
5           res += i;
6       }
7       return res;
8   }
```

Listing 2. The same example without generics

But it is legal in Java 5 for compatibility reasons as mentioned above: Otherwise it would not be possible to reuse existing class files that were compiled with Java 4. Usage of the raw type (among others) gives rise to an *unchecked* warning by the Java 5 compiler:

Note: Some input files use unchecked or unsafe operations.

The code in listing 1 does not produce any compilation warnings. Still the byte code for listing 1 is the same as for listing 2. Especially the cast to Integer is contained in the byte code. This has implications for a formal verification in the presence of *heap pollution*, and will be explained in detail in sections 5 and 6.

3   Heap Pollution

Heap pollution is described in JLS 3, 4.12.2.1:

It is possible that a variable of a parameterized type refers to an object that is not of that parameterized type. This situation is known as *heap pollution*. This situation can only occur if the program performed some operation that would give rise to an unchecked warning at compile-time.

Heap pollution can lead to a ClassCastException at run time. Listing 3 shows a simple example.

```
1    public int sum(List<Integer> li) {
2    int res = 0;
3    for(int i : li) res += i; // throws
4    return res;
5    }
6    public void example3() {
7    List li = new ArrayList<String>(); // raw type
8    li.add("foo");
9    List<Integer> lii = (List<Integer>)li; // ok
10   System.out.println(sum(lii));
11   }
```

Listing 3. An example for heap pollution

In line 7 a raw type is used and a list containing a string is created. In line 9 this list is assigned to a variable of type List<Integer>, causing heap pollution. The code compiles, but running example3() causes a ClassCastException in line 3. Line 9 does not cause a ClassCastException because the cast effectively checks whether the argument is of type List – the type parameter is *erased* and not available (and hence not checked) at run time. The byte code for line 3 contains an explicit cast to Integer as described in the previous section, causing the exception. The behavior of the code is the same if li is passed directly to the sum() method.

Heap pollution can occur even without involvement of the heap, and it is easy to write very obfuscated programs where it is difficult to guess whether they will compile, and what their run time behavior will be. Listing 4 contains an example for this.

```
 1  public class Example4<X>{
 2
 3      public X m(boolean flag){
 4      if(flag) return (X) "string";
 5      else return (X) Integer.valueOf(3);
 6      }
 7      public static void main(String[] args){
 8      Example4 ex = new Example4<String>();
 9      Example4<Integer> ex4 = ex; // raw type
10      Integer x = ex4.m(false);   // ok
11      Integer y = ex4.m(true);    // throws
12      }
13  }
```

Listing 4. Heap pollution without the heap

The example compiles. Method m in line 3 returns either a String or an Integer object. This is possible because the type variable X is erased at run time, and on the byte code level the method has the result type Object. Line 9 causes "heap pollution" because a raw type is used. In line 10 m returns an Integer, and the assignment to x works. Line 11 causes a ClassCastException, because a String is returned.

Of course, both examples produce "unchecked" warnings at run time. It is tempting to reason in the following manner: "Good programming practice will not create code that produces unchecked warning. Therefore, we exclude those programs from formal verification." However, that is not true. Except for very simple examples it is almost impossible to avoid unchecked warnings. For example, the Java Collection Framework produces 96 unchecked warnings. This means that a useful verification system must cope with them.

4 Java Verification in KIV

The KIV system has a calculus for the interactive verification of sequential Java programs. Before describing the specific features of generics concerning verification we give a short introduction to the KIV calculus.

The calculus is a sequent calculus for dynamic logic [12] based on algebraic specifications with a loose semantics. Dynamic logic extends predicate logic with two modal operators, box $[\,.\,]$ and diamond $\langle\,.\,\rangle$. Box and diamond contain a context (a store) st and a Java program running in this context. The context contains the Java heap with the objects, and additional information about static fields, initialization of classes, and the execution state to model exceptions. It is specified algebraically. The class and interface declarations are part of a global environment. The intuitive meaning of $\langle st;\,\alpha\rangle\,\varphi$ is: with initial store st the Java statement α terminates, and afterwards φ holds. φ is again a formula of dynamic logic, i.e. it may contain boxes or diamonds. The meaning of $[st;\,\alpha]\,\varphi$ is: if α terminates then afterwards φ holds. A sequent $\varphi_1,\ldots,\varphi_m \vdash \psi_1,\ldots,\psi_n$ consists of two lists of formulas (often abbreviated by Γ and Δ) divided by $\vdash$ and is equivalent to the formula $\varphi_1 \wedge \ldots \wedge \varphi_m \rightarrow \psi_1 \vee \ldots \vee \psi_n$. The formulas $\varphi_1,\ldots\varphi_m$ can be thought of as preconditions, while one of $\psi_1,\ldots,\psi_n$ must be proved. A Hoare triple $\{\varphi\}\alpha\{\psi\}$ can be expressed as $\varphi \vdash [st;\alpha]\psi$ or $\varphi \vdash \langle st;\alpha\rangle\,\psi$ if termination is included. Java's type system is not built into the calculus, but rather specified algebraically. Logically, Java types in KIV are simple algebraic data types. This makes it trivial to incorporate parameterized types, type variables, wildcards, and bounds.

The calculus essentially has one rule for every Java expression and statement, plus some general rules. It works by symbolic execution of the Java program from its beginning to its end (i.e. computation of strongest postcondition). This means it follows the natural execution of the program, which is very important for interactive proofs. Nested expressions and blocks are flattened to a sequence of simple expressions and statements that can be executed directly. Obviously, this flattening must obey the evaluation order of Java. The result of a sub expression is 'stored' with an assignment to a local variable. This is shown in the following example.

$$\Gamma \vdash \langle st; \texttt{x = m1(m2(y), m3());}\rangle\, x = 5$$

1. Here the arguments of the method call m1 must be evaluated first. This is done by introducing a new local variable x2, and a new assignment to x2:
2. $\Gamma \vdash \langle st; \texttt{x2 = \textbf{m2(y)};}\,\rangle\,\langle st; \texttt{x = m1(\textbf{x2}, m3());}\rangle\, x = 5$
   The sub expression is replaced by x2. Since the argument to m2 is a variable the method call can be evaluated. A proof rule for the method call basically replaces the method call by its body. If m2 is declared as
   int m2(**int** i) { **return** i + 1; }
   the following goal is obtained:
3. $\Gamma, i = y \vdash \langle st; \textbf{return}\ \texttt{i + 1;}\rangle\,\langle st; \textbf{target}(\texttt{x2})\rangle$
   $\qquad\qquad \langle st; \texttt{x = m1(x2, m3());}\rangle\, x = 5$

The formal parameter is bound to the actual parameter by the equation $i = y$. This is only possible if the actual argument is already fully evaluated, i.e. in KIV either a local variable or a literal.

The `target(x2)` statement (not part of Java, of course) acts as a catcher for the `return` statement, and assigns x2 to the returned value. For i + 1 another variable is introduced:

4. $\Gamma, i = y, i1 = i + 1 \vdash \langle st; x2 \; = \; i1; \rangle \; \langle st; x \; = \; m1(x2, \; m3()); \rangle \; x = 5$

   The assignment becomes an equation, and then the next sub expression can be flattened. If variable conflicts occur, then a renaming will also take place:

5. $\Gamma, i = y, i1 = i + 1, x2 = i1 \vdash \langle st; x \; = \; m1(x2, \; m3()); \rangle \; x = 5$

And so on. After a finite number of applications of the flattening rule a list of assignments is returned where every sub expression is either a local variable or a literal. Then a rule for the main expression (e.g. a method call) or statement is applicable.

As a last example we show the rule for an instance method invocation `e.m(e₁, ..., eₙ);`. Figure 1 shows a class hierarchy where class c_1 contains a method declaration m with a body α_1 that is overridden in class c_2 with another body α_2.

The compiler determines at compile time a suitable method declaration, and the method call is annotated with the computed method signature, i.e. the method name m and the formal parameter types of the declaration. The argument types are needed because of overloading. Java verification in the KIV

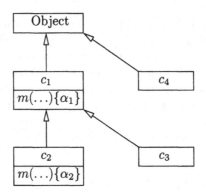

1. $\Gamma, mode(st) \neq normal \vdash \varphi, \Delta$
2. $\Gamma, e = null, mode(st) = normal \vdash$
   $\langle st; \textbf{throw new } \texttt{NullPointerException}(); \rangle \; \varphi, \Delta$
3. $\Gamma, e \neq null, mode(st) = normal \vdash classOf(e, st) \in \{c_1, c_2, c_3\}, \Delta$
4. $\Gamma, e \neq null, mode(st) = normal, classOf(e, st) \in \{c_1, c_3\},$
   $this' = e, \underline{z} = e_1, \ldots, e_n \vdash \langle st; \alpha'_1 \rangle \; \langle st; \textbf{target}(x) \rangle \; \varphi, \Delta$
5. $\Gamma, e \neq null, mode(st) = normal, classOf(e, st) \in \{c_2\},$
   $this' = e, \underline{z} = e_1, \ldots, e_n \vdash \langle st; \alpha'_2 \rangle \; \langle st; \textbf{target}(x) \rangle \; \varphi, \Delta$

   $\overline{\Gamma \vdash \langle st; x \; = \; \texttt{e.m}(e_1, \ldots, e_n); \rangle \; \varphi, \Delta}$

Fig. 1. Example class hierarchy and rule for instance method invocation

system uses as input an annotated abstract syntax tree of the Java program and class declarations; so every method call is annotated with the computed method signature, too. The dynamic method lookup for an instance method then works as follows: The run-time class of the invoking object is determined, and the class declaration is searched for a method declaration with an identical signature as the annotated signature. If one is found this is the method to invoke. Otherwise the super class is searched and so on. The proof rule in the KIV system works in the same manner.

The proof rule is only applicable if e and the arguments $e_1, \ldots, e_n$ are fully evaluated, i.e. local variables or literals obtained by the flattening rule. This ensures that no side effects can occur. Premise 1 ensures that the method call is evaluated at all, and not skipped due to an exception. Premise 2 throws a NullPointerException if e is null. Premise 3 ensures that the type of e is either c_1, c_2, or c_3. If e is a reference to an object with type c_1 or c_3 then method $m(\ldots)\{\alpha_1\}$ is invoked (premise 4); if the type of e is c_2 then method $m(\ldots)\{\alpha_2\}$ is invoked (premise 5). In both premises the parameters $e_1, \ldots, e_n$ are bound to new variables $\underline{z}$, a new variable $this'$ is introduced for this and bound to e, in the method body the formal parameters are replaced with the new variables yielding α_i', and the new statement $\mathbf{target}(x)$ is added that will catch a return statement and bind x to the returned value.

Instead of expanding the method call, pre- and postconditions can be used (proof by contract). The calculus is well suited for interactive proofs because it follows the evaluation order of the Java statements and expressions as described in the Java language specification. Other proof rules modify or access the heap, but they are not relevant with respect to the formal verification of generics. We refer the reader to other literature [24] [25] [10].

5   Method Invocation

Method invocation is a situation where generics influence the run-time behavior of Java, for two reasons:

1. Dynamic method lookup is more complicated than before because of type variables and instantiation.
2. Heap pollution can cause an Exception during *method invocation conversion* (JLS 3, section 5.3).

Both items are described in turn.

Dynamic method lookup. In the presence of generics, it can be very complicated to compute the correct method signature that is associated with a method call at compile time. The description in JLS 3 is 32 pages long as compared to 9 pages in JLS 2. As mentioned in the previous section this annotation process is outside of KIV's formal framework. The dynamic method lookup also becomes more complicated if the types of the signature contain type variables. Listing 5 contains an example. (The heap pollution in the example can be ignored for the moment.)

```
1  interface I<T> { public int m(T x) ; }
2
3  class C<X> implements I<Integer> {
4    public int m(Integer x) { return 6; } // overrides m in I
5    public int m(String  x) { return 8; } // does not
6  }
7  public class Example5 {
8
9    public static void main(String[] args) {
10       I<Object> o = new C();              // raw type
11       System.out.println(o.m(5));         // prints 6
12       System.out.println(o.m("foo"));     // throws
13    }
14 }
```

Listing 5. An example for dynamic method lookup

The program compiles. Since class C implements I<Integer> the method
m(Integer x) in line 4 implements the method m(T x) in interface I. The
two method calls in lines 11 and 12 are annotated with the method signature
m(T) because the type of the invoking expression is I. At run time, it is not
correct to search simply for a declaration with signature m(T). Rather, it must
be determined that the type variable T is instantiated with Integer in class C,
so in class C a method with signature m(Integer) must be searched. In other
classes that implement I the type variable may be instantiated with another
class, or not at all. The same is possible for subclasses of C that override m.

The proof rule for dynamic method lookup in KIV now works as follows:

– The annotation for the method call must also include the name of the class
  or interface containing the suitable method declaration, not only the method
  signature. In the example this is interface I.
– Given a run-time class C, searching for the method declaration is done as
  follows: It is computed in which manner C inherits the method m(T) from I.
  This is done by following the chain of implements (or extends) clauses
  downward from I to C. In this process a substitution for the type variable T
  is computed. Because C<X> implements I<Integer>, and I has type
  variable T, the substitution is T ← Integer.

It may be noted that the description of the dynamic method lookup in JLS
3 (15.12.4.4) is identical to JLS 2, and the complication with instantiation of
type variables is not mentioned. Another possibility for a proof rule would be to
annotate every method declaration with those method signatures it overrides or
implements. Then searching a class of a matching method signature would mean
to search the annotations as well. This is comparable to using a dispatch table
in a real implementation.

Method invocation conversion. JLS 3 states that the arguments of the method
call are evaluated from left to right (15.12.4.2), then method invocation

conversion takes place (15.12.4.3), then an additional check is performed that may throw a `ClassCastException` (15.12.4.3). This is not correct, because after evaluation of one argument unboxing takes place (if necessary), and only then the next argument is evaluated. The evaluation order is significant, because unboxing can cause a `NullPointerException` if the reference to unbox is `null`. However, the additional checks (casts) are performed only after all arguments have been evaluated and converted.

Listing 5 is also an example why an additional cast may be necessary. In line 12 the method m is called with a string. The actual method to invoke depends on the run-time class of the invoking expression and the method signature as computed at compile time. In the example it is `m(T)` in interface `I` which is overridden by the method `m(Integer)` in class `C` as described above. Since a string cannot be converted to an Integer, a `ClassCastException` must be thrown. The method `m(String)` does not implement `m(T)` in `I`, and is not used even though the argument is a `String`. On the other hand, the incompatibility cannot be determined at compile time because another class `D` could implement `I<String>`, and for an invoker of class `D` a `String` argument is perfectly valid.

1. $\Gamma, mode(st) \neq normal \vdash \varphi, \Delta$
2. $\Gamma, o = null, mode(st) = normal \vdash$
   $\langle st; \textbf{throw new } \text{NullPointerException}(); \rangle \varphi, \Delta$
3. $\Gamma, o \neq null, mode(st) = normal \vdash classOf(o, st) = C, \Delta$
4. $\Gamma, o \neq null, mode(st) = normal, classOf(o, st) = C, this = o, \vdash$
   $\langle st; \mathtt{x = (Integer)e;} \rangle \langle st; \textbf{return } 6; \rangle \langle st; \textbf{target} \rangle \varphi$

   $\overline{\Gamma \vdash \langle st; \mathtt{o.m(e);} \rangle \varphi}$

Fig. 2. Method call for `o.m(e)`

The proof rule for a method call now works as follows (Fig. 2):

1. All arguments must be either local variables or literals, and autoboxing has been applied if necessary. This guarantees that no side effects occur.
2. For a given run-time class of the invoker the correct method declaration to invoke is determined as described above, in the example `m(Integer x) {...}`.
3. For every parameter of this declaration and actual argument:
   (a) If the static type of the actual argument is a subtype of the parameter type, then simply an equation *formal parameter variable = actual argument* is generated.
   (b) Otherwise an assignment to the formal parameter variable is generated, and the actual argument is cast to the formal parameter type. In the example the assignment `x = (Integer)e;` (premise 4 in Fig. 2) is generated.
4. The method call is replaced by its body, and all generated assignments are added before the body, in the example `x = (Integer)e; return 6;` (premise 4 in Fig. 2)

The Java compiler introduces a so called *bridge method* (JLS 3, 15.12.4.5) at compile time that is called at run time and performs the casts. In the example the bridge method is added to class C: `m(Object o) {return m((Integer)o);}`. The proof rule has the identical behavior, but without additional transformations that are outside the formal framework.

6   Invalid Result Values

Section 15.5 of JLS 3 states rather cryptically

> *A run-time type error can occur only in these situations: [...] • In an implicit, compiler-generated cast introduced to ensure the validity of an operation on a non-reifiable type. [...]*

Because of heap pollution, the result of a method call (or a field access) can return a value that is not a subtype of (the erasure of) its static type (JLS 3, section 5.2). In these cases sometimes a `ClassCastException` is thrown. Listing 6 shows an example.

```
1   class Bag<E> {
2       public E content;
3       public Bag(E val) { content = val; }
4       public E get() { return content; }
5   }
6   public class Example6 {
7
8       static void mo(Object o) {
9       if (o instanceof String) System.out.println(1);
10      else System.out.println(2);
11      }
12      static void mi(Integer i) { System.out.println(i); }
13
14      public static void main(String[] args) {
15      Bag<Integer> bi = new Bag("foo"); // raw type
16      mo(bi.get());    // ok, prints 1
17      mi(bi.get());    // throws
18      }
19  }
```

Listing 6. An example for invalid return values

Line 15 creates heap pollution. In the following lines the static type of the variable bi is Bag<Integer> which means that the content field of bi should hold an Integer. However, it holds the string "foo". The method call bi.get() returns this string.

Line 16 does not raise an exception. This is surprising since the result of the method call bi.get() (the string) is not a subtype of its static type Integer.

However, the result value is used in a context where only an Object is required. Therefore it is not necessary to throw a ClassCastException (JLS 3 5.2 and 5.3). The string is passed to the method mo, and the method prints 1. Line 17 throws a ClassCastException because the result is used in a context that requires an Integer. This is a different situation than the method calls in listing 5 where bridge methods are used. The Java compiler guarantees this behavior by simply inserting casts into the byte code. The byte code always contains the casts, even when no "unchecked" warnings are issued because the heap pollution could stem from already compiled code.

What are the implications for the formal verification? One possibility would be to modify the source code during parsing and annotation. However, this would be outside the formal framework, and in interactive proofs it is desirable to be as close to the source code as possible. Therefore, these implicit (or "unchecked") casts are included in the calculus:

1. A new proof rule is introduced for "unchecked" casts.
2. The proof rules for field access and method call are applicable only if no "unchecked" casts are required.
3. The flattening rule is modified to keep track of the type required by the context.

In the same manner, a proof rule for autoboxing has been included in the calculus. The new proof rule for an "unchecked" cast is applicable for a method call x = e.m($e_1, \ldots, e_n$); (and similarly for a field access x = e.f) iff

- e and $e_1, \ldots, e_n$ are local variables (possibly introduced by flattening), and
- the declared return type of m (in constrast to the computed result type) is a type variable T, and
- the erasure of T is not a subtype of the static type of x. For a type variable or wildcard without bounds this means that the type of x is neither Object nor an unbounded type variable. For bounded type variables T extends C or wildcards ? extends C the erasure is C.

Then the proof rule simply introduces a cast to the static type of x. Fig. 3 shows the rules. Conversely, the proof rules for method calls and field access are only applicable if the "unchecked" rule is not applicable. The flattening rule guarantees that the "unchecked" rule is not applied a second time.

Line 16 in listing 6 contains an example that the context is used to decide whether a cast is added or not. Since the flattening rule transforms mo(bi. get()) into x = bi.get(); mo(x); the static type of x must be Object (the context type), not Integer (the computed result type of bi.get()). The modified flattening rule must use the context type where necessary.

$$\frac{\Gamma \vdash \langle st; x \ = \ (\mathrm{Ty}) \, e \, . \, m(e_1, \ldots, e_n); \rangle \, \varphi}{\Gamma \vdash \langle st; x \ = \ e \, . \, m(e_1, \ldots, e_n); \rangle \, \varphi} \qquad \frac{\Gamma \vdash \langle st; x \ = \ (\mathrm{Ty}) \, e \, . \, f; \rangle \, \varphi}{\Gamma \vdash \langle st; x \ = \ e \, . \, f; \rangle \, \varphi}$$

Fig. 3. The new "unchecked" proof rules

This finishes the description of implicit casts for result values. JLS 3 does not mention it, but the Java compilers treat an array access for an array of type E[] with E a type variable in the same manner as a field access or method call. This means an array access a[i] can also cause a ClassCastException.

7   Verification with Generics in KIV

The examples in the paper can be verified in KIV with the modified calculus. It turns out that generics have almost no effect on the specification and verification methodology used in KIV which is based on algebraic specifications and the proof of functional properties. This is illustrated with the following example: We want to prove that the sum method from listing 1 correctly computes the sum of some integers, $\sum$ *ints*. *ints* is an algebraically specified list of integers, and $\sum$ an algebraic function. The proof can only succeed if we know (or assume) that the input li to the sum method represents this list of integers, *isList(ints, li, st)*. *isList* is a predicate that "looks" into the heap *st*. The goal to prove is therefore

$$isList(ints,\ li,\ st),\ \ldots \vdash \langle st;\ \mathtt{i}\ =\ \mathtt{x.sum(li)};\ \rangle\ \mathtt{i} = \sum ints$$

This property is not trivial: The iterator (used by the enhanced for loop as in listing 2) must be implemented correctly; the hasNext method must eventually return false (for termination); the next method must successively return Integer objects (not null, and not other objects because of heap pollution) that represent the integers in *ints*; no integer over- or underflow may occur.

Essentially this means we need a very precise knowledge about the data structure represented by li in the heap – independent of whether generic types are used or not. Of course, we do not have this knowledge because it is not known which List implementation is used. Therefore, we must make assumptions about the methods iterator, hasNext, and next, and the predicate *isList* (proof by contract). Then, for a given List implementation we can specify *isList* and prove the assumptions. E.g., the assumption for next is:

$$isIterator(ints,\ iter,\ st),\ ints \neq [],\ \ldots$$
$$\vdash \langle st;\ \mathtt{o}\ =\ \mathtt{iter.next()};\rangle\ (\ \ isIntegerObject(ints.first,\ o,\ st)$$
$$\wedge\ isIterator(ints.rest,\ iter,\ st) \wedge \ldots)$$

Two auxiliary predicates are used: *isIterator(ints, iter, st)* is true if *iter* is an Iterator object that represents the integers *ints*. Then the next method returns an Integer object that represents the first value of *ints* (*isIntegerObject(ints.first, o, st)*, and by side effect the iterator has been modified so that it represents the *remaining* integers *ints.rest* (*isIterator(ints.rest, iter, st)*). Again, this is completely independent of generic types.

For a given List implementation (for example, the ArrayList of the Java collection framework) the predicates must be specified. This requires a look into the actual implementation (how the next method accesses the element to return etc.), and a class invariant about the iterator (the cursor field used by the iterator is not greater than the size field of the ArrayList which in turn is less than the length of the array holding the elements etc.). And it must be specified that all list elements are indeed Integer objects.

8 Conclusion

We have extended KIV's Java calculus to support the formal verification of Java generics. It may be mentioned that JLS 3 is sometimes cryptic, unclear, and possibly wrong for generics. The main design decision was not to modify the source code to verify, but to include the run-time effects of generics dynamically into the appropriate proof rules. The effects are: First, dynamic method lookup is more complicated than before (Listing 5); second, because of the possibility of heap pollution (Sect. 3) a method invocation may require additional checks (Listing 5); third, because of heap pollution the result of a method call or a field access can cause a ClassCastException (Listing 6). This has the subtle consequence that in addition to the static type of an expression the context (the expected or required type) of the expression becomes important. It is now possible to verify programs with "unchecked" warnings, and in the presence of heap pollution (for example, the programs in this paper).

Experience shows that the effects of generics on proofs in KIV are small because the additional casts cause little overhead, and because KIV's methodology relies on algebraic properties where static types play a negligible role. A possible direction for future work is a formal specification of a type correct Java program with generics, and a proof of type soundness.

References

1. Alves-Foss, J. (ed.): Formal Syntax and Semantics of Java. LNCS, vol. 1523. Springer, Heidelberg (1999)
2. Balser, M., Reif, W., Schellhorn, G., Stenzel, K., Thums, A.: Formal system development with KIV. In: Maibaum, T. (ed.) FASE 2000. LNCS, vol. 1783. Springer, Heidelberg (2000)
3. Barnett, M., Leino, K.R.M., Schulte, W.: The Spec# programming system: An Overview. In: Barthe, G., Burdy, L., Huisman, M., Lanet, J.-L., Muntean, T. (eds.) CASSIS 2004. LNCS, vol. 3362. Springer, Heidelberg (2005)
4. Barthe, G., Burdy, L., Charles, J., Grégoire, B., Huisman, M., Lanet, J.-L., Pavlova, M., Requet, A.: JACK: a tool for validation of security and behaviour of Java applications. In: FMCO: Proceedings of 5th International Symposium on Formal Methods for Components and Objects, vol. 4709. Springer, Heidelberg (2007)
5. Beckert, B., Hähnle, R., Schmitt, P. (eds.): Verification of Object-Oriented Software. LNCS (LNAI), vol. 4334. Springer, Heidelberg (2007)
6. Burdy, L., Cheon, Y., Cok, D., Ernst, M., Kiniry, J., Leavens, G.T., Leino, K.R.M., Poll, E.: An overview of JML tools and applications. International Journal on Software Tools for Technology Transfer 7(3) (2005)
7. Cok, D.R., Kiniry, J.R.: ESC/Java2: Uniting ESC/Java and JML. In: Barthe, G., Huisman, M. (eds.) CASSIS 2004. LNCS, vol. 3362. Springer, Heidelberg (2005)
8. Gosling, J., Joy, B., Steele, G.: The Java Language Specification. Addison-Wesley, Reading (1996)

9. Gosling, J., Joy, B., Steele, G., Bracha, G.: The Java (tm) Language Specification, 3rd edn. Addison-Wesley, Reading (2005)
10. Grandy, H., Bertossi, R., Stenzel, K., Reif, W.: ASN1-light: A Verified Message Encoding for Security Protocols. In: Software Engineering and Formal Methods, SEFM. IEEE Press, Los Alamitos (2007)
11. Grandy, H., Bischof, M., Schellhorn, G., Reif, W., Stenzel, K.: Verification of Mondex Electronic Purses with KIV: From a Security Protocol to Verified Code. In: FM 2008: 15th Int. Symposium on Formal Methods, vol. 5014. Springer, Heidelberg (2008)
12. Harel, D., Kozen, D., Tiuryn, J.: Dynamic Logic. MIT Press, Cambridge (2000)
13. Jacobs, B., Marché, C., Rauch, N.: Formal verification of a commercial smart card applet with multiple tools. In: Rattray, C., Maharaj, S., Shankland, C. (eds.) AMAST 2004. LNCS, vol. 3116. Springer, Heidelberg (2004)
14. Jacobs, B., Poll, E.: Java Program Verification at Nijmegen: Developments and Perspective. In: Futatsugi, K., Mizoguchi, F., Yonezaki, N. (eds.) ISSS 2003. LNCS, vol. 3233, pp. 134–153. Springer, Heidelberg (2004)
15. JML home page, http://www.jmlspecs.org/
16. Joy, B., Steele, G., Gosling, J., Bracha, G.: The Java (tm) Language Specification, 2nd edn. Addison-Wesley, Reading (2000)
17. Kiniry, J.: Recent advances in extended static checking. Technical report, KeY Symposium 2007 (2007), http://www.key-project.org/keysymposium07/slides/kiniry-esc.pdf
18. KIV homepage, http://www.informatik.uni-augsburg.de/swt/kiv
19. Leavens, G.T., Baker, A.L., Ruby, C.: Preliminary design of JML: A behavioral interface specification language for Java. ACM SIGSOFT Software Engineering Notes 31(3), 1–38 (2006)
20. Leavens, G.T., Kiniry, J., Poll, E.: A JML tutorial. Technical report, CAV 2007 Tutorial (2007), http://cav2007.org/Docs/Leavens.JML.ps4.pdf
21. Marché, C., Paulin-Mohring, C., Urbain, X.: The Krakatoa tool for certification of Java/Javacard programs annotated in JML. Journal of Logic and Algebraic Programming 58(1-2) (2004)
22. MasterCard International Inc. Mondex, http://www.mondex.com
23. Schmitt, P.H., Tonin, I.: Verifying the Mondex case study. In: Software Engineering and Formal Methods, SEFM. IEEE Press, Los Alamitos (2007)
24. Stenzel, K.: A formally verified calculus for full Java Card. In: Rattray, C., Maharaj, S., Shankland, C. (eds.) AMAST 2004. LNCS, vol. 3116, pp. 491–505. Springer, Heidelberg (2004)
25. Stenzel, K.: Verification of Java Card Programs. PhD thesis, Universität Augsburg, Fakultät für Angewandte Informatik (2005)
26. Sun Microsystems Inc. Java Card 2.2 Specification (2002), http://java.sun.com/products/javacard/
27. Ulbrich, M.: Software verification for Java 5. Diplomarbeit, Fakultät für Informatik, Universität Karlsruhe (in English, 2007)

Domain Axioms for a Family of Near-Semirings

Jules Desharnais[1] and Georg Struth[2]

[1] Département d'informatique et de génie logiciel, Université Laval, Canada
Jules.Desharnais@ift.ulaval.ca
[2] Department of Computer Science, University of Sheffield, United Kingdom
g.struth@dcs.shef.ac.uk

Abstract. Axioms for domain operations in several variants of Kleene algebras and their semiring reducts are presented. They provide abstract enabledness conditions for algebras designed for the verification and refinement of action systems, probabilistic protocols, basic processes and games. The axiomatisations are simpler, more uniform and more flexible than previous attempts; they are especially suited for automated deduction. This is further demonstrated through the automated verification of some classical refinement laws for action systems.

1 Introduction

Variants of Kleene algebras provide the basic operations for modelling the dynamics of discrete systems. Choices between actions or processes are modelled through addition, sequential composition through multiplication, finite and infinite iteration via fixed points. Additive identities capture deadlock or abortion; silent or ineffective actions correspond to multiplicative identities. A main benefit of the approach is its suitability for first-order automated deduction in applications where model checking or interactive theorem proving is usually employed.

Axiomatic variations are dictated by the semantics of application domains. Kleene algebras, for instance, capture partial program correctness under angelic choice [10] or trace models of reactive systems. Variants in which some axioms have been weakened admit predicate transformer models for total program correctness under demonic choice [16], expectation transformer models for probabilistic programs and protocols [11], and multirelational [7] or game-based models [8] for situations where angelic and demonic choices interact. Other variants of Kleene algebras provide algebraic semantics for parallel reactive systems modelled by action systems [3] or for basic process algebras [4].

A main source of variation is the interaction of choice with composition. For games and processes, for instance, a choice between the sequences xy and xz of actions x, y and z must be distinguished from a choice between y or z after execution of x, hence $x(y + z) \neq xy + xz$. Relation- or trace-based models, in contrast, require this distributivity law. Other applications might exclude that an infinite action x can be aborted after it has started, that is, $x0 \neq 0$. Again, this annihilation law certainly holds for binary relations.

In many of these applications, axiomatising a domain operator is essential. For Kleene algebras, domain has been defined as a map into an embedded Boolean algebra that models a state space [5]. In fact, it suffices to axiomatise domain on the semiring retract of the Kleene algebra. It turned out that this axiomatisation can essentially be reused for some weaker variants [13] and applied to demonic refinement algebras [15] and probabilistic Kleene algebras [12]. Operationally, domain provides enabledness conditions for programs or processes. Moreover, on Kleene algebras, domain induces modal operators and formalisms similar to dynamic logic. Recently, domain axioms for Kleene algebras have been provided in a one-sorted setting [6] which is simpler, more flexible and better suited for automated deduction. But is this new axiomatisation stable and robust enough to scale to weaker variants of Kleene algebras?

The present paper provides a positive answer. We adapt the new axiomatisation of domain semirings to demonic refinement algebras [16], probabilistic refinement algebras [11], basic process algebras [4] and other variants of Kleene algebras. Our first contribution is a systematic development of domain on families of near-semirings [14]. As in the semiring case, we provide axioms that make the algebras of domain elements into distributive lattices. Second, based on antidomain operations, we provide simple axiomatisations that induce Boolean domain algebras. It turns out that we can simply reuse the semiring domain axioms for demonic refinement algebras and probabilistic Kleene algebras. Third, we also consider codomain operations for all variants. The entire development and investigation is based on the automated theorem proving system (ATP system) Prover9 and the counterexample generator Mace4 [2]. We therefore do not display proofs we could automate, but provide an encoding for Prover9/Mace4 at a web site [1] from which all results in this paper can easily be reproduced. A fourth contribution is an application of our new axioms to the automated verification of some classical action system refinement laws [3,15].

2   From Near-Semirings to Semirings

To model actions or processes, we consider weak variants of semirings with different identities. A *near-semiring* [14] is a structure $(S, +, \cdot)$ such that $(S, +)$ and $(S, \cdot)$ are semigroups and all elements satisfy the *right distributivity* law

$$(x + y)z = xz + yz \ . \tag{1}$$

Here and henceforth, the multiplication symbol is omitted. A *pre-semiring* is a near-semiring in which all elements satisfy the *left pre-isotonicity* law

$$x + y = y \Rightarrow zx + zy = zy \ . \tag{2}$$

A *semiring* is a near-semiring in which all elements also satisfy the left distributivity law $x(y + z) = xy + yz$. Every semiring is also a pre-semiring. We will restrict our attention to *commutative* near-semirings without explicitly mentioning the commutativity law $x + y = y + x$. A near-semiring is *idempotent* if all elements satisfy $x + x = x$. We also consider different identities.

- δ satisfies the identity and left annihilation axioms $x + \delta = x$ and $\delta x = \delta$.
- τ satisfies the right identity axiom $x\tau = x$.
- 0 satisfies the δ-axioms and the right annihilation axiom $x0 = 0$.
- 1 satisfies the τ-axiom and the left identity axiom $1x = x$.

In the presence of both additive or both multiplicative identities, these entities coincide: $\delta = \delta 0 = 0$ and $\tau = 1\tau = 1$. We will not consider 0 in this paper.

Idempotent near-semirings $(S, +, \cdot)$, possibly with δ and τ, are also called *basic process algebras*. There, δ is called *deadlock* and τ the *silent action* [4]. Idempotent pre-semirings $(S, +, \cdot, 0, 1)$ arise as reducts of probabilistic Kleene algebras [11] by forgetting an operation of finite iteration, and as game algebras [8]. Idempotent semirings $(S, +, \cdot, \delta, 1)$ arise as reducts of demonic refinement algebras [16] by forgetting an operation of strong iteration (see Section 9). We will see that a uniform treatment of the last three variants can be achieved via pre-semirings $(S, +, \cdot, \delta, 1)$.

Explicit axioms for near-semirings and pre-semirings, as input for Prover9, can be found at a web site [1]. The following fact has been verified with Prover9.

Lemma 2.1. *The relation $\leq$ defined, for all elements x and y of an idempotent near-semiring, by $x \leq y \Leftrightarrow x + y = y$ is a partial order. The identity δ or 0 is the least element with respect to that order if it exists. Addition and right multiplication are isotone with respect to the order.*

Mace4 yields a 3-element counterexample to isotonicity of left multiplication for near-semirings and a 4-element one for those with δ and 1. By Lemma 2.1, every idempotent near-semiring can be ordered and $(S, +)$ is a semilattice.

3   Domain Semirings

An operation of domain for semirings has been defined in a companion paper [6]. A *domain semiring* is a semiring $(S, +, \cdot, 0, 1)$ extended by a function $d : S \rightarrow S$ that satisfies

$$x + d(x)x = d(x)x \ , \qquad (D1) \qquad\qquad d(x) + 1 = 1 \ , \qquad (D4)$$
$$d(xy) = d(xd(y)) \ , \qquad (D2) \qquad\qquad d(0) = 0 \ . \qquad (D5)$$
$$d(x + y) = d(x) + d(y) \ , \qquad (D3)$$

We call (D1), (D2) and (D3) the *basic domain axioms* and overload (D4) and (D5) also for τ and δ. Every domain semiring is automatically idempotent [6]. Mace4 easily shows that the domain axioms are irredundant, that is, counterexamples exist for each mutual implication.

The axioms can be abstracted from relational models, where the domain $d(x)$ of a binary relation x is the binary relation consisting of all ordered pairs (a, a) with $(a, b) \in x$ for some b. (D1) says that $d(x)$ does not restrict the execution of x. (D2) says that the enabledness of a sequence xy depends on y only through its enabledness condition. (D3) says that the enabledness condition for a choice between actions is the union of the enabledness conditions of the particular actions. (D4) says that all enabledness conditions are below 1 and (D5) says that enabling abort or deadlock yields abort or deadlock.

The set of domain elements of S is denoted by $d(S)$ and it has been shown that $d(S) = \{x \in S : d(x) = x\}$, whence domain elements are precisely the fixpoints of the domain operation. This can be used to show that the *domain algebra* $(d(S), +, \cdot, 0, 1)$ of a domain semiring S is a bounded distributive lattice. By $d(x) + d(y) = d(d(x) + d(y))$, e.g., domain elements are closed under addition.

The domain algebras of domain semirings can be turned into Boolean algebras by adding an antidomain operation $a : S \to S$ that satisfies

$$d(x) + a(x) = 1 , \qquad (3) \qquad d(x)a(x) = 0 . \qquad (4)$$

The resulting structures are called *Boolean domain semirings*. It can be shown that the antidomain of an element is precisely the Boolean complement of its domain, hence $a(x)$ models those states for which x is not enabled. Since $a^2(x) = d(x)$ holds, domain can be eliminated from all axioms and it follows that a semiring is a Boolean domain semiring if and only if it satisfies the *basic Boolean domain axioms*

$$a(x)x = 0 , \qquad \text{(BD1)} \qquad a^2(x) + a(x) = 1 . \qquad \text{(BD3)}$$
$$a(xy) + a(xa^2(y)) = a(xa^2(y)) , \qquad \text{(BD2)}$$

These considerations form the basis for axiomatising domain on near-semirings.

4   Domain Conditions

Before investigating domain on a family of near-semirings, we collect some natural conditions that each domain operation should satisfy. First of all, axiomatisations should respect our intuitions about domain. Second, as in the semiring case, they should induce distributive lattices or Boolean algebras.

Let S be a near-semiring. The main intuition behind domain is that a domain element $d(x)$ is a left preserver of $x \in S$ in the sense that $x \leq d(x)x$, as expressed by (D1), or even

$$x = d(x)x . \qquad (5)$$

Since 1 is also a left preserver of x (if it exists), $d(x)$ should even be the *least left preserver* of x. Hence, for all $x \in S$ and $p \in d(S)$,

$$x \leq px \Leftrightarrow d(x) \leq p . \qquad (6)$$

Similarly, antidomain elements should be *greatest left annihilators*, that is,

$$px = \delta \Leftrightarrow p \leq a(x) . \qquad (7)$$

All axiomatisations of domain should therefore respect (5) and (6); all axiomatisations of antidomain should respect (7).

To induce a lattice as a domain algebra, it is necessary and sufficient that each domain element satisfies, besides the basic domain axioms, the *lattice conditions*

$$d^2(x) = d(x) \ , \qquad (8) \qquad d(x)d(y) = d(y)d(x) \ , \qquad (12)$$
$$d(d(x) + d(y)) = d(x) + d(y) \ , \qquad (9) \qquad d(x) = d(x) + d(x)d(y) \ , \qquad (13)$$
$$d(d(x)d(y)) = d(x)d(y) \ , \qquad (10) \qquad d(x) = d(x)(d(x) + d(y)) \ . \qquad (14)$$
$$(d(x))^2 = d(x) \ , \qquad (11)$$

The first three identities are closure conditions, and, more precisely, they are necessary if the fixpoint characterisation of domain elements holds. The other conditions correspond to lattice axioms. In the presence of τ or 1, $d(\tau) = \tau$ or $d(1) = 1$ should hold as well. The condition $d(\delta) = \delta$ holds by axiom (D5).

In the presence of (3) and (4), the *Boolean conditions*

$$d(a(x)) = a(x) \ , \qquad (15) \qquad a(x)d(x) = \delta \qquad (16)$$

should also be checked, but condition (16) follows from (4) and (12). The first of the following conditions is needed for d-elimination; the second one is dual to (D3) and again very natural.

$$a^2(x) = d(x) \ , \qquad (17) \qquad a(x+y) = a(x)a(y) \ . \qquad (18)$$

Finally, for non-idempotent near-semirings, it must be checked that the resulting domain weak semiring is idempotent, otherwise addition does not model choice.

We call a domain near-semirings or Boolean domain near-semiring *healthy* if it satisfies the relevant conditions among (5) to (18). Further natural properties may arise in particular applications and these can be added as axioms if needed. Also, we always make sure that axiomatisations are *irredundant* in the sense that no axiom is entailed by the remaining ones. This can usually (but not necessarily) be established by Mace4 through finite counterexamples. In the case of pre-semirings, additional domain conditions have a substantial impact on domain algebras. These will be investigated in Section 6.

5   A Family of Domain Near-Semirings

We now consider domain or enabledness axioms for near-semirings with and without δ, τ and 1. The general recipe is as follows: Start with the basic domain axioms plus the domain axioms for the respective identities. Then add domain conditions until the axiomatisation is healthy and induces a distributive lattice. Finally, remove redundancies. Prover9 and Mace4 allowed us to considerably simplify this analysis and we do not display any proofs that could be automated.

We first axiomatise various domain near-semirings. We do not investigate all possible combinations of identities, but restrict ourselves to structures that have previously been considered in applications. Pre-semirings with 1, for instance, form the basis for probabilistic Kleene algebras, game algebras and demonic refinement algebras, but we do not investigate pre-semirings with τ.

A *domain near-semiring* is a near-semiring $(S, +, \cdot)$ extended by a domain function $d : S \to S$ that satisfies (5), (D2), (D3), (12) and (14).

Table 1. A Family of Domain Near-Semirings

		NS	NS$_\delta$	NS$^\tau$	NS$_\delta^\tau$	NS^1	NS$_\delta^1$	PS^1	PS$_\delta^1$
(D1)	$x \le d(x)x$					√	√	√	√
(D2)	$d(xy) = d(xd(y))$	√	√	√	√	√	√	√	√
(D3)	$d(x + y) = d(x) + d(y)$	√	√	√	√	√	√	√	√
(D4)	$d(x) \le \tau$			√	√				
(D4)	$d(x) \le 1$					√	√	√	√
(D5)	$d(\delta) = \delta$		√		√		√		√
(5)	$x = d(x)x$	√	√	√	√				
(12)	$d(x)d(y) = d(y)d(x)$	√	√	√	√	√	√		
(14)	$d(x) = d(x)(d(x) + d(y))$	√	√						

NS: near-semiring, PS: pre-semiring.

A *domain near-semiring with τ* is a near-semiring $(S, +, \cdot, \tau)$ extended by a function $d : S \to S$ that satisfies (5), (D2), (D3), (D4) and (12).

A *domain near-semiring with 1* is a near-semiring $(S, +, \cdot, 1)$ extended by a function $d : S \to S$ that satisfies the domain axioms (D1)-(D4) and (12).

A *domain pre-semiring* (with 1) is a pre-semiring $(S, +, \cdot, 1)$ extended by a function $d : S \to S$ that satisfies (D1)-(D4).

In each case a variant with δ is obtained by adding (D5). The explicit domain axioms for these structures are displayed in Table 1.

The following fact has been verified by Prover9 and Mace4.

Lemma 5.1. *All domain axiomatisations are healthy and irredundant.*

For all domain near-semirings without 1, (5) cannot be replaced by (D1), since in that case, (10) or idempotency would not be entailed. For near-semirings with 1, (D1) can be used. Healthiness implies the following facts.

Lemma 5.2. *Domain near-semirings are idempotent and can be ordered.*

Hence the approach applies to basic process algebras, probabilistic Kleene algebras, game algebras and demonic refinement algebras, which are all idempotent.

Lemma 5.3. *Domain elements of near-semirings are least left preservers.*

So all axiomatisations respect our basic intuitions about domain and enabledness. Mace4 can easily show that all classes considered are indeed distinct.

We now investigate the impact of healthiness on the domain algebra. First, we can characterise domain elements within the language of domain weak semirings.

Lemma 5.4. *An element of a domain near-semiring is a domain element if and only it is a fixpoint of the domain operation.*

Proof. Let S be a near-semiring with a healthy mapping d, whence in particular $d^2(x) = d(x)$ holds for all $x \in S$. We show that $x \in d(S)$ if and only if $x = d(x)$. First, every $x \in d(S)$ is the image of some $y \in S$, that is, $x = d(y)$. Therefore,

$d(x) = d(d(y)) = d(y) = x$ holds by healthiness. Second, $x = d(x)$ trivially implies that $x \in d(S)$. □

So (9) and (10) are indeed closure conditions for domain elements, and the domain algebras can easily be characterised.

Proposition 5.5. *Let S be a domain near-semiring. Then $(d(S), +, \cdot)$ is a distributive lattice. If the near-semiring has an additive (multiplicative) identity, it is the least (greatest) element of the lattice.*

Proof. The lattice conditions imply that $d(S)$ forms a lattice. The right distributivity axiom of near-semirings holds in particular for domain elements. By standard lattice theory, $d(S)$ is therefore a distributive lattice. The bound conditions could readily be checked with Prover9. □

Let us further discuss these results. We have seen that all near-semirings considered can be endowed with simple equational domain axioms that induce an order on the near-semiring and a domain algebra which is a distributive lattice. These axioms support our basic intuitions about domain and enabledness. In the case of pre-semirings with 1, which form the basis for probabilistic Kleene algebras, game algebras and demonic refinement algebras, the basic domain axioms of domain semirings [6] can entirely be reused.

There is, however, a crucial difference between domain semirings and domain for the weaker variants considered. Forward modal operators can be defined on a domain semiring S as $|x\rangle p = d(xp)$, for all $x \in S$ and $p \in d(S)$. The name "modal operator" is justified since $\lambda p.|x\rangle p$ is a strict and additive mapping, that is, it satisfies $|x\rangle 0 = 0$ and $|x\rangle(p+q) = |x\rangle p + |x\rangle q$. For weaker variants, $\lambda p.d(xp)$ need be neither strict nor additive. Prover9 and Mace4 could show that strictness holds only in the presence of the right annihilation law and additivity holds only in the presence of the left distributivity law. Therefore, none of the weak variants considered gives rise to a *modal* near-semiring; we do not obtain basic process algebras, probabilistic Kleene algebras, game algebras or demonic refinement algebras with modal operators from the domain axioms. This is an important negative result. The situation is different for backward diamonds which are based on an axiomatisation of codomain (cf. Section 8).

6   Boolean Domain Conditions

In domain semirings, domain algebras are strongly linked with maximal Boolean subalgebras [6]. Prover9 could show that this link still exists for domain pre-semirings with δ and 1, but not for near-semirings.

Proposition 6.1. *Let S be a domain pre-semiring with δ and 1. An element $x \in S$ is a domain element if some $y \in S$ satisfies $x + y = 1$ and $yx = \delta$.*

This statement does not hold in domain near-semirings with δ and 1; Mace4 presented a 5-element counterexample.

Corollary 6.2. *Elements x and y of a domain pre-semiring with δ and 1 are domain elements if $x + y = 1$, $xy = \delta$ and $yx = \delta$.*

Again, Mace4 presented a 5-element counterexample for near-semirings.

We say that an element x of a *weak semiring* near-semiring S is *complemented* if there exists some $y \in S$ such that $x + y = 1$, $xy = \delta$ and $yx = \delta$. We denote the set of all complemented elements in S by B_S.

Lemma 6.3. *Let $(S, +, \cdot, \delta, 1)$ be a domain pre-semiring. Then $(B_S, +, \cdot, \delta, 1)$ is a Boolean algebra.*

Proof. First, if x is complemented, then x is idempotent. Second, if x and y are complemented, then $xy = yx$. Third, if x and y are complemented, then so are $x + y$ and xy. The second fact has a 280-step proof, the third one a 212-step proof with Prover9. The first fact requires almost no time.   □

Lemma 6.3 has considerable impact on the structure of domain algebras.

Theorem 6.4. *Let $(S, +, \cdot, \delta, 1)$ be a domain pre-semiring. Then $d(S)$ contains the greatest Boolean subalgebra of S bounded by δ and 1.*

Again, Mace4 showed that Lemma 6.3 and Theorem 6.4 do not generalise to near-semirings. Also, the domain algebra of a domain pre-semiring with δ and 1 need not itself be Boolean.

7   A Family of Boolean Domain Near-Semirings

We now provide axioms for near-semirings with δ and τ or 1 which induce Boolean domain algebras. This situation corresponds perhaps most closely to the state spaces or propositional structures underlying practical applications, but as for semirings, Heyting domain algebras should also be possible [6].

A *Boolean domain pre-semiring* is a domain pre-semiring $(S, +, \cdot, \delta, 1)$ that satisfies the domain axioms (D1)-(D5) and that is extended by an *antidomain* operation $a : S \to S$ that satisfies (3) and (4).

Lemma 7.1. *Boolean domain pre-semirings are healthy.*

The proof of (18) with Prover9 has 168 steps. Corollary 6.2 and Theorem 6.4 imply the following fact.

Proposition 7.2. *The domain algebra of a Boolean domain pre-semiring is the maximal Boolean subalgebra of the pre-semiring of subidentities.*

Healthiness also implies that $a^2(x) = d(x)$, whence, as in the semiring case, domain can be eliminated from the axiomatisation and the following theorem could be shown automatically by Prover9.

Theorem 7.3. *A pre-semiring S is a Boolean domain pre-semiring if and only if it can be extended by an antidomain operation $a : S \to S$ that satisfies the basic Boolean domain axioms (BD1), (BD2) and (BD3).*

Moreover, Mace4 easily showed the following fact.

Lemma 7.4. *The axioms (BD1)-(BD3) are irredundant.*

Therefore, the basic Boolean domain axioms for semirings can be reused for probabilistic Kleene algebras, game algebras and demonic refinement algebras.

We now consider domain near-semirings. First, we turn to the case with δ and 1. A *Boolean domain near-semiring with δ and 1* is a domain near-semiring $(S, +, \cdot, \delta, 1)$ that satisfies the domain axioms (D1)-(D5) and (12) and that is extended by an *antidomain operation* $a : S \to S$ that satisfies (3), (4) and (15).

Lemma 7.5. *Boolean domain near-semirings with δ and 1 are healthy and irredundant.*

This could be shown by Prover9. Also, by Mace4, the Boolean domain semiring axioms alone are too weak. The following fact is an immediate consequence.

Proposition 7.6. *Boolean domain near-semirings with δ and 1 have Boolean domain algebras.*

However, this Boolean algebra need not always be maximal. Mace4 presented a 5-element counterexample to Corollary 6.2. Healthiness again implies that $a^2(x) = d(x)$, whence domain can be eliminated from the axiomatisation and the following theorem could be shown by Prover9.

Theorem 7.7. *A near-semiring $(S, +, \cdot, \delta, 1)$ is a Boolean domain near-semiring if and only if it can be extended by an antidomain operation $a : S \to S$ that satisfies the axioms (BD1)-(BD3) and (18).*

Moreover, Mace4 easily showed that these antidomain axioms are irredundant.

A *Boolean domain near-semiring with δ and τ* is a domain near-semiring $(S, +, \cdot, \delta, \tau)$ that satisfies (5), (D2), (D3), (D5) and (12) and that is extended by an *antidomain operation* $a : S \to S$ that satisfies (3), (4) and (15).

Lemma 7.8. *Boolean domain near-semirings with δ and τ are healthy and irredundant.*

This could be proved by Prover9, too. The following fact follows immediately.

Proposition 7.9. *Boolean domain near-semirings with δ and τ have Boolean domain algebras.*

Again, this Boolean algebra need not be maximal; there is a 5-element counterexample. Since healthiness implies that $a^2(x) = d(x)$, domain can be eliminated from the axiomatisation and the axioms can somewhat be simplified. However, the compaction obtained is not comparable to the stronger near-semirings and we therefore do not provide a deeper discussion.

The axioms for our family of Boolean domain near-semirings are summed up in Table 2. The ordering can be used because of Lemma 5.2. The first column is relevant for basic process algebras; the last column for probabilistic Kleene algebras, game algebras and demonic refinement algebras. The axiomatisation

Table 2. A Family of Boolean Domain Near-Semirings

		NS_δ^τ	NS_δ^1	PS_δ^1
(BD1)	$a(x)x = \delta$		✓	✓
(BD2)	$a(xy) \leq a(xa^2(y))$		✓	✓
(BD3)	$a^2(x) + a(x) = 1$		✓	✓
(18)	$a(x+y) = a(x)a(y)$		✓	
(5)	$x = d(x)x$	✓		
(D2)	$d(xy) = d(xd(y))$	✓		
(D3)	$d(x+y) = d(x) + d(y)$	✓		
(D5)	$d(\delta) = \delta$	✓		
(3)	$d(x) + a(x) = 1$	✓		
(4)	$d(x)a(x) = 0$	✓		
(12)	$d(x)d(y) = d(y)d(x)$	✓		
(15)	$d(a(x)) = a(x)$	✓		

NS: near-semiring, PS: pre-semiring.

in that case is precisely that of Boolean domain semirings [6] and the three basic Boolean domain axioms that need to be added to the semiring axioms are simpler and better suited for automated deduction than those of previous approaches [12,13,15], in which the Boolean algebra of states had to be axiomatised and embedded explicitly in a two-sorted setting.

8 Codomain

In the semiring case, domain and codomain are duals with respect to semiring opposition, which swaps the order of multiplication. Weaker variants break this symmetry and codomain therefore deserves special attention. Codomain is of independent interest because it induces an image operation which is useful, for instance, in the context of Hoare-style logics and for reachability analysis.

A *codomain semiring* is a semiring $(S, +, \cdot, 0, 1)$ extended by a function $d^\circ : S \to S$ that satisfies the basic codomain axioms

$$x + xd^\circ(x) = xd^\circ(x) , \qquad\qquad d^\circ(x) + 1 = 1 ,$$
$$d^\circ(xy) = d^\circ(d^\circ(x)y) , \qquad\qquad d^\circ(0) = 0 .$$
$$d^\circ(x+y) = d^\circ(x) + d^\circ(y) ,$$

We call an expression in the language of codomain near-semirings *dual* to an expression in the language of domain near-semirings if it is dual with respect to opposition, each term $d(x)$ is replaced by $d^\circ(x)$, and each term $a(x)$ is replaced by $a^\circ(x)$. Here, a° denotes the anticodomain operation. We refer to antidomain axioms as the duals of domain axioms. For instance, we write (D1°) for the dual of (D1), and likewise for the lattice and healthiness conditions.

Table 3. A Family of Codomain Near-Semirings

		NS	NS_δ	NS^τ	NS_δ^τ	NS^1	NS_δ^1	PS^1	PS_δ^1
	$x + x = x$	✓	✓	✓	✓				
(D1°)	$x \leq x d^\circ(x)$							✓	✓
(D2°)	$d^\circ(xy) = d^\circ(d^\circ(x)y)$	✓	✓	✓	✓	✓	✓	✓	✓
(D3°)	$d^\circ(x + y) = d^\circ(x) + d^\circ(y)$	✓	✓	✓	✓	✓	✓	✓	✓
(D4°)	$d^\circ(x) \leq \tau$			✓	✓				
(D4°)	$d^\circ(x) \leq 1$					✓	✓	✓	✓
(D5°)	$d^\circ(\delta) = \delta$		✓		✓		✓		✓
(5°)	$x = x d^\circ(x)$	✓	✓	✓	✓	✓	✓		
(12°)	$d^\circ(x)d^\circ(y) = d^\circ(y)d^\circ(x)$	✓	✓	✓	✓	✓	✓		
(14°)	$d^\circ(x) = d^\circ(x)(d^\circ(x) + d^\circ(y))$	✓	✓						
	$d^\circ(\tau) = \tau$			✓	✓				

NS: near-semiring, PS: pre-semiring.

Because of the lack of duality, the codomain axioms for our family of near-semirings differ from the domain axioms if healthiness is to be preserved. In particular, idempotency must sometimes be assumed.

A *codomain near-semiring* is an idempotent near-semiring $(S, +, \cdot)$ extended by a function $d^\circ : S \to S$ that satisfies (5°), (D2°), (D3°), (12°) and (14°).

A *codomain near-semiring with* τ is an idempotent near-semiring $(S, +, \cdot, \tau)$ extended by $d^\circ : S \to S$ that satisfies (5°), (D2°)-(D4°), (12°) and $d^\circ(\tau) = \tau$.

A *codomain near-semiring with* 1 is a near-semiring $(S, +, \cdot, 1)$ extended by $d^\circ : S \to S$ that satisfies (5°), (D2°)-(D4°) and (12°).

A *codomain pre-semiring* is a pre-semiring $(S, +, \cdot, 1)$ extended by $d^\circ : S \to S$ that satisfies (D1°)-(D4°).

Variants with δ are obtained by adding (D5°). Table 3 shows all axiomatisations.

The following statements could be proved by Prover9.

Lemma 8.1

(i) All axiomatisations are healthy and irredundant.

(ii) All codomain near-semirings are idempotent and can be ordered.

(iii) Codomain elements of codomain near-semirings are least right preservers.

(iv) An element of a codomain near-semiring is a codomain element if and only it is a fixpoint of the codomain operation.

Proposition 8.2. *Let S be a codomain near-semiring. Then $(d^\circ(S), +, \cdot)$ is a distributive lattice. If the near-semiring has an additive (multiplicative) identity, it is the least (greatest) element of the lattice.*

In Section 5 we saw that the domain operations on our family of near-semirings did not induce modal operators. Here the situation is different.

Proposition 8.3. *For every codomain near-semiring S, all $x \in S$ and all $p, q \in d^\circ(S)$ satisfy $d^\circ((p+q)x) = d^\circ(px) + d^\circ(qx)$, and $d^\circ(\delta) = \delta$ if this identity exists.*

Domain Axioms for a Family of Near-Semirings   341

Table 4. A Family of Boolean Codomain Near-Semirings

		NS^τ_δ	NS^1_δ	PS^1_δ
	$x \leq xa^\circ(a^\circ(x))$			✓
(BD2°)	$a^\circ(xy) \leq a^\circ(a^\circ(a^\circ(x))y)$			✓
(BD3°)	$a^\circ(a^\circ(x)) + a^\circ(x) = 1$			✓
	$a^\circ(x)a^\circ(a^\circ(x)) = \delta$			✓
(5°)	$x = xd^\circ(x)$	✓	✓	
(D2°)	$d^\circ(xy) = d^\circ(d^\circ(x)y)$	✓	✓	
(D3°)	$d^\circ(x + y) = d^\circ(x) + d^\circ(y)$	✓	✓	
(D5°)	$d^\circ(\delta) = \delta$	✓	✓	
(12°)	$d^\circ(x)d^\circ(y) = d^\circ(y)d^\circ(x)$	✓	✓	
(3°)	$d^\circ(x) + a^\circ(x) = 1$		✓	
(3°)	$d^\circ(x) + a^\circ(x) = \tau$	✓		
(4°)	$a^\circ(x)d^\circ(x) = \delta$	✓	✓	

NS: near-semiring, PS: pre-semiring.

So codomain on near-semirings is strict and additive, and it induces backward diamond operators $\langle x|p = d^\circ(px)$ defined via images.

In analogy to Boolean domain near-semirings, we now axiomatise an anti-codomain operation in order to obtain Boolean codomain algebras.

A *Boolean codomain near-semiring with δ and τ* is a codomain near-semiring $(S, +, \cdot, \delta, \tau)$ that satisfies (5°), (D2°), (D3°), (D5°) and (12) and that is extended by an *anticodomain operation* $a^\circ : S \to S$ satisfying (3°) and (4°). In particular, the near-semiring is idempotent. The definition of *Boolean codomain near-semiring with δ and 1* is analogous; both axiom sets are shown in Table 4.

A *Boolean codomain pre-semiring* is a codomain pre-semiring $(S, +, \cdot, \delta, 1)$ that satisfies (D1°)-(D3°), (D5°) and that is extended by an *anticodomain operation* $a^\circ : S \to S$ satisfying (3°) and (4°).

Lemma 8.4. *All axiomatisations satisfy the Boolean conditions (3°) and (4°); their axioms are irredundant.*

However, Boolean codomain near-semirings can be unhealthy. Mace4 showed that each class contains models that do not satisfy (7°) or (18°). This remains true for semirings with δ; the identity $x0 = 0$ is needed for healthiness. These counterexamples formally support a previous remark in the two-sorted setting for pre-semirings with δ and 1 [13]. Still we obtain the following result.

Proposition 8.5. *Boolean codomain near-semirings have Boolean domain algebras. Those of pre-semirings are maximal in the pre-semirings of subidentities.*

In the case of Boolean codomain near-semirings (with δ and 1), Mace4 presents a 16-element counterexample to Corollary 6.2, hence to maximality.

Proposition 8.6. *A pre-semiring S is a Boolean codomain pre-semiring if and only if it can be extended by an antidomain operation $a^\circ : S \to S$ that satisfies $x \leq xa^\circ(a^\circ(x))$, the axioms (BD2°),(BD3°) and $a^\circ(x)a^\circ(a^\circ(x)) = 0$*

These axioms are also displayed in Table 4. In sum, the development of codomain near-semirings is similar to that of domain near-semirings, but, due to the lack of duality with respect to opposition, slightly different and less compact axiomatisations arise. A significant difference is that—unlike for domain semirings—modal operators are induced by the codomain operations.

9   Automated Action System Refinement

To demonstrate the power of our axiomatisations for formal software development, we automatically verified some well-known action system refinement laws [3], the proofs of which have already been replayed manually with demonic refinement algebras [15] and the two-sorted domain axiomatisation [5].

Formally, a *demonic refinement algebra* [15] is a structure $(S, +, \cdot, \delta, 1, ^\omega)$ such that $(S, +, \cdot)$ is an idempotent semiring and the *strong iteration* operation $^\omega :$ $S \rightarrow S$ satisfies the unfold and the coinduction axiom

$$1 + xx^\omega = x^\omega \quad \text{and} \quad y \leq z + xy \Rightarrow y \leq x^\omega z \ .$$

von Wright's original axiomatisation also uses an operation of finite iteration that interacts with the strong variant [16]. Demonic refinement algebras model positively conjunctive predicate transformers over some state space, which themselves model demonically nondeterministic programs according to a weakest precondition semantics [16]. The law $1 + x^\omega x = x^\omega$ follows from the demonic refinement algebra axioms. Intuitively, strong iteration models a loop which is possessed by a demon, that is, which may be finite or infinite.

We define the *normaliser* $n(x)$ of an element x as

$$n(x) = x^\omega a(x) \ .$$

Intuitively, $n(x)$ relates the states in the domain $d(x)$ of an action x with states from which no further iteration is possible, hence with x-normal forms.

It is stipulated that an action x *excludes* an action y if $x = a(y)x$ [15]. But there is a more appealing equivalent definition for near-semirings $(S, +, \cdot, 0, 1)$: x excludes y iff $d(x)d(y) = 0$, that is, if they are not jointly enabled. It immediately follows that exclusion is commutative.

Action systems formalise parallel reactive systems as loops containing demonic choices between individual actions which terminate when no more action is enabled. In the algebraic semantics of demonic refinement algebras,

$$\text{do } x_0 \ [] \ldots [] \ x_{n-1} \text{ od} = n\left(\sum_{i=0}^{n-1} x_i\right) = \sum_{i=0}^{n-1} x_i^\omega \prod_{i=0}^{n-1} a(x_i) \ .$$

We first automatically verified the *action system leapfrog law* [3]

$$\text{do } xy \text{ od } x \leq x \text{ do } yx \text{ od}$$

for a loop without choice. In demonic refinement algebra it corresponds to

$$\mathsf{n}(xy)x \leq x\mathsf{n}(yx) .$$

Statements of comparable complexity usually require hypothesis learning and also here we could not prove the theorem in one full sweep within reasonable time. Therefore we started with a set of hypotheses from which explosive axioms like commutativity of addition have been discarded. We added further axioms or lemmas until Mace4 failed to detect a counterexample, that is, until we could expect that the hypotheses entail the goal. Then we ran the ATP system and, when this failed within reasonable time, tried another hypothesis set.

For proving the action system leapfrog we used the additional hypotheses $a(xy)x = a(xy)xa(y)$, which itself could be proved by Prover9 in 168 steps, left-isotonicity of multiplication and the sliding rule $x(yx)^\omega = (xy)^\omega x$, which has automatically been verified before [9]. Then Prover9 needed 52 steps and the equational proof extracted is simpler than that from the literature [15].

Second, we automatically verified the *action system decomposition law* [3]

$$\mathsf{do}\ x\ []\ y\ \mathsf{od} = \mathsf{do}\ y\ \mathsf{od}\ \mathsf{do}\ x\ \mathsf{do}\ y\ \mathsf{od}\ \mathsf{od} ,$$

which holds if x excludes y. In demonic refinement algebra we must prove that

$$x = a(y)x \Rightarrow \mathsf{n}(x+y) = \mathsf{n}(y)\mathsf{n}(x\mathsf{n}(y)) .$$

Following Solin and von Wright [15], we added $d(x)\mathsf{T} = x\mathsf{T}$ as a further hypothesis, where $\mathsf{T} = 1^\omega$ is the maximal element of the algebra.

Irredundancy of this identity could easily be established through a 5-element counterexample by Mace4, which answers a question by Solin and von Wright.

Now this additional hypothesis implies that $\mathsf{T} = \mathsf{n}(x)\mathsf{T}$, which could be shown by Prover9 in 56 steps. The equational proof is

$$\mathsf{T} = a(x)\mathsf{T} + d(x)\mathsf{T} = a(x)\mathsf{T} + x\mathsf{T} \leq \mathsf{n}(x)\mathsf{T} \leq \mathsf{T} ,$$

where the third step uses coinduction. Using this fact as a hypothesis together with the standard law $(x+y)^\omega = y^\omega(xy^\omega)^\omega$, which has already been automatically verified [9], again the sliding rule and commutativity of antidomain elements allowed Prover9 to show our claim in 56 steps. Surprisingly, the assumption $x = a(y)x$ instead of $d(x)d(y) = 0$ turned out to be beneficial here.

The property $d(x) \leq d(x\mathsf{n}(y))$ has been used in the previous more complex manual proof [15]. Using $\mathsf{T} = \mathsf{n}(x)\mathsf{T}$ again, we could find an instantaneous automated proof which yields a simpler equational argument:

$$a(x) = a(xd(\mathsf{T})) = a(x\mathsf{T}) = a(x\mathsf{n}(y)\mathsf{T}) = a(x\mathsf{n}(y)d(\mathsf{T})) = a(x\mathsf{n}(y)) .$$

In all these examples, using an ATP system therefore led to particularly simple proofs. Similar results for other domain near-semirings can be expected.

10   Conclusion

We have axiomatised domain operations that serve as enabledness conditions for variants of Kleene algebras with applications in program refinement, the analysis of probabilistic protocols, game theory and process algebra. The axioms obtained are simpler, more flexible and better suited for automation than previous approaches. They provide a basis from which further constraints imposed by the semantics of applications can be included. In the case of process algebras, for instance, the interaction of enabledness with parallel composition needs further investigation. We have also shown that the approach yields efficient automated proof support for applications in the refinement of parallel reactive systems.

The study of domain in weak Kleene algebras was strongly based on the ATP system Prover9 and the counterexample generator Mace4. These tools allowed us to drastically speed up the analysis, condense the presentation and dispense with routine technical proofs while even gaining in trustworthiness. The automated game of conjectures and refutations, the search for proofs and counterexamples, often took only a few seconds where humans would easily have spent several hours, and hardly more than a few minutes on a standard PC.

Beyond, that, the integration of algebraic methodology into off-the-shelf ATP technology could contribute towards bridging the gap between higher-order proof checking and model checking in software verification, and yield light-weight formal methods with heavy-weight automation.

The next step is to link the abstract algebraic level with concrete data (types) and their manipulation through assignment or communication. To achieve this as far as possible within ATP systems and to integrate appropriate decision procedures remains a challenge both for program analysis and theorem proving.

References

1. http://www.dcs.shef.ac.uk/~georg/ka
2. Prover9 and Mace4, http://www.cs.unm.edu/~mccune/prover9
3. Back, R.J.R., von Wright, J.: Reasoning algebraically about loops. Acta Informatica 36(4), 295–334 (1999)
4. Bergstra, J.A., Fokkink, W.J., Ponse, A.: Process algebra with recursive operations. In: Bergstra, J.A., Ponse, A., Smolka, S.A. (eds.) Handbook of Process Algebra, pp. 333–389. Elsevier, Amsterdam (2001)
5. Desharnais, J., Möller, B., Struth, G.: Kleene algebra with domain. ACM TOCL 7(4), 798–833 (2006)
6. Desharnais, J., Struth, G.: Domain semirings revisited. Technical Report CS-08-01, Department of Computer Science, University of Sheffield (2008); Accepted for Mathematics of Program Construction (MPC) (2008)
7. Furusawa, H., Tsumagari, N., Nishizawa, K.: A non-probabilistic model of probabilistic Kleene algebra. In: Berghammer, R., Möller, B., Struth, G. (eds.) Relations and Kleene Algebra in Computer Science. LNCS, vol. 4988, pp. 110–122. Springer, Heidelberg (2008)
8. Goranko, V.: The basic algebra of game equivalences. Studia Logica 75, 221–238 (2003)

9. Höfner, P., Struth, G.: Can refinement be automated? ENTCS 201, 197–222 (2007)
10. Kozen, D.: On Hoare logic and Kleene algebra with tests. ACM TOCL 1(1), 60–76 (2000)
11. McIver, A.K., Gonzalia, C., Cohen, E., Morgan, C.C.: Using probabilistic Kleene algebra pKA for protocol verification. J. Logic and Algebraic Programming 76(1), 90–111 (2008)
12. Meinicke, L., Solin, K.: Refinement algebra for probabilistic programs. ENTCS 201, 177–195 (2007)
13. Möller, B.: Kleene getting lazy. Sc. Computer Programming 65(2), 195–214 (2007)
14. Pilz, G.: Near-Rings: The Theory and Its Application. North-Holland, Amsterdam (1983)
15. Solin, K., von Wright, J.: Refinement algebra with operators for enabledness and termination. In: Uustalu, T. (ed.) MPC 2006. LNCS, vol. 4014, pp. 397–415. Springer, Heidelberg (2006)
16. von Wright, J.: Towards a refinement algebra. Sc. Computer Programming 51(1-2), 23–45 (2004)

Generating Specialized Rules and Programs for Demand-Driven Analysis*

K. Tuncay Tekle, Katia Hristova, and Yanhong A. Liu

SUNY Stony Brook, NY, USA
{tuncay,katia,liu}@cs.sunysb.edu

Abstract. Many complex analysis problems can be most clearly and easily specified as logic rules and queries, where rules specify how given facts can be combined to infer new facts, and queries select facts of interest to the analysis problem at hand. However, it has been extremely challenging to obtain efficient implementations from logic rules and to understand their time and space complexities, especially for on-demand analysis driven by queries.

This paper describes a powerful method for generating specialized rules and programs for demand-driven analysis from Datalog rules and queries, and further for providing time and space complexity guarantees. The method combines recursion conversion with specialization of rules and then uses a method for program generation and complexity calculation from rules. We compare carefully with the best prior methods by examining many variants of rules and queries for the same graph reachability problems, and show the application of our method in implementing graph query languages in general.

1 Introduction

Many complex analysis problems can be most effectively and easily described using a declarative language. The declarative specification makes it easy to understand the nature of the problem, without being distracted by implementation details. One way of writing a declarative specification is to write logic rules and queries.

Logic rules specify how given facts in a problem setting can be combined to infer new facts. For example, for program analysis, definitions of flow and dependence relations can be specified as rules; for model checking, definitions of system behaviors can be specified as rules; and for system security, access control policies can be specified as rules.

Once the specification of a problem is given by logic rules, queries can be used to select facts of interest to the analysis problem at hand. For program analysis, flow and dependence information involving particular program points of interest can be specified as queries; for model checking the properties to be checked can

---

* This work was supported in part by NSF under grants CCR-0306399 and CCF-0613913.

J. Meseguer and G. Roşu (Eds.): AMAST 2008, LNCS 5140, pp. 346–361, 2008.
© Springer-Verlag Berlin Heidelberg 2008

be specified as queries; and for system security, checking access to resources by users can be specified as queries. Queries can be used to filter the facts inferred by the rules, and moreover be a guide in the inference of the facts of interest. We use *on-demand analysis* to refer to an analysis that is expressed by a query, querying over facts that can be inferred from the rules.

Even when logic rules and queries are implemented in, say, a Prolog system, evaluated using various existing methods, or rewritten using methods such as magic set transformations to allow more efficient evaluation, such implementation is typically for fast prototyping. Furthermore, the running times of implementations using these methods can vary dramatically depending on the order of rules and the orders of hypotheses in rules, and even less is known about the space usage. Developing efficient implementations for answering queries on-demand for any given rules and queries with time and space guarantees is a nontrivial, recurring task.

This paper describes a powerful method for generating specialized rules and programs for demand-driven analysis from Datalog rules and queries, and for providing time and space complexity guarantees. Datalog [6] is an important logic-based language for specifying rules. Especially in recent years, Datalog-like rules have been used increasingly for expressing complex analysis problems, for example, pointer analysis and program analysis in general [16], model checking push-down systems [11], role-based access control [3], trust management [13], and information flow analysis [12]. Datalog-based languages are also important in graph queries [8,20] and semantic web applications [9] in general.

Given a set of rules and a kind of query, i.e., a query predicate with indications of which arguments will be bound, our method generates a set of rules and a program that is specialized for the kind of query, and produces complexity formulas for the time and space complexities of the generated program. The generated program for the specialized rules can take any set of given facts and any values of the bound parameters of the query predicate, and return the query result with the calculated time and space complexities. The method combines three transformation steps.

Recursion conversion: Transforms recursive rules into appropriate left or right linear recursive forms based on the kinds of queries, so that the connection between the queries and given facts can be established efficiently. Queries can then be answered equally efficiently for equivalent but slightly different recursive rules, which could otherwise differ asymptotically in running times.

Specialization: Specializes the transformed rules with respect to the kinds of query, so that bound parameters of the query predicate are used to restrict possible instantiations of the rules as much as possible. This is a drastically simplified form of partial evaluation [17] and may yield asymptotic improvements in running time.

Program generation and complexity calculation: Transforms specialized rules into efficient algorithms and data structures for the given analysis problem, and calculates the time and space complexities of the generated program. This uses the method developed previously [19] for bottom-up evaluation of Datalog rules.

The main contributions of this paper are not in each of the three transformation steps, but in their combination to produce efficient specialized rules and programs for on-demand analysis and to provide complexity guarantees. No less important is the evaluation of the method in precise comparison with the best prior methods whose effect on complexities are well-known to be difficult to understand. We also show the application of our method on graph query languages.

2 Language and Cost Model

We describe the Datalog language for defining rules and queries and give our cost model.

Datalog rules. *Datalog* is a declarative language for defining facts and rules that are used to infer new facts from given ones. A Datalog program is a finite set of clauses of the form: $p_1(x_{11}, ..., x_{1a_1}), ..., p_h(x_{h1}, ..., x_{ha_h}) \rightarrow p(x_1, ..., x_a).$, where h is a natural number, each p_i (respectively p) is a relation of a_i (respectively a) arguments, called a *predicate*, each x_{ij} and x_k is either a constant or a variable, and variables in x_k's must be a subset of the variables in x_{ij}'s. A predicate with arguments is called an *atom*. If $h = 0$, then there are no p_i's or x_{ij}'s, and x_k's must be constants, in which case $p(x_1, ..., x_a)$ is called a *fact*. An atom on the left hand side of a rule is called a *hypothesis*, and the atom on the right hand side is called the *conclusion*. Semantically, a rule of the form above says that if there is a substitution of variables in the rule with constants such that all of the hypotheses instantiated using the substitution are facts, then the instantiated conclusion is a fact.

Datalog queries. A query for a set of Datalog rules and facts is of the form $q(y_1, .., y_n)?$, where q is a predicate of n arguments. The meaning is to return all tuples of q that are given or can be inferred based on the rules, restricted by the constants in y_i's, if any. We denote constants by a,b,c, and variables by x,y,z.

Example. A canonical example of a Datalog program is the transitive closure of a relation, which can be expressed with two rules. We can think of the relation as the edges of a graph, and paths between any vertices as the set of transitive closure, then the specifications in Datalog would be the following:

$$\text{Doubly recursive: } \texttt{edge(x,y)} \rightarrow \texttt{path(x,y)}. \tag{1}$$
$$\texttt{path(x,z)}, \texttt{path(z,y)} \rightarrow \texttt{path(x,y)}.$$

$$\text{Right recursive: } \texttt{edge(x,y)} \rightarrow \texttt{path(x,y)}. \tag{2}$$
$$\texttt{edge(x,z)}, \texttt{path(z,y)} \rightarrow \texttt{path(x,y)}.$$

$$\text{Left recursive: } \texttt{edge(x,y)} \rightarrow \texttt{path(x,y)}. \tag{3}$$
$$\texttt{path(x,z)}, \texttt{edge(z,y)} \rightarrow \texttt{path(x,y)}.$$

These three programs can be proven by induction to infer the same **path** facts. The right- and left-recursive versions of the transitive closure concatenate edges from the vertex on the left, respectively right, with paths to the vertex on the right, respectively left. They are *linear* programs, i.e., there is at most one hypothesis in each rule that is recursive with its conclusion, however the doubly recursive program is not.

For these programs, there are 4 possible queries: path(x,y)? returns all pairs of vertices that have a path between them. path(a,y)? returns all vertices that are reachable from a. path(x,b)? returns all vertices that can reach b. path(a,b)? returns whether b is reachable from a.

Cost model. We use the cost model that resulted from the method in [19], which states the following: For any Datalog rule, the evaluation takes time proportional to the number of combinations of facts that make all hypotheses true. All input facts have to be read in, so the number of input facts must be added to the complexity. For example, for transitive closure, this is the number of edges. We use the following notation for complexity analysis. For queries regarding transitive closure, if the first argument is bound, it is denoted by a, and if the second argument is bound, it is denoted by b.

- V : number of vertices, P: number of paths, E: number of edges.
- $E(a)$: number of edges that are on any path from a to any vertex.
  $IE(a)$: number of edges that are on any path from any vertex to a.
- $o(a)$: outdegree of a, o: maximum outdegree of vertices.
  $i(a)$: indegree of a, i: maximum indegree of vertices.
- $R(a)$: number of vertices reachable from a, R: maximum number of vertices reachable from any vertex.
  $IR(a)$: number of vertices that reach a.

As an example, consider the program in (2). The evaluation of the first rule takes time $O(E)$, since all edges make the single hypothesis true. The second rule has two hypotheses, say we take all edges for the first hypothesis, then z becomes bound for the path predicate and the number of values that y can take is the maximum number of vertices reachable from any node. Therefore, a bound on the running time for this program is $O(E \times R)$.

3   Specialization and Complexity of Specialized Programs

Constants in the arguments of a query are called *static inputs*. For example, in the query path(a,x)?, a is a static input. Specialization uses static inputs to restrict the number of inferred facts by transforming the rules. Program specialization is also known as partial evaluation, and has been studied in logic programming [17], where it is sometimes called partial deduction.

Specialization for a set of Datalog rules S, and a query Q is obtaining another set of rules S' and a query Q' that satisfy the following: Every fact inferred as an answer to Q' during the evaluation of S' is a *projection* of a fact inferred as an answer to Q during the evaluation of S, where a *projection* of a fact is a selection of zero or more arguments from that fact up to a renaming of the predicate.

As an example, consider S being (3), and `path(a,y)?` being Q. Let S' be:

$$\text{edge(a,y)} \rightarrow \text{path}_{1a}\text{(y)}.$$
$$\text{path}_{1a}\text{(z)}, \text{ edge(z,y)} \rightarrow \text{path}_{1a}\text{(y)}. \tag{4}$$

and Q' be `path`$_{1a}$`(y)?`. The original query finds all vertices that are reachable from a by selecting the **path** facts whose first argument is a. Q' and S' do exactly that, and the answers to Q' are the vertices that are reachable from a. By inserting a as the first argument in the answers of Q', one trivially reconstructs the answers of Q.

To describe specialization, we need to define substitution. For a set of rules S, we denote the set of hypotheses of all rules by $h(S)$. We denote the conclusion of a rule r by $c(r)$. A *substitution* is a map from variables to constants. A substitution θ applied to a rule r, denoted $r\theta$, replaces the variables in r with constants according to θ. We say that an atom a' is an *instance* of an atom a if there is a substitution θ such that $a\theta = a'$; in case such a substitution exists, it is denoted $\text{subst}(a, a')$.

We specialize a set of Datalog rules with respect to a query via the fixpoint of a function f, which takes a set S of rules and a set A of atoms, and returns both of them with new elements added. At each step of computation, if there is an atom a in A, and a rule r in S for which a is an instance of the conclusion of r, then a new rule r', which is r updated with the substitution that makes a and the conclusion of r identical, is added to S and all hypotheses of r' are added to A. That is:

$$f(\langle S, A \rangle) = \langle S \cup S', A \cup h(S') \rangle \text{ where } S' = \{r\theta | a \in A, r \in R, \theta = \text{subst}(c(r), a) \neq undef\}.$$

Given a set of rules S, and a query Q, specialization computes the fixpoint of $f(S, Q)$ and returns the first component of the output pair as the desired set of specialized rules. The output of the function also has the original rules in the specialized set, therefore we need to remove them if they are not needed for the evaluation of the specialized query. An original rule r in the output is not needed, unless a hypothesis of a specialized rule is identical to the conclusion of r up to variable renaming. Once these rules are removed, we rewrite all atoms that have constant arguments to remove constants, and assign names based on the original predicate names and the places and values of bound arguments. We only rewrite the atoms whose predicates appear in the conclusion of some rule.

Specialization of (3) with respect to the query `path(a,y)?` yields:

$$\text{edge(a,y)} \rightarrow \text{path}_{1a}\text{(y)}.$$
$$\text{path}_{1a}\text{(z)}, \text{ edge(z,y)} \rightarrow \text{path}_{1a}\text{(y)}. \tag{5}$$

and the query `path`$_{1a}$`(y)?`. Given the same query, if one applies specialization to (1), the original unspecialized rules remain since the `path(z,y)` hypothesis of the second rule is identical to the conclusion of the original rules up to variable renaming. The original rules of (2) also remain after specialization for the same reason.

To make specialization independent of the values of the static input, we perform the following: For any query Q with n distinct static inputs, we generate n

fresh constants: say c1, ... ,cn, and replace the constants in Q with these fresh constants in order (i.e. the first distinct constant by c1, the second by c2, and so on). Next, we do specialization as described above for the given rules and rewritten Q. Note that, at this point, constants occur in the specialized rules only in the atoms for which no facts are derived by the rules. For any rule in the given set of rules, if a constant ci occurs in the rule, we replace it with a variable, say x, that does not occur in the rule, add ci(x) as a new hypothesis, where ci is a fresh predicate name to be used with ci, and add the fact ci(oci) to the set of rules, where oci is the ith original constant in the query. With this result, if another query Q' whose bound arguments are in the same places as Q is given, and Q''s ith constant is different than Q's, we retract the fact related to ci, and add a fact of ci that represents the new constant. For example, specialization of (3) with respect to the query path(a,x)? yields:

$$c(a).$$
$$c(x),\ edge(x,y)\ \rightarrow\ path_{1c}(y). \qquad (6)$$
$$path_{1c}(z),\ edge(z,y)\ \rightarrow\ path_{1c}(y).$$

and the query $path_{1c}(y)$?. If one wants to change the original query to path(b,x)?, it is not necessary to re-perform specialization, but just replace the fact c(a), with c(b).

Note that, for any set of rules, specialization does not result in different time complexities of the generated rules when the rule order within the set or the hypothesis order inside the rules is changed.

We have shown that specialization may result in a set with more specialized rules, however it may include unspecialized rules as well. Evaluating a purely specialized set of rules should be more advantageous. The purely specialized rules derived from (3), and the query path(a,x)? can be evaluated in linear time in the number of edges. Since the time is proportional to the combination of facts that make the hypotheses true, and z can only be assigned the vertices that can be reached from a as values, the evaluation takes time proportional to $E(a)$. Specialization of the programs (1) and (2) with respect to the same query is evaluated in asymptotically worse time since they include the original rules. Therefore, programs with the same semantics might have different execution times with respect to the same queries, even after specialization.

Differences in time complexity of the specialized programs can only result from the combination of the bound arguments in the query and the version of program that is being specialized, so we show such cases. If the left-recursive version is given and the left argument of the query is bound, or symmetrically if the right-recursive version is given and the right argument of the query is bound, the specialized versions have cost $O(E)$. For the doubly recursive version, no matter which arguments are bound, the complexity is $O(R \times P)$. The following are the complexities of evaluating programs with respect to queries with different bound arguments:

Bound argument	Time complexity		
	Left-rec.	Right-rec.	Doubly-rec.
None	$O(R \times E)$	$O(R \times E)$	$O(R \times P)$
First	$O(E(a))$	$O(R \times E)$	$O(R \times P)$
Second	$O(R \times E)$	$O(IE(b))$	$O(R \times P)$
Both	$O(E(a))$	$O(IE(b))$	$O(R \times P)$

4 Extension by Recursion Conversion

In the previous section, we showed that specialization might not obtain a more specialized set of rules for a given query. In general, for any set of unspecializable rules, another set of rules that infers the same set of facts may be specializable. For transitive closure, one needs to convert a particular form of recursion into another for the specialization to work. We give a general transformation which is applicable to transitive closure. Given the following set of rules:

$$p_1(x_1), \ .. \ , p_n(x_n) \rightarrow r(x).$$
$$r(y), \ r(z) \rightarrow r(x).$$

where x, x_n, y, z each denote one or more variables, y and z have common variables t, the uncommon ones are in different places in y than in z, and at the same place in x as in y or z, and the variables in t do not appear in x. Also p_i is not mutually recursive with r. Then the above rules are equivalent to both sets of rules below:

$$p_1(x_1),..,p_n(x_n) \rightarrow r(x). \qquad p_1(x_1),..,p_n(x_n) \rightarrow r(x).$$
$$p_1(y_1),..,p_n(y_n),r(z) \rightarrow r(x). \qquad r(y),p_1(z_1),..,p_n(z_n) \rightarrow r(x).$$

where each y_i (and z_i) is obtained by substituting the variables of x_i with the substitution that makes x and y (respectively z) identical.

All versions of transitive closure are instances of one of these schemas. Since they are all shown to be equivalent and there is a transformation method to transform from one to another, we exploit this fact before specialization.

We give a detailed complexity analysis of specialization extended with recursion conversion for transitive closure. Recursion conversion is also insensitive to hypothesis order or rule order. We just need to consider the main three versions of the transitive closure.

After applying the described transformations to any version of transitive closure, if any of the arguments is bound in the query, the program can be evaluated in $O(E)$ time, and if both arguments are free then the program can be evaluated in $O(R \times E)$ time. One can revise the $O(E)$ bound by more precise bounds as follows:

Bound argument	Time complexity for all three programs
None	$O(R \times E)$
First	$O(E(a))$
Second	$O(IE(b))$
Both	$O(\min(E(a), IE(b)))$

Recursion conversion as described is possible only for the given schema, i.e., doubly-recursive or linear Datalog programs, so it is of significance to convert a Datalog program into a linear one if possible. The question whether it is possible to perform such a transformation has been answered negatively in general, and a subset of Datalog programs have been shown to be convertible to linear ones [1].

For our purposes, any linearization procedure for a subset of Datalog is useful. If we obtain a program which obeys the schema for recursion conversion, we apply the recursion conversion to obtain different versions of the same program. We then apply our specialization algorithm to these different versions. After these steps, we can generate the program as in [19] and automatically analyze the time complexity of the bottom-up evaluation of each resulting program and choose the best one. In any of the steps if the transformation is not possible, we skip that step. The whole method can be summarized as: linearize (if possible), apply recursion conversion (if possible), specialize all versions, generate program, calculate complexity and choose the best. The algorithm is presented in Figure 1.

Algorithm *Demand-driven analysis*
Input: A set of Datalog rules S and a query Q
Output: A sequential program for the generation of answers to Q, with time complexity guarantees
1.   **if** any rule in S is linearizable
2.   **then** $S = \text{Linearize}(S)$
3. $RS \leftarrow \{S\}$
4.   **for** each predicate p in S that fits the recursion conversion schema
5.   **do** $S' = p$'s recursion type converted in S
6. $RS \leftarrow RS \cup \{S'\}$
7. $RSC = \{\}$: to keep rule sets with complexities
8.   **for** each set R of rules in RS
9.   **do** $R' \leftarrow R$ specialized for Q
10. $C \leftarrow$ Time complexity of evaluating R'
11. $RSC \leftarrow RSC \cup \{(R', C)\}$
12. Among all pairs in RSC, remove the ones that are provably worse in complexity than at least one pair.
13. **for** each pair (R, C) in RSC
14.   **do** generate program from R
15.   output C as the time complexity associated with it

Fig. 1. Algorithm for demand-driven analysis

The time complexity of the method is dominated by the specialization step, which has a super-exponential upper bound in the maximum arity of the predicates. In practice, the arity of the predicates is relatively small, 2-3 in many realistic Datalog programs and almost never exceeds 10. Thus, assuming a small constant for the maximum arity of predicates, the transformation takes linear time in the size of the set of rules, since for each rule, there is a constant number of different atoms that can unify with its conclusion, and specialization of a rule with respect to an atom takes time proportional to its size.

There are Datalog programs for which recursion conversion is not possible; and specialization cannot succeed in obtaining better running time. In this case, a transformation method such as magic sets may obtain asymptotic speedup with tighter complexity bounds, but the worst-case running times of programs transformed by both our method and magic sets are the same.

5 Comparison

This section discusses the power and limitations of our method in contrast to other work. We consider 12 versions of the transitive closure: the left, right and doubly-recursive programs, and for each program, different order of the two rules, and different order of hypotheses in the recursive rule. We denote the versions by three fields, the first being the recursion type (right, left, or doubly), the second being the order of rules (base-first or recursion-first), the third being the order of hypotheses (regular or inverse). Then for each version, we ask 4 different kind of queries: both arguments bound, only the first argument bound, only the second argument bound, and both arguments free. All results are summarized in Figure 2.

In this figure, we omit the order of rules, because the complexities and inferred facts remain the same for static filtering and magic sets, since they are bottom-up methods. For tabling, since termination is guaranteed, the complexities and inferred facts also remain the same. However, for Prolog evaluation, if the program does not terminate, there will be no inferred facts if the recursive rule is first, otherwise the evaluation will infer some facts, before it gets stuck in an infinite loop.

Method	Bound argument	Time complexity					
		Left-rec.		Right-rec.		Doubly-rec.	
		Regular	Inverse	Regular	Inverse	Reg.	Inv.
Prolog, cyclic gr	Any	Infinite					
Prolog, acyclic gr	Any	Infinite	Exponential	Exponential	Infinite	Infinite	
Tabling	None	$O(V^3)$	$O(V \times E)$	$O(V^3)$	$O(V \times E)$	$O(V^3)$	
	First	$O(E)$	$O(V \times E)$	$O(V^2)$	$O(V \times E)$	$O(V^3)$	
	Second	$O(V^3)$	$O(V^2)$	$O(V^3)$	$O(E)$	$O(V^3)$	
	Both	$O(E)$	$O(V^2)$	$O(V^2)$	$O(E)$	$O(V^3)$	
Static filtering	None	$O(V \times E)$		$O(V \times E)$		$O(R \times P)$	
	First	$O(R(a) \times o)$		$O(R \times E)$		$O(R \times P)$	
	Second	$O(R \times E)$		$O(IR(b) \times i)$		$O(R \times P)$	
	Both	$O(R(a) \times o)$		$O(IR(b) \times i)$		$O(R \times P)$	
Magic set	None	$O(V \times E)$		$O(V \times E)$		$O(V^3)$	
	First	$O(R(a) \times o)$	$O(E)$	$O(V \times R(a) \times o)$	$O(V \times E)$	$O(V^3)$	
	Second	$O(V \times E)$	$O(V \times IR(b) \times i)$	$O(E)$	$O(IR(b) \times i)$	$O(V^3)$	
	Both	$O(R(a) \times o)$	$O(E)$	$O(E)$	$O(IR(b) \times i)$	$O(V^3)$	

Fig. 2. A comparison of time complexities of computation using existing methods

Prolog. Prolog evaluation resolves subgoals in a top-down fashion. It has the general vulnerability that for any version of the transitive closure, for cyclic graphs, it will not terminate once it enters a cycle, because it will be doomed to resolve the same subgoals infinitely many times. Even when the input is restricted to acyclic graphs, it may still not terminate or it may terminate in exponential time. Prolog does not keep track of discovered vertices and discovers a vertex through all possible paths, which is exponential in the worst case. For versions whose first hypothesis is recursive in the recursive rule, the evaluation will be infinite with respect to all queries regardless of the graph structure. The doubly-recursive versions are always infinite; what differs is the generated facts due to the order of rules and hypotheses.

Tabling. Tabling adds memoization to Prolog evaluation to avoid repeating subgoals. It is guaranteed to be finite and be bounded by $O(V^3)$ for any version and query. If during tabled execution, one ever encounters a `path` call with both arguments free, the time complexity bound will be either $O(V \times E)$ or $O(V^3)$. If one encounters calls to `path` with both or one of the arguments bound, but bound to different values during the execution, then the time is $O(V \times E)$ or $O(V^3)$. If one only encounters calls to `path` with one of the arguments bound to the same value and the other argument free, then the time is $O(E)$ or $O(V^2)$. The criterion on obtaining the bounds in Figure 2 is the amount of data kept for each tabled predicate.

Static filtering and off-line partial evaluation. These are bottom-up procedures, and are not affected by the order of rules and hypotheses. Static filtering and partial evaluation work in essence as the specialization procedure described. Static filtering restricts, i.e. *filters*, the facts used during the evaluation using constants in the query. It is vulnerable to changes of the recursion type in the definition. For example, the method will be able to impose filters on the first argument for the rules in case the left-recursive version is used and the first argument is bound in the query, but will not be able to impose any filters on rules if such a query is asked to the right-recursive version. The doubly-recursive version is not *filterable*.

If static filtering yields linear time evaluation, it does so using less than all edges (except the time to read in all facts); more precisely speaking it only looks at edges reachable from a, which is bound by $R(a) \times o$. Symmetrically, using the right-recursive program with the second argument bound, the evaluation only considers edges that can reach b, which is bound by $IR(b) \times i$.

Dynamic filtering. Dynamic filtering is a version of filtering where the filters are set according to the underlying database during the evaluation. It is not easy to analyze, because the complexity measure may drastically change from one data set to another. As a simplistic overview, we can say that for dense graphs, dynamic filtering behaves exactly the same as static filtering; in contrast, for sparse graphs the filters imposed may remain fairly strict and the evaluation may be better than static filtering, although even for sparse graphs, the filters may reduce to those imposed by static filtering.

Magic set transformation. Generalized supplementary magic set transformation is a transformational method that is used to pass information from one hypothesis to another to mimick top-down evaluation. The resulting time complexity is not affected by the order of rules, but it is asymptotically affected by the version of recursion, and the order of hypotheses in the recursive rule. Another drawback of magic-set variants is that they produce programs that are significantly larger, continining new predicates, new rules and transformed rules with new hypotheses. The time complexity of the evaluation of the transformed programs are $O(E)$ or $O(V \times E)$ depending on how the transformation infers tuples of the given rules using supplementary predicates. For the transitive closure facts inferred, if the supplementary predicates can restrict one of the arguments to a specific value, then it is $O(E)$, otherwise it is $O(V \times E)$ for the left and right-recursive versions, and it is always $O(V^3)$ for the doubly-recursive versions regardless of the queries because no restrictions are possible for at least one of the two recursive hypotheses.

Our method. We have shown that, if any argument is bound in the query, we always obtain $O(E)$ time, which is not possible using other methods. We also present tighter bounds for our method in Figure 2. We believe that our method is strong because it is at least as efficient as other methods and better most of the time, when other methods fail to evaluate these rules efficiently with respect to a query. Also the rules that we generate are simpler, each rule becoming a specialized version of an original rule with respect to the bound arguments, and thus can be understood with respect to the original rules. Therefore, combining all the methods described, i.e., recursion conversion, specialization and program generation, prove to be a powerful method for efficient on-demand analysis.

A drawback of our method is that the context-free reachability queries [22] are not effectively specializable using our method, however we believe that this is not a major drawback since a solution to this problem would be a solution to the famous open problem for proving lower bounds on such problems.

6   Implementation and Applications

We have implemented the method and applied it to many problems including program analysis problems. Two examples are described below.

Implementation. The implementation consists of approximately 600 lines of Python code. Even though the running-time is super-exponential in the arity of predicates, since this number is generally small, in all the examples discussed below, the transformations are completed in under 1 second.

Application: strongly connected vertices. A small and illustrative example is computing pairs of vertices in the same strongly connected component. Suppose we use any version of transitive closure and we have the following additional rule: path(x,y), path(y,x) → sameSCC(x,y).

Given any argument bound, all prior methods discussed take cubic time in the number of vertices, since there are two subgoals where one has one argument bound, and the other has the other argument bound, therefore resulting in worst case for at least one of them. Our method generates a program that takes linear time in the number of edges.

Another interesting predicate is notSameSCC, whose facts are pairs of vertices that are not in the same strongly connected component, which can be obtained by negating either one of the hypotheses in the rule defining notSameSCC. First, if the negated predicate is the first one, then top-down evaluation methods will not be able to return correct answers due to negation as failure; and in case this program is rewritten using magic sets, the program does not even remain stratified, so the evaluation of the resulting program is inefficient.

Application: graph query examples.   Graph query languages [8,20,18] express graph analysis problems as queries on graphs. We take the examples from [18] for program analysis and model checking problems. For example, given a start point, to find the program points y such that an uninitialized variable x is used for the first time, one may write the following expression: y: [start] $(\neg(\text{def}(x)|\text{use}(x)))* \text{use}(x)$ [y].

Intuitively, this says that there is a path from start to y, such that the path consists of operations that are neither definitions nor uses of x, and the path ends with a use of x. This is transformed to the following set of rules [20]:

```
def(x1,x2,x)  →  deforuse(x1,x2,x).
use(x1,x2,x)  →  deforuse(x1,x2,x).
¬ deforuse(x1,x2,x)  →  notdef(x1,x2,x).
notdefs(x1,x2,x), notdef(x2,x3,x)  →  notdefs(x1,x3,x).
notdefs(start,x2,x), use(x2,y,x)  →  notdefsuse(start,y,x).
```

and a query notdefsuse(start,y,x)? would retrieve the answers. For the query notdefsuse(s,y,x)?, our method produces the following set of rules:

```
def(x1,x2,x)  →  deforuse(x1,x2,x).
use(x1,x2,x)  →  deforuse(x1,x2,x).
¬ deforuse(x1,x2,x)  →  notdef(x1,x2,x).
notdefs₁ₛ(x2,x), notdef(x2,x3,x)  →  notdefs₁ₛ(x3,x).
notdefs₁ₛ(x2,x), use(x2,y,x)  →  notdefsuse₁ₛ(y,x).
```

This program is much faster than the original program, since only the program points reachable from a particular point s is considered.

Moreover, our method does not require any modification in the presence of stratified negation and the complexity calculation remains the same since with stratified negation, negated hypotheses are looked up in the facts. In case the program is not stratified, we believe that our specialization method still keeps the semantics of the original program with respect to semantics such as well-founded semantics and stable model semantics.

Most graph query representations can automatically be translated into Datalog. This has been shown explicitly for GraphLog in [8]. We take examples from [18] and show the complexity results that our method yields for each of the problems.

We give a table of problems and associated complexities using our method in Figure 3. Shorthands like *undefvars*, *openfiles* are generally self-explanatory

Problem	Complexity
Uninitialized variables	$E(\text{start}) \times \text{undefvars}$
Live variables	$E(\text{end}) \times \text{usedvars}$
Available expressions	$E(\text{start}) \times \text{expr}$
Constant folding	$E(\text{start}) \times \text{def}$
Files	$E(\text{start}) \times \text{files}$
Freed memory	$E(\text{start}) \times \text{freedvars}$
Interrupts	$E(\text{start}) \times \text{savedvar}$
Security	$E(\text{start}) \times \text{openfiles}$
Deadlock avoidance	$E(\text{start}) \times \text{locks}^2$
Deadlocks	$\text{states} \times \text{outdegree}(\text{act}) + E(\text{start})$
Livelocks	$\text{action} \times \text{states} + E(\text{start})$

Fig. 3. Time complexities for solving analysis problems

Input	Vertices	Edges	Deadlock	Livelock
vasy0_1	289	1224	0.03s	0.01s
cwi1_2	1952	2387	0.09s	0.02s
vasy1_4	1183	4464	0.12s	0.03s
vasy5_9	5486	9676	0.30s	0.06s
cwi3_14	3996	14552	0.43s	0.13s
vasy8_24	8879	24411	0.71s	0.17s
vasy8_38	8921	38424	0.93s	0.25s
vasy10_56	10849	56156	1.35s	0.39s
vasy18_73	18746	73043	2.08s	0.65s

Fig. 4. Experimental results for model checking applications

abbreviations, denoting the number of undefined variables, and the number of files that are opened, respectively.

All the complexities in Figure 3 are asymptotically better than the results without specialization, which is $O(E \times V^n)$ in the worst case, where V is the number of vertices, and n is the number of variables in the query.

We conducted experiments for deadlock and livelock analysis using the VLTS benchmark[1]. Figure 4 shows the results obtained using the specialized rules automatically generated from the description of the problem using the graph query language described above. The first two columns show the vertices and edges in each input file, and the next two columns show the time taken by the analyses in seconds. The experiments were conducted using the Python 2.4.1 interpreter, on a Core 2 Duo 2.8GHz with 2 GB of free memory, running SuSE Linux.

The experiments verify the expected results from the time complexity analysis as they grow linearly with the size of the graph. The unspecialized rules for these analyses could only complete on the first input, and even an example as small as the second one could not be completed in 30 minutes. These applications involve computing reachable vertices from a given start node. We ran experiments on XSB [24] to perform the same task using different versions of transitive closure, and verified our bounds presented in Figure 2. For example, given (3) and a query with the first argument bound, the running time ranged from 1 millisecond for 5000 edges, to 7 milliseconds for 30000 edges, behaving linearly as expected.

---

[1] Available at: http://www.inrialpes.fr/vasy/cadp/resources

Given the inverse version of (2) for the same data and query, we obtained 830 milliseconds for 5000 edges, and 34280 milliseconds for 30000 edges, reflecting the $O(V \times E)$ bound.

The running times in Figure 4 parallel the results in [18], however they are worse by a constant factor of about 2.5, because our generated program is in Python and the results in [18] are obtained using programs in C++.

7 Related Work and Conclusion

Datalog has been extensively studied in the literature [6]. Bottom-up evaluation strategies originated from naïve evaluation and extended semi-naïve evaluation. Source-to-source transformations, such as magic set transformations [2,4] for faster query evaluation, try to mimic the benefits of top-down evaluation.

Although these methods offer a way of possibly faster evaluation, they do not have a succinct method for calculating the time complexity of the evaluation. A method that generates imperative programs from Datalog rules was developed by Liu and Stoller, and the time complexity bounds given by this method are tighter than the former [19].

Top-down evaluation methods have also been considered for the evaluation of Datalog programs. For recursive query processing, standard Prolog evaluation [21] is not feasible. An extension for Prolog evaluation called tabling, i.e., memoization, has been developed. A particular system that implements tabling is XSB and has been used for deductive databases [7,24]. One disadvantage for the evaluation of Datalog programs in a top-down fashion is that, there is no well-defined way for calculating the time complexity by only analyzing the rules.

Other methods for efficiently evaluating Datalog programs such as static filtering [15] and dynamic filtering [14] have also been proposed. These methods use special data structures for evaluating Datalog programs rather than using traditional evaluation engines. For static filtering, the computational complexity of the evaluation can be analyzed easily from the rules. For dynamic filtering, however, the computational complexity depends on input data therefore cannot be determined statically.

Using static filtering for the evaluation a Datalog program can be shown to be the same as using partial evaluation combined with the program generation method described. Partial evaluation for logic programming [17] is a general framework for taking static inputs into account for general logic programs. The specialization method that we describe in Section 3 is a simplified form of partial evaluation for Datalog programs.

Borrowing ideas from the theory of grammars for logic programming is natural since the evaluation of both involve similar components. We have incorporated one such idea [5] for our conversion between left-recursive and right-recursive programs. Grammar related ideas for Datalog programs can also be found in, e.g., [10]. Forms of recursion conversion have been discussed in other contexts as well. The conversion from doubly-recursive rules to rules with only one recursive hypothesis is a specific instance of linearization [23,25].

Our work distinguishes from the previous work in several aspects. Previous work generally focus on one aspect, such as specialization or evaluation alone. Our work combines several techniques: using recursion conversion to obtain different programs with the same semantics in order to specialize better, using specialization for on-demand evaluation, and using automatic program generation with complexity calculations. These together produce efficient specialized programs for demand-driven analysis and provide complexity guarantees specialized for each problem. We have extensively compared and contrasted our method with previous work, and showed that it outperforms previous methods in readability, efficiency, and usability: it generates specialized rules that are simpler than the original rules and are more efficient than using other methods, for a large class of Datalog programs such as the programs that are generated from the query language in [20], and the user just provides the set of rules and the query and our method produces specialized rules for efficient evaluation and generates a program ready to be executed.

References

1. Afrati, F.N., Gergatsoulis, M., Toni, F.: Linearisability on datalog programs. Theoretical Computer Science 308(1-3), 199–226 (2003)
2. Bancilhon, F., Ramakrishnan, R.: An amateur's introduction to recursive query processing strategies. In: Proc. of the 1986 ACM SIGMOD Intl. Conf. on Management of Data, pp. 16–52 (1986)
3. Barker, S., Leuschel, M., Varea, M.: Efficient and flexible access control via logic program specialisation. In: Proc. of the 2004 ACM SIGPLAN Workshop on Partial Evaluation and Semantics-based Program Manipulation, pp. 190–199 (2004)
4. Beeri, C., Ramakrishnan, R.: On the power of magic. J. Logic Programming 10(1/2/3&4), 255–299 (1991)
5. Brough, D.R., Hogger, C.J.: Grammar-related transformations of logic programs. New Generation Computing 9(2), 115–134 (1991)
6. Ceri, S., Gottlob, G., Tanca, L.: Logic Programming and Databases. Springer, Heidelberg (1990)
7. Chen, W., Warren, D.S.: Tabled evaluation with delaying for general logic programs. J. ACM 43(1), 20–74 (1996)
8. Consens, M.P., Mendelzon, A.O.: GraphLog: a visual formalism for real life recursion. In: Proc. of the 9th ACM SIGMOD-SIGACT-SIGART Symp. on Principles of Database Systems, pp. 404–416 (1990)
9. Gottlob, G., Koch, C.: Monadic datalog and the expressive power of languages for web information extraction. J. ACM 51(1), 74–113 (2004)
10. Greco, S., Saccà, D., Zaniolo, C.: Grammars and automata to optimize chain logic queries. Intl. J. Foundations of Computer Science 10(3), 349 (1999)
11. Hristova, K., Liu, Y.A.: Improved algorithm complexities for linear temporal logic model checking of pushdown systems. In: Proc. of 7th Intl. Conf. on Verification, Model Checking and Abstract Interpretation, pp. 190–206 (2006)
12. Hristova, K., Rothamel, T., Liu, Y.A., Stoller, S.D.: Efficient type inference for secure information flow. In: Technical Report DAR 07-35, Computer Science Department, SUNY Stony Brook (May 2007); A preliminary version of this work appeared in Proc. of the 2006 ACM SIGPLAN Workshop on Programming Languages and Analysis for Security

13. Hristova, K., Tekle, K.T., Liu, Y.A.: Efficient trust management policy analysis from rules. In: Proc. of the 9th ACM SIGPLAN Intl. Conf. on Principles and Practice of Declarative Programming (July 2007)
14. Kifer, M., Lozinskii, E.L.: A framework for an efficient implementation of deductive database systems. In: Proc. of the Advanced Database Symposium (1986)
15. Kifer, M., Lozinskii, E.L.: On compile-time query optimization in deductive databases by means of static filtering. ACM Trans. Database Systems 15(3), 385–426 (1990)
16. Lam, M.S., Whaley, J., Livshits, V.B., Martin, M.C., Avots, D., Carbin, M., Unkel, C.: Context-sensitive program analysis as database queries. In: Proc. of the 24th ACM SIGACT-SIGMOD-SIGART Symp. on Principles of Database Systems, pp. 1–12 (2005)
17. Leuschel, M.: Logic program specialisation. In: Hatcliff, J., Mogensen, T.Æ., Thiemann, P. (eds.) DIKU 1998. LNCS, vol. 1706, pp. 155–188. Springer, Heidelberg (1999)
18. Liu, Y.A., Rothamel, T., Yu, F., Stoller, S.D., Hu, N.: Parametric regular path queries. In: Proc. of the ACM SIGPLAN 2004 Conf. on Programming Language Design and Implementation, pp. 219–230 (2004)
19. Liu, Y.A., Stoller, S.D.: From datalog rules to efficient programs with time and space guarantees. In: Proc. of the 5th Intl. ACM SIGPLAN Conf. on Principles and Practice of Declarative Programming, pp. 172–183 (2003)
20. Liu, Y.A., Stoller, S.D.: Querying complex graphs. In: Proc. of the 7th Intl. Symp. on Practical Aspects of Declarative Languages, pp. 199–214 (2006)
21. Maier, D., Warren, D.S.: Computing with logic: logic programming with Prolog. Benjamin-Cummings Publishing Co. Inc., Redwood City (1988)
22. Melski, D., Reps, T.W.: Interconvertibility of a class of set constraints and context-free-language reachability. Theoretical Computer Science 248(1-2), 29–98 (2000)
23. Ramakrishnan, R., Sagiv, Y., Ullman, J.D., Vardi,: Proof-tree transformation theorems and their applications. In: Proc. of the 8th ACM SIGACT-SIGMOD-SIGART Symp. on Principles of Database Systems, pp. 172–181 (1989)
24. Sagonas, K.F., Swift, T., Warren, D.S.: XSB as a deductive database. In: Proc. of the 1994 ACM SIGMOD Intl. Conf. on Management of Data, p. 512 (1994)
25. Zhang, W., Yu, C.T., Troy, D.: Necessary and sufficient conditions to linearize double recursive programs in logic databases. ACM Trans. on Database Systems 15(3), 459–482 (1990)

Non Expansive ϵ-Bisimulations

Simone Tini

Dipartimento di Scienze della Cultura, Politiche e dell'Informazione
Università dell'Insubria, Como, Italy

Abstract. ϵ-*bisimulation* equivalence has been proposed in the literature as a technique to study the concept of *behavioral distance* between
probabilistic processes. In this paper we consider also two stronger equivalences: *action* ϵ-bisimulation and *global* ϵ-bisimulation. For each of these
three equivalence notions we propose an SOS transition rule format en-
suring the property of *non-expansiveness*. Non-expansiveness means that
if the behavioral distance between s_i and t_i is ϵ_i, then the behavioral distance between $f(s_1, \ldots, s_n)$ and $f(t_1, \ldots, t_n)$ is no more that $\epsilon_1 + \cdots + \epsilon_n$.
As expected, the stronger the ϵ-bisimulation considered, the (slightly)
weaker the constraints of the transition rule format.

1 Introduction

Many investigations on probabilistic concurrent processes are based on the classical notions of *equivalence* and *congruence*, and the underlying ideas of processes
having the same behavior and being inter-substitutable for each other [4,5,10,11,
14,15,23,24,25,26,28,29,32,38]. Several authors [1,2,13,16,17,19,21,33,34,35]
argue that this approach is too fragile when numerical values of probabilities
are based on statistical sampling, or are subject to error estimates, or appear in
models obtained as approximations of other, more accurate but less manageable,
models. In these cases it does not seem correct to consider processes that differ
for "very small" probability values just as processes that perform completely
different actions. What is needed is a notion of *distance* between process behaviors, so that two processes are considered *approximatively the same* when such
a distance is below a suitable bound. Then, a notion is needed to formalize the
intuition that processes being approximatively the same should be *approximatively inter-substitutable* each other. In [13,17] a notion of behavioral distance
expressed in terms of numerical values is called *non expansive* iff, given an operation f with n arguments, and processes $s_1, t_1, \ldots, s_n, t_n$ such that the distance
between s_i and t_i is ϵ_i, then the distance between $f(s_1, \ldots, s_n)$ and $f(t_1, \ldots, t_n)$
is bounded by $\epsilon_1 + \cdots + \epsilon_n$.

Two approaches have been proposed to measure the behavioral distance between processes. The approach of [13,16,17,33,34,35] is based on the notion
of *metric*, which, in the probabilistic processes setting, is defined as a function
that associates a numerical value called distance with each pair of processes.
The distance between two processes s and t depends on the distance between
the processes they can reach by performing the same action: The lower the probability to reach these processes, the smaller the contribution of their distance to

J. Meseguer and G. Roşu (Eds.): AMAST 2008, LNCS 5140, pp. 362–376, 2008.
© Springer-Verlag Berlin Heidelberg 2008

determine the distance between s and t. The approach of [1, 2, 19] considers the behavioral distance between two processes as bounded by ϵ if they are equated by an ϵ-bisimulation, namely an equivalence that relates two processes iff, for all actions a and equivalence classes C, the probabilities they have to perform a and to reach processes in C have difference $\leq \epsilon$. This notion of distance is "persistent", meaning that, since equivalent processes reach equivalent processes, the equivalence persists during their execution. On the contrary, in the metric approach it may happen that processes having distance ϵ have probability $< \epsilon$ to reach processes having distance greater than ϵ. The ϵ-bisimulation approach seems more appropriate when dealing with persistent properties is of interest. For instance, in [1, 2] several security properties for probabilistic processes based on ϵ-bisimulation have been studied, and in [20] it is argued that the persistency of these properties is determinant to let the system keep its security level when it is plugged into a dynamic untrusted context that can change the attack strategy at runtime.

In this paper we pursue the ϵ-bisimulation approach by introducing two stronger notions: *action ϵ-bisimulation* and *global ϵ-bisimulation*. These stronger notions are motivated by the fact that they are more robust under the point of view of compositionality, meaning that, as expected, the stronger the equivalence considered, the greater the set of operations f for which the equivalence is non expansive.

Since [18] a *transition rule format* is a set of syntactical constraints on the form of the rules that are used to give the semantics of a process algebra in the SOS style of [30]. Usually, these formats are used to ensure that an equivalence relation defined over processes is a congruence. In this paper we propose a rule format for each of the three notions of ϵ-bisimulation ensuring that all process algebra operations are non expansive for the ϵ-bisimulation considered. We show that some operations proposed in the literature respect the constraints of our formats, and we show, by means of some counterexamples, that these constraints cannot be relaxed in any trivial way. As expected, the stronger the ϵ-bisimulation considered, the weaker the constraints of the format.

2   Main Definitions

In this paper we consider the *generative* (or *full*) model of probabilistic processes [37], where a single probability distribution is ascribed to all moves of a process.

Let us use "$\{\!|$" and "$|\!\}$" as brackets for multisets.

Definition 1 (GPTS, [3, 4, 9, 37]). *A generative probabilistic transition system (GPTS) is a 4-tuple $(\mathcal{S}, Act, \mathcal{I}, T)$, where $\mathcal{S}$ is a set of states, Act is a set of actions, $\mathcal{I}$ is a set of indexes, and $T \subseteq \mathcal{S} \times Act \times (0, 1] \times \mathcal{I} \times \mathcal{S}$ is a set of transitions such that, for all states $s \in \mathcal{S}$:*

$$\sum \{\!| \, p \mid \exists a \in Act, \gamma \in \mathcal{I}, s' \in \mathcal{S} : (s, a, p, \gamma, s') \in T \, |\!\} \in \{0, 1\}$$

Indexes of transitions permit us to distinguish transitions leaving from the same state, reaching the same state, labeled with the same action and having the same probability [37]. Def. 1 requires that each state $s \in S$ be *probabilistic*, namely the sum of the probability of its outgoing transitions, if there are any, sum up to 1. Some authors admit that such a sum is a value q such that $0 \leq q \leq 1$, the interpretation being that $1 - q$ is the probability to have a deadlock.

Let $s \xrightarrow{a,p}_\gamma s'$ denote that $(s, a, p, \gamma, s') \in T$, $s \to s'$ that $s \xrightarrow{a,p}_\gamma s'$ for some a, p and γ, $s \to$ that $s \to s'$ for some s', and $s \not\to$ that $s \to s'$ holds for no s'.

Let us recall the *cumulative probability distribution function* [37] μ_G, which computes the total probability by which from a state s a set of states S can be reached through transitions labeled with an action a. Adopting the convention that the empty sum of probability is 0, μ_G is defined as follows.

Definition 2 (μ_G, [37]). $\mu_G : S \times Act \times 2^S \to [0,1]$ *is the function given by:* $\forall s \in S, \forall a \in Act, \forall S \subseteq S:$

$$\mu_G(s, a, S) = \sum \{\!| \, p \mid s \xrightarrow{a,p}_\gamma s' \text{ for some } \gamma \in \mathcal{I} \text{ and } s' \in S \, |\!\}$$

As usual, we shall write $\mu_G(s, S)$ for $\sum_{a \in Act} \mu_G(s, a, S)$.

For a relation $\mathcal{R} \subseteq S \times S$, let $\mathcal{R}^*$ denote the least equivalence relation containing $\mathcal{R}$. For an equivalence relation $\mathcal{R} \subseteq S \times S$, let $S/\mathcal{R}$ denote the set of its equivalence classes. Let us recall the definition of bisimulation of [37].

Definition 3 (Bisimulation, [37]). *An equivalence relation $\mathcal{R} \subseteq S \times S$ is a bisimulation if $(s_1, s_2) \in \mathcal{R}$ implies:*

$$\forall C \in S/\mathcal{R}, \forall a \in Act : \mu_G(s_1, a, C) = \mu_G(s_2, a, C)$$

As in the classic nondeterministic case, bisimulations are closed w.r.t. union.

The following definition is obtained by rephrasing those given in [1, 2, 19] for the reactive model of probabilistic processes.

Definition 4 (ϵ-bisimulation, [1,2,19]). *Given any $0 \leq \epsilon < 1$, an equivalence relation $\mathcal{R}_\epsilon \subseteq S \times S$ is an ϵ-bisimulation if $(s_1, s_2) \in \mathcal{R}_\epsilon$ implies:*

$$\forall C \in S/\mathcal{R}_\epsilon, \forall a \in Act : |\mu_G(s_1, a, C) - \mu_G(s_2, a, C)| \leq \epsilon$$

The idea in Def. 4 is that if two states are equated by some ϵ-bisimulation, then their behavioral distance is $\leq \epsilon$. Since Def. 4 and Def. 3 coincide when $\epsilon = 0$, the distance between states equated by some bisimulation is 0. Notice that ϵ-bisimulations are not closed w.r.t. union. Hence, we cannot give any notion of "the greatest" ϵ-bisimulation.

Let us introduce now two stronger notions of ϵ-bisimulation.

Definition 5 (Action ϵ-bisimulation). *Given any $0 \leq \epsilon < 1$, an equivalence relation $\mathcal{R}_\epsilon \subseteq S \times S$ is an* action ϵ-bisimulation *if $(s_1, s_2) \in \mathcal{R}_\epsilon$ implies:*

$$\forall a \in Act : \sum_{C \in S/\mathcal{R}_\epsilon} |\mu_G(s_1, a, C) - \mu_G(s_2, a, C)| \leq \epsilon$$

Def. 5 is strictly more demanding than Def. 4. For instance, the processes r and s graphically represented in Fig. 1 (see Table 1 for the meaning of operations) are equated by the ε-bisimulation $R = \{(r, s), (b \cdot 0, b \cdot 0), (c \cdot 0, c \cdot 0), (0, 0)\}^*$ (which is also an action 2ε-bisimulation), but by no action ε-bisimulation.

Definition 6 (Global ε-bisimulation). *Given any $0 \leq \epsilon < 1$, an equivalence relation $\mathcal{R}_\epsilon \subseteq \mathcal{S} \times \mathcal{S}$ is a global ε-bisimulation if $(s_1, s_2) \in \mathcal{R}_\epsilon$ implies:*

$$\sum_{a \in Act, C \in \mathcal{S}/\mathcal{R}_\epsilon} |\mu_G(s_1, a, C) - \mu_G(s_2, a, C)| \leq \epsilon$$

Def. 6 is strictly more demanding than Def. 5. In fact, if we come back to Fig. 1 and to relation $R = \{(r, s), (b \cdot 0, b \cdot 0), (c \cdot 0, c \cdot 0), (0, 0)\}^*$, it turns out that R is an action 2ε-bisimulation, but no global 2ε-bisimulation equating r and s exists (note that R is a global 4ε-bisimulation).

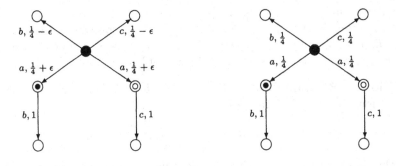

$r \equiv (a \cdot b \cdot 0 +^{\frac{1}{2}} a \cdot c \cdot 0) +^{\frac{1}{2}+2\epsilon} (b \cdot 0 +^{\frac{1}{2}} c \cdot 0)$ $s \equiv (a \cdot b \cdot 0 +^{\frac{1}{2}} a \cdot c \cdot 0) +^{\frac{1}{2}} (b \cdot 0 +^{\frac{1}{2}} c \cdot 0)$

Fig. 1. Pairs of states with the same color form an ε-bisimulation, an action 2ε-bisimulation, and a global 4ε-bisimulation

Intuitively, Def. 3 equates two processes if they have the same probabilistic branching structure. Def. 4, 5 and 6 admit that their branching structures are the same modulo an *approximation* (or *error*) ϵ. Def. 4 computes this value ϵ by considering the approximations introduced by each pair (a, C) separately. Def. 5 computes ϵ by considering the several actions a separately, and by summing the approximations introduced by a for all equivalence classes C. Finally, Def. 6 computes ϵ by summing the approximations introduced by all pairs (a, C).

2.1 Transition System Specifications

As usual, we assume a language whose abstract syntax is given by a *signature*, namely a set Σ of *operation symbols* together with an *arity* mapping ar such that $ar(f) \in \mathbb{N}$ for each $f \in \Sigma$. If $ar(f) = 0$, then f is called a *constant*. For a set of *variables* $\text{Var} = \{x, y, \ldots\}$, the set of (open) *terms* over Σ and Var is the least set such that: 1) each variable $x \in \texttt{Var}$ is a term; 2) $f(t_1, \ldots, t_{ar(f)})$ is a term when $f \in \Sigma$ and $t_1, \ldots, t_{ar(f)}$ are terms. Terms without variables are called closed terms, or *processes*. Let $vars(t)$ denote the set of the variables of a term t, defined inductively in the usual way. For a term t with $vars(t) = \{x_1, \ldots, x_n\}$ and terms $\{t_1, \ldots, t_n\}$, $t[x_1 \to t_1] \ldots [x_n \to t_n]$ is the term obtained by replacing each x_i in t with t_i.

The semantic model is a GPTS, whose states are processes, and whose transitions are inferred by a set of SOS rules [30] called *transition system specification* (TSS). We assume the standard ways [8, 36] to infer transitions from a TSS.

Definition 7 (Non-expansiveness). *An operation f is* non-expansive *(resp.: action non-expansive, global non-expansive) iff whenever r_i and s_i are equated by an ϵ_i-bisimulation (resp.: action ϵ_i-bisimulation, global ϵ_i-bisimulation) for each $1 \le i \le ar(f)$, then $f(r_1, \ldots, r_{ar(f)})$ and $f(s_1, \ldots, s_{ar(f)})$ are equated by an ϵ-bisimulation (resp.: action ϵ-bisimulation, global ϵ-bisimulation), where $\epsilon = \sum_{1 \le i \le ar(f)} \epsilon_i$.*

3   Rule Formats

For each ϵ-bisimulation introduced in the previous section, we present a transition rule format ensuring non-expansiveness. Let us begin with ϵ-bisimulation. We give first the constraints on the rules and, then, the constraints on the set of rules forming a TSS.

Given a set $I \subseteq \mathbb{N}$ such that $I = \{i_1, \ldots, i_{|I|}\}$ and $i_1 < \cdots < i_{|I|}$, and the set of indexes $\{\gamma_{i_1}, \ldots, \gamma_{i_{|I|}}\} \subset \mathcal{I}$, let $[\gamma_i]_{i \in I}$ denote the sequence $\gamma_{i_1}, \ldots, \gamma_{i_{|I|}}$.

Definition 8 (Safe transition rule). *A transition rule ρ for operation $f \in \Sigma$ is* safe *iff it is of the form*

$$\frac{\{x_i \xrightarrow{a_i, p_i}_{\delta_i} y_i \mid i \in I\} \quad \{x_j \not\to \mid j \in J\}}{f(x_1, \ldots, x_{ar(f)}) \xrightarrow{a, w_\rho \cdot \prod_{i \in I} p_i}_{(\rho, [\delta_i]_{i \in I})} t}$$

where:

1. *I and J are subsets of $\{1, \ldots, ar(f)\}$ such that $I \cap J = \emptyset$;*
2. *for each $i \in I$, p_i is a variable over $(0, 1]$ and δ_i is a variable over $\mathcal{I}$;*
3. *t is a term over Σ and $\{x_i \mid i \in \{1, \ldots, ar(f)\} \setminus I\} \cup \{y_i \mid i \in I\}$ in which:*
   (a) *each of the variables x_i with $i \in \{1, \ldots, ar(f)\} \setminus I$ appears at most once;*
   (b) *each of the variables y_i with $i \in I$ appears exactly once;*
4. *w_ρ is the weight of ρ and satisfies $0 < w_\rho \le 1$.*

Variables $\{x_i \mid i \in I\}$ are called *active variables*, transitions $\{x_i \xrightarrow{a_i, p_i}_{\delta_i} y_i \mid i \in I\}$ are called *active premises*, transitions $\{x_j \not\to \mid j \in J\}$ are called *negative premises*, the transition $f(x_1, \ldots, x_{ar(f)}) \xrightarrow{a, w_\rho \cdot \prod_{i \in I} p_i}_{(\rho, [\delta_i]_{i \in I})} t$ is called the *conclusion*, the term $f(x_1, \ldots, x_{ar(f)})$ is called the *source*, the term t is called the *target*, and a is called the *action* of ρ.

In Def. 8 we assume that the set of indexes $\mathcal{I}$ contains an index (ρ) for each rule ρ having a constant c as source. Moreover, given any rule ρ with active variables $\{x_i \mid i \in I\}$, and a set of indexes $\{\gamma_i \mid i \in I\} \subset \mathcal{I}$, we assume that also $(\rho, [\gamma_i]_{i \in I})$ is an index in $\mathcal{I}$.

First of all let us show by means of a counterexample why Def. 8 requires that each variable y_i with $i \in I$ must appear in the target term t.

Example 1. Let f be the operation having the following rule ρ_a^f for all $a \in Act$:

$$\frac{x \xrightarrow{a,p}_\delta y}{f(x) \xrightarrow{a,p}_{(\rho_a^f,\delta)} 0}$$

The processes r and s in Fig. 1 are equated by the ε-bisimulation $\{(r, s), (b \cdot 0, b \cdot 0), (c \cdot 0, c \cdot 0), (0, 0)\}^*$, but $f(r)$ and $f(s)$ are not equated by any ε-bisimulation. In fact, the probabilities they have to reach 0 through a differ by 2ϵ. Intuitively, the distance between $f(r)$ and $f(s)$ caused by the a moves to 0 is the sum of the distance between r and s caused by the a move to $b \cdot 0$ and the distance between r and s caused by the a move to $c \cdot 0$. To prevent this, we should replace the target 0 in each rule ρ_a^f with a term t containing y such that $t[y \to b \cdot 0]$ and $t[y \to c \cdot 0]$ are discriminated by all ε-bisimulations.

Let us show now why Def. 8 does not admit *duplication of variables*, namely, it requires that each variable y_i with $i \in I$ cannot appear twice (or more) in the target t. Similar counterexamples can be given to show why Def. 8 does not admit that any variable x_i with $i \in \{1, \ldots, ar(f)\} \setminus I$ appears twice in the target t, and that any variable x_i with $i \in I$ appears in t at all.

Example 2 (Duplication). Let f be the operation having the following rule ρ_a^f for each $a \in Act$:

$$\frac{x \xrightarrow{a,p}_\delta y}{f(x) \xrightarrow{a,p}_{(\rho_a^f,\delta)} g(y, y)}$$

Let g be the operation having the following rules ρ_a^g and $\rho_{a,b}^g$ for all $a, b \in Act$ with $a \neq b$, where $d \in Act$:

$$\frac{x_1 \xrightarrow{a,p_1}_{\delta_1} y_1 \quad x_2 \xrightarrow{a,p_2}_{\delta_2} y_2}{g(x_1, x_2) \xrightarrow{a,p_1 p_2}_{(\rho_a^g, \delta_1, \delta_2)} g(y_1, y_2)} \qquad \frac{x_1 \xrightarrow{a,p_1}_{\delta_1} y_1 \quad x_2 \xrightarrow{b,p_2}_{\delta_2} y_2}{g(x_1, x_2) \xrightarrow{d,p_1 p_2}_{(\rho_{a,b}^g, \delta_1, \delta_2)} g(y_1, y_2)}$$

All rules ρ_a^f admit duplication. Let $r \equiv a \cdot (b \cdot 0 +_{\frac{2}{3}} c \cdot 0)$ and $s \equiv a \cdot (b \cdot 0 +_{\frac{2}{3}+\epsilon} c \cdot 0)$. The relation $\{(r, s), (b \cdot 0 +_{\frac{2}{3}} c \cdot 0, b \cdot 0 +_{\frac{2}{3}+\epsilon} c \cdot 0), (0, 0)\}^*$ is an ε-bisimulation relating r and s, but $f(r)$ and $f(s)$ are related by no ε-bisimulation. This follows by the fact that, for instance, $g(b \cdot 0 +_{\frac{2}{3}} c \cdot 0, b \cdot 0 +_{\frac{2}{3}} c \cdot 0)$ and $g(b \cdot 0 +_{\frac{2}{3}+\epsilon} c \cdot 0, b \cdot 0 +_{\frac{2}{3}+\epsilon} c \cdot 0)$ reach $g(0, 0)$ through b with probability $4/9$ and $4/9 + 4/3\epsilon + \epsilon^2$, respectively.

Let us show why Def. 8 does not admit *double testing*, namely, two premises $x_i \xrightarrow{a_{i_1}, p_{i_1}}_{\delta_{i_1}} y_{i_1}$ and $x_i \xrightarrow{a_{i_2}, p_{i_2}}_{\delta_{i_2}} y_{i_2}$ cannot have the same variable x_i in the left side. Notice that, since events "x_i performs a_{i_1}" and "x_i performs a_{i_2}" are not independent, their probabilities p_{i_1} and p_{i_2} should be summed when computing the probability of the move of $f(x_1, \ldots, x_{ar(f)})$, as in [28]. However, since this is not the reason for which double testing cannot be admitted, in the example below we let p_{i_1} and p_{i_2} be composed with an arbitrary function h.

Example 3 (Double Testing). Let f be the operation having the following rules $\rho^f_{a,b}$, for a and b two actions in Act, and ρ^f_c, for all $c \in Act \setminus \{a, b\}$.

$$\frac{x \xrightarrow{a,p_1}_{\delta_1} y_1 \quad x \xrightarrow{b,p_2}_{\delta_2} y_2}{f(x) \xrightarrow{a,h(p_1,p_2)}_{(\rho^f_{a,b},\delta_1,\delta_2)} g(y_1,y_2)} \qquad \frac{x \xrightarrow{c,p}_{\delta} y}{f(x) \xrightarrow{c,p}_{(\rho^f_c,\delta)} y}$$

where $h : [0,1] \times [0,1] \to [0,1]$ is a function. Let g be the operation having the following rule $\rho^g_{a,b}$ for all actions $a, b \in Act$:

$$\frac{x_1 \xrightarrow{a,p_1}_{\delta_1} y_1 \quad x_2 \xrightarrow{b,p_2}_{\delta_2} y_2}{g(x_1,x_2) \xrightarrow{k(a,b),p_1 p_2}_{(\rho^g_{a,b},\delta_1,\delta_2)} g(y_1,y_2)}$$

where $k : Act \times Act \to Act$ is a function injective in $\{(b,b), (c,c), (b,c), (c,b)\}$. Double testing appears in rule $\rho^f_{a,b}$. Let $\hat{r} \equiv b \cdot 0 + \frac{1}{2} c \cdot 0$, $\hat{s} \equiv b \cdot 0 + \frac{1}{2} + \epsilon c \cdot 0$, $r \equiv a \cdot \hat{r} + \frac{1}{2} b \cdot \hat{r}$ and $s \equiv a \cdot \hat{s} + \frac{1}{2} b \cdot \hat{s}$. The relation $\{(r,s), (\hat{r},\hat{s}), (0,0)\}^*$ is an ϵ-bisimulation relating r and s, but no ϵ-bisimulation relates $f(r)$ and $f(s)$. In fact, both $f(r)$ and $f(s)$ have only one move, taking to $g(\hat{r},\hat{r})$ and $g(\hat{s},\hat{s})$, respectively. Now, $g(\hat{r},\hat{r})$ performs $k(b,b)$ with probability $1/4$, whereas $g(\hat{s},\hat{s})$ performs $k(b,b)$ with probability $1/4 + \epsilon + \epsilon^2$.

Notice that in the counterexample above the problem arises since both variables y_1 and y_2 appear in the conclusion of rule $\rho^f_{a,b}$. A partial form of double testing can be allowed, meaning that premises $\{x_i \xrightarrow{a_{i,j},p_{i,j}}_{\delta_{i,j}} y_{i,j} | j \in J\}$ can be admitted, provided that only one of the variables $y_{i,j}$ appears in the conclusion.

Let us show why Def. 8 does not admit *look ahead*, namely active premises viewing two consecutive moves $x_i \xrightarrow{a_i,p_i}_{\delta_i} y_i$ and $y_i \xrightarrow{b_i,q_i}_{\delta'_i} z_i$ of any argument of f.

Example 4 (Look Ahead). Let f be the operation having the following rules $\rho^f_{a_1,a_2}$ for all $a_1, a_2 \in Act$:

$$\frac{x \xrightarrow{a_1,p}_{\delta_1} y \quad y \xrightarrow{a_2,q}_{\delta_2} z}{f(x) \xrightarrow{g(a_1,a_2),pq}_{(\rho^f_{a_1,a_2},\delta_1,\delta_2)} z}$$

where $g : Act \times Act \to Act$ is a function injective in $\{(a,a), (a,b), (c,c)\}$. Let $r \equiv a \cdot (a \cdot 0 + \frac{1}{2} b \cdot 0) + \frac{1}{2} c \cdot c \cdot 0$ and $s \equiv a \cdot (a \cdot 0 + \frac{1}{2} + \epsilon b \cdot 0) + \frac{1}{2} + \epsilon c \cdot c \cdot 0$. Relation $\{(r,s), (a \cdot 0 + \frac{1}{2} b \cdot 0, a \cdot 0 + \frac{1}{2} + \epsilon b \cdot 0), (c \cdot 0, c \cdot 0), (0,0)\}^*$ is an ϵ-bisimulation, but $f(r)$ and $f(s)$ are equated by no ϵ-bisimulation. In fact, they perform $g(a,a)$ and reach 0 with probability $1/4$ and $1/4 + \epsilon + \epsilon^2$, respectively.

Let us show that Def. 8 cannot admit normalization of probability. Namely, rules cannot admit premises of the form $x_h \xrightarrow{A_h, q_h}$, meaning that the overall probability of the moves in the set $A_h \subset Act$ of the hth argument of f is q_h, where q_h is used to normalize the probability of the moves of $f(x_1, \ldots, x_{ar(f)})$ by multiplying their probability per factor $1/(1 - q_h)$.

Example 5 (Normalization). Let $A \subset Act$ and let $\_ \setminus A$ be the restriction operation having the following rule ρ_a^A for all actions $a \in Act \setminus A$:

$$\frac{x \xrightarrow{a,p}_\delta y \quad x \xrightarrow{A,q}}{x \setminus A \xrightarrow{a, \frac{p}{1-q}}_{(\rho_a^A, \delta)} y \setminus A}$$

Let $r \equiv a \cdot 0 + \frac{2}{3}(b \cdot 0 + \frac{1}{2} c \cdot 0)$ and $s \equiv a \cdot 0 + \frac{2}{3}(b \cdot 0 + \frac{1}{2} + 3\epsilon \; c \cdot 0)$. Relation $\{(r, s), (0, 0)\}^*$ is an ϵ-bisimulation, but no ϵ-bisimulation relates $r \setminus \{a\}$ and $s \setminus \{a\}$, since they perform b with probability $1/2$ and $1/2 + 3\epsilon$, respectively.

We can give now the constraints on the TSS.

Definition 9 (Safe TSS). *A safe TSS is formed by a set $\mathcal{R}$ of safe transition rules such that, for each operation $f \in \Sigma$, the set $\mathcal{R}^f$ of the rules in $\mathcal{R}$ for f is partitioned into (possibly infinite) sets $\mathcal{R}_1^f, \ldots, \mathcal{R}_n^f, \ldots$, such that:*

1. *Given two sets $\mathcal{R}_u^f \neq \mathcal{R}_v^f$, any rule $\rho_u \in \mathcal{R}_u^f$, and any rule $\rho_v \in \mathcal{R}_v^f$, there is an index $1 \leq i \leq ar(f)$ such that ρ_u contains an active premise $x_i \xrightarrow{a_i, p_i}_{\delta_i} y_i$ for some $a_i \in Act$ and ρ_v contains the negative premise $x_i \not\rightarrow$;*
2. *All rules in any $\mathcal{R}_u^f$ have the same active variables;*
3. *Given the set $I \subseteq \{1, \ldots, ar(f)\}$ such that $\{x_i \mid i \in I\}$ are the active variables of the rules in $\mathcal{R}_u^f$, and a set of actions $\{a_i \mid i \in I\}$, assume that $\rho_1, \ldots, \rho_m, \ldots$ are the rules in $\mathcal{R}_u^f$ having as active premises $\{x_i \xrightarrow{a_i, p_i}_{\delta_i} y_i \mid i \in I\}$. We require that $w_{\rho_1} + \cdots + w_{\rho_m} + \cdots = 1$;*
4. *For each action $a \in Act$, let $\mathcal{R}_u^{f,a}$ be the subset of the rules in $\mathcal{R}_u^f$ having a as action; the sum of the weights of the rules in any set $\mathcal{R}_u^{f,a}$ is less than or equal to 1.*

The first item in Def. 9 ensures that all moves of a process $f(t_1, \ldots, t_{ar(f)})$ can be derived by rules that are in the same set $\mathcal{R}_u^f$. Items 2 and 3 ensure that from a given set $\mathcal{R}_u^f$ we can infer either no move by $f(t_1, \ldots, t_{ar(f)})$, or moves by $f(t_1, \ldots, t_{ar(f)})$ with overall probability 1. Summarizing, items 1–3 ensure that the probability of the transitions of a process, if there are any, sum up to 1. This result has been proved in [28], where it is also shown that items 1–3 ensure that bisimulation is a congruence.

The last item has been introduced for ensuring non-expansiveness. We can show that it is mandatory by means of a counterexample.

Example 6. Let $Act = \{a, b, c\}$ and f be the operation having the following rules:

$$\frac{x \xrightarrow{a,p}_\delta y}{f(x) \xrightarrow{a,p}_{(\rho_a^f, \delta)} y} \qquad \frac{x \xrightarrow{b,p}_\delta y}{f(x) \xrightarrow{b,p}_{(\rho_b^f, \delta)} y} \qquad \frac{x \xrightarrow{c,p}_\delta y}{f(x) \xrightarrow{b,p}_{(\rho_c^f, \delta)} y}$$

The rules ρ_b^f and ρ_c^f violate Def. 9.4. Let us take the processes r and s in Fig. 1. They are related by the ϵ-bisimulation $\{(r,s),(b\cdot 0,b\cdot 0),(c\cdot 0,c\cdot 0),(0,0)\}^*$, whereas $f(r)$ and $f(s)$ cannot be related by any ϵ-bisimulation, since they reach 0 through b with probability $1/2 - 2\epsilon$ and $1/2$, respectively. Intuitively, f maps both b and c to b, so that the distance between $f(r)$ and $f(s)$ caused by b is the sum of the distance between r and s caused by b and that caused by c.

Table 1. Some operations respecting Def. 8 and Def. 9

$$a \xrightarrow{a,1}_{\rho_a} 0 \qquad\qquad a\cdot x \xrightarrow{a,1}_{\rho_a} x$$

$$\frac{x_1 \xrightarrow{a_1,p_1}_{\delta_1} y_1 \quad x_2 \xrightarrow{a_2,p_2}_{\delta_2} y_2 \quad \times \text{ injective}}{x_1 \mid x_2 \xrightarrow{a_1\times a_2, p_1\cdot p_2}_{(\rho_{a_1,a_2}^{\mid},\delta_1,\delta_2)} y_1 \mid y_2} \qquad \frac{x_1 \xrightarrow{a_1,p_1}_{\delta_1} y_1 \quad f \text{ injective}}{x_1[f] \xrightarrow{f(a_1),p_1}_{(\rho_{a_1}^{[f]},\delta_1)} y_1[f]}$$

$$\frac{x_1 \xrightarrow{a_1,p_1}_{\delta_1} y_1}{x_1\cdot x_2 \xrightarrow{a_1,p_1}_{(\rho_{a_1}^{\cdot 1},\delta_1)} y_1\cdot x_2} \qquad \frac{x_2 \xrightarrow{a_2,p_2}_{\delta_2} y_2 \quad x_1 \not\to}{x_1\cdot x_2 \xrightarrow{a_2,p_2}_{(\rho_{a_2}^{\cdot 2},\delta_2)} y_2}$$

$$\frac{x_1 \xrightarrow{a_1,p_1}_{\delta_1} y_1 \quad x_2 \xrightarrow{a_2,p_2}_{\delta_2} y_2}{x_1 +^p x_2 \xrightarrow{a_1,p_1\cdot p_2\cdot p}_{(\rho_{a_1,a_2}^{+1},\delta_1,\delta_2)} y_1} \qquad \frac{x_1 \xrightarrow{a_1,p_1}_{\delta_1} y_1 \quad x_2 \not\to}{x_1 +^p x_2 \xrightarrow{a_1,p_1}_{(\rho_{a_1}^{+3},\delta_1)} y_1}$$

$$\frac{x_1 \xrightarrow{a_1,p_1}_{\delta_1} y_1 \quad x_2 \xrightarrow{a_2,p_2}_{\delta_2} y_2}{x_1 +^p x_2 \xrightarrow{a_2,p_1\cdot p_2\cdot(1-p)}_{(\rho_{a_1,a_2}^{+2},\delta_1,\delta_2)} y_2} \qquad \frac{x_2 \xrightarrow{a_2,p_2}_{\delta_2} y_2 \quad x_1 \not\to}{x_1 +^p x_2 \xrightarrow{a_2,p_2}_{(\rho_{a_2}^{+4},\delta_2)} y_2}$$

$$\frac{x_1 \xrightarrow{a_1,p_1}_{\delta_1} y_1 \quad x_2 \xrightarrow{a_2,p_2}_{\delta_2} y_2}{x_1 \parallel^p x_2 \xrightarrow{a_1,p_1\cdot p_2\cdot p}_{(\rho_{a_1,a_2}^{\parallel 1},\delta_1,\delta_2)} y_1 \parallel^p x_2} \qquad \frac{x_1 \xrightarrow{a_1,p_1}_{\delta_1} y_1 \quad x_2 \not\to}{x_1 \parallel^p x_2 \xrightarrow{a_1,p_1}_{(\rho_{a_1}^{\parallel 3},\delta_1)} y_1 \parallel^p x_2}$$

$$\frac{x_1 \xrightarrow{a_1,p_1}_{\delta_1} y_1 \quad x_2 \xrightarrow{a_2,p_2}_{\delta_2} y_2}{x_1 \parallel^p x_2 \xrightarrow{a_2,p_1\cdot p_2\cdot(1-p)}_{(\rho_{a_1,a_2}^{\parallel 2},\delta_1,\delta_2)} x_1 \parallel^p y_2} \qquad \frac{x_2 \xrightarrow{a_2,p_2}_{\delta_2} y_2 \quad x_1 \not\to}{x_1 \parallel^p x_2 \xrightarrow{a_2,p_2}_{(\rho_{a_2}^{\parallel 4},\delta_2)} x_1 \parallel^p y_2}$$

Let us note that the operations in Table 1 respect Def. 8 and Def. 9. In the first row we have the constant a of [3] and the action-prefixing $a\cdot\_$ of [1,9,12,37]. In the second row we have the relabeling $\_[f]$ of [12,37], where f is a relabeling function $f: Act \to Act$, and the synchronous product $\_\mid\_$ of [21,37], where $\times$ is a function $\times: Act\times Act \to Act$. Note that if f and $\times$ would not be injective, then there would be at least two rules with the same action and weight 1 violating Def. 9.4. In the third row we have the sequential composition of terms $\_\cdot\_$ of [3]. Then, we have the probabilistic sum $\_+^p\_$ of [1,3,9,12,37]. If both arguments can move, then the first argument moves with probability p and the second with probability $1-p$. If only one argument can move, then it moves with probability 1. Rules for action a are partitioned in three sets, one without negative premises having two rules with weight p and $1-p$, one with the negative premise for the first argument, and the other with the negative premise for the second argument. Finally, we have the probabilistic interleaving $\_\parallel_p\_$ of [3], with a similar partitioning of rules into three sets.

Def. 8 and 9 present a format ensuring non-expansiveness of ϵ-bisimulations. Actually, these definitions present a format also for action ϵ-bisimulations and global ϵ-bisimulations. However, we can give two more general formats.

Definition 10 (Action safe TSS). *A transition rule ρ for operation $f \in \Sigma$ is action safe iff it is defined as in Def. 8, except that the constraint 3b is weakened as follows:*

- *3(b) each of the variables y_i with $i \in I$ appears* at most *once in* t.

An action safe TSS is a set $\mathcal{R}$ of action safe transition rules respecting the same constraints of Def. 9.

For instance, if we take the operation f in Example 1, which does not respect Def. 8, we note that it respects Def. 10. Example 1 creates problems with ϵ-bisimulations since the distance between processes r and s caused by the a-moves to $b \cdot 0$ and that caused by the a-moves to $c \cdot 0$ are considered separately when computing the distance between r and s, and are summed when computing the distance between $f(r)$ and $f(s)$ caused by the a moves to 0. This does not happen with action ϵ-bisimulation, since the distance between processes r and s caused by the a-moves to $b \cdot 0$ and that caused by the a-moves to $c \cdot 0$ are already summed when computing the distance between r and s caused by a.

Definition 11 (Global safe TSS). *A global safe TSS is a set $\mathcal{R}$ of action safe transition rules respecting the same constraints of Def. 9, except item 4 which is removed.*

For instance, if we take the relabeling operations $\_[f]$ in Table 1, we can remove the constraint on the injectivity of the relabeling function f. A non-injective f creates problems with action ϵ-bisimulations. For instance, let us assume that f maps both a and b to a, and let us take processes $r \equiv a \cdot c \cdot 0 +^{\frac{1}{2}} b \cdot d \cdot 0$ and $s \equiv a \cdot c \cdot 0 +^{\frac{1}{2}+\epsilon} b \cdot d \cdot 0$. We have that r and s are equated by the action ϵ-bisimulation $\{(r, s), (s, r), (c \cdot 0, c \cdot 0), (d \cdot 0, d \cdot 0), (0, 0)\}$, but $r[f]$ and $s[f]$ are equated by no action ϵ-bisimulation. The point is that the distance between processes r and s caused by a and that caused by b are considered separately when computing the distance between r and s, and are summed when computing the distance between $r[f]$ and $s[f]$ caused by a. This does not happen with global ϵ-bisimulation, since the distance between processes r and s caused by a and that caused by b are already summed when computing the distance between r and s.

We are now ready to state correctness of our three formats.

Theorem 1. *All operations in a safe (resp.: action safe, global safe) TSS are non expansive (resp.: action non expansive, global non expansive).*

4 Related and Future Work

In this paper we have studied the non-expansiveness of some notions of behavioral distance between probabilistic processes. We have worked within the generative model of probabilistic processes of [37], and the ϵ-bisimulation approach of [1, 2, 19] to measure the distance between processes.

Other notions of behavioral distance have been studied in the literature [13,16, 17,33,34,35] which are based on the notion of metrics and consider several models of probabilistic processes. Van Breugel and Worrell consider the generative model in [34] and the *reactive model* of [37] in [33, 35]. Desharnais et al. consider the reactive model in [17] and the *alternating model* of [23] in [16]. Deng et al. consider the *non alternating model* of [31], the reactive, and the generative model in [13].

A function $d : S \times S \to [0,1]$ is called a *pseudometric* iff, for all $s_1, s_2, s_3 \in S$, it holds that: $d(s_1, s_1) = 0$, $d(s_1, s_2) = d(s_2, s_1)$, and $d(s_1, s_3) \leq d(s_1, s_2) + d(s_2, s_3)$. In [13] it is proved that, given a pseudometric d, also the function $d' : S \times S \to [0,1]$ such that $d'(s_1, s_2)$ is defined as the solution of the following linear program is a pseudometric:

- maximize

$$\sum_{(a_i, s_i) \in Act \times S} x_i \left(\mu_G(s_1, a_i, \{s_i\}) - \mu_G(s_2, a_i, \{s_i\}) \right)$$

- subject to
  - $\forall i : 0 \leq x_i \leq 1$
  - $\forall i, j : x_i - x_j \leq \begin{cases} 1 & \text{if } a_i \neq a_j \\ d(s_i, s_j) & \text{if } a_i = a_j \end{cases}$

Definition 12 (State metric, [13]). *A pseudometric d is called a* state-metric *iff, for all $0 \leq \epsilon \leq 1$, $d(s_1, s_2) \leq \epsilon$ implies $d'(s_1, s_2) \leq \epsilon$.*

In this approach, the behavioral distance between s_1 and s_2 is $\leq \epsilon$ if there is a state metric d such that $d(s_1, s_2) = \epsilon$. In [13] it is proved that, if we take any relation $\mathcal{R} \subseteq S \times S$ and the pseudometric $d_\mathcal{R}$ such that $d_\mathcal{R}(s_1, s_2) = 0$, if $s_1 \mathcal{R} s_2$, and $d_\mathcal{R}(s_1, s_2) = 1$, otherwise, then it holds that $\mathcal{R}$ is a bisimulation iff $d_\mathcal{R}$ is a state-metric. Hence, the distance between states equated by some bisimulation is 0. This holds also in the ϵ-bisimulation approach. However, the ϵ-bisimulation and the metric approach behave differently with respect to persistency. ϵ-bisimulation is persistent, meaning that ϵ-bisimilar processes reach processes being, in turn, ϵ-bisimilar. This implies that processes having distance ϵ reach processes having the same distance ϵ. According to the metric approach, the distance $d(s_1, s_2)$ between s_1 and s_2 depends on the distance between the states that are reached from s_1 and s_2, the idea being that the lower the probability to reach these states, the smaller the contribution of their distance to determine $d(s_1, s_2)$. This notion of distance is not persistent, in the sense that, in general, states reached from s_1 and s_2 may have distance $> d(s_1, s_2)$. For instance, the processes r and r' in Fig. 2 have distance $\frac{7}{5}\epsilon$, but the processes $c \cdot 0 + \frac{1}{2} + 2\epsilon \, d \cdot 0$ and $c \cdot 0 + \frac{1}{2} \, d \cdot 0$ they reach through a have distance 2ϵ.

In general, the notions of distance behind the metric and the ϵ-bisimulation approaches are not comparable. For instance, let us consider once more the processes r and r' in Fig. 2. A metric assigning distance $\frac{7}{5}\epsilon$ to the pair (r, r') can be given, whereas no $\frac{7}{5}\epsilon$-bisimulation relates r and r', since the processes

$c \cdot 0 + \frac{1}{2} + 2\epsilon\, d \cdot 0$ and $c \cdot 0 + \frac{1}{2}\, d \cdot 0$ reached through a from r and r', respectively, are equated by a δ-bisimulation only if $\delta \geq 2\epsilon$. On the other side, let us consider the processes r, r', s, s', t, t' in Fig. 3. A global 2ϵ-bisimulation equating r and r' (and also the pair (s, s'), and the pair (t, t')) can be given, whereas any metric assigns to r and r' a distance not less than $\epsilon + \frac{21}{16}\epsilon$ (the distance between t and t' is at least ϵ, and the distance between s and s' is at least $\frac{7}{4}\epsilon$).

The notions of metrics and approximate bisimulation have been already investigated in [22], but in the model of *Metric Transition Systems*, where approximate bisimulation can be defined as a metric. We work in a different setting, since in Metric Transition Systems states are equipped with *observations* and both the state space and the observation space are equipped with metrics, but transitions do not carry any quantitative information.

Rule formats for probabilistic calculi have been already studied in [6,7] for the reactive case from a categorial perspective, and in [28] for both the generative

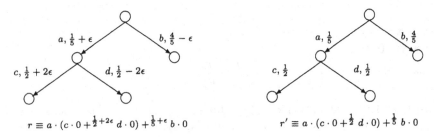

Fig. 2. Two processes having distance $\frac{7}{5}\epsilon$ in the metric approach and 2ϵ in the ϵ-bisimulation approach

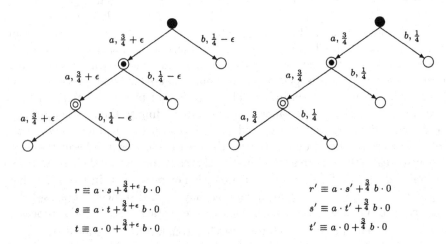

$$r \equiv a \cdot s + \frac{3}{4} + \epsilon\, b \cdot 0 \qquad\qquad r' \equiv a \cdot s' + \frac{3}{4}\, b \cdot 0$$
$$s \equiv a \cdot t + \frac{3}{4} + \epsilon\, b \cdot 0 \qquad\qquad s' \equiv a \cdot t' + \frac{3}{4}\, b \cdot 0$$
$$t \equiv a \cdot 0 + \frac{3}{4} + \epsilon\, b \cdot 0 \qquad\qquad t' \equiv a \cdot 0 + \frac{3}{4}\, b \cdot 0$$

Fig. 3. Two processes having distance 2ϵ in the global ϵ-bisimulation approach and at least $\epsilon + \frac{21}{16}\epsilon$ in the metric approach

and the reactive case. Formats of [6, 7, 28] ensure the congruence property of bisimulation, and have constraints weaker than those of the present paper. The reason is that several operations preserve bisimulation but are not non expansive w.r.t. ϵ-bisimulations.

Our work can be extended in several directions. Notions of ϵ-bisimulations can be given for the reactive, alternating and non-alternating model of probabilistic processes, and formats guaranteeing non-expansiveness of operations can be studied as well. In particular, the development for the reactive is very close to that we have considered. Notice that, since the overall probability of the transitions leaving from a state and labeled with a given action a, if there are any, is 1, the problems that have been considered in Example 1 do not emerge, thus implying that the format for ϵ-bisimulation can be slightly more general. Formats for non-expansiveness could be proposed also for the metric approach of [13, 16, 17, 33, 34, 35]. Moreover, the definition of non-expansiveness could be replaced by a weaker one, by replacing $\epsilon = \epsilon_1 + \cdots + \epsilon_{ar(f)}$ in Def. 7 with $\epsilon = h(\epsilon_1, \ldots, \epsilon_{ar(f)})$, for a suitable function h. If h is polynomial, the definition can be reasonable. In fact, if we assume that ϵ, being an approximation, is a value reasonably near to 0, all polynomial terms with degree > 1 could be treated as 0, and the only relevant terms are constants and terms of degree 1. Most of operations considered in counterexamples of the present paper that do not respect Def. 7 would respect such a modified version of non-expansiveness. Finally, let us note that in [27] a rule format for bisimulation in *stochastic* process calculi has been recently proposed. One could investigate whether defining notions of "error" and ϵ-bisimulation in such a setting is of interest, thus working on the format for the ϵ-bisimulation.

References

1. Aldini, A., Bravetti, M., Gorrieri, R.: A Process-algebraic Approach for the Analysis of Probabilistic Non-interference. J. Comput. Secur. 12(2), 191–245 (2004)
2. Aldini, A., Bravetti, M., Di Pierro, A., Gorrieri, R., Hankin, C., Wiklicky, H.: Two Formal Approaches for Approximating Noninterference Properties. In: Focardi, R., Gorrieri, R. (eds.) FOSAD 2001. LNCS, vol. 2946, pp. 1–43. Springer, Heidelberg (2004)
3. Baeten, J.C.M., Bergstra, J.A., Smolka, S.A.: Axiomatizing Probabilistic Processes: ACP with Generative Probabilities. Inf. Comput. 121(2), 234–255 (1995)
4. Baier, C., Hermanns, H.: Weak Bisimulation for Fully Probabilistic Processes. In: Grumberg, O. (ed.) CAV 1997. LNCS, vol. 1254, pp. 119–130. Springer, Heidelberg (1997)
5. Bandini, E., Segala, R.: Axiomatizations for Probabilistic Bisimulation. In: Orejas, F., Spirakis, P.G., van Leeuwen, J. (eds.) ICALP 2001. LNCS, vol. 2076, pp. 370–381. Springer, Heidelberg (2001)
6. Bartels, F.: GSOS for Probabilistic Transition Systems. In: Proc. Coalgebraic Methods in Computer Science. Electronic Notes in Theoretical Computer Science 65. Elsevier, Amsterdam (2002)
7. Bartels, F.: On Generalized Coinduction and Probabilistic Specification Formats. PhD Thesis, Vrije Univesiteit, Amsterdam (2004)

8. Bol, R.N., Groote, J.F.: The Meaning of Negative Premises in Transition System Specifications. J. ACM 43(5), 863–914 (1996)
9. Bravetti, M., Aldini, A.: Discrete Time Generative-reactive Probabilistic Processes with Different Advancing Speeds. Theor. Comput. Sci. 290(1), 355–406 (2003)
10. Christoff, I.: Testing Equivalences and Fully Abstract Models for Probabilistic Processes. In: Baeten, J.C.M., Klop, J.W. (eds.) CONCUR 1990. LNCS, vol. 458, pp. 126–140. Springer, Heidelberg (1990)
11. Cleaveland, R., Smolka, S.A., Zwarico, A.: Testing Preorders for Probabilistic Processes. In: Kuich, W. (ed.) ICALP 1992. LNCS, vol. 623, pp. 708–719. Springer, Heidelberg (1992)
12. D'Argenio, P.R., Hermanns, H., Katoen, J.P.: On Generative Parallel Composition. In: Proc. Int. Work. on Probabilistic Methods in Verification. Electr. Notes Theor. Comput. Sci. 22. Elsevier, Amsterdam (1999)
13. Deng, Y., Chothia, T., Palamidessi, C., Pang, J.: Metrics for Action-labelled Quantitative Transition Systems. In: Proc. Workshop on Quantitative Aspects of Programming Languages. Electr. Notes Theor. Comput. Sci, vol. 153(2), pp. 79–96. Elsevier, Amsterdam (2006)
14. Deng, Y., Palamidessi, C.: Axiomatizations for Probabilistic Finite-State Behaviors. In: Sassone, V. (ed.) FOSSACS 2005. LNCS, vol. 3441, pp. 110–124. Springer, Heidelberg (2005)
15. Deng, Y., Palamidessi, C., Pang, J.: Compositional Reasoning for Probabilistic Finite-State Behaviors. In: Middeldorp, A., van Oostrom, V., van Raamsdonk, F., de Vrijer, R. (eds.) Processes, Terms and Cycles: Steps on the Road to Infinity. LNCS, vol. 3838, pp. 309–337. Springer, Heidelberg (2005)
16. Desharnais, J., Gupta, V., Jagadeesan, R., Panangaden, P.: The Metric Analogue of Weak Bisimulation for Probabilistic Processes. In: Proc. IEEE Symp. on Logic in Computer Science, pp. 413–422. IEEE Press, Los Alamitos (2002)
17. Desharnais, J., Gupta, V., Jagadeesan, R., Panangaden, P.: Metrics for Labelled Markov Processes. Theor. Comput. Sci. 318(3), 323–354 (2004)
18. de Simone, R.: Higher-Level Synchronising Devices in Meije-SCCS. Theor. Comput. Sci. 37, 245–267 (1985)
19. Di Pierro, A., Hankin, C., Wiklicky, H.: Quantitative Relations and Approximate Process Equivalences. In: Amadio, R.M., Lugiez, D. (eds.) CONCUR 2003. LNCS, vol. 2761, pp. 498–512. Springer, Berlin (2003)
20. Focardi, R., Rossi, S.: Information Flow Security in Dynamic Contexts. J. Comp. Security 14(1), 65–110 (2006)
21. Giacalone, A., Jou, C.C., Smolka, S.A.: Algebraic Reasoning for Probabilistic Concurrent Systems. In: Proc. IFIP Work. Conf. on Programming, Concepts and Methods, pp. 443–458 (1990)
22. Girard, A., Pappas, G.J.: Approximation Metrics for Discrete and Continuous Systems. IEEE Trans. Automatic Control 52(5), 782–798 (2007)
23. Hansson, H., Jonsson, B.: A Framework for Reasoning about Time and Reliability. In: Proc. IEEE Real-Time Systems Symposium, pp. 102–111. IEEE Press, Los Alamitos (1989)
24. Jonsson, B., Larsen, K.G.: Specification and Refinement of Probabilistic Processes. In: Proc. IEEE Symp. on Logic in Computer Science, pp. 266–277. IEEE Press, Los Alamitos (1991)
25. Jonsson, B., Yi, W.: Compositional Testing Preorders for Probabilistic Processes. In: Proc. IEEE Symp. on Logic in Computer Science, pp. 431–443. IEEE Press, Los Alamitos (1995)

26. Jou, C.C., Smolka, S.A.: Equivalences, Congruences and Complete Axiomatizations for Probabilistic Processes. In: Baeten, J.C.M., Klop, J.W. (eds.) CONCUR 1990. LNCS, vol. 458, pp. 367–383. Springer, Berlin (1990)
27. Klin, B., Sassone, V.: Structural Operational Semantics for Stochastic Process Calculi. In: Proc. Int. Conf. on Foundations of Software Science and Computational Structures. LNCS. Springer, Berlin (to appear, 2008)
28. Lanotte, R., Tini, S.: Probabilistic Bisimulation as a Congruence. ACM Trans. Comput. Logic (to appear)
29. Larsen, K.G., Skou, A.: Bisimulation Trough Probabilistic Testing. Inf. Comput. 94(1), 1–28 (1991)
30. Plotkin, G.: A Structural Approach to Operational Semantics. J. Log. Algebr. Program, 17–139, 60–61 (2004)
31. Segala, R.: Modeling and Verification of Randomized Distributed Real-Time Systems. PhD Thesis, MIT, Technical Report MIT/LCS/TR-676 (1995)
32. Segala, R., Lynch, N.: Probabilistic Simulations for Probabilistic Processes. In: Jonsson, B., Parrow, J. (eds.) CONCUR 1994. LNCS, vol. 836, pp. 481–496. Springer, Berlin (1994)
33. van Breugel, F., Worrell, J.: An Algorithm for Quantitative Verification of Probabilistic Transition Systems. In: Larsen, K.G., Nielsen, M. (eds.) CONCUR 2001. LNCS, vol. 2154, pp. 336–350. Springer, Berlin (2001)
34. van Breugel, F., Worrell, J.: Towards Quantitative Verification of Probabilistic Transition Systems. In: Orejas, F., Spirakis, P.G., van Leeuwen, J. (eds.) ICALP 2001. LNCS, vol. 2076, pp. 421–432. Springer, Berlin (2001)
35. van Breugel, F., Worrell, J.: A Behavioural Pseudometric for Probabilistic Transition Systems. Theor. Comput. Sci. 331(1), 115–142 (2005)
36. van Glabbeek, R.J.: The Meaning of Negative Premises in Transition System Specifications II. J. Log. Algebr. Program, 60–61, 229–258 (2004)
37. van Glabbeek, R.J., Smolka, S.A., Steffen, B.: Reactive, Generative and Stratified Models of Probabilistic Processes. Inf. Comput. 121(1), 59–80 (1995)
38. Yuen, S., Cleaveland, R., Dayar, Z., Smolka, S.A.: Fully Abstract Characterizations of Testing Preorders for Probabilistic Processes. In: Proc. Int. Conf. on Concurrency Theory. LNCS, vol. 863, pp. 497–512. Springer, Berlin (1994)

A Hybrid Approach for Safe Memory Management in C

Syrine Tlili, Zhenrong Yang, Hai Zhou Ling, and Mourad Debbabi*

Computer Security Laboratory (CSL)
Concordia Institute for Information Systems Engineering
Concordia University, Montreal, Quebec, Canada
{s_tlili,zhenr_ya,ha_ling,debbabi}@ciise.concordia.ca

Abstract. In this paper, we present a novel approach that establishes a synergy between static and dynamic analyses for detecting memory errors in C code. We extend the standard C type system with effect, region, and host annotations that are relevant to memory management. We define static memory checks to detect memory errors using these annotations. The statically undecidable checks are delegated to dynamic code instrumentation to secure program executions. The static analysis guides its dynamic counterpart by locating instrumentation points and their execution paths. Our dynamic analysis instruments programs with in-lined monitors that observe program executions and ensure safe-fail when encountering memory errors. We prototype our approach by extending the GCC compiler with our type system, a dynamic monitoring library, and code instrumentation capabilities.

1 Introduction

Security was not part of the design of the C language, thus programming with C is error-prone. In fact, among the main objectives of C are performance and portability. Therefore, it provides programmers with low-level control over memory allocation, deallocation, and layout. Unfortunately, this flexibility and wide control given to programmers are an enormous source of several security flaws.

In this paper, we focus on memory errors in C code that may result in buffer overflow, denial of service, code injection, memory leaks, etc. Both static analysis techniques and runtime verification techniques can be used to detect memory errors. Static analysis operates at compilation time and offers the advantage of detecting errors at early stages of software development. However, the conservative nature of static analysis is prone to generate false alarms. Moreover, some of the memory errors require runtime information in order to be discovered. On the other hand, dynamic analysis detects runtime errors during program execution. It yields precise analysis results but comes with a notable performance cost.

* This research is the result of a fruitful collaboration between CSL (Computer Security Laboratory) of Concordia University, DRDC (Defense Research and Development Canada) Valcartier and Bell Canada under the NSERC DND Research Partnership Program.

J. Meseguer and G. Roşu (Eds.): AMAST 2008, LNCS 5140, pp. 377–391, 2008.
© Springer-Verlag Berlin Heidelberg 2008

Undecidability is a reality in static analysis that we face very often, especially with imperative programming languages. For instance in C, pointer analysis such as aliasing is statically undecidable. To remedy this issue, the solution is to resort to dynamic analysis while leveraging the information gathered during the static analysis. Therefore, there is a desideratum that consists in designing and implementing hybrid approaches that establish a synergy between static and dynamic analyses to detect safety and security violations.

Pioneering and interesting contributions have been made in [1,2,3]. They combine static and dynamic analyses for detecting memory errors in C source code. Most of these approaches require modifications to the source code and to the data structures' memory layout. These modifications result in binary compatibility issues of the analyzed code. Moreover, these techniques define a static analysis that relies heavily on the dynamic counterpart to decide on the safety of memory operations. For instance, CCured [1] does not consider control flow analysis and alias analysis that can help reducing the number of runtime checks.

In this paper, we define a hybrid approach that establishes a modular synergy between static and dynamic analyses for detecting memory errors. By modular, we mean that no tight coupling is needed between the two analyses in a sense that each analysis can be applied separately to verify memory safety of programs. The synergy is achieved through an effect-based interface in order to remedy static undecidability and to reduce the number of runtime checks.

The core idea involves a two-phase analysis, in which the first phase performs a flow-sensitive type analysis to ensure memory safety. We define a type system for the C language that propagates lightweight region, effect, and host annotations relevant for memory management. These annotations are used by our defined static checks to detect memory errors. Statically undecidable checks are considered by the dynamic analysis of the second phase.

The theoretical model underlying our dynamic analysis is inspired by the formalism of *Team Edit Automata* [4]. This is an extension of the well-established model of edit automata [5]. The latter is an automata-based approach for modeling monitors that enforce security properties for dynamic analysis. It gives the possibility to insert and suppress actions in the program and to halt program execution when facing a security violation. The *Team Edit Automata* model combines the powerful enforcing capabilities of edit automata into a component-interactive architecture. It allows us to specify correlative security properties in software program more accurately. We adapt this model for ensuring memory safety in C code. A team edit automaton is used to monitor the states and interaction of each dynamically allocated memory block and its referencing pointers. The monitors report errors and safely halt programs at their runtime.

The effects [6] collected during type analysis provide an interface to interact with our dynamic analysis. It guides code instrumentation by locating statically undecidable memory operations, so as to reduce the number of runtime checks. We characterize these undecidable cases with *dunno points* that define the needed runtime check, the pointer to check, the program point and the execution paths of the suspected operation. In fact, we do not use fat pointers that modify memory layouts of data structures and cause binary compatibility issues such as in [1,2].

The main contributions of this paper are the following:

- A new type system based on lightweight region, effect, and host annotations for detecting memory errors in C source code. We endow our type system with static checks that use these annotations to verify and ensure the safety of pointer usages.
- A new program monitoring technique for detecting memory errors in C programs based on the *Team Edit Automata* model [4].
- A synergy between static analysis and dynamic analysis where the generated effect annotations are used to guide code instrumentation.
- A prototyped GCC extension that statically type-checks C programs for memory errors and allows for general-purpose code instrumentation for the sake of dynamic analysis.

This paper is organized as follows: Section 2 introduces the annotations of our type system. Section 3 describes the typing rules. Section 4 outlines the static memory checks performed during our type analysis. Section 5 presents the code instrumentation for ensuring memory safety. Section 6 is dedicated to the synergy between the static and the dynamic analyses through the effect-based interface. Preliminary experiments and a case study are presented in Section 7. We discuss the related work in Section 8 and conclude this paper in Section 9.

2 Security Annotations

We illustrate our analysis on an imperative language, presented in Figure 1, that captures the essence of the C language. Expressions e comprise lvalues and rvalues. The rvalues include integer scalar n, dereferencing expression $*r_v$, and pointer arithmetic e op e'. The lvalues l_v are access paths to memory locations through variables and dereferenced pointers. The statements s include

$$
\begin{array}{lll}
\textit{Expressions} & e & ::= l_v \mid r_v \\
\textit{Rvalues} & r_v & ::= n \mid *r_v \mid e\ op\ e' \\
\textit{Lvalues} & l_v & ::= x \mid *l_v \\
\textit{Statements} & s & ::= s_1; s_2 \mid \textbf{if } b \textbf{ then } s_1 \textbf{ else } s_2 \mid \textbf{while } b \textbf{ do } s \\
& & \mid\ free(l_v) \mid l_v = malloc(e) \mid l_v = e \\
\textit{Declared Types} & \kappa & ::= void \mid int \mid ref(\kappa) \\
\textit{Inferred Types} & \tau & ::= void \mid int_\eta \mid ref_\rho(\kappa)_\eta \mid if_\ell(\tau, \tau') \\
\textit{Regions} & r & ::= \emptyset \mid \varrho \mid \rho \mid \{\rho_1, \dots, \rho_n\} \\
\textit{Hosts} & \eta & ::= \emptyset \mid [malloc] \mid [dangling] \mid [wild] \mid [\&\tau] \\
\textit{Effects} & \sigma & ::= \emptyset \mid \sigma; \sigma' \mid if_\ell(\sigma, \sigma') \mid rec_\ell(\sigma) \mid alloc(\rho, \ell) \mid dealloc(r, \ell) \\
& & \mid\ arith(r, \ell) \mid read(r, \tau, \ell) \mid assign(r, \tau, \ell)
\end{array}
$$

Fig. 1. Type algebra for an imperative language

the control flow constructs (sequencing, conditionals, and loops), the deallocation operation $free(l_v)$, the allocation operation $l_v = malloc(e)$, and assignment
operations. We extend the standard C type system with annotations relevant to
memory safety that we outline in the following paragraphs.

The domain of inferred types decorates the declared types with effect, region,
and host annotations inserted at the outermost level. Moreover, we define a
conditional type construct $if_\ell(\tau, \tau')$ to capture the types of an expression after
a branching condition at program point ℓ. The type τ is assigned on the true
branch, whereas the type τ' is assigned on the false branch. These types are
equal modulo region and host annotations.

The domain of regions, ranged over by r, is intended to abstract dynamic
memory locations and variables' memory locations. Region variables with unknown values are ranged over by ϱ. Values drawn from this domain are ranged
over by ρ. We use the notation $\{\rho_1, \ldots, \rho_n\}$ to represent the disjoint union of
regions a pointer may refer to at a given program point. A pointer type $ref_\rho(\kappa)_\eta$
is annotated with its memory location ρ.

The host annotation η indicates the content and the status of its corresponding memory location. The element $malloc$ denotes an allocated pointer to an
uninitialized value. The element $dangling$ defines a freed memory location. The
element $wild$ indicates unallocated pointer or uninitialized integer value. The
element $\&\tau$ stands for a region holding a value of type τ.

The annotations are initially inferred at declaration time. We define the "$\,\hat{}\,$"
operator: given a declared type κ, it infers a type $\tau = \hat{\kappa}$ with a host annotation
set to $[wild]$ and an unknown region ϱ. On the other hand, the "$\,\bar{}\,$" operator
suppresses all the annotations of inferred types to recover their corresponding
declared types. For conditional types it yields the following: $\overline{if_\ell(\tau, \tau')} = \bar{\tau} = \bar{\tau}'$.

The domain of effects captures the side effect of memory operations. We use
$\emptyset$ to denote the absence of effects. The term $\sigma; \sigma'$ denotes the sequencing of σ
and σ'. Each effect records the program point ℓ where it is produced. The effect
$if_\ell(\sigma, \sigma')$ refers to a branching condition at program point ℓ, where the effects σ
and σ' are produced at the true branch and the false branch, respectively. The
effect $rec_\ell(\sigma)$ stands for a recursive effect generated in a loop construct at program point ℓ. The effects $alloc(\rho, \ell)$ and $dealloc(r, \ell)$ denote memory allocation
and deallocation, respectively. The effect $arith(r, \ell)$ captures pointer arithmetics.
The effects $read(r, \tau, \ell)$ and $assign(r, \tau, \ell)$ represent reading and assigning a value
of type τ, respectively. The collected effects define a tree-based model of the program that abstracts memory operations with control-flow and alias information.
We use this model to establish a synergy with the dynamic analysis as defined
in Section 6.

3 Flow-Sensitive Type System

In this section, we present the typing rules of our imperative language. The main
intent of these rules is to apply static checks in order to ensure memory safety.
Some memory operations can not be statically guaranteed to be safe. As such,

we resort to dynamic analysis to monitor the execution of these operations and prevent runtime errors as detailed in Section 6. The typing judgements of our type system are the following:

- The judgement for expressions $\mathcal{E} \vdash \ell, e : \tau, \sigma$ states that under typing environment $\mathcal{E}$ and at program point ℓ, the expression e has type τ and the evaluation of e yields the effect σ.
- The judgement for statements is of the form $\mathcal{E} \vdash \ell, s, \mathcal{E}', \sigma$ which expresses that under typing environment $\mathcal{E}$ and at program point ℓ, the execution of statement s produces the effect σ and yields a new environment $\mathcal{E}'$.

The environment $\mathcal{E}$ is constructed at variable declaration, it maps variables to inferred types with host annotation initialized to $[wild]$ and unknown region variable ϱ. These annotations are flow-sensitive and are allowed to change from one program statement to another. Moreover, we resort to flow-sensitive alias analysis to change the annotations of aliases that are indirectly modified at each program statement. We define the recursive algorithm $updEnv()$, used in statements typing rules, for updating the environment $\mathcal{E}$ with new type annotations of a directly assigned variable and all its aliases. For space constraint, we do not give the algorithm of the $updEnv()$ function.

For precision sake, we consider control-flow statements so as to infer types for each execution path of the program. We define hereafter, the rule (cond) that derives types for each conditional branch:

$$(\text{cond}) \ \frac{\mathcal{E} \vdash \ell, b : bool, \emptyset \quad \mathcal{E} \vdash \ell', s_1, \mathcal{E}', \sigma_1 \quad \mathcal{E} \vdash \ell'', s_2, \mathcal{E}'', \sigma_2}{\mathcal{E} \vdash \ell, \text{if } b \text{ then } s_1 \text{ else } s_2, \mathcal{E}' \ \mathbb{M}_\ell \ \mathcal{E}'', if_\ell(\sigma_1, \sigma_2)}$$

The merge operator $\mathbb{M}_\ell$ is as following:

$$(\mathcal{E} \ \mathbb{M}_\ell \ \mathcal{E}')(x) = \begin{cases} \mathcal{E}(x) & \text{if } x \notin \text{Dom}(\mathcal{E}'), \\ \mathcal{E}'(x) & \text{if } x \notin \text{Dom}(\mathcal{E}), \\ if_\ell(\mathcal{E}(x), \mathcal{E}'(x)) & \text{if } x \in \mathcal{E}(x) \cap \mathcal{E}'(x). \end{cases}$$

The $if_\ell(\mathcal{E}(x), \mathcal{E}'(x))$ construct states that x is of type $\mathcal{E}(x)$ at the true branch and of type $\mathcal{E}'(x)$ at the false branch. The loop statement is typed as a recursive condition statement.

4   Static Memory Checks

We focus on the typing rules for pointer dereferencing, pointer deallocation, and pointer assignment. A detailed description of our typing rules is given in [7]. To facilitate the understanding of the typing rules, we first define the following auxiliary functions: (1) $regionof(\tau)$ that returns the region annotations of type τ, (2) the function $hostof(\tau)$ that returns the host annotation of type τ, (3) and the function $storedType(\tau)$ that extracts the actual type of a pointer from its host annotation.

4.1 Safe Dereferencing of Pointers

The rule (deref) returns the actual type referred to by a pointer as defined in Figure 2. The dereference is guarded by the $safeDeref()$ check that fails for $void$

$$\text{(deref)} \quad \frac{\mathcal{E} \vdash \ell, e : \tau, \sigma \quad safeDeref(e, \tau, \sigma, \ell) \quad \bar{\tau} = ref(\_) \quad r = regionof(\tau) \quad \tau'' = storedType(\tau)}{\mathcal{E} \vdash \ell, *e : \tau'', (\sigma; read(r, \tau'', \ell))}$$

$$safeDeref(e, ref_\rho(\kappa)_\eta, \sigma, \ell) = (\kappa \neq void) \wedge (\eta \notin \{wild, dangling\}) \wedge (arith(\rho, \ell) \notin \sigma)$$

$$safeDeref(e, if_\ell(\tau, \tau'), \sigma, \ell) = safeDeref(e, \tau, \sigma, \ell) \wedge safeDeref(e, \tau', \sigma, \ell)$$

Fig. 2. Typing rule for safe pointer dereferencing

pointers, freed pointers, unallocated pointers, and null pointers. Since we do not perform static bounds checking, it also fails for arithmetic pointers that have an effect $arith(r, \ell)$ related to their regions. We issue a *dunno point* to indicate that runtime bounds checking is required as described in Section 6.

4.2 Safe Assignment

The rule (assign) defined in Figure 3 assigns a value to a memory or a variable lvalue. The assignment is guarded by the $safeWrite()$ that fails if the declared

$$\text{(assign)} \quad \frac{\mathcal{E} \vdash \ell, l_v : \tau, \sigma \quad \mathcal{E} \vdash \ell, e : \tau', \sigma' \quad safeWrite(e, \tau', \tau, \ell) \quad r = regionof(\tau) \quad \mathcal{E}' = updEnv(\mathcal{E}, l_v = e, \ell)}{\mathcal{E} \vdash \ell, l_v = e, \mathcal{E}', (\sigma; \sigma'; assign(r, \tau', \ell))}$$

$$safeWrite(e, \tau', \tau, \ell) = (hostof(\tau') = [\&\tau'']) \wedge (\bar{\tau} = \bar{\tau}' = \bar{\tau}'')$$

$$safeWrite(e, if_\ell(\tau', \tau''), \tau, \ell) = safeWrite(e, \tau', \tau, \ell) \wedge safeWrite(e, \tau'', \tau, \ell)$$

Fig. 3. Typing rule for safe assignment

types of the right operand and the left operand are not the same. It also fails for uninitialized right operands. The $updEnv()$ propagates the type annotations from the right operand to the left operand and updates the annotations of the left operand aliases accordingly.

4.3 Safe Memory Deallocation

The (free) rule in Figure 4 conservatively deallocates all memory locations in r pointer l_v may refer to. The $safeFree()$ check fails for unallocated, dangling

$$\text{(free)} \quad \frac{\mathcal{E} \vdash \ell, \, l_v : \tau, \sigma \quad safeFree(l_v, \tau, \sigma, \ell) \quad \bar{\tau} = ref(\_)}{\mathcal{E} \vdash \ell, \, free(l_v), \mathcal{E}', (\sigma; dealloc(\rho, \ell))}$$
$$r = regionof(\tau) \quad \mathcal{E}' = updateEnv(\mathcal{E}, free(l_v), \ell)$$

$$safeFree(e, ref_\rho(\kappa)_\eta, \sigma, \ell) = (\eta \neq \{wild, dangling\}) \wedge (alloc(\rho, \_) \in \sigma)$$
$$safeFree(e, if_\ell(\tau, \tau'), \sigma, \ell) = safeFree(e, \tau, \sigma, \ell) \wedge safeFree(e, \tau', \sigma, \ell)$$

Fig. 4. Typing rule for safe memory deallocation

and null pointers. It also fails for region ρ that is not dynamically allocated, i.e, the effect $alloc(\rho, \_)$ is not present in the current effect model σ. The call to $updateEnv()$ yields a new environment $\mathcal{E}'$ where the host annotation of l_v and of all its aliases is set to $[dangling]$.

4.4 Static Analysis Limitations

As for all static analysis approaches, our type analysis faces undecidability issues for the following cases:

- Undecidability occurs when the static security checks are performed on an expression of type $\tau = if_\ell(\tau, \tau')$. We conservatively entail that all types defined in the conditional type τ must pass the security check. If one of the types fails our analysis is undecidable and generates a *dunno point* to indicate that a runtime check is needed to spot the potential vulnerable paths.
- False positives occurs when the detected vulnerable paths are actually infeasible. In fact, our analysis is path-insensitive and does not prune infeasible paths. As such, a failed check may result in a false positive alert. For precision sake, we generate *dunno points* to indicate that dynamic analysis is needed to verify the feasibility of vulnerable paths spotted during the static analysis.

5 Dynamic Analysis

This section introduces the details of our dynamic analysis techniques. It outlines respectively the definition of *Team Edit Automata* and its application for detecting memory management errors in our dynamic analysis phase.

5.1 Automata-based Program Monitoring

We use program monitors based on the *Team Edit Automata* model introduced in our previous publication [4]. In brief, a team edit automaton consists of one or multiple component edit automata. Each component checks a security property of a particular program element such as pointers. The capabilities of the component edit automata include: (1) *Error Report* of a runtime error, (2) *Suppression* of illegal actions and halt of the program if necessary, and (3) *Insertion* of remedial actions in the monitored program.

5.2   Coping with Memory Errors

We define two types of component edit automata to specify the legal behavior of pointers and dynamic allocated memory, respectively. At program execution, each dynamically allocated memory block is monitored by a component edit automaton, so is each pointer variable. We consider a dynamic memory block and its referencing pointers as a unit by grouping their corresponding component edit automata into a team edit automaton.

The nodes of an automaton represents its state. Each transition of an automaton has a (I&C/O) label that denotes an input action I with a guard condition C and an output action O. An input action can either be the execution of a memory operation from the analyzed code or a communication action between automata that form a team. The output action defines the monitoring capabilities of the automata. It can either be halting harmful execution with an eventual error reporting or a safe execution of the monitored action with an eventual communication action to interact with the team automata. We use the notation A_i to define the output communication action of an automaton.

5.3   Monitoring Dynamic Memory Blocks

The component edit automaton modeling dynamically allocated memory blocks is illustrated in Figure 5. The automaton starts monitoring a dynamic memory block when it's allocated on heap. If the memory block is going to be deallocated (input action a_7), the automaton emits the deallocation action then inserts an $A_2 = invalidatePtr$ communication action. The latter invalidates all pointers referring to the freed block. Upon memory reading (input action a_4), the memory initialization guard c_3 must hold true. Similarly, upon memory writing (input action a_3), communication action $A_1 = setInitialized(addr)$ is inserted into the automaton output to update the initialization status of the written address. The life cycle of the automaton stops when no more pointers reference the memory block.

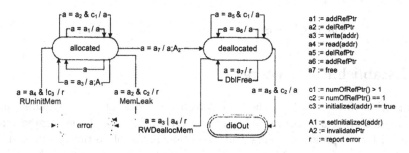

Fig. 5. Component edit automaton modeling dynamic memory blocks

In order to detect illegal access to uninitialized and out-of-bounds memory locations, we use a bitstream to bookkeep the initialization status of the dynamically allocated memory blocks. Each byte of allocated memory has a corresponding bit to record its current initialization status. The four memory checks applied by the monitors of the memory block automaton are the following: (1) *DblFree* detects double-free error, (2) *RUninitMem* detects reading access to uninitialized memory, (3) *RWDeallocMem*: detects access to freed memory, and (4) *MemLeak*: detects memory leak.

5.4 Monitoring Pointers

The component edit automaton modeling pointers is illustrated in Figure 6. The automaton starts monitoring a pointer variable once it is declared and stops when the pointer variable exits its declaration scope. Whenever the pointer is assigned to reference a memory block (input action a_3), the automaton emits this action and inserts communication action $A_1 = addRefPtr(addr)$ to inform the corresponding dynamic memory block. Similarly, once the pointer is freed (input action a_4) or set to null pointer (input action a_2), the automaton inserts action $A_2 = delRefPtr$ to withdraw itself from the team edit automata of the referenced memory block. The two memory checks applied by a pointer edit automaton are: (1) *DerefNullPtr*: detects null pointer dereference error, and (2) *DerefWildPtr*: detects wild (uninitialized or freed) pointer dereference error.

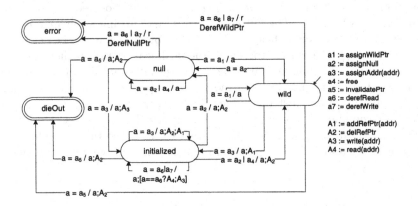

Fig. 6. Component edit automata modeling pointers

6   Establishing a Synergy

This section illustrates the synergy between the static and the dynamic analyses for detecting and preventing memory errors. We use the generated effect model to locate program points and execution paths of statically undecidable memory operations. The effect model defines the novelty of our hybrid approach in a sense that it allows us to collect relevant information for dynamic analysis without using fat pointers as in CCured [1], SafeC [2], and Cyclone [3]. Hence, our approach does not have binary compatibility issues encountered when using fat pointers as in the aforementioned tools.

6.1   Locating Dunno Points

Statically undecidable cases defined in Section 4 are captured by *dunno points* that we define as a four tuple $\langle dynCheck, e, \ell, T \rangle$: (1) the first element is a tag that describes the needed runtime check, (2) the second element is the program expression that needs to be monitored, (3) the third element indicates the program point of the suspected operation, (4) the last element represents the set of vulnerable execution paths.

The function *runtimeVerif()*, defined in Figure 7, takes as input the set of failed static checks and the generated effect model Σ of the whole analyzed program. It outputs a set of *dunno points* where code instrumentation is needed. We define the function *DfsPath()* that takes as argument a region ρ, a program point ℓ and the effect model Σ. It performs a Depth-First-Search (DFS) traversal of the tree-based model Σ to extract all execution paths to program point ℓ, where region ρ is accessed. The function *runtimeVerif()* outputs the following set of *dunno points*:

- $\langle Wild, e, \ell, T \rangle$: check if pointer e is referring to a valid memory location before dereferencing at program point ℓ for all execution paths in T.
- $\langle Bounds, e, \ell, T \rangle$: check if pointer e is not out-of-bounds before dereferencing at program point ℓ for all execution paths in T.
- $\langle DblFree, e, \ell, T \rangle$: check if pointer e has already been freed before freeing at program point ℓ for all execution paths in T.
- $\langle StkFree, e, \ell, T \rangle$: check if pointer e refers to a dynamic memory location before freeing at program point ℓ for all execution paths in T.
- $\langle InitRv, e, \ell, T \rangle$: check if right-hand-side operand e has an initialized value at program point ℓ for all execution paths in T.

Notice that we establish a modular synergy where the static analysis is not coupled with a specific dynamic analysis. It defines an interface to communicate *dunno points* that can be used by any code instrumentation approach to detect more vulnerabilities in C source code. In what follows, we illustrate how our dynamic analysis defined in Section 5 uses the *dunno points* to instrument the analyzed source code with execution monitors.

6.2   Instrumenting with Dunno Points

In order to reduce the number of runtime checks in the analyzed code, our dynamic analysis only considers statically undecidable memory operations. We illustrate in Figure the *dunno points* produced by our static analysis and the corresponding dynamic analysis strategies for each type of memory errors in C source code. As we mentioned previously, the *dunno points* include a set T of

Function $runtimeVerif(check(e, \tau, \_, \ell), \Sigma) =$
    case τ **of**
    $if_\ell(\tau', \tau'') \Rightarrow$ **if** $check(e, \tau', \_, \ell)$ **then** $runtimeVerif(check(e, \tau'', \_, \ell), \Sigma)$
              else $runtimeVerif(check(e, \tau', \_, \ell), \Sigma)$
    else $\Rightarrow$ **let** $\rho = regionof(\tau)$, $T = DfsPath(\rho, \ell, \Sigma)$
          in
              case $check(\_)$ **of**
                  $safeRead(e, \tau, \sigma, \ell)$ $\Rightarrow$ **if** $(arith(\rho, \ell') \in \sigma)$
                                        then $\langle Bounds, e, \ell, T \rangle$
                                        else $\langle Wild, e, \ell, T \rangle$
                  $safeFree(e, \tau, \sigma, \ell)$ $\Rightarrow$ **if** $(alloc(\rho, \ell') \in \sigma)$
                                          then $\langle DblFree, e, \ell, T \rangle$
                                        else $\langle StkFree, e, \ell, T \rangle$
                $safeWrite(e, \tau, \tau', \ell) \Rightarrow \langle InitRv, e, \ell, T \rangle$
          end
    end

Fig. 7. The function $runtimeVerif$ extracts the set of *dunno points* where code instrumentation is required

Interfacing Static and Dynamic Analyses		
Memory Errors	**Dunno Points**	**Dynamic Monitors**
deref_unalloc	$\langle Wild, e, \ell, T \rangle$	instrument monitors along T: detect with *DerefWildPtr*, *RWDeallocMem*, and *DerefNullPtr*
deref_OOB	$\langle Bounds, e, \ell, T \rangle$	instrument monitors along T: detect with *RUninitMem*
assign_uninit	$\langle InitRv, e, \ell, T \rangle$	instrument monitors along T: detect with *RUninitMem*
double_free	$\langle DblFree, e, \ell, T \rangle$	instrument monitors along T: detect with *DblFree*
free_unalloc	$\langle StkFree, e, \ell, T \rangle$	instrument monitors along T: record all dynamic memory allocation and detect with address hash failure

Fig. 8. Interface between static and dynamic analyses

program traces that lead to the suspected memory operations. We instrument monitoring codes along the traces T to check program actions such as memory allocation, deallocation, and pointer dereferencing, etc.

7 Preliminary Experiments

In this section we present the preliminary version of our tool used to conduct small-scale experiments. We also illustrate our approach through a sample code.

7.1 Extending the GCC Compiler

We prototyped the dynamic analysis of our approach as an extension to the GCC compiler for the C programming language. Our implementation is based on the

GCC core distribution version 4.2.0. The implementation of our dynamic analysis consists of two parts. Firstly, the program monitors are written in $C++$ and built into our shared library named `SecgccInstrSharedLib.so` with C interfaces. Secondly, we added a code instrumentation pass to the GCC optimization phase. The instrumentation is accomplished by injecting function calls to our analysis library on the intermediate representation of the monitored programs. We defined a simple language to specify the instrumentation guide, that enables us to instrument codes at function call, function exit, variable declaration, variable read, variable write, end of variable life cycle, and pointer dereference. To enable our dynamic analysis, we pass -ftree-security-instrument as a command-line option to the extended GCC compiler. We took the package gzip version 1.2.4. to conduct experimental performance measurements of our dynamic analysis. The code instrumentation is done by inserting function `SecInstr_Allocate` before all malloc function calls to bookkeep allocated memory blocks, and inserting function `SecInstr_Deallocate` before all the free function calls. These two aforementioned instrumental functions belong to the shared library `SecgccInstrSharedLib.so`, which is used to detect memory errors in C code.

We compressed the tar file of the linux kernel version 2.6.0 (linux-2.6.0.tar) of size 178.7 MB using the gzip program and the gunzip program part of the gzip package. The overhead induced by our instrumented code is presented in our experiments results in Table 1. For now, we are prototyping our type analysis in order to reduce the number of needed runtime checks and enhance the performance of the instrumented code. We are able to conduct small case study with our complete hybrid approach as illustrated later in this section. The static analysis is enabled with the -ftree-type-inference command-line option. It generates warnings when memory errors are detected. Statically undecidable operations, i.e. *dunno points*, are stored in external files as an instrumentation guide.

7.2   Case Study

We use the sample code of Figure 9 to illustrate our approach. The console output (a) in Figure 10 is generated by our static analysis. The static phase also generates the instrumentation guide given in part (b) of Figure 10.

All memory allocations are guarded by the `Secinstr_Allocate` monitors in order to bookkeep the dynamically allocated memory blocks and detect out-of-bounds access. The static *dunno point* at line 15 indicates that a bound checking is required for the memory access via buf1. As such, the run-time monitor `Secinstr_PointerDeref` is injected before buf1 dereference. The dereferences of

Table 1. Preliminary experiments results

Compression tool	Compression time original tool	Compression time instrumented tool	Ratio
gzip	14000 ms	20000 ms	1.428
gunzip	4000 ms	5000 ms	1.25

```
 1: #include <stdio.h>              17: x = argc * 10;
 2:                                 18:
 3: int main(int argc, char *argv[])  19: free(buf1);
 4: {                               20: buf2 = (int*)malloc(BUFSIZE);
 5:   int i,x;                      21:
 6:   const int BUFSIZE = 10;       22: *buf4 = &x;
 7:   int *buf1, *buf2, *buf3;      23:
 8:   int ** buf4;                  24: if (argc % 2 == 0)
 9:                                 25: {
10:   buf1 = (int*)malloc(BUFSIZE);  26:   free(buf2);
11:   buf4 = (int**)malloc(sizeof(int*));  27:   buf3 = *buf4;
12:   for (i = 0; i < BUFSIZE; ++i)  28: }
13:   {                             29:
14:     i -= 2;                     30: free(buf2);
15:     *(buf1+i) = i;              31: free(buf3);
16:   }                             32: return 0;
                                    33:}
```

Fig. 9. Example to illustrate our approach

```
L15: DUNNO <BOUNDS,buf1,15,
     alloc@10->loop@12->
     arith@15->deref@15>
L19: Safe Free of buf1
L22: Safe Assign to buf4
L26: Safe Free of buf2
L27: Safe Deref of buf4
L27: Safe Assign to buf3
L30: DUNNO <DBLFREE,buf2,30,
     alloc@20->free@26->
     free@30>
L31: Error Illegal Free buf3

        (a)
```

```
inscope "main" after callfunc
  (test.c::10::malloc)
  inject "Secinstr_Allocate"
  exposeargs exposereturn;
inscope "main" after callfunc
  (test.c::11::malloc)
  inject "Secinstr_Allocate"
  exposeargs exposereturn;
before derefptr (test.c::15::buf1)
  inject "Secinstr_PointerDeref";
inscope "main" after callfunc
  (test.c::20::malloc)
  inject "Secinstr_Allocate"
  exposeargs exposereturn;
inscope "main" before callfunc
  (test.c::26::free)
  inject "Secinstr_Deallocate"
  exposeargs noexposereturn;
inscope "main" before callfunc
  (test.c::30::free)
  inject "Secinstr_Deallocate"
  exposeargs noexposereturn;

        (b)
```

Fig. 10. Dunno points generated by the type analysis

buf4 at line 22 and line 27 are statically stated to be safe and do not require run-time monitoring. For the free operations, only the deallocation of buf2 on line 30 should be checked for double free error. The free operation of buf3 is unsafe and should be removed since buf3 is referring to the memory region of variable x.

8   Related Work

Detecting security property violations at runtime can be accomplished by various means. For example, the Debug Malloc Library (Dmalloc) [8] is a drop-in replacement for the system free and malloc family functions. The replacing functions keep track of the program dynamic memory management actions and detect illegal memory accesses. Purify [9] and Valgrind [10] monitor each memory access and detect memory leaks. Unlike our approach, these tools do not interact with static analysis in order to decrease the number of runtime checks. Moreover, they use a mark and sweep technique for detecting memory leaks that make them unsuitable for usage during production time. Mprof [11] is a dynamic tool for detecting memory leaks, however it does not perform any memory access checks. The literature contains several proposals on hybrid approaches. The approach defined in [12] is used to detect buffer overflows and does not provide checks to detect the dereference of dangling pointers nor memory leaks. Other approaches such as CCured [1] and SafeC [2] combine static and dynamic analysis for memory and type errors. CCured and SafeC use fat pointers to retain in memory temporal and bounds information required for runtime checks. Changing the data representation in memory results in compatibility problems of these tools with external libraries. Our approach does not have compatibility problems since we do not modify memory layouts of objects. Both CCured and SafeC do not provide execution paths that lead to runtime errors as we do. Therefore, our analysis can be used to guide path coverage for testing purposes. Cyclone [3] and Vault [13] are safe alternatives for the C language that prevent memory and type errors.

9   Conclusion

In this paper, we presented a novel approach that combines static and dynamic analysis for detecting memory errors in C source code. The static analysis extends the C type system with effect, region, and host annotations that are relevant to secure memory management. We defined security checks based on these annotations to detect illegal memory operations. The checks resort to dynamic analysis when runtime information is required for accurate analysis. We used program monitors to dynamically verify memory manipulation. Our approach reduces the runtime overhead of the monitored programs, in that the monitoring codes are instrumented only when static analysis is undecidable. The interface between the static and dynamic analyses is an effect-based model. It provides a modular synergy between the two analyses where each one enhances the other. We prototyped our approach as extensions to GCC, the de facto standard C compiler. In our future research work, we plan to augment the static phase with interprocedural analysis in order to detect more vulnerabilities in large software.

References

1. Necula, G.C., McPeak, S., Weimer, W.: CCured: Type-Safe Retrofitting of Legacy Code. In: Symposium on Principles of Programming Languages, pp. 128–139 (2002)
2. Austin, T.M., Breach, S.E., Sohi, G.S.: Efficient Detection of all Pointer and Array Access Errors. In: PLDI 1994: Proceedings of the ACM SIGPLAN 1994 conference on Programming language design and implementation, pp. 290–301. ACM Press, New York (1994)

3. Grossman, D., Morrisett, G., Jim, T., Hicks, M., Wang, Y., Cheney, J.: Region-based Memory Management in Cyclone. In: PLDI 2002: Proceedings of the ACM SIGPLAN 2002 Conference on Programming language design and implementation, pp. 282–293. ACM Press, New York (2002)
4. Yang, Z., Hanna, A., Debbabi, M.: Team Edit Automata for Testing Security Property. In: The Third International Symposium onInformation Assurance and Security, 2007. IAS 2007, pp. 235–240 (2007)
5. Ligatti, J., Bauer, L., Walker, D.: Edit Automata: Enforcement Mechanisms for Run-time Security Policies. Int. J. Inf. Sec. 4(1-2), 2–16 (2005)
6. Debbabi, M., Aidoud, Z., Faour, A.: On the Inference of Structured Recursive Effects with Subtyping. Journal of Functional and Logic Programming 1997(5) (1997)
7. Tlili, S., Debbabi, M.: Type and Effect Annotations for Safe Memory Access in C. In: Proceedings of the The Third International Conference on Availability, Reliability and Security, ARES 2008, Technical University of Catalonia, Barcelona, Spain, March 4-7, 2008, pp. 302–309. IEEE Computer Society Press, Los Alamitos (2008)
8. Watson, G.: Dmalloc - Debug Malloc Library, http://dmalloc.com/
9. Hasting, R., Joyce, B.: Purify: Fast Detection of Memory Leaks and Access Errors. In: Proceedings of the Winter USENIX Conference, pp. 125–136 (January 2002)
10. Seward, J., Nethercote, N.: Using Valgrind to Detect Undefined Value Errors with Bit-Precision. In: Proceedings of the USENIX 2005 Annual Technical Conference, Anaheim, California, USA, pp. 17–30 (April 2005)
11. Zorn, B.G., Hilfinger, P.N.: A Memory Allocation Profiler for C and Lisp Programs. Technical report, Berkeley, CA, USA (1988)
12. Aggarwal, A., Jalote, P.: Integrating Static and Dynamic Analysis for Detecting Vulnerabilities. In: Proceedings of the 30th Annual International Computer Software and Applications Conference (COMPSAC 2006), Washington, DC, USA, pp. 343–350. IEEE Computer Society Press, Los Alamitos (2006)
13. Fahndrich, M., DeLine, R.: Adoption and Focus: Practical Linear Types for Imperative Programming. In: PLDI 2002: Proceedings of the ACM SIGPLAN 2002 Conference on Programming language design and implementation, pp. 13–24. ACM Press, New York (2002)

Service Specification and Matchmaking Using Description Logic*
An Approach Based on Institutions

M. Birna van Riemsdijk, Rolf Hennicker, Martin Wirsing,
and Andreas Schroeder

Ludwig-Maximilians-Universität München, Germany

Abstract. We propose a formal specification framework for functional aspects of services. We define services as operations which are specified by means of pre- and postconditions, for the specification of which we use extensions of description logic. The (extensions of) description logic and the specification framework itself are defined as institutions. This gives the framework a uniformity of definition and a solid algebraic and logical foundation. The framework can be used for the specification of service requests and service providers. Given a signature morphism from request to provider, we define when a service request is matched by a service provider, which can be used in service discovery. We provide a model-theoretic definition of matching and show that matching can be characterized by a semantic entailment relation which is formulated over a particular standard description logic. Thus proofs of matching can be reduced to standard reasoning in description logic for which one can use description logic reasoners.

1 Introduction

Service-oriented computing is emerging as a new paradigm based on autonomous, platform-independent computational entities, called *services*, that can be described, published, and dynamically discovered and assembled. An important part of a service is its public interface, which describes the service and should be independent of the technique used for implementing it. A service's interface can describe various aspects of the service, such as the service's location and communication protocols that can be used for interacting with the service.

In this paper, we confine ourselves to the investigation of those parts of a service's interface that describe the *functionality* offered to a service requester. Not all service specification approaches support this (see, e.g., WSDL [4]). Services that *are* endowed with such functional descriptions are often called *semantic web services* [17]. Semantic web services facilitate more effective (semi-)automatic service discovery and assembly, since the services' functional descriptions can be

* This work has been sponsored by the project SENSORIA, IST-2005-016004, and by the GLOWA-Danube project, 01LW0602A2.

J. Meseguer and G. Roşu (Eds.): AMAST 2008, LNCS 5140, pp. 392–406, 2008.

taken into account. In particular, such descriptions can be used for *matchmaking*, i.e., for finding a matching service provider for a particular service request.

Various techniques have been proposed for specifying semantic web services (see, e.g., [17,18,16,12,8,21]). What most approaches have in common is that they suggest the use of *logical knowledge representation languages* for describing both service providers and service requests. Also, most approaches ([8] is an exception), including the approach we take in this paper, view semantic web services as *operations*, i.e., they can be invoked with some input, perform some computation and possibly return some output.

Where approaches for specifying semantic web services differ, is mostly the *kind* of knowledge representation language proposed, and the level of *formality*. In particular, in [12,21], a formal service specification approach using first-order logic is presented, and in [17,18] the use of so-called *semantic web markup languages* for service specification is proposed, but no formal specification language or semantics is defined. In this paper, we are interested in a formal approach to service specification, based on semantic web markup languages.

Semantic web markup languages are languages for describing the meaning of information on the web. The most widely used semantic web markup language is the Web Ontology Language (OWL) [20]. OWL is a family of knowledge representation languages that can be used for specifying and conceptualizing domains, describing the classes and relations between concepts in these domains. Such descriptions are generally called *ontologies* [9].

The formal underpinnings of the OWL language family are formed by *description logics* [1]. Description logics are formal ontology specification languages and form decidable fragments of first-order logic. Research on description logics has yielded sound and complete *reasoners* of increasing efficiency for various description logic variants (see [1] for more background). The fact that description logics come with such reasoners is an important advantage of using description logic for specifying services, since these reasoners can then be used for matchmaking.

In this paper, we propose a formal framework for specifying the functionality of services. Services are viewed as operations and we specify them using a particular description logic that corresponds to an expressive fragment of OWL, called OWL DL. As it turns out, we need to define several extensions of this description logic for its effective use in service specification. The formal tool that we use for defining the description logic, its extensions, and also the service specification framework itself, is *institutions* [7,22]. The notion of an institution abstractly defines a logical system, viewed from a model-theoretic perspective. Institutions allow to define the description logics and the specification framework in a uniform and well-structured way.

In addition to defining a service specification framework, we also provide a model-theoretic definition of when a service request is *matched* by a service provider specification, and show that matching can be characterized by a semantic entailment relation which is formulated over our basic description logic. Proofs of matching can thus be reduced to standard reasoning in description logic, for which one can use description logic reasoners.

The organization of this paper is as follows. In Section 2, we define the description logic upon which we base our service specification framework. We informally describe the approach we take in this paper in some more detail in Section 3. Then, in Section 4, we define the extensions of the description logic of Section 2 that are needed for service specification, followed by the definition of the service specification framework in Section 5. The definition and characterization of matching are presented in Section 6, and we conclude the paper in Section 7.

2   The Description Logic $\mathcal{SHOIN}^+$

In this section, we present the description logic $\mathcal{SHOIN}^+$, on which we base our service specification framework. The logic $\mathcal{SHOIN}^+$ is based on $\mathcal{SHOIN}^+(\mathbf{D})$ [11]. $\mathcal{SHOIN}^+(\mathbf{D})$ is the logic $\mathcal{SHOIN}(\mathbf{D})$, extended with a particular construct that was needed in [11] to show that OWL DL ontology entailment can be reduced to knowledge base satisfiability in $\mathcal{SHOIN}(\mathbf{D})$. That construct also turns out to be useful for service specification. In this paper, we will omit datatypes and corresponding sentences from $\mathcal{SHOIN}^+(\mathbf{D})$ since it does not affect the essence of the presented ideas and would only complicate the presentation. This leaves us with the logic $\mathcal{SHOIN}^+$.

We will define $\mathcal{SHOIN}^+$ as an institution. Loosely speaking, an institution is a tuple $Inst = \langle Sig_{Inst}, Sen_{Inst}, Mod_{Inst}, \models_{Inst,\Sigma} \rangle$, where Sig_{Inst} is a category of signatures, Sen_{Inst} is a functor that yields for each signature from Sig_{Inst} a set of sentences, Mod_{Inst} is a functor yielding a category of models for each signature from Sig_{Inst}, and $\models_{Inst,\Sigma}$ for each signature $\Sigma \in |Sig_{Inst}|$ is a satisfaction relation specifying when a model of $|Mod_{Inst}(\Sigma)|$ satisfies a sentence of $Sen_{Inst}(\Sigma)$. Moreover, for each signature morphism $\sigma : \Sigma \to \Sigma'$, sentence $\phi \in Sen_{Inst}(\Sigma)$, and model $\mathcal{M}' \in |Mod_{Inst}(\Sigma')|$, the so-called satisfaction condition should hold: $\mathcal{M}' \models_{Inst,\Sigma'} \sigma(\phi) \Leftrightarrow \mathcal{M}'|_\sigma \models_{Inst,\Sigma'} \phi$, where $\mathcal{M}'|_\sigma$ is the reduct of $\mathcal{M}'$ with respect to σ. For details, we refer to [7,22]. For all institutions defined in this paper, the details, in particular model morphisms and the proof of the satisfaction condition, are provided in [25].

We now define the institution $\mathcal{SHOIN}^+ = \langle Sig_{S+}, Sen_{S+}, Mod_{S+}, \models_{S+,\Sigma} \rangle$. The definition is similar to the way OWL DL, the semantic web markup language corresponding to $\mathcal{SHOIN}(\mathbf{D})$, was defined as an institution in [14]. We illustrate our definitions using a running example of a service GA for making garage appointments, which allows to make an appointment with a garage within a given day interval. Such a service is part of the automotive case study of the SENSORIA project[1] on service-oriented computing.

The basic elements of $\mathcal{SHOIN}^+$ are concept names N_C, role names N_R, and individual names N_i, which together form a $\mathcal{SHOIN}^+$ signature $\langle N_C, N_R, N_i \rangle$. They are interpreted over a domain of elements called individuals. A concept name is interpreted as a set of individuals, a role name as a set of pairs of individuals, and an individual name as a single individual.

---

[1] http://sensoria-ist.eu

Definition 1. *(SHOIN$^+$ signatures: Sig$_{S+}$)* A $\mathcal{SHOIN}^+$ signature Σ is a tuple $\langle N_C, N_R, N_i \rangle$, where N_C is a set of concept names, $N_R = R \cup R^-$, where R is a set of (basic) role names and $R^- = \{r^- \mid r \in R\}$, is a set of role names, and N_i is a set of individual names. The sets N_C, N_R, and N_i are pairwise disjoint. A $\mathcal{SHOIN}^+$ signature morphism $\sigma_{S+} : \Sigma \to \Sigma'$ consists of a mapping of the concept names of Σ to concept names of Σ', and similarly for role names and individual names.

A simplified signature Σ^{GA} for our garage appointment service GA can be specified as follows: $N_C = \{\text{Appointment}, \text{Day}, \text{WDay}, \text{WEDay}, \text{Hour}, \text{String}\}$, $N_R = \{\text{after}, \text{before}, \text{hasDay}, \text{hasHour}\}$, $N_i = \{1, 2, \ldots, 24, \text{mon}, \text{tue}, \ldots, \text{sun}\}$. The concept names WDay and WEDay stand for weekday and weekend day, respectively. The role names "after" and "before" will be used to express that a particular (week or weekend) day or hour comes before or after another day or hour, and "hasDay" and "hasHour" will be used to express that an appointment is made for a particular day and hour, respectively.

The main building blocks of $\mathcal{SHOIN}^+$ sentences are (composed) concepts, which can be constructed using concept names, individual names, and role names. For example, the concept $C_1 \sqcap C_2$ can be formed from the concepts C_1 and C_2, and is interpreted as the intersection of the interpretations of C_1 and C_2. Similarly, $C_1 \sqcup C_2$ denotes the union of the interpretations of C_1 and C_2. The concept $\exists r.C$ denotes all the individuals that are related to an individual from concept C over the role r, and several other composed concepts can be constructed.

Concepts, individual names, and role names are then used to construct sentences. For example, $C_1 \sqsubseteq C_2$ denotes that C_1 is a subconcept of C_2, and $a : C$ denotes that the individual represented by the individual name a belongs to concept C. The construct that $\mathcal{SHOIN}$ is extended with to form $\mathcal{SHOIN}^+$ is $\exists C$, which means that the interpretation of concept C is not empty. Definition 2 only contains those concepts and sentences that are used in the example. For a complete definition, we refer to [25].

Definition 2. *(SHOIN$^+$ sentences: Sen$_{S+}$)* Let $\Sigma = \langle N_C, N_R, N_i \rangle \in |Sig_{S+}|$ be a $\mathcal{SHOIN}^+$ signature, and let $A \in N_C$, $r \in N_R$, and $a, a_1, a_2 \in N_i$. The sentences $Sen_{S+}(\Sigma)$ are then the axioms ϕ as defined below.

$$C ::= A \mid \top \mid \bot \mid \neg C \mid C_1 \sqcap C_2 \mid C_1 \sqcup C_2 \mid \{a\} \mid \exists r.C \mid \forall r.C$$
$$\phi ::= C_1 \sqsubseteq C_2 \mid r_1 \sqsubseteq r_2 \mid a : C \mid r(a_1, a_2) \mid \exists C$$

A $\mathcal{SHOIN}^+$ model or interpretation $\mathcal{I}$ is a pair $\langle \Delta^{\mathcal{I}}, \cdot^{\mathcal{I}} \rangle$ where $\Delta^{\mathcal{I}}$ is a domain of individuals, and $\cdot^{\mathcal{I}}$ is an interpretation function interpreting concept names, role names, and individual names over the domain.

Definition 3. *(SHOIN$^+$ models: Mod$_{S+}$)* Let $\Sigma = \langle N_C, N_R, N_i \rangle \in |Sig_{S+}|$ be a $\mathcal{SHOIN}^+$ signature, where $N_R = R \cup R^-$ as specified in Definition 1. A model (or interpretation) $\mathcal{I}$ for $\mathcal{SHOIN}^+$ is a pair $(\Delta^{\mathcal{I}}, \cdot^{\mathcal{I}})$ consisting of a non-empty domain $\Delta^{\mathcal{I}}$ of individuals and an interpretation function $\cdot^{\mathcal{I}}$ which maps each concept name $A \in N_C$ to a subset $A^{\mathcal{I}} \subseteq \Delta^{\mathcal{I}}$, each basic role name $r \in R$ to a binary relation $r^{\mathcal{I}} \subseteq \Delta^{\mathcal{I}} \times \Delta^{\mathcal{I}}$, and each individual name $a \in N_i$ to an element $a^{\mathcal{I}} \in \Delta^{\mathcal{I}}$. The interpretation of an inverse role $r^- \in R^-$ is $(r^-)^{\mathcal{I}} = \{(y, x) \mid (x, y) \in r^{\mathcal{I}}\}$.

The $\mathcal{SHOIN}^+$ satisfaction relation is defined by first defining the interpretation of composed concepts, and then defining when an interpretation satisfies a sentence.

Definition 4. *($\mathcal{SHOIN}^+$ satisfaction relation: $\models_{S^+, \Sigma}$)* Let $\Sigma \in |Sig_{S^+}|$ be a $\mathcal{SHOIN}^+$ signature and let $\mathcal{I} = (\Delta^{\mathcal{I}}, \cdot^{\mathcal{I}}) \in |Mod_{S^+}(\Sigma)|$ be a Σ-model. The satisfaction relation $\models_{S^+, \Sigma}$ is then defined as follows, and is lifted to sets of sentences in the usual way.

$$
\begin{array}{llll}
\top^{\mathcal{I}} & = \Delta^{\mathcal{I}} & (C_1 \sqcap C_2)^{\mathcal{I}} = C_1^{\mathcal{I}} \cap C_2^{\mathcal{I}} \\
\bot^{\mathcal{I}} & = \emptyset & (C_1 \sqcup C_2)^{\mathcal{I}} = C_1^{\mathcal{I}} \cup C_2^{\mathcal{I}} \\
(\neg C)^{\mathcal{I}} & = \Delta^{\mathcal{I}} \setminus C^{\mathcal{I}} & \exists r.C^{\mathcal{I}} & = \{x \in \Delta^{\mathcal{I}} \mid \exists y : (x, y) \in r^{\mathcal{I}} \text{ and } y \in C^{\mathcal{I}}\} \\
\{a\}^{\mathcal{I}} & = \{a^{\mathcal{I}}\} & \forall r.C^{\mathcal{I}} & = \{x \in \Delta^{\mathcal{I}} \mid \forall y : (x, y) \in r^{\mathcal{I}} \Rightarrow y \in C^{\mathcal{I}}\}
\end{array}
$$

$$
\begin{array}{ll}
\mathcal{I} \models_{S^+, \Sigma} C_1 \sqsubseteq C_2 \Leftrightarrow C_1^{\mathcal{I}} \subseteq C_2^{\mathcal{I}} & \mathcal{I} \models_{S^+, \Sigma} r(a_1, a_2) \Leftrightarrow (a_1^{\mathcal{I}}, a_2^{\mathcal{I}}) \in r^{\mathcal{I}} \\
\mathcal{I} \models_{S^+, \Sigma} a : C \quad \Leftrightarrow a^{\mathcal{I}} \in C^{\mathcal{I}} & \mathcal{I} \models_{S^+, \Sigma} \exists C \quad \Leftrightarrow \exists x : x \in C^{\mathcal{I}}
\end{array}
$$

A set of description logic sentences can be used to specify relationships between concepts, and properties of individuals. Such a set of sentences is often called an ontology. We define an ontology formally as a so-called $\mathcal{SHOIN}^+$ presentation. Presentations over an arbitrary institution are defined as follows [22]. If $Inst = \langle Sig_{Inst}, Sen_{Inst}, Mod_{Inst}, \models_{Inst, \Sigma} \rangle$ is an institution where $\Sigma \in |Sig_{Inst}|$, then the pair $\langle \Sigma, \Phi \rangle$ where $\Phi \subseteq Sen_{Inst}(\Sigma)$ is called a presentation. A model of a presentation $\langle \Sigma, \Phi \rangle$ is a model $M \in |Mod_{Inst}(\Sigma)|$ such that $M \models_{Inst, \Sigma} \Phi$. Then $\mathbf{Mod}_{Inst}(\langle \Sigma, \Phi \rangle) \subseteq |Mod_{Inst}(\Sigma)|$ is the class of all models of $\langle \Sigma, \Phi \rangle$.

Definition 5. *($\mathcal{SHOIN}^+$ ontology)* A $\mathcal{SHOIN}^+$ ontology is a presentation $\langle \Sigma, \Omega \rangle$, where $\Sigma \in |Sig_{S^+}|$ and $\Omega \subseteq Sen_{S^+}(\Sigma)$. Its semantics is the class of Σ-models satisfying the axioms in Ω, i.e., $\mathbf{Mod}_{S^+}(\langle \Sigma, \Omega \rangle)$.

Part of the ontology Ω^{GA} for our garage appointment service GA can be specified as follows, where the $\mathcal{SHOIN}^+$ signature is Σ^{GA} as defined above (we refer to [25] for the complete definition of the running example). The concept "$\exists$hasDay.Day" consists of all individuals that are related to some individual of the concept "Day" over the role "hasDay". The axiom "$\exists$hasDay.Day $\sqsubseteq$ Appointment" specifies that these individuals should belong to the concept "Appointment", i.e., only appointments can have a day associated to them. Here and in the following we use $C \equiv C'$ as a shorthand notation for $C \sqsubseteq C', C' \sqsubseteq C$ where C and C' are concepts.

{ $\exists$hasDay.Day $\sqsubseteq$ Appointment, $\exists$hasHour.Hour $\sqsubseteq$ Appointment, $\exists\neg$Appointment,
  WDay $\sqcup$ WEDay $\equiv$ Day, mon : WDay, ..., fri : WDay, sat : WEDay,
  sun : WEDay, 1 : Hour, ..., 24 : Hour, after(mon, mon), after(mon, tue), ...,
  after(1, 1), after(1, 2), after(2, 2), after(1, 3), after(2, 3) ...,
  before(mon, mon), before(tue, mon), ...}

3 Overview of the Approach

The description logic $\mathcal{SHOIN}^+$ as defined in the previous section forms the basis for the specification of services in our framework. In this section, we present the general idea of how we propose to use $\mathcal{SHOIN}^+$ for the specification of services.

As in, e.g., [17,18,16,12,21], we see services as operations with input and output parameters that may change the state of the service provider if the service is called. In order to define the semantics of services, we thus need to represent which state changes occur if the service is called with a given input, and which output is returned. A semantic domain in which these aspects are conveniently represented are so-called labeled transition systems with output (LTSO), which are also used as a semantic domain for the interpretation of operations in [10,3].

An LTSO consists, roughly speaking, of a set of states and a set of transitions between these states, labeled by the name of the operation (which is a service in our case) by which the transition is made, and the actual input and output parameters. In our setting, the states are $\mathcal{SHOIN}^+$ interpretations. That is, we represent a service provider state as a $\mathcal{SHOIN}^+$ interpretation, and interpret services as operating on these states. The actual inputs and outputs of services are interpretations of variables (treated here as individuals).

It is important to note that using $\mathcal{SHOIN}^+$ for service *specification* does not mean that the service provider needs to be *implemented* using $\mathcal{SHOIN}^+$. Techniques for implementing services and for describing the relation of its implementation with its specification are, however, outside the scope of this paper.

In our framework, states are thus $\mathcal{SHOIN}^+$ interpretations. The general idea is then that the pre- and postconditions of a service are specified in $\mathcal{SHOIN}^+$. However, in order to be able to express pre- and postconditions properly, we do not use $\mathcal{SHOIN}^+$ as it is, but define several extensions. That is, in the precondition one often wants to specify properties of the input of the service, and in the postcondition properties of the input and output of the service. For this, it should be possible to refer to the *variables* forming the formal input and output parameters of the service. However, $\mathcal{SHOIN}^+$ does not facilitate the use of variables. For this reason, we use an extension of $\mathcal{SHOIN}^+$ with variables, called $\mathcal{SHOIN}^+_{Var}$, where variables refer to individuals.

Moreover, in the postcondition one typically wants to specify how the state may change, i.e., to specify properties of a transition. Hence, we need to be able to refer to the source and target states of a transition. For this purpose, we define an extension of $\mathcal{SHOIN}^+_{Var}$ called $\mathcal{SHOIN}^{+bi}_{Var}$ which allows both the use of variables and reference to the source and target states of a transition.

All necessary extensions of $\mathcal{SHOIN}^+$ are defined as institutions, and we define their semantics through a reduction to $\mathcal{SHOIN}^+$. This reduction allows us to use description logic reasoners for computing matches between a service request and service provider, which will be explained in more detail in Section 6. Although the extensions can be reduced to $\mathcal{SHOIN}^+$, we use the extensions rather than (an encoding in) $\mathcal{SHOIN}^+$ to let our approach be closer to the formalisms of [10,3], and to our intuitive understanding of the semantics of services.

4   Extensions of $\mathcal{SHOIN}^+$

In this section, we present the extensions of $\mathcal{SHOIN}^+$ that we use for the specification of pre- and postconditions. We do not provide the complete definitions.

The first extension is $\mathcal{SHOIN}^+_{Var}$, which extends $\mathcal{SHOIN}^+$ with variables. A $\mathcal{SHOIN}^+_{Var}$ signature is a pair $\langle \Sigma, X \rangle$ where Σ is a $\mathcal{SHOIN}^+$ signature and X is a set of variables. Sentences of $\mathcal{SHOIN}^+_{Var}$ are then defined in terms of $\mathcal{SHOIN}^+$ sentences, by adding X to the individuals of Σ, which is a $\mathcal{SHOIN}^+$ signature denoted by Σ_X.

Models of a $\mathcal{SHOIN}^+_{Var}$ signature $\langle \Sigma, X \rangle$ are pairs $(\mathcal{I}, \rho)$, where $\mathcal{I}$ is a Σ-interpretation, and $\rho : X \to \Delta^{\mathcal{I}}$ is a valuation assigning individuals to the variables. The semantics of $\mathcal{SHOIN}^+_{Var}$ sentences is then defined in terms of the semantics of $\mathcal{SHOIN}^+$ sentences by constructing a $\mathcal{SHOIN}^+$ interpretation $\mathcal{I}_\rho$ from $(\mathcal{I}, \rho)$, in which variables are treated as individual names that are interpreted corresponding to ρ. A similar construction, in which variables are treated as part of the signature, can be found in the institution-independent generalization of quantification [5].

The second extension is $\mathcal{SHOIN}^{+bi}_{Var}$, which is an extension of $\mathcal{SHOIN}^+_{Var}$ and allows both variables and references to source and target states of a transition. The $\mathcal{SHOIN}^{+bi}_{Var}$ signatures are the $\mathcal{SHOIN}^+_{Var}$ signatures, but sentences of a signature $\langle \Sigma, X \rangle$ are defined in terms of the sentences of $\mathcal{SHOIN}^+$ by adding for each concept name A of Σ a concept name $A@pre$, and similarly for role names.

Models are triples $(\mathcal{I}_1, \mathcal{I}_2, \rho)$, where $\mathcal{I}_1$ and $\mathcal{I}_2$ are $\mathcal{SHOIN}^+$ interpretations and ρ is a valuation. We require that the domains and the interpretations of individual names are the same in $\mathcal{I}_1$ and $\mathcal{I}_2$, i.e., individual names are constants. These restrictions are also typical for temporal description logics [15]. The idea of the semantics is then that a concept name $A@pre$ in a $\mathcal{SHOIN}^{+bi}_{Var}$ sentence refers to A in $\mathcal{I}_1$, and a concept name A refers to A in $\mathcal{I}_2$, and similarly for role names. On this basis we define the satisfaction relation by a reduction to $\mathcal{SHOIN}^+$.

Definition 6. *($\mathcal{SHOIN}^{+bi}_{Var}$ institution)*   The institution $\mathcal{SHOIN}^{+bi}_{Var} = \langle Sig_{\mathcal{S}^{+bi}_{Var}}, Sen_{\mathcal{S}^{+bi}_{Var}}, Mod_{\mathcal{S}^{+bi}_{Var}}, \models_{\mathcal{S}^{+bi}_{Var}, \Sigma} \rangle$ is defined as follows:

- The $\mathcal{SHOIN}^{+bi}_{Var}$ signatures are the $\mathcal{SHOIN}^+_{Var}$ signatures, $\langle \Sigma, X \rangle$, i.e., $Sig_{\mathcal{S}^{+bi}_{Var}} = Sig_{\mathcal{S}^+_{Var}}$.
- Let $\langle \Sigma, X \rangle$ be a $\mathcal{SHOIN}^{+bi}_{Var}$ signature. The $\mathcal{SHOIN}^{+bi}_{Var}$ sentences are then defined as $Sen_{\mathcal{S}^{+bi}_{Var}}(\langle \Sigma, X \rangle) \triangleq Sen^+_{\mathcal{S}}(\Sigma^{bi}_X)$ where Σ^{bi}_X is a $\mathcal{SHOIN}^+$ signature extending Σ_X (see above) by concepts names $A@pre$ for all concept names A in Σ and by role names $r@pre$ for all role names r in Σ.
- A $\mathcal{SHOIN}^{+bi}_{Var}$ model is a triple $(\mathcal{I}_1, \mathcal{I}_2, \rho)$ where $\mathcal{I}_1, \mathcal{I}_2 \in |Mod_{\mathcal{S}^+}(\Sigma)|$, $\mathcal{I}_1 = (\Delta^{\mathcal{I}_1}, \cdot^{\mathcal{I}_1})$, $\mathcal{I}_2 = (\Delta^{\mathcal{I}_2}, \cdot^{\mathcal{I}_2})$, $\Delta^{\mathcal{I}_1} = \Delta^{\mathcal{I}_2}$, and $a^{\mathcal{I}_1} = a^{\mathcal{I}_2}$ for all $a \in N_i$, and $\rho : X \to \Delta$ is a valuation where $\Delta \triangleq \Delta^{\mathcal{I}_1}(= \Delta^{\mathcal{I}_2})$.
- For each $\mathcal{SHOIN}^{+bi}_{Var}$ signature $\langle \Sigma, X \rangle \in |Sig_{\mathcal{S}^{+bi}_{Var}}|$, the satisfaction relation $\models_{\mathcal{S}^{+bi}_{Var}, \langle \Sigma, X \rangle}$ is defined as follows by means of a reduction to $\models_{\mathcal{S}^+, \Sigma^{bi}_X}$. Let

$(\mathcal{I}_1, \mathcal{I}_2, \rho) \in Mod_{S_{Var}^{+bi}}(\langle \Sigma, X \rangle)$ and let $\hat{\mathcal{I}}_\rho \in Mod_{S+}(\Sigma_X^{bi})$ be defined as follows:

$\Delta^{\hat{\mathcal{I}}_\rho} = \Delta^{\mathcal{I}_1}(= \Delta^{\mathcal{I}_2})$, $\cdot^{\hat{\mathcal{I}}_\rho} = \cdot^{(\mathcal{I}_2)_\rho}$ for concept names A, role names r, and individual names a of Σ, and $\cdot^{\hat{\mathcal{I}}_\rho} = \cdot^{(\mathcal{I}_1)_\rho}$ for concept names $A@pre$ and role names $r@pre$, where $(\mathcal{I}_1)_\rho$ and $(\mathcal{I}_2)_\rho$ are the extension of $\mathcal{I}_1$ and $\mathcal{I}_2$, respectively, to variables as defined above.

We now define $(\mathcal{I}_1, \mathcal{I}_2, \rho) \models_{S_{Var}^{+bi}, \langle \Sigma, X \rangle} \phi \triangleq \hat{\mathcal{I}}_\rho \models_{S+, \Sigma_X^{bi}} \phi$ for $\phi \in Sen_{S_{Var}^{+bi}}(\langle \Sigma, X \rangle)$ and thus by definition also $\phi \in Sen_{S+}(\Sigma_X^{bi})$.

5   Service Specification Using Description Logic

Having defined suitable extensions of $\mathcal{SHOIN}^+$, we continue to define our service specification framework. The definitions are inspired by approaches for the formal specification of operations in the area of object-oriented specification [10,3], although these approaches are not based on institutions.

In the context of semantic web services specified using description logics, services are generally assumed to operate within the context of an ontology (see, e.g., [8]). The ontology defines the domain in which the services operate by defining the relevant concepts and relations between them. Moreover, a service provider will often provide multiple services, which all operate in the context of the same ontology. We call a bundling of services together with an ontology a *service package*. We define a service as an operation that has a name and that may have input and output variables as follows.

Definition 7. *(service)* A service $serv = servName([X_{in}]) : [X_{out}]$ consists of a service name $servName$, and sequences of input and output variables $[X_{in}]$ and $[X_{out}]$, respectively, such that all x in $[X_{in}]$ and $[X_{out}]$ are distinct. We use $var_{in}(serv)$ and $var_{out}(serv)$ to denote the sets of input and output variables of $serv$, respectively.

A garage appointment service can be represented by $makeAppointment(name, from, to) : app$. This service takes a name of a client and two days in between which the appointment should be made, and returns the appointment that it has made.

Now, we formally define service packages as an institution, for which we need the following general preliminaries [22]. Let $Inst = \langle Sig_{Inst}, Sen_{Inst}, Mod_{Inst}, \models_{Inst, \Sigma} \rangle$ be an institution where $\Sigma \in |Sig_{Inst}|$. For any class $\mathcal{M} \subseteq |Mod_{Inst}(\Sigma)|$ of Σ-models, the theory of $\mathcal{M}$, $Th_\Sigma(\mathcal{M})$, is the set of all Σ-sentences satisfied by all Σ-models in $\mathcal{M}$, i.e., $Th_\Sigma(\mathcal{M}) = \{\phi \in Sen_{Inst}(\Sigma) \mid \mathcal{M} \models_{Inst, \Sigma} \phi\}$. The closure of a set Φ of Σ-sentences is the set $Cl_\Sigma(\Phi) = Th_\Sigma(\mathbf{Mod}_{Inst}(\Phi))$. A theory morphism $\sigma : \langle \Sigma, \Phi \rangle \to \langle \Sigma', \Phi' \rangle$ is a signature morphism $\sigma : \Sigma \to \Sigma'$ such that $\sigma(\phi) \in \Phi'$ for each $\phi \in \Phi$.

A service package signature Σ_{SP} is a pair $(\langle \Sigma, \Omega \rangle, Servs)$ where $\langle \Sigma, \Omega \rangle$ is a $\mathcal{SHOIN}^+$ ontology and $Servs$ is a set of services. An SP signature morphism

σ_{SP} from an SP signature Σ_{SP} to SP signature Σ'_{SP} then defines that there is a theory morphism from the ontology sentences of Σ_{SP} to those of Σ'_{SP}.

The sentences of an SP institution are used to specify the services and are of the form $\langle serv, \mathsf{pre}, \mathsf{post}\rangle$. Here, $serv$ is the service that is being specified, and pre and post are the pre- and postconditions of the service, respectively. We now use the extensions of $\mathcal{SHOIN}^+$ as defined in Section 4 for the definition of pre and post. That is, the precondition is specified by means of $\mathcal{SHOIN}^+_{Var}$ sentences, where the variables that may be used are the variables of the input of $serv$. The postcondition is specified by means of $\mathcal{SHOIN}^{+bi}_{Var}$ sentences, which means that the postcondition can refer to the source and target states of a transition, and the variables that may be used are the variables of the input and output of $serv$.

The models of service packages are non-deterministic total labeled transition systems with output (see also Section 3). A transition system in our framework is a pair $\mathcal{T} = (Q, \delta)$. Q is the set of states, which are in our case $\mathcal{SHOIN}^+$ interpretations that satisfy the ontology of the service specification, i.e., the ontology is treated as an invariant that the specified service always fulfills. The set δ is the transitions between states. Each transition $t \in \delta$ has a source and a target state from Q. Furthermore, t is labeled with the service through which the transition is made, together with a valuation of the input variables of the service, expressing which are the actual input parameters of the service call. Any transition t is equipped with a valuation of the output variables, expressing which are the actual output parameters of the service call. Loosely speaking, a transition system $\mathcal{T} = (Q, \delta)$ satisfies a sentence $\langle serv, \mathsf{pre}, \mathsf{post}\rangle$, if in all interpretations $\mathcal{I} \in Q$ in which pre holds, all transitions from $\mathcal{I}$ to some $\mathcal{I}' \in Q$ through service $serv$ satisfy post.

Definition 8. *(service package (SP) institution)* The institution $SP = \langle Sig_{SP}, Sen_{SP}, Mod_{SP}, \models_{SP, (\langle \Sigma, \Omega\rangle, Servs)}\rangle$ is defined as follows:

- An SP signature is a pair $(\langle \Sigma, \Omega\rangle, Servs)$ where $\langle \Sigma, \Omega\rangle$ is a $\mathcal{SHOIN}^+$ ontology (see Definition 5), and $Servs$ is a set of services. An SP signature morphism $\sigma_{SP} : (\langle \Sigma, \Omega\rangle, Servs) \rightarrow (\langle \Sigma', \Omega'\rangle, Servs')$ consists of a theory morphism $\sigma_\Omega : \langle \Sigma, Cl_\Sigma(\Omega)\rangle \rightarrow \langle \Sigma', Cl_{\Sigma'}(\Omega')\rangle$, and a mapping of each service $serv \in Servs$ to a service $serv' \in Servs'$, such that for each mapping from $serv$ to $serv'$ it holds that $serv$ and $serv'$ have the same number of input variables and the same number of output variables.
- An SP sentence is a triple $\langle serv, \mathsf{pre}, \mathsf{post}\rangle$, where $serv$ is a service, and $\mathsf{pre} \subseteq Sen_{\mathcal{S}^+_{Var}}(\langle \Sigma, X_{in}\rangle)$, $\mathsf{post} \subseteq Sen_{\mathcal{SHOIN}^{+bi}_{Var}}(\langle \Sigma, X_{in,out}\rangle)$, where here and in the following $X_{in} = var_{in}(serv)$, $X_{out} = var_{out}(serv)$, and $X_{in,out} = var_{in}(serv) \cup var_{out}(serv)$.
- An SP model for this signature is a non-deterministic total labeled transition system with outputs $\mathcal{T} = (Q, \delta)$, where $Q \subseteq \mathbf{Mod}_{S+}(\langle \Sigma, \Omega\rangle)$ is a set of states and δ is a set of transitions between states, defined as follows. Let $Label = \{(serv, \rho_{in}) \mid serv \in Servs, \rho_{in} : var_{in}(serv) \rightarrow \Delta\}$, where $\Delta = \bigcup\{\Delta^{\mathcal{I}} \mid \mathcal{I} \in Q\}$ and let $Output$ be the set of valuations $\rho_{out} : X \rightarrow \Delta$ where X is an arbitrary set of variables. Then $\delta \subseteq Q \times Label \times (Q \times Output)$ such

that for all $(\mathcal{I}, (serv, \rho_{in}), (\mathcal{I}', \rho_{out})) \in \delta$ we have $\rho_{in} : var_{in}(serv) \to \Delta^{\mathcal{I}}$ and $\rho_{out} : var_{out}(serv) \to \Delta^{\mathcal{I}'}$, and $\mathcal{T}$ is total, i.e., for all $\mathcal{I} \in Q$ it holds that for all $l \in Label$ there is an $\mathcal{I}', \rho_{out}$ such that $(\mathcal{I}, (serv, \rho_{in}), (\mathcal{I}', \rho_{out})) \in \delta$.
The reduct $\mathcal{T}'|_{\sigma_{SP}}$ where $\mathcal{T}' = (Q', \delta')$ is $(Q'|_{\sigma_{Ont}}, \delta'|_{\sigma_{SP}})$, where $Q'|_{\sigma_{Ont}} = \{\mathcal{I}'|_{\sigma_{Ont}} \mid \mathcal{I}' \in Q'\}$, and $\delta'|_{\sigma_{SP}}$ are all transitions $(\mathcal{I}_1|_{\sigma_{Ont}}, (serv, \rho_{in}|_{\sigma_{Var}^+}), \mathcal{I}_2|_{\sigma_{Ont}}, \rho_{out}|_{\sigma_{Var}^+})$ such that there is a transition $(\mathcal{I}_1, (\sigma_{SP}(serv), \rho_{in}), \mathcal{I}_2, \rho_{out}) \in \delta'$.

- Let $\Sigma_{SP} = (\langle \Sigma, \Omega \rangle, Servs)$ be an SP signature, and let $\mathcal{T} = (Q, \delta) \in Mod_{SP}((\langle \Sigma, \Omega \rangle, Servs))$. We define $\mathcal{T} \models_{SP, \Sigma_{SP}} \langle serv, \text{pre}, \text{post} \rangle$ iff for all $(\mathcal{I}, (serv, \rho_{in}), \mathcal{I}', \rho_{out}) \in \delta$ the following holds, where $X_{in} = var_{in}(serv)$ and $X_{in,out} = var_{in}(serv) \cup var_{out}(serv)$: If $(\mathcal{I}, \rho_{in}) \models_{S_{Var}^+, \langle \Sigma, X_{in} \rangle}$ pre then $(\mathcal{I}, \mathcal{I}', \rho_{in,out}) \models_{S_{Var}^{+bi}, \langle \Sigma, X_{in,out} \rangle}$ post. We use $\rho_{in,out}$ to denote the merging of the two valuations ρ_{in} and ρ_{out} to one valuation in the obvious way.

We now define a service package specification as an SP presentation, i.e., it consists of an SP signature and a set of SP sentences, and its semantics is the class of all its models.

Definition 9. *(service package specification)* A service package specification is a presentation $\langle \Sigma_{SP}, \Psi_{SP} \rangle$ where $\Sigma_{SP} \in |Sig_{SP}|$ and $\Psi_{SP} \subseteq Sen_{SP}(\Sigma_{SP})$ such that for each $serv \in Servs$ where $\Sigma_{SP} = \langle Ont, Servs \rangle$ there is exactly one sentence of the form $\langle serv, \text{pre}, \text{post} \rangle$ in Ψ_{SP}. Its semantics is the class of Σ_{SP}-models satisfying the axioms in Ψ_{SP}, i.e., $\mathbf{Mod}_{SP}(\langle \Sigma_{SP}, \Psi_{SP} \rangle)$.

A service package specification where the only service is the service *makeAppointment* considered above, then consists of the signature Σ^{GA} and ontology Ω^{GA} as defined in Section 2, and the following specification Ψ_{SP}^{GA} for the garage appointment service. We use "String *name*" instead of only the variable "*name*" as input, which is an abbreviation for adding "*name*: String" to the precondition, and similarly for the other inputs and for the output (in which case it abbreviates part of the postcondition).

The specification says that the only appointment made through calling the service is the appointment *app* which is returned, the (week)day on which the appointment should take place is in between *from* and *to* which have been passed as parameters, and the time of day of the appointment is between 8 and 16.

makeAppointment(String *name*, WDay *from*, WDay *to*) : Appointment *app*
  pre after(*from*, *to*)
  post Appointment $\sqcap \neg$(Appointment@*pre*) $\equiv \{app\}$,
    app : $\exists$hasDay.($\exists$after.$\{from\}$), *app* : $\exists$hasDay.($\exists$before.$\{to\}$),
    app : $\exists$hasHour.($\exists$after.$\{8\}$),   *app* : $\exists$hasHour.($\exists$before.$\{16\}$)

6 Matching Service Requests and Service Providers

Service package specifications can be used for specifying service providers. These service provider specifications can then be used by service requesters to determine whether a particular service provider matches their request, which can also be formulated as a service package specification. In this section, we make this matching precise by providing a model-theoretic definition of when a service request specification is matched by a service provider specification. Moreover, we provide a characterization of matching by semantic entailment over $\mathcal{SHOIN}^+$, which can be proven using standard description logic reasoners.

Our definition of matching is based on the idea that the service provider should be a *refinement* of the service request. That is, the service request specifies the behavior that the service provider is allowed to exhibit, and the specified behavior of the service provider should be within these boundaries. The idea is thus to define matching model-theoretically as inclusion of the model class of the provider specification in the model class of the request specification.

However, we cannot define this model class inclusion directly in this way, since we want to allow the request and the provider to be specified over different signatures. This is naturally facilitated through the use of institutions, by defining matching on the basis of a signature morphism from request to provider. In the semantic web community, techniques are being developed for aligning different ontologies [6], which could be applied in our setting for obtaining a signature morphism. Given a signature morphism from request to provider specification, we define matching as the inclusion of the reduct of the model class of the provider specification in the model class of the request specification.

Definition 10. *(matching)* Let $\langle \Sigma_{SP}^R, \Psi_{SP}^R \rangle$ and $\langle \Sigma_{SP}^P, \Psi_{SP}^P \rangle$ be service package specifications of request and provider, respectively, where $\sigma_{SP} : \Sigma_{SP}^R \to \Sigma_{SP}^P$ is an *SP* signature morphism. Then, the request is matched by the provider under σ_{SP} iff

$$\mathbf{Mod}_{SP}(\langle \Sigma_{SP}^P, \Psi_{SP}^P \rangle)|_{\sigma_{SP}} \subseteq \mathbf{Mod}_{SP}(\langle \Sigma_{SP}^R, \Psi_{SP}^R \rangle).$$

Now that we have defined matching model-theoretically, our aim is to be able to prove matching by proving particular logical relations between the ontologies and pre- and postconditions of the provider and request specifications.

The general idea is that for a particular service specification, the precondition of the provider should be weaker than the precondition of the request if the specification matches, since it should be possible to call the service at least in those cases required by the request. For the postcondition it is the other way around. The provider should at least guarantee what the request requires, i.e., the postcondition of the provider should be stronger than that of the request. These conditions are frequently used in the context of behavioral subtyping in object-oriented specification [13]. Moreover, we may assume that the provider ontology holds, because it is the provider's service which is actually executed. Also, in order to prove entailment of the request postcondition by the provider postcondition, we can assume additionally that the request precondition holds. Intuitively, this is allowed since we can assume that the requester will guarantee that he satisfies his precondition, if he calls the service. These considerations lead to the following theorem.

Theorem 1. *(characterization of matching by semantic entailment)*   Let $\langle \Sigma_{SP}^R, \Psi_{SP}^R \rangle$ and $\langle \Sigma_{SP}^P, \Psi_{SP}^P \rangle$ be service package specifications of request and provider, respectively, where $\langle \Sigma_{SP}^{P}, \Psi_{SP}^{P} \rangle$ is consistent, i.e., $\mathbf{Mod}_{SP}(\langle \Sigma_{SP}^{P}, \Psi_{SP}^{P} \rangle) \neq \emptyset$, and where $\sigma_{SP} : \Sigma_{SP}^{R} \to \Sigma_{SP}^{P}$ is an SP signature morphism. Then, the request is matched by the provider under σ_{SP} according to Definition 10, iff the following holds.

Let $\Sigma_{SP}^{R} = (\langle \Sigma^{R}, \Omega^{R} \rangle, Servs^{R})$ and $\Sigma_{SP}^{P} = (\langle \Sigma^{P}, \Omega^{P} \rangle, Servs^{P})$. Then for all $\langle serv^{R}, \mathsf{pre}^{R}, \mathsf{post}^{R} \rangle \in \Psi_{SP}^{R}$ two conditions hold for $\langle serv^{P}, \mathsf{pre}^{P}, \mathsf{post}^{P} \rangle \in \Psi_{SP}^{P}$, where $serv^{P} = \sigma_{SP}(serv^{R})$, $\sigma_{S+} : \Sigma^{R} \to \Sigma^{P}$, $X_{in} = var_{in}(serv^{P})$ and $X_{in,out} = var_{in}(serv^{P}) \cup var_{out}(serv^{P})$:[2]

1. $\sigma_{S+}(\mathsf{pre}^{R}) \cup \Omega^{P} \models_{S+, \Sigma_{X_{in}}^{P}} \mathsf{pre}^{P}$
2. $\sigma_{S+}(\mathsf{pre}^{R})@pre \cup \Omega^{P}@pre \cup \mathsf{post}^{P} \cup \Omega^{P} \models_{S+, \Sigma_{X_{in,out}}^{P}{}^{bi}} \sigma_{S+}(\mathsf{post}^{R})$

The sentences $\Omega^{P}@pre$ are obtained from Ω^{P} by adding $@pre$ to all concept names and role names, and similarly for $\sigma_{S+}(\mathsf{pre}^{R})@pre$.

The proof can be found in [25]. Note that we do not use the request ontology Ω^{R} in this characterization since it is the provider's service which is actually executed. However, as mentioned above, Ω^{R} is plays a key role in proving a match, since a theory morphism from Ω^{R} to the provider ontology Ω^{P} is required for a signature morphism from request to provider. This theory morphism can be proven by showing that $\Omega^{P} \models_{S+, \Sigma} \sigma_{S+}(\Omega^{R})$, where Σ is the $\mathcal{SHOIN}^{+}$ signature of Ω^{P}. Also, we require that the provider specification is consistent, since otherwise it would match with any request specification according to Definition 10, but the relation between invariants and pre- and postconditions might be such that no match can be derived according to Theorem 1.

It is also important to note that, while the pre- and postconditions are specified over the signatures $\mathcal{SHOIN}_{Var}^{+}$ and $\mathcal{SHOIN}_{Var}^{+bi}$, respectively, we interpret them here as $\mathcal{SHOIN}^{+}$ sentences over the signatures $\Sigma_{X_{in}}^{P}$ and $\Sigma_{X_{in,out}}^{P}{}^{bi}$, respectively. This is possible since the sentences and semantics of $\mathcal{SHOIN}_{Var}^{+}$ and $\mathcal{SHOIN}_{Var}^{+bi}$ have been defined by a reduction to $\mathcal{SHOIN}^{+}$ over the respective $\mathcal{SHOIN}^{+}$ signatures. $\mathcal{SHOIN}^{+}(\mathbf{D})$ entailment can further be reduced to satisfiability in $\mathcal{SHOIN}(\mathbf{D})$ [11], for which a sound and complete reasoner with acceptable to very good performance exists [19].

To illustrate matching, we take the garage appointment service package specification of Section 5 as a service provider specification. We define a service request specification CA, representing a car requesting a garage appointment, as follows. The signature Σ^{CA} is defined by $N_C = \{\text{Termin, Tag, Zeichenkette}\}$, $N_R = \{\text{nach, vor, hatTag}\}$, $N_i = \{1, 2, \dots, 24, \text{montag, dienstag}, \dots, \text{sonntag}\}$. These are the notions also occurring in Σ^{CA} in German. Part of the sentences of the ontology, Ω^{CA}, are the following:

$\{ \exists \text{hatTag.Tag} \sqsubseteq \text{Termin, montag} : \text{Tag, dienstag} : \text{Tag}, \dots, \text{sonntag} : \text{Tag},$
$\quad \text{nach(montag, montag), after(montag, dienstag)}, \dots,$
$\quad \text{nach}(1, 1), \text{nach}(1, 2), \text{nach}(2, 2), \text{nach}(1, 3), \text{nach}(2, 3) \dots,$
$\quad \text{vor(montag, montag), vor(dienstag, montag)}, \dots \}$

---

[2] We use $\sigma_{S+}(\Omega)$ as a shorthand notation for $Sen_{S+}(\sigma_{S+})(\Omega)$.

The requester is looking for a service $terminVereinbaren(name, von, bis) : ter$, specified as follows:

terminVereinbaren(Zeichenkette $name$, Tag von, Tag bis) : Termin ter
   pre nach(dienstag, von), nach(bis, dienstag)
   post hatTag(ter, dienstag)

In order to determine whether the service request CA is matched by the service provider GA, we need to define a signature morphism $\sigma : \Sigma_{SP}^{CA} \to \Sigma_{SP}^{GA}$. Using an appropriate signature morphism from the German notions of Σ^{CA} to the corresponding English ones of Σ^{GA},[3] it can be shown that the request is matched by the service provider (see [25]). The request specifies a service that makes an appointment on Tuesday if *from* and *to* are set to Tuesday, but it does not matter at what time.

7 Related Work and Concluding Remarks

Regarding related work, we mention that in [2], an approach to service specification using description logic is presented that is also based on a specification of pre- and postconditions using description logic. That paper, however, considers services for which the input parameters have already been instantiated by individual names, it does not consider output of services, and it requires strong restrictions on the kind of description logic formulas used in pre- and postconditions. Moreover, it does not provide a (model-theoretic) definition of matching with accompanying characterization. Rather, it investigates several reasoning tasks that are indispensable subtasks of matching, and focuses on solving the frame problem in this context.

In this paper, we have proposed a formal specification framework for specifying the functionality of services using description logic, based on institutions. We have defined extensions of description logic and the service specification framework itself as institutions. Using this framework, we have provided a model-theoretic definition of when a service request specification is matched by a service provider specification, allowing the request and provider specification to be defined over different signatures. We have shown that matching can be characterized by a semantic entailment relation which is formulated over a particular standard description logic. Therefore, proofs of matching can be reduced to standard reasoning in description logic for which one can use efficient, sound and complete description logic reasoners.

In future work, we would like to investigate adding a more abstract layer for facilitating service discovery, where not all details with respect to input and output of the service are specified. Such more abstract specifications could be used in the first phase of a two-phase approach to service discovery (see also [21]), and the approach presented in this paper would be used in the second phase. Another topic for future research is investigating an institution-independent generalization of this approach, which allows the service specification framework to

---

[3] And using the complete ontologies.

be based on arbitrary institutions, rather than on description logic. Also, the integration of our approach with specifications of dynamic interaction protocols of services can be investigated (cf. e.g. [23,24]).

Moreover, more extensive experimentation with the framework will have to show what kind of services are effectively specifiable using description logic. In particular, we aim to relate our approach to the well-known OWL-S [16] ontology for service specification, which is defined in the OWL language. As in this work, OWL-S views services as operations and proposes the use of pre- and postconditions for their specification. However, OWL-S does not specify how and in what language to define pre- and postconditions, it does not come with a model-theoretic interpretation of service specifications, and matching is not formally defined and characterized.

Acknowledgements. We would like to thank the anonymous referees for many valuable comments and suggestions.

References

1. Baader, F., Calvanese, D., McGuinness, D.L., Nardi, D., Patel-Schneider, P.F.: The description logic handbook: Theory, implementation, and applications. Cambridge University Press, Cambridge (2003)
2. Baader, F., Lutz, C., Milicic, M., Sattler, U., Wolter, F.: A description logic based approach to reasoning about web services. In: Proceedings of the WWW 2005 Workshop on Web Service Semantics (WSS 2005) (2005)
3. Bidoit, M., Hennicker, R., Knapp, A., Baumeister, H.: Glass-box and black-box views on object-oriented specifications. In: Proceedings of the 2nd International Conference on Software Engineering and Formal Methods (SEFM 2004), pp. 208–217 (2004)
4. Chinnici, R., Moreau, J.-J., Ryman, A., Weerawarana, S.: Web services description language (WSDL) version 2.0 part 1: Core language, W3C recommendation June 26, 2007 (2007), http://www.w3.org/TR/wsdl20/
5. Diaconescu, R.: Herbrand theorems in arbitrary institutions. Information Processing Letters 90, 29–37 (2004)
6. Euzenat, J., Shvaiko, P.: Ontology Matching. Springer, Berlin (2007)
7. Goguen, J., Burstall, R.: Institutions: Abstract model theory for specification and programming. Journ. of the ACM 39(1) (1992)
8. Grimm, S., Motik, B., Preist, C.: Matching semantic service descriptions with local closed-world reasoning. In: Sure, Y., Domingue, J. (eds.) ESWC 2006. LNCS, vol. 4011, pp. 575–589. Springer, Heidelberg (2006)
9. Gruber, T.R.: Towards principles for the design of ontologies used for knowledge sharing. In: Guarino, N., Poli, R. (eds.) Formal Ontology in Conceptual Analysis and Knowledge Representation, Deventer, The Netherlands. Kluwer Academic Publishers, Dordrecht (1993)
10. Hennicker, R., Knapp, A., Baumeister, H.: Semantics of OCL operation specifications. Electronic Notes in Theoretical Computer Science, Workshop OCL 2.0:Industry Standard or Scientific Playground 102, 111–132 (2004)
11. Horrocks, I., Patel-Schneider, P.F.: Reducing OWL entailment to description logic satisfiability. Journal of Web Semantics 1(4), 345–357 (2004)

12. Keller, U., Lausen, H., Stollberg, M.: On the semantics of functional descriptions of web services. In: Sure, Y., Domingue, J. (eds.) ESWC 2006. LNCS, vol. 4011, pp. 605–619. Springer, Heidelberg (2006)
13. Liskov, B.H., Wing, J.M.: A behavioral notion of subtyping. ACM Transactions on Programming Languages and Systems 16(6), 1811–1841 (1994)
14. Lucanu, D., Li, Y.F., Dong, J.S.: Semantic web languages – towards an institutional perspective. In: Futatsugi, K., Jouannaud, J.-P., Meseguer, J. (eds.) Algebra, Meaning, and Computation. LNCS, vol. 4060, pp. 99–123. Springer, Heidelberg (2006)
15. Lutz, C., Wolter, F., Zakharyaschev, M.: Temporal description logics: A survey. In: Proceedings of the Fifteenth International Symposium on Temporal Representation and Reasoning. IEEE Computer Society Press, Los Alamitos (2008)
16. Martin, D., Paolucci, M., McIlraith, S., Burstein, M., McDermott, D., McGuinness, D., Parsia, B., Payne, T., Sabou, M., Solanki, M., Srinivasan, N., Sycara, K.: Bringing semantics to web services: The OWL-S approach. In: Cardoso, J., Sheth, A.P. (eds.) SWSWPC 2004. LNCS, vol. 3387, pp. 26–42. Springer, Berlin (2005)
17. McIlraith, S.A., Son, T.C., Zeng, H.: Semantic web services. IEEE Intelligent Systems 16(2), 46–53 (2001)
18. Paolucci, M., Kawamura, T., Payne, T.R., Sycara, K.P.: Semantic matching of web services capabilities. In: Horrocks, I., Hendler, J. (eds.) ISWC 2002. LNCS, vol. 2342, pp. 333–347. Springer, Heidelberg (2002)
19. Sirin, E., Parsia, B., Grau, B.C., Kalyanpur, A., Katz, Y.: Pellet: A practical OWL-DL reasoner. Journal of Web Semantics 5(2), 51–53 (2007)
20. Smith, M.K., Welty, C., McGuinness, D.L.: OWL web ontology language guide, W3C Recommendation, February 10, 2004 (2004),
    http://www.w3.org/TR/owl-guide/
21. Stollberg, M., Keller, U., Lausen, H., Heymans, S.: Two-phase web service discovery based on rich functional descriptions. In: Franconi, E., Kifer, M., May, W. (eds.) ESWC 2007. LNCS, vol. 4519, pp. 99–113. Springer, Heidelberg (2007)
22. Tarlecki, A.: Institutions: An abstract framework for formal specifications. In: Astesiano, E., Kreowski, H.-J., Krieg-Brückner, B. (eds.) Algebraic Foundations of Systems Specification, pp. 105–130. Springer, New York (1999)
23. Wirsing, M., Clark, A., Gilmore, S., Hölzl, M., Knapp, A., Koch, N., Schroeder, A.: Semantic-Based Development of Service-Oriented Systems. In: Najm, E., Pradat-Peyre, J.-F., Donzeau-Gouge, V.V. (eds.) FORTE 2006. LNCS, vol. 4229, pp. 24–45. Springer, Heidelberg (2006)
24. Wirsing, M., De Nicola, R., Gilmore, S., Hölzl, M., Tribastone, M., Zavattaro, G.: SENSORIA Process Calculi for Service-Oriented Computing. In: Montanari, U., Sannella, D., Bruni, R. (eds.) TGC 2007. LNCS, vol. 4661, pp. 30–50. Springer, Heidelberg (2007)
25. van Riemsdijk, M.B., Hennicker, R., Wirsing, M., Schroeder, A.: Service specification and matchmaking using description logic: An approach based on institutions [extended version]. Technical Report 0802, LMU Munich (2008)

System Demonstration of Spiral: Generator for High-Performance Linear Transform Libraries

Yevgen Voronenko, Franz Franchetti, Frédéric de Mesmay, and Markus Püschel*

Department of Electrical and Computer Engineering
Carnegie Mellon University, 5000 Forbes Ave, Pittsburgh, PA 15213, USA
{yvoronen, franzf, fdemesma, pueschel}@ece.cmu.edu

Abstract. We demonstrate Spiral, a domain-specific library generation system. Spiral generates high performance source code for linear transforms (such as the discrete Fourier transform and many others) directly from a problem specification. The key idea underlying Spiral is to perform automatic reasoning and optimizations at a high abstraction level using the mathematical, declarative domain-specific languages SPL and $\sum$-SPL and a rigorous rewriting framework. Optimization includes various forms of parallelization. Even though Spiral provides complete automation, its generated libraries often run faster than any existing hand-written code.

Keywords: Linear transform, discrete Fourier transform, FFT, domain-specific language, program generation, rewriting, matrix algebra, automatic performance tuni, multithreading, SIMD vector instructions.

1 Introduction

The advent of mainstream parallel platforms has made the development of high performance numerical libraries extremely difficult. Practically every off-the-shelf computer has multiple processor cores, SIMD vector instruction sets, and a deep memory hierarchy. Compilers cannot optimize numerical code efficiently, since the necessary code transformations often require domain knowledge that the compiler does not have. Consequently, the library developer is forced to write multithreaded code, use vector instructions through C language extensions or assembly code, and tune the algorithm to the memory hierarchy. Often, this process is repeated once a new platform is released. Automating high performance library development is a goal at the core of computer science.

Some advances have been made towards this goal, in particular in two performance-critical domains: linear algebra and linear transforms. One example is FFTW [1], a widely used library for the discrete Fourier transform (DFT). FFTW partially automates the development process, by using a special "codelet generator" [2] to generate code for small fixed size transform functions, called "codelets". However, all top-level recursive routines are still hand-developed and vectorization and parallelization are also performed manually.

---

* This work was supported by NSF through awards 0325687, 0702386, by DARPA through the DOI grant NBCH1050009 and the ARO grant W911NF0710416, and by an Intel grant.

J. Meseguer and G. Roşu (Eds.): AMAST 2008, LNCS 5140, pp. 407–412, 2008.

We demonstrate Spiral, a system which takes domain-specific source code generation to the next level, by *completely* automating the library development process. Spiral enables the generation of the *entire* library, similar to FFTW, including the necessary codelet generator, given only a specification (in a domain-specific language) of the recursive algorithms that the library should use. Further, the library is vectorized and parallelized for highest performance. These capabilities extend our earlier work [3].

Even though Spiral achieves complete automation, the runtime performance of its generated libraries is often faster than any existing human-written code.

The framework underlying Spiral is built on two mathematical domain-specific languages, called SPL [4] (Signal Processing Language) and $\sum$-SPL [5]. These languages are derived from matrix algebra and used to represent and manipulate algorithms using rewriting systems. The rewriting is used to generate algorithm variants, to automatically parallelize [6] and vectorize [7] algorithms, and to discover and generate the library structure [8]. The latter includes the set of mutually recursive functions that comprise the library, and the set of required codelets.

2 Background

A linear transform is a matrix-vector multiplication $y = Mx$, where x, y are the input and output vectors, respectively, and M is the fixed transform matrix. For example, the DFT is given by the matrix $M = \mathbf{DFT}_n = \left[\omega_n^{k\ell}\right]_{0 \le k, \ell < n}$, with complex $\omega_n = e^{-2\pi i/n}$.

SPL. Many fast Fourier transform algorithms (FFTs) exist, and can be represented as factorizations of $\mathbf{DFT}_n$ into products of structured sparse matrices [9]. This representation forms the core of Spiral's domain-specific mathematical language SPL [4]. For example, the Cooley-Tukey FFT is a divide-and-conquer algorithm that for $n = km$ can be written as

$$\mathbf{DFT}_n = (\mathbf{DFT}_k \otimes I_m)D_{n,m}(I_k \otimes \mathbf{DFT}_m)L_k^n. \tag{1}$$

Evaluating $y = \mathbf{DFT}_n x$ by successively multiplying x with factors of (1) reduces the overall arithmetic cost. Above, I_n is the $n \times n$ identity matrix, $D_{n,m}$ is a diagonal matrix, and L_k^n is a stride permutation matrix, which precise form is irrelevant here. Most important in this formalism is the tensor (or Kronecker) product $\otimes$ of matrices, defined as

$$A \otimes B = [a_{k\ell} \cdot B]_{k,\ell}, \quad A = [a_{k\ell}]_{k,\ell}.$$

Tensor products of the form $A \otimes I$ and $I \otimes A$ are special, because they naturally express loops with independent iterations and special data layouts.

(1) is called a *breakdown rule* in Spiral [3], it is best understood by visualizing the nonzero pattern of the factor matrices, done here for $k = m = 4$. In the leftmost factor, all the 1st, 2nd, ..., mth, entries of the small diagonals constitute one $\mathbf{DFT}_k$, respectively.

$$\tag{2}$$

Recursive application of (1) for a two-power $n = 2^t$ yields an $O(n \log(n))$ algorithm, terminated by $\mathbf{DFT}_2$, which is computed by definition. For prime sizes other FFT algorithms are needed. Note that SPL is declarative: only the structure of the algorithm is described; not how exactly it is computed.

$\sum$-**SPL** . In order to generate looped code, we developed a lower-level representation, called $\sum$-SPL [5]. $\sum$-SPL like SPL is a structured sparse matrix factorization, however, it breaks down tensor products into iterative sums of products of smaller, rectangular matrices. Iterative sums serve as explicit representation of loops.

For example, if A is $n \times n$:

$$I_k \otimes A = \begin{bmatrix} A \\ & \ddots \\ & & A \end{bmatrix} = \begin{bmatrix} A \\ & \\ & \end{bmatrix} + \cdots + \begin{bmatrix} \\ & \\ & A \end{bmatrix}$$

$$= S_0 \, A \, G_0 + \cdots + S_{k-1} \, A \, G_{k-1} = \sum_{j=0}^{k-1} S_j \, A \, G_j,$$

$$G_j = \begin{bmatrix} & I_n & \end{bmatrix} \quad (I_n \text{ in } j\text{th block}), \quad S_j = G_j^\top .$$

$\sum$-SPL admits several optimizations not possible with SPL, in particular it enables the merging of tensor products (loops) with permutations, which converts them into a readdressing of the input data.

3   Library Generation

The library generation process in Spiral is shown in Fig. 1. The input to the system is a set of transforms and associated breakdown rules. For example, it could be just $\mathbf{DFT}_n$ and (1). The process has two stages, library structure and library target, which we explain next. The output is the library implemented in C++.

Library structure. One main goal of the *library structure* stage is to determine the minimum set of mutually recursive functions that computes the given transforms. We call this set the *recursion step closure*, and each function is called a *recursion step*. Each recursion step is represented by a $\sum$-SPL formula. The transform specification, e.g., $\mathbf{DFT}_n$, is also a (trivial) $\sum$-SPL formula and a recursion step.

This stage generates formulas and optimizes them using rewrite rules, which among other things perform loop merging, vectorization and parallelization.

When a breakdown rule is applied to a transform it decomposes the transform into smaller transforms. Even if the smaller transforms are still DFTs (as in (1)), the $\sum$-SPL optimizations will merge these DFTs with additional operations (e.g. strided data loads and stores, scaling, etc.) thus changing the interface and creating new types of recursion steps. Breakdown rules applied to these new steps may spawn others. This process is continued until we find a finite set of mutually recursive recursion steps. This set is the recursion step closure.

As an example, Fig. 2 shows the recursion step closure generated for the DFT with breakdown rule (1). Four recursion steps are needed and the arrows capture the associated call graph.

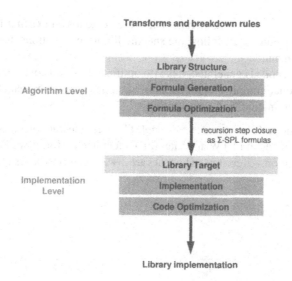

Fig. 1. Library generation process in Spiral

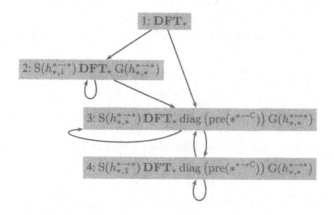

Fig. 2. Recursion step closure for $\mathbf{DFT}_n$, generated from (1), represented as a call graph. For readability, we replace all parameters of $\sum$-SPL formulas by "*".

In addition to the general size recursive implementations of recursion steps (which call other recursion steps), the library structure stage also generates fixed size *base case* implementations. Each such base case is equivalent to a codelet in FFTW. The number of recursion step types with base cases is equivalent to the number of codelet types in FFTW. As Spiral discovers the codelet types automatically, it readily obtains the codelet generator, which becomes a call to the $\sum$-SPL compiler on the appropriate $\sum$-SPL formula with the known transform size inserted.

Library target. In this stage, the recursion step closure and $\sum$-SPL implementations are mapped to the target language C++. This stage must take care of generating auxiliary initialization code, which allocates temporary buffers, precomputes the necessary constants, and more.

The system can be used to generate code which extends an existing library. In this case, the auxiliary code must follow the specific library conventions, for example, for memory management.

After the initial code is generated, it is also optimized using a combination of rewrite rules and traditional compiler optimizations, such as constant propagation, common subexpression elimination, and loop unrolling.

Performance. The performance of two example libraries, generated using Spiral, is shown in Fig. 3 and compared to FFTW and Intel IPP (Integrated Performance Primitives) on a dual-core workstation. All compared libraries are 2-way vectorized and support threading,

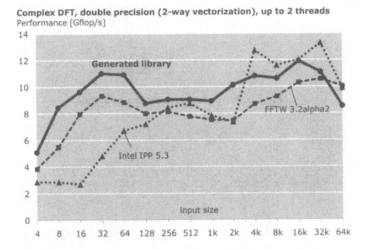

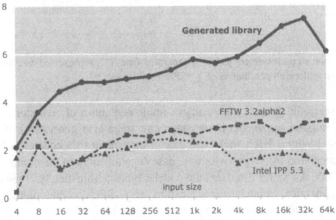

Fig. 3. Performance of automatically generated libraries compared to hand-written libraries (FFTW uses generated code for small fixed size transforms). Double precision, using SSE2 and up to 2 threads. Platform: dual-core 3 GHz Intel Xeon 5160 with 4 MB of L2 cache running Linux. Generated libraries are in C++ and are compiled with Intel C/C++ Compiler 10.1.

and the plots show maximum performance between 1 and 2 threads. While both FFTW and IPP achieve excellent performance for the DFT, they are less optimized for the less widely used DCT-2. Library generation, on the other hand, automates the tedious implementation and optimization process, and thus achieves uniform performance across a wide variety of transforms. The generated DFT library achieves a speedup over IPP and FFTW, due to using a specialized variant of (1) which reduces the number of vector shuffles. The generated DCT-2 library uses a "native" DCT-2 algorithm, instead of the suboptimal, but easy to implement, conversion to the DFT, used in FFTW and probably in IPP.

4 Demonstration

We will demonstrate several key components of Spiral, including a live run of generating a fully vectorized and parallelized DCT-2 library. In detail, we will show:

- An example of formula generation and formula rewriting;
- Generation of straightline and looped code from a sample $\sum$-SPL formula;
- An example of code rewriting;
- Generation of the recursion step closure;
- Compilation of the recursion step closure into a library implementation.

5 Conclusions

Automating high performance library development is a problem at the core of computer science. We demonstrate a system that achieves this goal for the domain of linear transforms. The system is based on a set of techniques from different disciplines including linear algebra, algorithms, programming languages, generative programming, rewriting systems, and compilers. Properly applied, these techniques makes high-performance library generation feasible, efficient, and rigorous.

References

1. Frigo, M., Johnson, S.G.: The design and implementation of FFTW3. Proceedings of the IEEE 93(2), 216–231 (2005); special issue on Program Generation, Optimization, and Adaptation
2. Frigo, M.: A fast Fourier transform compiler. In: Proc. PLDI, pp. 169–180 (1999)
3. Püschel, M., Moura, J.M.F., Johnson, J., Padua, D., Veloso, M., Singer, B.W., Xiong, J., Franchetti, F., Gačić, A., Voronenko, Y., Chen, K., Johnson, R.W., Rizzolo, N.: SPIRAL: Code generation for DSP transforms. Proceedings of the IEEE 93(2), 232–275 (2005)
4. Xiong, J., Johnson, J., Johnson, R., Padua, D.: SPL: A language and compiler for DSP algorithms. In: Proc. PLDI, pp. 298–308 (2001)
5. Franchetti, F., Voronenko, Y., Püschel, M.: Loop merging for signal transforms. In: Proc. PLDI, pp. 315–326 (2005)
6. Franchetti, F., Voronenko, Y., Püschel, M.: FFT program generation for shared memory: SMP and multicore. In: Proc. Supercomputing (2006)
7. Franchetti, F., Voronenko, Y., Püschel, M.: A rewriting system for the vectorization of signal transforms. In: Proc. High Perf. Computing for Computational Science (VECPAR) (2006)
8. Voronenko, Y.: Library Generation for Linear Transforms. PhD thesis, Department of Electrical and Computer Engineering, Carnegie Mellon University (2008)
9. Van Loan, C.: Computational Framework of the Fast Fourier Transform. SIAM, Philadelphia (1992)

The Verification of the On-Chip COMA Cache Coherence Protocol

Thuy Duong Vu[1], Li Zhang[2], and Chris Jesshope[2]

[1] Sectie Software Engineering
[2] Computer Systems Architecture Group,
University of Amsterdam,
The Netherlands
{tdvu,zhangli,jesshope}@science.uva.nl

Abstract. This paper gives a correctness proof for the on-chip COMA cache coherence protocol that supports the Microgrid of microthreaded architecture, a multi-core architecture capable of integrating hundreds to hundreds of thousands of processors on single silicon chip. We use the Abstract State Machine (ASM) as a theoretical framework for the specification of the on-chip COMA cache coherence protocol. We show that the protocol obeys the Location Consistency model proposed by Gao and Sakar.

Keywords: on-chip COMA cache coherence protocol, verification, location consistency, Abstract State Machine.

1 Introduction

A number of computer system architecture and implementation issues as long wire delay, heat dissipation, memory synchronization, etc., have driven the computer architecture to an inevitable transition from single-core to multicore processor design. The Microgrid of microthreaded [13,3,4,12] architecture is designed to possess thousands of on-chip simple processing cores , while providing the scalable throughput both on and off chip. The microthreaded architecture could perform explicit context switch during long latency operations as memory accesses without wasting the processor time.

The shift from off-chip to on-chip multiprocessing allows the cache coherence to operate at a higher clock rate. In addition, the capability of tolerating long memory access latency in the microthreaded architecture helps us revive a paradigm used in earlier parallel computers, such as the Kendal Square KSR1 [5]. We introduce a Cache Only Memory Architecture (COMA) [8] for the on-chip cache system. In COMA, all the memory modules can be considered as large caches, called Attraction Memory (AM). Data is stored by cacheline but the line has no fixed location to find. Similar to COMA, in on-chip COMA, a certain piece of data can be replicated and migrated dynamically between caches. A main difference between the on-chip COMA and traditional COMA is that the traditional COMA system will hold all data in the system without a backing

J. Meseguer and G. Roşu (Eds.): AMAST 2008, LNCS 5140, pp. 413–429, 2008.

store, while the on-chip COMA has a backing store for data off chip, where an interface is provided for storing incoming data. The readers are referred to [16] for more detail.

Although the on-chip COMA has some similar property and structure as the traditional COMA, the underlying consistency models and supporting cache coherence protocol are largely different. To balance the programming complexity and execution efficiency, a number of memory consistency models [11] had been proposed before. The most commonly used memory consistency model is the *sequential consistency* (SC) model given by Lamport [15]. In this model, memory operations performed by the processors are *serialized*. Since SC requires all the processors to observe the write requests in some unique order, thus the atomic broadcast communication is generally required for implementing SC, which may severely impair the cache throughput and execution efficiency. Furthermore, the assumption of the universal order poses fundamental obstacles to defining a scalable and efficient view of the memory consistency in computer system. A number of more relaxed consistency models of the SC model such as *release consistency, lazy release consistency, entry consistency* and *dag consistency* have been proposed in [8,14,1,2]. *Location Consistency* (LC) proposed by Gao and Sakar in [6,7], is considered the weakest memory model to date. In the LC model, memory operations performed by processors need not be seen in the same order by all processors, and therefore, there can be many multiple legal values for a memory location at the same time. The on-chip COMA cache coherence protocol is designed to obey this consistency model. In its cache system, multiple legal values of a memory location are stored in different caches. This reduces the consistency-related traffic in the network of the cache coherence protocol significantly, since a read operation can read a legal value from a local cache or from the main memory (in the case that there are no legal values available in the caches).

In this paper, we give a correctness proof for the design of the on-chip COMA cache coherence protocol. We show that our protocol does not rely on the memory coherence assumption, and therefore, it does not satisfy the SC and SC-derived models. However, it obeys the LC model of Gao and Sakar. Indeed, our protocol is strictly stronger than the LC model. We will use the *Abstract State Machine* (ASM) [9,10] as a theoretical framework for the specification and verification of our protocol.

2   Location Consistency

In this section, we follow Gao and Sakar [6,7] to define the location consistency with respect to the microthreaded architecture.

2.1   Programming Model

Our programming model consists of two memory operations and two synchronization operations whose descriptions are as follows:

Memory read: If thread T_i needs to read a value from memory location L, it performs a $\mathrm{read}(T_i, L)$ operation, which is also represented by the notation $\mathrm{read}\, L$ in thread T_i's instruction sequence.

Memory write: If thread T_i needs to write the value v on location L then it must wait for all read operations issued by T_i and its subthreads on location L to be complete and then performs a $\mathrm{write}(T_i, v, L)$ operation, which is also represented by the notation $L := v$ in thread T_i's instruction sequence.

Thread creation: If thread T_i needs to create a family of threads then it must wait for all write operations issued by T_i and its subthreads to be complete and then performs a $\mathrm{create}(T_i, \mathcal{F})$ operation where $\mathcal{F}$ is a sequence of threads. This operation is represented by the notation $\mathrm{create}(\mathcal{F})$ in T_i's instruction sequence. We note that every thread T_j of $\mathcal{F}$ is a *subthread* of T_i, and all subthreads of T_j are also subthreads of T_i.

Barrier synchronization: If thread T_i needs to identify the termination of a specified family of threads, it performs a $\mathrm{sync}(T_i, \mathcal{F})$ operation where $\mathcal{F}$ is the specified family. This operation is represented by the notation $\mathrm{sync}(\mathcal{F})$ in thread T_i's instruction sequence. The subsequent instructions after $\mathrm{sync}(\mathcal{F})$ in thread T_i must wait until all write operations of the threads in $\mathcal{F}$ and their subthreads are complete.

2.2 State Update for a Memory Location

In the LC model, the state of a memory location is a partial ordered set of memory and synchronization operations. Given a memory location L, the state of L is a *partially ordered multiset* (pomset) $\mathrm{state}(L) = (S, \prec)$, where S is a multiset and $\prec$ is a partial order on S. Each element of S is a memory operation or a synchronization involving location L. Two elements in multiset S can have the same value, however, they can be distinguished by the partial order. For two operations $e_1, e_2 \in S$ such that $(e_1, e_2) \in \prec$, we say that e_1 is a *predecessor* of e_2. Initially, the state of a memory location is the empty set. For an operation e, we denote $\mathrm{thread}(e)$ as the thread involved in operation e, i.e. $\mathrm{thread}(e) = T_i$ where $e \in \{\mathrm{write}(T_i, v, L), \mathrm{read}(T_i, v, L), \mathrm{create}(T_i, \mathcal{F}), \mathrm{sync}(T_i, \mathcal{F})\}$.

The state of a memory location L is updated when a memory operation on the location L or a synchronization operation is performed. This new operation is inserted to the current multiset of the state. The *precedence relation* (the partial order $\prec$) is updated by the following rules:

1. All operations in the multiset from the same thread with the new operation are considered as the predecessors of that new operation.
2. The thread creation operation creating the thread containing the new operation is a predecessor of that new operation.
3. If this new operation is a barrier synchronization operation then all operations issued by the threads involved in the barrier synchronization operation are predecessors of that new operation.

Let L be a memory location with the current state $(S, \prec)$. The state update of L with operation e is defined as follows. $S:=S \cup \{e\}$; and moreover:

$$\prec := \mathtt{trans}(\; \prec \cup \{(e', e) \,|\, e' \in S \wedge e' \neq e : \mathtt{thread}(e') = \mathtt{thread}(e)\}$$
$$\cup \{(e', e) \,|\, e' \in S : e' = \mathtt{create}(T_i, \mathcal{F}') \wedge \mathtt{thread}(e) \in \mathcal{F}'\}$$
$$\cup \{(e', e) \,|\, e = \mathtt{sync}(T_j, \mathcal{F}) \wedge e' \in S : \mathtt{thread}(e') \in \mathcal{F}\})$$

The function $\mathtt{trans}$ is to maintain the transitive property of the precedence relation $\prec$: $\mathtt{trans}(\prec) = \prec \cup \{(e_1, e_2) \,|\, \exists e_1, e_2, e' \in S : (e_1, e') \in \prec \wedge (e', e_2) \in \prec\}$.

2.3   State Observability for a Memory Location

The state of a memory location in the LC model can be observed via read operations. Let L be a memory location with $\mathtt{state}(L) = (S, \prec)$, and $r \in S$ a read operation on L. The **most recent predecessor write** with respect to r is a write operation $w \prec r$ such that there is no other write operation $w' \in S$ satisfying $w \prec w' \prec r$. The read operation r reads a **legal** value v if there is a write operation w such that $w = \mathtt{write}(T, v, L)$, and

1. w is the most recent predecessor write with respect to r, or
2. r and w are unordered, i.e. $(w, r) \notin \prec$.

The set $V(r)$ is the set of all legal values returned by r.

We now recall the definition of the Location Consistency from [7] as follows: A multiprocessor system is **location consistent** if, for any execution of a program on the system, the operations of the execution are the same as those for some location consistent execution of the program; and moreover, for any read operation R with target location L of any execution of a program on the system, R always returns a legal value.

3   The On-Chip COMA Cache Coherence Protocol

This section briefly introduces the on-chip COMA cache coherence protocol that supports our programming model. Threads are distributed to processors for their execution. One or more threads can be executed on a processor. Each processor may cache values for many memory locations in a cache consisting of a number of cachelines. The value of a memory location is cached in a cacheline. Note that the values of a memory location stored in different caches can be different, since they are not updated at the same time. For simplicity, we assume that a cache is connected to one processor, and a cacheline stores the value of one memory location only.

Thus in our protocol, caches are connected in a directed ring network which has a *directory* to hold the information about all the data available on the ring. The design of the ring networks is based on the properties of the microthreaded architecture. Due to its capability of tolerating long latency operations, the microgrid has less requirement on latency and higher requirement

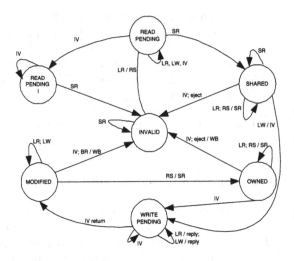

Fig. 1. The on-chip COMA cache coherence protocol

on bandwidth. The low cost ring structure, which can easily broadcast data and invalidation requests, meets both the requirement of COMA and the microgrid CMP. Details can be found in [16]. Only the directory has the access to the main memory. Hence, any loading data from or writing back to the main memory must be handled through this node. The on-chip COMA cache coherence protocol is based on MOSI variations in which a cacheline have four main states MODIFIED, OWNER, SHARED and INVALID, and three temporary states READ PENDING, READ PENDING I and WRITE PENDING (see Fig. 1) whose descriptions are given below:

- INVALID: If a cacheline is in an INVALID state then it has no valid data;
- MODIFIED: If a cacheline is in a MODIFIED state, it has the exclusiveness of the data.
- OWNER: If a cacheline is in an OWNER state, it has the ownership of the data, and there can be another cacheline in the system that has a valid data;
- SHARED: If a cacheline is in a SHARED state, it has a valid data but no ownership of the data.
- READ PENDING: If a cacheline is in a READ PENDING state, it is waiting for a valid data to be loaded;
- READ PENDING I: If a cacheline is in a READ PENDING I state, it has received an invalidation request while waiting for a valid data to be loaded. When it gets a valid data, its state will become INVALID;
- WRITE PENDING: If a cacheline is in a WRITE PENDING state, it is waiting for the exclusiveness of the data.

A cache can handle two kinds of requests: local requests and network requests. Local requests are memory operations issued by processors, while network requests (or messages) occur during the communication between caches, and have a higher priority to be considered than local ones. When a cache receives a local request to read or write a data, it will check whether all cache entries are occupied or not. If yes, it has to eject a cacheline for loading or writing a new data. We note that since caches are connected in a directed ring, network requests can only be sent or passed to the next cache on the ring. The types of requests of the on-chip COMA cache coherence protocol are:

- LR (Local Read): the type of a read operation issued by a processor;
- LW (Local Write): the type of a write operation issued by a processor;
- RS (Remote Read to SHARED state): issued by a cache to ask for a valid data when it receives a LR request but it has no valid data;
- SR (to SHARED state) Read Reply: issued by a cache when it receives a RS request and has a valid data;
- IV (InValidation): issued by a cache when it receives a LW request. It wants to become the ownership of the data, and therefore, tries to invalidate all other data on the ring network;
- WB (Write Back to main memory): issued by a cache to write back a dirty data (whose cacheline is in a MODIFIED or OWNER state) to the main memory before the ejection of the cacheline;
- eject: issued by a cache to notice the directory that one of its cachelines in a SHARED state has been ejected.

The next section will describe the on-chip COMA cache coherence protocol in more detail.

4   The Specification of the Protocol

This section specifies the on-chip COMA cache coherence protocol in the Abstract State Machine (ASM) framework [9,10]. The protocol is considered as an ASM whose transition rules represent the behavior of the protocol.

4.1   Vocabulary

We assume the existence of a fixed set Thread of threads, a fixed set Processor of processors, a fixed set Location of memory locations, a fixed set Operation of operations, a fixed set Message of messages, and a fixed set Data of data values. The undefined value or attribute of an object is specified as undef.

For a thread T, there is an attribute proc $\in$ Processor to characterize the processor where T is distributed to. Let Type = {LR, LW, CRE, SYNC, RS, SR, IV, WB, eject}. An operation $e \in$ Operation has four attributes type $\in$ Type, thread $\in$ Thread, val $\in$ Data and loc $\in$ Location to characterize the type, the thread, the data and the memory location involved in the operation. For instance, for a write operation $e = \text{write}(T, v, L)$, $e.\text{type} = $ LW, $e.\text{thread} = T$, $e.\text{val} = v$ and $e.\text{loc} = L$.

By the assumption, for a processor there is only one cache, and vice versa. We can assume that messages are issued by processors as well. Hence, a message

$m \in$ Message has three attributes type $\in$ Type, val $\in$ Data and loc $\in$ Location to characterize the type, the data and the memory location involved in the message. Moreover, it has an attribute source $\in$ Processor to characterize the processor who originally sends out the request. We denote the empty message as noMess. For each processor P and for each location $l \in$ Location, the pair (P, l) represents a unique cacheline whose description is given by the following functions:

- state$(P, l) \in \{$undef, INVALID, MODIFIED, OWNER, READ PENDING, READ PENDING I, WRITE PENDING$\}$ to indicate the current state of the cacheline (P, l). Initially, state$(P, l) =$ undef;
- cacheValid?(P, l) to indicate whether the cacheline (P, l) has a valid or not. Initially, cacheValid?$(P, l) =$ false;
- cacheVal(P, l) to indicate the value stored in the cacheline (P, l). Initially, cacheVal$(P, l) =$ undef;
- cacheDirty?(P, l) to indicate whether the cacheline (P, l) holds a dirty data or not. Initially, cacheDirty?$(P, l) =$ false;
- Eject$(P, l) = \{$state$(P, l) :=$ undef, cacheDirty?$(P, l) :=$ false, cacheValid?(P, l) := false, cacheVal(P, l) : $=$ undef, state$(P, P.$curOp.loc$) :=$ INVALID$\}$ to evict the cacheline (P, l) from the cache of P;
- Invalidate$(P, l) = \{$state$(P, l) :=$ INVALID, cacheDirty?$(P, l) :=$ false, cacheValid?$(P, l) :=$ false, cacheVal$(P, l) :=$ undef$\}$ to invalidate the cacheline (P, l).

A processor $P \in$ Processor has the following attributes:

- cacheOccupied? $\in \{$true, false$\}$ to determine whether all cache entries of P are occupied or not, monitored by the execution environment;
- id $\in \mathbb{N}$ to indicate the index of P;
- neighbor $\in$ Processor $\cup \{$dir$\}$ to indicate the next node of P on the ring network;
- ejectee $\in$ Location to indicate the location to be ejected when all cache entries of P are occupied, monitored by the execution environment satisfying the condition that state$(P, P.$ejectee$) \neq$ undef;
- Return $\in$ Data $\times$ Location to return a read value asked by a LR request;
- curMess $\in$ Message to indicate the current network request of P;
- curOp $\in$ Operation to indicate the current operation performed by P, monitored by the execution environment;
- nextOp $\in$ Operation to indicate the next operation performed by P, monitored by the execution environment.

The notation dir denotes the directory which has the following attributes:

- MMVal : Location $\rightarrow$ Data to determine the value of a location stored in the main memory;
- neighbor $\in$ Processor to indicate the next node of dir on the ring network;
- curMess $\in$ Message to indicate the current network request of dir;

- cacheCounter : Location $\to \mathbb{N}$ to determine the numbers of valid caches for a memory location on the ring network. Initially, for all $l \in$ Location, dir.cacheCounter(l) = 0. This counter is updated as follows. When the directory receives an IV request, meaning that someone wants to become the ownership of the data, the counter is set to 1. When the directory receives a RS (or SR) request from (or for) a processor whose cacheline is not in READ PENDING I state, meaning that someone wants to have a valid data, the counter is increased by 1. When the directory receives a WB (or eject) request, meaning that someone who has a valid data has been ejected, the counter is decreased by 1.

There are also two auxiliary functions needed for the specification of the protocol:

- SendMess(P, messType, val, l) = {if messType = SR then mess.source := P.curMess.source else mess.source = proc, mess.type := messType, mess.val := val, mess.loc := l, P.neighbor.curMess := mess, P.curMess := noMess} to send a message from node P to its next node (P.neighbor) on the ring;
- PassMess(P) = {P.neighbor.curMess = P.curMess, P.curMess := noMess} to pass the current message of node P to its next node (P.neighbor).

4.2 Transition Rules

The behavior of the on-chip COMA protocol is represented as an ASM *module* whose *transition rules* are given in Table 1, Table 2, Table 3, Table 4, Table 5, Table 6 and Table 8. We will sometimes shorten macros such as self.curMess| cacheOccupied?|ejectee|neighbor|curOp|nextOp|id|MMVal|cacheCounter by curMess, cacheOccupied?, ejectee, neighbor, curOp, nextOp, id, MMVal and cacheCounter.

Table 1. Transition rule responding LR requests

```
if curMess = noMess & curOp.type = LR then
  if state(self, curOp.loc) = undef then
    if cacheOccupied? then
      if cacheDirty?(self, ejectee) and neighbor.curMess = noMess then
        SendMess(self, WB, cacheVal(self, ejectee), ejectee)
        Eject(self, ejectee)
      if state(self, ejectee) = SHARED and neighbor.curMess = noMess then
        SendMess(self, eject, cacheVal(self, ejectee), ejectee)
        Eject(self, ejectee)
      if state(self, ejectee) = INVALID then
        Eject(self, ejectee)
    else state(self, curOp.loc) := INVALID
  else
    if cacheValid?(self, curOp.loc) then Return(cacheVal(self, curOp.loc), curOp.loc)
    if state(self, curOp.loc) = INVALID then
      if neighbor.curMess = noMess then
        SendMess(self, RS, _, curOp.loc)
        state(self, curOp.loc) := READ PENDING
        curOp := nextOp
    else curOp := nextOp
```

Table 2. Transition rule responding LW requests

```
if curMess = noMess & curOp.type = LW then
  if state(self, curOp.loc) = undef then
    if cacheOccupied? then
      if cacheDirty?(self, ejectee) and neighbor.curMess = noMess then
        SendMess(self, WB, cacheVal(self, ejectee), ejectee)
        Eject(self, ejectee)
      if state(self, ejectee) = SHARED and neighbor.curMess = noMess then
        SendMess(self, eject, cacheVal(self, ejectee), ejectee)
        Eject(self, ejectee)
      if state(self, ejectee) = INVALID then
        Eject(self, ejectee)
    else state(self, curOp.loc) := INVALID
  else
    cacheVal(self, curOp.loc) := opVal
    cacheValid?(self, curOp.loc) := true
    if state(self, curOp.loc) = WRITE PENDING then curOp := nextOp
    else if neighbor.curMess = noMess then
      SendMess(self, IV, _, curOp.loc)
      state(self, curOp.loc) := WRITE PENDING
      curOp := nextOp
```

With reference to Table 1, we first explain how a processor P reacts when it receives a LR (Local Read) request. As mentioned earlier, network requests have higher priority to be considered than the local ones. Thus, this local read request is only considered in the case that there is no network request available for P, i.e. P.curMess = noMess. If there is no cache entry set up for the memory location involved in the request yet (state(P, P.curOp.loc) = undef), then P first checks whether all cache entries are occupied or not. If yes (P.cacheOccupied? = true), P has to eject a cacheline determined by the execution environment (P.ejectee with state(P, P.ejectee) $\neq$ undef). If the ejectee has a dirty data then this data is written back to the main memory by sending a WB (Write Back) message to the directory. If the ejectee has a valid (but not dirty) data then P also sends out a eject message to notice the directory. If the ejectee is in a pending state then the removal is also pending. P then removes the ejectee, and sets up another cacheline for the location concerned (state(P, P.curOp.loc) = INVALID). If this cacheline has a valid data, then P just sends back the value stored in the cacheline. The read operation is considered *complete*. If it has no valid data and its state is INVALID, then P sends a RS request to other processors to ask for a valid data.

In Table 2, we now explain how a processor P reacts when it receives a LW (Local Write) request. Similar to the previous case, this request is only considered by the processor and when no network request is available. Moreover, P also has to set up a cacheline for writing the new data as in Table 1 in the case that there is no place for that yet. If there is already an available cacheline, P just overwrites the data. If the cacheline is not waiting for the exclusiveness of the data (i.e. it is not in a WRITE PENDING state), P then sends out a IV request to other processors to ask for the exclusiveness of the data. The state of the cacheline becomes WRITE PENDING. We impose the following condition on all write operations to avoid *useless* reads for a thread:

Table 3. Transition rule responding RS requests

```
if curMess.type = RS then
    if curMess.source = self and cacheValid?(self, curMess.loc) then
        Return(cacheVal(self, curMess.loc), curMess.loc)
        if state(self, curMess.loc) = READ PENDING then state(self, curMess.loc) := SHARED
        if state(self, curMess.loc) = READ PENDING I then Invalidate(self, curMess.loc)
        curMess := noMess
    else if neighbor.curMess = noMess then
        if self = dir then
            if cacheCounter(curMess.loc) = 0 then
                SendMess(self, SR, MMVal(curMess.loc), curMess.loc)
            else PassMess(curMess)
            if state(curMess.source, curMess.loc) = READ PENDING then
                cacheCounter(curMess.loc) := cacheCounter(curMess.loc) + 1
        else if cacheValid?(self, curMess.loc) then
            SendMess(self, SR, curMess.val, curMess.loc)
            if state(self, curMess.loc) = MODIFIED then state(self, curMess.loc) := OWNER
        else PassMess(curMess)
```

Table 4. Transition rule responding SR requests

```
if curMess.type = SR then
    if curMess.source = self then Return(curMess.val, curMess.loc)
        if state(self, curMess.loc) = READ PENDING then
            state(self, curMess.loc) := SHARED
            cacheVal(self, curMess.loc) := curMess.val
            cacheValid?(self, curMess.loc) := true
        if state(self, curMess.loc) = READ PENDING I then Invalidate(self, curMess.loc)
        curMess := noMess
    else if neighbor.curMess = noMess then
        if self = dir and state(curMess.source, curMess.loc) = READ PENDING then
            cacheCounter(curMess.loc) := cacheCounter(curMess.loc) + 1
        else if state(self, curMess.loc) ∈ {READ PENDING, READ PENDING I} then
            cacheVal(self, curMess.loc) := curMess.val
            cacheValid?(self, curMess.loc) := true
        PassMess(curMess)
```

Condition 1. *For every processor P, if the current operation of P is a write operation (P.curOp $= w$) then all the read operations performed by w.thread and its subthreads on the same location (w.loc) must be complete.*

Table 3 presents the transition rules for a node P on the ring network when it receives a RS (Remote Read to Shared state) request. If P originally sent out the request and has a valid data then P just sends back the value stored in its cache. If the cacheline concerned is currently in a READ PENDING state then its state becomes SHARED; otherwise it will be invalidated. All the read operations performed by P on the same location are considered *complete*. If P is the directory and there are no caches on the ring network having a valid data (P.cacheCounter(curMess.loc) $= 0$) then it sends out the value stored in the main memory together with the read reply SR. The counter of valid caches for the location involved in the message is increased by 1 if the cacheline who requested the data is in a READ PENDING state. If P is a processor who has a valid data then it sends out the data together with the reply SR. The state of the cacheline concerned is set to OWNER if it is MODIFIED in the current step. In the remaining cases, it just passes the message to the next node on the ring.

Table 5. Transition rule responding IV requests

```
if curMess.type = IV then
  if curMess.source = self then
    if state(self, curMess.loc) = WRITE PENDING then
        state(self, curMess.loc) := MODIFIED
        cacheDirty?(self, curMess.loc) := true
    curMess := noMess
  else if neighbor.curMess = noMess then
    if state(self, curMess.loc) = WRITE PENDING and id < curMess.source.id then
      Invalidate(self, curMess.loc)
    else if state(self, curMess.loc) = READ PENDING then
      state(self, curMess.loc) = READ PENDING I
    else if state(self, curMess.loc) ∉ {undef, READ PENDING I} then
      Invalidate(self, curMess.loc)
    else if self = dir then cacheCounter(curMess.loc) := 1
    PassMess(curMess)
```

Table 6. Transition rule responding WB requests

```
if curMess.type = WB then
  if self = dir then
    MMVal(curMess.loc) := curMess.val
    cacheCounter(curMess.loc) := cacheCounter(curMess.loc) − 1
    curMess := noMess
  else if neighbor.curMess = noMess then
    if state(self, curMess.loc) ∈ {READ PENDING, READ PENDING I} then
      cacheVal(self, curMess.loc) := curMess.val
      cacheValid?(self, curMess.loc) := true
    PassMess(curMess)
```

In Table 4, transition rules reacting SR (to Shared state Read Reply) requests for a node P are given. If P is waiting for this reply then it just sends back the data involved in the reply. The state of the cacheline concerned becomes SHARED if it was READ PENDING, and becomes INVALID otherwise. All the read operations performed by P on the same location are considered *complete*. If P is waiting for a valid data (state(self, curMess.loc) ∈ {READ PENDING, READ PENDING I}), then P just overwrites the data. If P is the directory and the cacheline requested this reply is in a READ PENDING state, then the counter of valid caches for the memory location involved in the message is increased by 1. P then passes the message to the next node on the ring network.

Table 5 presents transition rules reacting IV (Invalidation) requests for a node P. If P originally sent out the request and is waiting for the exclusiveness of the data then it has the exclusiveness of the data. The state of the cacheline concerned becomes MODIFIED. All the write operations performed by P on the same location are considered *complete*. If P did not sent out the request but it is also waiting for the exclusiveness of the data then a *racing situation* occurs. In this case, we compare the indexes of P and the processor who originally sent out the request. If P has a smaller index then it has to give up the exclusiveness of the data. The state of the cacheline concerned becomes INVALID. If P is waiting for a valid data, then the state of the cacheline concerned becomes READ PENDING I. In the remaining defined states, the state is reset to INVALID. Finally, if P is the directory then the counter of valid caches for the location involved in the message is reset to 1.

Table 7. Transition rule responding `Eject` messages

```
if curMess.type = eject then
    if self = dir then
        cacheCounter(curMess.loc) := cacheCounter(curMess.loc) − 1
        curMess := noMess
    else if neighbor.curMess = noMess then
        if state(self, curMess.loc) ∈ {READ PENDING, READ PENDING I} then
            cacheVal(self, curMess.loc) := curMess.val
            cacheValid?(self, curMess.loc) := true
        PassMess(curMess)
```

Table 8. Transition rules responding `create` and `sync` operations

```
if curMess = noMess & curOp = create(F) then curOp := nextOp
if curMess = noMess & curOp = sync(F) then curOp := nextOp
```

With reference to Table 6, we explain how a node P reacts when it receives a `WB` (Write Back to the main memory) request. If P is the directory, then P updates the memory value with the data involved in the message. The counter of valid caches for the location concerned is decreased by 1. If P is waiting for a valid data, then P also updates the cached value with the data value involved in the `WB` message. The state of the cacheline concerned remains the same. P then passes the message to the next node on the ring. Similarly, Table 7 presents transition rules for a node P when it receives a `eject` message. The only difference between the two tables is that in Table 7, P does not update the value stored in the main memory.

In Table 8, we provide transition rules for a processor P in the case that its current operation is a thread creation or a synchronization operation. We impose the following conditions to ensure that these operations are treated in the right order.

Condition 2. *1. For every processor P, if the current operation of P is a creation operation (P.curOp $= c$) then all the write operations performed by the creating thread c.thread and its subthreads must be complete.*

2. For every processor P, if the current operation of P is a synchronization operation (P.curOp $= \text{sync}(F)$) then all the write operations performed by the threads in F and their subthreads must be complete.

5   The On-Chip COMA Cache Coherence Protocol Obeys LC

In this section, we show that the on-chip COMA cache coherence protocol obeys the LC model, i.e. a read operation r always returns a value belonging to the set $V(r)$ defined as in Section 2.

By the ASM Lipari Guide [10], we lose no generality by proving correctness of an arbitrary linearization of a run of a distributed ASM. Hence, let ρ be a linearization of an arbitrary distributed run of the on-chip COMA cache coherence protocol, and let $\prec_m$ be the linear order on the moves of ρ. We adapt the definition of state update for a memory location in Section 2.2 as follows. When the current operation of a processor P concerning with a memory location L is updated by a move $P.\text{curOp} := P.\text{nextOp}$ in ρ, the state of memory location L is updated as $S := S \cup \{P.\text{curOp}\}$. We say that:

1. A processor P performs a read r at a move P_r if $P.\text{curOp} = r$;
2. A processor P completes a read r and reads value v for r at a move C_r if $\text{cacheValid?}(P, r.\text{loc})$ at P_r, $C_r = P_r$ and $v = \text{cacheVal}(P, r.\text{loc})$, or C_r is the first move after P_r at which $P.\text{curMess.source} = P$, $P.\text{curMess.loc} = r.\text{loc}$, $P.\text{curMess.type} = \text{RS}$ and $v = \text{cacheVal}(P, r.\text{loc})$; or $P.\text{curMess.type} = \text{SR}$ and $v = P.\text{curMess.val}$;
3. A processor P performs a write w at a move P_w if $P.\text{curOp} = w$;
4. A processor P completes any write w at a move C_w if it is the first move after P_w at which $P.\text{curMess.source} = P$, $P.\text{curMess.loc} = w.\text{loc}$ and $P.\text{curMess.type} = \text{IV}$;
5. A processor P performs a thread creation c at a move P_c if $P.\text{curOp} = c$;
6. A processor P performs a synchronization s at a move P_s if $P.\text{curOp} = s$.

Lemma 1. *Let w be a write operation, and o a memory operation on a location L satisfying that $w \prec o$, and w and o are not issued by the same thread. Then w must be complete before the execution of o, i.e. $C_w \prec_m P_o$.*

Proof. Since $w \prec o$, $w.\text{thread} \neq o.\text{thread}$ and by the definition of state update for a memory location in Section 2.2, we consider two possibilities:

1. There is an operation $c = \text{create}(T, \mathcal{F})$ such that $w.\text{thread} = T$ and $w \prec c \prec o$. Let P_w, P_c and P_o be the moves at which w, c and o are performed in ρ, respectively. Then $P_w \prec_m P_c \prec_m P_o$. It follows from Transition rule in Table 8 and Condition 2 that w must be complete before the next operation of c is performed. Hence, w must be complete before the move O.
2. There is an operation $s = \text{sync}(T, \mathcal{F})$ such that $w.\text{thread} \in \mathcal{F}$ and $w \prec s \prec o$. Again, it follows from Transition rule in Table 8 and Condition 2 that w must be complete before the execution of o.

Lemma 2. *In ρ, let C_r be a move at which a processor P completes a read r and reads value v for r. Then v is defined.*

Proof. We prove only for the case that $P.\text{curMess.type} = \text{RS}$ at C_r. The other cases are obvious. In this case, P had no valid data at P_r, and then it sent out a RS request for a valid data (by Transition rules in Table 1). Later, this request comes back to P at move C_r. We show that $\text{cacheValid?}(P, r.\text{loc})$ at C_r. It follows from Transition rules in Table 3 that there was no processor from P to dir, and there was at least one processor from dir to P having a valid data when the RS request arrived at dir. Since the RS request comes back to P, the processors having a valid data had been ejected when the RS request arrived to them. By Transition rules in Table 1 and Table 2, they had to send a WB or a eject message to notice the directory before their ejection. These messages can update the data stored in the cacheline $(P, r.\text{loc})$, according to Transition rules in Table 6 and Table 7. Hence there exists a move M such that $P_r \prec_m M \prec_m C_r$ and cacheValid?$(P, r.\text{loc})$ at M. It follows from Transition rules in Table 2, Table 3 and Table 5 that state$(P, r.\text{loc}) \in$ {READ PENDING, READ PENDING I, WRITE PENDING} between moves P_r and C_r. This implies that cacheValid?$(P, r.\text{loc})$ at C_r.

Finally, we prove our main theorem as follows.

Theorem 1. *In ρ, let C_r be a move at which a processor P reads value v for a read operation r. Then v is a legal value returned by r.*

Proof. Let w be the write operation that writes the value v ($v = w.\text{val}$). There are two cases:

1. w and r are unordered, i.e. $(w, r) \notin \prec$. Then $v \in V(r)$.
2. w and r are ordered. It follows from Condition 1 that $w \prec r$. We show that w is the most recent predecessor write with respect to r, i.e. there does not exist a write operation w' such that $w \prec w' \prec r$. We prove by contradiction. Assume that there is a write operation w' satisfying $w \prec w' \prec r$. If w' and r are performed by the same thread, and therefore, by the same processor then $C_{w'} \prec_m P_r$, otherwise v would be written by w', not w. If w' and r are performed by different threads then by Lemma 1, we also get that $C_{w'} \prec_m P_r$. With the transition rules in Table 1, Table 3 and Table 4, we consider the following subcases:

   (a) P reads the value v from a cache. Since after the completion of w', there is still processor P that has a valid data written by w, $C_{w'} \prec_m C_w$. This is a contradiction, since w must be complete before the move $P_{w'}$ in the case that w and w' are performed by different threads (by Lemma 1), or w must be complete before or at the same time as the completion of w' in the case that w and w' are performed by the same thread (by Transition rules in Table 5).
   (b) P reads the value v from the main memory, i.e. w was written back to the main memory. Since $C_{w'} \prec P_r$, w' was also written back to the main memory when the RS request for the value v from P arrived at the directory dir. Otherwise, dir.cacheCounter$(r.\text{loc}) \geq 1$ (by Transition rules in Table 5), and therefore, P would not read the value stored in the main memory. Since $w \prec w'$, v is written by w'. This contradicts the assumption that v is written by w.

Hence, there does not exist a write operation w' satisfying $w \prec w' \prec r$, or w is the most recent predecessor write with respect to r. Thus, $v \in V(r)$.

6 Relation with the Standard Consistency Models

6.1 Our Consistency Model Is Weaker Than SC Model

Sequential consistency requires all memory operations to be executed in some sequential order, and the operations with in a process to be executed in program order. In the context of microthreaded architecture, adapting location consistency model, memory accesses to different locations do not conform to any order. To illustrate the model's discontentment of SC, we recall the standard example from [6] as follows.

Example 1. Let threads T_1 and T_2 be distributed to two different processors. T_1 first writes 1 to the shared variable x and then reads the value of the shared variable y. Symmetrically, T_2 writes 1 to the shared variable y and then read the value of x. Note that initially, $x = y = 0$.

```
X:=0; Y:=0; /* initial values */
T1:                          T2:
w1: x := 1;                  w2: y := 1;
r1: read Y;                  r2: read x;
```

Under the SC and SC-derived models, the operations from T_1 and T_2 are seen in the same order by both processors. Hence, the case that both read operations r_1 and r_2 return 0 is prohibited by the SC and SC-derived models. However, this can happen according to the on-chip COMA cache coherence protocol. Here, r_1 and r_2 can just return the initialized values of x and y which are 0.

6.2 Our Model Is Stronger Than the Strong LC Model

After proving our on-chip COMA system complies with LC model, in this section, we show that our system is not strongly LC consistent [6]. Here, we consider the following example.

Example 2. Thread T_0 creates two separate thread families consisting of T_1, T_2 and T_3, T_4 accordingly. Threads T_1 and T_2 perform write operations on location L, and T_3 and T_4 perform read operations of L. We assume threads T_1, T_2, T_3 and T_4 are running on different processors.

```
T0:                 T1:       T2:       T3:            T4:
create(T1,T2);      L:=1;     L:=2;     r0: read L;    r1: read L;
sync(T1,T2);
create(T3,T4);
sync(T3,T4);
```

Under the strong location consistency definition, r_0 and r_1 can return different values from any of the two indeterministic writes in T_1 and T_2. However, in our system, after the synchronization on T_1 and T_2, only one of the two values written by T_1 and T_2 will be alive. Thus, the $r0$ and $r1$ cannot observe different values left by the two write operations. Hence, we conclude that our memory system implementing location consistency is not strongly location consistent.

7 Concluding Remarks

In this paper, the on-chip COMA cache coherence protocol has been formally specified in the ASM framework. We gave a correctness proof for the coherence protocol. Furthermore, we showed that our memory system is weaker than the SC and SC-derived models. It complies with location consistency but it is not strongly location consistent. Our work is a part of a project investigating microthreading in a collaboration between the Computer Systems Architecture group and Sectie Software Engineering at the University of Amsterdam[1].

References

1. Bershad, B., Zekauskas, M., Sawdon, W.: The Midway distributed shared memory system. In: Proceedings of the IEEE COMPCON (1993)
2. Blumofe, R.D., Frigo, M., Joerg, C.F., Leiserson, C.E., Randall, K.H.: An analysis of DAG-consistent distributed shared-memory algorithms. In: Proceedings og the 18th Annual ACM Symposium on Parallel Algorithms and Architectures, pp. 297–308 (1996)
3. Bolychevsky, A., Jesshope, C.R., Muchnick, V.: Dynamic sheduling in rics architectures. IEE Proceedings Computers and Digital Techniques 143(5), 309–317 (1996)
4. Bousias, K., Hasasneh, N.M., Jesshope, C.R.: Instruction-level parallelism through Microthreading-a scalable Approach to chip multiprocessors. The Computer Journal 49 (2), 211–233 (2006)
5. Corporation. K.s.r.: Ksr1 technical summary. Technical report (1992)
6. Gao, G.R., Sarkar, V.: Location consistency: Stepping beyond memory coherence barrier. In: Int'l Conf. Parallel Processing, vol. 2, pp. 73–76 (1995)
7. Gao, G.R., Sarkar, V.: Location consistency - A new memory model and cache consistency protocol. IEEE Transactions on Computers 49(8), 798–813 (2000)
8. Gharachorloo, K., Lenoski, D., Laudon, J., Gibbons, P., Gupta, A., Hennessy, J.: Memory consistency and event ordering in scalable shared-memory multiprocessors. In: Proceedings of the 17th Annual International Symposium on Computer Architecture, pp. 15–26 (1990)
9. Gurevich, Y.: Elvolving algebras 1993: Lipari guide. In: Börger, E. (ed.) Specification and Validation Methods, pp. 9–36. Oxford University Press, Oxford (1995)
10. Gurevich, Y.: May 1997 draft of the asm guide. Technical Report CSE-TR-336-97, EECS Department, University of Michigan (1997)
11. Hennessy, J.H., Patterson, D.A.: Computer Architecture: A Quantitative Approach (2006)
12. Jesshope, C.R.: Microthreading a model for distributed instruction-level concurrency. Parallel Processing Letters 16 (2), 209–228 (2006)
13. Jesshope, C.R., Luo, B.: Micro-threading: A new approach to future risc. In: ACAC 2000, pp. 31–41. IEEE Computer Society Press, Los Alamitos (2000)

---

[1] The work presented in this paper is supported by NWO (Netherlands Organisation for Scientific Research) in the "Foundations for Massively Parallel on-chip Architectures using Microthreading" project.

14. Keleher, P., Cox, A.L., Zwaenpoel, W.: Lazy release consistency for software distributed shared memory. In: Proceedings of the 29th Annual International Symposium on Computer Architecture, pp. 13–21 (1992)
15. Lamport, L.: How to make a multiprocessor computer that correctly executes multiprocess programs. IEEE Transactions on Computers 28(9), 690–691 (1979)
16. Zhang, L., Jesshope, C.R.: On-chip coma cache-coherence protocol for microgrids of microthreaded cores. In: Euro-Par 2007 Workshops: Parallel Processing, vol. 4854, pp. 38–48. Springer, Heidelberg (2008)

Author Index

Lecture Notes in Computer Science

Sublibrary 2: Programming and Software Engineering

For information about Vols. 1– 4530
please contact your bookseller or Springer

Vol. 4839: O. Sokolsky, S. Taşıran (Eds.), Runtime Verification. VI, 215 pages. 2007.

Vol. 4834: R. Cerqueira, R.H. Campbell (Eds.), Middleware 2007. XIII, 451 pages. 2007.

Vol. 4829: M. Lumpe, W. Vanderperren (Eds.), Software Composition. VIII, 281 pages. 2007.

Vol. 4824: A. Paschke, Y. Biletskiy (Eds.), Advances in Rule Interchange and Applications. XIII, 243 pages. 2007.

Vol. 4821: J. Bennedsen, M.E. Caspersen, M. Kölling (Eds.), Reflections on the Teaching of Programming. X, 261 pages. 2008.

Vol. 4807: Z. Shao (Ed.), Programming Languages and Systems. XI, 431 pages. 2007.

Vol. 4799: A. Holzinger (Ed.), HCI and Usability for Medicine and Health Care. XVI, 458 pages. 2007.

Vol. 4789: M. Butler, M.G. Hinchey, M.M. Larrondo-Petrie (Eds.), Formal Methods and Software Engineering. VIII, 387 pages. 2007.

Vol. 4767: F. Arbab, M. Sirjani (Eds.), International Symposium on Fundamentals of Software Engineering. XIII, 450 pages. 2007.

Vol. 4765: A. Moreira, J. Grundy (Eds.), Early Aspects: Current Challenges and Future Directions. X, 199 pages. 2007.

Vol. 4764: P. Abrahamsson, N. Baddoo, T. Margaria, R. Messnarz (Eds.), Software Process Improvement. XI, 225 pages. 2007.

Vol. 4762: K.S. Namjoshi, T. Yoneda, T. Higashino, Y. Okamura (Eds.), Automated Technology for Verification and Analysis. XIV, 566 pages. 2007.

Vol. 4758: F. Oquendo (Ed.), Software Architecture. XVI, 340 pages. 2007.

Vol. 4757: F. Cappello, T. Herault, J. Dongarra (Eds.), Recent Advances in Parallel Virtual Machine and Message Passing Interface. XVI, 396 pages. 2007.

Vol. 4753: E. Duval, R. Klamma, M. Wolpers (Eds.), Creating New Learning Experiences on a Global Scale. XII, 518 pages. 2007.

Vol. 4749: B.J. Krämer, K.-J. Lin, P. Narasimhan (Eds.), Service-Oriented Computing – ICSOC 2007. XIX, 629 pages. 2007.

Vol. 4748: K. Wolter (Ed.), Formal Methods and Stochastic Models for Performance Evaluation. X, 301 pages. 2007.

Vol. 4741: C. Bessière (Ed.), Principles and Practice of Constraint Programming – CP 2007. XV, 890 pages. 2007.

Vol. 4735: G. Engels, B. Opdyke, D.C. Schmidt, F. Weil (Eds.), Model Driven Engineering Languages and Systems. XV, 698 pages. 2007.

Vol. 4716: B. Meyer, M. Joseph (Eds.), Software Engineering Approaches for Offshore and Outsourced Development. X, 201 pages. 2007.

Vol. 4709: F.S. de Boer, M.M. Bonsangue, S. Graf, W.-P. de Roever (Eds.), Formal Methods for Components and Objects. VIII, 297 pages. 2007.

Vol. 4680: F. Saglietti, N. Oster (Eds.), Computer Safety, Reliability, and Security. XV, 548 pages. 2007.

Vol. 4670: V. Dahl, I. Niemelä (Eds.), Logic Programming. XII, 470 pages. 2007.

Vol. 4652: D. Georgakopoulos, N. Ritter, B. Benatallah, C. Zirpins, G. Feuerlicht, M. Schoenherr, H.R. Motahari-Nezhad (Eds.), Service-Oriented Computing ICSOC 2006. XVI, 201 pages. 2007.

Vol. 4640: A. Rashid, M. Aksit (Eds.), Transactions on Aspect-Oriented Software Development IV. IX, 191 pages. 2007.

Vol. 4634: H. Riis Nielson, G. Filé (Eds.), Static Analysis. XI, 469 pages. 2007.

Vol. 4620: A. Rashid, M. Aksit (Eds.), Transactions on Aspect-Oriented Software Development III. IX, 201 pages. 2007.

Vol. 4615: R. de Lemos, C. Gacek, A. Romanovsky (Eds.), Architecting Dependable Systems IV. XIV, 435 pages. 2007.

Vol. 4610: B. Xiao, L.T. Yang, J. Ma, C. Muller-Schloer, Y. Hua (Eds.), Autonomic and Trusted Computing. XVIII, 571 pages. 2007.

Vol. 4609: E. Ernst (Ed.), ECOOP 2007 – Object-Oriented Programming. XIII, 625 pages. 2007.

Vol. 4608: H.W. Schmidt, I. Crnković, G.T. Heineman, J.A. Stafford (Eds.), Component-Based Software Engineering. XII, 283 pages. 2007.

Vol. 4591: J. Davies, J. Gibbons (Eds.), Integrated Formal Methods. IX, 660 pages. 2007.

Vol. 4589: J. Münch, P. Abrahamsson (Eds.), Product-Focused Software Process Improvement. XII, 414 pages. 2007.

Vol. 4574: J. Derrick, J. Vain (Eds.), Formal Techniques for Networked and Distributed Systems – FORTE 2007. XI, 375 pages. 2007.

Vol. 4556: C. Stephanidis (Ed.), Universal Access in Human-Computer Interaction, Part III. XXII, 1020 pages. 2007.

Vol. 4555: C. Stephanidis (Ed.), Universal Access in Human-Computer Interaction, Part II. XXII, 1066 pages. 2007.

Vol. 4554: C. Stephanidis (Ed.), Universal Acess in Human Computer Interaction, Part I. XXII, 1054 pages. 2007.

Vol. 4553: J.A. Jacko (Ed.), Human-Computer Interaction, Part IV. XXIV, 1225 pages. 2007.

Vol. 4552: J.A. Jacko (Ed.), Human-Computer Interaction, Part III. XXI, 1038 pages. 2007.

Vol. 4551: J.A. Jacko (Ed.), Human-Computer Interaction, Part II. XXIII, 1253 pages. 2007.

Vol. 4550: J.A. Jacko (Ed.), Human-Computer Interaction, Part I. XXIII, 1240 pages. 2007.

Vol. 4542: P. Sawyer, B. Paech, P. Heymans (Eds.), Requirements Engineering: Foundation for Software Quality. IX, 384 pages. 2007.

Vol. 4536: G. Concas, E. Damiani, M. Scotto, G. Succi (Eds.), Agile Processes in Software Engineering and Extreme Programming. XV, 276 pages. 2007.